BIRDS' MODERN INSURANCE LAW

BIRDS' MODERN INSURANCE LAW

TENTH EDITION

by
JOHN BIRDS, LL.M.
Emeritus Professor, School of Law
University of Manchester
Honorary Professor, School of Law
University of Sheffield

SWEET & MAXWELL

First edition 1982
Second edition 1988
Third edition 1993
Fourth edition 1997
Fifth edition 2001
Sixth edition 2004
Seventh edition 2007
Eighth edition 2010
Ninth edition 2013

Published in 2016 by Thomson Reuters (Professional) UK Limited
trading as Sweet & Maxwell, Friars House, 160 Blackfriars Road,
London SE1 8EZ (Registered in England & Wales,
Company No 1679046. Registered Office and address for service:
2nd Floor, 1 Mark Square, Leonard Street, London EC2A 4EG)

For more information on our products and services, visit
www.sweetandmaxwell.co.uk

Typeset by Servis Filmsetting Ltd, Stockport, Cheshire
Printed and Bound in Great Britain by CPI Group (UK) Ltd, Croydon, CR0 4YY

No natural forests were destroyed to make this product;
only farmed timber was used and re-planted.

A CIP catalogue record for this book is available from the British Library.
ISBN: 978-0-414-05567-4

Thomson Reuters and the Thomson Reuters logo are trademarks of Thomson Reuters.
Sweet & Maxwell is a registered trademark of Thomson Reuters (Legal) Limited.

Crown copyright material is reproduced with the permission of the Controller of
HMSO and the Queen's Printer for Scotland.

PREFACE

There have been relatively few cases of note since the previous edition of this book, but, as those already familiar with the subject will know, there have been some very important legislative changes. The most important of these are in the Insurance Act 2015, making notable changes to the law governing good faith, disclosure, warranties and other terms, and fraudulent claims. Many of these changes, taken together with the changes already made to consumer insurance in 2013, represent significant reform of principles first established well over three centuries ago and they have necessitated a fair amount of rewriting and reordering of the material in Chs 7 and 9 in particular. I have pruned some of the previous material that will no longer be relevant when the provisions of the Act are in force, but retained some references thereto given that the Act will apply only prospectively. While the contents of the Act are to be welcomed as providing a much fairer basis for key aspects of insurance contract law, they are not all free from difficulties of interpretation and most of them can be excluded by contract terms in non-consumer insurances. These factors seem certain to give rise to litigation as time goes by.

Other changes include the replacement of the Unfair Terms in Consumer Contracts Regulations by Pt 2 of the Consumer Rights Act 2015 and the introduction of the new MIB Agreement on Uninsured Drivers. I had hoped to be able to include detail of the Law Commissions' final recommendations, on insurable interest, arising out of their lengthy law reform exercise, but despite the Commissions' hope that these would be published by the end of 2015, they appear unlikely now to appear until late in 2016.

The volume of new material means that the length of this book has increased yet again. I have noted that there are also almost 50 per cent more pages than were contained in the first edition in 1982!

As always I am extremely grateful to the publishers. Particular thanks also go to Peter Tyldesley for some very valuable comments and to colleagues with whom I worked on the Project for the Restatement of European Insurance Contract Law, which resulted in the *Principles of European Insurance Contract Law*. My exposure to how other European legal systems approach aspects of the subject was particularly thought-provoking and valuable, even if few references to that work actually appear in a book which basically remains a text on UK insurance law.

I have endeavoured to make the book up to date to December 2015.

John Birds
February 2016

TABLE OF CONTENTS

TABLE OF CASES

TABLE OF STATUTES

TABLE OF STATUTORY INSTRUMENTS

TABLE OF EUROPEAN LEGISLATION

Chapter 1

Introduction: The Nature and Definition of Insurance and Insurance Law

1.0

The contract of insurance is basically governed by the rules which form part of the general law of contract, but equally there is no doubt that over the years it has attracted many principles of its own to such an extent that it is perfectly proper to speak of a law of insurance. The aim of this book is to present those principles in a fairly conventional doctrinal way.[1] Some of them owe their existence to the fact that the documents of the standard insurance contract, principally the proposal form and the policy, have long been drafted in a fairly uniform way. The effect of this will be seen throughout this book. In addition, the reasons for many of the principles of insurance can be found by looking at the history of insurance and of the insurance contract. A detailed examination of this history would be inappropriate in a book of this size,[2] but a brief excursus is useful to set the scene.

1.1 History

The origins of the modern insurance contract are to be found in the practices adopted by Italian merchants from the fourteenth century onwards, although there is little doubt that the concept of insuring was known long before then. Maritime risks, the risk of losing ships and cargoes at sea, instigated the practice of medieval insurance and dominated insurance for many years. The habit spread to London merchants but not, it appears, until the sixteenth century. At first, there were no separate insurers. A group of merchants would agree to bear all of their risks among themselves. For a long time, the common law played little or no part in the regulation of disputes concerning insurance. For this purpose merchants in 1601 secured the establishment by statute of a chamber of assurance that was outside the normal legal system. However, with the appointment of Lord Mansfield as Lord Chief Justice in the mid-eighteenth century, the common law courts took an interest in insurance contracts. Lord Mansfield applied principles derived from the law

---

[1] For an excellent, more contextual, critique, see Malcolm Clarke, *Policies and Perceptions of Insurance Law in the Twenty-First Century* (Oxford: OUP, 2005).

[2] See for more detail, Holdsworth, "The early history of the contract of insurance" (1917) 17 Col. L.R. 85; G. Clayton, *British Insurance* (London: Elek Books Ltd, 1970).

merchant as well as more traditional common law concepts to the solution of disputes over insurance, and by the time of his retirement in 1788, the jurisdiction of the courts over insurance matters had been established.

Marine insurance retained its prominent position for some considerable time, and from the late seventeenth century onwards was increasingly transacted at a coffee house in the City of London owned by a man called Lloyd. There developed the practice that the merchant wishing insurance would pass round to the people willing to provide it, who were gathered there, a slip of paper on which he had written the details of the ship, voyage and cargo, etc. Those willing to accept a proportion of the risk initialled the slip. When the total amount of insurance required was underwritten, the contract was complete.[3] From this practice comes the term "underwriter" which, of course, is still in use today, and the name of the owner of the coffee house attached itself to the institution. Lloyd's of London[4] is now itself a Corporation formed with statutory authority, and it has long since ceased to operate from a coffee house, but it is notable that the members still conduct their business in much the same way as it was done in the coffee house.[5] The influence of Lloyd's on insurance and insurance law has been very significant; for example, the standard Lloyd's marine insurance policy was adopted as the statutory form in the Marine Insurance Act 1906.[6] On the other hand, there have long been numerous other companies and associations transacting the business of insurance.[7]

The principles developed in regard to marine insurance have by and large been applied to the other types of insurance that developed subsequently.[8]

---

[3] For a more detailed legal analysis of this, see Ch.5.

[4] See further 1.2.4.

[5] Until fairly recently, members of Lloyd's had to be individuals whose liability was unlimited, but severe problems in the late 1980s and early 1990s led to limited liability companies being allowed to be members, and in financial terms at least they now dominate the Lloyd's market.

[6] However, this is rarely used today.

[7] See 1.3 for a brief description of those bodies allowed to act as insurers.

[8] This was perhaps the major reason for the unsatisfactory nature of some of the principles of insurance law, at least as they applied in theory, if not always in practice, to consumer contracts. There is obviously a vast difference between the circumstances surrounding a marine policy in the early days of insurance and those surrounding the modern mass-produced motor, household, etc. policies. An explanation for the courts' and, until recently, the legislature's failure to intervene and correct these unsatisfactory rules may lie in the fact that Britain has long had a comprehensive social security insurance system, although some might now say that it has in recent years lost much of its comprehensiveness. In contrast, in the US, where such a system was of a more recent origin and much less extensive, and where therefore private insurance was and is much more important in providing basic protection, the courts have been very active in intervening to protect the position of insureds: see Hasson, "The special nature

The first of these was fire insurance, its birth stimulated by the Great Fire of London in 1666. This was followed by life and personal accident insurance, the latter growing rapidly in tandem with the growth of the railways and industrialisation in the nineteenth century. The twentieth century saw such development that it is now possible to insure almost every conceivable event or thing against the risk of loss or damage. Nevertheless, the law governing all these insurances is basically the same. Marine insurance law was codified in the Marine Insurance Act 1906 and some of its principles are peculiar to it. This book is not specifically concerned with marine insurance,[9] but on occasion reference will be made to sections of the 1906 Act and to marine cases where they establish a principle of general applicability or provide authority for a principle which is also valid for non-marine insurance. In many ways the law governing non-marine insurance contracts is still based on case law, but there have been some statutory inroads, including, most importantly, by the Consumer Insurance (Disclosure and Representations) Act 2012 and the Insurance Act 2015.[10] However, it is important to note at this stage that the law "in the books" is not the law that has always been applied in practice, especially so far as consumer insurance contracts are concerned. The 2012 and 2015 Acts mentioned above have produced important reforms of insurance law in a domestic context from the work of the Law Commissions and there may also be reforms at a European level. These matters are considered in a general way at the end of this chapter.

1.2   Some Classifications of Insurance

The insurance industry today transacts vast amounts of business, not just in Britain but overseas. The risks that it covers can be classified in several different ways. It is worthwhile explaining two of these classifications because they relate to some important legal distinctions.

1.2.1 First and third party insurance

First, one can distinguish first party insurance, under which someone insures their own life, house, factory or car, etc. from third party or liability insurance,

---

of the insurance contract: a comparison of the American and English law of insurance" (1984) 47 M.L.R. 505.

[9] For an excellent account, see Howard Bennett, *The Law of Marine Insurance,* 2nd edn (Oxford: OUP, 2006).

[10] See also, in particular, in respect of life insurance (see Ch.19) and insurances which are compulsory (see Chs 21 and 22). There have been general reforms of the law of contract that affect insurance contracts, particularly what is now Pt 2 of the Consumer Rights Act 2015 and the Contracts (Rights of Third Parties) Act 1999. These are examined at the appropriate places in later chapters.

that is, someone insuring against their potential liability in law to pay damages to another. Of course, first and third party aspects may well be combined in the same policy. The law reflects this difference, first by demanding that some third party insurances should be compulsory,[11] and secondly by recognising that in practice, third party insurance involves the third party as much as the insured person. Often in practice, for example, the victim of a car accident may talk in terms of claiming from the negligent driver's insurer rather than from the driver, which in law is the correct way of expressing the position. The law has deemed that in certain cases the third party should be protected from the strict contractual rights and liabilities between insured and insurer. Although this book is not concerned with the economics of insurance, it is worth pointing out that in general the third party insurance system is much more expensive and less efficient to operate than first party insurance. This factor, among others, has led some commentators to conclude that in certain areas, especially road and work accidents involving personal injury or death, the present system of third party insurance backing up a system of liability in tort should be replaced by first party insurance. The latter could be run by private insurers, but more logically perhaps should be taken over by the state as part of the social security system.[12] It must be admitted that such a development appears highly unlikely.

1.2.2 Life and other insurances

A second classification, which is well recognised in law and in insurance practice, distinguishes between life insurance on the one hand and all other forms of insurance on the other. There is a great variety of forms of life insurance, ranging from pure, whole life insurance, an undertaking to pay a certain sum on the death of the life insured whenever this occurs, to endowment policies whereby the insured receives a sum if he survives beyond a certain age, and to modern devices which combine an element of life insurance with the more substantial element of investment in securities or property.[13] Whatever the

---

[11] See Chs 21 and 22.

[12] See generally, e.g. Peter Cane, *Atiyah's Accident Compensation and the Law*, 7th edn (Cambridge: CUP, 2006); *Report of the Royal Commission on Civil Liability and Compensation for Personal Injury* (1978), Cmnd.7054 (*The Pearson Report*). For an interesting study of the impact of liability insurance on the development of the tort of negligence, see Davies, "The end of the affair: duty of care and liability insurance" (1989) 9 L.S. 67.

[13] As long as there is a life insurance element, even if that may be no more than the surrender value of the contract at any time, the contract is one of life insurance for the purposes of the regulatory statutes (see Ch.2) and the Life Assurance Act 1774 (see Ch.3): *Fuji Finance Inc v Aetna Life Insurance Ltd* [1996] 4 All E.R. 608. That in practice many life insurance policies are in reality investments was recognised by the incorporation of many forms of life insurance within the investor protection

type of life policy, the uncertainty which, as will be seen shortly, is a necessary feature of all insurances is of a different nature from the uncertainty in other insurances. Death is certain; the uncertainty is as to when it will occur. On the other hand, for example, the property insured against loss by fire may never burn down, the motor insured may never be involved in an accident. Accordingly, contracts of life insurance and related ones such as personal accident insurance, are regarded simply as contracts for contingency insurance, in other words, contracts to pay an agreed sum of money when the event insured against occurs. Non-life insurance contracts are, in general, contracts to indemnify the insured only in respect of the loss suffered if it is actually suffered and only to the amount of the loss suffered.[14] We shall return to this distinction at the relevant points throughout this book.

1.2.3 Terminology

There are one or two related points concerning the terminology of insurance. It is sometimes said that the proper description of the contract that insures a life is life assurance and this is indeed a common, though not universal, usage. The reason is simply that death is assured of happening, the risks covered by other insurances are not. The usage is not universal though, and we shall in general use the terms "insurance" and "insured" in all cases.[15] Often in practice, the person who actually contracts with an insurer is referred to as the policyholder, but this is not a usage that we tend to follow.

1.3 Types of Insurer

We shall see in the next chapter that the business of providing insurance is closely regulated by or on behalf of government. It is appropriate here to outline the principal types of business that are allowed to engage in insurance.

With the exception of Lloyd's, insurers must be a company registered under the Companies Act,[16] an industrial and provident society or a body corporate established by charter or Act of Parliament. Virtually all large non-life insurers and composite insurers[17] have long adopted the ordinary registered company form. A number of the long-established life insurers

---

framework established by the Financial Services Act 1986, since replaced by the Financial Services and Markets Act 2000, as briefly described in Ch.2.

[14] Valued policies, where the insured is entitled to a stated sum regardless of the exact measure of his loss, are rare but possible in non-marine insurance; see 15.8.

[15] Some commentators and judges use the term "assured" in relation to any type of insurance.

[16] The Companies Act 2006 or one of its predecessors.

[17] That is, insurers offering both long-term (life) and other insurance business.

are mutual insurers incorporated by charter or statute.[18] A small number of industrial and provident societies still operate the form of life insurance known as industrial life assurance, the essential characteristic of which is that premiums are collected at the insureds' homes on a regular basis.

Lloyd's is a unique organisation and operates as such on a worldwide basis,[19] although strictly there is no insurer called Lloyd's. The Corporation of Lloyd's, which is established under the Lloyd's Acts 1871–1982, does not itself transact insurance business nor does it have any liability on policies issued by Lloyd's underwriters.[20] It is concerned to control the membership of Lloyd's, to provide facilities for the conduct of members' business and, in part, to regulate the Lloyd's market under the Lloyd's Acts, although there is now a substantial element of general statutory regulation.[21] Insurance at Lloyd's is effected with individual underwriters, for many years grouped into syndicates. Working members run the day-to-day business of the syndicates, the "names" (who constitute the majority of the underwriters) being passive investors. Except for those who invest on a limited liability basis, each underwriter is potentially liable without limit on the insurance contracts entered into on his/her behalf. The liability of Lloyd's underwriters is several not joint.[22]

---

[18] In recent years many have "demutualised" and become public listed companies. Mutual insurance, in the form of clubs owned by ship owners, is also common in the marine insurance market; the clubs themselves will usually be ordinary limited companies registered in the UK or elsewhere.

[19] It operates overseas through agency arrangements.

[20] Problems at Lloyd's in the early 1990s led to considerable litigation regarding the legal relationships involved, in particular as to whether the Corporation of Lloyd's owes any duty of care to its "names"; see *Ashmore v Corp of Lloyd's* [1992] 2 Lloyd's Rep. 1; above *(No.2)* [1992] 2 Lloyd's Rep. 620.

[21] Under Pt XIX of the Financial Services and Markets Act 2000, as amended by the Financial Services Act 2012; see Ch.XII of the Financial Services and Markets Act 2000 (Regulated Activities) Order 2001. Following disastrous losses in the early 1990s, a complicated scheme was introduced in effect to save the whole institution. Legal challenges to the validity of the scheme were rejected in *Society of Lloyd's v Leighs* [1997] C.L.C. 1398 and *Society of Lloyd's v Fraser* [1999] 1 Lloyd's Rep. I.R. 156, and an action by dissentient names claiming that Lloyd's fraudulently induced them to become underwriters failed. Among the many other cases concerning the problems at Lloyd's and the attempts to resolve them, see especially the House of Lords' decision in *Society of Lloyd's v Robinson* [1999] 1 W.L.R. 756, which, among other things, approved the judicial description of the Lloyd's market given in *Napier* and *Ettrick v Kershaw* [1997] L.R.L.R. 1 at [7]–[8].

[22] Lloyd's Act 1982 s.8(1), relied upon by the House of Lords in *Touche Ross & Co v Baker* [1992] 2 Lloyd's Rep. 207 holding that, in the absence of anything to the contrary in the policy, a "discovery extension" clause in a professional indemnity policy issued by a group of insurers could be exercised against one Lloyd's syndicate notwithstanding that it was not exercised against the other insurers involved.

1.4 Reinsurance

A further important feature of insurance is the fact that, for many years, insurers have themselves insured against the risks to which they are subject, by means of what is called reinsurance.[23] There are many different ways in which reinsurance can be effected, any detailed description of which is beyond the scope of this book,[24] but there are two basic forms. The first is facultative reinsurance, which in essence is the reinsurance of a particular risk with either party being free to decide whether or not to enter into the contract. The second is treaty reinsurance, under which both parties may be bound in respect of the reinsurance of risks of the sort covered by the treaty, but there are variants in respect of which the reinsured in particular may have a degree of choice as to which risks to cede. Whatever the type of reinsurance effected, the basic principles of law that apply to a contract of insurance, including the principles of utmost good faith and indemnity, also apply to reinsurance contracts.[25] What are also of particular importance are the terms that dictate the extent to which the reinsurance contract incorporates the terms of the underlying insurance contract, those that bind the reinsurers to indemnify the reinsured regardless of whether or not the latter was strictly liable under the original contract,[26] and those concerned with the notification of claims and the control of claims.

1.5 The Legal Definition of Insurance

An essential task at this stage is to attempt to formulate a legal definition or at least an explanation of the meaning of the contract of insurance.[27] As has been pointed out judicially,[28] this is not an easy matter. The statutes dealing with the regulation of insurance business[29] have never contained a definition, no doubt because of the risk of inadvertently excluding contracts that should be within their scope.[30] One effect of this, though, must be that it gives the

---

[23] Reinsurers themselves may further reinsure, in which case the proper term is retrocession.

[24] For an account, see *MacGillivray on Insurance Law*, 13th edn (London: Sweet & Maxwell, 2015), Ch.35.

[25] Indeed many of the leading cases have arisen out of disputes surrounding a reinsurance contract rather than an insurance contract.

[26] Often called "follow settlements" clauses.

[27] See Purves [2001] J.B.L. 623.

[28] *Department of Trade and Industry v St Christopher Motorists' Association Ltd* [1974] 1 All E.R. 395; *Medical Defence Union v Department of Trade* [1979] 2 All E.R. 421 at 429.

[29] See Ch.2.

[30] See *Department of Trade and Industry v St Christopher Motorists' Association Ltd* [1974] 1 All E.R. 395 at 396–7. Like its predecessors, and despite the fact that it includes

regulators[31] a considerable discretion. This discretion can be challenged effectively only by a body going to court in order to seek a declaration that it is not carrying on insurance business or having to defend an application by the regulator for a declaration that it is or a petition by the regulator to wind up the company. Apart from the desirability of defining the scope of what the law of insurance applies to, clearly the fundamental reason for any attempt to define the meaning of insurance contract is because the business of providing insurance under contracts of insurance is closely regulated. We shall briefly consider the nature of this regulation in the next chapter.

However, there are other reasons. Insurance law has its peculiar principles, for example the doctrine of utmost good faith,[32] and it may be necessary to know whether a contract is one of insurance in order to know whether this doctrine applies. Furthermore, a statute may include within or exempt from its operation "contracts of insurance" without defining these. One obvious case is the exemption of such contracts from the Unfair Contract Terms Act 1977.[33] More recently, the Consumer Insurance (Disclosure and Representations) Act 2012 applies to consumer insurance contracts, defining "consumer" but not "contract of insurance". Similarly, there is no definition of "contract of insurance" in the Insurance Act 2015.

As it happens, almost all the decided cases that have considered this problem have been concerned to discover whether or not a business was subject to regulation as insurance. Others have been concerned with tax statutes and one or two only with principles peculiar to the insurance contract.[34] It will be assumed, for the present, that a definition can be found which works for all purposes; we shall then briefly consider whether, in fact, it might not be useful to have different definitions for different purposes.

1.6   A Definition for Regulatory Purposes

It is suggested that a contract of insurance is any contract having as its principal object[35] one party (the insurer) assuming the risk of an uncertain

---

all types of insurance within its scope (see s.424 and Sch.2), the Financial Services and Markets Act 2000 does not attempt a definition as such. The Perimeter Guidance issued by the FCA gives guidance, although this has in part been criticised: see *MacGillivray on Insurance Law*, 13th edn (London: Sweet & Maxwell, 2015), para.1–009.

[31] The Prudential Regulation Authority (PRA) and the FCA.

[32] See Chs 7 and 8.

[33] Sch.1, para.1(a): see 1.7.

[34] One area that has given rise to litigation and to difficulties is that of distinguishing contracts of insurance from contracts of guarantee. It is clear that what the contract is called does not matter. The leading case is *Seaton v Heath* [1899] 1 Q.B. 782, and see Blair, "The conversion of guarantee contracts" (1966) 39 M.L.R. 522.

[35] For discussion of the need for a "principal object" in contracts containing both

event,[36] which is not within its control, happening at a future time, in which event the other party (the insured) has an interest, and under which contract the insurer is bound to pay money or provide its equivalent if the uncertain event occurs.[37] It would follow that anyone who regularly[38] enters into such contracts as the party bearing the risks is carrying on insurance business for the purposes of the statute regulating insurance business. Several aspects of this definition merit closer attention.

1.6.1 Legal entitlement

First, there must clearly be a binding contract, and the insurer must be legally bound to compensate the other party. It is not enough that there is a right to be considered for a benefit that is truly only discretionary. In *Medical Defence Union v Department of Trade*,[39] the plaintiff was a company whose members were practising doctors and dentists. Its business consisted primarily of conducting legal proceedings on behalf of members and indemnifying them against claims made against them in respect of damages and costs. However, under its constitution, its members had no right to such benefits, merely the right to request that they be given assistance or an indemnity. It was held that the company was not carrying on insurance business. The contracts between it and its members were not contracts of insurance because to be that a contract must provide for the right of the insured to money or money's worth on the happening of the uncertain event. The right to request assistance was not such a right.

1.6.2 Uncertainty

Secondly, the uncertainty that is a necessary feature of insurance, as we have already seen, is in most cases as to whether or not the event insured against will occur. In life insurance, it is as to the time when it will occur.[40]

"insurance" and "non-insurance" elements, see the comments of Warren J in *Digital Satellite Warranty Cover Ltd* [2011] EWHC 122 (Ch) at [84] to [86] and the discussion in *MacGillivray on Insurance Law*, 13th edn (London: Sweet & Maxwell, 2015), paras 1–008 to 1–009.

[36] It is clear that the uncertain event need not be adverse to the other party, though in cases other than certain endowment and annuity policies, it will be. See *Gould v Curtis* [1913] 3 K.B. 84, qualifying the definition given in the leading case of *Prudential Insurance Co v IRC* [1904] 2 K.B. 658, and the discussion by Megarry VC in *Medical Defence Union v Department of Trade* [1979] 2 All E.R. 421 at 427–428.

[37] English law regards a contract of indemnity insurance as amounting to a promise by the insurer to hold the insured harmless; see further 15.1.

[38] Although regularity may not be necessary: see 2.4.

[39] *Medical Defence Union v Department of Trade* [1979] 2 All E.R 421.

[40] See *Gould v Curtis* [1913] 3 K.B. 84.

1.6.3 Insurable interest

Thirdly, the other party, the insured, must have an insurable interest in the property or life or liability that is the subject of the insurance. This requirement will be examined in detail in Ch.3.

1.6.4 Control

Fourthly, it seems essential that the event insured against be outside the control of the party assuming the risk. No English case has directly considered this point, but it has been raised in two cases when it was not necessary for decision.[41] The potential problem can be illustrated by considering the case of a manufacturer which contractually guarantees its products to its consumers.[42] The example may be taken of a washing machine manufacturer which undertakes to repair any fault arising from defective manufacture within a year of purchase. The manufacturer has clearly undertaken to provide a service in money's worth in assuming the risk of an uncertain event in which the consumer clearly has an interest. Yet surely it has not entered into a contract of insurance as most people would understand it. It is suggested that the answer is to introduce the element of control.[43] In the example, all that the manufacturer has done is to guarantee to put things right that it has put wrong in the first place, that is defects in manufacture. Therefore, its guarantee is not a contract of insurance.[44] On the other hand, however, someone who, in return for a consideration, guarantees a product against certain risks that are not within his control because they are not his products, nor has he sold them, is, it is thought, entering into contracts of insurance.[45] The same would be true if a manufacturer did more than simply guarantee

---

[41] *Department of Trade and Industry v St Christopher Motorists' Association Ltd* [1974] 1 All E.R. 395 at 401; *Medical Defence Union v Department of Trade* [1979] 2 All E.R. 421 at [424].

[42] For other problems regarding guarantees, especially in the context of the EC Directive on Consumer Guarantees, see Twigg-Flesner, "Consumer product guarantees and insurance law" [1999] J.B.L. 279.

[43] Perhaps "control" is a misleading term, as in practice a manufacturer may have very little actual control over its warranted products. An alternative formulation might be whether the alleged insurer is in fact responsible for producing the event giving rise to the claim for indemnity.

[44] See the American cases cited in Hellner, "The scope of insurance regulation: what is insurance for the purposes of regulation?" (1963) 12 Am. J. Comp. L. 494 at 505.

[45] See *Re Sentinel Securities Plc* [1996] 1 W.L.R. 316, where a "guarantee" to repair double glazing and other home improvement products if the original supplier went out of business was held to constitute insurance and *Re Digital Satellite Warranty Cover Ltd* [2011] EWHC 122 (Ch), affirmed [2011] EWCA Civ 1413 and [2013] UKSC 7.

its products against manufacturing defects, for example, if it undertook to replace them if they were damaged from specified causes.[46] Associations which provide a repair or recovery service for car owners upon breakdown should also be regarded as providing insurance, assuming that their members have a right to their services and not just a right to be considered.[47]

1.6.5 Provision of money's worth

Fifthly, there seems no reason in principle why it should be necessary for the insurer to have to undertake to pay money on the occurrence of the uncertain event, and there is clear authority that the provision of something other than money is enough, provided that it is of money's worth. In *Department of Trade and Industry v St Christopher's Motorists' Association Ltd*,[48] the defendant undertook to provide its members with chauffeur services should they be disqualified from driving due to being convicted of having more than the permitted level of alcohol in the blood. It was held that this constituted insurance. The fact that the benefits were not in money was irrelevant.[49] As was pointed out in the subsequent case of *Medical Defence Union v Department of Trade*, it is neither sufficient nor accurate to say that the provision of services is

---

[46] Above at 505–506. The leading US case is perhaps State ex rel. *Duffy v Western Auto Supply Co* 134 Ohio St. 163 (1938). The New York Insurance Law, s.41, among others, incorporates the control test into its definition of insurance contracts. However, the use of this test has been criticised; see, e.g. Hellner, "The scope of insurance regulation: what is insurance for the purposes of regulation?" (1963) 12 Am. J. Comp. L. 494, especially at 500–502. If such a manufacturer were held to be entering into contracts of insurance, that does not necessarily imply that it is carrying on the business of insurance for the purposes of the Financial Services and Markets Act 2000; see Megarry VC in *Medical Defence Union v Department of Trade* [1979] 2 All E.R. 421 at 431–432. It should be noted that were this the result, the manufacturer is not strictly entitled to carry on any other commercial business (R.1.5.13 of the Prudential Sourcebook for Insurers, made by the regulators under s.141(1) of the Financial Services and Markets Act 2000) which would obviously be ridiculous. See also Parkash, (1985) *L.S.G.* 3547.

[47] This is recognised by the fact that the activities of such associations are exempt from the control of the regulators under the Financial Services and Markets Act 2000 (Regulated Activities) Order 2001 art.10.

[48] *Department of Trade and Industry v St Christopher's Motorists' Association Ltd* [1974] 1 All E.R. 395. It should be noted that by the time the case was heard, the defendant had in fact made arrangements for insurance that were satisfactory to the Department of Trade, so that they did not appear in court. Such insurance was in fact probably contrary to public policy (see Ch.12), and is no longer sold in this country.

[49] This decision was followed in *Re Sentinel Securities Plc* [1996] 1 W.L.R. 316 (the benefit provided by the insurer was the repair of defects in double-glazing and other home improvements). See also *Fuji Finance Inc v Aetna Life Insurance Co* [1995] Ch. 122 at 130.

enough.[50] It is better to say that it must be the provision of something that is clearly worth money, whether that be a right to valuable services, a right to advice[51] or a right to have an item of property repaired or replaced.

1.6.6 Other requirements

Certain authorities suggest, however, that the above definition may not be sufficiently comprehensive. *Hampton v Toxteth Co-operative Society*[52] and *Hall D'Ath v British Provident Association*[53] both appear to suggest that there can be no insurance business carried on in the absence of a clearly stipulated premium and a policy. In *Hampton v Toxteth Co-operative Society*, membership of a local co-operative society was expressed to confer the right to a sum of money on the death of a member's spouse, the sum to be calculated by reference to the member's purchases from the society over a certain period. This was held not to constitute the provision of life insurance, so that the society was not required to deposit the sum of £20,000 under the relevant regulating statute, the Assurance Companies Act 1909. It is clear that the majority of the Court of Appeal[54] did regard the absence of a policy as crucial; the decision may also have turned upon the fact that under the rules of the society as the court read them, there was no enforceable contractual right to the sums concerned. It has already been seen how this is essential.

The absence of a policy was probably crucial because the 1909 Act, in ss.1 and 30, expressly referred to the carrying on of insurance business under policies of insurance. *Hampton v Toxteth Co-operative Society*[55] can therefore be read as turning on a point of statutory construction.[56] The current statutory

---

[50] *Medical Defence Union v Department of Trade* [1979] 2 All E.R. 421 at 428.

[51] It was also said in *Medical Defence Union v Department of Trade* [1979] 2 All E.R. 421 at 430, that a right to advice and assistance conferred on members of a club should involve the "insurer" in additional expenses, rather than being merely part of the general costs of running the club for the benefit of members generally. Megarry VC therefore added "or the provision of services to be paid for by the insurer" to "money or money's worth".

[52] *Hampton v Toxteth Co-operative Society* [1915] 1 Ch 721.

[53] *Hall D'Ath v British Provident Association* (1932) 48 L.T.R. 240.

[54] Phillimore LJ gave a strong dissent.

[55] The same must be true of *Hall D'Ath v British Provident Association*.

[56] This also distinguishes the earlier case of *Nelson v Board of Trade* (1901) 84 L.T. 565, where tea merchants who offered married women who bought their tea over a certain period annuities on the deaths of their husbands were held to be subject to the Life Assurance Companies Act 1870. Although the word "policies" appeared in that Act, this was only part of the relevant definition; the other part referred simply to the granting of annuities upon human life, with no reference to the necessity for a policy.

descriptions of insurance[57] refer merely to contracts of insurance,[58] and it is suggested therefore, that these older cases are not relevant to the construction of the modern statute and to a modern definition of insurance at least for regulation purposes.[59] It would indeed be most strange if a business could escape from regulation as insurance merely by introducing less formality, even if in all respects the contracts it entered into fell within a definition of the sort that has been given here. The legislature has deemed that insurers should be more closely scrutinised as regards their financial situation than most other businesses, because of the importance of insurance, the risks involved, and the need to ensure that insured persons do not suffer at the hands of reckless or fraudulent insurers.

1.6.7 A wider view

It may indeed be arguable that there should be no great concern to find a formal definition of insurance for regulation purposes. It could be enough to say that any transaction that looks like insurance by displaying the necessary characteristics of assumption and distribution of risk, and which is transacted on a reasonable scale, should be the subject of regulation.[60] On this view, technical questions as to the enforceability of the right by the insured, and whether or not the benefit that has been promised is worth money, may be irrelevant. If, in fact, the "insurer" regularly dispenses real benefit, that person should be regarded as an insurer. As has been pointed out with respect to the Medical Defence Union,[61] it is extremely rare for that body to refuse assistance to its members, and it is unlikely that any member faced with an allegation of negligence would deny getting good value from the company. There are strong arguments that such a body is in the business of insuring to such an extent that the protection of its members requires that it be subject to statutory regulation.

---

[57] Financial Services and Markets Act 2000 Sch.2 and the Financial Services and Markets Act 2000 (Regulated Activities) Order 2001 Sch.1.

[58] Note, though, that the Treasury has power, under s.424 of the Financial Services and Markets Act 2000, to specify the meaning of "policy" for the purposes of that Act.

[59] Whether or not the *Hampton* case might be used as the basis for a definition for other purposes is discussed briefly below.

[60] See especially, for a full and persuasive argument on these lines, to which the text does no justice at all, the article by Hellner, "The scope of insurance regulation: what is insurance for the purposes of regulation?" (1963) 12 Am. J. Comp. L. 494 at 505.

[61] Roberts (1980) 43 M.L.R. 85; Merkin (1979) 1 *Liverpool Law Review* 125.

1.7   Definition for Other Purposes

If, in order to qualify as insurance for the purposes of regulation, it is sufficient that a transaction displays the necessary characteristics, the question
arises whether a similar description will suffice for other purposes. Take, for
example, the sort of deal that involves the assumption of risk outside the control of the party assuming the risk, but which is not described as insurance
and which, perhaps, most people would not think of as insurance. As well
as the examples given earlier, an actual instance involved a manufacturer of
engine lubricants who, when it sold these, also guaranteed that the purchaser's car would not break down from any cause for a certain period. Clearly
this went beyond risks that were within its control. Could such a manufacturer claim, for example, that its contracts are exempt from the statutory
control of exclusion clauses in the Unfair Contract Terms Act 1977, because
they are contracts of insurance? It is suggested that it should not be able to
do so.[62] For regulation purposes, for the reasons mentioned, a wide definition of insurance should be used which would indeed catch this sort of case.
However, the Unfair Contract Terms Act exemption was clearly intended to
apply to contracts of insurance as normally understood and described.[63] The
policy of the Act dictates that anything which does not choose to identify
itself as insurance cannot claim the advantage of the exemption. It is suggested therefore, that for this purpose, and perhaps for the purposes of applying the special rules of insurance law such as the doctrine of utmost good
faith, there is merit in the views expressed in the *Hampton* case and others that
the transactions are accompanied by the usual incidents of insurance, namely
some sort of policy[64] and an identifiable premium.

It is thought that the same reasoning should apply to any statute that
applies to a contract of insurance without defining it, for example the Third
Parties (Rights against Insurers) Act 1930,[65] the Consumer Insurance
(Disclosure and Representations) Act 2012 and the Insurance Act 2015.

1.8   Practice and Reform

It was mentioned earlier that the law in the books, that is the strict doctrinal insurance contract law, has not always applied in practice. This factor,

---

[62] In any event, such a manufacturer will be subject to Pt 2 of the Consumer Rights
Act 2015 because, as will be seen, this applies to contracts of insurance, although
the scope of its application is not wholly clear.

[63] Because the insurance industry promulgated Statements of Practice in return; see
below.

[64] Although it is not suggested that it is necessarily called a "policy".

[65] This will be replaced by the Third Parties (Rights against Insurers) Act 2010; see
Ch.20.

together with many calls for reform of the doctrinal law, led to the Law Commissions undertaking a widespread review of the law which, as we have already seen, has already led to statutory reform. It is appropriate here to review these and associated developments in a general way, while leaving more detailed consideration of practice and reform to the appropriate later chapters.

1.9   Commercial v Consumer Insurance Law

It is probably fair to say that developments since the latter part of the 20th century led to a situation where key aspects of insurance contract law were in practice different depending on whether the insured was acting as a consumer or was in business. These related particularly to the pre-contractual duties imposed on a prospective insured when applying for insurance and to some of the obligations traditionally imposed on the insured under standard contracts, the detailed law on which is examined in Chs 6 to 9.[66] Because these duties have long been recognised as being capable of operating unfairly on consumers, statutory reform was recommended on a number of occasions, most notably perhaps by the Law Commission in 1980.[67] Until recently, rather than changing strict legal doctrine, successive British governments have by and large sanctioned reform by what can be called "self-regulation"[68] under the measures that are described below.

That said, however, there was already some doctrinal protection afforded to consumers. Thus the sale of both life insurance and most forms of non-life insurance is regulated by the Financial Conduct Authority (FCA) under the Financial Services and Markets Act 2000.[69] In particular, the rules in the Insurance Conduct of Business Sourcebook (ICOBS) impose a range of

---

[66] However, traditionally in Britain there has been no control of policy terms and conditions, in contrast with the position in many other countries, especially those with a civil law system. It may well be that a general freedom from state control has led to benefits for insurance consumers in terms of both the cover provided and its costs. For a useful, although now dated, study, comparing the British system with the much more regulatory German system, see the Institute for Fiscal Studies, "Insurance: Competition or Regulation?" Report Series No.19 (1985).

[67] Report No.104, Cmnd. 8064. See Birds, "The reform of insurance law" [1982] J.B.L. 449.

[68] For a more detailed account, see Birds, "Self-regulation and insurance contracts", *New Foundations for Insurance Law* edited by F. D. Rose, (Rothman, 1987), Ch.1. For an interesting study of the agreements, many of them modifying the legal rules, under which the insurance industry operates, see Lewis, "Insurers' agreements not to enforce strict legal rights: bargaining with government and in the shadow of the law" (1985) 48 M.L.R. 275.

[69] As amended by the Financial Services Act 2012. Detailed consideration of this protection in respect of life insurance is outside the scope of this book, but there are some brief references in later chapters.

statutory duties on insurers and intermediaries[70] and in particular require that insurers cannot unreasonably reject a claim and incorporate what were previously "rules" contained in the Statement of General Insurance Practice discussed below. The ICOBS rules are examined further in Ch.2. Further, we must also note the potential impact of Pt 2 of the Consumer Rights Act 2015, replacing the Unfair Terms in Consumer Contracts Regulations 1999.[71] This will be considered further at appropriate parts throughout this book, including the question of whether or not they impose a general requirement of "fairness" on the terms of consumer insurance contracts.[72] For the present, it suffices to note the general requirement applicable to any insurance contract with a consumer[73] that the insurer must ensure that any written term of a contract is transparent, that is expressed in plain and intelligible language and legible.[74] This has given statutory force to the increasing trend of recent years towards insurance policies drafted in "plain English".

The impact of these various devices was such that it seemed proper to speak of a "consumer insurance law" separate from that which applying to insurance contracts effected by commercial persons or organisations. The enactment of the Consumer Insurance (Disclosure and Representations) Act 2012 and the Insurance Act 2015 makes it quite clear that, in some respects at least, there is now a doctrinal distinction.

1.9.1 Self-regulation and complaints mechanisms for consumers

As far as self-regulation is concerned, there were a number of important developments. The first devices were the Statement of General Insurance Practice and the Statement of Long-term Insurance Practice, initially introduced in 1977[75] and later revised in 1986, under which most insurers undertook not

---

[70] The predecessor to ICOBS (the Insurance Conduct of Business Rules or ICOB) was effective from early 2005 and replaced a self-regulatory device that was known as the General Insurance Standards Council (GISC); see Burling, "The impact of the GISC" [2001] J.B.L. 646. This in turn replaced from 2000 the ABI's Code of Practice for All Intermediaries (Including All Employees of Insurance Companies) Other than Registered Brokers, which was first issued in 1988 and slightly revised in 1994. The latter applied only to insurance intermediaries, whereas the GISC code applied and the Conduct of Business Sourcebook apply also to insurers.

[71] SI 1999/2083, which itself replaced SI 1994/3159 and implements EC Directive 93/13.

[72] See Chs 6 and 13.

[73] Any individual acting for purposes which are outside their trade, business, craft or profession: the Consumer Rights Act 2015, s.2(3).

[74] Consumer Rights Act 2015 s.68.

[75] This was in return for the exemption of insurance contracts from the Unfair Contract Terms Act 1977. See Birds (1977) 40 M.L.R. 677.

to exercise some of their legal rights against their individual policyholders. The Statements of Practice, which were primarily concerned with the consequences of non-disclosure, misrepresentation and breach of warranties and conditions, were not strictly legally binding,[76] although there can be no doubt that a large majority of insurers generally observed their terms[77] and they were certainly enforced by the complaints mechanisms described below. The Statements were withdrawn on the introduction of the FCA's rules on the conduct of business, but what they contained can still influence, for example, the decisions of the Financial Ombudsman Service (FOS).

Perhaps the most significant self-regulatory device, which operated for the last two decades of the twentieth century, was the Insurance Ombudsman Bureau (IOB), which provided an important complaints mechanism for individual insurance consumers.[78] Although the IOB no longer exists, having been replaced by a statutory body—the Financial Ombudsman Service— about which more will be said shortly, its impact on consumer insurance was so significant that a brief description is still worthwhile.[79]

Concern that the consumer of insurance was getting a somewhat raw deal led three of the biggest insurers to set up the IOB in 1981,[80] and its membership ultimately comprised general insurers covering more than 90 per cent of private non-life policyholders. The service was free to complainants

---

[76] The point was discussed in *James v CGU Insurance Plc* [2002] Lloyd's Rep. I.R. 206 at 219, although that was in the context of a commercial policy where clearly they did not apply.

[77] Note, though, that in respect of the original 1977 Statements, it took some considerable time for some insurers to comply; see the report of the Scottish Consumer Council, *Forms without Fuss*, 1981. For a more recent, although now itself somewhat dated, survey of compliance with the Statements, see *Cadogan and Lewis*, (1992) 21 Anglo-American L.R. 123.

[78] The literature on the IOB and the other similar private Ombudsmen schemes includes James, "The Insurance Ombudsman," Ch.2 in Private Ombudsmen and Public Law (Dartmouth, 1997); Birds, "The reform of insurance law" [1982] J.B.L. 449; Birds and Graham, "Complaints mechanisms in the financial services industry," (1988) 7 C.J.Q. 313; Birds and Graham, *Complaints against Insurance Companies* (University of Sheffield, 1992), reprinted with amendments in [1993] Consum. L. J. 77; Morris and Hamilton, "The Insurance Ombudsman and PIA Ombudsman: a critical comparison" (1996) 47 N.I.L.Q. 119 and Merricks, "The jurisprudence of the Ombudsman" [2001] J.B.L. 654. The IOB published Annual Reports and regular case digests, which provided a fascinating picture of the operation of the modern insurance industry.

[79] For a fuller description, see the 5th edition of this work at pp.5–7. The IOB had a rival—Personal Insurances Arbitration Services (PIAS)—which a minority of insurers used, but very little was known about PIAS as there were no reports on its operation published, mainly because each case was treated as a private arbitration subject to the ordinary rules about arbitration.

[80] See Tyldesley, "The Insurance Ombudsman Bureau: the early history" (2003) 18 Insurance Research and Practice 34.

and the Ombudsman could make awards of up to £100,000 that were bind-ing on member companies, but not on the complainant. The Ombudsman's original terms of reference required him to make decisions in accordance with "good insurance practice" as well as in accordance with the law, and these were later amended so as to require him to make decisions that were "fair and reasonable in all the circumstances". Among other things, this led to the Ombudsman applying flexible remedies when the insured was in breach of his duty of disclosure[81] and sometimes disallowing reliance by insurers on unreasonable terms. Although the IOB was a highly successful institution, its existence was not entirely free from controversy and whether or not the Ombudsman was sufficiently accountable from a public law per-spective was highlighted when it was held by the Court of Appeal that the Ombudsman's decisions were not amenable to judicial review.[82] On the other hand, of the self-regulatory measures that existed in insurance law, the most far-reaching benefits to consumers were almost certainly due to the Insurance Ombudsman.

The statutory FOS is effected under Pt XVI of the Financial Services and Markets Act 2000.[83] There is no doubt that this scheme has clear advantages over its predecessor, not least because it is a compulsory scheme and if neces-sary its awards can be enforced through the courts. Further, the FOS has the statutory right to demand information.[84] The range of insurance consumers that can complain to the ombudsman is wider. It includes small businesses[85] as well as individual consumers, and persons for whose benefit an insurance contract was taken out or a person on whom the legal right to benefit from a claim under a contract of insurance has been devolved by contract, statute or subrogation. The first category clearly includes, for example, a beneficiary under a group life insurance policy and a person named or described as enti-tled to benefit under a household insurance policy effected by their spouse or parent. The second would appear to include someone who has obtained rights under the Third Parties (Rights against Insurers) Acts 1930 or 2010[86] or Pt IV of the Road Traffic Act 1988.[87] Like the IOB, its services are free to complainants. Further, it determines complaints by reference to what is "fair

---

[81] See Ch.7.
[82] *R. v Insurance Ombudsman Bureau, Ex p. Aegon Insurance* [1994] C.L.C. 88. For criti-cism of this decision, see Morris, "The Insurance Ombudsman and judicial review" [1994] L.M.C.L.Q. 358 and James, above, Chs 1 and 2.
[83] See *http://www.financial-ombudsman.org.uk/* [Accessed 27 December 2015].
[84] Financial Services and Markets Act 2000 s.231.
[85] Described as "micro businesses", which are businesses employing fewer than 10 people and having a turnover or annual balance sheet not exceeding £2 million.
[86] See Ch.20.
[87] See Ch.21.

and reasonable in all the circumstances of the case".[88] This is repeated and amplified in the Dispute Resolution Rules issued under the Act, which state that in considering what is fair and reasonable in all the circumstances of the case, the Ombudsman will take into account the relevant law, regulations, regulators' codes and guidance and standards, relevant codes of practice and, where appropriate, what is considered to have been good industry practice at the relevant time.[89] This clearly included the provisions of, for example, the Statements of Insurance Practice. In addition the FOS can hear complaints about the selling of insurance by brokers and other intermediaries. The basic limit on awards is £150,000, but the Ombudsman can recommend that the respondent pay more if he considers that fair compensation requires this and can also award costs reasonably incurred by the complainant. It is not possible for a complainant to accept an award of £150,000 and then sue in court for any loss over that amount. Instead he must reject the award and claim the whole amount in legal proceedings.[90]

A possible disadvantage of the statutory scheme is that the FOS deals with complaints from customers across the whole financial services industry and concern has been expressed that the volume of complaints will lead to its having to rely more on issuing general guidance than dealing with individual complaints with the same amount of attention that the IOB could give.[91] However, it has to be said that there seems to be no evidence of this having happened. Perhaps more significant is the limit on the FOS' compulsory jurisdiction, certainly as regards claims made under policies insuring homes.

1.10   Law Reform

The existence of the various self-regulatory and statutory devices briefly reviewed here meant that there was a body of consumer insurance soft law distinct in part from that applicable to commercial insurances. However,

---

[88] Financial Services and Markets Act 2000 s.228(2).

[89] The Rules also require insurers to have and operate appropriate and effective internal complaint handling procedures, that their literature refers to the FOS, and that they co-operate fully with the Ombudsman. A challenge to the Ombudsman's right to decide on this basis failed in *R. v Financial Ombudsman Services Ltd, Ex p. IFG Financial Services Ltd* [2005] EWHC 1153 (Admin).

[90] *Clark v In Focus Asset Management & Tax Solutions Ltd* [2014] EWCA Civ 118. This may be regarded as unfortunate and a disincentive to use the FOS where the value of a claim may exceed the £150,000 maximum. With respect, the reasoning of the Court of Appeal is not wholly convincing; see Merkin, *Insurance Law Monthly*, July 2014.

[91] For a very useful review, see James and Morris, "The new Financial Ombudsman Service in the United Kingdom—has the second generation got it right?" in *International Perspectives on Consumer Access to Justice*, eds Rickett and Telfer (CUP, 2003), pp.167–195.

there seemed a strong case for actual legal reform of aspects of insurance contract law,[92] and arguably this needed to be done for commercial as well as consumer insurance contracts. The very fact that the law was often not applied in practice might by itself be regarded as a compelling argument for change. Some years after the Law Commission's 1980 Report,[93] in 1997, the National Consumer Council issued a report urging reform,[94] based in part on the pioneering reforms introduced in Australia some years ago[95] as well as reflecting concerns expressed and recommendations made by other consumer bodies. In 2002, the British Insurance Law Association added its voice to this and urged that the Law Commission be given the opportunity to examine the case for reform again.[96]

1.10.1 Law Commissions' project

This pressure bore fruit and the English and Welsh and Scottish Law Commissions have been engaged on the task of reviewing many aspects of insurance contract law, although the scope of their project became somewhat narrower than originally conceived as it developed.[97] The draft Bill in their first Report[98] was enacted more or less verbatim as the Consumer Insurance (Disclosure and Representations) Act 2012. A further Report[99] was published in 2014 and most of its contents were enacted in the Insurance Act 2015. The detail of these Acts is considered in the appropriate subsequent chapters.[100] They were aiming to publish a final Report, dealing in particular with insurable interest, in 2015.

---

[92] Note that the liquidator of a failed insurance company would be bound to apply the law, not practice, in dealing with outstanding claims.

[93] See Report No.104, Cmnd.8064. See Birds, "The reform of insurance law" [1982] J.B.L. 449.

[94] *Insurance Law Reform: the Consumer Case for a Review of Insurance Law.*

[95] Insurance Contracts Act 1984.

[96] See the report issued in September 2002 by BILA. Note also the authoritative calls for reform by senior members of the judiciary, especially Longmore and Rix LJJ, in lectures reproduced as appendices to this report, and Longmore, "An Insurance Contracts Act for a new century?" [2001] L.M.C.L.Q. 356.

[97] See generally at *http://www.lawcom.gov.uk/project/insurance-contract-law/* [Accessed 27 December 2015].

[98] *Consumer Insurance Law: Pre-Contract Disclosure and Misrepresentation*, 2009, Law Com. No.319, Scot Law Com. No.219.

[99] *Insurance Contract Law: Business Disclosure, Warranties, Insurers' Remedies for Fraudulent Claims, and Late Payment*, 2014, Law Com. No.353, Scot Law Com. No.238.

[100] For commentary on the Law Commissions' various recommendations at the relevant time, see Soyer, ed., *Reforming Marine and Commercial Insurance Law* (2008), Informa and the articles in the January 2013 special issue of the *Journal of Business Law.*

1.10.2 European developments

Another important factor in terms of law reform is what might emanate at a European level.[101] The original reference to the Law Commission that resulted in the 1980 Report was principally influenced by the fact that the European Commission had produced a draft Directive that would have sought to harmonise key aspects of insurance contract law. This was thought to be necessary in order to move towards a genuine single European market for insurance. In the event, as described in the next chapter, the European law-makers concentrated on harmonising the regulatory rules regarding insurance business and creating freedom of establishment and freedom of services for insurance providers; the idea of a harmonised insurance contract law disappeared off the agenda. However, in order to truly create a single market, the importance of some degree of harmonisation or at least providing a framework that is an alternative to national laws, an optional legal regime, was recognised again,[102] and a group of European insurance lawyers worked on a Restatement of European Insurance Contract Law.[103] As well as being to some extent a self-standing project in that it was established originally outside any official EU framework, this group was part of the Joint Network on European Private Law,[104] established by the EC Commission under the sixth framework programme. The ultimate aim was to produce a Common Frame of Reference of European Contract Law, which, as well as containing provisions on general contract law, would cover two specific types of contracts, namely sales and insurance.[105] The Restatement Group drafted the Common Frame of Reference on Insurance Contract Law. Having first delivered the basic principles to the European Commission, a more complete version containing comments and notes was published in

[101] See the discussions about whether or not there should be a code on a Europe-wide basis: Basedow, "The case for a European insurance contract code" [2001] J.B.L. 569; Croly and Merkin, "Doubts about insurance codes" [2001] J.B.L. 587; Clarke, "Doubts from the dark side—the case against codes" [2001] J.B.L. 605. For an interesting comparison between English and German insurance law in a European context, see Rühl, "Common law, civil law, and the single European Market for insurances" (2006) 55 I.C.L.Q. 879.

[102] See the Communication from the Commission to the European Parliament and the Council—A more coherent European Contract Law—an Action Plan, COM (2003) 68 (12 Feb), 47–49 and 74.

[103] See *http://restatement.info/* [Accessed 27 December 2015] and Clarke and Heiss, "Towards a European insurance contract law? Recent developments in Brussels" [2006] J.B.L. 600.

[104] See *http://www.copecl.org* [Accessed 27 December 2015].

[105] See Annex I of the Communication of the EC Commission of 11 October 2004, COM [2004] 651 final.

2009.[106] This has been followed by a second edition containing, in addition, rules for some particular categories of insurance contract.[107] However, the prospect of some sort of legislation at the European level seems to have diminished somewhat recently, if not disappeared for the foreseeable future, and, perhaps unfortunately, the work of the Restatement Group may, in the end, be no more than an academic exercise, however useful that might be for some purposes.

---

[106] Basedow, Birds, Clarke, Cousy, Heiss, eds. *Principles of European Insurance Contract Law*. (Munich: Sellier, European Law Publishers, 2009).
[107] Basedow, Birds, Clarke et al eds. *Principles of European Insurance Contract Law*, 2nd edn (Munich: Sellier, European Law Publishers, 2015).

Chapter 2

The Regulation of Insurance

2.0   Introduction

Of the two parties to a simple contract of insurance,[1] the law requires of the insured only that he has an insurable interest in what he insures[2] and that he has the usual capacity to contract.[3] In contrast, a body can act as an insurer only if it satisfies the regulatory requirements established by detailed and complex legislation. These requirements exist because of the very nature of most insurance business. The insured entrusts his money to the insurer, but in return receives only a promise of payment in the event of specified events happening. Regulation has long been necessary in order to ensure so far as possible that insurers are able to meet their promises, that is that they will remain solvent.

However, the detail of the system of financial regulation is beyond the scope of this book.[4] It has also been the subject of many changes since it was first introduced in 1870. Often changes have followed a major failure of an insurer and the latest, referred to briefly below, has resulted from the banking crisis that started in 2007, since banks and other financial service providers are regulated under broadly the same system as insurers. Much of the detail of the system is also based on European Union requirements, with a succession of Directives designed to promote freedom of establishment and, subsequently, freedom of services across Europe. These have now been consolidated in the so-called Solvency II Directive 2009/138/EC. This chapter gives a very brief description of these requirements as they control the provision of insurance business and also considers the rules in the Insurance Conduct of Business Sourcebook that apply both to insurers and to intermediaries.

---

[1] Although there are only two parties to the contract, much insurance business, both in terms of entering into contracts and subsequent dealings thereon, is effected through the agency of an intermediary. The law relating to agency in insurance is considered in Ch.12; the regulation of insurance intermediaries is considered later in this chapter.

[2] This is considered in detail in Ch.3, but note that there are situations where interest is not required at least at the time of contracting.

[3] The detailed law on capacity may be found in any standard text on the law of contract.

[4] For a detailed description, see *Regulation of Insurance in the UK, Ireland and the EU* (London: Sweet & Maxwell). An annotated version of the legislation may be found in the *Encyclopedia of Insurance Law* (London: Sweet & Maxwell).

Financial regulation is now governed by the Financial Services and Markets Act 2000 (the 2000 Act), as amended by the Financial Services Act 2012, and the detailed rules made by the Treasury and the regulatory bodies.[5] There are two regulators: the Prudential Regulation Authority (PRA) acting under the control of the Bank of England and the Financial Conduct Authority (FCA). The PRA has responsibility for the financial regulation of insurance business and the FCA for the conduct of insurance business.

2.1   The Financial Regulation of Insurance Business

The 2000 Act brought the regulation of insurance business under the same umbrella as the regulation of other financial services,[6] although the system retained the features of the system that existed under the previous specific legislation, not least because most of the requirements stem from EU law.[7] An important feature of the 2000 legislation is that it brought Lloyd's of London fully within the regulatory umbrella. The 2000 Act itself provides only the broad structure under which the financial services industry is regulated. It has been augmented by a large volume of secondary legislation and by the PRA and FCA's Handbook, made under Pt X, Ch.1 of the Act. The Handbook is divided into a number of blocks. Those relevant to the regulation of insurance companies under the Act, and the individual components that are also relevant, are as follows.

High Level Standards. This block includes the rules relating to Principles for Businesses; Senior Management Arrangements, Systems and Controls; Threshold Conditions; Statements of Principle and Code of Practice for Approved Persons; The Fit and Proper Test for Approved Persons.

Prudential Standards. This block includes the General Prudential Sourcebook and the Prudential Sourcebook for Insurers.

Business Standards. This block includes the Conduct of Business Sourcebook and the Insurance: Conduct of Business Sourcebook.

Regulatory Processes. This block includes the rules relating to Supervision and Decision Procedure.

---

[5] The copious rules, regulations and other documents are available at *http://fshandbook.info/FS/html/handbook* [Accessed 27 December 2015].

[6] The regulation of the selling of most types of life insurance was already under the same umbrella.

[7] An important feature of modern commercial life is the trend toward "bancassurance", whereby insurance and banking functions are in effect offered by the same financial services group (although legally they have to be distinct entities). This is a Europe-wide if not global occurrence, as is perhaps indicated by the use of the convenient French term.

Redress. This block includes the rules relating to Dispute Resolution: Complaints and Compensation.

2.2   The Development of State Control

State control of insurers began in 1870.[8] It followed the failure some two years previously of two sizeable life insurance companies. The pattern was repeated for many years in the sense that subsequent revisions and extensions of control generally followed some major insurance collapse, which drew attention to the defects in the existing law or the way that it was applied. For example, the circumstances surrounding the liquidation of the Fire, Auto and Marine Insurance Company in the mid-1960s led to a substantial amendment (by Pt II of the Companies Act 1967) of the system then established under the Insurance Companies Act 1958. Even more disastrous was the failure of the "cut-price" motor insurer, the Vehicle and General, in 1971, when overnight approximately one million motorists found themselves without cover.[9] As a result, the 1958 Act was further amended by the Insurance Companies Amendment Act 1973. The legislation was then consolidated in the Insurance Companies Act 1974. However, this Act was premature because it almost immediately had to be amended in order to take account of requirements emanating from the first EC Directive.[10] Since then, the story has been one of changes due to further EU measures; these are briefly described below.[11] In the event that the system of regulation fails to prevent the insolvency of an insurer, measures exist to compensate policyholders; these are briefly described below.

2.3   The Impact of EU Law

As already indicated, EU law has had a significant effect on the regulation of insurance business.[12] The first directives were concerned to establish freedom

---

[8] Life Assurance Companies Act 1870. This and amending statutes until the 1930s required only that insurers deposit a sum of money with the court as security.

[9] The Department of Trade, then in charge of insurance regulation, was severely criticised over this by a Tribunal of Inquiry: 1972 H.C. Papers 133. See Chapman, "The Vehicle & General affair: some reflections for public administration in Britain" (1973) *Public Administration* 273.

[10] The Directive regarding Freedom of Establishment in Non-Life Insurance, No. 73/239 (23 July 1973), concerning the right of insurers from one EC Member State to establish branches or agencies in other Member States. This was followed by the Establishment Directive on Life Business, No. 79/267 (5 March 1979).

[11] For an excellent account, see Andrew McGee, *The Single Market in Insurance: Breaking Down the Barriers* (Dartmouth: 1998).

[12] For a very helpful description of the development of European law in this respect, see *Digital Satellite Warranty Cover Ltd v Financial Services Authority* [2013] UKSC 7 at [7]–[15].

of establishment within the Community, initially with regard to non-life insurance business and then with regard to life insurance. Later directives were concerned with freedom of services across Europe. The various directives are now implemented together by the 2000 Act[13] and the Financial Services and Markets Act 2000 (EEA Passport Rights) Regulations 2001.[14] All the Directives have been consolidated in Directive 2009/138/EC, the so-called Solvency II Directive as amended by Directive 2014/51/EU.[15] Despite this, it seems that true freedom of services, in the sense that insurers from one state sell insurance to persons in another state, has not really happened, at least as far as consumers are concerned. This is probably at least partly attributable to the fact that the directives provide for the applicable law to be that of the consumer's habitual residence and it seems unlikely that insurers are willing to adjust their contracts to cover all the different laws applicable. This factor has led to the increased possibility of some degree of an alternative optional regime of insurance contract law, as discussed in Ch.1.

2.3.1 Freedom of establishment

As far as non-life insurance was concerned, the first directive[16] introduced a uniform system of solvency margins[17] calculated as a percentage of annual premiums or claims (whichever gave the higher result)[18] and prescribed a procedure to be followed in the event that an insurer failed to show possession of the necessary margin.[19] It gave insurers from one Member State the right to establish branches or agencies in other Member States and prescribed, in broad outline, the authorisation procedure to be followed in such cases.[20] There were also provisions[21] as to the regime to be applied to branches and agencies of insurers with their head offices outside the EU (the authorisation of such insurers remaining discretionary). The provisions of the first life directive[22] were in many ways similar to those of the non-life directive. The principle of a solvency margin was again introduced, though in this case based on the insurer's mathematical reserves.[23] The most difficult problem that had to be resolved in the negotiations leading to this directive

---

[13] Sections 31 and 37, and Schs 3 and 4.
[14] SI 2001/2511.
[15] This will be implemented on 1 January 2016.
[16] No.73/239.
[17] The UK had adopted a solvency margin system some years before.
[18] Art.16.
[19] Arts 20 and 22.
[20] Arts 10–12.
[21] Arts 23–29.
[22] No.79/267.
[23] See art.18.

was the existence of "composite" life and non-life insurers in the UK; in contrast, the majority of Member States require life assurance to be carried on by "specialist" life companies not involved in any other class of business. The outcome was that no new composites could be authorised in the UK. Existing composites could continue and set up branches or agencies in other Member States for the conduct of non-life business. If, however, they wish to do life business elsewhere in the Community, they must set up subsidiaries.[24]

2.3.2 Freedom of services

Substantial changes were made to the British legislation then in force in order to implement freedom of services within the EU and the EEA. The Non-life Insurance Services Directive[25] gave non-life insurers, licensed to write insurance business in any EU Member State, the right to offer "large risks"[26] across national frontiers without the need for authorisation. This was followed by the Second Life Directive.[27] These were quickly superseded when in July 1992, the Council of Ministers adopted the Third Non-Life Directive[28] and the Third Life Directive.[29] These took freedom of services to its logical conclusion by introducing the single European licence. An insurer authorised in any Member State is automatically allowed to sell most types of non-life insurance anywhere else in the community, either through a branch or agency in the host state or via direct selling in the host state. The home state controls all its activities and its solvency.[30]

The UK implemented the Third Directives with effect from 1 July 1994. In consequence, as regards EU insurers, there is a distinction between the insurer who carries on business, which requires the company to have a UK

---

[24] Art.13.

[25] No.88/357.

[26] There are three types of large risks, namely (1) broadly, marine, aviation and transit business, (2) credit and suretyship insurance where the policy holder carries on business and (3) property, pecuniary and liability insurances relating to a business carried on by the insured where the business meets two out of three criteria: (a) 250 employees, (b) an annual turnover of 12 million ECU, and (c) a balance sheet total of 6.2 million ECU.

[27] No.90/619.

[28] No.92/49.

[29] No.92/96. The three life insurance directives were consolidated by Directive 2002/83/EC.

[30] Although there is provision for the host state to take action where the home state defaults in so doing. The Directive also requires that no new system of what is called "material control", that is any system for the prior approval of policy terms and premium rates, can be introduced. States that previously had such a system can retain it, but insurers authorised in a Member State that does not exercise such control will not be required to submit policy terms and premium rates to the authorities of any host state that does exercise such control.

branch, and the insurer who merely offers insurance in the UK, but who carries out the relevant paperwork elsewhere; the latter is merely a provider of insurance and not carrying on insurance business in the UK.

An EU insurance company wishing to carry on direct insurance business in the UK[31] must be authorised in its home state in accordance with the relevant provisions of the first Insurance Directives, and its supervisory authority must provide the PRA with a notice containing details of it and a certificate attesting to its margin of solvency and indicating the classes of business for which it is authorised. The details required are the name of the company and its authorised agent, the address of its UK branch, a scheme of operations prepared in accordance with any requirements of its supervisory authority and, in the case of a motor insurer, confirmation that it has become a member of the Motor Insurers' Bureau (MIB).[32] In addition, either the PRA must have informed the supervisory authority of the conditions which, in the general good, must be complied with by the company in carrying on insurance business through the branch, or two months must have lapsed from the date of receipt of the notice and certificate.

EU insurers wishing to provide insurance in the UK must similarly be authorised to provide the relevant class or classes of business in their home state and are subject to generally similar conditions. So, their supervisory authority must provide a notice and a certificate, the only material difference being that in this case there will be no branch details or authorised agent.

In respect of any EU insurer operating in the UK market, the PRA has many of the general powers that it has in relation to UK companies. Specifically, it has the power to prevent the disposal of assets by the insurer, powers to obtain information, the general power to protect policyholders if requested to do so by the home state supervisor, a general power to intervene for the breach of any relevant legal provision and the power to withdraw recognition.

2.4   Authorisation to Carry on Insurance Business

Insurers are authorised by reference to the classes of general insurance business and long-term insurance business defined in Sch.1 to the Financial Services and Markets Act 2000 (Regulated Activities) Order 2001 (the Regulated Activities Order).[33] There is a general prohibition, in s.19, on carrying on a regulated activity in the UK unless the person in question is an

---

[31] The requirements for insurers wishing to effect reinsurance business are similar.
[32] As to the MIB, see Ch.21.
[33] SI 2001/544, as amended. There are 18 classes of general business and 9 classes of long-term business.

authorised or exempt person.[34] By s.22, an activity is a regulated activity if it is an activity of a kind specified by the Treasury, which is carried on by way of business and relates to an investment of a specified kind. Schedule 2 to the Act includes "rights under a contract of insurance" as an indicative regulated activity and this is confirmed by art.75 of the Regulated Activities Order. Article 10 of the Regulated Activities Order amplifies this by separately specifying "effecting a contract of insurance as principal" and "carrying out a contract of insurance as principal" as regulated activities. The words "carrying out" connote some element of continuity, as opposed to mere isolated transactions,[35] but it has been held on the construction of a similar statutory prohibition that a single transaction may afford sufficient evidence of "carrying on business".[36] Further, it was held that the equivalent prohibition in s.2 of the Insurance Companies Act 1982 was contravened by the negotiation of a prospective insurance contract without authorisation.[37]

The separate specification, in art.10 of the Regulated Activities Order, of "effecting" and "carrying out" contracts of insurance reflects the fact that insurance business contains two principal elements, first, the negotiation and conclusion of contracts and, secondly, the execution of those contracts by, in particular, paying claims.[38] It also makes it clear that if either or both these activities take place in the UK, business is being carried on here.[39] On the other hand, if neither activity takes place here, business is not carried on here and the fact that insured property or insured persons may be located in the UK is irrelevant.[40] In this respect, UK law is sharply distinguished from that of many other countries, where its ambit is determined by the "situs of the risk"—a concept unknown to our law. Activities in the UK that are customarily those undertaken by insurance brokers acting as such were held not to

---

[34] For the consequences of acting without permission, see ss.20 and 23; no transaction is void or unenforceable, but there is a limited right to compensation for anyone who suffers loss as a result of the contravention. Contravening the general prohibition is a criminal offence. For discussions of these remedial consequences, see *Whiteley Insurance Consultants* [2008] EWHC 1782 (Ch); [2009] Lloyd's Rep. I.R. 212.

[35] See *Smith v Anderson* (1880) 15 Ch D 247 at 277.

[36] *Cornelius v Phillips* [1918] A.C. 199.

[37] *R. v Wilson* [1997] 1 All E.R. 119.

[38] See *Re AA Mutual Insurance Co Ltd* [2004] EWHC 2430 (Ch); [2005] 2 BCLC 8 at [14].

[39] In the earlier insurance companies legislation, "effecting and carrying out" appeared as one phrase, although this was interpreted disjunctively: *Bedford Ins Co Ltd v Instituto de Resseguros do Brasil* [1985] Q.B. 966; *Stewart v Oriental Fire & Marine Ins Co Ltd* [1985] Q.B. 988; *Phoenix General Ins Co of Greece SA v Administration Asiguraliror de Stat* [1988] Q.B. 216. See also Lord Goff of Chieveley in *Scher v Policyholders Protection Board* [1994] 2 A.C. 57 at 99; see also Lord Donaldson MR in the Court of Appeal in the latter case at 70.

[40] See *Re United General Commercial Ins Corp* [1927] 2 Ch 51.

be evidence of the carrying on of insurance business in a decision under the former legislation.[41] The specific inclusion of the phrase "as principal" in the current legislation reinforces this. However, someone who ostensibly acts as agent for an insurer from which it had no authority or on behalf of unnamed and non-existent insurers is carrying on a regulated activity.[42]

People are authorised under the 2000 Act if they have a Pt IV permission, are an EEA firm with passport rights or are otherwise authorised by or under the Act. There are two general exemptions. The first relates to trades unions and employers' organisations providing provident or strike benefits exclusively for their own members.[43] The second exempts a former Lloyd's underwriter who ceased to be an underwriting member of Lloyd's before 24 December 1996 from needing authorisation to carry out contracts of insurance.[44] The Society of Lloyd's is an authorised person under the Act.[45] Insurers who were authorised under ss.3 or 4 of the 1982 Act continue to be authorised under the 2000 Act.[46] Vehicle breakdown insurance does not require authorisation.[47]

Application for Pt IV permission to carry on a regulated activity, including insurance, under s.40 of the 2000 Act must be made in accordance with the Threshold Conditions in the High Level Standards part of the Handbook. An application may not cover both long-term and general business unless the applicant's business will be restricted to reinsurance or the general business is restricted to accident and/or health insurance, and it must specify the classes of business to be carried on. Schedule 6 to the 2000 Act specifies the threshold conditions that, under s.41, the regulator must ensure that an applicant will satisfy. As they apply to insurance business, they are as follows:

1.   The applicant must be a body corporate, a registered friendly society or a member of Lloyd's.

2.   The insurer's head office and registered office must be within the UK.

---

[41] *Re a Company (No.007816 of 1994)* [1995] 2 B.C.L.C. 539. It would clearly be otherwise if the brokers were authorised to take all effective decisions, including underwriting decisions: see *A Re Company (No.007923 of 1994) (No.2)* [1995] 1 B.C.L.C. 594 and *Secretary of State for Trade and Industry v Great Western Assurance Co SA* [1997] 2 B.C.L.C. 685, on appeal from the first-mentioned decision.

[42] *Re Whiteley Insurance Consultants* [2008] EWHC 1782 (Ch); [2009] Lloyd's Rep. I.R. 212.

[43] The Financial Services and Markets Act 2000 (Exemption) Order 2001 (SI 2001/1201), made under s.38 of the 2000 Act, para.43.

[44] Above, para.46.

[45] Section 315(1).

[46] The Financial Services and Markets Act 2000 (Transitional Provisions) (Authorised Persons, etc.) Order 2001 SI/2636 art.14.

[47] Regulated Activities Order art.12.

3. If the insurer has close links with another person, being either a parent or subsidiary of another[48] or where there is a 20 per cent shareholding by one company in the other, the Authority must be satisfied that these links are not likely to prevent effective supervision of the insurer.

4. The resources of the insurer must be adequate in relation to the regulated activities in question.

5. The applicant must be a fit and proper person, having regard to connections with any other person, the nature of the regulated activity and the need to ensure that its affairs are conducted soundly and prudently. Enquiries by the regulator will be on a case-by-case basis and relevant issues include whether the insurer conducts its business with integrity and in compliance with proper standards, has a competent and prudent management and conducts its affairs with the exercise of due care, skill and diligence.

2.5   Continuing Requirements

The legislation and rules made under it impose a number of continuing requirements on insurers, the most important of which are as follows.

2.5.1 Maintaining solvency margins

The concept of the solvency margin has been central to insurance company supervision for many years. Simply, insurers are required to maintain a minimum amount whereby their assets exceed their liabilities. It is hoped that, by this means, insurers will never approach actual insolvency. The actual calculation of the margin required is a complex business, involving, in addition, the application of statutory requirements as to the valuation of assets and liabilities.

2.5.2 Non-insurance activities

There is an important prohibition in the *Prudential Sourcebook for Insurers*. Rule 1. 5.13 states that an insurer must not carry on any commercial business in the UK or elsewhere other than insurance business and activities directly arising from that business. However, contravention of rules made by the Authority is not an offence[49] nor does it make any transaction void or

---

[48] As defined in the Companies Act 2006 Pt 38; see s.420(1) of the 2000 Act.
[49] Section 138E(1).

unenforceable.[50] This clarifies a point that was uncertain under the statutory provision replaced by the rule.[51]

2.5.3 Localisation and matching of assets

There is power for the regulator to make regulations to introduce into the law the provisions of the EU Directive requiring that the reserves of an insurer required to meet known and estimated liabilities must be covered by assets situated in the country where the business is carried on.

2.5.4 Accounts, actuarial investigations and statements

More detailed accounts are required of insurance companies than of registered companies generally, and these must be deposited with the regulator. Companies that carry on long-term business are subject to actuarial investigation every year, and must appoint their own qualified actuary. All companies are required to prepare periodical statements of business in respect of each class of insurance business they underwrite.

2.5.5 Separation of assets

Companies that combine long-term and general insurance business must maintain separate funds in respect of the different kinds of business, and the assets representing the long-term fund are available only for that business and, on a winding up, are available only to meet liabilities attributable to that business. In addition, a company is prohibited from declaring a dividend when its long-term liabilities exceed its long-term assets. These are important provisions aimed obviously at protecting the policyholders with life insurance.

2.5.6 Changes in management and control

There are detailed provisions in Pt XII of the 2000 Act laying down the procedures to be followed when someone acquires, increases or reduces their control of an authorised person including an insurer.

---

[50] Section 138E(2). A private person who suffers loss as a result of a contravention may have an action for damages for breach of statutory duty: s.138D.

[51] The provision was s.16 of the Insurance Companies Act 1982, which made no provision for the effect of breach. In *Fuji Finance Inc v Aetna Life Insurance Co Ltd* [1997] Ch 173, reversing [1995] Ch 122, differing views were expressed as to whether or not a contract entered into in breach of s.16 was unlawful and unenforceable on public policy grounds.

2.6   The Protection of Policyholders

In the event that the regulatory structure established to ensure the solvency of insurance companies fails, there has for some years been a mechanism to ensure that policyholders are largely protected financially. Originally this was by virtue of the provisions of the Policyholders Protection Acts 1975 and 1997.[52] This particular legislation, though, was replaced by the general scheme for compensating consumers of failed financial services providers under Pt XV of the 2000 Act.[53] Like the scheme under the 1975 and 1997 Acts, it does not apply to protect the policyholders of insurance companies that acted without authorisation, nor does it apply to Lloyd's policyholders.

Section 212 of the 2000 Act requires the regulator to establish a body corporate, the scheme manager, to exercise the functions under Pt XV; this body is Financial Services Compensation Scheme Ltd (FSCS). Section 213 requires the regulator to establish the scheme where "relevant persons", including authorised insurers, are unable, or are likely to be unable, to satisfy claims against them. Sections 214–217 indicate the rules that may be made to give effect to the scheme, and these are contained in the Compensation part of the Redress part of the PRA/FCA Handbook. The scheme is funded by levies on authorised firms in accordance with the detailed rules in Ch.13 of the Compensation Rules.

A person is entitled to compensation where an insurer has failed only where continuation of cover cannot be secured. With respect to long-term insurance, FSCS must make arrangements to secure continuity of such insurance where it is reasonably practicable to do so and one of the following has occurred:

(a)   the insurer has passed a resolution for a creditors' voluntary winding up;

(b)   the insurer's home state regulator has determined that it appears unable to meet claims and has no early prospect of being able to do so;

(c)   a liquidator or administrator, or provisional liquidator or interim manager has been appointed;

(d)   the court has made an order for winding up or administration; or

(e)   a voluntary arrangement has been approved.

---

[52] The original Act was introduced following the spectacular and very public failure of a large life insurance company. It has been used quite a lot; e.g. it seems that there have been over 30 relevant failures since 1990.

[53] With transitional provisions governing claims made before the commencement of the 2000 Act.

The arrangements contemplated may be securing or facilitating the transfer of the long-term business to another insurer or securing the issue of substitute policies by another insurer.[54]

Different rules apply as regards any type of insurance issued by an insurer in financial difficulties. This is defined as where an insurer is in provisional liquidation, has been proved in winding up proceedings to be unable to pay its debts or is the subject of an application under s.895 of the Companies Act 2006 for a compromise or arrangement to reduce or defer payment of the liabilities or benefits under its policies, or where the regulator determines that it is unlikely to be able to satisfy claims protected under the scheme. Here, FSCS must take such measures to safeguard insureds on such terms (including terms reducing or deferring payment of any liabilities or benefits) as it considers appropriate if, in its opinion, the cost is likely to be less than the cost of paying compensation. These measures may amount to transferring the insurance business to another insurer or assisting the insurer in difficulties to enable it to continue to effect or carry out contracts of insurance. However, before taking these measures in respect of a long-term insurance contract, FSCS must reduce the insured's interest in the contract to 90 per cent of what would otherwise have been payable and similarly reduce the amount of future premiums.

The persons who may benefit from compensation or continuity of cover under the scheme are called "eligible claimants". As far as long-term insurance is concerned, this category comprises any person other than directors or managers (and their close relatives) of the insurer in default, bodies corporate in the same group, five per cent shareholders of the insurer or of any body corporate in the same group, the auditors of the insurer in default or of any body corporate in the same group or the appointed actuary of the insurer in default, persons who in the opinion of the FSCS are responsible or have contributed to the insurer's default, and persons whose claim arises from transactions in connection with which they have been convicted of an offence of money laundering.

As far as general insurance is concerned, claims under a reinsurance contract, a Lloyd's policy and an insurance contract relating to aircraft, ships, goods in transit, aircraft liability, and liability of ships or credit are totally excluded. Subject to this, eligible claimants are essentially:

(1)   private persons;

(2)   any business qualifying as small at the date of commencement of the contract[55];

---

[54] The statutory provisions governing the transfer of insurance business are described in *MacGillivray on Insurance Law*, 13th edn (London: Sweet & Maxwell, 2015), Ch.36.

[55] Basically any business with an annual turnover of less than £1 million.

(3) a large partnership in respect of a relevant general insurance contract entered into before 1 December 2001;

(4) a third party whose claim arises under the Third Parties (Rights against Insurers) Act 1930[56]; and

(5) any person in respect of a liability subject to compulsory insurance, that is under the Riding Establishments Act 1964, the Employers' Liability (Compulsory Insurance) Act 1969[57] and the Road Traffic Act 1988.[58]

A person is eligible for compensation or continuity of cover in respect of a protected claim, which is a claim under a protected contract of insurance. It is irrelevant that a policy evidencing the contract has not been issued, if the FSCS is satisfied that a person is insured under a contract with an insurance undertaking. The Compensation Rules distinguish between contracts issued after and before 1 December 2001.[59]

Contracts issued after this date must relate to a protected risk or commitment under one of the following three types of contract. The first is a contract issued by an insurer in default through an establishment in the UK where the risk or commitment is situated in an EEA State, the Channel Islands or the Isle of Man. The second is a contract issued by an authorised insurance company through an establishment in another EEA State where the risk or commitment is situated in the UK. The third is a contract issued through an establishment in the Channel Islands or the Isle of Man where the risk or commitment is situated in the UK, the Channel Islands or the Isle of Man.[60]

Where a contract was issued before 1 December 2001 but the insurer defaults thereafter, it qualifies for protection if: (1) it was a relevant general insurance contract, a contract of credit insurance or a long-term insurance contract; and (2) either: (a) it was a "UK policy at the beginning of the liquidation" for the purposes of the Policyholders Protection Act 1975; or (b) if it is a contract of employer's liability insurance entered into before 1 January 1972[61] and the claim was agreed after the default of the insurer, the risk or commitment was situated in the UK. UK policies under the 1975 Act are policies under which at any time the performance by the insurer of any of its

---

[56] See Ch.20. The Act is due to be replaced by the 2010 Act with the same title, as explained in that chapter.

[57] See Ch.22.

[58] See Ch.21.

[59] The date when the 2000 Act was brought into force.

[60] There are detailed rules determining where a risk or commitment is situated.

[61] The date the Employer's Liability (Compulsory Insurance) Act 1969 came into force.

obligations under the contract evidenced by the policy would constitute the carrying on by the insurer of insurance business of any class in the UK. This means that a policy is a UK policy if, had any of the obligations under the contract evidenced by the policy been performed at the relevant time, such performance would have formed part of an insurance business which the insurer was authorised to carry on in the UK, whether or not such obligation(s) would have been performed in the UK.[62] Thus, in *Scher v Policyholders Protection Board*, it was held that professional indemnity policies issued to doctors, dentists and lawyers in North America, which were placed and administered in the UK, were UK policies, even though the indemnities were payable in North America. The performance of the contract had to be looked at as a whole and it was not possible to separate the payment of proceeds from the other obligations of the insurers.

The FSCS is obliged to treat the following liabilities of an insurance undertaking as giving rise to claims under a protected contract of insurance:

(a) if the contract has not commenced, premiums paid to the insurance undertaking;

(b) proceeds of a long-term insurance contract that has matured or been surrendered but which have not yet been passed to the claimant;

(c) the unexpired portion of any premium in relation to relevant general insurance contracts; and

(d) claims by persons entitled to the benefit of a judgment under s.151 of the Road Traffic Act 1988.

As far as the amount of compensation is concerned, 100 per cent of the whole claim must be paid in respect of a liability subject to compulsory insurance. As regards claims under the Third Parties (Rights against Insurers) Act in respect of employer's liability insurance before it was compulsory, 90 per cent of the claim must be paid. In all other cases of general insurance, 100 per cent of the first £2,000 and 90 per cent of the remainder of the claim must be paid. In respect of long-term insurance, 100 per cent of the first £2,000 must be paid together with at least 90 per cent of the remaining value of the policy, including future benefits declared before the date of the insurer's default. The same principle applies to cases where continuity of insurance cover is secured.

---

[62] *Scher v Policyholders Protection Board (No.2)* [1994] 2 A.C. 57.

2.7   Regulating the Conduct of Insurance Business

The requirements considered hitherto in this chapter have been concerned with seeking to ensure that insured persons are protected against insurers that get into financial difficulties. As was indicated in Ch.1, the scope of regulation under the 2000 Act was enlarged in 2005 when the Insurance Conduct of Business Rules (ICOB) were introduced; these were replaced in 2008 by the Insurance Conduct of Business Sourcebook (ICOBS).[63] ICOBS is more principles-based and less detailed than ICOB was. These rules apply to general insurance, which is essentially non-life insurance, and to what is called pure protection insurance, which are essentially life insurance contracts of a short-term duration and with no surrender value.[64] The particular impetus for this was the need to implement the Insurance Mediation Directive,[65] requiring the statutory regulation of insurance intermediaries, but the rules go further than that and apply generally to the conduct of general insurance business, on the ground that customers of insurers selling directly should receive the same level of protection, although some of the detailed provisions apply only to insurers and some only to intermediaries.[66] Distinctions are also made in a number of the rules between the requirements in dealing with retail customers (that is mainly private individuals) and commercial customers. It has been plausibly argued[67] that ICOBS represents a significant reform of insurance contract law, although, rather curiously, without reference to many of the general criticisms of insurance law that have been made over the years.[68]

After its general application provision (ICOBS 1), ICOBS contains

(1)   general matters, including rules on communications with customers and prohibiting unfair inducements (ICOBS 2);

---

[63] It is noteworthy that a breach of these rules may be actionable under s.138D of the 2000 Act, which provides an action for breach of statutory duty for "private persons" who suffer loss through breach of FCA rules by an authorised person. See the excellent discussion of this and the regime generally by McMeel, "The FSA's insurance conduct of business regime: a revolution in (consumer) insurance law?" [2005] L.M.C.L.Q. 186, although that account deals with the position under ICOB rather than ICOBS. Time will tell whether s.138D confers a significant weapon available against an insurer. The detailed ICOBS rules and commentary thereon can be found in the *Encyclopedia of Insurance Law*.

[64] ICOBS does not apply to commercial insurances of large risks, reinsurance and group policies. Most forms of life insurance are covered by the rules on investments generally and covered by the general Conduct of Business Sourcebook.

[65] 2002/92/EC. There was also the need to implement the Directive on distance marketing of financial services (2002/65/EC).

[66] Note also the statutory complaints mechanism for many insurance customers, as described in 1.9.1.

[67] See McMeel, [2005] L.M.C.L.Q. 186.

[68] As to reform generally, see 1.10.

(2) rules regarding distance communications, implementing the relevant EU Directive[69] (ICOBS 3);

(3) general requirements for insurance intermediaries, including disclosure of their status and regarding the disclosure of fees and commission (ICOBS 4);

(4) rules on identifying client needs and advising (ICOBS 5);

(5) rules on product information to ensure that customers have the necessary information to make an informed choice about whether or not to buy a specific insurance contract and whether a contract continues to meet their needs (ICOBS 6);

(6) rules conferring cancellation rights on retail customers (ICOBS 7); and

(7) rules regarding the handling of claims, including rules restricting insurers' rights to repudiate a claim for non-disclosure, misrepresentation or breach of warranty (ICOBS 8).

Some of the more significant detailed provisions that are not referred to in later chapters are as follows. Firms must take reasonable steps to ensure that all communications with all customers are clear, fair and not misleading.[70] Firms must take reasonable steps to ensure that they do not offer, give, solicit or accept inducements which may conflict to a material extent with their duties to their customers; this is particularly directed at, for example, situations concerning insurers and intermediaries.[71] Exclusions of liability under the rules are prohibited.[72] There are specific provisions about distance contracts with retail customers, including ensuring that a paper copy of the terms and conditions must be provided at the customer's request.[73] Distance contracts are any where there is no face to face dealing, which will apply to all situations where negotiations are conducted on the telephone or over the internet, something that is increasingly common these days. Intermediaries must not disclose their fees to their retail customers,[74] and commercial customers are entitled to know the amount of commission that an intermediary would receive.[75]

---

[69] 2002/92/EC. There was also the need to implement the Directive on distance marketing of financial services (2002/65/EC).
[70] ICOBS 2.2.
[71] ICOBS 2.3.
[72] ICOBS 2.5.
[73] ICOBS 3.1.16.
[74] ICOBS 4.3.
[75] ICOBS 4.4.

There are rules about what is called "financial promotion", which means the advertising and marketing of insurance to ensure that it is fair, clear and not misleading.[76] The rules on advising and selling standards will apply especially to intermediaries who must, among other things, disclose the basis on which they recommend a particular insurance product on the basis of an analysis of the market, from a limited number of insurers or from a single insurer and who are under a duty to seek out information from a customer about their circumstances and objectives. These will clearly be relevant in assessing whether an intermediary can be liable for negligent advice.[77] The product disclosure requirements of ICOBS 6 and the cancellation rights conferred by ICOBS 7 are considered in Ch.5.

The restrictions on the legal rights of insurers in ICOBS 8 are considered in Ch.9.[78] More generally the rules provide detailed requirements on claims handling to ensure that they are handled fairly and settled promptly. Insurers must provide all customers with reasonable guidance to help them to make a claim and appropriate information on its progress.[79] Retail customers are given specific protection, which is briefly considered in Ch.14.

---

[76] ICOBS 2.2. See also the general prohibition on financial promotion other than by authorised persons under s.21 of the 2000 Act.

[77] See Ch.12.

[78] Note here the general rule that insurers must not unreasonably reject a claim: ICOBS 8.1.1.

[79] ICOBS 8.1.1.

CHAPTER 3

INSURABLE INTEREST

3.0

Insurable interest is a basic requirement of any contract of insurance unless it can be, and is, lawfully waived. At a general level, this means that the party to the insurance contract who is the insured or policyholder must have a particular relationship with the subject matter of the insurance, whether that is a life or property or a liability to which he might be exposed. The absence of the required relationship will render the contract illegal, void or simply unenforceable, or prevent a claim under it, depending on the type of insurance. We have already stressed how there are many essential differences between life and other insurances,[1] and the law regarding insurable interest is one situation where the differences can be crucial. A brief examination of the history of the insurable interest requirement[2] reveals this.

3.1   History of the Requirement

Simply, a contract of life insurance was enforceable at common law despite the absence of any relationship between the insured and the life insured, and even in the face of judicial reluctance. The reason for this was that wagers in general were legally enforceable[3] and thus the courts had no option but to enforce wagers in the form of life insurance contracts. An increase in these practices, which were clearly distasteful[4] and which indeed could serve as an inducement to murder, led to growing concern and, ultimately, legislative action in the form of the Life Assurance Act 1774 (the 1774 Act).

As far as other types of insurance were concerned, namely indemnity contracts, there was abundant authority recognising as valid marine policies without interest,[5] which, as has been seen earlier, were the other common

---

[1] See 1.2.1 and 1.2.2.

[2] For more detail, see *MacGillivray on Insurance Law*, 13th edn (London: Sweet & Maxwell, 2015), Ch.1.

[3] See, e.g. *March v Piggott* (1771) 2 Burr. 2862, a bet as to which father of the parties would live longer. In certain instances wagers were not enforceable, particularly where public policy intervened or where the matter was regarded as a waste of the court's time.

[4] See the preamble to the Life Assurance Act 1774.

[5] See *MacGillivray on Insurance Law*, 13th edn (London: Sweet & Maxwell, 2015), para.1–20.

form of insurance at the time. However, statute, in the form of the Marine Insurance Act 1745, put a stop to this practice. The exact position with regard to non-marine indemnity policies is not clear. By analogy with life and marine policies, the mere fact of there being no interest, at least at the date of the contract, should not have affected the validity of such policies. However, as such contracts were and are, in most cases,[6] contracts only to indemnify the insured against a loss he actually suffers, the insured could only recover if he showed that he had suffered a loss, in other words that he had an interest at the time of loss.[7] Further, there is authority concerning a fire policy on buildings,[8] which precedes any statutory requirement, that interest was required by the common law both at the date of the contract and at the date of the loss.

In any event, the legislature intervened with a series of statutes, finally rendering all contracts by way of gaming or wagering void under s.18 of the Gaming Act 1845, although this provision was repealed by s.334(1) of the Gambling Act 2005. The details of the relevant provisions will be examined shortly, but it is useful at this stage briefly to summarise how the various statutory provisions apply to the various types of insurance:

(i) marine policies are now governed by the Marine Insurance Act 1906, by s.4 of which such policies without interest are void[9];

(ii) life policies and policies providing for the payment of fixed sums in the event of personal injury are governed by the 1774 Act and a failure to show interest renders a policy illegal[10];

(iii) all other policies except those on "goods and merchandises"[11] used to be regarded as covered by the Life Assurance Act, despite the misleading short title, but this is not now regarded as the modern position[12];

(iv) in respect of policies on goods, there is clearly no statutory requirement of insurable interest as such. The provision that used to strike down any goods policy which was really a wager[13] has been

---

[6] See further Ch.13.
[7] *Lynch v Dalzell* (1729) 4 Bro.P.C. 431.
[8] *Sadler's Co v Badcock* (1743) 2 Atk. 554.
[9] But not illegal: *Edwards (John) & Co v Motor Union Insurance Co* [1922] 2 K.B. 249.
[10] *Harse v Pearl Life Assurance Co* [1904] 1 K.B. 558; see 3.4.1.
[11] Section 4 of the 1774 Act expressly exempts these.
[12] Though it can still be regarded as a controversial question and is considered further later.
[13] See e.g. *Newbury International Ltd v Reliance National (UK) Ltd* [1994] 1 Lloyd's Rep. 83.

repealed,[14] but it seems that the Marine Insurance Act 1788 still technically requires that every goods policy contain the name of a person interested therein.[15]

It is conventional to examine quite separately the detail of the requirement of insurable interest in life and similar insurances on the one hand and in property and other indemnity insurances on the other, and this is the basic way in which this chapter will proceed. However, it should be pointed out that the decision of the Court of Appeal in *Feasey v Sun Life Assurance Corp of Canada*[16] adopted an approach to the question of the meaning of insurable interest that appears, at least in part, to merge the requirements. This decision is examined in detail later.[17] Further, one general point should be stressed at this stage, which is that the strict legal requirements may in some instances be honoured more in the breach than the observance, particularly in the field of life insurance. Illustrations of this are certain policies insuring the lives of children and some group insurances of employees. There is no justification for this state of affairs and detailed examples and suggestions for reform will be made at the appropriate stages. The Law Commissions have been examining insurable interest as part of their project and further space is devoted to this question later in this chapter.

3.2   Insurable Interest in Life Insurance[18]

Section 1 of the Life Assurance Act 1774 requires the insured to have an insurable interest in the life insured. The other relevant provisions of the Act require the names of persons interested to be inserted in the policy (s.2) and declare that when the insured has an interest, he can recover no more than the amount of the value of his interest (s.3). These provisions raise four basic questions: the time at which interest is required; the nature of insurable interest; attempted evasions and the meaning of s.2; and the effect of a policy without interest.

---

[14] The provision (the Gaming Act 1845 s.18) was repealed by the Gambling Act 2005 s.334(1).

[15] This Act applied to land policies on goods as well as marine policies. It was repealed by the 1906 Act but only in so far as it related to marine risks (see Sch.2). It is a matter for doubt how far the requirement is ever consciously heeded. Certainly purely oral insurance policies on goods are recognised as valid despite it (see Ch.5).

[16] *Feasey v Sun Life Assurance Corp of Canada* [2003] EWCA Civ 885; [2003] Lloyd's Rep. I.R. 637.

[17] See 3.5.

[18] Life insurance for these purposes includes any insurance where there is some cover provided in the event of the death of the life insured, even if the cover is no greater than the surrender value of the policy at any time: *Fuji Finance Inc v Aetna Life Insurance Ltd* [1996] 4 All E.R. 608.

3.3 The Time When Interest is Required in Life Insurance

It is convenient to consider this first, simply because it is the most straight-forward question. There can be little doubt that s.1 of the Act on its own can be read as requiring interest at the time a policy is effected, but no more. However, s.3 of the Act, which refers to the insured recovering only the value of his interest, might be thought to require interest at the time of loss, that is at the date of the death of the life insured. This was the decision in the old case of *Godsall v Boldero*,[19] which held, in effect, that a policy by a creditor on the life of his debtor was an indemnity policy because s.3 permitted recovery in language appropriate to the concept of indemnity against a loss.

However, *Godsall v Boldero* was overruled in the landmark case of *Dalby v India and London Life Assurance Co*,[20] a decision that has stood unchallenged for many years and which established, beyond doubt, that it is necessary for the insured to have an interest only at the time the policy is effected. The *Dalby* case was not strictly a case of life insurance, but rather of the reinsurance of a life policy.[21] The claimant was the director of a company which had insured the life of the Duke of Cambridge, and which reinsured the risk with the defendant. The original policies were cancelled, but the claimant kept paying the premiums on the reinsurance policy until the Duke died. The defendant then denied liability on the ground that the claimant had no interest in the Duke's life at the date of his death, having himself nothing to pay out on it. The Exchequer Chamber found for the claimant, holding that s.3 of the 1774 Act applied only to require the insured to value his interest at the date of effecting the policy. As s.1 was satisfied, because the claimant did have interest at the time he reinsured, and as there was no common law requirement that the claimant prove interest at the date of loss, he was enti-tled to recover.

While there are difficulties with regard to the construction of s.3, which looks as though it refers to the time of loss, and while the decision in *Dalby* could lead to certain mischief to which we shall refer, there is no doubt that the decision is totally justifiable. To hold the contrary would be against justice and fair dealing, as the premiums paid on a life policy are calculated on actuarial principles according to the probable duration of the life. They are fixed just as the sum payable on death is fixed. There is no comparison

---

[19] *Godsall v Boldero* (1807) 9 East 72, followed in *Henson v Blackwell* (1845) 4 Hare 434.

[20] *Dalby v India and London Life Assurance Co* (1854) 15 C.B. 365. In fact the insurers in *Godsall v Boldero* repented and paid out, following the outcry against them after the decision: see Lord Blackburn in *Burnand v Rodocanachi* (1882) 1 App.Cas. 333 at 340–341.

[21] See also on this, following *Dalby, Southern Cross Assurance Co Ltd v Australian Provincial Assurance Association Ltd* (1935) 53 C.L.R. 618 (High Court of Australia).

with the assessment of a risk under an indemnity policy, even though it can hardly be denied that certain life policies are intended in effect to indemnify against a possible loss, a point we shall return to. To allow an insurer who has assessed the risk under a life policy in the usual way to resile from its bargain for these reasons would be quite absurd. Further, many forms of life insurance today are in reality investments where the actual insurance element is a relatively minor part of the benefits provided, and there is very little expectation that death will occur during the currency of the policy.[22]

3.3.1 Consequences of Dalby

However, the decision in *Dalby* has consequences that may be regarded as mischievous. These will arise only where the insured is not also himself the life insured or where an insured assigns[23] a policy on his own life to a party with no interest. An example will illustrate the point. As will be seen, creditors may insure their debtors' lives for the amount of their debts. Indeed it is not uncommon for financiers to effect group policies on their debtors. The debt may be repaid shortly thereafter, yet the creditor may keep up the policy until the debtor dies, which may be many years later. Is there not an element of wagering here? One of the reasons for requiring insurable interest has been said[24] to be the removal of an inducement to murder the life insured; yet the creditor has a strong motive for murder.[25] In essence, this sort of policy is surely intended to indemnify creditors against the loss they may suffer by debtors not repaying their debts before they die, and the same can be said of other common types of policy, for example, by employers on the lives of their employees.[26] It could be suggested that once the insured ceases to have an interest in the life insured, the latter should have the option of taking over the policy for his own benefit, subject to some compensation to the insured

---

[22] For an example of the latter point, see *Fuji Finance Inc v Aetna Life Insurance Ltd* [1996] 4 All E.R. 608, where the sum insured on death was the same as the surrender value of the policy at any time, and the potential return if the switching of investments had continued as successfully as it had been effected up to the date the policy was surrendered, was the gross national product of the UK for 460,000 years! The policy was surrendered for a mere £1,100,000!

[23] As to assignment of a life policy, see 19.2.

[24] See *Worthington v Curtis* [1875] 1 Ch. D. 419; McGovern, "Homicide and succession to property," (1969) 68 Mich.L.Rev. 65 at 78.

[25] Of course one would hope that the creditor would be deterred by the criminal consequences, but not all murders are solved. Should the civil law permit the survival of an inducement to murder?

[26] See the Canadian case of *Re Chatiam and Packall Packaging Inc* (1998) 38 O.R. (3d) 401, where the principle was applied in a case of "key man" insurance and the Ontario Court of Appeal refused to compel the insured to transfer the policy to the employee.

in respect of the premiums he has paid.[27] Thus, in effect, the consent of the life insured would be necessary for the continuation of a policy where interest had ceased. This is an area that would merit careful reconsideration, although there is no indication that the Law Commissions will recommend any change to this aspect of the law.

3.4 The Nature of Insurable Interest in Life Insurance

Despite stipulating that an interest is required, the 1774 Act does not say, in so many words, exactly what constitutes an insurable interest in a life. However, the provisions of s.3, to which we have already adverted, indicate that it means a pecuniary or financial interest, because the section refers to "the amount of the value of the interest of the insured". In general this has been the approach adopted by the courts.

There are two cases, though, where insurable interest is presumed and where s.3 is regarded as inapplicable, the reason being that they are outside the mischief of wagering that the 1774 Act was passed to prevent.[28] Insurances on the insured's own life[29] or on the life of a spouse[30] or civil partner[31] are automatically valid regardless of the amount insured. This presumption probably extends to the fiancé(e) insuring the life of his or her fiancé(e).[32] However, it does not extend to other family relationships.

Apart from in these cases, the requirement of pecuniary interest means that the law was very strict, and, indeed, no doubt stricter than common practice would indicate. Essentially, the insured must show that he would suffer financially by the loss of a legal right on the death of the life insured and it was only the amount of likely loss that can be covered. This approach was perhaps best illustrated by examining separately family relationships, other than that of husband and wife, from other relationships, and we shall continue to proceed on this basis. However, we must note at this stage that

---

[27] An alternative would be to confine recovery by the insured to the surrender value of the policy at the time interest ceases.

[28] *Griffiths v Fleming* [1909] 1 K.B. 805 esp. at 821. Because of the lack of, or the lack of the need for, a pecuniary interest in one's own life, it has been held that there is no loss recoverable in a negligence claim against a person who fails, in breach of duty, to effect a policy: *Lynne v Gordon Doctors & Walton, The Times*, 17 June 1991.

[29] *Wainewright v Bland* (1835) 1 Moo. & R. 481.

[30] *Griffiths v Fleming* [1909] 1 K.B. 805 and see *Murphy v Murphy* [2004] Lloyd's Rep. I.R. 744 at 751. cf. the Married Women's Property Act 1882 s.11, (see 19.3.1) which allows a married woman to insure her own and her husband's life.

[31] Civil Partnerships Act 2004 s.253.

[32] This was certainly the view of one Insurance Ombudsman; see the Annual Report of the Insurance Ombudsman Bureau for 1989, paras 2.31–2.35. It is suggested that the presumption should also apply to an unmarried couple living together.

the decision in *Feasey v Sun Life Assurance Corp of Canada*[33] indicates an alternative approach, which will be considered in detail shortly, and therefore that the following account must be read with that in mind.

3.4.1 Family relationships

So far as family relationships are concerned, it is clear that a child who is a minor would have an insurable interest in the lives of his or her parents, if they are legally obliged to support the child, as the child would clearly therefore suffer financially, by the loss of a legal right on their death. Whether or not there is such a legal obligation is unclear. There is no such obligation under English common law,[34] but statutory procedures may lead to such an obligation. For example, if a maintenance order has been made, compelling a parent to provide for a child, the child must have an insurable interest in the parent's life. In all cases, though, there is the problem of valuing the interest as required under s.3 of the 1774 Act. It may be that an unlimited interest could be presumed as in the case of spouses. Insurance by a minor child on the life of a parent is surely outside the mischief of the Act. However, on principle and authority,[35] an adult child can have no such insurable interest unless he can prove some legal obligation arising on the death of his parent. In *Harse v Pearl Life Assurance Co Ltd*,[36] a son insured the life of his mother who lived with him and kept house for him. The insurance was expressly declared to be "for funeral expenses". It was held by the Court of Appeal that the policy was illegal for lack of interest, there being no legal obligation on the son to bury his mother when she died, and she not being legally bound to keep house for him. The existence of a legal obligation of any sort must in practice be extremely unlikely. In all these cases, of course, there is no objection to a parent insuring his or her own life and even naming a child as beneficiary, provided that the insurance is genuinely own-life, a point to which we shall return.

The converse situation of a parent insuring the life of a child raises interesting problems, for there is no doubt that such insurances are effected in practice. *Halford v Kymer*[37] was long regarded as authority for the fact a parent would not usually have the necessary interest, except possibly to cover

---

[33] *Feasey v Sun Life Assurance Corporation of Canada* [2003] EWCA Civ 885; [2003] Lloyd's Rep. I.R. 637.

[34] *Bazeley v Forder* (1868) L.R. 3 Q.B. 559. In Scots Law, there is such an obligation, which extends quite widely throughout the family; see *MacGillivray on Insurance Law*, 13th edn (London: Sweet & Maxwell, 2015), para.1–105.

[35] *Shilling v Accidental Death Insurance Co* (1857) 2 H. & N. 42; *Harse v Pearl Life Assurance Co Ltd* [1904] 1 K. B. 558.

[36] *Harse v Pearl Life Assurance Co Ltd* [1904] 1 K.B. 558.

[37] *Halford v Kymer* (1830) 10 B. & C. 724.

funeral expenses,[38] because there was no other financial loss arising. There can be no other legal obligation on a parent to incur expenditure on the death of a child. Even if an adult child were supporting their parent, there was no obligation and hence no interest,[39] and it goes without saying that the parent who was not being supported would have no interest. It appears that in practice parents do insure the lives of their children. One example[40] is a personal accident policy taken out when the family is travelling. Clearly such insurance is justified on the ground that extra expense would be incurred if the child died away from home. But as there was no obligation to incur such expense, it was difficult to see strictly how there was insurable interest in this sort of case, and even if there were, under s.3 of the 1774 Act, the amount recoverable would be only the actual costs likely to be incurred which should be valued when the policy was effected. On this basis, it could be argued that some statutory authorisation of these insurances, to a carefully defined extent, was essential. However, the approach of the majority of the Court of Appeal in *Feasey v Sun Life Assurance Corp of Canada*[41] to the question of the meaning of insurable interest indicates an alternative approach and it is note-worthy that in this case the court doubted the authority of *Halford v Kymer*.

Outside the context of parent and child, there is one curious case[42] hold-ing that a de facto guardian had an insurable interest in the life of her infant step-sister, on the ground that she had promised the child's dying mother that she would take care of her and thus incurred expenditure. This decision simply cannot be supported in the absence of an obligation on the child to repay the guardian, so that the latter would suffer financial loss in the event of the child's prior demise; such an obligation is surely most unlikely in prac-tice. This case has never been overruled but there is a Privy Council decision to the opposite effect on similar facts.[43]

---

[38] While there used to be an obligation to bury one's children, this may now in fact be obsolete, as local authorities are now obliged to bury any person who dies in their area; see *MacGillivray on Insurance Law*, 13th edn (London: Sweet & Maxwell, 2015), para.1–096. Insurance of funeral expenses used to be permissible in the area of industrial life assurance.

[39] See *Halford v Kymer* (1830) 10 B. & C. 724.

[40] Another might be school fees insurance, depending upon how it is effected. The problems here have their parallels in cases involving trusts or alleged trusts of life policies. These cases are considered in Ch.19.

[41] *Feasey v Sun Life Assurance Corp of Canada* [2003] EWCA Civ 885; [2003] Lloyd's Rep. I.R. 637; see below.

[42] *Barnes v London, Edinburgh & Glasgow Life Assurance Co Ltd* [1892] 1 Q.B. 864.

[43] *Anctil v Manufacturer's Life Insurance Co* [1899] A.C. 604; see also the comments of the Court of Appeal in *Griffiths v Fleming* [1909] 1 K.B. 805 at 819 and of Lord Alvestone CJ in *Harse v Pearl Life Assurance Co* [1903] 2 K.B. 92 at 96, doubting the decision in *Barnes*.

3.4.2 Business relationships

In respect of relationships of a business character, insurance may be effected by, for example, creditors on the lives of their debtors, employers on the lives of their employees, or vice versa, and partners on the lives of their partners. In all these cases, however, the amount of interest is limited again to the pecuniary interest of the insured. The point is nicely illustrated by the old case of *Hebdon v West*.[44] A bank clerk insured his employer's life with two insurers, one policy being for £5,000, the other for £2,500. The clerk had a contract of employment for seven years at a salary of £600 per annum, and he owed his employer £4,700, the latter having promised that he would not call in the debt during his lifetime. When his employer died, the clerk received the £5,000 from the first insurer. The refusal of the second insurer to honour its contract was upheld by the court. It was accepted that the insured had an insurable interest in his employer's life to the extent of what he was contractually entitled to under his contract of employment, that is a maximum of £4,200, because he stood to suffer this loss by the loss of a legal right. However, he had no interest by virtue of the promise not to call in the debt as he had provided no consideration and hence the promise was not legally enforceable.[45] As his interest was more than satisfied by the payment of the first insurer,[46] the second was not liable.

Perhaps more than the decisions involving family relationships, the decision in *Hebdon v West* illustrates that, in substance and despite what has often been said, the effect of s.3 of the 1774 Act is to render this sort of life insurance in law a contract of indemnity, the difference from the normal indemnity principle being that the measure of the insured's loss is judged at the time the policy is effected rather than at the time of loss. The result is hardly just, particularly when compared with that in the decision in *Dalby*. *Hebdon* was not a case of gaming or wagering and the insurer had received premiums based, one assumes, on usual actuarial considerations.

It seems most unlikely that in practice the decision is applied. Provided that the insured has an interest in the life insured, a valuation of that interest

---

[44] *Hebdon v West* (1863) 3 B. & S. 579. Although the judge at first instance in *Feasey v Sun Life Assurance Corp of Canada* [2002] EWHC 868; [2003] Lloyd's Rep. I.R. 529 was critical of this decision, the Court of Appeal ([2003] EWCA Civ 885; [2003] Lloyd's Rep. I.R. 637), rightly it is submitted, regarded it as probably correct.

[45] Quaere whether the promise might not now be binding under the doctrine of promissory estoppel.

[46] It is interesting to speculate as to whether the first insurer could have recovered the "excess" he had paid. As it was money paid under a mistake of law, it would once have been irrecoverable, but as the common law has now effectively abolished the distinction between mistakes of law and of fact (see 10.2.3), it would presumably now be recoverable.

within the strict confines of s.3 is often unlikely. Take, for example, the case of an employer insuring the life of an employee, a common practice particularly under group insurance policies. As a matter of strict law, the employer's interest will be only the value of the services that it will lose if the employee dies.[47] While, in the case of a most valuable employee with a lengthy service contract, that may be a substantial sum, in the case of a less exalted employee, it can be at most the equivalent of the period of notice that the employee must lawfully give to determine their employment. In fact employees are insured for sums that may bear no relation to the strict legal value. Two relatively modern cases illustrate this, although in neither was the point the subject of any dispute between the parties.[48] In *Green v Russell*,[49] an employee architect was one of a group insured by the employer. The sum insured was £1,000. In law the employer received the money when the employee was killed and the latter's representatives had no claim.[50] It is difficult to believe that that figure was strictly the pecuniary interest of the employer. Similarly, in *Marcel Beller Ltd v Hayden*,[51] the relevant facts involved a group policy. Here the insurable interest point was adverted to, and the learned judge commented[52] that it was not in question that the insured employers had an insurable interest in their deceased employee's life. While this is perfectly correct, the amount of that interest may not strictly have been the £15,000 for which the employee was insured, but the point was simply not considered. It cannot be said that a section of a statute that is so obviously ignored serves any useful purpose.

3.5 A New Approach to the Meaning of Insurable Interest?

We have already indicated at several points in this chapter that the Court of Appeal decision in *Feasey v Sun Life Assurance Corp of Canada*[53] suggests

---

[47] *Simcock v Scottish Imperial Insurance Co* (1902) 10 S.L.T. 286.

[48] See also the sums involved in *Fuji Finance Inc v Aetna Life Insurance Ltd* [1996] 4 All E.R. 608, referred to in 3.7, where the insured was the company, which insured the life of its controller.

[49] *Green v Russell* [1959] 2 Q.B. 226.

[50] See below at 19.3.4. The Law Commission (Law Com. 242, 1996, paras 12.23 and 12.24) cited this case as an example of where their recommendations to reform the law of privity of contract might still not entitle the employee's representatives to claim directly on the policy. These recommendations were implemented in the Contracts (Rights of Third Parties) Act 1999; see 4.5.

[51] *Marcel Beller Ltd v Hayden* [1978] Q.B. 694. See further at 13.6.1.

[52] Above at 697.

[53] *Feasey v Sun Life Assurance Corp of Canada* [2003] EWCA Civ 885; [2003] Lloyd's Rep. I.R. 637. See Havenga, "Liberalising the requirement of an insurable interest in (life) insurance", (2006) 18 S. Afr. Mercantile LJ 259.

that the question of the meaning of insurable interest should be approached rather differently today, and it is appropriate at this stage to give detailed consideration to this decision. *Feasey* arose out of an insurance effected by a P and I Club, insuring members of the club in respect of their liabilities for personal injury or death suffered by employees of members and others on board their vessels. Originally the club reinsured their own liabilities under a conventional reinsurance with a Lloyd's syndicate (number 957). There could be no insurable interest problems under that sort of arrangement since anyone, including an insurer, has an unlimited insurable interest against legal liabilities that they might incur. However, in 1995, because of changes in the Lloyd's rules regarding liability insurance, the reinsurance between the club and Syndicate 957 was changed, in effect becoming what looked like a first party rather than a third party insurance. Syndicate 957 agreed to pay a fixed sum to the club in respect of relevant injuries and death, the sort of arrangement that looks like classic life and personal accident insurance. It was not tied to the amount of the legal liability of the members of SM, but Langley J at first instance[54] held, and the majority in the Court of Appeal upheld this point of construction, that the policy was in effect a sort of hybrid. It was not an insurance that operated only once the liability of SM was established, rather cover for losses that SM might incur once liability was established. Reaching this result depended on rather tortuous reasoning that it is not necessary to review here, although it has to be said that the dissenting judgment of Ward LJ is rather more convincing on this point. In his view, this was simply a reinsurance personal accident policy.[55] However, even if it was properly construed as a hybrid, so that a double contingency, death or bodily injury and potential liability therefore, was the subject matter of the insurance, Ward LJ still differed as to whether or not SM had an insurable interest.

All members of the court treated the case as governed by the Life Assurance Act 1774, so, if the club had no interest, the policy was illegal and void. However, there was reference to authorities concerning insurable interest in property insurance and all of the judges opined that there ought to be some alignment between contingency insurances and indemnity insurances. All were also agreed that it was the duty of the court to try and find an insurable interest.[56] An argument that s.1 of the 1774 Act was concerned only with form and that a policy was enforceable provided that it was

---

[54] *Feasey v Sun Life Assurance Corp of Canada* [2002] EWHC 868 (Comm); [2002] Lloyd's Rep. I.R. 807.

[55] See *Feasey v Sun Life Assurance Corp of Canada* [2003] EWCA Civ 885; [2003] Lloyd's Rep. I.R. 637 at 669–670.

[56] Citing the well-known dictum of Brett MR in *Stock v Inglis* (1884) 12 QBD 564 at 571.

not one of gaming or wagering was also rejected.[57] The leading judgment
of Waller LJ contains an interesting and, in some respects, slightly novel
way of categorising insurable interest. Having reviewed some of the classic
nineteenth century cases,[58] he considers that the key question is what is the
proper subject matter of the insurance and hence whether or not the insured
has an insurable interest in that subject matter.[59] On this basis he groups the
authorities into four categories. The first is straightforward insurances of an
item of property, exemplified by decisions such as *Lucena v Craufurd*[60] and
Macaura v Northern Assurance Co Ltd,[61] which we examine below. Here the
law is strict, the insured having to show a recognised interest in the property in order to show insurable interest. Second are cases where the subject
matter is a defined life,[62] where the law is equally strict and there must be
a pecuniary loss flowing from a legal obligation suffered on the death of the
life insured. The third group is cases where according to the proper construction of the policy its subject matter is an adventure, not simply a particular
item of property.[63] Fourthly "are policies in which the court has recognised
interests which are not even strictly pecuniary".[64] In this category, which he
regards as covering the facts of the case, Waller LJ places the life cases where
interest is presumed, namely insurances on one's own life and the life of a
spouse, as well as some property insurance cases where, he says, "But even in
the case of property something less than a legal or equitable or even simply
a pecuniary interest has been thought to be sufficient".[65] Dyson LJ's concurring judgment is to similar effect, but, as already indicated, there is a strong
dissent from Ward LJ to which further reference is made below.

As far as insurable interest in life and related insurance is concerned, this
decision might be regarded as validating some of the problem situations to

---

[57] Only Waller LJ considered an argument based on s.2 as amended by s.50 of the
Insurance Companies Amendment Act 1973. He appears to suggest (at 652–3)
that a policy describing the lives assured by a class, as the policy in question did,
could in some way dispense with the requirement of s.1. This is an interesting
point, although it seems to go beyond the normal view of s.50, namely that it was
simply intended to facilitate group policies; see below.

[58] *Lucena v Craufurd* (1806) 2 Bos. & P.N.R. 269; *Dalby v The India and London Life
Assurance Co* (1854) 15 C.B. 364 and *Hebdon v West* (1863) 3 B. & S. 579.

[59] See in particular his summary of the principles that he discerns from the cases at
[2003] Lloyd's Rep. I.R. 659 at 659–660, which is cited at 4.2.2.

[60] Above.

[61] *Macaura v Northern Assurance Co Ltd* [1925] A.C. 619.

[62] Exemplified by decisions such as *Halford v Kymer* (1830) 10 B. & C. 725; *Law v The
London Indisputable Life Policy Co* (1855) 1 K. & J. 223; *Simcock v Scottish Imperial
Insurance Co* (1902) 10 S.L.T. 286 and *Harse v Pearl Life Assurance Co* [1903] 2 K.B.
92, as well as *Dalby* and *Hebdon v West*.

[63] See, for example, *Wilson v Jones* (1867) L.R. 2 Ex. 139, mentioned in 3.10.2.

[64] [2003] Lloyd's Rep. I.R. at 657.

[65] These cases are examined in Ch.4.

which we have already referred, although it clearly does not challenge the traditional approach in straightforward insurances of the life of another. We shall consider other aspects of it later.

3.6   Attempted Evasions and Section 2

Section 1 of the Life Assurance Act 1774 does not require simply that the insured has an interest in the life insured. It also stipulates that any person "for whose use, benefit, or on whose account" a policy is made must have an interest, and by s.2,[66] the names of the insured and any beneficiaries must be inserted in the policy, on pain of the policy being illegal. The purpose behind these provisions is clearly to prevent evasions of the basic requirement so that if, for example, A appears to insure his own life, but in fact B is insuring A's life, or the insurance is for B's benefit, B must have an interest and B's name must appear in the policy. The word "benefit" in this context must not be read too widely. The fact that a man, in insuring his own life, intends ultimately to benefit his wife and children, as must be common, does not mean that his wife and children must have an interest under s.1 and be named under s.2. Only if the direct purpose of effecting the policy is to confer an immediate benefit on another[67] can the requirement be applicable.

A strict application of s.2 can lead to unjust results. In *Evans v Bignold*,[68] a wife appeared to insure her own life. In fact the insurance was effected because her husband borrowed money from the trustees of a will under which the wife was entitled to money when she became 21. The trustees insisted on the husband providing security, and the surety insisted that he insure his wife's life. The husband was not named in the policy. It was held that he should have been, as a person interested, under s.2, and the failure to do so meant that the policy was illegal. In fact, of course, he had an insurable interest in his wife's life, so s.1 was satisfied, and the result is unnecessary.

It is suggested that s.2 is, in fact, superfluous. If A insures his own life for the benefit of B, but B has an insurable interest, whether or not B is named in the policy should not affect its validity, as there is no element of gaming or wagering. If B has no interest in A's life, the policy is illegal under s.1, even if B is expressly named in the policy. If B is not named, and on the face of it the policy appears to be effected by A on her own life, the court can nonetheless enquire into the realities of the situation and find such a policy illegal under s.1 if it was really intended for B who has no interest. In *Shilling v Accidental Death Insurance Co*,[69] a father effected a policy on his own life,

---

[66] Subject to the Insurance Companies Amendment Act 1973 s.50, discussed below.
[67] As in *Evans v Bignold* (1869) L.R. 4 Q.B. 622, discussed below.
[68] *Evans v Bignold* (1869) L.R. 4 Q.B. 622.
[69] *Shilling v Accidental Death Insurance Co* (1857) 2 H. & N. 42.

but the evidence showed that it was his son who was entirely instrumental in the transaction and who paid the premiums, and that the policy was for the benefit of the son, as the father immediately afterwards executed a will in his favour. It was held that in reality the policy was taken out by the son on the life of his father, in which he had no insurable interest. It was, therefore, illegal under s.1.[70]

However, as will be seen in detail later,[71] there is no bar to an insured's assigning a policy of life insurance to someone without interest. This would appear to be the easiest legal solution to the problem of cases without interest. Provided that A who effects a policy on his own life does so genuinely, when he has done so, he can assign the policy to whomsoever he pleases (to B) and there is no need at all for B to have an interest in A's life nor to have her name inserted under s.2. The line appears to be a very fine one between A taking out a policy in order to benefit B, and A bona fide effecting a policy with an intention of assigning the benefit but with no particular assignee in mind. The first case would fall foul of s.2 if B's name were not inserted and of s.1 if it was really a case of B insuring A's life in which she had no interest. The second is perfectly valid.[72]

It has already been pointed out that s.2 of the 1774 Act appears superfluous. In certain instances it was clearly also a most inconvenient nuisance, particularly in respect of group policies, for example, a policy taken out by an employer to cover the whole of, or the whole of a class of, its employees. If the policy were solely for the employer's benefit, then of course s.2 would not apply. But if the policy were effected for the benefit of the employees, they would all have had to be named in it. Because of the inconvenience, s.50 of the Insurance Companies Amendment Act 1973 now provides that, in such a case, s.2 of the 1774 Act does not invalidate a policy for the benefit of unnamed individuals within a class or description if the class or description is stated in the policy and every member is identifiable at any time.[73]

3.7   The Effect of a Life Policy Without Interest

There is a difference between the wording of ss.1 and 2 of the 1774 Act. Failure to comply with s.2 renders the policy unlawful, but s.1 says merely that policies without interest "shall be null and void to all intents and purposes whatsoever". Despite this, there is clear authority[74] that a breach of s.1 does render a policy illegal. The usual practical consequence of this concerns

---

[70] It would also have failed s.2.

[71] See Ch.19.

[72] *M'Farlane v Royal London Friendly Society* (1886) 2 T.L.R. 755.

[73] As to the effect of s.50 favoured by Waller LJ in *Feasey v Sun Life Assurance Corp of Canada*, see fn.57.

[74] *Harse v Pearl Life Assurance Co Ltd* [1904] 1 K.B. 558.

the recovery of premiums paid on an illegal policy if the insurer in fact takes the point.[75] Except in such cases, of which in any event there is no modern reported example,[76] insurers do not often raise the point for the obviously sensible reason that to do so in respect of a policy on which premiums had been duly paid could rightly attract unfavourable publicity. It is noteworthy, though, that the insurers did successfully plead that a contract of life insurance was void for lack of insurable interest[77] in the relatively recent decision in *Fuji Finance Ltd Inc v Aetna Life Insurance Ltd*,[78] in order that they could resist a claim for damages for breach of contract.[79]

If insurers have paid out under an illegal policy and there is a dispute between rival claimants to the money, the illegality is ignored.[80] If an insurer did not pay, not because of illegality but relying upon some other defence, the court should raise the illegality point and refuse to enforce the contract on this ground.[81]

3.8   Reforming Insurable Interest in Life Insurance

The strict law on insurable interest in life insurances is clearly out of touch with reality in many respects, as has been pointed out in the preceding account, and despite the somewhat novel approach in *Feasey v Sun Life Assurance Corp of Canada*. It is suggested that a general reform is necessary, which might well follow the useful precedent that was set by the Australian Insurance Contracts Act 1984.[82] Although this legislation was subsequently amended and the requirement of interest abolished altogether in 1995,[83] it provides an interesting precedent which assumed that a requirement of interest was still desirable, but set out a list of relationships in respect of which it was permissible for one person to insure the life of another.

The Law Commissions have given detailed consideration to the law on

---

[75] This is dealt with in Ch.8.

[76] Note, though, the case that went to the Ombudsman described in fn.32, where the insured argued for the return of his premiums on the ground that the policy he had effected was illegal for lack of interest.

[77] Or at least that the interest was substantially more than permitted by s.3. Strictly, the whole policy must have been void and illegal, but the insurers had paid the surrender value at the time they terminated it.

[78] *Fuji Finance Ltd Inc v Aetna Life Insurance Ltd* [1996] 4 All E.R. 608.

[79] The insurers had terminated the contract because of the phenomenal success of the life insured in "switching" the linked investments. The insured claimed that this was in breach of contract.

[80] *Worthington v Curtis* (1875) 1 Ch. D. 419; *Carter v Renouf* (1962) 36 A.L.J.R. 67.

[81] For example, *Gedge v Royal Exchange Assurance Corp* [1900] 2 Q.B. 214.

[82] ss.18 and 19. See also Merkin (1980) 9 Anglo-American L.R. 331 and Tarr (1986) 60 A.L.J. 613.

[83] The Life Insurance (Consequential Amendments and Repeals) Act 1995.

insurable interest as a key part of their reform project. They produced an Issues Paper in January 2008.[84] In this they were tentatively of the view that a requirement of insurable interest should be retained, principally in order to deter gambling in the guise of insurance.[85] However, they thought that the categories of interest should be broadened by extending the situations where natural affection would support it and tentatively proposed that this would include co-habitants, people dependent on their parents or guardians and parents in the lives of their adult children. They asked for views on the issues of parents insuring the lives of their minor children and fiancés and fiancées, siblings and grandparents/grandchildren insuring each others' lives. In all such cases interest would be unlimited in amount. As far as non-family interests were concerned, they tentatively proposed that the category of insurable interest supported by a legal pecuniary loss should be amended by relaxing the test applied, so that the requirement would be that the insured had a reasonable expectation of pecuniary or economic loss on the death of the life insured, rather than a pecuniary interest recognised by law. While rejecting the view that the consent of the life insured should be the sole basis for interest, they tentatively proposed that consent of the life insured should provide an alternative ground for establishing insurable interest, where the insured and the life to be insured do not fit within the categories of natural affection or a reasonable expectation of loss.

The December 2011 Consultation Paper[86] indicated that they remain convinced of the need for a requirement of interest but of the broader nature mentioned above. Presumed cases of interest would, though, only be extended to the insurances of minor children to a modest amount and co-habitants who have lived together for five years or more immediately prior to the insurance being taken out. Trustees of pension schemes and employers effecting group insurance for their members/employees should have an unlimited interest. Section 2 of the 1774 Act would be abolished and a contract without interest would be void but not illegal. They no longer supported the idea of the consent of the life insured providing an alternative basis for interest.

The lack of any consensus among consultees resulted in this area not being included in the Commissions' 2014 Report should be produced in a final Report on insurable interest in 2016.[87] If these proposals do become formal recommendations, then some will see them as a welcome, if rather modest, set of changes. It may well be right to limit the insurance of minor children by reference to a defined sum, but it could be argued that, as far as insuring

---

[84] This contains some very useful material including comparative material.

[85] This was clearly one of the original driving forces behind the 1774 Act.

[86] LCCP 201/SLCDP 152.

[87] A further Issues Paper (no.10) was produced in March 2015.

the life of an adult is concerned, outside group insurances, a simple requirement of consent would suffice to ensure compliance with the policy behind
insurable interest.

3.9   Insurable Interest in Property Insurance

We now turn to consider the question of insurable interest in property
insurances. This requires a consideration of exactly why the law imposes the
requirement, as well as looking at exactly what it means. The meaning of
insurable interest in the context of the other sort of indemnity insurances,
namely liability insurances, is in reality irrelevant, since anyone has an insurable interest in their potential legal liability.

3.9.1 Statutory or contractual requirement

The first issue here concerns the extent to which, if at all, the 1774 Act
applies.[88] It clearly does not apply to insurances of goods, for these are
expressly exempted by s.4. Whether or not it applies to insurances of real
property is a question of some difficulty that has occasioned opposing views.[89]
In one Court of Appeal case, *Re King*,[90] it was stated, obiter, that the Act did
apply, while a more recent dictum of the same court in *Mark Rowlands Ltd v
Berni Inns Ltd*[91] is to the contrary effect. In the latter case, where the insurer
of a landlord was arguing that the landlord's unnamed tenant could not
benefit from the insurance because the tenant was not named in the policy
as required by s.2, Kerr LJ stated that "this ancient statute was not intended
to apply, and does not apply to indemnity insurances, but only to insurances

---

[88] There was no doubt that s.18 of the Gaming Act 1845 applied to all such insurances (*Macaura v Northern Assurance Co Ltd* [1925] 2 A.C. 619), but that section has
been repealed (see 3.1) and in any event it was much easier to satisfy than the strict
requirement of insurable interest.

[89] The question of whether it applies to intangible personal property does not appear
ever to have arisen for decision.

[90] *Re King* [1963] Ch. 459 at 485 (per Lord Denning MR). *MacGillivray and
Parkington on Insurance Law Relating to All Risks*, 8th edn (London: Carswell, 1988),
para.153 relied on this dictum in support of the application of the Act to real
property insurance, but now (*MacGillivray*, 13th edn, paras 1–161—1–162) takes
the opposite view. The dictum was ignored in *Ivamy's Fire and Motor Insurance*, at
175–181, putting the opposite view. Clarke, *The Law of Insurance Contracts*, 4th
edn (LLP Professional Publishing, 2002), paras.4–4A, points out that, whatever
the strict legal position, insurance practice has largely ignored the Act. See also the
Australian High Court decision in *British Traders' Insurance Co v Monson* (1964) 1 1.
1 C.L.R. 86.

[91] *Mark Rowlands Ltd v Berni Inns Ltd* [1986] Q.B. 211. The ratio of this case concerned an insurer's subrogation rights; see 17.14.

which provide for the payment of a specified sum upon the happening of an insured event".[92] More recently, in *Siu Yin Kwan v Eastern Insurance Co Ltd*,[93] the Privy Council followed the opinion of Kerr LJ in holding that s.2 did not apply to a policy of liability insurance. It was said that the words "event or events" were not apt to describe an insured's potential liability and that s.2 must take colour from the short title and preamble to s.1. "By no stretch of imagination could indemnity insurance be described as 'a mischievous kind of gaming'. Their Lordships are entitled to give s.2 a meaning which corresponds with the obvious legislative intent."[94]

While it must be recognised that the decision in *Siu Yin Kwan* could be interpreted as having resolved the issue, it is respectfully submitted that the reasoning and the authorities, especially those relied upon by Kerr LJ in *Mark Rowlands Ltd* are not wholly convincing,[95] and it is thought that the matter still merits some discussion. The strongest support for the modern view comes perhaps from the decision in *Mumford Hotels Ltd v Wheeler*,[96] a case where a tenant unnamed in a landlord's insurance policy was held entitled to compel the landlord to use insurance moneys for reinstatement, this right being implied from the terms of the lease.[97] On the other hand, a literal reading of ss.1 and 2 seems clearly to suggest that, with the reference to "other event or events", they comprehend real property insurance, even if, as was clearly only the strict ratio of *Siu Yin Kwan*, they may not be apt to refer to liability insurance. Although it may be admitted that indemnity insurances of real property were not within the primary mischief the Act was designed to prevent, since the principal reason was to prohibit wagering on lives and, well before the Act was passed, there was authority that the common law required an insurable interest in insurances on buildings at the time of the policy,[98] it seems unlikely that there were in existence in 1774 non-indemnity, that is valued, insurances on buildings which could be caught by the Act. Given that s.4 expressly exempted marine and goods policies and that it is unlikely that in 1774 forms of insurance other than life, marine, goods and buildings insurance existed, the words "other event or events" could literally incorporate ordinary insurances of real property. It is also notable that when passing later legislation, Parliament seems to have assumed that the 1774 Act had a

---

[92] *Mark Rowlands Ltd v Berni Inns Ltd* [1986] Q.B. 211 at 227.
[93] *Siu Yin Kwan v Eastern Insurance Co Ltd* [1994] 1 All E.R. 213. The case is considered further at 4.6.1.
[94] Above at 224, per Lord Lloyd of Berwick.
[95] Although Kerr LJ made no reference to the dictum in *Re King*, the Privy Council did, dismissing Lord Denning's view on the ground that his observation was obiter and the point was not argued.
[96] *Mumford Hotels Ltd v Wheeler* [1964] Ch. 117.
[97] This case is discussed further in 16.3.
[98] *Sadler's Co v Badcock* (1743) 2 Atk. 554.

wider application than Kerr LJ's dictum would allow.[99] Further, reliance on the short title of the 1774 Act seems somewhat misplaced as that was only "added" a century after the Act was passed.

The application of s.1 to real property insurances would cause no problems, and there is an attractive construction of s.2 which would remove the difficulties posed in the recent decisions. This was propounded in the Australian case of *Davjoyda Estates Ltd v National Insurance Co of New Zealand*,[100] and is to the effect that s.2 applies only when the insured himself has no interest to satisfy s.1 but is insuring on behalf of another with an interest who must therefore be named. This construction is consistent with the mischief that the 1774 Act was designed to prevent and does remove the inconvenience of having to list all the persons interested in an insurance. It is perhaps a pity that it was not considered in *Mark Rowlands Ltd* or *Siu Yin Kwan*.[101]

However, there is a problem in applying s.3 to real property insurances. This provides that where the insured has an interest, no greater sum can be recovered from the insurer than the amount of the value of his interest. It thus appears to imply that even where another person would be named in the policy, in accordance with s.2, and that other person's interest is insured, only the value of the insured's interest can strictly be recovered. If, for example, a tenant insures the house and names his landlord as interested, recovery is limited to the value of the tenant's interest, which may be much less than the value of the property or the sum insured.[102] Furthermore, s.3 is unnecessary in the case of property insurances for these are usually contracts of indemnity and the insured can recover only the value of his interest at the date of loss. This principle clearly existed before the 1774 Act was passed.

---

[99] See especially s.148(7) of the Road Traffic Act 1988, discussed further at 21.3.1, where the words "Notwithstanding anything in any enactment" seem apt to refer to the 1774 Act by allowing enforcement of a motor policy by anyone named in the policy, notwithstanding that the actual insured has no insurable interest in a named person's liability. The fact that case law reached the same result (see 4.3) does not destroy the force of this point. In fact in many of the cases on "waiver" of insurable interest (see 3.11 and Ch.4), it seems to have been assumed that the 1774 Act applied to all insurances except those on goods, as the argument has often turned on the meaning of "on goods" rather than on any wider point such as that propounded in *Mark Rowlands Ltd* and *Siu Yin Kwan*. See especially *Williams v Baltic Insurance Association of London* [1924] 2 K.B. 282.

[100] *Davjoyda Estates Ltd v National Insurance Co of New Zealand* (1967) 65 S.R (N.S.W.) 381 at 428, per Manning J. This construction was cited with approval by the Australian Law Reform Commission, Report No.20, para.112, although Australia solved any problems in this area by a wide-ranging reform.

[101] It is also inconsistent with the dictum in *Re King*!

[102] The point was not considered in *Re King* but there the tenant insured had an interest to the full value of the property, because he had covenanted to repair.

A possible solution to this problem would be to read s.3 as not applying to property insurances, as not being within the mischief that the Act was passed to prevent,[103] or as no more than confirmation of the principle of indemnity in property insurance.

It is respectfully suggested, therefore, that there are arguments, not wholly convincingly rebutted by *Mark Rowlands Ltd* and *Siu Yin Kwan*, that ss.1 and 2 do, as a matter of strict law, apply to real property insurance. This does seem unnecessary, even if one can be confident that a court is likely to follow the dicta in those decisions. The principle of indemnity will ensure that no one profits from a loss in respect of which they have no interest. To make the point absolutely clear, the 1774 Act needs to be repealed in this respect.

Even if the Act does not apply to real property insurance, there is, as already mentioned above, a common law requirement of interest at the date of contract[104] and this seems to mean insurable interest in the strict sense which will be described below. Further, in all cases of insurances of property, insurable interest is prima facie required at the date of loss, simply because such insurances are only contracts to indemnify the insured against a loss actually suffered.[105] This is merely a necessary incident of the contract and as such can be, and sometimes is, dispensed with.[106]

3.10   The Meaning of Insurable Interest in Property Insurances

We can now turn to consider exactly what constitutes an insurable interest in property, regardless of whether or when it is statutorily or contractually required. As with life insurance, the law in this country is stricter than is probably necessary.[107] The starting-point is the classic decision in the marine insurance case of *Lucena v Craufurd*.[108] Here the Crown Commissioners insured a number of enemy ships that had been captured by British vessels

---

[103] This would perhaps be consistent with balancing literal and mischief constructions of the Act. To read "the insured" in s.3 as comprehending the insured and any interested person whose name is inserted in the policy would be misleading, because there is one clear case where, by statutory authority (Fires Prevention (Metropolis) Act 1774 s.83, see Ch.16) a person interested in real property may compel the insurer to expend the insurance moneys on reinstatement, regardless of whether or not the person was named in the policy and regardless of the insured's strict entitlement.

[104] *Sadler's Co v Badcock* (1743) 2 Atk. 554.

[105] *Macaura v Northern Assurance Co Ltd* [1925] A.C. 619.

[106] See 3.11.

[107] For a useful critique, see Harnett and Thornton, "Insurable interest in property; a socio-economic re-evaluation of a legal concept" (1948) 48 Col.L.R. 1162.

[108] *Lucena v Craufurd* (1806) 2 B. & P.N.R. 269.

but were still on the high seas. The statute giving them authority empowered them to take charge of such ships only when they reached British ports. A number of the ships were lost at sea before reaching port. Whether or not the Commissioners had an insurable interest in them caused a great division of opinion, and was debated by the judges before the House of Lords whose decision was that there was no interest, at the time of loss the Commissioners having no present proprietary right to the ships. In the classic words of Lord Eldon,[109] insurable interest is "a right in the property, or a right derivable out of some contract about the property, which in either case may be lost upon some contingency affecting the possession or enjoyment of the party". A complete modern definition would add interest created by the existence of a legal obligation to bear any loss arising from destruction of, or damage to, the insured property.[110]

3.10.1 Factual expectation of loss?

A wider "factual expectation" test had been propounded by some of the judges, although it was clearly not accepted by the House of Lords. This wider test was expressed by Lawrence J as follows[111]:

> "A man is interested in a thing to whom advantage may arise or prejudice happen from the circumstances which may attend it and whom it importeth, that its condition as to safety or other quality should continue . . . To be interested in the preservation of a thing is to be so circumstanced with respect to it as to have benefit from its existence, prejudice from its destruction."

Curiously, this dictum was cited by Kerr LJ in *Mark Rowlands Ltd v Berni Inns Ltd*,[112] even though that it does not represent prevailing British law is obvious from many decisions, particularly that of the House of Lords in *Macaura v Northern Assurance Co Ltd*,[113] which is discussed below.[114] It is also arguable that this dictum has been read in isolation from other parts of the judgment of Lawrence J, which overall seems consonant with the views of Lord Eldon in the House of Lords.[115] That it should perhaps represent the law is another

---

[109] Above at 321.

[110] *Glengate-KG Properties Ltd v Norwich Union Fire Insurance Society* [1996] 1 Lloyd's Rep. 613 at 624.

[111] *Lucena v Craufurd* (1806) 2 B. & P.N.R. 269 at 302.

[112] *Mark Rowlands Ltd v Berni Inns Ltd* [1986] Q.B. 211 at 228.

[113] *Macaura v Northern Assurance Co Ltd* [1925] A.C. 619.

[114] See also *Glengate-KG Properties Ltd v Norwich Union Fire Insurance Society* [1996] 1 Lloyd's Rep. 613, also discussed below.

[115] Legh-Jones, *The Modern Law of Marine Insurance*, ed. D. Rhidian Thomas (2002) Ch.4; *MacGillivray*, 13th edn, para.118.

question.[116] In *Feasey v Sun Life Assurance Corp of Canada*,[117] Waller LJ referred to the fact that the dictum had been cited in later cases, but was content to assume that the law remained strict in straightforward property insurance situations.

3.10.2 Proprietary or contractual right

As the law stands, therefore, a mere expectation or even a moral certainty of loss should particular property be destroyed, is not enough. There must be a present right to a legal or equitable interest or a right under contract. A remainderman whose interest is vested has an insurable interest,[118] but the person with a contingent interest does not, nor does the beneficiary of property under the will of a dying testator.[119] The contingency may not happen; testators may, in theory, revoke their wills. In a famous American case,[120] a turnpike company insured a bridge spanning a stream that connected two parts of the company's road, but the company had no legal or equitable interest in the bridge, and it was held that they had no insurable interest in it. The risk that a person might become liable for negligently causing damage to someone else's property does not of itself give him an insurable interest in that property, as opposed to an interest in his potential liability.[121]

In *Macaura v Northern Assurance Co Ltd*,[122] the sole shareholder of a limited company, who was also a substantial creditor of the company, insured in his own name timber owned by the company. The House of Lords held that he had no insurable interest in the timber that had been subsequently destroyed by fire. As a shareholder he had no right to the property owned by the company, the latter being a separate legal person, even though his shares

---

[116] See 3.12. The wider test has been adopted judicially by the Canadian Supreme Court in *Constitution Insurance Co of Canada v Kosmopoulos* (1987) 34 D.L.R. (4th) 208, which decided that the time had come to refuse to follow any more the *Macaura* case. It has also been adopted legislatively in the Australian Insurance Contracts Act 1984 s.17. For discussion, see Birds [1987] J.B.L. 309; Wolfe [1989] S.L.T. 103; Clarke, *The Law of Insurance Contracts*, para.4.3; Birds, "Insurable Interests", Ch.4 in *Interests in Goods*, Palmer and McKendrick (eds), 2nd edn, (1998); Hasson (1995) 33 OHLJ 680 at 681–683.

[117] *Feasey v Sun Life Assurance Corp of Canada* [2003] EWCA Civ 885; [2003] Lloyd's Rep. I.R. 637 at 654.

[118] Per Lord Eldon in *Lucena v Craufurd*, above, at 314.

[119] Above at 325.

[120] *Farmers' Mutual Insurance Co v New Holland Turnpike Road Co*, 122 Pa. 37 (1888).

[121] *Deepak Fertilisers and Petrochemical Corp v ICI Chemicals and Polymers Ltd* [1999] 1 Lloyd's Rep. 387 at 399–400; see further, 4.2.2.

[122] *Macaura v Northern Assurance Co Ltd* [1925] A.C. 619. This decision has been followed regularly in modern Scottish cases: *Arif v Excess Insurance Group Ltd* 1987 S.L.T. 473; *Mitchell v Scottish Eagle Insurance Co Ltd* 1997 S.L.T. 2; *Cowan v Jeffrey Associates* 1999 S.L.T. 757.

would fall in value in the event of the destruction of the company's property. This was merely a moral certainty of loss. Similarly, as creditor, as Macaura had no right to the company's property in the sense of a mortgage or charge over it, or some other proprietary security interest,[123] he had no interest in it. One may wonder whether this is not too narrow a view. In both the above capacities, the insured did have a real economic interest in the company's property, and of course he could so easily have put matters right by arranging for the company to insure the timber.[124] It should be noted, though, that a shareholder can insure his shares against loss of value due to the failure of an adventure that his company is embarked upon,[125] and a creditor may insure against his debtor's insolvency,[126] so that the practical results of the decision in *Macaura* can be substantially mitigated.

The more recent decision of the Court of Appeal in *Glengate-KG Properties Ltd v Norwich Union Fire Insurance Society*[127] was concerned with the interpretation of the phrase "the interest of the insured" in a policy covering the insured owner of a building against consequential loss following a fire or other insured peril. The issue was whether or not the insured could recover for the loss of architects' plans that were owned by the architects although they might one day have been acquired by the insured. All the members of the Court of Appeal held that the insured had an interest in the plans, notwithstanding the lack of a proprietary interest in them, but it is clear that the majority regarded that interest as being to insure in respect of consequential loss and not to insure the plans themselves.[128]

---

[123] For example the statutory right in *Moran Galloway & Co v Uzielli* [1905] 2 K.B. 555.

[124] Note that the insurer initially resisted Macaura's claim on the ground of fraud; although the allegation failed, this may have influenced their resistance. In the US shareholders do have an insurable interest in their companies' property; see Vance, *Handbook on the Law of Insurance*, 2nd edn (West Publishing Co, 1930) at 175. In Canada, the *Kosmopoulos* case concerned a "one-man" company and as already noted the Supreme Court decided that the time had come to depart from the narrow English law exemplified by *Macaura v Northern Assurance*. *Macaura v Northern Assurance* was distinguished in a marine case (*The Moonacre* [1992] 2 Lloyd's Rep. 501), where the bailee of a boat had full control of it and hence an insurable interest, although it was owned by "his" company. Although *The Moonacre* was cited by Waller LJ in *Feasey v Sun Life Assurance Corp of Canada* [2003] EWCA Civ 637; [2003] Lloyd's Rep. I.R. 637 at 657 as support for his wider view of insurable interest, as Ward LJ pointed out (above at 674), it is supportable on traditional grounds.

[125] *Wilson v Jones* (1867) L.R. 2 Ex. 139.

[126] *Waterkeyn v Eagle Star Insurance Co* (1920) 5 Ll.L.R. 42.

[127] *Glengate-KG Properties Ltd v Norwich Union Fire Insurance Society* [1996] 1 Lloyd's Rep. 614.

[128] See especially the judgment of Auld LJ at 623–4. Sir Iain Glidewell (at 625–6) took the view that the owners of the property could have insured the plans, applying the broad test of Lawrence J literally. This decision was cited by Waller

3.10.3 Possession of property

One other point of general interest which arises out of the *Macaura* case is that possession of property by itself is not enough to found insurable interest. The timber in question was standing on Macaura's land. There must be some right of enjoyment of the property or some legal liability in respect of it. However, it would only be on facts as unusual as those in *Macaura v Northern Assurance*,[129] where the insured had no right to enjoy the timber, that possession would not give interest. There is authority that finders can insure the property they have found,[130] on the ground that possession in English law is a good root of title generally defeasible only by the true owner. What is clear beyond doubt is that possession with legal liability, such as that of a bailee, gives the possessor an insurable interest and, as we shall see, the courts have generally adopted a generous approach to the insurable interest of the various contractors and sub-contractors working on a construction project.

3.10.4 Sales of goods

The party to a contract for the sale of goods who either has property in the goods or bears the risk of their loss has an insurable interest.[131] So far as hire purchase agreements are concerned, the owner of the goods will retain an insurable interest so long as the property or the right to repossess the goods remain vested in that owner.[132] The hirer will also have an interest as bailee, in addition to a likely obligation to insure the goods.[133]

LJ in *Feasey v Sun Life Assurance Corp of Canada* [2003] EWCA Civ 885; [2003] Lloyd's Rep. I.R. 637 as illustrative of his fourth category of insurable interest (see further 3.5 and 4.2.2).

[129] Compare *Boehm v Bell* (1799) 8 T.R. 154: the captors of a ship had an interest because of the rights and duties attaching.

[130] *Stirling v Vaughan* (1809) 11 East 619.

[131] *Inglis v Stock* (1885) 10 App. Cas. 263. It seems unlikely that an innocent purchaser of stolen goods, without good title to them, has an insurable interest: *Chadwick v Gibraltar General Insurance Co* (1981) 34 O.R. (2d) 488; *Thompson v Madill* (1986) 13 C.C.L.I. 242; see Hasson, (1983–84) 8 Canadian Business Law Journal 114. The Insurance Ombudsman, however, took a different view; see the Annual Report of the Insurance Ombudsman Bureau for 1991, para.2.25.

[132] Even if the owner's right is liable to be defeated because of failure to comply with the statutory requirements of the Consumer Credit Act 1974.

[133] The Insurance Ombudsman decided (Annual Report for 1991, para.2.25) that a buyer under a conditional sale agreement had an insurable interest in the full value of the goods. Clearly such buyers have an insurable interest, although the extent of their interest should depend on their liability under the agreement. If, for example, they are relieved of liability in the event of a theft, their recovery should be limited (see 3.10.6), unless they can recover for the benefit of the owner under the principles described in Ch.4.

3.10.5 People living together

Whether or not spouses, or other co-habitants, have an insurable interest in what is solely the property of the other has never been decided. In principle the answer should be in the negative unless the non-owner has possession that is sufficient to insure, in other words where use of the property is shared.[134] But, for example, a husband without a claim to ownership or possession can hardly have an insurable interest in his wife's jewellery, though there may be other ways in which the law permits him in effect to insure it, as we shall see later.

3.10.6 Limited interests in property

The other categories of legal or equitable interest that will support insurable interest include the interests of mortgagor and mortgagee, vendor and purchaser, landlord and tenant and trustee and beneficiary. But once the insured is not the sole, unencumbered owner of property, whether real or personal, the question of the extent of his interest becomes of importance. This does not turn upon any statutory requirement of insurable interest, but stems from the fact that such insurances are contracts of indemnity. Anyone who has a proprietary interest in property may insure it up to its full value; any statutory requirement is thereby satisfied. However, contractually the insured must have an interest at the time of loss and the value of his interest is crucial. He can prima facie recover only sufficient to indemnify himself.[135]

For example, any tenant of property has an insurable interest in it and can therefore insure it for up to its full value. If he is merely a weekly tenant with no obligation to insure or repair, his recovery is limited to the value of his insurable interest, which can at most be the equivalent of four week's rent, assuming the premises to be a dwelling house.[136] If he has a fixed term lease under which he is liable to pay the full rent regardless of the destruction of the property, he will have an interest at the time of loss to that extent. If he is under an obligation to insure or to repair, his interest will be the full value of the property. Conversely, in all cases, it seems that the landlord's interest as reversioner extends to the full value of the property, even where the tenant

---

[134] *Goulstone v Royal Insurance Co* (1858) 1 F. & F. 276.

[135] The authority which, it is suggested, most clearly explains the distinction between the existence of an insurable interest and the value of it is the Australian case of *Davjoyda Estates v National Insurance Co of New Zealand* (1967) 65 S.R. (N.S.W.) 381.

[136] Because of the statutory requirement of four weeks' notice to terminate such a lease (Protection from Eviction Act 1977 s.5).

is liable to repair, because of the risk of the tenant failing to comply with his obligation.[137]

The same points can be made in respect of all the other categories of limited owners that have been mentioned. Each has sufficient legal or equitable interest to insure, but they will prima facie recover only what they have lost. A mortgagee will recover only the value of his outstanding debt,[138] while the vendor of land may recover nothing if he can still enforce the contract of sale against his purchaser.[139] Insurance by those with a limited interest in property raises the further question whether there are any circumstances when they can recover more than the value of their interest in the property, in order to account for the balance to another. This will be considered in Ch.4.

The insured is not necessarily confined to recovering the value of his proprietary interest in the property. He has an insurable interest in an expectancy based upon his proprietary interest, for example, in the profits he would expect to make from his ownership or occupation of the property.[140] This, however, has to be insured quite separately; the usual indemnity policy on property will not indemnify against consequential losses.[141]

3.10.7 A broader category of interest?

We have already seen how, in the decision in *Feasey v Sun Life Assurance Corp of Canada*,[142] Waller LJ identified a category of insurable interest that was broader than that applied in straightforward cases of property insurance. As this was at least partly dependant on decisions that are examined in detail in the next chapter, we will examine this question again after considering those decisions.

3.11   Waiver of Insurable Interest

If the Life Assurance Act 1774 applies to insurances of real property, it is clear that the statutory requirement imposed thereby cannot be dispensed with, but, as we have already seen,[143] that Act is unlikely now to be regarded

---

[137] Important subrogation issues may arise; see Ch.17.

[138] *Westminster Fire Office v Glasgow Provident Investment Society* (1888) 13 App. Cas. 699.

[139] This question is discussed later in Chs 11 and 17.

[140] *City Tailors Ltd v Evans* (1922) 91 L.J.K.B. 379; *Bestquest Ltd v Regency Care Group Ltd* [2003] Lloyd's Rep. I.R. 392 at [21]. In this situation, it may not be necessary to have an insurable interest in the property itself: see *Glengate-KG Properties Ltd v Norwich Union Fire Insurance Society* [1996] 1 Lloyd's Rep. 613, discussed above.

[141] See 13.8.

[142] *Feasey v Sun Life Assurance Corp of Canada* [2003] EWCA Civ 885; [2003] Lloyd's Rep. I.R. 637.

[143] In 3.9.1.

as applicable to any indemnity insurances. Therefore the requirement of insurable interest is merely implied into the contract as a consequence of the principle of indemnity, where it applies only at the time of loss.[144] *Macaura v Northern Assurance Co*,[145] which we have discussed above, illustrates this quite neatly. The insurers had initially referred the dispute to arbitration pursuant to a term in the policy. The insured argued that having done so they were precluded from alleging that the contract was void for want of insurable interest. It was held that the insurers were not alleging that the contract was void for failure to comply with any statutory obligation. They recognised the contract as valid, but denied (successfully) that the insured had at the time of loss the interest necessarily required in such a contract of indemnity.

On principle, there is no reason why, in an appropriate case, this contractual requirement should not be waived or dispensed with,[146] provided that there is no element of wagering involved, and there are clear authorities to this effect. In *Prudential Staff Union v Hall*,[147] the claimant was an association of employees that insured with Lloyd's against any loss suffered by any of its members of money held by them as agents or collectors of their employer. Clearly the association had no insurable interest in its members' liabilities, yet this was held to be no bar to its enforcing the insurance contract, the 1774 Act being inapplicable[148] and the contractual undertaking of the insurer to pay the association waiving any requirement of insurable interest.[149] Similarly, in *Thomas v National Farmers' Union Mutual Insurance Society*,[150] the tenant of a farm insured the hay and straw thereon which was destroyed by fire, but after his lease had ended. The policy provided that it ceased to cover all property insured which passed from the insured "otherwise than by operation of law". The hay and straw had become the landlord's property on the expiration of the lease but only by operation of law owing to a provision in the Agricultural Holdings Act 1948. Thus, although the tenant no longer had any property in the goods, and thus no insurable interest, this was "by operation of law" and the insurer was contractually liable to pay him. We shall consider in Ch.4 what exactly the obligation of the insured in cases like these is with respect to the insurance money he receives.

---

[144] This does not appear to be the case with regard to marine insurance because of s.4 of the 1906 Act.

[145] *Macaura v Northern Assurance Co* [1925] A.C. 619.

[146] But compare Clarke, *The Law of Insurance Contracts*, 4th edn (LLP Professional Publishing, 2002), para.4.1.D.

[147] *Prudential Staff Union v Hall* [1947] K.B. 685.

[148] Money is goods for these purposes, although it would not be for the purposes of the Sale of Goods Act. The modern trend already mentioned would seemingly now dispense with the need to enquire as to the applicability of the 1774 Act.

[149] In fact the action failed as it was held that the plaintiff suffered no loss.

[150] *Thomas v National Farmers' Union Mutual Insurance Society* [1961] 1 W.L.R. 386.

These cases concerned insurances of goods, and this was once regarded as necessary requirement.[151] However, there seems no reason why the principle should not apply to insurances of any property, although in practice it may not often arise outside the context of goods insurance. This question is considered further in the next chapter.

3.12 Reforming Insurable Interest in Property Insurance

We have already mentioned some aspects in which the law relating to insurable interest is arguably in need of reform. Indeed it may be questioned whether the concept is needed at all in property insurances, as the principle of indemnity will ensure that an insured recovers no more than the value of his loss, however that is calculated.[152] The Law Commissions' Issues Paper of January 2008 pointed out that the law is probably unnecessarily complex and outdated and in need of reform. It stressed a number of uncertainties, including the somewhat difficult analysis of the majority of the Court of Appeal in the *Feasey* case,[153] the fact that the effect on insurance of the repeal of s.18 of the Gaming Act 1845 was seemingly not considered and that there remains an argument that the Life Assurance Act 1774 applies to insurances of buildings. They also considered whether a requirement of insurable interest is necessary for the definition of an insurance contract, something that has regulatory and taxation implications, among other things. At that time they saw no need for a requirement for interest in indemnity insurances, where the principle of indemnity would continue to operate. In this respect they wanted to know views on whether insurers should be obliged to check whether or not an insured has a reasonable expectation or chance of a loss when taking out a policy. As insurers are, and would be, entitled to ask questions about a proposed insured's interest in property to be insured, this hardly seemed necessary.

The December 2011 Consultation Paper was, perhaps unfortunately, more conservative. In response to arguments that insurable interest is an integral part of the definition of an insurance contract[154] and distinguishes insurance from gambling, the Commissions proposed to retain the requirement and that the law should provide that an insurance contract was void

---

[151] As mentioned, it was discussed in *Prudential Staff Union v Hall*. It was also considered in *Williams v Baltic Insurance Association of London Ltd* [1924] 2 K.B. 242, where it was held that a liability policy on a motor vehicle was a policy on goods. Statute has since made this aspect of the decision in *Williams* redundant; see the Road Traffic Act 1988 s.148(7) (see 21.3.1).

[152] This is considered in Ch.15.

[153] See 3.5 and 4.2.2.

[154] But this argument is somewhat weakened by the fact that in certain situations the requirement of interest can be waived: see 3.11 and 4.3.

for lack of insurable interest unless there was a real possibility that a party would acquire some form of interest during the life of the contract. As now, the insured must show interest at the time of loss in order to make a claim. The idea of a contract being void in the circumstances they described is perhaps a little curious and there still seems an argument that interest should be required only at the time of loss.[155] As far as the meaning of interest is concerned, the Commissions canvassed a number of options, including (1) providing a statutory definition along the lines of the factual expectation test discussed earlier in this chapter and (2) leaving the matter for development by the courts. As regards the latter, they clearly considered that the courts are now adopting a wider definition than the traditional case law would indicate.[156] Some remain to be convinced that these modern cases do in fact support this, especially in the face of House of Lords' authority to the contrary. For clarity it is thought that a broad statutory definition would be the best solution.

Because of a lack of consensus among stakeholders, the Commissions did not produce any recommendations in their 2014 Report. Instead they issued a further Issues Paper (no.10) in March 2015 and stated that they expected to produce their final recommendations in 2015. However, they will not in fact be published until later in 2016.

---

[155] Arguably this is unnecessary as the principle of indemnity in effect restricts the amount of a claim to the measure of the insured's interest.

[156] Especially by reference to cases such as *Feasey*.

CHAPTER 4

INSURANCE OF THIRD PARTIES' INTERESTS

4.1   Introduction

This chapter considers the not uncommon situations when a person insures property or, indeed, against legal liability when they have a limited interest or indeed no interest themselves in the property or potential liability, and where they are in effect insuring for the benefit of a third party. The issues that arise are closely concerned with questions of insurable interest discussed in the previous chapter. Some of these situations may properly be described as situations of co-insurance or composite insurance. Common examples include a bailee insuring goods for the benefit of the owner as well as himself, contractors' insurance where the principal insured expressly insures the various parties who may be engaged on the project, a household policy that is expressed to cover the property of all occupants of the household not just that belonging to the actual insured, a policy taken out by a mortgagor of property that is expressed to insure the mortgagee's interest, and liability insurances where the cover extends to insurance against the liability of, among others, employees of the insured.[1] Policies of composite insurance may now be construed as containing, in effect, separate contracts of insurance between the insurer and each co-insured.[2] This will be important in determining whether actions by one co-insured can affect the rights of another co-insured, and this question is discussed elsewhere.[3]

For the present, the principal questions to be considered are when a limited owner, or indeed someone without insurable interest in particular property, can recover on an insurance policy for the benefit of a third party, and when such a third party may be able to make a direct claim on the policy. The third party may or may not be named or described in the policy. It is convenient to consider insurances of goods separately from insurances of real

---

[1] Note that the appropriate wording in the policy must be clearly capable of being construed as covering an alleged co-insured: see *Talbot Underwriting Ltd v Nausch, Hogan & Murray Inc* [2006] EWCA Civ 889; [2006] Lloyd's Rep. I.R. 531, which is discussed in 4.6.1.

[2] See *Samuel & Co Ltd v Dumas* [1924] A.C. 421; *General Accident Fire & Life Assurance Corp v Midland Bank Ltd* [1940] 2 K.B. 388; *New Hampshire Insurance Co v MGN Ltd* [1997] L.R.L.R. 24; [1996] C.L.C. 1728; *Arab Bank Plc v Zurich Insurance Co* [1999] 1 Lloyd's Rep. 262 (noted Birds [1999] J.B.L. 151); *FNCB Ltd v Barnet Devanney (Harrow) Ltd* [1999] Lloyd's Rep. I.R. 459.

[3] See 7.11.

property, partly because, as we have seen in the previous chapter, it has been most clearly recognised in goods insurance that the requirement of insurable interest can be waived.

4.2 Insurance on Goods—the Insured With an Interest

If the insured has a limited interest in the goods insured, but has insured them for their full value, which is perfectly permissible, as we saw in the previous chapter, he may, in certain cases, be entitled to recover the full value upon a loss, holding the balance on trust for the third party or parties entitled to the other interest or interests in the goods. Indeed, if he himself has suffered no loss, he may recover the full value for the third party. The essential requirements are that the insured does have an interest in the goods and that, as a matter of construction of the insurance contract, the policy does cover more than that limited interest. It is a question primarily of what the parties intend as derived from the construction of the contract, rather than from extrinsic evidence of actual intention.[4]

4.2.1 The bailee cases

In *Waters v Monarch Fire and Life Assurance Co*,[5] the claimants were flour and corn factors who effected a floating policy over the goods in their warehouse, whether their own or those held "in trust or on commission". A fire destroyed all the goods in the warehouse at a particular time. It was held that the claimants were entitled to recover the full value of the goods; they would retain sufficient to cover their own interest and were trustees[6] for the owners of the goods as to the rest. It was clear from the words of the policy cited above that it covered the interests of the owners. The fact that the latter were unaware of the policy was irrelevant. By contrast, in *North British & Mercantile Insurance Co v Moffat*,[7] tea merchants insured chests of tea stored in their warehouses, which were their own or "in trust or on commission for which they are responsible". Fire destroyed certain chests that had been

---

[4] *Hepburn v A Tomlinson (Hauliers) Ltd* [1966] A.C. 451; contra, *British Traders' Insurance Co Ltd v Monson* (1964) 111 C.L.R. 86. In *Alfred McAlpine Construction Ltd v Panetown Ltd* [2000] 3 W.L.R 946 at 1006, Lord Millett referred to the underlying rationale of this rule as being uncertain. Note, though, the comments of David Donaldson QC in *Ramco Ltd v Weller Russell & Laws Insurance Brokers Ltd* [2009] Lloyd's Rep. I.R. 27 at [30] as regards the bailee cases.

[5] *Waters v Monarch Fire and Life Assurance Co* (1856) 5 E. & B. 870. See also *London & NW Railway Co v Glyn* (1859) 1 E. & E. 652.

[6] As to whether or not they were trustees in the strict sense, see 4.4.

[7] *North British & Mercantile Insurance Co v Moffat* (1871) L.R. 7 C.P. 25. See also *Engel v Lancashire & General Ass Co Ltd* [1925] Com. Cas. 202.

resold by the insured. It was held that, because property in those chests had passed to the purchasers, the insured had no interest in them. They could not recover for the purchasers because the words "for which they are responsible" qualified both the phrases "in trust" and "on commission". They would have been entitled to recover only for those third parties to whom they were in some way liable. In *Ramco (UK) Ltd v International Insurance Co of Hannover Ltd*,[8] the Court of Appeal confirmed that these words limited the interest of the bailee.[9]

The leading case now is *Hepburn v A Tomlinson (Hauliers) Ltd.*[10] Carriers took out insurance on a quantity of tobacco that was stolen in circumstances imposing no legal liability on them. The policy was clearly expressed to be a goods in transit policy, that is, an insurance of the goods as such while they were being transported from one place to another, and not one simply insuring the carriers' potential legal liability. The owners of the goods were expressly named and the terms of the policy were those appropriate to a first party and not a liability policy. In these circumstances the House of Lords held that the carriers were entitled to recover the full value of the tobacco for the benefit of the owners.[11] There was no wagering involved, the carriers did have an interest in the goods, because of their potential legal liability in respect of them if they were negligent, and the only question for decision was whether they intended to insure as it appeared from the construction of the contract.

4.2.2 Other cases

The principle of *Waters* and *Hepburn* is most easily applicable to the situation where a bailee or carrier, for reasons of commercial convenience, insures goods on behalf of their owner as well as on the bailee's own behalf.[12] It has, though, also been applied, expressly for reasons of "commercial convenience", to an insurance of contract works under a contractor's all risks policy and to the insurances of a ship and of an oil well under construction.

---

[8] *Ramco (UK) Ltd v International Insurance Co of Hannover Ltd* [2004] EWCA Civ 675; [2004] Lloyd's Rep. I.R. 606.

[9] In the subsequent case of *Ramco Ltd v Weller Russell & Laws Insurance Brokers Ltd* [2008] EWHC 2202 (QB); [2009] Lloyd's Rep. I.R. 27, the brokers who arranged the cover for the insured were held liable in negligence for not having secured wider cover.

[10] *Hepburn v A Tomlinson (Hauliers) Ltd* [1966] A.C. 451.

[11] As to whether or not there was double insurance if the owners had also insured, see 18.2.3.

[12] The reference to commercial convenience should not be read as implying that the principle is applicable only to commercial insurances. There is no reason why it should not apply, on appropriate facts, to e.g. a private hire of goods; see *Guardian Royal Exchange Assurance of New Zealand Ltd v Roberts* [1991] N.Z.L.R. 106.

In *Petrofina Ltd v Magnaload Ltd*,[13] it was held that an insurance effected by
the owners and main contractors covering the construction of an extension
to an oil refinery, under which all the sub-contractors working on the site
were included within the definition of "the insured", inured to the benefit
of each and every sub-contractor in respect of all the property insured.
Arguably this point was unnecessary for the decision as the issue was
not whether the principal insured could recover for the benefit of a third
party, but whether or not the insurer could exercise subrogation rights in
the name of the principal insured against the negligent sub-contractors
responsible for the loss[14]; it was surely not necessary to find that the sub-
contractors had an interest in the whole works in order to disallow subrogation. Further it is arguable that on the construction of the policy, the
sub-contractors were not insured in respect of the whole contract works
because the words "for which they are responsible" were expressed to limit
the property insured,[15] and this was the view of the Court of Appeal in
Ramco (UK) Ltd v International Insurance Co of Hannover Ltd,[16] which doubted
this aspect of the decision in *Petrofina*.

The principle in *Petrofina* was followed in *Stone Vickers Ltd v Appledore
Ferguson Shipbuilders Ltd*[17] and *National Oilwell (UK) Ltd v Davy Offshore
Ltd*.[18] In *Stone Vickers*, the suppliers of the propeller for a new ship claimed
the protection of a policy effected by the principal contractors and in
National Oilwell, the suppliers of a component for a floating oil production
facility claimed to be insured under the contractors' policy. In both cases,
the judge engaged in a lengthy analysis of the insurable interest of the
suppliers, although again it may be thought that this should be unnecessary for real point in issue, namely whether the insurers have subrogation
rights. The "Petrofina principle"—that the various parties involved in a
construction project have a pervasive interest—was approved by the Court
of Appeal in *Co-operative Retail Services Ltd v Taylor Young Partnership Ltd*,[19]

---

[13] *Petrofina Ltd v Magnaload Ltd* [1984] 1 Q.B. 127.

[14] As to this aspect of the case, see 17.14.1. As will be seen there, the modern tendency is to deal with the issue of whether or not subrogation rights are excluded
by reference to the contract between the co-insureds rather than to the insurance
contract.

[15] See further Birds [1983] J.B.L. 497.

[16] Above at [26] to [30].

[17] *Stone Vickers Ltd v Appledore Ferguson Shipbuilders Ltd* [1991] 2 Lloyd's Rep. 288. The
decision was reversed by the Court of Appeal, [1992] 2 Lloyd's Rep. 578, on the
question of the construction of the policy in question. The relevance of insurable
interest issues was therefore not considered in their judgment.

[18] *National Oilwell (UK) Ltd v Davy Offshore Ltd* [1993] 2 Lloyd's Rep. 582.

[19] *Co-operative Retail Services Ltd v Taylor Young Partnership Ltd* [2000] 2 All E.R. 865.
The decision in this case was upheld by the House of Lords ([2002] UKHL 17;
[2002] 1 W.L.R. 1419), but without reference to this reasoning.

where again the issue concerned the potential subrogation rights of the insurer.[20]

On the other hand, another Court of Appeal decision cast some doubt on the reasoning employed in these decisions.[21] In *Deepak Fertilisers and Petrochemicals Corporation v ICI Chemicals & Polymers Ltd*,[22] the issue was the liability of a firm of consulting engineers for an explosion at a methanol production plant that occurred after the construction of the plant.[23] It was held that the engineers, who were a co-insured under the policy in question, did not have an insurable interest in the plant at the time of the explosion. It was accepted that they had such an interest while the plant was under construction because, if it were destroyed or damaged by any of the insured perils, their opportunity to perform their job and earn their retainer might be lost. But after completion any loss they would suffer could only be caused by their own actionable breach of contract or negligence, which was appropriately insured by liability insurance and not property insurance. Thus, as the loss occurred after completion of the project and their work, they no longer possessed an insurable interest.

It is thought that this is a much sounder approach to the question of the interest of a co-insured than that taken in the earlier cases, and that it destroys some of the reasoning on which they were based or at least limits their effect. It suggests that in a construction situation, the risk of being held liable for causing damage to the contract works does not of itself create a valid insurable interest for the purpose of an insurance of those works, and seems more in line with the traditional view of what constitutes an insurable interest in property, as explained earlier. On the other hand, the Court of Appeal did not address the question of the extent of interest, which, it is thought, could still be relevant.[24]

The different approaches suggested by these construction insurance cases are reflected in the different approaches adopted by the more recent Court of Appeal decision in *Feasey v Sun Life Assurance Corporation of Canada*.[25] Giving

---

[20] See also *Hopewell Project Management Ltd v Ewbank Preece Ltd* [1998] 1 Lloyd's Rep. 448. As already indicated, subrogation in these co-insurance situations is more fully considered later; see 17.14.1.

[21] This decision was not cited in *Co-operative Retail Services Ltd v Taylor Young Partnership Ltd*.

[22] *Deepak Fertilisers and Petrochemicals Corp v ICI Chemicals & Polymers Ltd* [1999] 1 Lloyd's Rep. 387 at 399. For a general critique, see Olubajo, "Pervasive insurable interest: a reappraisal", (2004) 20 Const. LJ 45.

[23] Again, the case was a subrogation action brought in the name of the principal insured, the owners of the plant, and it is discussed further at 17.14.1.

[24] See the comments in 3.10.6.

[25] *Feasey v Sun Life Assurance Corp of Canada* [2003] EWCA Civ 885; [2003] Lloyds' Rep. I.R. 637. See also the analysis, obiter, in *O'Kane v Jones* [2003] EWHC 2158 (Comm); [2004] 1 Lloyd's Rep. 389, which took a similarly broad view.

the leading majority judgment, Waller LJ relied on the broader concept of insurable interest indicated by most of them in support of his view that there is a fourth category of insurable interest. In his view, where the construction of the policy permits and the insurance is not properly simply one insuring against the liability of someone such as a sub-contractor, insurable interest can exist that is not strictly pecuniary. His summary of the appropriate principles that he gleaned from the authorities is expressed as follows[26]:

> "(1) It is from the terms of the policy that the subject of the insurance must be ascertained; (2) It is from all the surrounding circumstances that the nature of an insured's insurable interest must be discovered; (3) There is no hard and fast rule that because the nature of an insurable interest relates to a liability to compensate for loss, that insurable interest could only be covered by a liability policy rather than a policy insuring property or life or indeed properties or lives; (4) The question whether a policy embraces the insurable interest intended to be recovered is a question of construction. The subject or terms of the policy may be so specific as to force a court to hold that the policy has failed to cover the insurable interest, but a court will be reluctant so to hold. (5) It is not a requirement of property insurance that the insured must have a 'legal or equitable' interest in the property as those terms might normally be understood. It is sufficient for a sub-contractor to have a contract that relates to the property and a potential liability for damage to the property to have an insurable interest in the property. It is sufficient under section 5 of the Marine Insurance Act for a person interested in a marine adventure to stand in a 'legal or equitable relation to the adventure.' That is intended to be a broad concept."

Although this view might now be taken to state the legal position,[27] it is submitted that, however much it may lead to some sensible results, it is not without difficulties. The dissenting judgment of Ward LJ offers a much more conventional analysis of insurable interest and reads at least as logically as that of Waller LJ. He recognises that there is binding House of Lords' authority[28] that requires interest to be supported by a proprietary interest as well as an expectation of harm and doubts the authority of some of the construction cases in this respect. This fascinating difference of opinion is something that, it is to be hoped, is resolved before too long, either by the Supreme Court or by legislative reform of the meaning of insurable interest.[29]

---

[26] Above at 659–660. Waller LJ was critical of the analysis proffered in *MacGillivray*, 11th edn, although the dissenting judge, Ward LJ, preferred it.

[27] Whether or not it strictly does in the case of property insurance is an interesting issue. The case itself, as we have seen at 3.5, did not involve property insurance.

[28] *Lucena v Craufurd* (1806) 2 Bos. & P.N.R. 269 and *Macaura v Northern Assurance* [1925] A.C. 619; see 3.10.

[29] This is something that ought to result from the work of the Law Commissions: see 3.12.

4.3 Insurance on Goods—the Insured Without an Interest

Turning to the case of insurance of goods where the insured himself has no interest in them, as we have already seen, there is clear authority that the insured can recover if the contract admits of the construction that the requirement of insurable interest was waived.[30] In *Williams v Baltic Insurance Association of London*,[31] the claimant effected a motor policy on his car including cover against liability to third persons injured by use of the car. The policy was also expressed to cover any friend or relative of the insured driving with his consent. The claimant's sister, driving the car with consent, negligently injured some people who recovered damages from her. The question was whether or not the insured could recover an indemnity in respect of these damages on his sister's behalf. Plainly, he had no insurable interest in his sister's legal liability, but, equally, the wording of the policy was expressed to cover that liability, so that the principal question was whether or not it was necessary for the claimant to have an insurable interest. Roche J held that the policy did not fall foul of the prohibition then in force[32] on gaming and wagering.[33] As the common law did not require insurable interest in such a case, except as a consequence of the principle of indemnity, the very application of which was in issue, he was able to construe the contract as waiving any requirement of interest (and hence the principle of indemnity) because the policy expressly extended to the sister's liability.[34]

4.4 Third Party's Right to the Money

It is clear that the insured who is entitled to and does recover for the benefit of a third party, whether they have an interest themselves or not, is obliged to account to the latter, although until relatively recently it had not been finally decided exactly what was the basis for this.[35] The point arose directly in *Re E Dibbens & Sons Ltd*.[36] Here, Harman J rejected the argument that the insured is a trustee, holding, correctly it is suggested, that references to

---

[30] *Prudential Staff Union v Hall* [1947] K.B. 685; *Thomas v National Farmers' Union Mutual* [1961] 1 W.L.R. 386; see 3.11.

[31] *Williams v Baltic Insurance Association of London* [1924] 2 K.B. 282.

[32] Under the Gaming Act 1845 s.15, now repealed as described in 3.1.

[33] He also held that the policy was one on goods and thus did not fall within the Life Assurance Act 1774, although, as we have seen in 3.9.1, this question would seemingly not be relevant today.

[34] The decision was confirmed by statute in cases of compulsory motor insurance; see the Road Traffic Act 1988 s.148(7); see 21.3.1.

[35] The matter was left open by the House of Lords in *Hepburn v Tomlinson* [1966] A.C. 451.

[36] *Re E Dibbens & Sons Ltd* [1990] B.C.L.C. 577.

"trust" in the earlier cases,[37] which were made by common law judges, were not to be read literally.[38] He held that bailees who had contracted for insurance of the goods with their owners were to be regarded as under a fiduciary duty to insure and hold any proceeds for the bailors.[39] Such bailors could thus claim insurance moneys as against the insured's insolvent estate. However, if there was no contractual agreement to insure, the bailors had no proprietary claim to the proceeds and in an insolvency were left to their claims as general creditors.[40]

4.5   Third Party's Right to Claim Directly

The next question is whether the third party has a direct claim against the insurers in the event of the insured himself being unwilling or unable to claim.[41] The traditional answer, based on the doctrine of privity of contract, was that he would be able to do so only if he could show specific statutory authority[42] or that the insured contracted as trustee or agent for him.[43]

---

[37] Including *Waters v Monarch*.

[38] See also *DG Finance Ltd v Scott* [1999] Lloyd's Rep. I. R. 387, referring to Lord Diplock in *The Albazero* [1977] A.C. 774 at 845.

[39] The compatibility of a fiduciary relationship with a contract had been confirmed in *Barclays Bank Ltd v Quistclose Investments Ltd* [1970] A.C. 567.

[40] See further, Adams, "The insured insolvent hire-purchaser" [1991] J.B.L. 291.

[41] Some of the issues, especially in the context of co-insurance, are discussed in Birds, "Insurable Interests", Ch.4 in *Interests in Goods*, Palmer and McKendrick (eds), 2nd edn (1998), which in this respect draws heavily on some Australian literature (especially Nicholson, "Conundrums for co-insureds", (1990) 3 Ins. LJ 218 and (1991) 4 Ins. LJ 126; Brownie, "Composite insurance", (1991) 4 Ins. LJ 250; Derrington and Ashton, *Law of Liability Insurance*, at 69–91). However, this was written before the enactment of the Contracts (Rights of Third Parties) Act 1999, discussed below.

[42] As is the case in respect of compulsory motor insurance: s.148(7) of the Road Traffic Act 1988; see 23.3.1.

[43] See *Vandepitte v Preferred Accident Insurance Corp of New York* [1933] A.C. 70, where the doctrine of privity was applied to a situation on all fours with *Williams v Baltic Insurance Association*, above, except that the writ was issued by the third party not the insured, and *DG Finance Ltd v Scott*. The latter case involved a hirer insuring goods, as obliged to do under the contract of hire, but declining to claim for their loss (being bankrupt and disinterested by the relevant time). The owner, a finance company that had leased the goods, sought to make a direct claim against the insurers on the basis of trust, but this was rejected for reasons briefly considered below; agency was not pleaded. It is clear that the parties, and the Court of Appeal, accepted the prima facie application of the privity rule. See Price, (1996) 59 M.L.R. 738. Note that the Australian High Court dispensed with the doctrine of privity in this sort of context: *Trident General Insurance Co v McNiece Bros Pty Ltd* (1988) 165 C.L.R. 107. See now the Australian Insurance Contracts Act 1984, s.48. The English courts might possibly have dispensed with privity in the context of construction insurance: in *Petrofina Ltd v Magnaload Ltd* [1984] Q.B. 127, which has

However, as regards contracts of insurance entered into or renewed after 11 May 2000, the Contracts (Rights of Third Parties) Act 1999 may give the third party the right to claim directly.[44] Thus we must examine the relevant provisions of this Act first, before examining whether the traditional exceptions of trust and agency could apply if for some reason the Act is inapplicable.

It is important to note first that the parties to a contract can exclude the operation of the Act, and it may well be the case that insurers insert an appropriate exclusion in a wide range of insurance contracts. However, subject to that, a third party can enforce a contract term that confers a benefit on him if either (a) the contract expressly provides that he may,[45] or (b) if the term purports to confer a benefit on him, unless it appears from a proper construction of the contract that the parties did not intend the term to be enforceable by him.[46] The third party must be identified in the contract by name, as a member of a class or as answering to a particular description.[47] Broadly speaking, though, any defences that the insurer might have to a claim by the insured, for example based on non-disclosure or breach of a warranty or condition, are available against the third party.[48] It seems clear that, in the absence of an exclusion, the third party in the sort of situations that we have been considering here, particularly insurances by bailees and construction insurance, would be able to enforce the contract under the Act. Even in the absence of an express provision to that effect, there would seem little difficulty in satisfying limb (b) of the test.

been considered above, the tenor of Lloyd J's judgment could be read as supporting the view that he would have permitted a direct action by the third party sub-contractor. Curiously this was not cited in *Trident*, above, although both cases arose from the same sort of background. A dictum of Kerr LJ in *Mark Rowlands Ltd v Berni Inns Ltd* [1986] Q.B. 211 at 226 could be read as dispensing with the strict requirements of privity. He said: "Provided that a person with a limited interest has an insurable interest in the subject matter of the insurance . . . there is no principle of law which precludes him from asserting that an insurance effected by another person was intended to enure for his benefit to the extent of his interest in the subject matter". However, this can equally be read as merely giving the third party rights against the insured, not the insurer, and this was not a co-insurance case. It might also be read as support for the use of agency doctrines to escape the privity problem and as such is supported by more recent authorities discussed below.

[44] This Act implemented the recommendations of the Law Commission: Privity of Contract: Contracts for the Benefit of Third Parties, Law Com. No.242, 1996. On the Law Commission Report and its implications for insurance, see Bowyer, "Contracts (Rights of Third Parties) Bill and insurance" [1997] J.B.L. 230.

[45] Section 1(1)(a).

[46] Section 1(1)(b) and (2). Note that there is a presumption of enforceability.

[47] Section 1(3). There is no need for the third party to be in existence at the time of the contract. As to variations in the contract, see s.2.

[48] Section 3.

However, as mentioned, insurers may, and, it is thought, quite often do, exclude the operation of the Act, and there may well be cases that arise for some time concerning contracts effected before the date on which the Act came into effect. For these reasons, it is still necessary to consider the alternative bases on which a third party might rely. As far as trust is concerned, although there are dicta referred to above which could have been read as supporting this, the decision in *Re Dibbens* would seem to preclude this in many cases.[49] More promising is the possible application of agency principles.

4.6   Use of Agency Principles

The use of agency will depend on the application of general principles of agency law, which are briefly described in Ch.13. If the insured was given actual authority to insure, then the third party can clearly claim if the agency was disclosed, and this may not be too difficult to show in a case where the insured himself has a limited interest.[50] Further, it may be possible to use the doctrine of the undisclosed principal, as explained below. If the insured did not have actual authority to insure, the conventional view was that the third party could ratify and claim on the contract only if he did so before loss,[51] but this view may now be wrong.[52] The modern decisions that have raised these two possibilities merit detailed consideration as in part they are not free from difficulty.[53]

---

[49] If an insured does insure as trustee, the third party, as beneficiary, could sue the insurer, joining the insured as defendant: *Vandepitte v Preferred Accident Insurance Corp of New York* [1933] A.C. 70.

[50] For example if the insured is known to be a bailee, an insurance of goods by him must be at least partly for the benefit of the owner. In the *Waters* case (1856) 5 E. & B. 870 at 881, Lord Campbell CJ seemed to treat the question as one of agency, as well as referring to "trust".

[51] *Grover & Grover Ltd v Mathews* [1910] 2 K.B. 401. The absence of express authority and hence the need for ratification is likely in practice to be much more of a problem where the insured himself has no interest, e.g. a householder's policy may cover the property of the insured and members of her family permanently living with her. It is by no means certain that, for example, a spouse or child would be aware of this until a loss was suffered. Note that the third party in *Williams v Baltic Insurance Assoc of London* [1924] 2 K.B. 282 did ratify before the loss (see the finding of the arbitrators reported at 284), but curiously did not herself sue the insurers.

[52] *National Oilwell (UK) Ltd v Davy Offshore Ltd* [1993] 2 Lloyd's Rep. 213. An appeal in this case was settled after it had been argued but, unfortunately, before judgment was given by the Court of Appeal.

[53] See further [1994] J.B.L. 386.

4.6.1 Undisclosed agency

In *Siu Yin Kwan v Eastern Insurance Co Ltd*,[54] Hong Kong shipping agents (R) purportedly effected employers' liability insurance on behalf of ship owners (A). Some members of a vessel owned by the latter were killed in circumstances entitling them to claim compensation from A, but A was wound up and the representatives of the deceased sought to recover from the insurers, E.[55] E resisted the claim on the basis that R had acted as undisclosed agents for A and that the doctrine of the undisclosed principal was inapplicable to insurance contracts.[56] Based on the finding that R had clearly had actual authority to effect the insurance on behalf of A, the Privy Council held that the doctrine of the undisclosed principal was applicable to insurance contracts, they being not sufficiently personal to preclude the operation of the doctrine.[57]

"Since the contract in the present case is an ordinary commercial contract, [A] were entitled to sue as undisclosed principal unless [R] should have realised that [E] were unwilling to contract with anyone other than themselves."[58]

As the proposal form questions were answered as if they referred to A, and fully answered, there was nothing expressly or impliedly to exclude A's rights to sue as undisclosed principal. The Privy Council then dismissed the separate argument for the insurers[59] to the effect that the contract of insurance is such a personal one as to preclude the operation of the doctrine of the undisclosed principal. It was clear that the actual identity of A was a matter of indifference to E as they received full information on the proposal form. However,

---

[54] *Siu Yin Kwan v Eastern Insurance Co Ltd* [1994] 1 All E.R. 213.

[55] Under the Hong Kong equivalent of the Third Parties (Rights against Insurers) Act 1930 (see Ch.20).

[56] A point was also raised on the applicability of the Life Assurance Act 1774; see 3.9.1.

[57] The facts of the case are hardly typical of undisclosed agency, because E knew that R were shipping agents and not the owners of the vessel, but the Privy Council was obliged to treat the case in this way because the trial judge had specifically ruled against inferring knowledge to E that A was the true insured. Many "ordinary" cases will in fact be of unnamed rather than undisclosed agency so that the problems discussed here will not arise. For example, a household policy covering the property of members of the insured's family must be so regarded and any arguments relating to non-disclosure of material facts relating to an unnamed co-insured not known by the insured can be met by the argument that the insurers have waived the requirement of disclosure.

[58] *Siu Yin Kwan v Eastern Insurance Co Ltd* [1994] 1 All E.R. 213 at 221, per Lord Lloyd of Berwick, applying a dictum of Diplock LJ in *Teheran-Europe Co Ltd v S T Bolton (Tractors) Ltd* [1968] 2 Q.B. 545 at 555.

[59] Based on *Peters v General Accident Fire and Life Assurance Corp Ltd* [1937] 4 All E.R. 628; see 11.4.

the judgment went further, holding that insurance contracts can never be so personal as to deny the operation of the undisclosed principal doctrine.

The result of what looks more a case of an unnamed than an undisclosed principal seems entirely justified since it is clear that the insurers were sufficiently aware of all material circumstances concerning the risk. However, it is respectfully submitted that the rejection of the broader arguments for the insurers concerning the personal nature of the insurance contract is open to challenge. Rather curiously, there seems to have been no reference to the special nature of insurance contracts as contracts of the utmost good faith.[60] As a general rule, full completion of the proposal form does not of itself satisfy the requirement of full disclosure.[61] Of course, if the insured acting as agent in fact knows of material facts which he fails to disclose, the contract would be voidable, as the undisclosed principal doctrine requires that any defence which the third party may have against the agent is available against his principal.[62] However, what if the insured does not know of highly material facts relating to the alleged undisclosed principal and does not disclose them for that reason? Unless the insurer can be regarded as having waived any requirement of disclosure of such facts, it surely cannot be the case that the "true" insured would be allowed to step in and enforce the contract, although it must be recognised that there will be many situations where waiver can operate.[63]

The decision in *Talbot Underwriting Ltd v Nausch, Hogan & Murray Inc*[64] both confirmed the possible application of the principle of undisclosed agency but also made clear some limitations on its application. For present purposes the complex facts can be summarised as follows. A barge that had been constructed in China was towed to a shipyard (S) in Singapore for completion, outfitting, commissioning and testing. The contract between the owners of the barge and S required the owners to arrange builders' all risks insurance to include S as a co-insured, although not to be named as a co-insured. Despite being given instructions to this effect, the brokers who negotiated the insurance failed to arrange for this and it was held that the actual wording of the policy was not nearly clear enough to permit a construction that S was in fact a co-insured. The Court of Appeal also held that S was not entitled to enforce the contract of insurance as an undisclosed principal. While the owners (and

---

[60] This is surely implicit in the rule that non-marine indemnity insurance contracts cannot be assigned; see 11.4.

[61] Or the duty of fair presentation as it has become, in business insurance contracts, under the Insurance Act 2015; see Ch.7.

[62] As confirmed by Lord Lloyd [1994] 1 All E.R. 213 at 220.

[63] See the comments in fn.57.

[64] *Talbot Underwriting Ltd v Nausch, Hogan & Murray Inc* [2006] EWCA Civ 889; [2006] Lloyd's Rep. I.R. 531. See also *O'Kane v Jones* [2003] EWHC 2158; [2004] 1 Lloyd's Rep 389.

the brokers acting on their behalf) clearly had actual authority to insure on behalf of S and it was accepted that undisclosed agency had to be available in such a situation, this was subject to consideration of "whether the terms of the contract or the circumstances surrounding it were such as to make it clear that the insurers were willing to contract only with the person or persons identified as the assureds . . .".[65]

Here the fact that a number of insureds were named, but S was not, was critical:

> "When a vessel enters a shipyard for completion and fitting out the persons most immediately interested in her safety are the owner and the shipyard. Other parties with commercial interests in her may also be adversely affected if she suffers loss or damage and it is not surprising, therefore, to find that the assureds in the present policy include other companies within the same group as the owner and even joint venturers. In this context the absence of any reference to the shipyard and its sub-contractors is striking, particularly when it is borne in mind that their inclusion as co-assureds would have a significant effect on the insurers' rights of subrogation[66] and therefore on the risk. Bearing in mind the context in which this policy was issued, I have come to the conclusion that the omission of any reference to the yard or its sub-contractors is not neutral but must be regarded as a positive indication that the insurers were not willing to contract with them. I am satisfied that this is a case, therefore, in which the terms of the contract by implication exclude any right on the part of [S] to sue on it as an undisclosed principal."[67]

The court then went on to consider arguments regarding non-disclosure although their comments here are clearly obiter given that S's claim to be an insured failed. While, it was said, in many cases the identity of an undisclosed principal would be a matter of indifference to the insurers, it would be surprising if it was so in a case such as this one given that it might affect potential subrogation rights of the insurers.

"The fact that the law generally recognises the right of an undisclosed principal to sue and be sued on a contract does not relieve the nominal insured from the duty to make full disclosure of all material circumstances in each case, including any which may relate to his undisclosed principal. That is essential to ensure a fair presentation of the risk to the insurer."[68]

It is submitted that this recent decision clarifies the application of undisclosed agency in these cases in a welcome and sensible way. It stresses that the terms of the policy and the surrounding circumstances are of crucial importance. In many cases of this sort, involving complex commercial

---

[65] Above per Moore-Bick LJ at [26]. See also [34].

[66] As to this, see Ch.17.

[67] Above at [35] and [36].

[68] Above at [43].

considerations with the potential for insurers having subrogation rights in the event of a loss being caused by an undisclosed insured, the identity of the latter will often be material. If the policy and circumstances are clear that someone other than the named insureds are entitled to benefit under the policy, the doctrine of undisclosed agency can be used, although, as we have already pointed out, this is hardly undisclosed agency in the strict sense, but rather unnamed agency. If insurers chose to contract on this basis then they must be taken to have regarded the actual identity of the undisclosed insured as unimportant. What perhaps is not wholly clear is the effect on a truly genuine case of an undisclosed principal where the named insured makes full disclosure but is unaware of material facts that are known to the undisclosed insured.

4.6.2 Ratification

As indicated earlier, *National Oilwell (UK) Ltd v Davy Offshore Ltd* was a construction case. Here Colman J used both the doctrine of the undisclosed principal and the doctrine of ratification as support for a co-insured being able to make a direct claim on the insurance contract. The use of undisclosed agency seems subject to the comments already noted, but the clarification of the application of ratification is, it is thought, most welcome. Colman J summarised the position as follows:

> "Where at the time when the contract of insurance was made the principal assured or other contracting party had no actual authority to bind the other party to the contract of insurance, but the policy is expressed to insure not only the principal assured but also a class of others who are not identified in that policy, a party who at the time when the policy was effected could have been ascertained to qualify as a member of that class can ratify and sue on the policy as co-assured if at that time it was intended by the principal assured or other contracting party to create privity of contract with the insurers on behalf of that particular party."[69]

Perhaps as important are the views of Colman J on the question of the timing of ratification. The earlier leading authority is the decision in *Grover & Grover Ltd v Mathews*,[70] where the claimants insured their piano factory through an agent at Lloyd's. Without consulting them, the agent wrote

---

[69] *National Oilwell (UK) Ltd v Davy Offshore Ltd* [1993] 2 Lloyd's Rep. 582 at 596–7. Evidence as to intention may be provided by the terms of the policy itself, by the terms of any contract between the principal assured or other contracting party and the alleged co-assured or by any other admissible material showing what was subjectively intended by the principal assured.

[70] *Grover & Grover Ltd v Mathews* [1910] 2 K.B. 401.

seeking renewal of the policy when it expired. A fire happened after this expiry and after the agent wrote, but before the claimants knew what the agent had done. When they did find out, they purported to ratify his acts. It was held that the insurers were not liable. While ratification after loss has long been regarded as permissible in marine insurance,[71] Hamilton J regarded this rule as anomalous and not to be extended to non-marine insurance.[72] It is arguable that this case is wrong in principle and that it conflicts with other authority.[73] Recognising the force of criticisms like this, in *National Oilwell*, Colman J would have been prepared[74] to allow ratification after loss in such a situation. It is to be hoped that a case arises soon when there is the opportunity actually to overrule *Grover & Grover v Mathews*.

4.7   Insurance on Real Property

We have seen in Ch.3 that a court is unlikely now to hold that the Life Assurance Act 1774 (the 1774 Act) applies to insurances of real property.[75] If it were to do so, then the insured without an interest in the property insured could not recover for the benefit of another simply because the policy would be illegal under s.1, but it seems that in any event the common law reaches the same result.[76] If the insured has an interest, it seems highly unlikely that a court would now hold that s.2 was applicable to require the naming of the third party,[77] and, in any event, the construction of the section propounded in *Davjoyda Estates Ltd v National Insurance Co of New Zealand*[78] would provide an alternative and sensible solution to this problem.

However, whether or not the 1774 Act applies, it seems less likely in respect of real property insurances, as compared with insurances on goods, that a policy will be open to a construction that allows the insured to recover for the benefit of a third party or allows the third party himself to sue on the policy. It must be stressed that we are here concerned with this limited

---

[71] *Williams v North China Insurance Co* (1876) 1 C.P.D. 757.

[72] He regarded himself as bound by the *Williams* case in which, he said, the court had recognised the anomaly of the rule. With respect, this is a curious reading of the *Williams* case.

[73] For example a dictum in *Waters v Monarch Fire & Life Assurance Co*.

[74] Strictly this comment was clearly obiter as the third party failed to show that they were actually insured in the circumstances of the case.

[75] See 3.9.1.

[76] *Sadler's Co v Badcock* (1743) 2 Atk. 554; see 3.1

[77] See 3.9.1.

[78] *Davjoyda Estates Ltd v National Insurance Co of New Zealand* (1967) 65 S.R. (N.S.W.) 381; see 3.9.1. In Canada, where the 1774 Act clearly does not apply, there are a number of authorities applying the *Waters* principle to insurances of real property on appropriate facts; see e.g. *Commonwealth Construction Co v Imperial Oil* (1976) 69 D.L.R. (3d) 558.

question, the answer to which is not necessarily the same as the answer as to whether or not the third party has an interest in any insurance moneys actually recovered or as to whether he can use the compulsory reinstatement provisions of the Fires Prevention (Metropolis) Act 1774.[79] Just because, for example, the terms of a lease can be construed to entitle the tenant to the benefit of money received by his insured landlord[80] does not necessarily mean that the landlord was entitled under the insurance contract to recover for the benefit of the tenant nor that the tenant could sue on the insurance contract if the landlord chose not to.

Bearing this in mind, the same basic principle of construction as applies to insurances of goods for the benefit of third parties will apply to insurances of real property. Thus the contract as properly construed must reveal an intention to cover the third party's interest,[81] and the insurance will have to be of the full value of the property rather than merely of the interest of the insured as limited owner.[82] This seems to be fairly likely where the relationship between the insured and the third party is that of trustee and beneficiary[83]

---

[79] As to this, see Ch.16 and especially the decision in *Lonsdale & Thompson Ltd v Black Arrow Group Plc* [1993] 3 All E.R. 648, discussed in 16.2.3.

[80] As in, for example, *Mumford Hotels Ltd v Wheeler* [1964] Ch. 117 (see 16.3) and, it seems, *Mark Rowlands Ltd v Berni Inns Ltd* [1986] Q.B. 211; see 3.9.1. See also *Beacon Carpets Ltd v Kirby* [1985] Q.B. 755, fn.86 below. Compare *Re King* [1963] Ch. 459.

[81] *Hepburn v Tomlinson* [1966] A.C. 451; see 4.2.1. Compare the decision of the High Court of Australia in *British Traders Insurance Co v Monson* (1964) 111 C.L.R. 86, where, wrongly, the matter was said to turn upon whether or not the insured could show that he intended to insure for the benefit of the third party. Clearly though the decision in that case was correct. A tenant proposing to purchase the freehold of the property insured it for its full value and as freehold owner, making no mention of the landlord's interest. However, the purchase fell through before the fire that damaged the property. It was held that the tenant could recover only sufficient to indemnify him for his loss and nothing for the benefit of his landlord.

[82] Note that there is no rule of law requiring an insured to specify his interest in the insured property, although normally this would be required by the terms of the proposal form or stated in the policy.

[83] See *Davjoyda Estates Ltd v National Insurance Co of New Zealand* where the plaintiff company entered into a contract to purchase land as agent for another company and insured the land; the insurers were aware of the true principal, but the latter was not named in the policy. Before completion, fire damaged the property. Applying the analogy of the "bailee cases" (see 4.2.1) and getting round the problem posed by s.2 of the 1774 Act in the way described at 3.9.1, it was held that the plaintiff insured as trustee for the other company and could recover the full value of the property. On the construction of the policy, what was insured was the property itself and not merely the limited interest of the insured; there was no presumption of law, merely of fact, that an insured insures only his own interest and in the case of insurance by a trustee, he must also be insuring the interest of the beneficiary since their interests are essentially the same and of necessity the proceeds are held on the same trusts as the property is held.

or mortgagor and mortgagee[84]; in the first case, the interests of the parties are similar, whereas in the second there is most likely to be a noting of both interests on the insurance policy. It seems less likely to be the case where the interests of the parties are quite distinct, as where they are vendor and purchaser[85] or landlord and tenant. In *Re King*,[86] the Court of Appeal refused to apply the analogy of the "bailee cases" to an insurance by a tenant who had covenanted to repair and reinstate. The case involved a dispute between landlord and tenant, the insurer not being involved. The tenant had a full insurable interest and could not be said to be insuring for the benefit of the landlord; the latter in fact was also named in the policy, but this was held to be merely to ensure that the landlord was able to control the receipt of the moneys and insist on reinstatement.[87]

[84] See, e.g. *Hepburn v Tomlinson* [1966] A.C. 451 at 481–482, per Lord Pearce.

[85] *Rayner v Preston* (1881) 18 Ch. D. 1; see 11.1.1.

[86] *Re King* [1963] Ch. 459.

[87] Compare *Beacon Carpets Ltd v Kirby* [1985] Q.B. 755, where the relevant provisions in both the lease and the insurance policy were quite different. Again the dispute was between landlord and tenant, the insurer being quite unconcerned having paid out the insurance moneys. See also an interesting unreported Irish case, *Church and General Insurance Co v Connolly*, noted (1983) 5 D.U.L.J. (n.s.) 291, where a tenant at will recovered under a fire policy for the benefit of its landlord. The arrangement was a very informal letting of premises used as a youth centre and quite unlike the usual formal lease. The 1774 Act was held not to apply to Ireland.

CHAPTER 5

FORMALITIES AND FORMATION OF THE INSURANCE CONTRACT

5.0

This chapter is concerned with a number of matters, some of which at least involve merely the application of general requirements of the law of contract to the particular context of the insurance contract; others arise from regulatory requirements imposed by the Financial Conduct Authority (FCA), which mostly stem from requirements imposed by EU Directives. While we are first concerned with questions as to the formation of the contract and the formalities required, it is convenient to consider also a number of related matters, namely temporary cover and cover notes, and the law concerning the duration, renewal, cancellation and surrender of insurance contracts.

5.1 Formation of the Insurance Contract

The insurance contract is no exception to the general rule requiring offer, acceptance, agreement, consideration and an intention to create legal relations in order to find a binding legal contract.[1] The last two requirements, however, will invariably be satisfied automatically and need not be considered further.

5.1.1 Offer and acceptance

An offer to enter into an insurance contract may be made by a prospective insured or by an insurer. At the initial stage,[2] it will in practice be made by the proposed insured,[3] usually, but by no means necessarily, by means of completing a proposal form.[4] Proposal forms are standard mass-produced documents

---

[1] See generally Edwin Peel, *Treitel on the Law of Contract*, 14th edn (London: Sweet & Maxwell, 2015), Chs 2 to 5. As to the information which statute requires insurers to supply to all prospective insurers, see 5.2.

[2] Compare the position on renewal, discussed later at 5.7.

[3] For an illustration, see *Rust v Abbey Life Assurance Co* [1979] 2 Lloyd's Rep. 334.

[4] Proposal forms are not used in all classes of business nor often in respect of temporary cover (see later). In *Adie v The Insurance Corp* (1898) 14 T.L.R. 544, the offer by the insured took the form of a letter attaching his old policy from a different insurer. In addition, the form is often now completed initially at any rate in a telephone conversation or online. As to the latter, see below.

prepared by insurers. The insurer may simply accept the offer made or may "accept" it with qualifications, in which case the "acceptance" may in law amount to a counter-offer.[5] This analysis may not be appropriate for contracts made online. The insured could be regarded as making an invitation to treat rather than an offer when filling out an online proposal form. The insurer would make the offer by quoting the premium and inviting the insured to accept it, and the insured would accept by clicking the appropriate button.[6] Assuming for the present that there appears to have been an offer and an unqualified acceptance of that offer, the question arises as to what must be comprised in this agreement for there to be a binding insurance contract.

5.1.2 Agreement on material terms

It was once suggested in the House of Lords[7] that both parties must agree all the terms and conditions of the contract. Clearly there are certain essential matters on which there must be accord, namely, the amount of the premium[8]; the nature of the risk, including the subject matter of the insurance[9]; and the duration of the risk.[10] But otherwise it is suggested that the better view, despite the authoritative dictum already referred to, is that these matters are the only ones upon which agreement is required, for the reason that the proposer for insurance is deemed to have applied for the usual form of policy issued by the insurer in respect of the particular type of insurance in question. The proposer is thus deemed to have agreed to the usual terms and conditions to be found in the insurer's policy.[11] In *General Accident Insurance*

---

[5] An alternative view could be that the completion of the proposal form by the insured is an invitation to treat, the insurer makes the offer of insurance and the insured accepts by paying the premium.

[6] There are other potential problems with online contracting. For example it increases the risk of the proposer making misrepresentations because of mis-keying, and the opportunity for thorough checking of the form is perhaps more limited. Any problems with regard to understanding the insurance being offered and the information that insurers must provide (see 5.2) ought, at least in theory, to be dealt with by the fact that the insured will have a statutory cancellation right as described in 5.3. Note that in December 2009, the ABI published guidance to ensure that consumers have a positive experience when buying insurance online; this is available at *https://www.abi.org.uk/~/media/Files/Documents/Publications/Public/Migrated/Motor/ABI%20guide%20to%20ensuring%20positive%20customer%20experiences%20of%20buying%20insurance%20online.pdf* [Accessed 28 December 2015].

[7] *Alliss-Chalmers Co v Fidelity & Deposit Co of Maryland* (1916) 114 L.T. 433 at 434.

[8] In the case of an ordinary risk, however, the amount may be deemed to be in accordance with the insurer's usual tariff. The premium need not actually be paid.

[9] *Beach v Pearl Assurance Co Ltd* [1938] I.A.C. Rep. 3.

[10] See generally *Murfitt v Royal Insurance Co* (1922) 38 T.L.R. 334 at 336.

[11] *General Accident Insurance Corp v Cronk* (1901) 17 T.L.R. 233; *Rust v Abbey Life* [1979] 2 Lloyd's Rep. 334.

Corporation v Cronk,[12] the proposal form that the applicant completed did not contain some terms that were in the policy he subsequently received. He declined to pay the premium, arguing that the sending of the policy with different terms was merely a counter-offer that he chose not to accept. It was held that he was liable for the premium for the reasons already outlined. In practice nowadays, apart from the situation when an application is made orally, for example for a cover-note,[13] no difficulty is likely to arise on this point, as invariably proposal forms stipulate that the proposer's offer is subject to the insurer's usual terms and conditions.

5.1.3 Counter-offer

It may well be that the insurer does not simply accept the proposer's offer, but states that acceptance is subject to payment of the first premium. It is clear that in law this generally amounts to a counter-offer,[14] so that there is no binding contract until the premium is in fact paid.[15] As a matter of general principle, until this act of acceptance, either party should be free to withdraw. However, the law appears to be that the insurer's act constitutes a counter-offer which the proposer may decline to accept but which the insurer cannot revoke, unless there is a change in the risk involved between the time of the original offer and the insured's acceptance by payment of the premium. In other words, the insurer is bound by its counter-offer so long as the risk remains the same. If the risk changes, the tender of the premium by the insured constitutes a new offer that the insurer is at liberty to reject. In *Canning v Farquhar*,[16] a proposal for life insurance was "accepted" on 14 December, on the terms that no insurance was to take effect until the first premium was paid. The premium was tendered on 9 January but four days previously the proposer had fallen and suffered serious injuries from which he subsequently died. The Court of Appeal ruled that the insurer was not bound, the majority[17] reasoning along the lines already discussed.[18] However, it may

---

[12] *General Accident Insurance Corp v Cronk* (1901) 17 T.L.R. 233.

[13] See 5.6.

[14] It may even be merely an invitation to treat, whereupon the proposer must make a new offer on this basis: *Locker v Law Union and Rock Insurance Co Ltd* [1928] 1 K.B. 554.

[15] *Canning v Farquhar* (1886) 16 Q.B.D. 727 at 733.

[16] *Canning v Farquhar* (1886) 16 Q.B.D. 727. See also *Harrington v Pearl Life Assurance Co* (1914) 30 T.L.R. 613.

[17] Lindley and Lopes LJJ.

[18] Lord Esher MR decided the case primarily upon the ground that tender of the premium could never be acceptance of an offer by the insurers, even if there had been no change in risk. The tender would be an offer by the proposer requiring to be accepted by the insurers. With respect, this must be incorrect. The insurer's letter of 14 December was more than a mere statement of intent or invitation to treat.

be that the insurer is estopped from denying that there is a binding contract. This will be the case if, for example, the policy contains a statement that the premium has been paid, as in *Roberts v Security Co Ltd*,[19] where this overrode a condition that the insurance was not effective until the premium was paid.

5.1.4 Changes in risk

If there are any material changes in the risk between the date of proposal and the date of the conclusion of the contract, then these must be disclosed to the insurer in accordance with the general duties imposed on proposers.[20] Failure to do so may render the contract voidable at the option of the insurer. If, in *Canning v Farquhar*, the insurer had accepted the premium tendered, not knowing of the insured's fall, they would have been able to avoid liability for this reason. However, this principle applies only so long as there is no contract in existence. If, for example, the insurer accepts the insured's offer unconditionally, it is thereupon bound, even if the contract provides that the risk will not run until the premium is paid.[21] Non-disclosure of a change in the risk before the premium is paid will not give a remedy to the insurer, although it would not be liable for any loss occurring before the premium was paid.

5.1.5 Communication of acceptance

It is a general rule of the law of contract that acceptance of an offer is not effective until communicated to the offeror; this rule obviously applies to the insurance contract. There are some well-established exceptions to this rule, however, three of which appear of particular relevance in the context of insurance. First, where an offer is unilateral, acceptance is constituted simply by performance in accordance with the terms of the offer. There are one or two examples of this in the insurance field. It used not to be uncommon for

---

This is not to deny, of course, that such a reply by insurers to a proposal could not in an appropriate case be construed as merely an invitation to treat if matters other than the mere payment of the premium were left open; see e.g. *Locker v Law Union*.

[19] *Roberts v Security Co Ltd* [1897] 1 Q.B. 111; see 5.1.5.

[20] As regards a consumer insured, it will be the duty not to make a misrepresentation under the Consumer Insurance (Disclosure and Representations) Act 2012; as regards a non-consumer insured, it will be the duty to make a fair presentation of the risk under the Insurance Act 2015; see Ch.7.

[21] See *MacGillivray*, 13th edn, paras 4–040 to 4–044. This position is unlikely in practice. A provision that the risk does not run is perhaps most likely to be construed as meaning that no contract is in force. It has indeed been held that there is a strong presumption, in the case of life insurance, that no contract comes into existence until the premium is paid and the policy issued: *Southern Cross Assurance Co Ltd v Australian Provincial Assurance* (1939) 39 S.R. (N.S.W.) 174.

newspapers and diaries to offer accident insurance to people who having bought the article, filled in the relevant coupon. A modern example of such coupon insurance is cover against death or injury during aeroplane fights that can be purchased at airport counters. There can be no doubt that in law the provision of such insurance is a unilateral offer by the insurer which the proposer accepts simply by filling in the relevant details requested on the form.

The second exception to the communication of acceptance rule, which can be of some importance, is where a policy is issued under seal. Assuming that the insurer's acceptance is unconditional, or that any condition as to prepayment of the premium is waived, if the acceptance takes the form of the signing and sealing of a policy,[22] there is no requirement of communication to the insured. In *Roberts v Security Co Ltd*,[23] the plaintiff filled in a proposal form for burglary insurance on 14 December. On 27 December, the directors of the insurer fixed the company's seal to the policy accepting the proposal, which provided that it was effective from 14 December. On the night of 26 December, obviously before he knew of the insurer's acceptance, since it had not then taken place, the insured suffered a loss. It was held that the insurer was liable.

Thirdly, the rule requiring communication of acceptance obviously implies that silence or delay does not constitute acceptance. While this is certainly prima facie the case, an insured who acts in reliance on an offer from an insurer will be regarded as having accepted it even in the absence of express communication.[24] In *Rust v Abbey Life Assurance Co Ltd*,[25] the proposer for a form of linked life policy retained the policy for seven months before disputing that she was bound by it. She alleged that she had never intended to enter into that sort of contract and had been misled by the insurer's agent. It was found that the nature of the contract had been fully explained to her and that she was bound by it. Even if she had not made an offer to the insurer, which the latter had accepted by issuing the policy, which the court considered was the case,[26] the insurer's issue of a policy was an offer that she had accepted by doing and saying nothing for seven months.

---

[22] See generally *MacGillivray*, 13th edn, Ch.5.

[23] *Roberts v Security Co Ltd* [1897] 1 Q.B. 111; a condition that the policy was not effective until the premium was paid was waived by a recital that the premium had been paid.

[24] See, e.g. *Taylor v Allon* [1966] 1 Q.B. 304, discussed at 5.6.2.

[25] *Rust v Abbey Life Assurance Co Ltd* [1979] 2 Lloyd's Rep. 334.

[26] Following *Adie v The Insurance Corp* (1898) 14 T.L.R. 544, and *General Accident v Cronk* (1901) 17 T.L.R. 233.

5.2   Statutory Disclosure Requirements

There are significant disclosure requirements imposed by the Insurance Conduct of Business Sourcebook (ICOBS),[27] some of which were required by the Third EC Insurance Directives[28] and some by the Directive on the distance marketing of financial products.[29] The background to these was explained in Ch.2, but it is important here to give some of the detail.[30] This account, which deals with the requirements for general insurance,[31] deals first with the requirements imposed as a result primarily of the Distance Marketing Directive and then describes the product information requirements, including those imposed under the non-life Insurance Directive.

5.2.1 Distance marketing requirements

A distance contract is essentially one concluded over the internet, by telephone or by post. It will therefore be found in a great number of consumer insurance situations. Distance marketing disclosure is governed by ICOBS 3. The information required[32] must be provided in good time before conclusion of the contract and in a clear and comprehensible manner.[33] Customers must be provided with all the contractual terms and conditions and the information listed below in writing or in another durable medium available and accessible to them in good time before the conclusion of any distance contract, unless the contract has been concluded at the customer's request using a means of communication that does not enable the provision of the information in that form in good time before the conclusion of the contract.[34] In the latter case, the information must be provided immediately after the conclusion of the contract. Where a contract is concluded by telephone, only abbreviated information (see Annex 3 to ICOBS 3) has to be provided during the telephone conversation, but the basic obligation to provide the full information still applies before the conclusion of the contract unless the exception described above applies.[35]

---

[27] As to the scope of ICOBS, see 2.7. For critical discussion of the requirements, see Loacker, *Informed Insurance Choice? Insurer's Pre-contractual Information Duties in General Consumer Insurance*, Edward Elgar, 2015.

[28] See also the rules therein regarding advertising and marketing, referred to above.

[29] 2002/65/EC.

[30] ICOBS itself should be consulted for all the detail and for the guidance it gives as to the scope of the rules.

[31] The requirements in respect of life insurance are briefly described in Ch.17.

[32] Which must be produced by the insurer and provided by it if there is no intermediary involved: see ICOBS 6.

[33] ICOBS 3.1.3 and 3.1.5.

[34] ICOBS 3.1.10 and 3.1.15.

[35] ICOBS 3.1.14.

The key information required (this is not the complete list) is the following (Annex 2 to ICOBS 3):

(1) The name and the main business of the firm, the geographical address at which it is established and any other geographical address relevant for the consumer's relations with the firm.

(2) Where the firm has a representative established in the consumer's EEA State of residence, the name of that representative and the geographical address relevant for the consumer's relations with the representative.

(3) An appropriate statutory status disclosure statement, namely a statement that the firm is on the Financial Services Register and its FCA registration number.

(4) A description of the main characteristics of the service the firm will provide.

(5) The total price to be paid by the consumer to the firm for the financial service, including all related fees, charges and expenses, and all taxes paid through the firm or, when an exact price cannot be indicated, the basis for the calculation of the price enabling the consumer to verify it.

(6) Notice of the possibility that other taxes or costs may exist that are not paid through the firm or imposed by it.

(7) Any limitations on the period for which the information provided is valid, including a clear explanation as to how long a firm's offer applies as it stands.

(8) The arrangements for payment and for performance.

(9) Details of any specific additional cost for the consumer for using a means of distance communication.

(10) The existence or absence of a right to cancel under the cancellation rules and, where there is such a right, its duration and the conditions for exercising it, including information on the amount which the consumer may be required to pay (or which may not be returned to the consumer) in accordance with those rules, as well as the consequences of not exercising the right to cancel.

(11) The minimum duration of the contract.

(12) Information on any rights the parties may have to terminate the contract early or unilaterally under its terms, including any penalties imposed by the contract in such cases.

(13) Practical instructions for exercising any right to cancel, including the address to which any cancellation notice should be sent.

(14) The EEA State or States whose laws are taken by the firm as a basis for the establishment of relations with the consumer prior to the conclusion of the contract.

(15) Any contractual clause on law applicable to the contract or on the competent court, or both.

(16) In which language, or languages, the contractual terms and conditions and the other information in this Annex will be supplied, and in which language, or languages, the firm, with the agreement of the consumer, undertakes to communicate during the duration of the contract.

(17) How to complain to the firm, whether complaints may subsequently be referred to the Financial Ombudsman Service and, if so, the methods for having access to it, together with equivalent information about any other applicable named complaints scheme.

(18) Whether compensation may be available from the compensation scheme, or any other named compensation scheme, if the firm is unable to meet its liabilities, and information about any other applicable named compensation scheme.

5.2.2 Product information requirements

This is covered by ICOBS 6. There are disclosure requirements related to general insurance contracts,[36] and then more detailed requirements relating to protection policies.[37] There is a general requirement[38] that a firm takes reasonable steps to ensure that customers are given appropriate information about policies in good time and in a comprehensible form so that they can make informed decisions about the arrangements proposed. This may be provided to consumers in a policy summary (as described in ICOBS 6, Annex 2) but this is not a requirement except for protection policies. The non-life

---

[36] These are accident and sickness policies and all forms of indemnity insurance.

[37] No detail is given here of the latter. They differ to some extent as between pure protection contracts (primarily life insurance with no surrender value or where benefits are only payable on death) and payment protection policies (non-investment insurance contracts with elements of a general insurance contract and the benefits of which are described as enabling policyholders to protect their ability to continue to make payments due to third parties, or can reasonably be expected to be used in this way). In so far as life insurance contracts are governed by the Life Insurance Directive, more can be found in Ch.19.

[38] ICOBS 6.1.5.

Directive requirements are in ICOB 6.2.2, 6.2.3 and 6.2.4. Before a contract is concluded, the customer who is a natural person must be told (1) the law applicable to the contract where the parties do not have a free choice or, where they do, the law the insurer proposes to choose and (2) the arrangements for handling complaints including, where appropriate, the existence of the FOS, without prejudice to the right to take legal proceedings. If the insurer is an EEA firm, it must inform any customer, before any commitment is entered into, of the EEA State in which the head office or branch with which the contract is to be concluded is situated. The contract, or any other document granting cover, together with the insurance proposal where it is binding on the customer, must state the address of the head office or branch. Consumers must be told of the right to cancel a policy, which is described below, in good time before the conclusion of the contract.[39]

5.3   Statutory Cancellation Rights

Cancellation rights given to either insurer or insured under an express term of the policy are considered later in this chapter. Here we are concerned with the statutory cancellation rights conferred by ICOBS in respect of general insurance contracts.[40] These were required in respect of distance contracts,[41] but the regulator took the opportunity to give them to all retail customers. In essence, apart from in respect of short-term contracts and travel insurance, ICOBS 7 requires that all general insurance consumers must be offered the right to cancel for the 14 day period from the later of the conclusion (or renewal) of the contract and the consumer receiving the contractual terms and conditions and any other pre-contractual information required by ICOBS.[42] If the consumer is not told of the right to cancel under ICOBS 7, then there is no time limit. The consumer does not have to give reasons and the notice is deemed served on the day it is sent. Where a consumer exercises the right to cancel, the insurer must repay any premium paid without delay and no later than 30 days after receiving notice of cancellation, subject to the consumer paying for services actually provided by the insurer, provided that he was told of what it might cost if he cancelled. This might be, for example, a situation where a motor policy is cancelled but the insured has already made a claim, which has been partly indemnified by the insurer providing a hire car.

---

[39] ICOBS 6.2.5.

[40] For life contracts, see Ch.19.

[41] Because of the Directive on distance marketing of financial services (2002/65/EC).

[42] There is a longer 30 day period for a pure protection contract, which is essentially term life insurance (this is not covered by the rules applying to most forms of life insurance). For the exceptions for short-term contracts, including travel insurance where the cover is for less than a month, see ICOBS 7.1.3.

5.4 Formalities

Subject to one or two exceptions,[43] there is no general requirement of English law that an insurance contract be in any particular form. Indeed, an oral agreement, provided that it can be proved, is binding, provided that there is the necessary agreement on the material terms.[44] In practice, of course, apart from cases of temporary cover, insurance contracts are invariably recorded in a policy, but there is no legal need for this,[45] unless it is a term of the insurer's acceptance that they are not liable until a policy has been issued. The areas where there are particular formalities are those of life insurance and compulsory motor insurance. Consideration of these can be found in Chs 19 and 21, respectively.

5.5 Forming the Contract at Lloyd's

Where the insurer is a member of Lloyd's, there are sufficient peculiarities concerning the procedure adopted in the formation of a contract to justify brief[46] separate consideration. We adverted in Chs 1 and 2 to the special position of Lloyd's underwriters, whose procedure for the consideration of an offer for insurance involves the submission of a slip with details of the risk etc. to each relevant underwriter in turn. It should be noted that the proposer cannot do this, but instead must act through a Lloyd's broker.[47] The legal conundrum is simply when the contract is concluded. Is each underwriter bound when he has accepted the offer by initialling the slip, even though later underwriters might decline the offer or amend its terms, or is there a contract only once the whole of the offer, the full amount of insurance requested, has been accepted?

It has been authoritatively decided by the Court of Appeal[48] that underwriters are bound from the moment they initial the slip, despite the fact that in theory this could lead to odd legal results, for example if a later underwriter accepts on different terms. Strictly therefore the insured may have separate contracts with different underwriters rather than the one whole

---

[43] Especially marine policies (Marine Insurance Act 1906 s.22) and guarantee policies (Statute of Frauds 1677 s.4).

[44] *Murfitt v Royal Insurance Co* (1922) 38 T.L.R. 334.

[45] See *Scher v Policyholders Protection Board* [1993] 3 All E.R. 384 at 396 per Lord Donaldson MR.

[46] For a fuller account, see *MacGillivray*, 13th edn, Ch.37.

[47] See Ch.12. Brokers may have authority to grant temporary cover: *Praet v Poland* [1960] 1 Lloyd's Rep. 416; see further below.

[48] *General Reinsurance Corp v Forsakringsaktiebolaget Fennia Patria* [1983] Q.B. 856; contra *Jaglom v Excess Insurance Co Ltd* [1972] Q.B. 250. See also *Eagle Star Insurance Co Ltd v Spratt* [1971] 2 Lloyd's Rep. 116.

insurance contract. In reaching this conclusion, the Court of Appeal applied the well-established customs of the London insurance market.[49]

It also seems from the Court of Appeal's judgment[50] that the insured has no right to cancel a contract with an underwriter who has accepted his offer if a later underwriter refuses to accept the offer, so that the insured is only partially covered, or "accepts" it on terms unacceptable to the insured. Again in theory this could lead to odd results, though no doubt in practice disputes would rarely arise.

5.6 Temporary Cover and Cover Notes

It is, of course, common practice in many different types of insurance, but most commonly in motor insurance, for insurers to agree to temporary cover upon first receipt of a proposal, pending full consideration and possible acceptance of the offer, and issue of a policy. Such "cover notes", as they are usually called, are undoubtedly fully effective contracts of insurance.[51] There is a comparative dearth of legal authority concerning them, but a number of important legal questions arise which are examined in the following paragraphs.

5.6.1 Authority to issue cover notes

Whereas invariably only the insurer can accept an offer for a full contract of insurance, authority to conclude a binding cover note will often be vested in an agent. Some of the relevant agency principles are examined in detail in Ch.12. In this context, it is necessary merely to say that, regardless of whether or not an insurer has expressly conferred authority on an agent to issue cover notes, the fact that an agent is entrusted with blank cover notes or their equivalent appears sufficient to confer upon him either implied actual authority or apparent authority.

In *Mackie v European Assurance Society*,[52] M insured his mill and warehouse through W, at the time an agent for the Commercial Union. Subsequently W became an agent of the defendant. M's policy with the Commercial Union expired and he asked W for a new one. W gave him a cover note, in the form of a receipt, for a month in the name of the defendant. Despite the fact that

---

[49] If the contract is subsequently incorporated into a policy, as will normally be the case, the letter constitutes the contract and the slip is not admissible as an aid to construction of it: *Youell v Bland Welch & Co Ltd* [1992] 2 Lloyd's Rep. 127.

[50] Compare the views of Staughton J at first instance in the *General Reinsurance* case: [1982] Q.B. 1022.

[51] *Mackie v European Assurance Society* (1869) 21 L.T. 102.

[52] *Mackie v European Assurance Society* (1869) 21 L.T. 102.

at the time M did not realise that the insurer was different,[53] and despite the fact that the defendant no longer transacted fire business, Mallins VC, in a judgment notable for its criticism of the defendant's attitude, held that there was a binding temporary contract of insurance between the parties. Having provided W with cover notes, the defendant had conferred authority on him to bind them. The principle must apply to any agents entrusted with cover notes, even if they are brokers and normally agents of the insured.[54]

An agent not entrusted with blank cover notes will not usually be regarded as having authority to bind the insurer.[55] The decision in *Murfitt v Royal Insurance Co*,[56] where an agent was held to have implied actual authority to enter into temporary oral contracts of fire insurance, must be regarded as exceptional. The judge stressed that the facts were special, because the agent in question had been giving such cover orally for two years with the knowledge and consent of his superiors. However, it would appear that the position of brokers may be different. There is a clear dictum[57] that they have implied authority to issue interim contracts of insurance in a case where the only acknowledgement by the broker was oral. This appears to be a clear recognition of a common practice whereby insurers do confer such authority on brokers. It must be stressed, however, that this can apply only where there is a pre-existing arrangement between insurer and broker.

5.6.2 Conclusion of the temporary contract

In the ordinary case, this should be a simple matter, the contract being concluded by the insurer or its agent's temporary acceptance of the proposer's offer, provided that the material terms are agreed, as discussed earlier. It will then last for the stated period or until earlier termination by the insurer if, as is usual, this is permitted, or upon being superseded by a formal policy. There can be no objection, sufficient terms being agreed, to the conclusion of a temporary contract by telephone.[58] It should be noted, however, that as a cover note is a proper contract of insurance, the proposer is under the pre-contractual disclosure duties now contained, for consumers, in the Consumer Insurance (Disclosure and Representations) Act 2012 and, for non-consumers, in the Insurance Act 2015.[59]

---

[53] Though this should be irrelevant; M merely wanted to be insured.
[54] See *Stockton v Mason* [1978] 2 Lloyd's Rep. 430, discussed in 12.2.
[55] *Dicks v SA Mutual Fire & General Insurance Co* [1963] (4) S.A. 501.
[56] *Murfitt v Royal Insurance Co* (1922) 38 T.L.R. 334.
[57] *Stockton v Mason* [1978] 2 Lloyd's Rep. 430 at 431, per Lord Diplock.
[58] Which is good news for the large number of people who initially insure in this way with "direct" insurers. Of course the requirements of ICOBS with regard to distance contracts described earlier will apply.
[59] *Mayne Nickless Ltd v Pegler* (1974) 1 N.S.W.L.R. 228, criticised in (1977) 40 M.L.R.

There is one contrasting situation where, it seems, this analysis of an offer by the proposer being accepted by the insurer will not apply. This is where the insurer offers temporary cover upon the termination of a formal contract. In practice this appears to be confined to motor insurance in order to enable the insured to satisfy the compulsory insurance requirements of the Road Traffic Act 1988.[60] What happens is that the insurer, sometimes by way of a slip attached to the motor insurance certificate, alternatively by the notice sent out inviting renewal of the policy, offers to cover the insured for a short period, usually 15 days, upon expiry of the old policy.[61] Any legal problem surrounding this is likely to arise only when the insured neither renews his old policy nor effects a new one with a different insurer in time. This was the case in *Taylor v Allon*,[62] where the insured's policy with insurer A expired on 5 April, but he possessed the sort of temporary slip described. He had decided to change his insurer to B, and from B he obtained new cover from 16 April. However, he drove his car on 15 April, and was charged with driving without insurance.[63] The Divisional Court held that he had been rightly convicted of that offence. Obviously he was not insured by B on 15 April. A's cover note was, it was held, merely an offer by A to insure him from the expiry of the policy, which was binding only if he accepted it.[64] On the facts there was no evidence that the insured accepted that offer. Clearly the insured had not expressly communicated his acceptance to A, though the court was prepared to assume that this was the sort of situation where the usual rule as to communication of acceptance did not apply. However, even on this assumption, acceptance by conduct was necessary and there was no evidence of this, which would usually be by the insured's driving his car in reliance upon the offer.

5.6.3 Terms incorporated into the cover note

The question next arises as to what are the terms of the contract constituted by a cover note. Here the question of when the contract is concluded may be crucial. Obviously, the material terms[65] must be agreed, but it may be important to know whether conditions regarding the

---

79 (Birds); *Marene Knitting Mills v Greater Pacific General Insurance Ltd* [1976] 2 Lloyd's Rep. 631. As to the duties, see Ch.7.

[60] See Ch.21.

[61] This temporary extension is normally only in respect of the compulsory requirements.

[62] *Taylor v Allon* [1966] 1 Q.B. 304.

[63] Under what is now Road Traffic Act 1988 s.143.

[64] Even though A stated in evidence that they regarded themselves as bound to the insured.

[65] See 5.1.2.

claims process, for example, contained in the insurer's standard policy are incorporated.

The careful insurer will ensure that its acceptance of the insured's offer is expressly made subject to its usual terms and conditions for the class of insurance in question.[66] Alternatively, the cover note may be issued following completion of a proposal form that incorporates the relevant terms.[67] However, it might be thought that this is unnecessary, by virtue of the rule examined earlier that a proposer's offer for insurance is deemed to be for the usual form of policy issued by the insurer. It would appear, though, that this rule does not apply to cover notes.

In *Re Coleman's Depositories Ltd and Life & Health Assurance Association*,[68] a company applied for a policy of employer's liability insurance. They completed a proposal form on 28 December and on that day received a cover note with no reference to any conditions. The insurers accepted the offer by the sealing of a policy on 3 January, which was expressed to run from 1 January, and which was delivered to the company on 9 January. On 2 January, one of the insured's employees was injured. At the time his condition was not considered dangerous, but he subsequently developed dangerous symptoms and died on 15 March. On 14 March, the insured gave notice of a possible claim against them to the insurers. The latter denied liability on the ground that the insured had failed to give immediate notice of the claim as required by a condition in the policy. By a majority, the Court of Appeal held that the insured was not bound by this condition, reasoning that it could not apply until communicated to the insured, which was not until 9 January, and after the injury to the employee.[69] Although there is an obvious element of justice in the decision, the reasoning is not easy to follow. If the insured was simply relying upon the cover note, and indeed the policy was not executed until after the accident, although it was stated to apply retrospectively, there is a case for saying that as it did not contain any reference to conditions, and in particular the condition requiring notice, the insured was not bound by any. Even this, however, runs contrary to the decisions in cases like *General Accident v Cronk*,[70] and there are contrary authorities.[71] However, the insured had relied upon the terms of the policy in agreeing initially to go

---

[66] See, e.g. *Dawson v Monarch Insurance Co of New Zealand* [1977] 1 N.Z.L.R. 372.

[67] See, e.g. *Houghton v Trafalgar Insurance Co Ltd* (1953) 2 Lloyd's Rep. 18.

[68] *Re Coleman's Depositories Ltd and Life & Health Assurance Association* [1907] 2 K.B. 798. See also *Insurance Corp International Ltd v American Home Assurance Co* (1974) 42 D.L.R. (3d) 46.

[69] The court was also of opinion that in any event the condition was not a condition precedent to liability. On this distinction, see Ch.9.

[70] *General Accident v Cronk* (1901) 17 T.L.R. 233; see 5.1.2.

[71] For example *Wyndham Rather Ltd v Eagle Star & British Dominions Insurance Co Ltd* (1925) 21 L.I.L. Rep 214.

to arbitration and there was no suggestion that they were not suing on the policy. In these circumstances, it is difficult to see how they could deny that they were bound by other terms in the policy, it being irrelevant that they may not have had actual knowledge of them at the relevant time.

While *Re Coleman* must stand as clear authority for the proposition that conditions imposing obligations on the insured apply to cover notes only when expressly incorporated, it is perhaps safe to assume that it has survived largely unchallenged only because, since then, insurers have always stipulated expressly that their cover notes incorporate their policy terms. In any event, it must be the case that terms of the usual policy defining the scope of the cover are impliedly incorporated into the cover note.

It may be that the insured is able to argue that a contract was concluded before the written cover note or any incorporation by reference on a proposal form was made available to him. The facts of the Australian case of *Mayne Nickless Ltd v Pegler*[72] illustrate this quite neatly. The insured purchased a car and the vendor immediately arranged for insurance, seemingly by telephone. The insured later received a cover note bearing the date of purchase of the car and incorporating the insurer's usual terms. The case was decided upon other grounds, but it must be at least arguable that a binding insurance contract was concluded orally by telephone before the insured was aware of any express terms. The point was not argued, but if this is the correct legal analysis, and the situation may arise commonly in motor insurance, it is difficult to see, consistently with the decision in *Coleman*, how an insurer can rely upon express incorporation of policy conditions, unless of course there is mention of this when the oral contract is being concluded.

The cover note in the *Pegler* case also stated that it was "subject to . . . a satisfactory proposal for your insurance". It was held that the effect of this was to enable the insurer to avoid liability under the cover note because of a misstatement in the proposal form subsequently completed by the insured. The proposal was not "satisfactory". With respect, it might be argued that the phrase simply warned the insured as to the need to complete a proposal form before a formal policy could be issued, or simply that "satisfactory" meant proper in the formal sense rather than in the sense of everything being absolutely correct. There was at least some ambiguity that was surely sufficient to invoke the contra proferentem rule.[73] Further, the effect of the decision is that if a proposal form is never completed, which may be for quite innocent reasons, for example, a subsequent accident[74] or the insured's decision to approach another insurer, the cover note is technically worthless. It is suggested that in a case where such a qualification is attached to a cover note,

---

[72] *Mayne Nickless Ltd v Pegler* (1974) 1 N.S.W.L.R. 228.
[73] See 13.3.4.
[74] See (1977) 40 M.L.R. 79 at 82.

the court should disregard it on the grounds that it may render the protection allegedly provided useless.

5.6.4 Termination of the cover note and its relationship with a subsequent policy

Finally, it is necessary to consider when the contract contained in a cover note comes to an end, otherwise than by the expiry of its stated period. In practice, it may well provide that the insurer can terminate it, and there can be no objection to an insurer's acting in reliance upon such an express right, although the insured must receive notice of cancellation. In the absence of such a right, a cover note would clearly not be terminable until it duly expired.[75]

It must frequently be the case, however, that a formal policy is issued before the cover note's expressed duration has run. Here it would appear that the policy takes over from the date it is issued, but not before. Even if the policy is expressed to be retrospective, it must be arguable that a claim arising before its issue falls under the cover note only.[76] This can only be of any real consequence, however, if there is a relevant difference between the terms of the cover note and the policy, which, as has been seen, is not very likely nowadays.

5.7　Duration and Renewal of Insurance Policies

The question of the length of an insurance contract is a matter for the policy itself to provide. There are no rules of law. However, it is safe to state as a general rule that the life contract is quite different from other insurance policies. There must be at least a presumption that a life contract is entire, is one contract, existing until the death of the life assured, or a specified fixed date in the case of an endowment or term policy.[77] So, provided that the premiums due are properly paid,[78] the insurer cannot refuse to renew a life policy, nor can it allege non-disclosure of material facts that happen after the contract is first concluded. We shall advert to this question later when considering "days of grace".

In contrast, most other policies are of limited duration, normally of one year, though, of course, there is no bar to the agreement of a policy for a

---

[75] *Smith v National Mutual Fire Insurance Co Ltd* [1974] 1 N.Z.L.R. 278.

[76] See *Re Coleman*. Rather oddly in that case, as we have seen, the insured appeared to be suing on the policy rather than the cover note.

[77] *Stuart v Freeman* [1903] 1 K.B. 47 at 53–54 and 55; compare *Pritchard v Merchants' and Tradesmen's Mutual Life Assurance Co* (1858) 3 C.B. (N.S.) 622 at 643.

[78] *Pritchard v Merchants' and Tradesmen's Mutual Life Assurance Co.*

shorter or longer term. But upon expiry of such a policy, if the parties choose to renew the contract, the renewal is clearly in law a fresh contract[79] and thus, for example, the duty of disclosure arises again.[80]

5.7.1 Cancellation under a policy term

Many non-life policies contain a condition entitling either party to cancel them upon giving notice to the other party, usually of seven or 14 days, but a clause permitting immediate cancellation would no doubt be valid. Some such conditions may require the insurer who seeks to cancel to show cause, but this is not essential and an absolute right to cancel is enforceable.[81] That such a right is capable of being abused, though it is an open question how often it may be abused, is evident from the cases.

In *Sun Fire Office v Hart*,[82] the Privy Council upheld the cancellation of a fire policy under a clause providing for termination by the insurers "from any . . . cause whatever" after the insured had suffered several fires and had received an anonymous letter threatening arson.[83] More extreme perhaps are the facts in the Indian case of *General Assurance Society v Chandermull Jain*.[84] There the insured's property was covered against loss or damage by flood. The River Ganges, which ran near the insured's property, had already started to flood further up its course when the insurers served notice of cancellation. The Supreme Court of India held that the insurers were perfectly justified in taking this action, there being nothing unreasonable about unrestricted cancellation rights,[85] provided that cancellation is effected before the risk insured against has run. This is a question of fact; presumably there

---

[79] *Stokell v Heywood* [1897] 1 Ch. 459. For a useful discussion of whether the practice of assuming acceptance of a renewal is or should be consistent with general requirements regarding the formation of a contract, see Barron, "Acceptance by silence and insurance contracts" [2009] J.B.L. 633.

[80] *Lambert v Co-operative Insurance Society* [1975] 1 Lloyd's Rep. 465; see Ch.8.

[81] *Sun Fire Office v Hart* (1889) 14 App. Cas. 98.

[82] *Sun Fire Office v Hart* (1889) 14 App. Cas. 98.

[83] The Court of Appeal of Grenada had refused to uphold the clause, saying that it would permit cancellation for any reason, which would be absurd. The Privy Council justified their decision partly on the ground that the insured could go elsewhere. This must be somewhat unrealistic. What insurer would insure at anything like the same premium an insured who has been threatened with arson, and the fact of cancellation must be a material fact which should be disclosed to any subsequent insurer, which again is hardly likely to dispose it to look kindly on the insured.

[84] A.I.R. (1966) S.C. 1644.

[85] The insured had a similar right of cancellation that, it was said, complimented the insurer's. This is ridiculous. The insured who cancels does not jeopardise the position of the insurer who can retain at least the premium appropriate for the risk it has borne. As the facts of the case show, the insured may very easily be substantially harmed by the insurer's cancellation.

has to be some danger to the property insured before a cancellation would be illegitimate.

It should be noted that usually, upon cancellation, the insured is entitled under the standard condition to a pro rata return of premium. In the absence of such an express right, he would not be entitled to anything, the risk having run.[86]

One would imagine that nowadays insurers only rarely exercise their cancellation power arbitrarily,[87] but, even if this is so, there would appear to be an unanswerable case for the restriction of such rights, particularly in the field of motor insurance, where insurance is compulsory.[88] What is needed is a guaranteed minimum period of notice before cancellation can take effect, in order to enable the insured to seek fresh cover, and, particularly, a require-ment that the insurer have good reason to cancel.[89]

5.7.2 Life policies

Life policies do not, of course, contain cancellation clauses of the same kind but commonly, at least apart from term assurance, they do contain provisions enabling the insured to terminate the policy. They may permit the insured to surrender the policy after a certain number of years, so that the insured then receives a lump sum, the surrender value, or they may provide for the policy to become paid-up, so that no more premiums are due, but the benefits pay-able on death are reduced to the appropriate sum according to the amount of premium actually paid. At the early stages of a life policy, these values are inevitably low and may be much less than the value of the premiums paid, the insurer having to take account of his administrative costs. What these entitlements are must be provided in writing to the insured,[90] but the law does not prescribe any minimum entitlements.[91]

---

[86] See Ch.10.

[87] A modern reported example of what appears to have been a fairly arbitrary cancel-lation is *JH Moore v Crowe* [1972] 2 Lloyd's Rep. 563. The dispute concerned the consequences of a cancellation.

[88] Compare the position in the US: see (1969) *Duke Law Journal* 327.

[89] In a consumer contract, a cancellation condition might be regarded as an unfair term under Pt 2 of the Consumer Rights Act 2015; see 6.1.

[90] Under the FCA's Conduct of Business Sourcebook (COBS).

[91] As, for example, in the Australian Life Insurance Act 1945–1973 ss.95–99 and Sch.6.

5.7.3 Renewal and days of grace

Apart from life policies, there is no right to renew an insurance contract in the absence of a term of the contract to that effect.[92] At common law an insurer was not under any general obligation to send out a renewal notice,[93] or any form of warning that a policy is about to expire, though this was common practice and now ICOBS 5.3 requires that insurers do take reasonable steps, not less than 21 days before expiry of the policy, to send out notices inviting renewal or informing a consumer insured that it is not prepared to renew. There is a similar obligation as regards commercial insureds in ICOBS 5.4, except that there is no specific time limit, rather this must be done "in good time". An insurer does not need any reason for not renewing.[94] As we have seen, the renewal of a non-life policy constitutes the effecting of an entirely new contract.

In practice of course insurers do generally renew, and they may allow "days of grace" after the expiry of the old contract, for the renewal premium to be paid. The precise effect of such a period depends upon the wording of the policy in question, but as a general rule, as this is a concession, it is unlikely that the insured is protected while the premium remains unpaid, so that a loss before payment would not be covered. It must also be doubtful whether an insured could, after a loss, insist upon renewal by tendering the premium within the days of grace and thus purporting to accept the insurer's offer.[95] However, there does appear to be a clear exception in the case of life

---

[92] For an example, see the policy in *Kirby v Cosindit Spa* [1969] 1 Lloyd's Rep. 75; compare *Jones Construction v Alliance Assurance Co Ltd* [1961] 1 Lloyd's Rep. 121 and *Webb v Bracey* [1964] 1 Lloyd's Rep. 465.

[93] *Simpson v Accidental Death Insurance Co* (1857) 2 C.B. (N.S.) 257.

[94] Query whether an insurer should have, for the reasons suggested in connection with cancellation. In theory problems could arise when, as is common in motor insurance, an insured has the right to a "no claims" or "loyalty" bonus entitling him to a discount on the normal premium. For example, an insurer may promise that the bonus will adhere if the insured makes no more than a limited number of claims over a period of some years, that is spanning several legally separate contracts. The question may arise as to how such a promise is legally enforceable. A possible solution is that the insurer makes a standing offer to continue to insure, subject no doubt to there being no unacceptable or undisclosed material changes in risk; this would of course be contrary to the usual legal position governing non-life contracts, as explained above. Another possibility might be an enforceable collateral contract, so that the insured would be entitled to damages, namely the extra cost of other insurance, if the insurer unjustifiably failed to renew, but not actually to any right to a new contract of insurance. It is conceivable perhaps that the insurer failing to renew in these circumstances would be in a breach of a general duty to act with the utmost good faith (see Ch.8), but this would probably not give the insured an effective remedy.

[95] cf. *Canning v Farquhar* (1886) 16 Q.B.D. 727, discussed in 5.1.3.

policies that permit days of grace. As these are continuing policies, subject to lapse only upon non-compliance with conditions as to payment of premium, payment within the days of grace, but not of course afterwards,[96] is effective, even if the loss, that is the death of the life assured, has already occurred.[97] The only situation where this would not be the position is where the insurer has the right not to accept payment of the premium after the renewal date,[98] but in this case it is hardly correct in any event to speak of there being days of grace.

[96] *Pritchard v Merchants' and Tradesmen's Mutual Life Assurance Society* (1858) 3 C.B. (N.S.) 622.

[97] *Stuart v Freeman* [1903] 1 K.B. 47.

[98] *Simpson v Accidental Death Insurance Co* (1857) 2 C.B. (N.S.) 257.

CHAPTER 6

INSURERS' REPUDIATIONS OF POLICIES AND LIABILITY— GENERAL CONSIDERATIONS

6.0

Lying at the heart of insurance contract law are those situations where an insurer can lawfully refuse to pay a claim. This may arise because what has happened is simply not within the scope of the policy in question, a matter of construing the provisions that describe the cover and any exceptions to it, which is dealt with in Ch.13. Alternatively, the insurer may successfully allege lack of insurable interest or public policy in support of its refusal to pay; the former has already been dealt with in Ch.3 and the latter is considered separately, later, in Ch.14.

More importantly, for present purposes, there is a range of situations when an insurer's refusal to pay is by reason of its claim that the contract is void or voidable or properly repudiated or that it is discharged from liability or can repudiate liability without denying the validity of the actual contract. The substantive detail of the most important grounds upon which such claims can be made is considered in the next two chapters, but, because this is an area where general principles are easier to state than to apply, this chapter gives an overview of the grounds upon which an insurer can claim such a refusal and of the reforms to the law introduced by the Consumer Insurance (Disclosure and Representations) Act 2012 and the Insurance Act 2015. Some of these grounds arise from circumstances surrounding the initial application for, or renewal of, a contract, which in itself justifies their consideration at an early stage in this book; these are principally claims arising out of a failure to disclose or a misrepresentation of material facts. Others arise from allegations of breaches of warranty or condition contained in the body of the insurance policy. It should be noted in this context that there are no overriding rules of law as to how a particular term in an insurance contract is to be classified. Insurers have complete freedom as to the terms they use and what any term is in any particular contract will depend on how the particular insurer concerned has chosen to draft its contract. Further, it has to be said that the legal distinctions between warranties, conditions precedent and mere conditions, which are adverted to below, are sometimes confusing, and the questions involved are some of the most difficult to resolve in insurance law.

6.1   Unfair Terms in Consumer Insurance Contracts

Where any of the above grounds arises as a result of a term of the contract,[1] their operation may be affected by the operation of Pt 2 of the Consumer Rights Act 2015,[2] controlling unfair terms where the insured is a "consumer".[3] As indicated earlier,[4] these provisions apply to insurance contracts, but a crucial question in determining their impact on the issues we are concerned with here is the meaning and applicability of the exclusion from assessment of fairness now contained in s.64. This covers a term that "specifies the main subject matter of the contract" provided that it is transparent and prominent; these are commonly referred to as "core terms".[5] Transparency means that a term must be expressed in plain and intelligible language and be legible. Prominence[6] means that a term must be brought to the consumer's attention in such a way that the average consumer[7] would be aware of it. It is clear that a condition in an insurance contract that is concerned solely with some obligation on the insured following the occurrence of a loss cannot be such a term and is therefore liable to be set aside on the ground that it is unfair. On the other hand, the true insurance warranty, as explained below, imposes an obligation on the insured to control the risk run by the insurer. Therefore, it could possibly be regarded as a term specifying the main subject matter of the contract and, if it is in plain and intelligible language and prominent, outside the scope of the Act.[8]

---

[1] This will not be the case where a policy is void or voidable by reason of some general legal principle, such as non-disclosure or misrepresentation, but will be where an insurer may not be liable because of the operation of a warranty or condition in the contract.

[2] Replacing, from 1 October 2015, the Unfair Terms in Consumer Contracts Regulations 1999 (SI 1999/2083) (the 1999 Regulations), which themselves replaced the Unfair Terms in Consumer Contracts Regulations 1994 (SI 1994/3159). These provisions implement the EC Directive 93/13 on Unfair Terms in Consumer Contracts.

[3] "Consumer" is defined in s.2(3) as an individual who is acting for purposes that are mainly outside that individual's trade, business, craft or profession. This could give rise to some interesting issues in an insurance context, for example insurance of a motor vehicle that is used for domestic and business purposes.

[4] See 1.9.

[5] This exclusion is expressed differently from how it was in reg.6(2)(a) of the 1999 Regulations, in particular by the use of the word "specifies" rather than "defines", but it seems unlikely to make a difference in practice. Note that, as far as insurance contracts are concerned, these various wordings seem narrower than what was permitted by the EC Directive. The Directive in its preamble excludes insurance terms "which clearly define or circumscribe the insured risk". As to the views of the ECJ on the relevant paragraph of the Directive with respect to contracts of insurance, see *Van Hove v CNP Assurances SA, Case C-96/14.*

[6] There was no specific requirement of prominence in the earlier Regulations.

[7] A consumer who is reasonably well-informed, observant and circumspect.

[8] Certainly most of the obligations imposed by warranties could be rewritten as exclusions of the insurer's liability, and plain, intelligible exclusions must be outside

Whatever the true scope of the Act,[9] a matter which ultimately will have to be decided by the courts, a term will be regarded as unfair if, "contrary to the requirement of good faith [it] causes a significant imbalance in the parties' rights and obligations arising under the contract, to the detriment of the consumer".[10] Assessment of fairness must take account of the nature of the subject matter of the contract and refer to all of the circumstances existing when the term was agreed and to all the other terms of the contract.[11] Schedule 2 contains an indicative and illustrative list of terms that may be regarded as unfair, although this list is not exhaustive.

This obviously has an impact on consumer insurance contracts. However, even if the provisions apply to insurance warranties or conditions affecting the risk, it does not follow that they can be struck down as unfair. For example, a common requirement on an insured to take reasonable care of insured property[12] may well be quite fair in the circumstances of the contract. What would clearly not survive the provisions, in so far as any such terms still exist in consumer insurance contracts, are conditions which impose unreasonable deadlines on the insured, for example in giving notice of a loss,[13] and, possibly, terms which give the insurer complete control over the actions of an insured following an insured loss, for example some of the standard terms in liability insurance policies.[14] However, even such terms which are deemed to be reasonable and therefore fair may still be subject to judicial scrutiny. Such conditions would normally be conditions precedent to the insurer's liability to pay the claim, but before that remedy will be granted, the insurer must prove genuine prejudice.[15]

---

the control of the Regulations; see 13.1.1. There is very little case law on this subject but the decision in *Bankers Insurance Co Ltd v South* [2003] EWHC 380 (QB); [2004] Lloyd's Rep. I.R. 1 seems to confirm this.

[9] See the very thorough discussion of the point in the Law Commissions' Issues Paper on Warranties (2006), Pt 4.

[10] Section 62(4). Note that the wording of this test differs slightly from the wording under the previous Regulations. Under these, individually negotiated terms could not be assessed for fairness, but they can now be, although this is unlikely to be of relevance to consumer insurance contracts.

[11] Section 62(5).

[12] See 13.2.2.

[13] See 14.6.

[14] See 20.2.

[15] See *Bankers Insurance Co Ltd v South* [2003] EWHC 380 (QB); [2004] Lloyd's Rep. I.R 1. Prejudice was proved here due to the seriousness of the insured's breach and his lengthy delay in notifying the insurer of his accident. See also *Parker v NFU Mutual Insurance Society Ltd* [2012] EWHC 2156 (Comm), considered in 14.7.

6.2   Void Contracts

In certain, although rather rare, situations an insurance contract may be void.[16] The most obvious example is a contract that is void by reason of illegality.[17] It is also conceivable, although perhaps unlikely in practice, that an insurance contract could be void for mistake.[18] For present purposes,[19] an insurance contract may be illegal and void for one of the following two reasons:

(1)   the contract may have been entered into to achieve a purpose which is illegal or contrary to public policy; or

(2)   the contract may be vitiated by the unlawful use of property.

There are few examples of these situations. One example of (1) would be a contract of insurance on the property of an enemy agent.[20] Another at common law is a contract entered into by an unauthorised insurer.[21] The most likely example of (2) comes from marine insurance law, where there is a principle that an unlawful voyage renders the marine insurance contract unlawful. The same principle presumably applies in theory to non-marine insurance contracts, so that if the property insured is always used unlawfully,[22] the insurance contract would be void, but it is clear that occasional or temporary illegal use does not have this effect. In *Leggate v Brown*,[23] for example, the use of a tractor in circumstances prohibited by the Road Traffic Act, but covered by the insured's motor policy, was held not to render that policy illegal.

---

[16] Insurers sometimes claim that a policy is "void", e.g. for non-disclosure, even using the word as a verb as in "The policy is voided", in situations where strictly this is an incorrect usage. They mean that a policy is voidable or that the insurer is given an automatic discharge from liability or that it has the right to treat the contract as repudiated.

[17] This is different from the situation where performance of an insurance contract may be illegal on public policy grounds; as already indicated, this is dealt with later in Ch.12.

[18] As to mistake, see, e.g. Peel, *Treitel on Law of Contract*, Ch.8.

[19] Illegality may also arise by reason of lack of insurable interest; as already indicated, this has been considered in Ch.3.

[20] At a time of war, the legislature often makes express provision as to the illegality of insurance contracts effected in this country on enemy property, etc.

[21] *Phoenix General Insurance Co of Greece SA v Administratia Asiguraliror de Stat* [1986] 2 Lloyd's Rep. 552. Statute now makes express provision for this situation; see 2.4.

[22] It may not be possible to recover in respect of property obtained unlawfully, but this is a consequence of public policy (see Ch.12) and does not affect the validity of the insurance contract.

[23] *Leggate v Brown* (1950) 66(2) T.L.R. 281.

6.3 Voidable or Discharged Contracts

Of particular importance in insurance law are those areas of law which have the effect of giving the insurer (or, sometimes, the insured) the option to avoid the contract in its entirety or which achieve a similar result by reason of either an automatic discharge of the insurer from liability or the insurer having the right to treat the contract as repudiated.[24] Strictly, the only circumstances in which an insurance contract is voidable are where one party can avoid by reason of the other's fraud or non-disclosure or misrepresentation of material facts or some other breach of the duty of utmost good faith. These circumstances are examined in detail in the next chapter.[25] As explained there, the law has been significantly affected as far as consumer insurance contracts are concerned by the Consumer Insurance (Disclosure and Representations) Act 2012 and as far as other insurance contracts are concerned, though less significantly, by the Insurance Act 2015. As already noted, it is strictly incorrect to talk about a policy being void in these circumstances.

A distinct situation was where the liability of the insurer was automatically discharged, which used to be the effect of a breach by the insured of a warranty.[26] A warranty in insurance law is essentially a term involving a promise by the insured that controls the risk run by the insurer.[27] In this respect, insurance law usage regarding the warranty as a fundamental term in an insurance contract differs from the position in general contract law, where a warranty is normally regarded as a relatively minor term, the breach of which only ever entitles the innocent party to damages.[28] Full

[24] For a more detailed attempt to explore these and other issues regarding the termination of an insurance contract, see Ch.4 in Birds, *Termination of Contracts*, eds Birds, Bradgate and Villiers, (Cambridge: CUP, 1995), although this should now be read with caution as it is somewhat dated and, in part, has been rendered irrelevant, except from a historical perspective, by provisions in the Insurance Act 2015.

[25] For an interesting discussion of the nature of the obligation of utmost good faith in the context of arts 5, 7 and 11 of the Lugano Convention, see *Agnew v Länsförsäkringsbolagens AB* [2000] 2 W.L.R. 497.

[26] *Bank of Nova Scotia v Hellenic Mutual War Risks Association (Bermuda) Ltd, (The Good Luck)* [1991] 2 W.L.R. 1279, briefly discussed in Ch.9. Strictly this remains the position until 12 August 2016, when the Insurance Act 2015 comes into force and the changes will only apply to contracts entered into, varied or renewed on or after that date.

[27] Not all such terms, though, will necessarily be warranties; see below.

[28] As in the Sale of Goods Act 1979. Of course the term "warranty" may be used in other senses, e.g. as meaning guarantee (manufacturers' warranties, etc.). The fact that modern case law in contract generally (see, e.g. *Schuler v Wickman* [1974] A.C. 235) has reconsidered the whole question of the relationship between and description of the terms of a contract seems almost irrelevant to insurance contract law. Cases in the latter area generally proceed along their own lines, see *The Good Luck* [1991] 2 W.L.R. 1279 and *Cox v Orion Insurance Co Ltd* [1982] R.T.R. 1 (see 9.11),

consideration of warranties is given in Ch.9. For the present it suffices to say that under the Insurance Act 2015, a breach of warranty only suspends the liability of the insurer for the duration of the breach. However, it is possible in a non-consumer contract for this to be excluded and for the contract itself to provide for automatic discharge.

6.4   Repudiating the Contract or Claim

In addition to warranties, insurance contracts invariably contain what they describe as "conditions". Indeed, what in one policy may be covered by a warranty may in another fall under the heading or description of condition. Having said that, it is probably safe to say that if something is described as a warranty, it will normally be held to be such[29] and the same result will follow in respect of terms where a breach is expressly described as giving rise to avoidance of the policy as a whole or discharging the insurer from all liability.[30]

What is clear is that an insurance contract can provide for a condition to have the same effect as a condition in general contract law, namely that on breach, the insurer can treat the whole contract as repudiated. This will normally be done by making performance of the condition precedent to any liability of the insurer. However, it does seem clear that repudiation is allowed only if there is a causal connection between the breach and the loss for which the insured has made a claim.[31] In this respect there is a clear distinction from the warranty, where a breach is in law actionable regardless of any such causal connection.[32] A term with a slightly less significant effect is the condition that is merely precedent to the insurer's liability to pay for a particular claim.[33] A less common term is a "mere" condition, namely a condition that is not declared to be precedent to anything. On breach of such a term, the

---

where the Court of Appeal considered the effect of conditions precedent in an insurance contract without reference to general contract principles. However, there have recently been signs that the courts are now prepared to review such terms along general contract law principles. See Ch.9 for a detailed discussion.

[29] Though by no means always; see 9.8.

[30] These are of course strictly incorrect usages, as already explained, at least as a matter of the general law.

[31] See 9.9.

[32] See 9.2. This remains the position under the Insurance Act.

[33] The insurer can repudiate liability for a claim for breach of this sort of condition while affirming the contract generally; see e.g. *Mint Security Ltd v Blair* [1982] 1 Lloyd's Rep. 188; compare the ruling in *West v Motor Accident Insurance Union* [1954] 1 Lloyd's Rep. 461; [1955] 1 All E.R. 800, discussed at 9.2, although, as suggested there, this decision may not be supportable in the light of the decision in *The Good Luck* [1991] 2 W.L.R. 1279.

insurer is entitled only to claim damages for such loss as it has suffered.[34] Apart from those matters that may also be the subject of warranties, namely those matters that affect the risk run by the insurer, the usual matters covered by conditions are duties to be performed by the insured, often upon the making of a claim. It is this sort of term that is clearly potentially subject to the statutory controls on unfair terms, as already discussed.

Another term which has a similar consequence to a condition precedent, but which is conceptually different, is the suspensive condition, often known as a condition or clause descriptive of, or delimiting, the risk. Its effect is that the insurer is not on risk, and therefore not liable for any loss, while the term is not being complied with, but the risk attaches or reattaches, as the case may be, when the term is being complied with. It thus operates in the same way as an exception contained in the body of a policy. It differs from a warranty in the traditional sense in that it cannot lead to a complete discharge of the insurer and from a condition precedent in that a breach does not entitle the insurer to repudiate the contract. However, as the effect of the Insurance Act is to make a breach of warranty only suspensory, the distinction between warranties and suspensive conditions becomes almost irrelevant.

6.5   Loss of the Right to Avoid or Repudiate

Finally, there are a number of circumstances in which an insurer may lose the right to rely upon a non-disclosure or misrepresentation, or a breach of warranty or condition. This can arise by application of the doctrines of waiver (or affirmation) or estoppel. The essence of the matter is that the insurer, by what it says or does, leads the insured to believe that it will not insist upon its strict legal rights. The law then precludes the insurer from doing so. Waiver and estoppel may be conceptually different. This is a question more fully discussed later,[35] as indeed are the principles surrounding the application of these doctrines. Other illustrations of cases of waiver and estoppel will be found in the following chapters. Chapter 8 discusses the question of whether the insurers' duty of good faith can preclude their reliance on a non-disclosure or misrepresentation.

6.5.1 Indisputable policies

Sometimes insurers provide that their policies are to become indisputable after they have been in force for a particular time. In practice this is only

---

[34] Although if the amount of the insurer's damages equals the amount of the insured's claim, the result will be the same as if it were a condition precedent. See generally 14.5.

[35] See Ch.12.

likely to apply to life policies. The effect of an indisputability clause is that the insurer cannot rely upon defences that would entitle it to avoid the policy, or liability under it, from its inception.[36] Thus it will apply to non-disclosure, misrepresentation and certain breaches of warranty, but not, for example, to conditions or the coverage or definition of risk in the policy.[37] Furthermore, it cannot be relied upon to cure the lack of an insurable interest whose absence renders the policy illegal and void.[38] In addition, an indisputability clause never precludes the insurer from alleging that a policy was obtained by fraud.

---

[36] *Anstey v British Natural Premium Life Assurance Ltd* (1909) 99 L.T. 765.
[37] See, e.g. Cardozo J in *Metropolitan Life Insurance Co v Conway* 252 N.Y. 449, 169 N.E. 642 (1930). In some American states, indisputability clauses are compulsory. Compare the Australian Life Insurance Act 1954 s.84, which is to the same effect. The Law Commissions considered whether a similar position should apply in the UK and recommended that it should not: see Consumer Insurance Law: Pre-Contract Disclosure and Misrepresentation, Law Com No.319, Scot Law Com No.219, para.10.20 and following.
[38] *Anctil v Manufacturers' Life Insurance Co* [1899] A.C. 604.

CHAPTER 7

UTMOST GOOD FAITH—THE DUTIES OF THE INSURED

7.0 Introduction

As was described briefly in the last chapter, an insurer traditionally had the right in law to avoid the contract of insurance in its entirety if the insured was guilty of fraud, non-disclosure or misrepresentation before the contract was entered into; this may be described as the pre-contractual duty of the insured. It may also have a remedy in the case of a breach of good faith during the contract, although as will be seen, the law has never imposed a general duty of disclosure during the contract.[1] Questions of fraud and misrepresentation are common to all contracts, although certainly nowadays misrepresentation in insurance law is governed by specific statutory rules. Non-disclosure and a breach of a continuing duty of utmost good faith are peculiar to a class of contracts—those said to be uberrimae fidei or of the utmost good faith—of which the insurance contract is the prime example. The principle of utmost good faith does not have consequences just for the proposer or insured. Insurers are also subject, at least in theory, to a similar duty. This question and the extent to which it might be used to restrict the insurer's traditional right of avoidance are given separate consideration in Ch.8.

The traditional law was one of the central issues examined by the Law Commissions in their insurance contract law project and the first result of that[2] was in the substantial modification of the requirement of utmost good faith in consumer insurance contracts by the Consumer Insurance (Disclosure and Representations) Act 2012 (the 2012 Act).[3] This Act largely enacted as doctrinal law the practices developed by the Financial Services Ombudsman and partly reflected in the FCA's Insurance Conduct of Business Sourcebook, both in terms of the scope of the duties imposed on the insured and the remedies for breach of those duties. Further reforms,[4] applying to both consumer and non-consumer insurance contracts, were made by the Insurance Act 2015 (the 2015 Act).[5] In this regard, s.14(2) of the 2015

---

[1] This may be effected by express terms, as we shall see in 7.13.

[2] *Consumer Insurance Law: Pre-contract Disclosure and Misrepresentation*, Law Com No.310, Scot Law Com No.219, Cm 7758.

[3] Referred to in this chapter as "the 2012 Act".

[4] As recommended in *Insurance Contract Law: Business Disclosure; Warranties; Insurers' Remedies for Fraudulent Claims; and Late Payment*, Law Com No.353, Scot Law Com No.238, Cm 8898.

[5] Referred to in this chapter as "the 2015 Act". Given that we now have these two

Act[6] provides that any rule of law to the effect that a contract of insurance is a contract based on the utmost good faith is modified to the extent required by the provisions of the two Acts.[7]

Despite the above, there are, it is thought, at least five reasons why it still seems necessary to describe the law before these reforming statutes, what in this chapter is referred to as "the traditional law". First, it is arguable that the new law cannot be properly understood without knowledge of the mischiefs that it was designed to overcome. Secondly, although the traditional law will have very little relevance to consumer contracts that are indemnity contracts, given the date on which the 2012 Act came into force, it will still apply to many life insurance contracts taken out before that date, i.e. 6 April 2013. Thirdly, the law under the 2015 Act takes effect only as regards contracts entered into, renewed or varied on or after 12 August 2016 and one can be confident that disputes arising out of contracts effective before that date will continue to arise for some time to come. Fourthly, it is possible in a non-consumer contract to exclude the operation of the 2015 Act, so that in effect contract terms can be used to "resurrect" the traditional law. Fifthly, the 2015 Act does not make fundamental changes so far as non-consumer contracts are concerned and most of the traditional law remains relevant as regards such contracts.

For these reasons, this chapter gives a description of the traditional law on misrepresentation and non-disclosure[8] before looking at the statutory provisions, and those aspects of the traditional law thought to be still relevant, in 7.4 and following.

7.1   Fraud—the Traditional Law

This topic can be disposed of quickly; more detailed discussion can be found elsewhere.[9] Proposers are guilty of fraudulent misrepresentations if they knowingly make statements that are false, without belief in their truth or recklessly as to whether they are true or false.[10] They are guilty of fraudulent non-disclosure if they wilfully conceal from the insurer any material fact that they

---

reforming statutes, an account of previous recommendations for reform no longer seems appropriate. A brief account was given in para.7.18 of the ninth edition of this book.

[6] Section 14(1), abolishing avoidance as an automatic remedy for breach of the duty of utmost good faith, is considered further later.

[7] Section 2(5) of the 2012 Act made similar provision but that subsection is repealed by s.14(4) of the 2015 Act since it is replaced by s.14(2) applying to both consumer and non-consumer contracts.

[8] Although in much less detail than in earlier editions.

[9] See, e.g. *MacGillivray on Insurance Law*, 13th edn (London: Sweet & Maxwell, 2015), Ch.16.

[10] *Derry v Peek* (1889) 14 App. Cas. 337.

know the insurer would wish to be aware of. In addition to the right to avoid a contract entered into by an insured who has been fraudulent, the insurer may also have the right to claim damages in the tort of deceit, and can in addition retain any premium paid.[11] A clause purporting to protect insureds from the consequences of their fraud is unenforceable on public policy grounds.[12]

7.2   Misrepresentation—the Traditional Law

An insurer can avoid an insurance contract if it was induced to enter into it by a misrepresentation of fact made by the proposer that was false in a material particular, whether the proposer acted negligently or quite innocently.[13] The onus of proof as regards inducement, described as "always difficult for an insurer or reinsurer to discharge",[14] is on the insurer and the right to avoid differs little from that attaching generally in the law of contract.[15] Historically, misrepresentation in the strict sense was not of particular importance in the insurance context. This is partly because the extreme width of the duty to disclose material facts, as described below, meant that often non-disclosure subsumed questions of misrepresentation. Cases frequently failed to distinguish between the two defences taken by an insurer and indeed it appeared to be standard practice for an insurer, where possible, to plead both defences. While this may be conceptually unsatisfactory,[16] it was well established, the rationalisation being that it was part of the insured's duty of good faith to answer correctly questions on a proposal form.[17] On the other

---

[11] See *Chapman and others, assignees of Kennet v Fraser B R Trin*. 33 Geo. 111.

[12] *HIH Casualty & General Ins Ltd v Chase Manhattan Bank* [2003] UKHL 6; [2003] Lloyd's Rep. I.R. 230. The House of Lords left open the question as to whether a clause could protect the insured in the event of dishonest misrepresentation or non-disclosure by his agent to insure.

[13] See s.20 of the 1906 Act (repealed and replaced, as far as consumer insurance contracts are concerned, by the 2012 Act and replaced, as far as non-consumer contracts are concerned, by provisions of the 2015 Act with effect from 12 August 2016). Note that the Insurance Conduct of Business Sourcebook required an insurer to pay a claim despite an innocent misrepresentation: see 7.17.1.

[14] See Longmore J in *Sirius International Insurance Corp v Oriental Insurance Corp* [1999] Lloyd's Rep. I.R. 343 at 354.

[15] See, e.g. Peel, *Treitel, Law of Contract*, Ch.9. Until the decision of the House of Lords in *Pan Atlantic Insurance Co v Pine Top Insurance Co* [1994] 3 All E.R. 581, it was unclear whether or not "inducement" was an element of misrepresentation in the law of insurance contracts, especially because s.20 does not refer to it.

[16] See Hasson (1975) 38 M.L.R 89.

[17] *Everett v Desborough* (1829) 5 Bing. 503. A further reason for the relative unimportance of misrepresentation was that statements on a proposal form were often made into contract terms by the device known as the "basis of the contract clause", as briefly described in 9.2.1. Both the 2012 and 2015 Acts (in consumer and non-consumer insurances, respectively) have abolished this device.

hand, there is clearly a distinction between an innocent misrepresentation, where the proposer does not know the truth, and an innocent non-disclosure, where the proposer knows the truth but does not appreciate that he should disclose the fact in question. It seems, however, that this distinction does not matter.[18]

Most of the legal questions that arise in the context of misrepresentation, in particular the need for the misrepresented fact to be material, how materiality is judged, inducement and the possibility of excluding the remedies for a misrepresentation, are the same as apply to non-disclosure and these will be fully discussed later in this chapter. A representation of fact made before the original contract is not impliedly re-made on renewal.[19] However, in *Synergy Health (UK) Ltd v CGU Insurance Plc*,[20] a statement made four months before renewal, that the insured would install an intruder alarm within an agreed time, which proved to be false, was impliedly misrepresented on renewal.

Section 2(2) of the Misrepresentation Act 1967, giving the court a discretion to award damages in lieu of avoidance, could in theory operate as a restriction on the insurer's right to avoid for misrepresentation in a consumer case,[21] but this would appear now to be academic given the provisions of the 2012 Act.

7.2.1 Representations of opinion

The statements made by the proposer may not be representations of fact but only representations of opinion. This is likely always to be the case as regards insurances effected by individual consumers[22] and is also quite common nowadays in commercial insurance proposal forms. A representation of opinion

---

[18] *Pan Atlantic Insurance Co v Pine Top Insurance Co* [1994] 3 All E.R. 581, discussed further below. See Birds and Hird, (1996) 59 M.L.R. 285. There were signs, however, that the courts would no longer allow the defence of non-disclosure to succeed when the insured had allegedly made what can only be an innocent misrepresentation. See *Economides v Commercial Union Assurance Co Plc* [1999] 3 All E.R. 636.

[19] *Limit No.2 Ltd v Axa Versicherung AG* [2008] EWCA Civ 1231; [2009] Lloyd's Rep. I.R. 396.

[20] *Synergy Health (UK) Ltd v CGU Insurance Plc* [2010] EWHC 2583 (Comm); [2011] Lloyd's Rep. I.R. 500.

[21] It was held in *Highlands Insurance Co v Continental Insurance Co* [1987] 1 Lloyd's Rep. 109 that it would never be used in a commercial insurance context. This view was supported by Rix LJ in *HIH Casualty & General Insurance Co Ltd v Chase Manhattan Bank* [2001] Lloyd's Rep. 703 at [116].

[22] The Statement of General Insurance Practice provided that the declaration at the foot of a proposal form should make it clear that the form was completed only to the best of the proposer's knowledge and belief. Although the Statement is no longer operational, this remains the common practice.

has been described as a statement as regards which, as it appears or should appear to the person to whom the statement is made, the speaker does not have sufficient information to guarantee its accuracy.[23] Even if the representor is an expert, if there could be another, reasonable interpretation, then the statement may still be of opinion. The opinion must be based upon a genuine belief, but in insurance law, unlike in general contract law, [24] that belief need only be honest and the representor is not required to have reasonable grounds on which to base it. This was the decision of the Court of Appeal in *Economides v Commercial Union Assurance Co Plc*, [25] where the insured honestly under-estimated the value of the contents of his flat, relying on the advice of his father. His parents had come to live with him in the flat and brought valuables worth some £30,000, although it would appear that no one realised this. The contents were only insured for £16,000 at the time of the loss, which arose from a burglary when more than £30,000 worth of valuables were stolen. The court applied a literal interpretation of s.20(5) of the Marine Insurance Act—"a representation as to a matter of expectation or belief is true if it be made in good faith"—rejecting the insurers' argument, relying on both general contract and insurance law cases,[26] that the requirement of reasonable grounds was to be implied into s.20(5). Although the decision was criticised,[27] it clearly became settled law,[28] and the same construction will no doubt be given to s.3(3)(c) of the 2015 Act.[29]

7.3   Utmost Good Faith and Non-Disclosure— the Traditional Law

As already mentioned, the contract of insurance is the primary illustration[30] of a class of contracts described as uberrimae fidei, that is, of the utmost good faith. In its original version, s.17 of the Marine Insurance Act 1906 (the 1906

---

[23] *Hubbard v Glover* (1812) 3 Camp 313 at 314–315, per Lord Ellenborough.

[24] See Bennett, "Statements of fact and statements of opinion in insurance contract law and general contract law" (1998) 61 M.L.R. 886.

[25] *Economides v Commercial Union Assurance Co Plc* [1997] 3 All E.R. 636.

[26] *Smith v Land & House Property Corp* (1884) 28 Ch. D. 7 at 15 per Bowen LJ; *Brown v Raphael* [1958] 2 All E.R. 79 at 83 per Lord Evershed MR; *Credit Lyonnais Bank Nederland v Export Credit Guarantee Dept* [1996] 1 Lloyd's Rep. 200 at 216 per Longmore J; *Ionides v Pacific Fire and Marine Insurance Co* (1871) L.R. 6 Q.B. 674 at 683–684 per Blackburn J; *Highlands Insurance Co v Continental Insurance Co* [1987] 1 Lloyd's Rep. 109 at 112–113 per Steyn J.

[27] See Bennett, above and Hird [1998] J.B.L. 279.

[28] See the dictum of Longmore LJ in *Limit No.2 Ltd v Axa Versicherung AG* [2008] EWCA Civ 1231; [2009] Lloyd's Rep. I.R. 396 at [4].

[29] See 7.5.1.

[30] Others are family arrangements and contracts to take shares in public companies, the disclosure obligations in the latter case being imposed largely by statute.

Act), which represents the law applicable to all insurance contracts, puts it as follows:

> "A contract of marine insurance is a contract based upon the utmost good faith, *and, if the utmost good faith be not observed by either party, the contract may be avoided by the other party.*"

Note that, when the 2015 Act is in force,[31] the words italicised will be repealed. As a result of this principle, the law developed to require the potential parties to it to volunteer to each other, before the contract was concluded, information that was material. A very important issue is whether, and to what extent, a duty of good faith applies throughout the contract, but this is discussed at various stages later in this chapter and elsewhere.[32] As indicated, the principle of utmost good faith in terms of a pre-contractual duty of disclosure applies to insurers as well as insureds, but for the present we concentrate on the duty it imposes on the proposer or insured; its impact on insurers is considered in Ch.8.

The basic effect of the duty, before its modification by the 2012 and 2015 Acts, can be stated quite simply and was expressed in s.18 of the 1906 Act.[33] An applicant for insurance was under a duty to disclose to the insurer, prior to the conclusion of the contract,[34] but only up to this date, all material facts (or circumstances in the wording of s.18) within his knowledge that the latter did not or was not deemed to know. A failure to disclose, however innocent, entitled the insurer to avoid the contract ab initio, although in some consumer cases the Insurance Conduct of Business Sourcebook required the payment of a claim.[35] On avoidance the contract was deemed never to have existed.[36] The

---

[31] From 12 August 2016.

[32] See 7.15 in the context of a general duty on the insured, Ch.8 as regards the duty of the insurer and 14.12 in the context of fraudulent claims. The duty of disclosure did not depend on an implied term in the insurance contract: see 8.1.

[33] Section 18(1) provided: "Subject to the provisions of this section, the assured must disclose to the insurer, before the contract is concluded, every material circumstance which is known to the assured, and the assured is deemed to know every circumstance which, in the ordinary course of business, ought to be known by him. If the assured fails to make such disclosure, the insurer may avoid the contract." It was repealed, so far as consumer contracts were concerned, by the 2012 Act and is repealed and replaced for non-consumer contracts by the 2015 Act.

[34] The exact date when this occurs (see Ch.4) may therefore be of the greatest importance.

[35] See 7.17.1. This has become generally applicable for consumer insurances under the 2012 Act.

[36] This was not an easy question. For example, *Mackender v Feldia AG* [1967] 2 Q.B. 590 appeared to have decided to the contrary, and there is an argument that avoidance meant the parties being restored substantially to the position that they would have been in if no contract had been made: see *Brit Syndicates v Italaudit SpA* [2006]

insurer had to show inducement[37] and to avoid within a reasonable time of becoming aware of the non-disclosure and avoidance was effective as soon as the insurer's election to avoid was communicated to the insured,[38] although the right to avoid might be lost by affirmation. The duty arose whenever a fresh contract was concluded and, most importantly, this included upon a renewal of any contract except that of life insurance; this point has already been considered in an earlier chapter.[39] A number of important issues arise from this description and these are examined under the following headings. The very different obligation on a consumer insured under the 2012 Act is described in 7.4 and following. The rewriting of the duty for non-consumer insurances by the 2015 Act is described in 7.5 and following.

7.3.1 The rationale for the rule

In the leading case that established the duty of disclosure in insurance contracts, *Carter v Boehm*,[40] Lord Mansfield said[41]:

> "Insurance is a contract upon speculation. The special facts, upon which the contingent chance is to be computed, lie most commonly in the knowledge of the insured only: the under-writer trusts to his representation, and proceeds upon the confidence that he does not keep back any circumstance in his knowledge, to mislead the under-writer into a belief that the circumstance does not exist, and to induce him to estimate the risque as if it did not exist."

There can be no doubt that the contract of insurance is a special one in the terms that Lord Mansfield expressed, but two comments can at this stage be made about his formulation of the doctrine of non-disclosure. First, it is by no means certain that he was intending to lay down as broad a doctrine as subsequent cases established,[42] although this is an academic question today given the statutory reforms. Certainly the United States courts developed a

Lloyd's Rep. I.R. 483 and the discussion in *MacGillivray on Insurance Law*, 13th edn, para.17–030.

[37] See *Pan Atlantic Insurance Co v Pine Top Insurance Co* [1994] 3 All E.R. 581, discussed in 7.9.1, where this was implied into s.18(1).

[38] *Brotherton v Aseguradora Colseguros SA* [2003] EWCA Civ 705; [2003] Lloyd's Rep. I.R. 758.

[39] See 5.7.

[40] *Carter v Boehm* (1766) 3 Burr. 1905. Rather curiously in *Banque Financiere de la Cite v Westgate Insurance Co Ltd* [1990] 1 Q.B. 665, affirmed [1991] 2 A.C. 249, it was held that the duty of disclosure is equitable in origin, and this view was repeated in *Pan Atlantic Insurance Co v Pine Top Insurance Co* [1994] 3 All E.R. 581. See further at 8.1 and see generally the excellent analysis by Bennett [1999] L.M.C.L.Q. 165.

[41] *Carter v Boehm* (1766) 3 Burr. 1905 at 1909.

[42] See Hasson, "The doctrine of uberrima fides in insurance law: a critical evaluation" (1969) 32 M.L.R. 615.

much narrower duty of disclosure from the same source.[43] It is also noteworthy that Lord Mansfield regarded his principle of good faith as he called it as applying to all contracts.[44] He could hardly have been referring to the broad duty of disclosure as it became. Secondly, it is important to remember that *Carter v Boehm* involved a contract entered into at a time when communications were poor and insurers were not equipped with means easily to discover all the information they needed to know by the asking of questions of the proposer. It must be concluded that the justification for an all-ranging duty of disclosure with the drastic sanction of avoidance of the contract was not so apparent in modern times and indeed for some time this was accepted by insurers themselves in respect of insurances effected by individuals.[45] This has now been recognised by the 2012 Act as we shall see later.

There are also indications in modern cases dealing with business insurance that the courts were to some extent formulating a rather stricter test as the basis for establishing a non-disclosure. As the Law Commissions pointed out[46]: "It is now common for the courts to describe the policyholder's duty in terms of making a fair presentation of the risk". This, they argue, "is a more limited concept than 'every material circumstance'",[47] citing the following dictum of Clarke J in *Garnat Trading & Shipping (Singapore) Pte Ltd v Baominh Insurance Corporation*[48]:

> "A minute disclosure of every material circumstance is not required. The assured complies with the duty if he discloses sufficient information to call the attention of the underwriter to the relevant facts and matters in such a way that, if the latter desires further information, he can ask for it. A fair and accurate presentation of a summary of the material facts is sufficient if it would enable a prudent underwriter to form a proper judgment, either on the presentation alone, or by asking questions if he was sufficiently put upon enquiry and wanted to know further details, whether to accept the proposal and, if so, on what terms."

While one can agree that this approach is a fairer one than some earlier decisions would perhaps indicate, and it is in effect that adopted by the 2015 Act, it did seem little more than applying the doctrine of waiver, as discussed in 7.6.2.

---

[43] *Vance on Insurance* (3rd edn) at 370 and following; *Sebring v Fidelity Phoenix Insurance Co* 225 N.Y. 382 (1931).

[44] See (1766) 3 Burr. 1905 at 1910.

[45] It was also accepted by the House of Lords when they restated the test of materiality in *Pan Atlantic Insurance Co v Pine Top Insurance Co* [1994] 3 All E.R. 581 (see 7.8).

[46] *Insurance Contract Law: the Business Insured's Duty of Disclosure and the Law of Warranties*, LCCP 204, SLSDP 155, June 2012 at 5.12.

[47] See 5.13.

[48] *Garnat Trading & Shipping (Singapore) Pte Ltd v Baominh Insurance Corp* [2012] EWHC 2578 (Comm); [2011] 1 Lloyd's Rep. 589.

7.3.2 Statements of Fact

The duty of disclosure and the duty not to misrepresent examined earlier require that statements made by the proposer be of facts not opinion. A misstated opinion is actionable only if not given in good faith.[49] However, the distinction between questions of fact and questions of opinion is not always an easy one to make. This point can be illustrated particularly by the example of proposals for life insurance, where proposers may very well not know highly material facts regarding their health, because they are not experts, or if they do know something, may very well fail to appreciate its significance. In *Joel v Law Union & Crown Insurance Co*,[50] a statement as to the health of the proposer, made by her, was regarded as a statement of opinion. This accords with common sense, as the proposer who is not a medical expert or told specifically by such an expert of facts as to his health, cannot be expected to give more than an opinion. However, in a later case[51] concerning a similar issue, a proposer who failed to disclose a visit to a specialist was held to be guilty of non-disclosure of a material fact, even though he did not know that there was anything seriously wrong with him. Thus, although a mere statement as to health without more is a statement of opinion, at least where the proposer does not know any relevant facts, if a proposer for life insurance has consulted a doctor in more than an ordinary way, the fact of consultation will almost certainly be a material fact requiring to be disclosed.

7.3.3 Good faith and utmost good faith

It has long been clear that whether or not the proposer knows that he is under a duty to disclose is totally irrelevant. Innocent non-disclosure is as actionable as negligent non-disclosure or fraudulent concealment, as all the cases assume. Similarly, the insured's opinion as to the materiality of non-disclosed facts is irrelevant even though he may well have acted in good faith. As has been pointed out, it is the law that a person may act in perfect good faith within the ordinary meaning of the phrase, yet still be held not to have acted in the utmost good faith in the legal sense.[52] These points apply to the modern law affecting non-consumer insurance as much as they do to the traditional law.

---

[49] *Anderson v Pacific Fire & Marine Insurance Co* (1872) L.R. 7 C.P. 65, and see the earlier discussion of *Economides v Commercial Union Assurance Plc* [1997] 3 All E.R. 636.

[50] *Joel v Law Union & Crown Insurance Co* [1908] 2 K.B. 863. See also *Life Association of Scotland v Forster* [1873] 1 Macph. 351.

[51] *Godfrey v Britannic Assurance Co Ltd* [1963] 2 Lloyd's Rep. 515.

[52] See, e.g. McNair J in *Roselodge Ltd v Castle* [1966] 2 Lloyd's Rep. 113 at 129.

7.4 Consumer Insurance Contracts—the Modern Law

As was mentioned earlier, the law was substantially reformed as regards consumer insurance contracts by the Consumer Insurance (Disclosure and Representations) Act 2012, which came into force on 6 April 2013.[53] It only applies to contracts entered into or renewed after that date, so it does not apply to ordinary indemnity contracts entered into before 6 April 2013, although it is increasingly unlikely that disputes will arise under such contracts. Perhaps more importantly, it will never apply to most life insurance contracts entered into before that date.[54]

The Act was the product of a long period of consultation and effectively enacts the approach that the Financial Conduct Authority (previously the Financial Services Authority) and the Financial Ombudsman Service have taken, in respect of the ICOBS rules and the approach of the Ombudsman in relevant disputes.[55] A "consumer" for this purpose means an individual contracting "wholly or mainly for purposes unrelated to the individual's trade, business or profession".[56] There will no doubt be borderline cases, for example someone taking out a motor policy that covers business as well as private use or a household policy taken out by someone who runs their business from home.

7.4.1 Duty to take reasonable care

Section 2 contains the first key point of the Act. It abolishes the pure duty of disclosure and the application of ss.18 to 20 of the 1906 Act as far as consumer contracts are concerned.[57] In this context there is no longer a concept

[53] See the Consumer Insurance (Disclosure and Representations) Act 2012 (Commencement Order) 2013 (SI 2013/450).

[54] As seen earlier (see 5.7) ordinary life insurance contracts are entire and run until death or an earlier insured event such as the reaching of a certain age.

[55] For this reason, the detail of ICOBS and the approach of the Ombudsmen are not considered in detail in this edition, although technically they will continue to govern some contracts, especially life insurance contracts, for a good few years yet. More detail of these and of the non-statutory ABI Code of Practice for Long-term Insurance can be found in the eighth edition of this book at 7.17.1 to 7.17.3. Note that, as well as dealing with non-disclosure and misrepresentation, the Act abolishes the device of the basis of the contract clause, as described in 9.5. See generally *Consumer Insurance Law: Disclosure, Representations and Basis of the Contract Clauses*, ed. Tyldesley, Bloomsbury, 2013 and for commentary on the Act, Lowry and Rawlings, (2012) 75 M.L.R. 1099.

[56] See s.1. Note that it does not matter for the purposes of the Act whether the insurer is acting with authorisation under the FSMA 2000.

[57] This is also the case as regards marine insurance contracts taken out by a consumer: s.11. The 2015 Act repeals those sections but retains the substance of them, as will be seen.

of a "material circumstance" or a "material fact". In place of the previous law, the Act imposes a duty on a consumer to take reasonable care not to make a misrepresentation to the insurer, which includes a failure to comply with the insurer's request to confirm or amend previously given information. So in essence, it is only mis-statements on a proposal form[58] or in answer to questions posed on the telephone or electronically that are actionable in the situation of an original proposal for insurance. The "failure to comply" is aimed particularly at the situation on renewal, for example if the insurer chooses to resend a proposal form to the insured and ask if any of the information thereon has changed. It remains to be seen whether this leads to lengthier proposal forms than have been common in some situations.

Under s.3, reasonable care is judged by the standard of a reasonable consumer in the light of all the relevant circumstances, namely an objective test and not whatever might be the opinion of the actual consumer proposer, the actual insurer or a reasonable insurer. The section gives examples of what the "relevant circumstances" might be: (a) the type of policy in question and its target market; (b) any relevant explanatory material or publicity produced or authorised by the insurer; (c) how clear and how specific the insurer's questions were; (d) on renewal or variation, how clearly the insurer communicated the importance of answering questions or the possible consequences of failure to answer; and (e) whether or not an agent was acting for the consumer. In addition, account must be taken of any particular characteristics or circumstances of the actual consumer that the insurer knows or ought to know. A dishonest misrepresentation will always be regarded as made without reasonable care.

Section 3 is clearly the most interesting part of the Act. It, like much of the Act, is deliberately "principles based", explained by the Law Commissioner responsible at the time as follows[59]:

> "The Bill has been drafted to provide high-level overarching principles. It sets out a framework to deal with the problems but does not seek to lay down guidance. We do not deal with, for example, underwriting processes and practices in any particular detail. We were conscious that it is 105 years since the Act was passed and we hope that this Bill might last, if not quite so long, then for a reasonable period of time in future. Our view was that trying to lay down detailed guidance covering every eventuality, particularly those that might relate to scientific and information technology matters, would quickly become out of date and the Bill would become ossified, so we tried to set out principles rather than detailed practices. On the reasonable assumption that detailed rules—for

---

[58] Whether on paper or online.

[59] The oral evidence presented by David Hertzell to the House of Lords Special Public Bill Committee considering what became the 2012 Act, cited in Tyldesley at p.329.

example, around inappropriate questions—should come via guidance from the insurance industry, from targeted legislation such as the Equality Act or, as appropriate, from the [FCA]."

7.4.2 Remedies for breach

Remedies are covered by ss.4 and 5 and Sch.1, and it should be noted immediately that there is a remedy for breach of the duty to take reasonable care only if a misrepresentation was a "qualifying misrepresentation". The definition of this does not encompass an innocent or reasonable misrepresentation so that, even if such a misrepresentation could be regarded as breaching the duty, the insurer has no remedy for breach. This is another of the most notable differences from the previous law.

To be a "qualifying misrepresentation", the insurer must have been induced to enter into the contract or a variation of the contract or do so on different terms and the misrepresentation must be either (a) deliberate or reckless or (b) careless. A deliberate or reckless misrepresentation is where the consumer both knew that, or did not care whether, the misrepresentation was untrue or misleading and knew that, or did not care whether, the subject matter was relevant to the insurer. In such a case, the insurer can avoid the contract, refuse any claim and retain the premium unless that would be unfair to the consumer.[60]

As regards a careless misrepresentation, the insurer can avoid the contract and reject any claims if it would not have entered into the contract at all. Otherwise, if the insurer would have entered into the contract on different terms (except as regards the amount of premium), the contract is to be treated as if entered into on those terms. So, if, for example, the insurer would have imposed a particular term, say regarding security precautions, had the insured not misrepresented that the current precautions were working properly, a claim for loss which would not have been covered had that term been included can be rejected. If a higher premium would have been charged, then the insurer pays the proportion of claim that premium actually paid bears to the higher premium that would have been charged. In both these instances, other than in respect of a life insurance contract, the insurer may terminate the contract. Termination, rather than avoidance, is used here so that the remedy is prospective and thus the insurer would remain potentially liable for a prior claim.

---

[60] There is no guidance as to when it would be unfair to the consumer.

7.4.3 Group insurance

Section 7 of the Act contains a fairly complex provision concerning group insurance to ensure that where a group policy is effected for benefit of one or more consumers, and a consumer provides information to the insurer (directly or indirectly), the scheme of the Act applies and a breach by one consumer does not affect the contract so far as other consumer beneficiaries are concerned. The insurer here may have a remedy against the policyholder.

7.4.4 Life insurance

There is a second special provision, s.8, concerning insurance on life of another. It assumes that the life insured is not a party to insurance contract. Here, information provided by the life insured is treated as if provided by the person who is the party to the contract and it will be the life insured's knowledge etc. that is relevant for determining whether there is a breach of duty and the type of breach.

7.4.5 Agency

Many consumer insurance contracts are effected through an intermediary, whether that be a traditional agent or broker or through an online agent. As explained in Ch.12, it is not always easy to know whether an agent is in law agent of the insured or of the insurer, something that has caused particular problems over the years. Rather than laying down binding rules, the Act provides, in s.9 and Sch.1, rules for the purposes of the Act only.[61] The importance of these lies in deciding whether or not the knowledge of an agent is to be imputed to the insurer in accordance with the principles described in 12.4.

An agent is taken to be the insurer's agent in three situations: (a) when they do something in their capacity as an appointed representative of the insurer, (b) when they collect information from the consumer having been expressly authorised to do so by the insurer and (c) when they enter into the contract as the insurer's agent having been given express authority to do so.

Otherwise it is presumed that an intermediary is acting as the insured's agent unless, in the light of all the relevant circumstances, the contrary appears. The Act then lists factors that may be relevant to determine this. Those tending to confirm that an intermediary is acting for the consumer are where (a) the agent undertakes to give impartial advice to the consumer, (b) the agent undertakes to conduct a fair analysis of the market, and (c) the consumer pays the agent a fee. Those tending to confirm the contrary are where (a) the agent places insurance with only a small proportion of the insurers

---

[61] Which is why we deal with them here rather than in the later chapter.

who provide the relevant type of insurance, (b) the insurer provides the relevant insurance through only a limited number of agents, (c) the insurer permits the agent to use the insurer's name in providing the agent's services, (d) the insurance in question is marketed under the name of the agent, and (e) the insurer asks the agent to solicit the customer's custom.

7.4.6 Comment

It is thought that the 2012 Act produces a generally clear and balanced solution to the problems under previous law so far as consumers are concerned. There appear to be very few difficulties in interpretation, something that arguably contrasts quite strongly with the 2015 Act, to which we now turn.

7.5   Non-consumer Insurance Contracts—the Modern Law

As indicated earlier, Pt 2 of the 2015 Act, which follows the recommendations of the Law Commissions,[62] rewrites the principles governing non-disclosure and misrepresentation in non-consumer contracts, and is effective as regards contracts entered into, varied or renewed on or after 12 August 2016. There is no fundamental reform of the law, although there are not insignificant changes in some respects. In particular a duty of disclosure is retained, but both a failure to disclose and a misrepresentation are subsumed under what is now termed a "duty of fair presentation" and a breach of the duty does not necessarily entitle the insurer to avoid the contract. The key provision is s.3(1), by which, before a contract of insurance is entered into, the insured must make to the insurer a fair presentation of the risk.

This rewritten duty will apply to any person or body who is not a consumer. Thus it will apply to an individual who is a sole trader, a company or partnership that is a small business (as well obviously as medium and large businesses) and to a body such as a charity. Whether this is a totally fair outcome is perhaps debatable, as it could be argued that a small business, for example a person with a trade such as an electrician or a plumber, whether or not they conduct that trade through the medium of a limited company, is as deserving of protection as a consumer. Some of these people may be entitled to complain to the Financial Ombudsman Service,[63] which

---

[62] See Pt 2 of their Report, *Insurance Contract Law: Business Disclosure; Warranties; Insurers' remedies for Fraudulent Claims; and Late Payment* (Law Com No.353, Scot Law Com No.238, 2014, Cm 8898), hereafter referred to as the "2014 Report". For commentary on the Act, see Merkin and Gürses, "The Insurance Act 2015: rebalancing the interests of insurer and assured" (2015) 78 M.L.R. 1004.

[63] See 1.9.1.

may be expected to apply the law reasonably, but it is perhaps a pity that the Law Commissions bowed to pressure from the insurance industry in this regard.[64]

Because the duty of fair presentation was intended to be, and clearly is, a rewriting of the traditional law, to be read alongside the traditional case law, this part of the chapter will describe the duty by reference, where appropriate, to that case law.

7.5.1 The duty of fair presentation of the risk

As indicated above, the duty of fair presentation comprises both a duty of disclosure and a duty not to make a misrepresentation.[65] As far as disclosure is concerned, it includes, by s.3(3)(b), a requirement to make the disclosure in a manner which would be reasonably clear and accessible to a prudent insurer. By s.3(4), disclosure must be of every material circumstance which the insured knows or ought to know or, failing that, disclosure which gives the insurer sufficient information to put a prudent insurer on notice that it needs to make further enquiries for the purpose of revealing those material circumstances. While the first part of s.3(4) in effect repeats what was in s.18(1) of the 1906 Act and clearly includes constructive knowledge,[66] the second part reflects the case law developments described in 7.3.1. The purpose of this second part is to dispense with the need for "data dumping", that is the inclusion by the insured of a large amount of what might in part be unnecessary information in case any of it were in fact found to be material. What an insured knows or ought to know is considered further in 7.5.2, and the exceptions to the duty of disclosure in s.3(5) in 7.6 and following. Materiality is considered in 7.7 and following.

As far as representations are concerned, s.3(3)(c) states that every material misrepresentation as to a matter of fact must be substantially correct and every material representation as to a matter of expectation or belief must be made in good faith. The notable difference from s.20 of the 1906 Act is the inclusion of "substantially", described in s.7(5) as where a prudent insurer would not consider the difference between what is represented and what is actually correct to be material; again this reflects what is seen as the modern development in the case law of not requiring every single detail to be correct.

---

[64] On the other hand, had they not done so, it is unlikely that the Bill that became the 2015 Act would have been regarded as sufficiently uncontroversial to be put through Parliament under the special procedure for uncontroversial Law Commission Bills.

[65] By s.7(1), a fair presentation need not be contained in only one document or oral presentation.

[66] As under s.18 of the 1906 Act and so held by McNair J in *Australia and New Zealand Bank v Colonial and Eagle Wharves Ltd* [1960] 2 Lloyd's Rep. 241 at 252.

Section 7(6) states that a representation may be withdrawn or corrected before the contract of insurance is entered into; this seems almost to be stating the obvious. The requirement that representations as to expectation or belief be made in good faith mirrors s.20(3) of the 1906 Act and will no doubt be construed in accordance with the decision in *Economides v Commercial Union Assurance Plc*, described in 7.2.1.

7.5.2 Knowledge of the insured

What the insured knows or ought to know for the purpose of the duty of fair presentation under s.3(4) is amplified by s.4, although it should be noted that, by s.6,[67] as well as actual and constructive knowledge, an individual is deemed to know matters which he suspected and of which he would have had knowledge but for deliberately refraining from confirming them or enquiring about them.[68]

Section 4 is complex, especially because of the somewhat difficult issues that can arise when the insured is an organisation such as a public company, where a large number of individuals will have knowledge of facts that may be material to an insurance taken out by the organisation. What it covers has not been the subject of very much previous law in the insurance context, but the Law Commissions were anxious that it was dealt with in order to produce a more or less complete code.[69]

Section 4(2) provides that an insured who is an individual knows only what he or she knows and what is known to any individuals who are responsible for the insured's insurance. Section 4(3) provides that an insured who is not an individual knows only what is known to one or more of the individuals who are part of the insured's senior management or responsible for the insured's insurance. The inclusion of the word "only" is to ensure that these statutory rules replace the common law rules as to when the knowledge of an agent is imputed to their principal. An individual is responsible for an insured's insurance if they participate on behalf of the insured in the process of procuring the insurance, whether as the insured's employee or agent, as an employee of the insured's agent or in any other capacity.[70] As well as, for example, a broker or other intermediary, this clearly includes a person whose job within the insured's business is to deal with insurance matters.[71] "Senior management"

---

[67] This also applies to knowledge of the insurer.

[68] This is often called "blind-eye" knowledge. Note that s.6(2) preserves the general rule of the common law that knowledge of a fraud by an agent is not attributed to his principal.

[69] Part 8 of the Law Commissions' 2014 Report contains detailed discussions and illustrations.

[70] Section 4(8)(b).

[71] If a broker failed to disclose information, that would be regarded as negligence and

means the individuals who play significant roles in the making of decisions about how the insured's activities are to be managed or organised.[72] There has been much discussion about what this means. It must cover the members of a company's board of directors or the equivalent in non-corporate bodies, but probably does not extend to managers lower down the management structure as they would be unlikely to make decisions about *how* the insured's activities are to be managed or organised. However, their knowledge might be caught by the provision in s.4(6) which is discussed below.

Section 4(4) and (5) deals with confidential information. An insured is not deemed to know confidential information known to an individual if the individual is, or is an employee of, the insured's agent and the information was acquired by the agent or an employee of the agent through a business relationship with a person who is not connected with the contract of insurance.[73] The latter means anyone other than the insured and any other persons covered by the insurance and, if the insurance is a reinsurance, the insured under, and other persons covered by, the underlying insurance contract. This will apply principally to brokers who hold confidential information relating to one client that could be material to the insured who is a different client. This is not information that the insured is deemed to know. On the other hand, the insured will be deemed to know information that their broker knows that was obtained from another client but which is not confidential.

Section 4 deals separately with what can be called constructive knowledge. Any insured, that is whether an individual or an organisation, ought to know what should reasonably have been revealed by a reasonable search of information available to the insured, whether by making enquiries or by any other means (s.4(6)).[74] This includes information held within the insured's organisation or by any other person, such as the insured's agent or a person for whom cover is provided by the contract of insurance.[75] A key issue here is whether the test is subjective or objective. The case law on the equivalent provision in s.18(1) of the 1906 Act, which was much less expansive, took the view that the insured was deemed to know only what he would be expected to know in the course of his own business, making allowance for its imperfect organisation.[76] The Law Commissions appear to

the insured would have a remedy against them; see Ch.12. However, the knowledge of another person within a broking firm or company would not be attributed as the definition only covers individuals who act for the insured.

[72] Section 4(8)(c).
[73] Employee in this context means anyone working for the agent regardless of whether or not they are technically an employee; see s.4(8)(a).
[74] This would cover something like a database search.
[75] Section 4(7).
[76] *Australia & Colonial Bank v Colonial and Eagle Wharves* [1960] 2 Lloyd's Rep. 241

have intended an objective test,[77] but it remains to be seen how this will actually be interpreted.

7.6   What Need Not be Disclosed

There have long been exceptions to the duty to disclose material circumstances. These are now codified in s.3(5) as circumstances which diminish the risk, which are known or ought to be known to the insurer or are presumed to be known to the insurer or of which the insurer waives disclosure. Note that these exceptions apply only to the duty of disclosure and s.3(5) makes it clear that there will be a duty if the insurer makes a specific enquiry, where an incorrect answer will be a matter of misrepresentation.[78] These exceptions are discussed in more detail in the following paragraphs.

7.6.1 Knowledge of the insurer

As it does for the knowledge of the insured, the Act makes explicit, albeit less complex, provision as to what is the knowledge of the insurer. Note that by s.6,[79] as well as actual and constructive knowledge, an individual is deemed to know matters which he suspected and of which he would have had knowledge but for deliberately refraining from confirming them or enquiring about them.[80] Section 5(1) describes actual knowledge as covering only when something is known to one or more of the individuals who participate on behalf of the insurer in the decision whether to take the risk and, if so, on what terms (whether this is as the insurer's employee or agent, as an employee of the insurer's agent or in any other capacity). This provision in effect concerns the knowledge of the underwriter(s) in question.

By s.5(2), an insurer ought to know something only if either an employee or agent of the insurer knows it and ought reasonably to have passed on the relevant information to an individual mentioned in s.5(1) or the relevant information is held by the insurer and is readily available to an individual mentioned in s.5(1). The first category here is intended to include things like information held by the claims department and reports produced for assessing the risk, for example medical or surveying reports.[81]

at 252; *Simner v New India Assurance Co* [1995] L.R.L.R. 240 at 253–255; see *MacGillivray*, 13th edn, para.17–014.

[77] See the 2014 Report at paras 87–91, where the issue is discussed in great detail and the commentary in *MacGillivray*, 13th edn, paras 20–036 to 20–038.

[78] It may be, though, that the insurer will find it difficult to prove inducement.

[79] This also applies to knowledge of the insured.

[80] This is often called "blind-eye" knowledge. Note that s.6(2) preserves the general rule that knowledge of a fraud by an agent is not attributed to his principal.

[81] See the 2014 Report at paras 10–43 to 10–54.

The second is intended to require underwriters to search information available to them, for example information in the insurer's electronic records, provided they have access to it. This is an important proviso, as within some insurers the underwriting department may not have access to the records of the claims department. It will be a question of fact as to what is "readily available".

The inclusion of the word "only" in both s.5(1) and 5(2) means that any general common law rules on the attribution of knowledge are inapplicable in this context. So cases holding that an insurer was deemed to have the knowledge that its agent had if that knowledge was acquired by the agent acting in the scope of its authority, actual or ostensible[82] would no longer be decided on that basis, although they can still provide useful illustrations of what s.5(1) may cover. For example, in *Ayrey v British Legal & United Provident Assurance Co*,[83] the district manager of the insurer knew that the insured, who effected a life policy and was by occupation and on the proposal form described as a fisherman, was also a member of the Royal Navy Reserve. It was held that this knowledge was imputed to the insurer who could not therefore rely upon its non-disclosure by the insured. In *Blackley v National Mutual Life Association of Australasia*,[84] the agent knew before the contract was concluded that the life insured had a brain tumour that had just been operated upon. Again this knowledge was imputed to the insurer.[85]

An insurer's presumed knowledge covers two things, as now contained in s.5(3). The first is what is a matter of common knowledge; *Carter v Boehm* itself was a case where the insurers could not rely upon the non-disclosure because, it was held, the material facts were a matter of common knowledge. The insurance was of a fort in Sumatra by the Governor of the then colony. The material fact was that the fort was likely to be attacked by the French. It was held that the underwriters in London should have known that as well as the insured; indeed it was said that they were more likely to know. Another good example is the dangers of asbestos, of which insurers have been held presumed to know.[86] The second type of presumed knowledge is something which an insurer offering insurance of the class in question to insureds in the

---

[82] A more detailed description of basic principles of agency law is given in Ch.12.

[83] *Ayrey v British Legal & United Provident Assurance Co* [1918] 1 K.B. 136.

[84] *Blackley v National Mutual Life Association of Australasia* [1972] N.Z.L.R. 1038. The judgments in the New Zealand Court of Appeal contain a very comprehensive review of the principles governing the imputation of an agent's knowledge to his principal.

[85] See also *Woolcott v Excess Insurance Co* [1978] 1 Lloyd's Rep. 533, which is considered in 12.2.

[86] *Canadian Indemnity Co v Canadian Johns-Manville Co* (1990) 72 D.L.R. (4th) 478, Canadian Supreme Court.

field of activity in question would reasonably be expected to know in the ordinary course of business.[87]

7.6.2 Waiver

Waiver of the duty of disclosure raises a number of points. First are those that arise from the fact that in many cases insurance is effected following the completion by the proposer of a proposal form on which a great deal of information is in practice solicited. The fact that many questions are expressly asked does not relieve proposers of their duty to disclose facts outside the scope of the questions,[88] and indeed the questions may also show that the insurers regard certain matters as material,[89] but in some cases the form of questions asked may reduce the scope of the duty of disclosure. Similarly, if the proposer leaves a blank to a question which is accepted without inquiry by the insurer, this will normally be taken as a waiver by the insurer of any duty of disclosure in respect of the matters covered by the question.[90] This would not be the case, however, if in the circumstances, the blank space implies a negative answer to the question. If this is so, and a negative answer is incorrect, there will be a breach of duty by the insured.

Waiver as a result of the form of questions asked will usually arise where an express question asks for some details of certain facts or types of facts.[91] Disclosure of other details will be waived if it is felt that a reasonable person reading the proposal form would consider that the insurer did not seek the other details.[92] For example, a question asking the proposer for details of previous losses he has suffered within a five-year period would waive disclosure of losses outside that period even though such losses might well be material

---

[87] It may be that an insurer is presumed to know information readily available online; see the discussion, in the context of s.18 of the 1906 Act, in *Sea Glory Maritime Co v Al Sagr National Insurance Co (The Nancy)* [2013] EWHC 2116 (Comm) at [170] to [179].

[88] *Glicksman v Lancashire & General Assurance Co* [1927] A.C. 139; *Schoolman v Hall* [1951] 1 Lloyd's Rep. 139.

[89] *Hazel v Whitlam* [2004] EWCA Civ 1600; [2005] Lloyd's Rep. I.R. 168. See also *McNealy v Pennine Insurance Co Ltd* [1978] 2 Lloyd's Rep. 18, which is discussed in 12.6.3.

[90] *Roberts v Avon Insurance Co* [1956] 2 Lloyd's Rep. 240.

[91] *McCormick v National Motor Accident Insurance Union Ltd* (1934) 49 Ll.L.R. 361 at 363 per Scrutton LJ; *Schoolman v Hall* [1951] 1 Lloyd's Rep. 139 at 143 per Asquith LJ.

[92] See *Doheny v New India Assurance Co Ltd* [2004] EWCA Civ 1705; [2005] Lloyd's Rep. I.R. 251, especially at [14] to [20] and [37]. Even though the view expressed here was obiter, it is clearly authoritative. Longmore LJ was also at pains to stress that the principle was not confined to consumer insurance situations. See also *WISE (Underwriting Agency) Ltd v Grupo Nacional Provincial SA* [2004] EWCA 962, which is discussed below.

facts according to the usual test. Similarly, a question asking about the claims history of the proposer in relation to the type of insurance for which he is applying might well be regarded as waiving any duty of disclosure of losses or claims in respect of other types of insurance that in some circumstances might be regarded as material facts.[93]

There has been some discussion in modern cases about whether the insurer is in fact obliged to ask questions before an argument based on waiver can be made. This issue was discussed by Law Commissions in their June 2012 Consultation Paper.[94] They referred in particular to the judgement of Rix LJ in *WISE (Underwriting Agency) Ltd v Grupo Nacional Provincial SA*,[95] who linked the issue with that of fair presentation of the risk, and suggest that the duty of good faith on an insurer[96] may require it to ask questions. Any development along these lines seems unlikely given the terms of the 2015 Act, although the Law Commissions did consider that the rewriting of the duty of disclosure as part of a duty of fair presentation would result in there being less reliance on the concept of waiver.

7.7   The Test of Materiality

Much of the criticism of the wide-ranging nature of the duty of disclosure was directed at the central question of the test for determining materiality. Traditionally, a circumstance was material for the purposes of both non-disclosure and misrepresentation if it was one that would influence the judgment of a reasonable or prudent insurer in deciding whether or not to accept the risk or what premium to charge. This test was conclusively adopted for non-marine insurance purposes in *Lambert v Co-operative Insurance Society*,[97]

---

[93] In *Hair v Prudential Assurance Co Ltd* [1983] 2 Lloyd's Rep. 667, it was held that the effect of a general warning on a proposal form of the need for disclosure, of the sort then required by the Statements of Insurance Practice, was to waive the proposer's need to do any more than answer the questions put to him. However, this seems to be going too far (see [1984] J.B.L. 163).

[94] *Insurance Contract Law: the Business Insured's Duty of Disclosure and the Law of Warranties*, LCCP 204, SLSDP 155, especially 5.38 ff.

[95] *WISE (Underwriting Agency) Ltd v Grupo Nacional Provincial SA* [2004] EWCA 962. They also cite Lord Mansfield's views in *Carter v Boehm* (1766) 3 Burr. 1905.

[96] This is discussed further in Ch.8. Rix LJ was a notable proponent of there being such a duty. His judgment in the *WISE* case was a dissenting one. The majority judgments of Longmore and Peter Gibson LJJ proceeded along more conventional lines.

[97] *Lambert v Co-operative Insurance Society* [1975] 2 Lloyd's Rep. 485. See Merkin (1976) 39 M.L.R. 478. Some earlier non-marine cases, e.g. *Joel v Law Union* [1908] 2 K.B. 863, suggested a test depending on the opinion of the reasonable insured. The Court of Appeal in *Lambert* did not like having to reach their decision and thought that the law should be changed. See also *Kelsall v Allstate Insurance Co Ltd, The Times*, 20 March 1987, where the test was accepted, but was modified by an

the Court of Appeal holding that its statutory formulation in these terms in s.18 of the 1906 Act[98] was a codification of the common law applicable to all insurance contracts. Despite some indications to the contrary, it is thought that in respect of a pure non-disclosure[99] the view of the particular insurer is not relevant if a circumstance is not objectively material.[100] Although no longer relevant in a consumer insurance situation, such as the *Lambert* case, as we have seen, this core test is retained in the 2015 Act, with minor modification, for non-consumer insurances. Now, s.7(3) states that a "circumstance or representation is material if it would influence the judgement of a prudent insurer in determining to rake the risk and, if so, on what terms". The modification is that the last phrase replaces the more limited reference to premium and also encompasses clearly the possibility of the prudent insurer including particular terms in the contract. The 2015 Act also introduces a description of the word "circumstance" so that it includes any communication made to, or information received by, the insured.[101]

However, "influence the judgment", a phrase used in both the new and old statutory formulation, is capable of at least two interpretations. One is that the non-disclosed circumstance must have had a decisive influence on the judgment of the prudent insurer. Another is that all that is required is that the prudent insurer would have wished to know about the circumstance when reaching its decision. Surprisingly, perhaps, until relatively recently no case had adopted a definitive view on this matter. The first occasion when it was properly raised and decided was in *Container Transport International Inc v Oceanus Mutual Underwriting Association (Bermuda) Ltd*.[102] Here it was held the phrase meant merely that a prudent insurer would have wanted to know of the circumstance when making its decision; "judgement" was construed as meaning "the formation of an opinion", not the final decision. It was arguable, however, that the decision was based on a misreading of earlier authorities,[103] and it certainly seems to impose a particularly heavy burden on the insured.

express provision in the contract, "no known adverse facts", which had the effect of requiring the insured to disclose only facts known by him, as a reasonable man, to be adverse.

[98] See fn.33, above.

[99] As opposed to answering specific questions.

[100] See the discussion in *MacGillivray*, 13th edn, para.17–039

[101] Section 7(2).

[102] *Container Transport International Inc v Oceanus Mutual Underwriting Association (Bermuda) Ltd* [1984] 1 Lloyd's Rep. 467. See also *Highlands Insurance Co v Continental Insurance Co* [1987] 1 Lloyd's Rep. 109, where the judge felt bound to follow the decision in a non-marine misrepresentation case, though clearly with some misgivings.

[103] See the excellent article by Brooke, "Materiality in Insurance Contracts" [1985] L.M.C.L.Q. 437 analysing all the earlier cases, especially the Privy Council case of

In *Pan Atlantic Insurance Co v Pine Top Insurance Co Ltd*,[104] the House of Lords had the opportunity to rule authoritatively on the question, and, by a bare majority of three to two, they decided to follow the *CTI* ruling.[105] Although this could be regarded as unfortunate, and the dissenting opinion of Lord Lloyd in favour of the decisive influence test seems to read as persuasively as the leading majority judgment of Lord Mustill, the question is clearly now settled.[106] However, in order to mitigate what their Lordships recognised was the potential harshness of this aspect of the law, they introduced an additional requirement of inducement into the test of materiality. We will consider this, which has now been confirmed by statute, separately later.

7.7.1 Evidence of materiality

Because the test of materiality depends initially on the opinion of a reasonable insurer, the courts have long been prepared to accept the opinion of other insurers as evidence of whether or not particular circumstances are material.[107] In some cases, such opinions appear to have been accepted very readily, but some of the more modern decisions emphasise that they are in no way binding on the court, which must decide the issue as a question of fact. For

Mutual Life Insurance Co of New York v Ontario Metal Products Co Ltd [1925] A.C. 344. This case concerned the construction of a Canadian statute which required, in respect of life insurance, not just that a misrepresentation be material but also that it induced the actual insurer to enter into the contract (cf. s.151(9) of the Road Traffic Act 1988 above, which contains the same requirement). As Brooke pointed out, the Privy Council was careful to distinguish these two points and was clearly of opinion as regards the first that a non-disclosed or misrepresentation fact must actually have influenced a reasonable insurer to decline the risk or to have stipulated for a higher premium in order to be material; see Lord Salveson at 351. See also the judgment of Lloyd J at first instance in the *CTI* case [1982] 2 Lloyd's Rep. 178. The *CTI* case was not followed in some other common law jurisdictions; see e.g. *Barclay Holdings (Australia) Pty Ltd v British National Insurance Co Ltd* (1987) 8 N.S.W.L.R. 514; see Ying [1990] J.B.L. 97. For a general review, see Clarke "Failure to disclose and failure to legislate: is it material?" [1988] J.B.L. 206 at 298.

[104] *Pan Atlantic Insurance Co v Pine Top Insurance Co Ltd* [1995] 1 A.C. 501.

[105] Note that the Court of Appeal in *Pan Atlantic* ([1993] 1 Lloyd's Rep. 443) had adopted a "middle way", requiring proof that a prudent insurer would have treated the fact as increasing the risk, even though ultimately it might not have rejected the risk or charged a higher premium.

[106] It is thought, though, that the adoption of the decisive influence test would have produced a fairer result; for a detailed critique, see Birds and Hird (1996) 59 M.L.R. 285.

[107] See, e.g. *Babatsikos v Car Owners' Mutual Insurance Co* [1970] 2 Lloyd's Rep. 314, for a general survey, but compare the comment of Lord Mansfield in *Carter v Boehm* (1766) 3 Burr. 1905 at 1918. For a general criticism, see Hasson (1969) 32 M.L.R. 615. See also Evans (1984) 12 Australian Bus. L. Rev. 4.

example, in *Roselodge Ltd v Castle*,[108] an insurer's evidence to the effect that it would be material to an application for insurance many years later that the proposer was caught stealing apples at the age of 12 was ridiculed by McNair J. Similarly, the judgment of Forbes J in *Reynolds v Phoenix Assurance Co*[109] is instructive. He rejected the arguments that if an insurer is telling the truth and it is held to be a reasonable insurer, the court must accept its evidence as conclusive. The evidence is expert evidence that assists the court but never binds it. This is particularly so, of course, where there is conflicting evidence from different insurers.

7.8   Examples of Material Circumstances

While the test to be applied to determine whether or not a circumstance is material is a question of law, the actual determination of the issue in any particular case involves the resolution of a question of fact.[110] As such, it is generally a question solely for the trial judge or arbitrator and not subject to appeal, and, furthermore, strictly no decision is actually binding in a later case under the doctrine of precedent.[111] In addition, it must be remembered that in any given case the actual insurer must also have been induced by the non-disclosure or misrepresentation of such a circumstance, although as regards many "traditional" material circumstances, this is unlikely to be a difficult requirement to satisfy.

In a new development, the 2015 Act now includes examples of things which may be material circumstances. Section 7(4) states that these are (a) special or unusual facts relating to the risk, (b) any particular concerns which led the insured to seek insurance cover for the risk, and (c) anything which those concerned with the class of insurance and field of activity in question would generally understand as being something that should be dealt with in a fair presentation of risks of the type on question. The Law Commissions regarded (c) as likely to be the most important. Whether this adds a great deal to the "prudent insurer" test may be a matter for debate and it still seems useful to describe and illustrate some of the categories of circumstances that have traditionally been regarded as material.

These relate in general either to the physical hazard, that is the property, life or liability insured, or to the moral hazard. Circumstances relating to the physical hazard are generally obviously material. In property insurance, they

---

[108] *Roselodge Ltd v Castle* [1966] 2 Lloyd's Rep. 113 at 132.

[109] *Reynolds v Phoenix Assurance Co* [1978] 2 Lloyd's Rep. 440 at 457–459.

[110] For example, *Glicksman v Lancashire & General Assurance Co* [1927] A.C. 139.

[111] For a recent example of an unsuccessful appeal on the question of materiality and inducement, see *Laker Vent Engineering Ltd v Templeton Insurance Ltd* [2009] EWCA Civ 62.

would include, for example, the nature, construction or use of an insured building, or whether it is particularly exposed to risk; in life insurance, they would include health or a high risk occupation or hobby, excessive consumption of alcohol,[112] or the results of any health tests known to the insured[113]; in liability insurance, they would include a bad accident record and loss record.[114]

7.8.1 Moral hazard

Moral hazard cases can perhaps traditionally be regarded as falling into three categories: (1) those relating to the insurance history of the applicant; (2) those relating to criminal convictions or dishonesty; and (3) those relating to the applicant's nationality or origins. However, category (3) is now of purely historical interest, as explained in 7.8.5.

The insurance history of the proposer includes both previous refusals to insure by other insurers as well as his claims history. In *Glicksman v Lancashire & General Assurance Co*,[115] G and his partner applied for burglary insurance. It was held that the fact that G had, when trading on his own, previously been refused insurance was material, regardless of the reasons for the previous refusal and of the fact that there was on the proposal form a question which elicited such information in a way which could have been interpreted as applying to a previous proposal made by the applicants together. The House of Lords, in deciding the case, was full of regrets, but really there was nothing

---

[112] *Mundi v Lincoln Assurance Co* [2005] EWHC 2678 (Ch); [2006] Lloyd's Rep. I.R. 353.

[113] For example, for HIV, or even genetic tests. While there can be no doubt that such facts are material as a matter of strict law, whether or not the insurance industry should always be entitled morally to know of them is another matter and one which has been much discussed in recent years. See Davey, "Future imperfect: human genetics and insurance" [2000] J.B.L. 587. At present there is a *Concordat and Moratorium on Genetics and Insurance* (available at *http://www. abi.org.uk/Information/Consumers/Health_and_Protection/Genetics.aspx* [Accessed 29 December 2015]), under which the ABI and government have agreed essentially that there is no requirement to disclose the results of genetic testing except in very limited circumstances approved by the Genetics and Insurance Committee. For a detailed examination, see Wilkinson, *Gene rummy*, unpublished PhD thesis, University of Manchester, 2009; see also Wilkinson, "Unjustified discrimination: is the moratorium on the use of genetic test results by insurers a contradiction in terms?", available at *http://www.springerlink.com/openurl.asp?genre=article&id=-doi:10.1007/s10728-009-0137-9* [Accessed 29 December 2015].

[114] See *New Hampshire Insurance Co v Oil Refineries Ltd* [2003] Lloyd's Rep. I.R. 386.

[115] *Glicksman v Lancashire & General Assurance Co* [1927] A.C. 139. See also *London Assurance v Mansel* (1879) 11 Ch. D. 363 for an example in life assurance and *Stowers v GA Bonus Plc* [2003] Lloyd's Rep. I.R. 402 regarding the refusal of a renewal.

their Lordships could do. Materiality was a question of fact, which had been conclusively decided by the arbitrator. It should be noted that, in vivid contrast, in marine insurance a previous refusal to insure is not material.[116]

Whether or not a previous refusal to insure in respect of a type of insurance other than that for which the proposer is applying is material is not so clear. In *Ewer v National Employers' Mutual & General Insurance Association*,[117] Mackinnon J clearly rejected such a wide proposition, but in *Locker & Wolf Ltd v Western Australian Insurance Co*,[118] a previous refusal of motor insurance was held material to a proposal for fire insurance, quite apart from the fact that there was a general question on the proposal form. It would appear that such a previous refusal may be material when it relates in a general way to the integrity of the proposer.[119] A mere refusal would therefore not be material, but a refusal based on the insurance history of the proposer, for example, as to his claims experience, might well be.[120]

Previous losses of the sort against which the proposer is seeking insurance are clearly material,[121] although in practice these will be solicited by express questions and, quite possibly, any duty to disclose outside the scope of the question will be waived.

7.8.2 Criminal history and dishonesty

Perhaps the most important fact affecting the moral hazard of the proposer, apart from insurance history, is any criminal history. Certainly many of the modern cases appear to have been concerned with this question and the fact that the insured is facing serious criminal charges may be as material as an actual conviction.[122] This too may be affected by legislation, in this instance the Rehabilitation of Offenders Act 1974. A number of cases involving mostly the insurance of valuables establish that criminal convictions for offences of dishonesty are normally material, including those that relate to "a dim and

---

[116] *Glicksman* in the Court of Appeal, [1925] 2 K.B. 593 at 608.

[117] *Ewer v National Employers' Mutual & General Insurance Association* [1937] 2 All E.R. 193 at 202–203

[118] *Locker & Wolf Ltd v Western Australian Insurance Co* [1936] 1 K.B. 408.

[119] *Locker & Wolf Ltd v Western Australian Insurance Co* [1936] 1 K.B. 408 at 414 per Slesser LJ.

[120] But what if the insurers were told of the claims experience, but not of the refusal based on it?

[121] For example, *Arterial Caravans Ltd v Yorkshire Insurance Co* [1973] 1 Lloyd's Rep. 169.

[122] See *North Star Shipping Ltd v Sphere Drake Insurance Plc* [2006] EWCA Civ 378; [2006] Lloyd's Rep. I.R. 519, distinguished in *Norwich Union Insurance Ltd v Meisels* [2006] EWHC 2811; [2007] Lloyd's Rep. I.R. 69.

distant past", 12 years[123] and, possibly, 20 years[124] prior to the insurance application. In *Roselodge Ltd v Castle*,[125] though, a conviction for bribery was held not material to the insurance of diamonds, though a smuggling conviction was material. It appears also, logically enough, that the mere commission of an offence may be material, even if the proposer is acquitted by a jury, provided, of course, that the insurer can prove to the satisfaction of the civil court that the proposer did commit the offence.[126] A wrongful conviction should also be disclosed.[127] Although judicial opinion has been divided as to whether proposers must disclose the fact of arrest where they were innocent,[128] the prevailing view is that allegations of serious criminal conduct and serious criminal charges should be disclosed.[129] In *Lambert v Co-operative Insurance Society*,[130] it was the convictions of the proposer's husband that were material facts. Although the result of this case has been criticised,[131] the offences were of dishonesty, and the insurance was an all risks one on jewellery, including some which was owned by the proposer's husband. In *Drake Insurance Plc v Provident Insurance Plc*,[132] it was common ground that a speeding conviction was material in motor insurance. It has also been held that a failure to disclose a material conviction to a previous insurer is itself a material fact that should be disclosed to a subsequent insurer.[133]

Woolcott v Sun Alliance & London Insurance[134] appears to be a more extreme example because here there was no obvious connection between the non-disclosed conviction and the sort of insurance applied for. The claimant proposed for fire insurance on his house through the building society to

---

[123] *Schoolman v Hall* [1951] 1 Lloyd's Rep. 139.

[124] *Regina Fur v Bossom* [1957] 2 Lloyd's Rep. 466.

[125] *Roselodge Ltd v Castle* [1966] 2 Lloyd's Rep. 113.

[126] *March Cabaret Club & Casino Ltd v London Assurance* [1975] 1 Lloyd's Rep. 169.

[127] Above.

[128] See 177. The opposite was held in *Reynolds v Phoenix Assurance Co Ltd* [1978] 2 Lloyd's Rep. 440 at 460.

[129] See especially *Brotherton v Aseguradora Colseguros SA* [2003] EWCA Civ 705; [2003] Lloyd's Rep. I.R. 758; *North Star Shipping Ltd v Sphere Drake Insurance Plc* [2006] EWCA Civ 378; [2006] Lloyd's Rep. I.R. 519. See 8.2 as to whether the insurer's remedy might be lost if the allegations prove to be unfounded or the insured is acquitted.

[130] *Lambert v Co-operative Insurance Society* [1975] 2 Lloyd's Rep. 465.

[131] Merkin (1976) 39 M.L.R. 478.

[132] *Drake Insurance Plc v Provident Insurance Plc* [2003] EWCA Civ 1834; [2004] Lloyd's Rep I.R. 277; see further in 8.2.

[133] *Joseph Fielding Properties (Blackpool) Ltd v Aviva Insurance Ltd* [2010] EWHC 2192 (QB); [2011] Lloyd's Rep. I.R. 238. This was so even though the conviction was spent under the Rehabilitation of Offenders Act 1974 (see 7.8.3) at the time of the proposal to the subsequent insurer; it had not been at the time of the proposal to the previous insurer.

[134] *Woolcott v Sun Alliance & London Insurance* [1978] 1 All E.R. 1253.

which at the same time he was making a mortgage application.[135] He failed to disclose the fact that he had been convicted of robbery some 12 years previously. It was held that the insurers could avoid the policy.[136] The learned judge appears to have accepted, without demur, the evidence called for the insurers that the fact related to Woolcott's moral hazard. With respect, it is not at all obvious why a convicted robber should be more risky in relation to the insurance of a building than anyone else, even though it must be accepted that Woolcott's conviction was serious. In contrast, in *Reynolds v Phoenix Assurance Co*,[137] after perhaps a more thorough review of the law, Forbes J held that a conviction for receiving was not a material fact in relation to fire insurance. Admittedly the matter was comparatively trivial and the insured was merely fined. It was held that the matter depended basically on the extent of the dishonesty and the age of the conviction. As the learned judge admitted, hard and fast rules cannot be laid down about this sort of case. This must be correct, even though it makes the application of the law somewhat uncertain, and the insured in the unenviable position of having to find evidence to challenge that of the insurers. One interesting comment in the judgment in *Reynolds* relates to the lack of experience among the experts called of actual disclosures by proposers of their previous convictions. Forbes J[138] understandably found this surprising in view of the large numbers of crimes dishonestly committed every year and the almost universal adoption of some form of insurance for buildings. Clearly he did not believe some of the more extreme evidence as to materiality put forward in that case.[139]

It seems, in summary, that any conviction relevant to the insurance sought will be regarded as material unless it is both trivial and old. An irrelevant conviction, that is one not directly germane to the risk, will affect the moral hazard of the proposer certainly when it is serious, presumably meaning punished by imprisonment or a substantial fine. An ancient trivial offence would not be material. It is less certain whether a recent unconnected trivial offence would be material. In the decided cases of relevance, the offences were all quite old.

---

[135] There was no proposal form; the insurance application was simply the answer to one question on the mortgage application form.

[136] But the building society that was also insured was able to recover as the policy was not a joint one. The question of the effect of a non-disclosure by one co-insured on the position of an innocent co-insured is discussed at 7.11.

[137] *Reynolds v Phoenix Assurance Co* [1978] 2 Lloyd's Rep. 440.

[138] Above at 460.

[139] See also 7.7.1. Today, this would clearly also affect the question of inducement.

7.8.3 Spent convictions

However, regardless of the above, an applicant for insurance is never bound to disclose a conviction which has become spent under the terms of the Rehabilitation of Offenders Act 1974 (the 1974 Act).[140] There are different periods laid down for rehabilitation depending on the seriousness of the sentence imposed. Most importantly, a conviction resulting in a sentence of two and a half years' imprisonment or more can never become spent. Otherwise, convictions with custodial sentences of between six months and two and a half years become spent after ten years and those of less than six months after seven years. In respect of other sentences, the period is five years, except in relation to absolute discharges (six months) and conditional discharges and probation (one year).

There is one provision, though, in s.7(3) of the 1974 Act, which gives the court a discretion to admit evidence as to spent convictions if the court is satisfied that "justice cannot be done in the case except by admitting it". The issue arose in earlier proceedings in *Reynolds v Phoenix Assurance Co*[141] because the offence already referred to came to light only after the case commenced and the insurers sought to amend their pleadings to allege its non-disclosure. The Act did not apply when the insured applied for the insurance in 1972, but it did when the matter came to trial. The Court of Appeal held that the pleadings should be amended on the ground that no prejudice would be caused to the insured. Whether or not the evidence of the conviction should be admitted was then a matter for the trial judge. Forbes J subsequently held that the evidence should be admitted, although this did not matter in the result as he held that the conviction was not material, as we have already seen.

It is unfortunate that in the *Reynolds* litigation the courts did not really decide the effect of s.7(3) on the duty of disclosure. They may have been influenced by the fact that the alleged non-disclosure took place before the 1974 Act existed. It can hardly be said to be just to admit evidence of spent convictions in relation to insurance effected after 1974 when, since that time, the proposer has been under no duty to disclose them.

7.8.4 Dishonesty

Proven dishonesty, even in the absence of a criminal conviction, may be a material fact. In *Insurance Corporation of the Channel Islands v Royal Hotel Ltd,*[142]

---

[140] See s.4(3)(a).

[141] *Reynolds v Phoenix Assurance Co* [1978] 2 Lloyd's Rep. 22.

[142] *Insurance Corp of the Channel Islands v Royal Hotel Ltd* [1998] Lloyd's Rep. I.R. 151. See also *Gate v Sun Alliance Insurance Ltd* [1995] L.R.L.R. 385; *Markel International*

a director of the insured, who was also its company secretary, had prepared false invoices in order to give the insured's bankers a more favourable impression of its profitability. Although these had not been used by the time of the insurance proposal, and no criminal offence had actually been committed, it was held that this kind of dishonesty was material. This seems unobjectionable and is in line with the authorities already mentioned regarding allegations of criminality.

7.8.5 Anti-discrimination legislation

In the past, moral hazard would have been regarded as also encompassing factors like the nationality,[143] racial origins or gender of the proposer. However, legislation has over the years outlawed discrimination on many such grounds[144] and the matter is now covered by the Equality Act 2010, which consolidated earlier legislation as well as prohibiting other forms of discrimination. Prima facie, this Act prohibits discrimination in the provision of services on the grounds of age, disability, gender reassignment, marriage and civil partnership, race, religion or belief, sex and sexual orientation. There are, however, a number of exceptions so far as insurance is concerned. Primarily these are (1) insurance provided to employees and others as a consequence of employment under arrangements made by the employer for the insurer to provide the insurance; (2) regarding disability, if insurers act by reference to information that is both relevant to the assessment of the risk and from a source on which it is reasonable to rely, and it is reasonable to do so; and, subject to the important qualification below, (3) regarding sex, gender reassignment, pregnancy and maternity, anything reasonably done in relation to annuities, life and accident insurance where it is done by reference to actuarial or other data from a source on which it is reasonable to rely.

Where the Act allows discrimination by insurers, then failure to disclose a relevant condition can amount to non-disclosure of a material fact. So, under (3) above, insurers had the right to know the sex of a proposer for life insurance since they would be able to show actuarial data that women tend on the whole to live longer than men. However, this particular situation was complicated by the decision of the European Court of Justice in *Association Belge des Consommateurs Test-Achats ASBL v Conseil des Ministres*.[145] Here the court held that a provision in Directive 2004/113/EC, the Directive generally

---

Insurance Co v La Republica Cia Argentina de Seguros [2004] EWHC 1826 (Comm); [2005] Lloyd's Rep. I.R. 90 and *Sharon's Bakery (Europe) Ltd v Axa Insurance UK Plc* [2011] EWHC 210 (Comm); [2012] Lloyd's Rep. I.R. 164.

[143] A classic case was *Horne v Poland* [1922] 2 K.B. 364.

[144] Especially the Race Relations Act 1976 and the Sex Discrimination Act 1975.

[145] C-236/09, [2011] Lloyd's Rep. I.R. 296.

prohibiting gender discrimination, which exempted insurance where sex could be regarded as actuarially and statistically justified, was invalid. As a result, an amendment was made to the Equality Act[146] removing exception (3) as far as concerns contracts concluded on or after 21 December 2012.[147]

7.9   Remedies for Breach

Section 8 of and Sch.1 to the 2015 Act deal with the remedies the insurer has for a breach by the insured of the duty of fair presentation.

7.9.1 Inducement

Section 8(1) states that the insurer has a remedy against the insured for a breach of the duty of fair presentation only if it shows that, but for the breach, it would not have entered into the contract of insurance at all or would have done so only on different terms. This is the codification of the requirement introduced into the previous law by the House of Lords, in *Pan Atlantic Insurance Co v Pine Top Insurance Co*,[148] and as interpreted in subsequent case law. In effect, as well as being of a circumstance that a prudent insurer would want to know about, the non-disclosure or misrepresentation must be an effective cause of the insurer entering into the contract. Because this requirement is now statutory, it is unnecessary here to consider the reasoning process that led to its introduction.[149]

On the other hand, the case law since *Pan Atlantic* is clearly still relevant to the interpretation of s.8(1). The non-disclosure or misrepresentation does not have to be the sole cause.[150] In the judgment of the House of Lords there was a clear dictum that there was a presumption of inducement,[151] albeit a factual presumption and not a legal presumption, and this was followed by the subsequent Court of Appeal decision in *St Paul Fire & Marine Insurance Co (UK) Ltd v McDonnell Dowell Constructors Ltd*.[152] If a fact is obviously material,[153] the court may be justified in inferring that the insurers were induced

---

[146] The Equality Act 2010 (Amendment) Regulations 2012 (SI 2012/2992).

[147] This was the date from which the ECJ ruled that its decision would be effective.

[148] *Pan Atlantic Insurance Co v Pine Top Insurance Co* [1994] 1 A.C. 501.

[149] This and a brief critique can be found in para.7.10 of the previous (9th) edition of this book and the references therein.

[150] *St Paul Fire & Marine Insurance Co (UK) Ltd v McDonnell Dowell Constructors Ltd* [1995] 2 Lloyd's Rep. 116; *Assicurazioni Generali SpA v Arab Insurance Group* [2002] EWCA Civ 1642; [2003] 1 W.L.R. 577 at [59] and [87].

[151] See Lord Mustill [1994] 3 All E.R. at 610 and 617, although Lord Lloyd strongly disagreed, saying that this was "a heresy long since exploded" (p.637).

[152] Above.

[153] See earlier for examples of facts that have normally been regarded as material.

even where they do not give evidence and thus to this extent they can benefit from the presumption of inducement.[154] This will normally be the situation when other insurers' evidence as to materiality has been accepted.[155]

Otherwise, it is clear that the insurer must show that, had it known the non-disclosed or misrepresented circumstance, it would not have concluded the contract on the same terms or at all, because if it would have made the same contract, the non-disclosure or misrepresentation cannot have made any difference.[156] One way of doing this is to show that disclosure of the relevant circumstance would have led the insurer to ask further questions that, if answered correctly, would have led it to impose different terms.[157] A good illustration of the importance of the inducement requirement is the Court of Appeal decision in *Drake Insurance Plc v Provident Insurance Plc*.[158]

In 1996, K caused a road accident when driving her husband's (S) car. K and S had separate insurance covering K's liability. K's own policy, issued by Drake, covered her whilst she was driving any vehicle with the owner's consent. S's policy issued by Provident covered K as a named driver. Drake settled the claim brought against K by the injured third party and then sought a contribution from Provident.[159] Provident avoided its contract alleging non-disclosure by S of a speeding conviction incurred by K. It was common ground that the non-disclosure was objectively material, so Provident's case turned on the question of inducement. Provident's underwriting policy worked on a mechanical system of points, allocated according to particular risks. If a proposer had 16 points or fewer, then a normal pre-

---

[154] See *St Paul Fire & Marine Insurance Co (UK) Ltd v McDonnell Dowell Constructors Ltd* and *Assicurazioni Generali SpA v Arab Insurance Group*, above. See also *Bate v Aviva Insurance UK Ltd* [2014] EWCA Civ 334.

[155] See, for example, *Marc Rich & Co AG v Portman* [1996] 1 Lloyd's Rep. 430; *Aneco Reinsurance Underwriting Ltd v Johnson & Higgins* [1998] 1 Lloyd's Rep. 565; *Insurance Corp of the Channel Islands v Royal Hotel Ltd* [1998] Lloyd's Rep. I.R. 151; *International Management Group v Simmonds*, above and *Toomey v Banco Vitalicio Espana* [2004] Lloyd's Rep. I.R. 354. In some of the cases the court has accepted such evidence where the insurers have not done everything possible to enable it to hear the actual underwriter involved, an approach that was criticised by Yeo [2004] 10 J.I.M.L. 84.

[156] See especially *Assicurazioni Generali SpA v Arab Insurance Group*, above.

[157] *International Management Group v Simmonds* [2004] 2 Lloyd's Rep. I.R. 247. In another case it was held that a liability insurer had been induced by the non-disclosure of a claim for $5 million that had been made against the insured because the premium would have been raised, even if the precise amount of the increase could not be shown: *New Hampshire Insurance Co v Oil Refineries Ltd* [2003] Lloyd's Rep. I.R. 386.

[158] *Drake Insurance Plc v Provident Insurance Plc* [2003] EWCA Civ 1834; [2004] Lloyd's Rep I.R. 277. The case also raised important issues of the insurer's duty of utmost good faith which are addressed in 8.2.

[159] As to contribution, see Ch.16.

mium was charged. Over 16 points attracted an increase in premium of 25 per cent. An accident that was the fault of an insured attracted 15 points and a speeding conviction 10 points, so one of each automatically attracted the 25 per cent increase in premium. K had been involved in an earlier accident, which S had disclosed to Provident in February 1995 as K's fault, but by itself this did not affect the premium as it attracted only 15 points. However, on renewal in February 1996, S failed to disclose that when the accident was investigated, K was found not to be at fault. He also failed to disclose that K was convicted of speeding in 1995. Had both these facts been disclosed on renewal, the points tally would have been only 10, so a normal premium would again have been charged. As neither was disclosed, the tally was 25, so an increased premium was charged at renewal.

The Court of Appeal held that Provident had no right to avoid, as it had not been induced to enter the contract by reason of the non-disclosure of the speeding conviction. Had it been disclosed, Provident would have sought to charge a higher premium, which S would have queried and the mistake regarding K's accident would have come to light. Provident had to prove that the mistake would not have come to light had the speeding conviction been disclosed, which clearly it could not do.[160]

7.9.2 Remedies

Assuming that an insurer can show inducement, what its remedy will be purports first to depend on whether the breach of duty by the insured is a "qualifying breach", which may be either deliberate or reckless or not deliberate or reckless. Section 8(5) defines a qualifying breach as deliberate or reckless if the insured knew that it was in breach of the duty of fair presentation or did not care whether or not it was in breach of that duty, but the onus is on the insurer to prove either of these.[161] It should be noted that the 2015 Act, unlike the 2012 Act, does not distinguish between innocent and negligent breaches of duty, so that in a non-consumer insurance, an innocent breach of duty will give the insurer a remedy. It therefore seems somewhat curious that the 2015 Act bothers to contain and define the concept of a "qualifying breach".

If a qualifying breach was deliberate or reckless, the insurer may avoid the contract and refuse all claims and need not return any premium.[162] So the remedy here is identical to the previous law, although it is not certain that

---

[160] Whilst this approach is extremely advantageous for an insured, it has been pointed out that it comes perilously close to allowing the court to underwrite the policy itself: Merkin, *Insurance Law Monthly*, (2004) Vol.16 No.2.

[161] Section 8(6).

[162] Sch.1 para.2.

a reckless breach would have meant forfeiture of the premium. Any other breach has similar consequences to those in the 2012 Act.[163] If the insurer would not have entered into the contract on any terms had it known the truth, it may avoid the contract and refuse all claims, but must return the premium.[164] If it would have entered into the contract but on different terms, other than relating to the premium, the contract is treated as if it had been entered into on those terms if the insurer so requires.[165] So if a particular loss would have been excluded, the insurer will not be liable in that respect, although the contract remains in force. But if, say, the non-disclosed or mis-represented circumstance was quite irrelevant to the actual loss, so that any term would not have affected the insurer's liability for that loss, the insurer is liable. If a higher premium would have been charged, then the insurer pays the proportion of claim that premium actually paid bears to the higher premium that would have been charged.[166] Unlike the provisions of the 2012 Act, the 2015 Act says nothing about the further consequences of a breach of duty if the insurer is liable to pay either the whole or a proportion of a claim. This is left to the terms of the contract, and it seems likely that insurers will reserve the right to themselves to terminate the contract.

7.9.3 Excluding the remedies for breach

It is clear that the law, except in cases of fraud, will uphold clauses that exclude the remedies for breach of the duty of fair presentation or exclude or limit the scope of that duty. It is not uncommon for a policy to do so in situations of co-insurance, such as those considered below. Another very important context is where insurance is taken out by a bank as security for a loan, for example in order to finance the making of a film (known as film finance insurance). This was the type of insurance in issue in *HIH Casualty & General Insurance Ltd v Chase Manhattan Bank*.[167] Here, the contract in question contained what was described as a "truth of statement" clause, which provided, among other things, that the insured would not have any duty or obligation to make any representation, warranty or disclosure of any nature, express or implied (such duty and obligation being expressly waived by the insurers), and that any non-disclosure by the insured or by others would not be a ground for avoidance of the insurers' obligations. Neither the principle

---

[163] Sch.1 Pt 2 contains the remedies where there has been a breach of the duty of fair presentation on a variation of the contract. These are effectively the same as described in the text.

[164] Sch.1 para.4.

[165] Sch.1 para.5.

[166] Sch.1 para.6.

[167] *HIH Casualty & General Insurance Ltd v Chase Manhattan Bank* [2003] UKHL 6; [2003] Lloyd's Rep. I.R. 230.

of utmost good faith nor public policy invalidated such a provision, except where there was fraudulent concealment by the insured.[168]

7.9.4 Losing the right of avoidance by affirmation

The insurers will waive any right they may have to avoid for breach of the duty of fair presentation if they elect to continue with the contract and so affirm it. Relatively recent case law[169] has clarified the requirements in this respect. The insurers must have actual, not constructive, knowledge of the relevant circumstance and know that they have the right to avoid. They have a reasonable time for decision and there must be an unequivocal communication to the insured[170] by words or conduct that they have made an informed choice to affirm. An unequivocal communication depends on how a reasonable person in the position of the insured would interpret the insurer's word or conduct. Delay by itself is not sufficient but will count if the insured is prejudiced by it or it is explicable only on the basis that the insurers are affirming the contract. Otherwise any kind of conduct by the insurers that leads the insured reasonably to believe that the insurers intend to continue to insure him is sufficient. This can include failing to avoid and return the premium while refusing to pay a claim, making an interim payment, accepting a premium and giving instructions to the insured concerning the subject matter of the insurance.

7.10   Contracting-out of the 2015 Act

As was indicated earlier, it is possible in a non-consumer insurance contract to contract out of much of the Act, including Pt 2 on the duty of fair presentation. This is possible only if the requirements of s.17 are satisfied.[171] The insurer must take sufficient steps to draw a term to this effect, referred to in the Act as a "disadvantageous term", to the insured's attention before the contract is entered into or a variation is agreed, unless the insured or its agent had actual knowledge of it at that time, and the term must be clear and unambiguous as to its effect. By s.17(4), in determining whether these

---

[168] The House of Lords left open the question of whether a clause could be effective in the event of fraud by an agent to insure.

[169] *Insurance Corp of the Channel Islands v Royal Hotel Ltd* [1998] 1 Lloyd's Rep. I.R. 151; *Spriggs v Wessington Court School Ltd* [2004] EWHC 1432 (QB); [2005] Lloyd's Rep. I.R. 474. See also *Scottish Coal Co Ltd v Royal & Sun Alliance Plc* [2008] EWHC 880 (Comm); [2008] Lloyd's Rep. I.R. 718.

[170] Communication to the third party in the case of liability insurance is not enough: *Spriggs v Wessington Court School Ltd*, above.

[171] Section 16(2). Note the provisions of s.18, which import the same requirements into group insurance contracts.

requirements have been satisfied, the characteristics of insured persons of the kind in question and the circumstances of the transaction must be taken into account. The application of s.17(4) will clearly be of particular importance for those non-consumers who do not use the services of a broker or similar intermediary and may even, like many consumers, contract for insurance online.

As far as the duty of fair presentation is concerned, it will clearly be possible to exclude the duty of fair presentation completely or some part of the Act, for example by retaining the insurer's traditional right of avoidance in all circumstances. What will not be sufficient is simply to exclude the Act and rely on the previous law as encapsulated in ss.18 to 20 of the 1906 Act, as those provisions are repealed, together with any rule of law to the same effect.[172] However, in principle there would seem no objection to a contract term clearly providing for a pre-contractual duty to disclose material facts and not to make material representations, defined as under the traditional law (and in the 2015 Act), but, say, giving the right to avoid without the insurer having to show inducement. How often there will be exclusions seeking to take advantage of this freedom of contract remains to be seen. It is possible that a court might take the view that relying on an exclusion could amount to a breach of the insurer's duty of good faith; this is considered further in 8.2.

7.11   Non-Disclosure and Misrepresentation in Co-Insurance

Some interesting questions arise regarding non-disclosure and misrepresentation in co-insurance situations. In general these have not been affected by the statutory reforms examined earlier, the Law Commissions declining to make any recommendations in this context and stating that they would expect the courts to continue to approach this question in a flexible way.[173] As we have seen,[174] co-insurance, or composite insurance, arises when more than one party insures separate interests under the same policy, for example a mortgagor and mortgagee insuring their different interests in the same property, or the various parties involved in a construction project.

The question is whether, when one co-insured is guilty of a breach of the duty of fair presentation, the insurers are entitled to a remedy only against that co-insured, or against all those insured under the policy.[175] If the policy

---

[172] Section 21(2) and (3).

[173] This was referred to specifically in a document of 20 November 2014, produced by the Law Commissions when the Insurance Bill was under consideration in Parliament.

[174] See 4.1.

[175] If someone is simply a beneficiary under an insurance contract rather than a co-insured, then by s.4(7) of the 2015 Act, information they have is treated in effect as information known to the insured.

is one single contract, then the insurers would argue that they ought to be allowed a remedy against all the parties because they have been misled as to the overall risk, and, in principle, a remedy against one co-insured ought to be possible only if, on its true construction, the policy contains separate contracts.[176]

However, in *Woolcott v Sun Alliance & London Assurance*,[177] which concerned a single contract, the insurers were allowed to avoid under the former law against a mortgagor, despite the fact that they had indemnified the mortgagee in respect of its separate interest. It might have been argued that the insurers had waived the right to avoid the whole contract by paying the mortgagee, but this point was not raised. In *New Hampshire Insurance Company v MGN Ltd*,[178] the Court of Appeal similarly held that the insurers were not entitled to avoid against an innocent co-insured, where the various parties insured were the different members of a group of companies. The court relied on the House of Lords' decision in *P Samuel & Co Ltd v Dumas*.[179] This latter case concerned a claim brought by shipbrokers, the named assured on a marine hull policy, for the benefit of both the owners and the mortgagees of the insured ship. The vessel was scuttled by the owners without the knowledge of the mortgagees. The insurers argued that the policy was joint, but the House of Lords held that it was a composite policy, and, as such, the innocent co-insured could recover, despite the fraud of the owner. In the *New Hampshire* case, Staughton LJ, raised the crucial issue of whether the contract was single, or whether there were several contracts. He said:

"Technically, one ought to enquire whether . . . there was one contract or as many contracts as there were companies insured. And, if the former, can a contract be avoided for non disclosure as against one or some of the insured but not against others?"[180]

However, he felt that the court was relieved from having to tackle the issue because the principle established in *Samuel v Dumas* regarding wilful misconduct by a co-insured should equally apply to a non-disclosure. It is, however, clear from his remarks that he thought there were several separate contracts in this case. The decision is probably correct, at least in terms of justice; it cannot be fair to allow an insurer to avoid the whole contract or have

---

[176] Where a composite policy is a single contract, albeit that the insurer can undertake distinct obligations to the separate parties, then it is difficult to see how the insurer can avoid only against one party—see *Federation Insurance v Wasson* (1987) C.L.R. 303.

[177] *Woolcott v Sun Alliance & London Assurance* [1978] 1 All E.R. 1253; see 7.11.2.

[178] *New Hampshire Insurance Company v MGN Ltd* [1997] L.R.L.R. 24.

[179] *P Samuel & Co Ltd v Dumas* [1924] A.C. 431 (HL).

[180] *New Hampshire Insurance Co v MGN Ltd* [1997] L.R.L.R 24 at 57–58.

another remedy when only one single co-insured out of many has failed to disclose facts relevant to the risk. However, it does not adequately deal with the problem that Staughton LJ himself recognised, that of whether there is in fact one single contract or several contracts.

The issue was considered again in *Arab Bank Plc v Zurich Insurance Co.*[181] Here, the clients of a company that ran an estate agency recovered judgments in respect of negligent valuations by the managing director of the company, which they sought to recover from the latter's insurers under the Third Party (Rights against Insurers) Act 1930.[182] There was no question that the managing director, who was a co-insured under the policy, had failed to disclose the material fact that he had been involved in making fraudulent valuations. Rix J held that the insurers were not entitled to avoid the policy as against the company. It was common ground that the professional indemnity policy in question insured separate interests and was specifically worded to ensure that the dishonesty of one co-insured would not deny recovery by the others if they were not complicit in the deceit. This, together with provisions in the policy concerning subrogation and a general condition spelling out the penalties for innocent non-disclosure, provided a basis for the judge to hold that the insurers were liable to the innocent company.[183] However, he went on to say that in fact the policy in question involved a bundle of separate contracts between the insurers and the various co-insureds, and that the dishonesty of one did not allow total avoidance against all. He said that this ought to be the "prima facie" position under all composite policies, without meticulous examination of the terms. With respect, this seems too wide. It was not necessary for Rix J to tackle this issue; because of the particular contract in this case, he had ample ammunition to deny avoidance on its own terms. Whether there is one contract or several is crucial if this issue is to be resolved in accordance with legal principle; to say that as a matter of course all such insurances consist not of a single contract but of several contracts cannot be satisfactory.

It would appear, however, that this view was given at least tacit approval by the Court of Appeal in *FNCB Ltd v Barnet Devanney (Harrow) Ltd.*[184] This case concerned the placing of composite insurance by the defendant broker on behalf of the claimant bank and its mortgagor. The mortgagor was

---

[181] *Arab Bank Plc v Zurich Insurance Co* [1999] 1 Lloyd's Rep. 262. For a detailed examination of this decision, see Birds [1999] J.B.L. 151.

[182] As to the 1930 Act, see Ch.20.

[183] The insurers further argued that the managing director's knowledge of the fraud ought to be imputed to the company, but this argument was also rejected. The fraud of an agent is never imputed to his principal: see 12.4. It could be argued that even the policy provisions relied on by Rix J were not really support for his conclusion; see Birds [1999] J.B.L. 151.

[184] *FNCB Ltd v Barnet Devanney (Harrow) Ltd* [1999] Lloyd's Rep. I.R. 459.

found to have made a material non-disclosure and the insurer avoided the policy. The bank's claim was settled for less than the outstanding amount of the mortgage and it sought to recover the shortfall from the broker. The bank argued that the broker was in breach of duty in failing to ensure that a mortgagee protection clause was inserted into the policy. It was common practice at the time the insurance was effected in 1987 to insert such a clause, preserving an innocent mortgagee's rights under the policy in the event that the mortgagor could not effectively make a claim. The court at first instance refused to find the broker negligent, relying on the *New Hampshire* decision as having established that a mortgage protection clause was unnecessary, because the bank was protected from avoidance in any event. On appeal, the Court of Appeal found for the bank, saying that the *New Hampshire* decision could not apply to insurance contracts effected in 1987. The court did not, however, cast any doubt on the principle that all composite insurances are now to be regarded as containing separate contracts. While it could be argued that this is too important a principle to be dealt with in such a cursory fashion, it must be regarded as settled,[185] although it will often be subject to the proper construction of the terms of the policy.[186]

7.12   The Continuing Duty of Utmost Good Faith

Hitherto in this chapter we have examined the principle of utmost good faith, which, it will be recalled, was first expressed by Lord Mansfield in *Carter v Boehm*[187] and is codified in s.17 of the 1906 Act, in the context of its traditional imposition of a pre-contractual duty of disclosure on the insured, albeit now modified to a greater or lesser extent by the recent statutes; we will examine in the next chapter if and how it imposes a duty on the insurer. Our concern at this stage is the extent to which the principle has a continuing effect. Although referred to very occasionally in earlier case-law, it is really only in the last 30 years or so that this has become an important issue.

In providing that the remedy for breach of the principle was avoidance of the contract, which would mean from the beginning (ab initio), s.17 raised difficulties and debate, as a breach of the principle during the contract ought not normally to lead to retrospective avoidance of the whole contract. When the 2015 Act is in force, these difficulties largely disappear because the relevant words are omitted from s.17 by s.14(3)(a) of the 2015 Act and s.14(1)

---

[185] It might also be argued that the courts have allowed arguments based on commercial convenience to overcome properly thought-out principle in the situations where insurers seek to exercise subrogation rights against a co-insured. This question is fully discussed elsewhere in this book in Chs 4 and 17.

[186] For a recent example of such a situation, see the House of Lords' decision in *Brit Syndicates Ltd v Italaudit SpA* [2008] UKHL 18; [2008] Lloyd's Rep. I.R. 601.

[187] See 7.4.

provides that any rule of law permitting a party to a contract of insurance to avoid the contract on the ground that the utmost good faith has not been observed by the other party is abolished. Because of this, we do not any longer consider the problems of this nature that existed before the Act.[188]

It is clear that the section does have a continuing effect,[189] but the exact nature of this continuing duty of utmost good faith is not wholly clear. It was discussed in the case law most with regard to its effect on fraudulent claims, but in this respect has been rendered almost irrelevant because of the specific provisions regarding these in Pt 4 of the 2015 Act. These are considered later in Ch.14. In recommending retention of the principle but removal of the consequence of avoidance for breach, the Law Commissions considered that it could continue to be developed by the courts as and when appropriate.[190] One can say with some degree of certainty only that it will apply when an insured breaches an obligation to supply information to the insurer. In the leading case of *Manifest Shipping Co Ltd v Uni Polaris Shipping Co Ltd (The Star Sea)*,[191] Lord Hobhouse confirmed that "utmost good faith is a principle of fair dealing which does not come to an end when the contract has been made", although he did say that the "content of the obligation to observe good faith has a different application and content in different situations". *The Star Sea* decided as such only that any post contractual duty of good faith comes to an end once litigation proceedings have commenced. It was closely followed by two Court of Appeal decisions—*K/S Merc-Scandia XXXXII v Certain Lloyd's Underwriters (The Mercandian Continent)*[192] and *Agapitos v Agnew (The Aegeon)*,[193] although these cases were concerned with fraudulent claims and, as mentioned, these are now expressly dealt with in the 2015 Act.

What is not in doubt is that any general duty to disclose material circumstances is cast upon the insured only before the contract is concluded, renewed or varied, whether at common law as codified in the 1906 Act or under the terms of the 2012 and 2015 Acts, as examined earlier. At common law, there is no general duty to disclose material facts that occur during the period of insurance. The authority for this is the old case of *Pim v Reid*,[194] where the insured changed his trade and caused a large amount of highly

---

[188] They are considered in para.7.16 of the previous (9th) edition of this book.

[189] See *The Star Sea* [2001] UKHL 1; [2001] 2 W.L.R. 170, which is discussed below.

[190] Some might argue that it was not really necessary to retain it as insurers can draft express terms to deal with any problems if they wish.

[191] Above.

[192] *K/S Merc-Scandia XXXXII v Certain Lloyd's Underwriters (The Mercandian Continent)* [2001] EWCA Civ 1275; [2001] Lloyd's Rep. I.R. 802.

[193] *Agapitos v Agnew (The Aegeon)* [2002] EWCA Civ 247; [2002] Lloyd's Rep. I.R. 573.

[194] *Pim v Reid* (1843) 6 M. & G. 1.

inflammable material to be brought on to the insured premises. It was held that his non-disclosure of this fact to the insurer was not actionable. This basic common law position has more recently been confirmed by the Court of Appeal in *Kausar v Eagle Star Insurance Co Ltd*,[195] although specific "increase of risk" clauses very often appear as express terms of the contract and these are examined in 7.13 immediately below.

7.13   Increase of Risk Clauses

As mentioned above, certain contracts of insurance, most notably those of fire insurance, do, in practice, impose a duty on the insured to disclose facts occurring during the insurance that materially increase the risk.[196] The term that imposes such a duty is usually, though not necessarily, a promissory warranty. Although we shall be examining promissory warranties in general in Ch.9, it is appropriate here to consider this common type, since it clearly imposes a duty of disclosure similar to that imposed by virtue of the principle of utmost good faith.[197]

A simple increase of risk clause, as it may be called, only operates when the increase is permanent and habitual.[198] In *Shaw v Robberds*,[199] a fire policy was effected upon a granary which contained a kiln for drying corn. On one occasion, the insured allowed a third party to dry some bark in the kiln and this, in fact, occasioned the fire that brought about the dispute. It was held that the insurers were liable, despite the presence of an increase of risk clause. The change was merely temporary. It mattered not of itself that drying bark was a much more hazardous business than drying corn.

If, therefore, an insurer wishes to be notified of merely temporary increases in risk, it must insert express clauses to that effect.[200] It is also notable that a clause in fire policies on buildings may only relate to alterations to the building itself and not to any alteration of its contents that may increase the risk.[201] Insurers must also be careful when replacing the traditional clause

---

[195] *Kausar v Eagle Star Insurance Co Ltd* [1997] C.L.C. 129. And see the dictum of Lord Hobhouse in *The Star Sea* [2001] UKHL 1; [2001] 2 W.L.R. 170 at [48].

[196] There is evidence that such a duty is being imposed more widely by insurers, e.g. in household policies, and the need for clear wording to impose such a duty is illustrated by the decision in *Kausar*; see further below.

[197] For an excellent comparative survey, see Clarke, "Aggravation of risk during the insurance period" [2003] L.M.C.L.Q. 109.

[198] For a more recent example of the operation of the standard clause, see *Forrest & Sons Ltd v CGU Insurance Plc* [2006] Lloyd's Rep. I.R. 113.

[199] *Shaw v Robberds* (1837) 6 A. & E. 75. Compare *Farnham v Royal Insurance Co* [1976] 2 Lloyd's Rep. 437.

[200] See, e.g. *Glen v Lewis* (1853) 8 Ex. 607.

[201] *Exchange Theatre Ltd v Iron Trades Mutual Insurance Co Ltd* [1984] 1 Lloyd's Rep. 149; see [1984] J.B.L. 363.

by one worded in "plain English". In *Kausar v Eagle Star Insurance Co Ltd*,[202] a provision that stated: "You must tell us of any change of circumstances which increases the risk of injury or damage. You will not be insured under the policy until we have agreed in writing to accept the increased risk" was held ineffective when, in an insurance of a shop, the insured failed to tell the insurers that threats to damage the shop had been made by the tenants and (unlawful) sub-tenants.[203] This decision was distinguished more recently in *Ansari v New India Assurance Ltd*.[204] Here the key part of the relevant provision stated:

> "This insurance shall cease to be in force if there is . . . any material change in the facts stated in the proposal form . . . unless the insurer agrees in writing to continue the insurance."

The proposal form had stated that the premises insured were protected by an automatic sprinkler system, but at some point this had been turned off other than merely for maintenance or repair. Construing "material" as referring to changes of a kind that take the risk outside that which was in the reasonable contemplation of the parties when the policy was issued,[205] the Court of Appeal held that the provision operated to relieve the insurers of liability.

An analogous specific disclosure requirement often imposed in fire policies relates to the property being unoccupied for a specified period and requiring that fact to be reported to the insurer. Unoccupancy relates, it has been held, to the absence of a physical presence in the building insured.[206] If, in fact, no one is regularly and daily present therein, the building is unoccupied, unless the absence is merely temporary, for example, by reason of the insured being on holiday.[207]

---

[202] *Kausar v Eagle Star Insurance Co Ltd* [1997] C.L.C. 129.

[203] The result may be justifiable on the ground that this was not in any event a permanent increase in risk. See also *Scottish Coal Co Ltd v Royal & Sun Alliance Plc* [2008] EWHC 880 (Comm); [2008] Lloyd's Rep. I.R. 718.

[204] *Ansari v New India Assurance Ltd* [2009] EWCA Civ 93; [2009] Lloyd's Rep. I.R. 562.

[205] Rejecting the argument for the insurer that "material" was to be construed more widely in accordance with its meaning for pre-contractual disclosure purposes.

[206] *Marzouca v Atlantic and British Commercial Insurance Co Ltd* [1971] 1 Lloyd's Rep. 449.

[207] *Winicofsky v Army and Navy General Insurance Co* (1919) 88 L.J.K.B. 111.

CHAPTER 8

GOOD FAITH ON THE PART OF THE INSURER

8.0

We have seen in the previous chapter how the law traditionally imposed a strict duty of disclosure on the insured as a consequence of the principle of utmost good faith, albeit that this duty has been repealed or modified by the recent statutes. The question explored in this chapter is whether, and to what extent, that principle applies also to the insurer. As s.17 of the Marine Insurance Act 1906 imposes the principle on both parties, it might be thought that the answer to the question is a simple affirmative. While it is certainly true that the insurer does owe a duty of disclosure, we shall see that this duty is in reality somewhat limited in its application. The extent to which an insurer is subject to a wider duty of good faith is certainly not as clear.

8.1 The Insurer's Duty of Utmost Good Faith and Disclosure

It has long been said[1] that the requirement of utmost good faith applies to both parties to the insurance contract, in other words that it imposes a duty of disclosure on the insurer as much as on the insured. Until the important decision in *Banque Financière de la Cite SA v Westgate Insurance Co Ltd*,[2] this did not, however, seem to have any real significance. In this fascinating piece of litigation, there was a bold attempt by the judge at first instance, having applied such a duty on an insurer, to give it some real teeth by awarding damages for breach of the duty. However, while the Court of Appeal and House of Lords accepted that there was a duty, they held that the only remedy for breach was the traditional one of avoidance of the contract.[3]

---

[1] See the founding judgment of Lord Mansfield in *Carter v Boehm* (1766) 3 Burr. 1905; see also the judgment of Farwell LJ in *Bradley and Essex and Suffolk Accident Indemnity Society* [1912] 1 K.B. 415.

[2] *Banque Financière de la Cite SA v Westgate Insurance Co Ltd* [1991] 2 A.C. 249, affirming the Court of Appeal, [1990] 1 Q.B. 665, reversing the judgment at first instance, sub nom. *Banque Keyser Ullman SA v Skandia Insurance Co* [1987] 1 Lloyd's Rep. 69.

[3] Part of the problem with the case was that, wound up with the pure insurance aspects, in terms of utmost good faith and disclosure, was a claim in tort for, in effect, pure economic loss. It arose at the time when the higher courts were

Given that the Insurance Act 2015 repeals that part of s.17 that stated that a breach of utmost good faith gave the right to avoid, this decision must be read in the light of that. However, the principle of utmost good faith is retained so this is not simply an academic question.

A number of banks agreed to make some very substantial loans on condition that, inter alia, binding contracts of credit insurance had been issued before the money would be advanced. The manager of the firm of brokers responsible for arranging the insurance fraudulently issued cover notes to the banks in respect of the first loan representing that insurance cover was complete when in fact there was a shortfall. Some months later, the senior underwriter discovered what had happened and realised that there had been a substantial gap in the insurance coverage during those months, although by that time the gap had largely been filled. He failed to inform the banks of this and the banks made further loans. The whole scheme proved to have been a massive fraud by the borrower who defaulted in repaying any of the money. In addition to making a claim against the brokers, which was settled, the banks claimed on the insurance contracts. However, their claim was rejected[4] on the ground that the contracts contained a clause excluding the insurers' liability for "any claim or claims arising directly or indirectly out of or caused directly or indirectly by fraud attempted fraud misdescription or deception by any person firm organisation or company". They then sued the insurers for damages for the latter's failure to disclose to them the broker's fraud. At first instance, their claim was largely successful. The Court of Appeal allowed an appeal by one of the insurers involved, holding that, although there had been a breach by the insurers of the duty of disclosure, the only remedy for breach of the duty was avoidance of the contract and return of the premiums, not damages.

When one of the banks appealed to the House of Lords, the arguments proceeded along rather different lines. Their lordships held the losses suffered by the banks were not the consequence of any breach of a duty of disclosure

---

cutting back on the availability of tortious remedies for pure economic loss and may have suffered accordingly, with the special insurance attributes being in effect overlooked. The only other English case where the question of the remedy for a non-disclosure had been expressly considered previously was *Glasgow Assurance Corp v Symondson* (1911) 16 Com. Cas. 109 at 121, where Scrutton J stated that the only remedy was avoidance. However, this dictum was clearly obiter, although it was relied upon by the Court of Appeal in the *Banque Financière* case in support of their decision.

[4] In the litigation, the banks conceded that they could not claim on the contracts. This was perhaps unfortunate. Otherwise they might, for example, have argued that the effect of the insurers' non-disclosure was to preclude their relying on the exclusion clause by analogy with cases like *Curtis v Chemical Cleaning and Dyeing Co* [1951] 1 K.B. 805. However, they would still have had to overcome the causation problem, as resolved in the House of Lords; see below.

by the insurers. The brokers' fraud was not within the fraud exclusion clause since that fraud did not cause a claim under the policy to arise. The insurers could therefore not have repudiated liability on the ground of the brokers' fraud, nor could they have been under any duty to disclose it to the insureds since no negotiating party could be under a duty to disclose to the opposite party information that the agent of the opposite party had committed a breach of the duty he owed to his principal in an earlier transaction. So any failure to disclose that fraud did not cause the banks' loss. The sole cause of that was the fraud of the borrower, which was excluded under the policies. However, the House of Lords did approve of the reasoning of the Court of Appeal to the effect that an insurer is under a pre-contractual duty of disclosure to its insured but only in respect of matters that are material to the risk or to the recoverability of a claim. Breach of such a duty could not sound in damages, whether in contract or tort.

Even if the conclusion on causation was correct,[5] it has to be disappointing that the case establishes a rather narrow duty of disclosure on an insurer and a fairly ineffective remedy limited to avoidance and return of the premium. As far as the insurer's duty of disclosure is concerned, it seems to extend to disclosure of all facts known to the insurer which are material either to the nature of the risk sought to be covered or the recoverability of a claim under the policy which a prudent insured would take into account in deciding whether or not to place the risk for which he sought cover with that insurer.[6] The reasoning of the Court of Appeal, approved by the House of

---

[5] This is perhaps doubtful; see Trindade (1991) 107 L.Q.R. 24 and compare, in a different context, *Swingcastle v Alistair Gibson* [1991] 2 A.C. 223.

[6] This was how the Court of Appeal described it and this was expressly approved by Lord Bridge, with whom Lords Brandon and Ackner agreed. Lord Templeman did not consider it necessary to consider whether there was a duty of disclosure by reason of the obligation of an insurer to deal with the proposer of insurance with the utmost good faith. Lord Jauncey referred to the insurer's duty of disclosure in fairly narrow terms, as relating to facts which would reduce the risk such as the insurer's knowledge that the house which was the subject of a proposal had already been demolished, referring to the well-known example of Lord Mansfield in *Carter v Boehm* at 102, of the insurer insuring a ship for a voyage knowing that the ship had already arrived. It could not, in his view, extend to a situation of a broker's fraud which neither increased not decreased the risk to the insured. Nor was there any duty to disclose supervening facts that come to the knowledge of either party after conclusion of the contract, subject always to such exceptional cases as a ship entering a war zone or an insured failing to disclose all facts relevant to a claim. Presumably here he was thinking of *The Litsion Pride* [1985] 1 Lloyd's Rep. 437 (see 14.12), although the case was not cited by him. At first instance, Steyn J had referred to a much broader duty: "in a proper case, it will cover matters peculiarly within the knowledge of the insurers, which the insurers know that the insured is ignorant of and unable to discover, but which are material in the sense of being calculated to influence the decision of the insured to conclude the contract of

Lords,[7] as to why a breach of a duty of disclosure could not result in damages is unsatisfactory. That court, in rejecting Steyn J's adoption of the principle *ubi jus ibi remedium*, stated that to found a claim in damages it was necessary that there was a breach of contract, a tort, a breach of statute or a breach of a fiduciary relationship. Neither of the last two was applicable.[8] The duty of disclosure did not result from an implied term of the contract of insurance, so that there was no breach of contract. This seems acceptable.[9] The only final argument was that a breach of the obligation was itself a tort.[10] The Court of Appeal, and by adoption, the House of Lords, was disinclined to create such a novel tort. There was no authority in support, although it is unclear why this should be decisive,[11] and there were at least four further reasons. The first related to the supposed equitable origin of the relief for non-disclosure of material facts. This, with respect, seems quite rather strange reasoning. The duty of disclosure stems from the common law courts of Lord Mansfield.[12] The second referred to the fact that in relation to avoidance, the effect on the actual insurer (of non-disclosure by the insured) or the actual insured (of non-disclosure by the insurer) is irrelevant.[13] So there would be difficulties in translating this approach to a case where the insured is seeking damages. At the time this may have been correct, although it hardly seems an insuperable difficulty if the actual insured (or for that matter insurer) can prove an actual loss arising from the non-disclosure. In the light of *Pan Atlantic Insurance*

insurance. In considering whether the duty of disclosure is activated in a given case a Court ought in my judgment to test any provisional conclusion by asking the simple question: Did good faith and fair dealing require a disclosure?" [1987] 1 Lloyd's Rep. at 97.

[7] Especially at [1990] 1 Q.B. 773–781.

[8] Quaere perhaps whether more could have been made of the quasi-fiduciary nature of the insurance relationship, although this sort of argument would clearly have got nowhere in the House of Lords.

[9] It seems fairly clear, historically, that the principle of uberrima fides and the consequential duty of disclosure is inherent in the nature of the insurance contract and that it is not proper to talk of it as being based on an implied term in the usual contractual sense; cf., however, Matthews, "Uberrima fides in modern insurance law", in *New Foundations for Insurance Law*, ed. Rose (1987), at p.39.

[10] This was quite separate from the argument based on negligence, which of course failed also and, as indicated earlier, got very little mention in the House of Lords.

[11] There are modern cases where the judges have in effect created new torts to give a damages remedy where one was not available before; see e.g. *Seager v Copydex* [1967] 2 All E.R. 415; [1969] 2 All E.R. 718 and *Fraser v Thames Television* [1983] 2 All E.R. 101, awarding damages for breach of confidence. Further, in the area of insurance law, the House of Lords was quite content to create new law by introducing the requirement of inducement into the insured's duty of disclosure: *Pan Atlantic Insurance Co v Pine Top Insurance Co* [1994] 3 All E. R. 581; see 7.9.1.

[12] See 7.3.1, but it is a point which the House repeated in *Pan Atlantic*, above.

[13] Citing *Container Transport International v Oceanus Mutual Underwriting Association (Bermuda) Ltd* [1984] 1 Lloyd's Rep. 476; see 7.8.

Co Ltd v Pine Top Insurance Co,[14] holding that the effect of an insured's non-disclosure on the actual insurer is relevant, this point clearly does not stand.

The Court of Appeal's third reason was based on the fact that the Marine Insurance Act 1906 did not refer to damages being available for a breach of the requirement of utmost good faith (s.17) or a non-disclosure by the insured (s.18). With respect, this is very poor reasoning and it is surprising that the House of Lords was content to adopt it. The 1906 Act was merely a codification of the law as it had developed as at a particular date. In those circumstances, the statement that if Parliament had contemplated damages as a remedy, "it would surely have said so"[15] is, with respect, nonsense. This view is also reinforced by the decision in *Pan Atlantic Insurance Co Ltd v Pine Top Insurance Co*,[16] where the House of Lords did read words into the 1906 Act.[17] Finally, the court referred to the fact that the damages remedy would have to be reciprocal and would cause hardship because of the draconian nature of the duty of disclosure, not being dependent on fault at all. This is somewhat more convincing but not wholly so. After all, a party in breach of contract can be liable in damages to the other party without any fault or other blameworthiness at all.

In conclusion this case was, at least in part, very badly reasoned and leaves the distinct impression of a timid judiciary.[18] It was, inevitably, followed subsequently in *Aldrich v Norwich Union Life Insurance Co Ltd*,[19] where the Court of Appeal struck out a claim brought by Lloyd's names against an insurer who provided a plan that was in substance a guarantee for a Lloyd's underwriter and of which an endowment insurance policy was an integral element. The allegation was that the insurer failed to disclose substantial impending losses at Lloyd's. It was held that these facts were not material to the insurance and that in any event there was no duty on an insurer to disclose facts that might induce a person to enter into an insurance contract or a composite transaction of which an insurance contract formed part.[20] Further, there could not be a claim for damages. While *Banque Financière* might have heralded an exciting judicial development of

---

[14] *Pan Atlantic Insurance Co Ltd v Pine Top Insurance Co* [1994] 3 All E.R. 581; see 7.9.1.

[15] [1990] Q.B. at 781.

[16] *Pan Atlantic Insurance Co Ltd v Pine Top Insurance Co* [1994] 3 All E.R. 581.

[17] In holding that inducement was an implied requirement in ss.18 and 20. As we have seen in the last chapter, inducement is now a statutory element.

[18] For useful general comments, in addition to those already cited, see Kelly, "The insured's rights in relation to the provision of information by the insurer" (1989) 2 Ins. L.J. 45; Yeo, "Of reciprocity and remedies: duty of disclosure in insurance contracts" (1991) 11 L.S. 131; Fleming, (1992) 108 L.Q.R. 357.

[19] *Aldrich v Norwich Union Life Insurance Co Ltd* [2000] Lloyd's Rep. I.R. 1.

[20] Note though that Evans LJ, above, at 10–11, clearly reached this result with some reluctance.

a broad duty of good faith in insurance law, sadly that seems unlikely now to happen.

8.2   Good Faith as a Restriction on the Right of Avoidance

From the decisions just examined it might be thought that there is no effective duty of utmost good faith or even just good faith on the insurer. However, recent case law has raised the issue in a different context, namely whether or not the insurer's right to avoid for non-disclosure or misrepresentation, which was considered in the previous chapter, can be subject to a requirement that it exercises that right in good faith. That, of course, is now a much restricted right in both consumer and non-consumer insurance under the statutory reforms considered in the previous chapter, but in both cases there is still a right to avoid in the traditional sense in some circumstances. In addition, as discussed in 7.10, it is possible that, in a non-consumer insurance, an insurer might seek, by excluding the effect of the 2015 Act, to confer on itself by contract a right of avoidance in wider circumstances than under the Act, so the issue discussed here remains relevant.

Although there were some indications in previous cases to this effect,[21] the issue was first clearly raised and a clear view expressed in *Strive Shipping Corp v Hellenic Mutual War Risks Association*.[22] The issue arose again in *Brotherton v Aseguradora Colseguros SA (No.2)*.[23] In both these cases the insureds had failed to disclose to their insurers that, at the time of taking out the insurance, they were under investigation for alleged fraudulent activity. Subsequently, all the allegations were proven to be false. Nevertheless, it was held that the investigations were material. The insureds argued that in exercising the remedy of avoidance in this situation the insurers were in breach of their duty of utmost good faith. In *Strive Shipping*, Colman J's view was that the right of avoidance could be refused where it would be unconscionable,[24] but the argument was rejected by the Court of Appeal in *Brotherton*. It was held that the intelligence possessed by the insured and not disclosed to the insurer was, at the time of insuring, material, thereby allowing the insurer to avoid. It was not open to the insured to try and undermine that materiality at a later date.

In contrast a differently constituted Court of Appeal took a rather different

---

[21] *Pan Atlantic Insurance Co v Pine Top Insurance Co* [1995] 1 A.C. 501 at 555 per Lord Lloyd; *Kausar v Eagle Star Insurance Co Ltd* [2000] Lloyd's Rep. I.R. 154 at 157 per Staughton LJ.

[22] *Strive Shipping Corp v Hellenic Mutual War Risks Association* [2002] EWHC 203 (Comm); [2002] Lloyd's Rep I.R. 669.

[23] *Brotherton v Aseguradora Colseguros SA (No.2)* [2003] EWCA Civ 705; [2003] Lloyd's Rep I.R. 758.

[24] Above at [132].

view in *Drake Insurance Plc v Provident Insurance Plc*.[25] The facts of the case have been given in 7.9.1; it concerned a pre-contractual non-disclosure that actually benefited the insurer. Rix LJ, whilst accepting that there was no binding authority on the point, said that in his opinion an insurer seeking to avoid the contract could not blindly rely upon the remedy of avoidance but must show a good objective reason for doing so. It must also justify its avoidance by reference to the facts as they stood at the time of contracting. Clarke LJ agreed with this conclusion but Pill LJ dissented on this point. He said that what mattered was the actual presentation of the risk, not the reality of the position. It was accepted that it was not open to the court to overturn a valid avoidance by relying on a continuing duty of good faith—however, it was said that as a result of this duty, the insurer, must, at the time of avoidance, enquire whether there were good grounds for seeking it. Unhelpfully, there was no clear view on exactly when an insurer would be in breach by avoiding. Certainly it would be in breach if it attempted to avoid knowing that the facts relied upon did not exist, but whether it must go further than this, i.e. by making reasonable enquiries, is a moot point. On the facts, it was decided that the insurer was acting in bad faith by seeking to avoid. Whether or not this produces a fair result, it has to be pointed out that the reasoning is by no means clear and is in direct conflict with clear dicta of Mance LJ in *Brotherton*.[26] A right to avoid or rescind is not traditionally limited by any requirement of acting in good faith and it could be argued that this is a better view of the law as it is than that seemingly expressed in *Drake v Provident*. The argument on the other hand turns on the fact that, as we have seen, recent case-law has developed a continuing duty of good faith on both parties and there is no reason to deny the role of a doctrine of unconscionability in this situation. This argument ought to carry more weight if an insurer seeks to rely on a contractual right of avoidance.

8.3   Other Instances of a Requirement of Good Faith

Irrespective of a duty of disclosure imposed on the insurer and whether good faith can affect the insurer's right of avoidance, there are some limited but clear examples of case law imposing a duty on the insurer to act in good faith when exercising some of their contractual rights.[27] For example, it is

---

[25] *Drake Insurance Plc v Provident Insurance Plc* [2003] EWCA Civ 1834; [2004] Lloyd's Rep. I.R. 277.

[26] See especially [2003] Lloyd's Rep I.R. 758 at [29] to [34]. In *North Star Shipping Ltd v Sphere Drake Insurance Plc* [2006] EWCA Civ 378; [2006] Lloyd's Rep. I.R. 519, Waller LJ thought (at [17]) that the decision in *Drake v Provident* was likely to apply in very few cases.

[27] Note also the requirement under the FCA's Principles for Business, r.2.1.1, that a regulated firm must pay due regard to the interests of its customers and treat them

well-established that a liability insurer conducting the defence of proceedings against its insured must act in good faith[28] and it has fairly recently been held that in giving their consent to the relaxation of a term requiring the insured to maintain an intruder alarm the insurer must also act in good faith.[29] It is arguable that insurers exercising rights of subrogation, certainly under an express contractual provision, must act similarly.[30] The duty of good faith can more broadly be regarded as a duty that supports the implication of terms in the insurance contract when required to achieve the goal of fair dealing between the parties.[31] On the other hand, there does not appear to be a general duty on insurers to act in good faith when assessing and paying claims, or at least nothing that is effectively remediable in the event of breach.[32] It is clear that the principle has the potential for considerable further development, although it is impossible to predict with any certainty what exactly that might entail.

As part of their insurance law reform project, the Law Commissions' examined the question. Their Issues Paper 6[33] contained a very valuable review of the position and a provisional proposal of a statutory duty of good faith on insurers which would, inter alia, allow the payment of damages for unjustified delay in paying claims. However, ultimately, they merely recommend that good faith was enshrined as a general interpretive principle in insurance law, a shield not a sword, so that breach of that by itself would not give rise to any specific remedy, but the principle would allow appropriate case law development. In effect this has been done by the retention of s.17 of the 1906 Act subject, as we have seen, to the removal of avoidance as the remedy for breach.

---

fairly. Note also that there are clear instances when an insured must act in good faith regardless of any duty of disclosure, for example with regard to not prejudicing the insurer's right of subrogation; see 17.8.

[28] *Groom v Crocker* [1939] 1 K.B. 194; see 20.2.

[29] *Anders & Kern Ltd v CGU Insurance Plc* [2007] EWHC 377 (Comm); [2007] Lloyd's Rep. I.R. 555.

[30] See 17.13.

[31] *Goshawk Dedicated Ltd v Tyser & Co Ltd* [2006] EWCA Civ 379; [2007] Lloyd's Rep. I.R. 224 at [53].

[32] See the discussion in 15.1 about the measurement of loss when an insurer unjustifiably delays or refuses to make payment, but note that this should be remedied when the Enterprise Bill 2015 becomes law.

[33] *Damages for Late Payment and the Insurer's Duty of Good Faith* (March 2010).

CHAPTER 9

WARRANTIES AND CONDITIONS

9.0

This chapter is concerned with the terms of the contract of insurance other than those that describe the risk covered and exceptions to it. The nature of these terms was described in a general way in Ch.6. The contract of insurance will invariably in practice consist of not just the policy document itself, but also a completed proposal form or slip, and often, in addition, other documents including in some cases renewal notices. This contract may contain three sorts of relevant terms, namely warranties, conditions and clauses descriptive of the risk.[1] There is, however, no necessity for this, and it may be, for example, that a particular contract contains only conditions in the sense that they have been described earlier.[2]

The warranty is the most fundamental term and will therefore be considered first before we distinguish and describe clauses descriptive of the risk and conditions. The Insurance Act 2015 contains important reforms to the law in this area, without altering the basic nature of the relevant terms and the effect of these is considered at the appropriate points.[3] Given that the provisions of the Act apply only to contracts concluded, varied or renewed on or after 12 August 2016, and can be excluded in a non-consumer insurance contract, a brief account of the "traditional" law is retained.

9.1   Warranties

A warranty must be a term of the policy.[4] As will be explained further below, it is essentially a promise made by the insured. It has already been

---

[1] It will also contain exceptions to the risk, but these, whilst often similar in effect to some of these terms, operate differently.

[2] See 6.4.

[3] The Consumer Insurance (Disclosure and Representations) Act 2012, s.6, had already abolished the creation of warranties by means of a basis of the contract clause in consumer insurance contracts, and the Insurance Act 2015, s.9, in to the same effect for non-consumer insurance contracts with effect from 12 August 2016; see 9.2.1. Until the 2015 Act is in force from that date, in consumer cases an insurer's right to rely on a breach of warranty or condition is constrained by the Insurance Conduct of Business Sourcebook, r.8.1.2. See 9.12.

[4] This means it must be incorporated into the policy although it need not be written into the body of the policy itself. It could be attached to the policy, or even written in the margin: *Thompson v Weems* (1884) 9 App. Cas. 671. It cannot, however, be in

pointed out[5] that, upon breach of a warranty, traditionally, the insurer was discharged from all liability as from the date of the breach. This date would vary depending on the type of warranty, as explained shortly. Warranties had to be strictly complied with, and it was quite irrelevant that the breach was unconnected with a loss. One of the oldest cases illustrates this point very neatly. *De Hahn v Hartley*[6] involved a marine policy covering a ship and its cargo from Africa to its port of discharge in the West Indies. The insured warranted that the ship sailed from Liverpool with 50 hands on board. In fact it sailed with only 46 hands but it took on an extra six hands in Anglesey, very shortly out of Liverpool, and it thus had and continued to have 52 hands. It was held that the insurer could avoid all liability for breach of warranty, even though it was obvious that the breach had no connection with the loss that subsequently occurred when the ship was lost in the Atlantic Ocean. Under the provisions of the Insurance Act 2015, this, however, would no longer be the result in a case of this sort, as explained in detail in 9.7, below, although the Act does not abolish the rule of strict compliance.

9.2   Warranties as Promises

Warranties are essentially promises made by insureds relating to facts or to things that they undertake to do or not to do, as the case may be. They will invariably affect the risk to which the insurer is subject. There are three sorts of warranties: warranties as to present or past facts as at the date they are made; warranties as to the future; and warranties of opinion.

9.2.1 Warranties of past or present fact

Traditionally, warranties as to past or present facts would often arise as a result of a completed proposal form where that was declared to be the basis of the contract. By this means, representations made on that form could be converted into terms of the contract.[7] In a consumer insurance contract this has not been possible as regards contracts entered into, varied or renewed on or

---

a separate document, even if this is attached to the policy, unless it is incorporated into the policy: *Bean v Stupart* (1778) 1 Doug 11.

[5] See 6.3.

[6] *De Hahn v Hartley* (1786) 1 T.R. 343. See also the earlier case of *Pawson v Watson* (1778) 2 Cowp. 785. Both cases were decided by Lord Mansfield, clarifying and establishing the distinction between warranties and representations.

[7] The leading authority is the House of Lords' decision in *Dawsons Ltd v Bonnin* [1922] 2 A.C. 413, notable because it concerned what was an immaterial mis-statement converted into a warranty. That basis clauses are still in use in commercial policies is evident from the decision in *Genesis Housing Association Ltd v Liberty Syndicate Management Ltd* [2013] EWCA Civ 1173.

after 6 April 2013.[8] The same result will apply as regards non-consumer contracts entered into, varied or renewed on or after 12 August 2016.[9] Because of this, we no longer consider basis of the contract clauses, which were probably the most-criticised devices in insurance contract law, in any detail.[10]

However, although pre-contractual representations cannot be converted into warranties, there is no reason why their substance cannot form the basis of an express warranty that the insurers include in the policy and it is possible that a basis clause could still have some additional effect as discussed later in 9.6.

9.2.2 Continuing warranties

Warranties as to the future are known as continuing or promissory. They are continuing promises by the insured that facts will or will not exist in the future or will or will not continue to exist for the future. Common examples are warranties to maintain alarms or sprinkler systems in commercial fire policies and a warranty to maintain property in a reasonable condition, which may be found in all sorts of policies. As a result of the statutory provisions described above in 9.2.1, continuing warranties can no longer arise from the contents of a proposal form declared to be the basis of the contract. Before then, there was a body of case law concerned with the question of construing the language of statements or questions and answers on a proposal form in order to determine whether they were continuing warranties. This no longer seems relevant and further discussion here is unnecessary.[11]

9.2.3 Warranties of opinion

Warranties of opinion are less severe than warranties of facts because if the insured merely warrants that facts are or will be true to the best of his knowledge and belief, there will be a breach of warranty only if he dishonestly or recklessly supplies an incorrect answer. The insured must exercise due care when making his warranty, but that is sufficient.[12] As warranties of opinion would normally arise from a completed proposal form, they are unlikely to be found following the reforming statutory provisions.

---

[8] Consumer Insurance (Disclosure and Representations) Act 2012 s.6.
[9] Insurance Act 2015 s.9.
[10] This can be found in para.9.5 of the ninth edition of this book.
[11] Further discussion can be found in para.9.3.2 of the ninth edition of this book.
[12] *Huddleston v RACV Insurance Pty Ltd* [1975] V.R. 683; cf. *Mammone v RACV Insurance Pty Ltd* [1976] V.R. 617. See also *Macphee v Royal Insurance Co* 1979 S.L.T. 54.

9.3   Creation of Warranties

There are a number of ways in which warranties may be created. The policy
may create warranties by the use of the word "warranty" itself, such as in
the phrase "the insured warrants . . .", but even this may not be conclusive
if the court concludes that as a matter of construction the parties could not
have intended a warranty.[13] A provision whereby the contract is declared to
be void or voidable in certain circumstances probably has the same effect.[14]
A classic illustration here is the standard increase of risk clause in fire policies
that was discussed in Ch.7.[15] In addition, it must be open to the court to
conclude that on the construction of the policy, the wording of a particular
term gives rise to a warranty.[16]

9.3.1 Warranty or condition precedent?

The use of the phrase "condition precedent" can give rise to difficulties. As
has been seen,[17] there is a legal distinction between warranties and conditions
precedent to a particular liability, but in fact, what we have described as a
warranty may in a particular insurance policy be referred to as a condition
precedent, provided it imposes a promise relating to the risk and it is clear
that performance of the condition is precedent to the liability of the insurer
under the policy.[18] It seems clear that a general declaration making the terms
of the policy conditions precedent to the validity of the policy is not sufficient
to create warranties or fundamental terms of all of these terms, because by
their nature some of them will be of the sort that cannot conceivably be
regarded as precedent to the liability of the insurer, for example terms which
after indemnity confer rights on the insurer such as subrogation rights. We
consider the nature of conditions and conditions precedent further below.

---

[13] See e.g. *De Maurier (Jewels) Ltd v Bastion Insurance Co* [1967] 2 Lloyd's Rep. 550;
CTN Cash and Carry Ltd v General Accident Fire & Life Assurance Group Plc [1989] 1
Lloyd's Rep. 229 and the other authorities discussed in 9.6.

[14] The use of "void" or "voidable" was misleading because, traditionally, a breach of
warranty discharged the insurers from liability and did not render the contract void
or voidable. Despite this and notwithstanding that there is no longer an automatic
discharge from liability (see 9.7), it is thought that it is still proper to regard such
provisions as warranties. In *AC Ward & Sons Ltd v Catlin (Five) Ltd* [2008] EWHC
3585 (Comm), upheld [2009] EWCA Civ 1098; [2010] Lloyd's Rep. I.R. 301,
a general definition provision in a goods policy contained such wording and was
regarded as supporting the construction of terms beginning "it is warranted that
. . ." as true warranties.

[15] See 7.13.

[16] Law Com. No.104, 6.3.

[17] See 6.4.

[18] See the judgment of Lord Goff in *The Good Luck* [1991] 2 W.L.R. 1279 at 1294–5.

Insurers, though, cannot be blamed entirely for this confusion by reason of the wordings they adopt. Some of the decided cases are equally unclear. Judges have sometimes used the description "condition" when referring to what here is meant by "warranty". Even terms that are very similar to each other have attracted different appellations and different legal consequences in decided cases. Two contrasting examples will suffice. In *Conn v Westminster Motor Insurance Association*,[19] a term in a motor policy requiring the insured to maintain his vehicle in an efficient condition appears to have been regarded as a warranty in the proper sense. While the Court of Appeal did talk in terms of its being a condition precedent, they appear to have regarded the term as precedent to the validity of the policy because they held that upon any breach the insurers would be discharged from liability, which at the time was the consequence of a breach of warranty, although it would not now be so. In *WJ Lane v Spratt*,[20] on the other hand, a term in a goods in transit policy requiring the insured to take all reasonable precautions for the protection and safeguarding of the goods was regarded as a term breach of which could be relied upon only if there was a causal connection between the breach and a particular loss.[21] The ground for the distinction between what on the face of them appear to be the same sort of term is not obvious. It is suggested that this sort of conceptual confusion is not satisfactory even despite the reforms to the law of warranties which we consider below.

9.4 Interpretation of Warranties

Some mitigation of the strictness of the law of warranties was effected by the courts adopting strict rules of interpretation.[22] In particular, as it is usually the insurer who formulates the wording, in the event of any ambiguity, the warranty will be construed *contra proferentem*. The leading example is the decision of the House of Lords in *Provincial Insurance Co v Morgan*,[23] although it should be noted that the warranty in question arose from a proposal form and this, as we have seen, is no longer possible. A firm of coal merchants insured a lorry under a standard motor policy. Part of the completed proposal form,

---

[19] *Conn v Westminster Motor Insurance Association* [1966] 1 Lloyd's Rep. 407. See further at 21.3.6.

[20] *WJ Lane v Spratt* [1970] 2 Q.B. 480.

[21] In fact Roskill J referred to the term as a warranty, but it is clear that he was using the terms condition and warranty in the opposite sense to what is the usual practice and the practice adopted here. See also *Port-Rose v Phoenix Assurance Plc* (1986) 136 N.L.J. 33 (see 13.2.2), where a "condition" requiring the taking of reasonable care was held not to be actionable unless the breach caused the loss.

[22] Clearly, though, if the natural and ordinary meaning of a warranty is clear, it will be enforced: see, for example, *GE Frankona Reinsurance Ltd v CMM Trust No.1440* [2006] EWHC 429 (Admlty); [2006] Lloyd's Rep. I.R. 704.

[23] *Provincial Insurance Co v Morgan* [1933] A.C. 240.

which was the basis of the contract, read as follows: "State (a) the purposes in full for which the vehicle will be used; and (b) the nature of the goods to be carried. (a) Delivery of coal; (b) coal." One day the lorry was carrying some timber, as it did occasionally, as well as five hundredweight of coal. After the timber and three fifths of the coal had been delivered, and while the lorry was being driven to deliver the remaining coal, it was damaged in an accident. It was held that the insurers could not repudiate liability for breach of continuing warranty. The insured warranted only that the lorry would in general be used for carrying coal, which was complied with; he did not, on the wording of the question and answer, warrant that the vehicle would be used to carry only coal. "In insurance a warranty . . ., though it must be strictly complied with, must be strictly though reasonably construed."[24]

Another example of the reasonable interpretation of warranties is afforded by the cases concerning obligations imposed on a liability insured to take reasonable precautions. These are considered in Ch.20.

9.5   Warranties in a Multi-Section Policy

Many insurance contracts have more than one section and thus cover a number of different, often unrelated, risks. This is true of both consumer and non-consumer insurances.[25] Until the decision in *Printpak v AGF Insurance Ltd*,[26] it was not clear if a breach of warranty relating to one section of a policy could be relied upon in relation to a claim made another section. Here, the insured effected a "commercial inclusive" insurance with AGF. The policy comprised a number of sections, each offering a different type of cover. Under section A, the insured's stock and other goods were insured against destruction or damage by, inter alia, fire. There were several clauses in the policy purporting to be warranties. One of them, numbered P17, stated that the insured warranted that there was a burglar alarm on the premises which had been correctly installed and which would be properly

---

[24] Lord Wright at 253–254; and see his comments at 254–256. The other point that arises from the case is mentioned below in fn.34. See also the comment of Saville LJ in *Hussain v Brown* [1996] 1 Lloyd's Rep. 627 at 629–30 and the decision in *Pratt v Aigaion Insurance Co SA* [2008] EWCA Civ 1314; [2009] Lloyd's Rep. I.R. 225, where a warranty in a marine policy on a trawler requiring the owner or skipper to be "on board at all times" was not breached when the trawler was safely tied up in harbour with no one on board. It was to be read as relevant only when the vessel was being navigated. Apparently the parties regarded the term as one delimiting the risk rather than a warranty in the strict sense, but that made no difference to the question of construction, nor indeed to the insurer's attempt to avoid liability.

[25] For example, a standard household insurance is "sectionalised" in this way, one section dealing with the cover being provided for loss caused by fire or theft, etc., another with cover for public liability, and so on.

[26] *Printpak v AGF Insurance Ltd* [1999] Lloyd's Rep I.R. 542.

maintained and fully operational throughout the currency of the insurance. Condition 5 stated:

> "Any Warranty shall, from the time it is applied, continue to be in force during the whole currency of the Policy. Failure to comply with any Warranty shall invalidate any claim for loss, destruction, damage or liability which is wholly or partly due to or affected by such failure to comply."

A fire at the insured's premises caused damage to the stock and the insurers relied on, inter alia, a breach of warranty P17 to deny liability. It was common ground that the clause was a warranty that, by virtue of the fact that the alarm was not working at the time of the fire, had been broken. However, the courts accepted the argument for the insured that the various warranties did not apply to the whole of it. They held that section B of the policy provided cover for theft and because the P17 warranty was detailed at the end of that section only, by means of an endorsement, it was incorporated only into that section. Accordingly, breach of P17 could relieve the insurer only from liability for theft.

Both the judge at first instance and the Court of Appeal reached this conclusion by examining the content of other warranties in the policy. They all had the prefix P, but were at the end of the sections only to which they were relevant. One in particular was discussed at some length. Section C provided cover in respect of money. At the foot of that section, there was a clause, P20, which stated that the insured warranted that "each single transaction of money . . . shall be accompanied by a number of responsible adult persons . . .".[27] It was said that it was ridiculous to suppose that if on any one occasion only one person had accompanied a consignment of money to the insured's bank, then the insurer would be relieved from liability under all sections of the policy, including product and public liability.

This was clearly a sensible result and is a further example of how the courts, particularly in modern times, are concerned to construe warranties reasonably.[28] Hirst LJ stated: "In my judgment, it does not follow from the fact that the policy is a single contract that it is to be treated as a seamless contractual instrument."[29] It would appear that a multi-section policy will be regarded as in effect consisting of several different insurance contracts. This does not seem objectionable in principle.[30]

---

[27] If the transaction was over the sum of £2,500. The number of responsible adults was stated in the Policy Schedule to be two.

[28] See also the dictum of Saville LJ in *Hussain v Brown*, cited by Hirst LJ [1999] Lloyd's Rep. I.R. at 545–6.

[29] Above at 546.

[30] See the similar principle established in American case law, as described in Clarke, *The Law of Insurance Contracts,* 5th edn (Informa Subscriptions, 2002) 20-6C1.

9.6 Clauses or Warranties Descriptive of or Delimiting the Risk

In a number of cases the courts construed a term in an insurance contract, which at first sight looked like a warranty, as lesser term, variously described as a statement or clause descriptive of or delimiting the risk or as a suspensive condition.[31] This sort of term, relating to the use of insured property, would have a similar effect to an exception to the risk properly so-called,[32] in that the insurer would not be on risk while the term was not being complied with, but the risk would reattach when the term was being complied with. However, there was no need for the insurers to prove a causal connection between the "breach" of such a term and a loss. In the earlier cases, the term in question, relating to the use of the insured property, arose out a proposal form stated to be the basis of the contract and it may be that a degree of uncertainty about its exact extent[33] resulted in the court being generous to the insured in deciding it was not a warranty. If it had been the latter, the insurers would have been relieved from liability from the date of breach irrespective of whatever happened thereafter.[34] More recent cases, however, reached the same result in respect of terms in the body of the insurance policy, even where, sometimes, they were described as warranties.

As we will see, the effect of the reforms in the Insurance Act 2015 is to render the effect of a breach of warranty in the strict sense very similar to the effect of breach of a suspensive condition and it is difficult to see the need to construe a term in this way once the 2015 Act is in force and applicable. However, having said that, it should be noted that while s.6 of the 2012 Act and s.9 of the 2015 Act prohibit the use of a basis of the contract clause to convert a pre-contractual representation into a warranty, they do not seem as a matter of construction to preclude the use of that device to

---

[31] Sometimes the description "warranty describing (or delimiting) the risk" was used (see e.g. *De Maurier (Jewels) Ltd v Bastion Insurance Co* [1967] 2 Lloyd's Rep. 550 and *GE Frankona Reinsurance Ltd v CMM Trust No.1440* [2006] EWHC 429 (Admlty); [2006] Lloyd's Rep. I.R. 704). Although this seems a rather confusing appellation, it is consistent with marine insurance usage, where the term "warranted" is often used to describe what in effect are exceptions to the risk and not warranties in the strict sense.

[32] See Ch.13.

[33] In the sense that it was not clearly a continuing warranty and/or not sufficiently going to the root of the transaction.

[34] The classic early illustrations are *Farr v Motor Traders' Mutual Insurance Society* [1920] 3 K.B. 669 and *Roberts v Anglo-Saxon Insurance Co* [1927] K.B. 590. See also the decision of the Court of Appeal and the views of some of their Lordships in *Provincial Insurance Co v Morgan* [1932] 2 K.B. 70; [1933] A.C. 240.

create a suspensive condition.[35] For this reason, some case law is still worth consideration.[36]

In *De Maurier (Jewels) Ltd v Bastion Insurance Co*,[37] an all risks insurance effected by jewellers contained the following term[38]: "Warranted road vehicles fitted with locks and alarm systems approved by underwriters and in operation." The insured suffered two losses. At the time of the first, the locks on the car in question were not of the required sort; at the time of the second, there were no faults. At first the insurers repudiated the policy,[39] and hence liability for both losses, seemingly on the ground that a continuing warranty had been broken before the first loss. Subsequently, however, they admitted liability for the second loss. It was held that the insurers were not liable for the first loss, as the risk was suspended because the locks were not approved. The term cited, despite the presence of "warranted", was not a warranty in the full sense, but merely a warranty descriptive of the risk.

In *CTN Cash & Carry Ltd v General Accident Fire & Life Assurance Corp Plc*,[40] on renewal of a general commercial policy insuring the plaintiff's cash and carry business, the insurers inserted a term under which the insured "warranted" that certain anti-theft security measures would be complied with. It was held that this was a clause descriptive of the risk and not a warranty in the strict sense. A warranty in the strict sense is only a clause which goes "to the root of the transaction between the parties which ought to avoid or relieve the [insurers] from their liability under the policy".[41] Here, the "warranty" could relate only to two sections of a policy,[42] which was a general commercial policy with 12 sections in total. While the result of the case seems sensible, it does appear somewhat out of line with some of the leading cases on warranties, particularly on proposal form warranties, where insignificant or immaterial breaches did entitle the insurers to be completely discharged.[43] Furthermore, the device here was used not to protect the insured as in the earlier leading cases but

---

[35] This would only really be relevant where there was no relevant term in the body of the policy.

[36] More detailed consideration can be found in the ninth edition of this book at 9.8.

[37] *De Maurier (Jewels) Ltd v Bastion Insurance Co* [1967] 2 Lloyd's Rep. 550.

[38] This was contained in a slip, not on a proposal form as such, though the effect is the same.

[39] The remedy for breach of warranty at the time.

[40] *CTN Cash & Carry Ltd v General Accident Fire & Life Assurance Corp Plc* [1989] 1 Lloyd's Rep. 299. See [1989] J.B.L. 355.

[41] Bankes LJ in *Roberts v Anglo-Saxon Insurance Co* [1927] K.B. 590 at 591, cited by Macpherson J in the *Cash & Carry* case, above at 302.

[42] For example only those protecting the insured against the risk of theft of cash from the warehouse.

[43] See, especially, *Dawsons Ltd v Bonnin* [1922] 2 A.C. 413, which was perhaps the classic case on the basis of the contract clause; cf. the *Printpak* case discussed at 9.5.

for the benefit of the insurers, who had drafted the term using the word "warranted".[44]

A more recent decision is *Kler Knitwear Ltd v Lombard General Insurance Co Ltd*.[45] The claimant's renewal of its business policy in May 1998 was subject to the following endorsement:

> "It is warranted that within 30 days of renewal 1998 the sprinkler systems . . . must be inspected by an . . . approved engineer with all the necessary rectification work commissioned within 14 days of the inspection report being received".

General Condition 2 clearly stated that all warranties would attach and apply throughout the duration of the contract and that non-compliance with any of them would be bar any claim, other than one made during the renewal period itself. The premises suffered storm damage in October 1998. It transpired that no inspection of the sprinkler systems had been carried out within the prescribed 30 days, although the claimant contended that an inspection had taken place in August, approximately 90 days after renewal. Morland J decided that the clause contained in the endorsement, on its true construction, was not a warranty, but merely a "suspensive condition". The reasoning is, with respect, not wholly convincing. It was held that because a warranty was a "draconian term", then if underwriters wanted such protection they must "stipulate for it in clear terms".[46] With respect it is difficult to see how the insurer could have stipulated this in any clearer terms. The term itself was called a warranty and was drafted in clear and intelligible language, and the consequences of non-compliance were spelled out. It is difficult to have sympathy with commercial insureds who, in spite of every effort on the insurer's part to alert them to danger, still do not comply.

The learned judge also said that it "would be absurd and make no rational business sense for a claim for property damage to be barred if inspection of the sprinkler system was not carried out on time".[47] Expressed in this way, the point could be said to be irrelevant to the decision on the status of the term. Arguably this point goes to materiality and materiality is not relevant to warranties. A more satisfactory rationale would be to construe the appropriate term in the light of its commercial purpose, and it may indeed be that this is what Morland J was doing and that this was part of a trend to mitigate the harshness of the law on warranties. More recently, in *GE Frankona*

---

[44] As we have seen earlier, the quality of drafting in this area and the whole issue of categorisation of terms in insurance contracts leaves a lot to be desired.

[45] *Kler Knitwear Ltd v Lombard General Insurance Co Ltd* [2000] Lloyd's Rep I.R. 47.

[46] [2000] Lloyd's Rep I.R. 47 at 50; quoting Saville LJ in *Hussain v Brown* [1996] 1 Lloyd's Rep 627 at 630.

[47] Above at p.48.

Reinsurance Ltd v CMM Trust No 1440,[48] Gross J took the view, obiter, that a term "warranted vessel fully crewed at all times" was "delimiting" rather than "promissory", on the basis that this would meet the commercial purpose of the warranty.

Yet more recently, in *Sugar Hut Group Ltd v Great Lakes Reinsurance (UK) Plc*,[49] it was said that it may be easier to construe a "warranty" as a suspensive condition where the obligation by the insured is to comply with some deadline[50] rather than where there is a warranty as to a state of affairs.[51] Here, Burton J referred to the following passage from the judgment of Rix LJ in *HIH Casualty & General Insurance Ltd v New Hampshire Insurance Co*[52] as particularly helpful:

> "It is a question of construction, and the presence or absence of the word 'warranty' or 'warranted' is not conclusive. One test is whether it is a term that goes to the root of the transaction; the second, whether it is descriptive of or bears materially on the risk of loss; a third, whether damages would be an unsatisfactory or inadequate remedy. As Bowen LJ said in *Barnard v Faber* [1893] 1 QB 340 at 344: 'A term as regards the risk must be a condition'.[53] Otherwise the insurer is merely left to a cross-claim in a matter that goes to the risk itself, which is unbusinesslike : . . ."

In the *Sugar Hut* case, terms described as warranties and imposing safety precautions[54] in an insurance of nightclubs were held to be warranties in the true sense.

9.7 The Effect of a Breach of Warranty

It is with regard to this question that the Insurance Act 2015 has reformed the law of warranties and other terms by provisions in Pt 3 that apply to both consumer and non-consumer insurance contracts, although they may be excluded in the latter, as described below.

---

[48] *GE Frankona Reinsurance Ltd v CMM Trust No 1440* [2006] EWHC 429 (Admlty); [2006] Lloyd's Rep. I.R. 704. See also *Pratt v Aigaion Insurance Co SA* [2008] EWCA Civ 1314; [2009] Lloyd's Rep. I.R. 225, described in fn.24, where it was accepted by the parties that a "warranty" of a similar sort was merely delimiting.

[49] *Sugar Hut Group Ltd v Great Lakes Reinsurance (UK) Plc* [2011] EWHC 2636 (Comm); [2011] Lloyd's Rep. I.R. 198.

[50] Citing *Kler Knitwear*.

[51] *Sugar Hut Group Ltd v Great Lakes Reinsurance (UK) Plc* [2011] EWHC 2636 (Comm) at [41].

[52] *HIH Casualty & General Insurance Ltd v New Hampshire Insurance Co* [2001] Lloyd's Rep. I.R. 596 at [101].

[53] Clearly "condition" here means warranty as we have described it.

[54] Regarding the use of frying pans and burglar alarms. A similar result was reached in *AC Ward & Sons Ltd v Catlin (Five) Ltd* [2008] EWHC 3585 (Comm), upheld [2009] EWCA Civ 1098; [2010] Lloyd's Rep. I.R. 301.

Under the law until the 2015 Act is in force and applicable, a breach of warranty automatically discharges the insurer from liability, unless the insurer waives the breach.[55] This was the decision of the House of Lords in *Bank of Nova Scotia v Hellenic Mutual War Risks Association (Bermuda) Ltd, (The Good Luck)*,[56] applying the literal meaning of the words in the second sentence of s.33(3) of the Marine Insurance Act 1906.[57] The decision was subsequently applied in a non-marine case.[58] It is no longer necessary to go into any detail about the decision, the reasoning behind it or the difficulties with it.[59] It is sufficient to say that the Law Commissions thought that the fairest way to reform the law of warranties and mitigate the potential harshness of the law was to overturn this principle, together with a further limit on the application of terms that are not in fact relevant to the particular loss in respect of which the insured is making a claim.[60]

Section 10(1) abolishes the rule of automatic discharge and s.10(2) provides instead that an insurer has no liability in respect of any loss occurring, or attributable to something happening, after a warranty has been breached but before the breach has been remedied. However, under s.10(3), the insurer will not be discharged from liability if (a) because of a change of circumstances, the warranty ceases to be applicable to the circumstances of the contract, (b) compliance with the warranty is rendered unlawful by any subsequent law, or (c) if the insurer waives the breach of warranty. In addition, under s.10(4), the insurer will be liable in respect of losses occurring, or attributable to something happening, before the breach of warranty or, if the breach can be remedied, after it has been remedied. A breach is regarded as remedied in two situations (s.10(5)). The first, detailed in s.10(6), is where a warranty requires something to be done or not done, or a condition is to be fulfilled, or something is or is not to be the case and that requirement is not complied with, but the risk to which the warranty relates later becomes essentially the

---

[55] Waiver has to be by estoppel and not election: *HIH Casualty & General Insurance v AXA Corporate Solutions* [2002] EWCA Civ 1253; [2003] Lloyd's Rep I.R. 1. See also *Argo Systems FZE v Liberty Insurance (Pte)* [2011] EWHC 301 (Comm); [2011] 2 Lloyd's Rep. 61, reversed on the facts ([2011] EWCA Civ 1572).

[56] *Bank of Nova Scotia v Hellenic Mutual War Risks Association (Bermuda) Ltd, (The Good Luck)* [1991] 2 W.L.R. 1279. For comments, see Birds (1991) 107 L.Q.R. 540; Bennett [1991] J.B.L. 598; Clarke [1991] L.M.C.L.Q. 437.

[57] "If [a warranty] be not [exactly] complied with, then, subject to any express provision in the policy, the insurer is discharged from liability as from the date of the breach of warranty, but without prejudice to any liability incurred by him before that date." This sentence is repealed by the 2015 Act s.10(7).

[58] *Hussain v Brown* [1996] 1 Lloyd's Rep. 627.

[59] The detail can be found in the previous edition of this book at 9.2.

[60] So, for example, there is still no requirement that a warranty be material, no change in the principle that a warranty must be exactly complied with nor necessarily a causal requirement between breach and loss.

same as that originally contemplated by the parties. The second is in any other case if the insured ceases to be in breach of the warranty.

The Law Commissions' Explanatory Notes explain the inclusion of the words "attributable to something happening" in subs.(2) so as to cater for the situation when loss arises as a result of something that occurred during suspension of liability, but is not actually suffered until after the breach has been "remedied". They give the example[61] of a warranty requiring bottle of fine wines to be stored on their sides. The insured fails to do this with the result that the corks shrink and the wine becomes oxidized, but then seeks to remedy the breach by laying the bottles correctly. The loss of quality is attributable to something happening during the period of breach of warranty so the insurer is not liable for it.

The basic effect of these changes is to render a warranty more like a term delimiting the risk or suspensive condition, and in future, as already mentioned, it will be much less important, if necessary at all, to draw a distinction between those different types of term. In effect the warranty is converted into a term of a suspensory nature. It should be noted, however, that there is no definition of "warranty", so identification of whether or not a term is a warranty will be subject to the considerations described earlier.

9.7.1 Terms not relevant to the actual loss

The reform introduced by s.11 is potentially more significant in practice than that introduced by s.10, but its construction and application may cause more difficulties. A draft clause was included in the draft Bill appended to the Law Commissions' Report, but it was not contained in the original Bill presented to Parliament because of doubts as to whether it was sufficiently uncontroversial to be included in a Bill designed for the special procedure for uncontroversial Law Commission Bills. However, following debate in the Lords' Grand Committee, when it became clear that a provision of this sort would not be objectionable to stakeholders provided that it was less uncertain than the draft, what became s.11 was introduced at Report stage, but without any real Parliamentary discussion.[62]

Given that there appear to be some difficulties in construing s.11, we set it out in full:

> (1) *This section applies to a term (express or implied) of a contract of insurance, other than a term defining the risk as a whole, if compliance with it would tend to reduce the risk of one or more of the following—*

---

[61] Law Com. No.353/Scot Law Com. No.238, Cm.8898, Explanatory Notes, A.76, p.372.

[62] The Law Commissions did consult on the revised draft that became s.11.

(a)   loss of a particular kind,

(b)   loss at a particular location,

(c)   loss at a particular time.

(2)   If a loss occurs, and the term has not been complied with, the insurer may not rely on the non-compliance to exclude, limit or discharge its liability under the contract for the loss if the insured satisfies subsection (3).

(3)   The insured satisfies this subsection if it shows that the non-compliance with the term could not have increased the risk of the loss which actually occurred in the circumstances in which it occurred.

(4)   This section may apply in addition to section 10.

It is clear that s.11 further limits the effect of a breach of warranty, as well as applying to other terms, such as suspensive conditions or terms delimiting the risk and terms that are actually described as conditions precedent. The basic intention is to permit recovery despite a breach of warranty or other term designed to mitigate the risk, where the loss that in fact occurred was not one that the particular warranty or other term that was breached was designed to prevent. In the words of the Law Commissions' Explanatory Notes to their original draft[63]:

> "For example, breach of a warranty requiring a policyholder to have a fire safety system in place would result in suspension of the insurer's liability in respect of fire-related losses, but not in respect of flood losses. Breach of a condition that a building must retain a night watchman would mean that the insurer will have no liability for losses occurring at night, while a watchman should be present."

Those Notes continue:

> "A direct causal link between the breach and the ultimate loss is not required. That is, it is not relevant whether or not breach of the term actually caused or contributed to the loss which has been suffered. The clause is intended to provide that the insurer will not be liable for any loss falling within the particular category of loss with which the warranty or other term is concerned."

It is respectfully submitted that in at least two respects the operation of this provision is not entirely clear. There was concern that the original draft might apply to terms defining the risk as a whole, something now expressly excluded in subs.(1). The Law Commissions gave examples of terms defining the risk as a whole as those setting out (1) the use to which insured property

---

[63] Law Com. No.353/Scot Law Com. No.238, Cm.8898, A.85, p.373. For full discussion of their recommendation, see Ch.18 of the Report.

can be put, (2) the geographical limits of the policy, (3) the class of ship being insured and (4) the minimum age, qualifications or characteristics of a person insured.[64] While these examples are clear, there seem likely to be arguments over other terms. It seems clear that a term might define "the risk as a whole" but also at first sight be one that reduces the risk in one of the ways covered by s.11, for example a term in a motor policy that insures driving only for social, domestic and pleasure purposes. Such a term is probably, it is thought, one that is not subject to s.11, so that the insurers could rely on a breach if the car were being used for business purposes, but it might be argued that the risk as a whole is providing cover against the compulsory liability risks and the other usual incidents of a motor policy. More problematic may be a motor policy that covers the insured and any family member driving the vehicle who is 25 or older, and a loss arises when the vehicle is being used for a short time by the insured's 24-year-old child. Here the limiting term could be argued to apply to only a relatively narrow part of the risk as a whole. Assuming the insured in these hypothetical examples to be an individual consumer, s.11 will clearly be applicable and thus some difficult questions of interpretation seem likely to arise.

It is thought that s.11 cannot apply to terms drafted as exclusion clauses, as these are not terms that require compliance by the insured, although the Law Commissions took a different view when explaining their original draft.[65]

The effect of subs.(3) is clearly to lay on the insured the burden of showing that non-compliance with the term could not have increased the risk of the loss which actually occurred in the circumstances in which it occurred. The original draft in the Law Commissions' Report did not refer to which party bore the burden of proof. The Law Commissions[66] stated that the subsection should result in a more objective assessment of whether it is obvious that the breach could not have made any difference, with the onus on the insured to show this. The words "the circumstances" in subs.(3) are intended to require that the issue is looked at in a broad way. "There is less suggestion of causation in these words, as there would be if the court was required to consider 'the way' in which the loss occurred."[67]

It may be helpful to quote the examples that the Law Commissions gave of how they intended s.11 to operate[68]:

---

[64] This was stated in a "Stakeholder Note" that the Law Commissions produced in November 2014 between the Committee and Report stages of the Bill. It seems no longer to be available online.

[65] See Law Com No.353, Scot Law Com No.238 at 18.24.

[66] In the Note referred to in fn.63.

[67] Para.1.17 of the Note referred to in fn.64.

[68] Para.1.18 of the Note referred to in fn.64.

"(1)   There is a clause in the policy requiring the insured factory to install
         five-lever mortise locks on all doors. This is breached because the
         lock on one door (door A) only has three levers. Thieves break in
         through door A. The lock might have made a difference given the
         circumstances of the loss (which are that the door did not have
         the requisite lock, and the thieves broke in through it), so the
         insurer does not have to pay. The policyholder cannot argue that
         the thieves would have just found another way in, or that the crow-
         bar they used would have shattered the wood even with the right
         lock.

         Same warranty; same breach. Thieves break in through a window,
         or a different door (B) which does have the required lock. In these
         circumstances, it would not have made any difference if door A had
         had a different lock. The insurer should not escape liability based on
         the breach.

(2)   The insured warrants that the insured vehicle will be roadworthy.
         This is breached because the left front headlight is defective. The
         vehicle skids on black ice in the dark. Although the faulty headlight
         did not cause the accident, it is possible that it could have contrib-
         uted, given the circumstances of the loss (that is, that it was dark,
         and a headlight was defective). The insurer does not have to pay.

         Same warranty; same breach. The vehicle collides with a truck
         in broad daylight. There is no possibility that the defective head-
         light contributed to the accident given the circumstances in which
         it happened (it was daylight and the headlights would not have
         needed to be on even if they were working properly). The insurer
         should not escape liability based on the breach."

It is not absolute that s.11(3) does in fact dispense with arguments about
causation. It has both prospective—"could not have increased the risk"—and
retrospective—"loss which actually occurred in the circumstances in which
it occurred"—elements. It is not clear that the answer given in example (1)
quoted above, where thieves break a door down and the correct lock on that
door would not have made any difference, would be that given by the Law
Commissions, as the actual circumstances have to be looked at and, by itself,
a lock might not make any difference as to whether a door can be broken
down, although this would be fact-dependent. Clearly if the thieves gain
entry by unpicking the lock that is the incorrect type of lock, the loss would
not be covered.

    In conclusion, it seems likely that disputes concerning s.11 are likely to
reach the courts sooner rather than later.

9.7.2 Contracting-out in non-consumer insurance

The reforms in Pt 3 of the 2015 Act cannot be excluded in a consumer insurance contract or a variation thereof.[69] However, in non-consumer insurance contracts they can be excluded by contract terms that satisfy the transparency requirements of s.17.[70] The insurer must take sufficient steps to draw such a disadvantageous term to the insured's attention before the contract is entered into or a variation agreed, unless the insured or its agent had actual knowledge of it, and the term must be clear and unambiguous as to its effect. In determining whether these requirements have been met, the characteristics of insured persons of the kind in question and the circumstances of the transaction must be taken into account.

It will clearly be possible, therefore for a non-consumer contract to provide that a breach of warranty automatically discharges the insurer from liability and that a breach of any term will have similar effect regardless of any connection, whether causal or temporal, between breach and a loss. It seems likely that ss.10 and 11 will in practice be excluded in at least a large number of non-consumer contracts.

9.8　　　　　Conditions

It has already been pointed out that insurance policies almost universally list a number of terms of the contract under the heading "Conditions". While it is difficult to generalise, it is probably accurate to say that at least some of these terms do not relate directly to the risk covered or to statements of fact, but are in the nature of collateral promises or stipulations. Some "conditions" may, of course, be warranties in the sense described earlier in this chapter, as has been seen. One further important reason for distinguishing warranties from conditions other than those already considered, even when both terms might appear in the same part of a policy, is that it has been held that compliance by an insured with a condition may be dispensed with if it is unnecessary, for example, by reason of information which the insurer possesses from another source. The actual decision that seems to establish this[71] will be considered in a later chapter.[72] It can hardly apply to warranties properly so-called, which, as we have seen, must always be strictly complied with, even if the effects of a breach may now be modified by the provisions of the 2015 Act. In addition, a breach of condition was said to be actionable

---

[69] Insurance Act 2015 s.15. They can be excluded in a contract of settlement: subs. (3).
[70] Insurance Act 2015 s.16(2) and (3).
[71] *Lickiss v Milestone Motor Policies at Lloyd's* [1966] 2 All E.R. 972.
[72] See 14.7.1.

only if it caused the loss,[73] whereas, as we have seen, there was clearly no such requirement as regards warranties, albeit again that position is to some extent modified by the 2015 Act. It should also be noted at this stage that it has been held that breach of a condition precedent can only be waived by estoppel and not by election[74]; this is the same principle as applies to waiver of breach of warranty.[75] This is also considered in more detail later.[76]

9.9 Nature of Conditions

Conditions that are in the nature of collateral terms are of two kinds. First, there are promises or obligations imposed on the insured, primarily with regard to the claims procedure, which are not made fundamental to the validity of the contract. Second are conditions conferring rights on the insurer, often repeating or enlarging rights given by the general law. Examples here include conditions governing subrogation rights and the rights of insurers to control proceedings by or against their insureds, and conditions concerning double insurance. Detailed consideration of the usual obligations and rights conferred by this sort of condition will be given in subsequent chapters. The questions to be considered here are first the effect of conditions imposing obligations on the insured, namely whether they are precedent to the insurer's liability for a particular loss or whether upon breach the insurer has merely the right to claim damages for such loss as it has suffered,[77] and secondly the onus of proof where it is alleged that there has been a breach of such conditions.

9.10 Conditions Precedent or Mere Conditions

It can be particularly difficult to determine the exact status of terms requiring the insured to give prompt notice of any occurrence likely to give rise to a

---

[73] *WJ Lane v Spratt* [1970] Q.B. 480; see 9.4.1.

[74] *Kosmar Villa Holidays Plc v Trustees of Syndicate 1243* [2008] EWCA Civ 147; [2008] Lloyd's Rep. I.R. 489.

[75] See 9.7.

[76] See 14.11.

[77] It may not be easy for the insurer to prove the necessary causal link between breach of a mere condition and loss for it to be able to recover more than merely nominal damages: see *Porter v Zurich Insurance Company* [2009] EWHC 376 (HC); [2010] Lloyd's Rep. I.R. 373. In *Milton Keynes BC v Nulty* [2011] EWHC 2847 (TCC), a failure to give notice in time in breach of a mere condition in a liability policy was held to have lost the insurers the chance to prove that the insured had not been negligent. They were entitled to deduct 15 per cent from the sum due to the insured.

claim.[78] Such terms are common, and can often be the subject of litigation,[79] but are often differently labelled. The traditional analysis of claims conditions is either that they are conditions precedent to the bringing of a claim or that they are suspensive conditions or that they are merely procedural conditions, giving rise only to a claim for damages by the insurer.[80] It does seem, however, that such matters, which cannot objectively be regarded as fundamental to the validity of the contract, can be made fundamental by appropriate wording and in some ways equivalent to warranties in the sense we have described them. For example, in *Cox v Orion Insurance Co*,[81] the Court of Appeal held that a breach of a condition relating to the furnishing of particulars of loss entitled the insurer to treat the whole contract as repudiated because the policy contained a provision making its conditions "conditions precedent to any liability of the company to make any payment under this policy". In *Kazakstan Wool Processors v Nederlandsche Creditverzekering Maatschappij NV*,[82] there was a very wide ranging term requiring the insured to fulfil each and every obligation of the claims process which the insurer stipulated before it would pay out upon loss. The Court of Appeal held that such a term could be a condition precedent to all future liability under the policy.[83]

If there is no reference to the sorts of condition in question being precedent to the insurer's liability, then it is clear that a breach does not entitle the insurer to repudiate liability. The Court of Appeal in *Friends Provident Life & Pensions Ltd v Sirius International Insurance*[84] has confirmed that this is the position and rejected or overruled a number of decisions[85] where it had been

---

[78] For what constitutes likely in this context, see *Jacobs v Coster (T/A Newington Commercials Service Station) and Avon Insurance (Third Party)* [2000] Lloyd's Rep I.R. 506; *Layher v Lowe* [2000] Lloyd's Rep. I.R. 510.

[79] See the dictum of Potter LJ in *Virk v Gan Life Holdings Plc* [2000] Lloyd's Rep. I.R. 159 at 162, where he said that the issue of whether a particular term is a condition precedent to the liability of an insurer *usually arises* in the context of clauses in an insurance contract governing claims procedures . . ." (emphasis added).

[80] See e.g. Clarke, *The Law of Insurance Contracts*, 5th edn (Informa Subscriptions, 2002) para.26-2G.

[81] *Cox v Orion Insurance Co* [1982] R.T.R. 1.

[82] *Kazakstan Wool Processors v Nederlandsche Creditverzekering Maatschappij NV* [1999] Lloyd's Rep I.R. 596.

[83] Although the words "all liability under the policy" could not include liabilities which had already crystallised and been paid out. The court queried whether these were any longer "liabilities" as they had already been discharged.

[84] *Friends Provident Life & Pensions Ltd v Sirius International Insurance* [2005] EWCA Civ 601; [2006] Lloyd's Rep. I.R. 45, followed in *Ronson International Ltd v Patrick* [2005] EWHC 1767 (QB); [2005] All E.R. (Comm) 453 in the context of a notice term in the liability insurance section of a household insurance policy.

[85] *Alfred McAlpine Plc v BAI (Run-Off) Ltd* [2000] Lloyd's Rep I.R. 352; *K/S Merc-Scandia XXXXII v Certain Lloyd's Underwriters* [2001] EWCA Civ 1275; [2001] Lloyd's Rep I.R. 563 at [13] per Longmore LJ; *The Beursgracht* [2002] EWCA Civ

held that a condition that did not expressly provide as to its effect could be an innominate term[86] and that repudiation of a claim would be allowed if the breach demonstrated a clear intention by the insured not to continue to make a claim or if it caused the insurer serious enough consequences.[87] In restoring what had been the traditional view, as referred to above, the court stressed that it is easy for insurers to spell out the effect of a condition if they want to make performance of it precedent to their liability.[88]

Often, however, in any event policies will contain some general reference to their conditions being conditions precedent, if not a specific reference in a particular condition.[89] The only legal problem which then appears likely to arise is where there is a general declaration, but within a particular condition there are parts which cannot conceivably be precedent to the insurer's liability, perhaps because the obligation thereunder can only be performed after the insurer has paid or because a relevant part does not actually impose an obligation on the insured.

In *London Guarantee Co v Fearnley*,[90] for example, a fidelity policy effected by an employer to protect himself against the risk of embezzlement by an employee had a condition which required the insured to prosecute the employee suspected when a claim had been made and which provided that he should give all information and assistance to the insurer to enable the latter to obtain reimbursement from the employee of any sums which the insurer was liable to pay. Clearly the second part of this condition could not be precedent to the insurer's liability since it could only operate when that liability was established. Despite that, the majority of the House of Lords, with some hesitation, held that the first part was a condition precedent since the policy contained a general declaration to that effect and the two parts were separate and independent.

In contrast is the decision in *Bradley and Essex & Suffolk Accident Indemnity Society*.[91] This concerned a condition in a workmen's compensation policy taken out by a farmer, condition 5. There was a similar general declaration

---

2051; [2002] Lloyd's Rep. I.R. 335. See also the first instance decision in *Bankers Insurance Co Ltd v South* [2003] EWHC 380; [2004] Lloyd's Rep. I.R. 1, which is the only case where the insurers were able to avoid liability on the basis of a serious breach of an innominate term. In the other cases the views expressed were strictly obiter.

[86] As in *Hong Kong Fir Shipping Co Ltd v Kawasaki Kisen Kaisha Ltd* [1962] 2 Q.B. 26; [1962] 1 All E.R. 474 (CA).

[87] See Davey, "Insurance claims notification clauses: innominate terms and utmost good faith" [2001] J.B.L. 179.

[88] For comments, see Birds, "Innominate terms in insurance contract", [2006] J.B.L. 543, Lowry and Rawlings [2006] L.M.C.L.Q. 135.

[89] But not always, as we have seen.

[90] *London Guarantee Co v Fearnley* (1880) 5 App. Cas. 911.

[91] *Bradley and Essex & Suffolk Accident Indemnity Society* [1912] 1 K.B. 415.

to the effect that the conditions were precedent to the liability of the insurer. Condition 5 contained three sentences. The first provided that the premium was to be regulated by the amount of wages and salaries paid by the insured, the second required the keeping of a proper wages book and the third required the insured to supply information to the insurers regarding wages and salaries paid. The insured, who only had one employee, his son, failed to maintain a wages book and the insurer relied upon this to deny liability for a particular claim. By a majority, the Court of Appeal held that the insured was not guilty of a breach of a condition precedent. According to Cozens Hardy MR the first and third parts of condition 5 were incapable of being conditions precedent. While the second, the one in issue, could be,

> "I think the fifth condition is one and entire, and it is to my mind unreasonable to hold that one sentence in its middle is a condition precedent while the rest of the condition cannot be so considered. A policy of this nature, in case of ambiguity or doubt, ought to be construed against the office".[92]

The judgment of Farwell LJ is to the same effect, though his reasoning is much broader; he would have required that the insured be informed of and consent to conditions precedent to liability before the policy was effected before they could be binding. With respect, this is too wide, however laudable, to constitute the law, and it conflicts with other authority.[93] Fletcher Moulton LJ, dissenting, followed the decision in *Fearnley*, which he clearly regarded as conclusive.

Although one can applaud the Court of Appeal's determination to ensure that insurers frame their conditions precedent clearly and separately, it is difficult to distinguish the decision in the *Bradley* case from that in the earlier one. Perhaps all that can be said is that each decision turns on questions of construction and that other decisions are of small assistance unless the wording is identical.[94] It is probably fairly safe to suggest that a general declaration as to conditions precedent would normally be effective in so far as particular conditions or parts of them are clearly capable of being separated.

9.11   The Onus of Proof

In relation to an alleged breach of condition,

---

[92] Above at 422.

[93] See the cases concerning offer and acceptance in the insurance context, discussed in Ch.5.

[94] See MacKinnon LJ in *Welch v Royal Exchange Assurance* [1939] 1 K.B. 294 at 311 and Toulson J in *Kazakstan Wool Processors v Nederlandsche Creditverzekering Maatschappij NV* [1999] Lloyd's Rep. I.R. 596 at 601.

"it is axiomatic in insurance law that, as it is always for an insurer to prove an exception, so it is for him to prove the breach of a condition which would relieve him from liability for a particular loss".[95]

It is, however, possible for the wording of a policy to affect this, but it is clear that very clear words would be required to place the onus of proving that he complied with a condition on the insured.[96]

9.12   Practice in the Law of
Warranties and Conditions

The Insurance Conduct of Business Sourcebook contains restrictions on the rights of insurers to avoid liability for breach of warranty or condition as against consumer insureds. While this will become redundant, as far as warranties and other terms controlling the risk, once the provisions of the 2015 Act are in force, it, or the principle it contains, will remain relevant to breaches of claims conditions. Rule 8.1.1 having stated that a claim must not be unreasonably rejected, r.8.1.2 provides:

"A rejection of a consumer policyholder's claim is unreasonable, except where there is evidence of fraud, if it is for breach of warranty or condition unless the circumstances of the claim are connected to the breach and unless (for a pure protection contract):
(a) under a "life of another" contract, the warranty relates to a statement of fact concerning the life to be assured and, if the statement had been made by the life to be assured under an "own life" contract, the insurer could have rejected the claim under this rule; or
(b) the warranty is material to the risk and was drawn to the customer's attention before the conclusion of the contract."

The key point here is the requirement of a causal link, which of course is not the way in which the 2015 Act will control warranties and similar terms. As far as claims conditions are concerned, it has been held that insurers could not claim to be entitled to reject a claim where it would be unreasonable in breach of this standard.[97]

---

[95] Per Lord Goddard CJ in *Bond Air Services Ltd v Hill* [1955] 2 Q.B. 417 at 427.
[96] Above at 428.
[97] *Parker v NFU Mutual Insurance Society Ltd* [2012] EWHC 2156 (Comm); see further at 14.7. It was also held (and see *Bate v Aviva Insurance UK Ltd* [2013] EWHC 1687 (Comm)) that a breach of ICOBS would be actionable by the insured under s.138D of the Financial Services and Markets Act 2000.

CHAPTER 10

PREMIUMS

10.0

The premium is the consideration given by the insured in return for the insurer's undertaking to cover the risks insured against in the policy of insurance.[1] It need not, although, of course, it usually will, take the form of a money payment; for example, it could be the liability to contribute to the funds of a mutual society insuring its members, imposed by membership of that society. Furthermore, if a policy is under seal, and hence does not require consideration to support it, strictly no premium is necessary, but needless to say, this is hardly likely to arise. The amount of the premium is entirely a matter for the insurer and competition led to the end of agreed tariffs many years ago.[2] This can be contrasted with the position in some civil law countries where tariffs are standard, and with the position in some other countries where state approval of premium rates is required.[3]

In this chapter we consider first the payment of the premium and secondly, when the insured is entitled to a return of premium.

10.1   Payment of Premium

We have seen[4] that there is no general rule requiring the actual payment of the premium before the insurer is at risk, although this will frequently, particularly in life insurance, be required by a term of the policy. Prima facie, the proper mode of payment of premium is in cash, but of course it is just as common nowadays to find payment by cheque. The latter is only conditional on the cheque being honoured. Indeed, other modern forms of paying money are also, with the insurer's consent, frequently used. Predominant here are the systems of bank giro, standing order, direct debit and credit and debit cards, their use depending upon the type of insurance concerned. For example, a renewal notice for motor or property insurance will commonly contain a bank giro form for the insured's use if he chooses, while premiums

---

[1] *Lewis v Norwich Union Fire Insurance Co* [1916] A.C. 509 at 519.
[2] For a comprehensive criticism of the tariff system that used to exist in respect of fire insurance, see the Monopolies Commission Report on the Supply of Fire Insurance (HMSO 1972).
[3] See, e.g. Franson, "The prior-approval system of property and liability insurance rate regulations: a case study", (1969) 4 Wisconsin L.R. 1104.
[4] See 5.1.2.

on certain endowment policies, particularly those used in conjunction with a mortgage for house purchase, may well be paid by standing order or direct debit. There has been little case law on the use of such methods generally for payment for any goods or services, and no problems can arise unless the bank responsible is for some reason late in making payment or the insurer fails to pass on the appropriate mandate. It seems likely that, if the insured has sufficient funds in his account, the insurer who permits the use of one of these methods of payment would be held to be bearing the risk of any default by the bank, despite the fact that the bank is acting as agent of the insured rather than of the insurer.[5] If not, the bank would in any event be liable to the insured for any loss suffered.

10.2   Return of Premium

An insured is basically entitled to a return of premium where there has been a total failure of consideration[6] and any action to recover it is in restitution in what used to be called the action in quasi-contract for money had and received. If the insurer has been at risk in any way or for any period, there is no entitlement at common law to a recovery of any part of the premium paid. In *Wolenberg v Royal Co-operative Collecting Society*,[7] the insured had effected several policies of industrial assurance with different insurers to cover the cost of funeral expenses to be incurred on her mother's death. Having recovered that cost from one insurer, she sought to recover the premiums paid on the policy effected with the defendant. It was held that as the insurer had been at risk there could be no return of premiums, even though, by reason of the principle of indemnity, the plaintiff had no claim on the policy. *Wolenberg* was thus a case of over insurance. The same principle will apply to any situation where the insurer has been at risk at all, for example, where liability under the policy, though not the policy itself,[8] is avoided for breach of condition and where the policy is cancelled by either party after it has been in operation. In practice, the principle is sometimes expressly reversed, and usually, for example, the cancellation clause in a policy[9] will provide for a rateable return of premium following cancellation.

There are two broad heads of case where there will or may be a total

---

[5] This seems to be supported by *Weldon v GRE Linked Life Assurance Ltd* [2000] 2 All E.R. (Comm) 914, 14 April 2000, where it was held that the claimant had an arguable case for breach of an implied term of the insurance contract against an insurer who had negligently failed to implement a properly completed direct debit form and thus collect the premium.

[6] *Tyrie v Fletcher* (1777) 2 Cowp. 666.

[7] *Wolenberg v Royal Co-operative Collecting Society* (1915) 83 L.J.K.B. 1316.

[8] As to this distinction, see Ch.6.

[9] See Ch.5.

failure of consideration entitling insureds to recover their premiums. The first is where the policy is never concluded, is cancelled ab initio, or is void or voidable ab initio. The second, which was traditionally the less certain category, is where the policy is illegal.

10.2.1 Non-existent, cancelled and void or voidable policies

If an insured pays a premium in respect of a contract of insurance that is never concluded, he is obviously entitled to its return. The result is the same if a policy is cancelled, or a proposal withdrawn, under the statutory rules that allow cancellation.[10] A policy may theoretically be void for mistake[11] or because it is ultra vires the insurer,[12] or it may be voidable at the insurer's option for non-disclosure or misrepresentation,[13] or at the insured's option for misrepresentation or non-disclosure on the part of the insurer.[14]

Where a policy is avoided ab initio by the insurer, it seemed, although there was no clear non-marine insurance case-law authority, that the insured is entitled to recover premiums paid in all cases except where his non-disclosure or misrepresentation was fraudulent.[15] In effect this is the situation now made clear by the statutory reforms in the Consumer Insurance (Disclosure and Representations) Act 2012[16] for consumer insurance and the Insurance Act 2015[17] for non-consumer insurance.

It must be a fairly rare occurrence where an insured is entitled, and wants, to avoid a policy for misrepresentation of fact by the insurer, but a notable instance is the case of *Kettlewell v Refuge Assurance Co*.[18] Here the insured was minded to let lapse the life policy she had with the defendant insurers, but she was persuaded to continue with it by the false representation of an agent of the defendant that after four more years, she would obtain a free policy, that is, that the policy would remain in force but she would have no more premiums to pay. The Court of Appeal held that the insured had the right to

---

[10] See 5.3 and 19.1.

[11] Although this is unlikely; see 6.2.

[12] Even though the ultra vires doctrine will not now have this effect where the insurer is a registered company (Companies Act 2006 s.39), it could still apply to insurers taking other corporate forms.

[13] See Chs 6 and 7.

[14] See Ch.8.

[15] *Chapman, assignees of Kennet v Fraser* B.R. Trin. 33 Geo. 111; *Anderson v Fitzgerald* (1853) 4 H.L. Cas. 484.

[16] See Sch.1, paras 2 and 5, although note that return of premiums following avoidance for a deliberate or reckless misrepresentation can be allowed if it would be unfair on the consumer for the insurer to retain them.

[17] See Sch.1, paras 2 and 4. There is no equivalent to the qualification mentioned in the preceding footnote regarding unfairness.

[18] *Kettlewell v Refuge Assurance Co* [1908] 1 K.B. 545; affirmed [1909] A.C. 243.

avoid the policy and recover the premiums paid since the date of the misrepresentation as money had and received,[19] it being irrelevant that the defendant had been at risk during the period that the premiums were paid and the policy in effect, albeit voidable. Avoidance by the insured operated ab initio.

10.2.2 Illegal policies

Where a policy is void because of illegality, different considerations may apply. It should be noted that here we are concerned with contracts that are themselves illegal, not those situations where recovery under a valid policy is illegal for reasons of public policy.[20] In the latter case, the premium is never recoverable.

While there are a number of circumstances which could, in theory, render an insurance contract illegal,[21] easily the most common, and that which gave rise to the problems in this area, was illegality due to lack of insurable interest required by statute.[22] The general rule with regard to illegal contracts, whether of insurance or otherwise, was that the court would not entertain any action in respect of them. Further, in terms of restitutionary remedies, the law has always traditionally treated mistakes of fact and mistakes of law differently. In the insurance arena, according to s.1 of the Life Assurance Act 1774, a contract without the requisite insurable interest is illegal.[23] The contract is also void for what is a mistake of law. Premiums paid under such an illegal life policy were not recoverable unless the parties were not considered to be in *pari delicto*, that is not equally blameworthy.[24] The law presumed, as a general principle, that everyone knew the law. However, in the general

---

[19] Lord Alverstone CJ considered that the money was also recoverable as damages in an action in deceit (above at 550). Buckley LJ rested his decision on another ground entirely, considering that there had not been a total failure of consideration since the insured had had the right to enforce the contract until she avoided it. According to him, the money was recoverable as obtained by the insurers only by the fraud of their agent.

[20] For the distinction, see Ch.6, and for avoidance on public policy grounds, see Ch.14.

[21] See Ch.6. Note that the insured has a statutory right, where the insurer is acting without authorisation, to recover the premiums: s.26(2) of the Financial Services and Markets Act 2000. The common law reached the same result: *Re Cavalier Insurance Co Ltd, Re* [1989] 2 Lloyd's Rep. 430.

[22] For example the Life Assurance Act 1774; see Ch.3.

[23] See generally Ch.3.

[24] This would be where there was some element of fraud or trickery on the part of the insurer or its agent, but there were problems concerning the sufficient degree of improper conduct. See *British Workmen's & General Assurance Co v Cunliffe* (1902) 18 T.L.R. 502; *Harse v Pearl Life Assurance Co* [1904] 1 K.B. 558; *Hughes v Liverpool Victoria Legal Friendly Society* [1916] 2 K.B. 482.

restitution law case of *Kleinwort Benson Ltd v Lincoln City Council*,[25] the House of Lords cast doubt on this principle. Whilst their Lordships did not dismiss the distinction between mistakes of fact and mistakes of law entirely, they effectively did so by holding that money paid under a contract that was void for mistake of law could be recovered via a restitutionary claim in the same way as money paid under a mistake of fact had always been so. They recognised that given the vast body of law now in existence it was fatuous to assume that laymen are in a position to know all of it, which is clearly true.

The Law Commission has stated that it is reasonably clear that a party who enters into an illegal contract, as a result of a mistake of facts constituting the illegality, may be granted restitution.[26] This is true regardless of the state of mind of the other party, who may also be under the same mistake, and therefore the parties are technically in *pari delicto*. As the effect of the decision in *Kleinwort Benson* is to assimilate claims for mistake of law with claims for mistake of fact, then, provided the mistake masks the illegality, money paid under a contract that is illegal because of a mistake of law must be recoverable. If a contract of insurance is illegal because of lack of insurable interest, the premiums paid by the insured ought to be recoverable on the same basis. The only defence for the insurer would be that of change of position and it is difficult to see how this could ever arise.

---

[25] *Kleinwort Benson Ltd v Lincoln City Council* [1998] 4 All E.R. 513.
[26] Law Commission Consultation Paper 154, paras 2.38–2.39.

CHAPTER 11

ASSIGNMENT

11.0 Introduction

A number of very important questions in insurance law and practice arise under the general heading of Assignment. Essentially, though, there are three distinct, but closely related topics involved. The first concerns the effect of an assignment by the insured of the subject matter of his insurance policy. The second is the assignment of the benefit of a contract of insurance and the third concerns the assignment of a contract of insurance itself. Various points within these topics overlap, but the basic distinctions are crucial. We shall consider each one in turn. We are not concerned in this chapter with assignment in the context of life insurance. This is a suitably self-contained topic more aptly considered in the later chapter (Ch.19) on life insurance.

11.1 Assignment of the Subject Matter of Insurance

The point that arises here concerns insurance of property when that property is sold or otherwise disposed of by the insured. It has been most often considered in connection with the sale and purchase of land, and for this reason we shall concentrate initially on this area, but the principles established in the cases are equally applicable to dealings with personal property. The assignment of the subject matter of an insurance policy cannot operate to assign the insurance. Once contracts for the sale of land are exchanged, the purchaser obtains an equitable interest in the property, although the vendor retains the legal estate. At this stage, both parties clearly have an insurable interest in the property and, in practice, both may well be insured.[1] On completion of the purchase, or, where the title to the land is registered, upon registration of the purchaser as proprietor, the legal estate vests in the purchaser and obviously the vendor ceases to have an insurable interest.[2] If the property is then lost or damaged, the vendor can recover nothing for this reason.

11.1.1 Claim by the purchaser

If, between contract and completion, the purchaser does not insure, the question arises as to whether, in the absence of an assignment of the benefit of the

---

[1] See further below.
[2] *Ecclesiastical Commissioners v Royal Exchange Assurance Corp* (1895) 11 T.L.R. 476.

vendor's policy, which we shall consider shortly, he can claim the benefit of the vendor's policy. It is clear that the vendor can recover, as he still has an insurable interest to the extent of his unpaid interest in the property, but the suggestion, in one of the cases that supports this,[3] that he holds any money received for the benefit of the purchaser was soon dispelled by the decision in the leading case of *Rayner v Preston*.[4]

Here fire destroyed the property that was the subject matter of the insurance policy effected by P, after P had contracted to sell it to R. Despite this, the contract was completed in accordance with the general rule in conveyancing of real property,[5] that the property is at the purchaser's risk from the date of contract, and P received the full agreed purchase price from R. P also received money from his insurers and the action was brought by R claiming that the assignment of the property to him operated also to assign the benefit of the insurance. R argued that, following the contract of sale, P held the land and the insurance contract on trust for him. By a majority, the Court of Appeal denied R's claim, holding that the insurance contract was merely collateral to the main contract and that the relationship between vendor and purchaser of land was not generally that of trustee and beneficiary. In the absence of an express assignment of the insurance policy or moneys, which was not in issue, there was no reason to say that P held the money for R.[6] As a result of this decision, P was of course in effect paid twice for the property, but his liability to repay the insurance moneys was subsequently established in *Castellain v Preston*,[7] a decision which is examined further in Ch.17.

11.1.2 Consequences of Rayner v Preston

The effect of the decision in *Rayner v Preston* may, as we shall see, be mitigated by an assignment of the benefit of the policy, but this may not be possible, for example, because the insurers refuse their required consent. If so, the decision hardly appears justifiable, because it requires that, if the risk lies with the purchaser, it is advisable that both vendor and purchaser insure, the former at least to the amount he is unpaid, and the latter at least to the amount of the full purchase price for which he will remain liable. This is surely wasteful, and it can hardly matter greatly from the insurer's point of view, if, the property insured is destroyed and the insured has an insurable interest, to whom the

---

[3] *Collingridge v Royal Exchange Assurance Corp* (1877) 3 Q.B.D. 173.
[4] *Rayner v Preston* (1881) 18 Ch D 1.
[5] This rule may now be varied by contract; see below.
[6] Note though that R could perhaps have used the provisions of the Fires Prevention (Metropolis) Act 1774 to compel reinstatement: James LJ (1881) 18 Ch D at 15. This point is discussed below in 16.2.3.
[7] *Castellain v Preston* (1883) 11 Q.B.D. 380.

policy monies go.[8] This point is reinforced by the fact that fire policies do often contain a condition giving the purchaser the benefit of the insurance in this sort of case.[9] Insurers have thus recognised the harshness of *Rayner v Preston*, and would presumably rely on it only rarely. Despite this, it must not be forgotten that vendor and purchaser do have different interests, and the vendor will generally be concerned to recover in total only the market value of the property, whereas the purchaser will probably want sufficient to rebuild. We shall take up this point again.

Considerations like those mentioned in the last paragraph led the Law Commission[10] to undertake a review of the law relating to the question of the risk under a contract for the sale of land. The consequences of their review are considered below.

11.1.3 Position of the vendor

We have already noted that after completion of the contract for the sale of land, or, indeed, upon receiving full payment,[11] the vendor can no longer recover because he no longer has any insurable interest, unless very exceptionally, he is allowed to and did insure for the benefit of the purchaser.[12] Indeed his policy will lapse automatically once the subject matter disappears.[13] This applies equally to the insurance of goods which are sold. In the case of a sale of specific goods, the contract itself may operate as a conveyance of the property,[14] in which case the seller will be able to insure only if he retains actual possession, s.39 of the Sale of Goods Act 1979 giving him a lien for the price despite the transfer of ownership. However, once the seller surrenders possession, the policy will lapse. Thus in *Rogerson v Scottish Automobile & General Insurance Co Ltd*,[15] the insured had a motor policy covering a particular car. He exchanged that car for a new one of a similar type without informing his insurers. The House of Lords held that thereupon his policy lapsed.

---

[8] Unless, of course, there is some material fact about the purchaser of which the insurers are entitled to be told.

[9] It is thought that such a provision would also have the effect of disallowing the insurer from exercising subrogation rights in the vendor's name against the purchaser; see 17.14.

[10] Transfer of Land: Passing of Risk from Vendor to Purchaser, Working Paper No.109, 1988; Transfer of Land: Risk of Damage after Contract of Sale, Report No.191, 1990.

[11] *Ziel Nominees Pty Ltd v VACC Insurance Co Ltd* (1976) 50 A.L.J.R. 106.

[12] See the discussion in Ch.4.

[13] *Rogerson v Scottish Automobile & General Insurance Co Ltd* (1931) 48 T.L.R. 17.

[14] Sale of Goods Act 1979 s.18, r.l. It is open to the parties to agree to the contrary, which often happens in practice.

[15] *Rogerson v Scottish Automobile & General Insurance Co Ltd* (1931) 48 T.L.R. 17. See also *Tattersall v Drysdale* [1935] 2 K.B. 174.

It should be noted, though, that this applies only where the insurance policy has a defined subject matter. Most policies do and must have, simply in order to satisfy the requirement of insurable interest, but it is perfectly possible for a liability policy to exist covering the insured against defined heads of liability to third parties without tying it to particular property. For example, a third party motor policy need not be referable to any particular vehicle; it could cover the insured when driving any vehicle. In *Boss v Kingston*,[16] the insured held a policy insuring the third party liabilities in respect of his own described motorcycle, and when he was driving a motorcycle not belonging to him with the owner's consent. He sold his motorcycle, but kept up his policy. One day he drove a friend's motorcycle, and was charged with driving without insurance.[17] The magistrates convicted him on the ground that his policy had automatically lapsed when he sold his motorcycle, following the *Rogerson* case, but the Divisional Court held that there was no such automatic lapse. The policy was merely a third party policy and it was not necessarily attached to any property. However, reluctantly they held that the insured had been rightly convicted. On the construction of the policy it had lapsed when the insured sold his motorcycle, simply because it contained conditions precedent to the insurer's liability which could not be complied with if the motorcycle was no longer owned by the insured.

More recently, in *Dodson v Peter H Dodson Insurance Services*,[18] the Court of Appeal distinguished *Boss v Kingston*, casting doubt on the reasoning therein, and held that the matter is dependent on the proper construction of the policy. A standard extension covering the insured as regards third party liability while driving any vehicle was held in effect to be independent of the cover provided in respect of the named vehicle and unaffected by the usual obligations relating to the insured vehicle. Thus the insurance did not automatically lapse. In practice, this will be confined to motor policies and the standard extensions therein.[19]

In the case of the sale of goods insured where property does not pass at the time of the contract for sale, principally of unascertained goods, there should be no problems. Property[20] and risk[21] will usually remain with the vendor who can therefore recover if the goods are damaged or destroyed. The purchaser can have no interest in claiming the benefit of any insurance. Once property passes, and the price is paid, the insurance will lapse.

---

[16] *Boss v Kingston* [1963] 1 W.L.R. 99.
[17] Under the Road Traffic Act 1988 s.145; see Ch.21.
[18] *Dodson v Peter H Dodson Insurance Services* [2001] Lloyd's Rep. I.R. 278.
[19] As to these extensions, see 21.3.1.
[20] Sale of Goods Act 1979 s.18, r.5.
[21] Sale of Goods Act 1979 s.20.

11.2 Assignment of the Benefit of an Insurance Policy

If the assignment of the subject matter of an insurance policy does not of itself assign any benefit under the policy to the assignee, the question next arises as to whether or not it is possible to assign the benefit itself. It must be stressed that we are not here considering the assignment of the policy or contract, but merely of the right to recover any benefits payable under it. There is no doubt that this benefit is a chose in action, one of those intangible pieces of property which can be assigned either at law, under s.136 of the Law of Property Act 1925, or in equity.[22] To bind the insurer, and make the latter directly liable to pay the assignee, notice will have to be given to it so that the assignment is legal. Otherwise the assignee can proceed only by suing the assignor to compel him to claim from the insurer. Such an assignment can take place before or after a loss[23] and the consent of the insurer is irrelevant.[24] The insured is simply saying that the proceeds from any claim he has or may have are to go to a third party.

However, the assignee will recover only what the assignor/insured is entitled to, that is the measure of the latter's insurable interest, and he will take subject to any rights the insurer may have, for example, to avoid the policy or liability for non-disclosure or breach of warranty. For these reasons, express assignment of the benefit may not avail the purchaser to the extent he would wish in the sort of case of which *Rayner v Preston*[25] is an example.

11.3 Statutory Assignment

Section 47 of the Law of Property Act 1925 appears to have been introduced to remove the need for this sort of express assignment where the parties are the vendor and purchaser of property, whether land or goods. It was clearly intended to overrule the decision in *Rayner v Preston* and provides, by subsection (1):

> "Where after the date of any contract for sale or exchange of property, money becomes payable under any policy of insurance maintained by the vendor in respect of any damage to or destruction of property included in the contract, the money shall, on completion of the contract, be held by or receivable by the

---

[22] A mortgagor's covenant to insure operates as an equitable assignment in favour of the mortgagee: *Colonial Mutual General Insurance Co Ltd v ANZ Banking Group (New Zealand) Ltd* [1995] 3 All E.R. 987. For a fuller description of the assignment of choses in action, see Treitel, *Law of Contract*, Ch.16.

[23] cf. *Tailby v Official Receiver* (1888) 13 App. Cas. 523; *Peters v General Accident Fire & Life Assurance Corp Ltd* [1937] 4 All E.R. 628, per Goddard J.

[24] *Re Turcan* (1888) 40 Ch D 5.

[25] *Rayner v Preston* (1881) 18 Ch D 1; see 11.1.2.

vendor on behalf of the purchaser and paid by the vendor to the purchaser on completion of the sale or exchange, or as soon thereafter as the same shall be received by the vendor."

By subsection (2), the section has effect subject to (a) any stipulation to the contrary contained in the contract; (b) any requisite consents of the insurer; and (c) the payment by the purchaser of the proportionate part of the premium from the date of the contract. Qualification (a) must refer to the contract of sale not the contract of insurance.

The first point to note is that the section does not give the purchaser any direct rights against the insurer, as an express assignment under s.136 would. Secondly, and fundamentally, the question arises as to what s.47 purports to assign. Is it the contract of insurance itself or merely any benefits payable under it? In the absence of any judicial authority, it is suggested that there is no reason to regard the section as purporting to effect an assignment of the policy, as it refers merely to the money becoming payable under any contract of insurance. If this is so, the next question is as to the meaning of the second requirement (b above) in subs.(2). The ordinary understanding of "any requisite consents" would surely be "any consents as are actually required in the policy", but this is not the view that some have taken.[26] It is often stated that the requirement specifies the need for the express consent of the insurer. It is true that in practice this is usually impliedly given by the standard clause in fire policies on buildings to which we have already referred.[27] But it is submitted that, in fact, the consent of the insurer is required only if it is expressly required. The section does not say that it operates "only with the consent of the insurer", and there seems no reason to construe it other than in accordance with its literal meaning. As we have already argued, s.47 does not purport to assign the contract of insurance itself, in which case the consent of the insurer would be necessary.[28] It must not be forgotten though, that if the consent of the insurer is, in fact, required, it may well be very difficult for the purchaser to discover this.

It is thought, therefore, that s.47 overruled the decision in *Rayner v Preston* in all but those cases where the insurers' consent is required and is not obtained. However, it appears that in practice it is generally excluded in contracts for the sale of land, and, in any event, in the majority of cases, it would not be safe for a purchaser to rely upon the section even it is not excluded. In the case of contracts for the sale or exchange of land, the purchaser is entitled only to that to which the vendor is entitled; in the words of s.47(1), only money that "becomes payable" to the vendor is impressed with the

[26] See, e.g. *Emmet on Title*, 19th edn (London: Sweet & Maxwell) at 42–43.
[27] At 11.1.2.
[28] See 11.4.

trust. Thus the insurer may have a defence to the vendor's claim and, in any event, the amount of the vendor's insurable interest, the amount which he is entitled to claim, may, following the contract of sale, be less than the full value of the property or the cost of its reinstatement. If the risk has passed to the purchaser, the vendor's loss can only be the amount for which he has contracted to sell the property less the deposit he has already received from the purchaser.

11.3.1 The Law Commission review

The rule that the risk of loss, in the case of sales of land, lies on the purchaser from the time of contract, which underlies the decision in *Rayner v Preston*,[29] together with the uncertainties surrounding the true scope of s.47, led to the result in standard conveyancing practice that the purchaser effected his own insurance upon exchange of contracts. Because the vendor would retain his own insurance to protect his own insurable interest, the result was the same property being insured twice against essentially the same risks. Arguments were made that reform of the law was necessary,[30] principally on the ground that the situation was unnecessarily wasteful. It also potentially gave rise to double insurance problems.[31]

The matter was referred to the Law Commission, which produced a working paper[32] arguing for a change in the law so that, in effect, the risk would remain with the vendor until completion.[33] The Commission did not consider that there should be any change to insurance rules as such. This provisional view was supported by the vast majority of respondents and confirmed in the final Report published in 1990.[34] However, by the time that Report was published, there had been a change in the standard contractual conditions applying to the vast majority of conveyancing transactions. The effect of these was the same as the effect of the Law Commission's recommendation and so the Commission concluded that, for the time being at least, there was no need for any change to be effected by statute.

These contractual conditions were the relevant parts (clause 5) of the

---

[29] *Rayner v Preston* (1881) 18 Ch D 1; see 11.1.2.
[30] See e.g. Aldridge (1974) 124 N.L.J. 966; Adams and Aldridge, *Law Society's Gazette*, 16 April 1980.
[31] See Ch.18.
[32] No.109; see fn.10, above.
[33] Their provisionally preferred solution was actually that by statute the vendor would be contractually obliged to convey the property in the physical condition in which it was at the date of the contract, but for most purposes this has the same effect as altering the rule on the passing of risk.
[34] Law Com No.191. This was subject to the possibility of the parties being free to contract out of the new rule.

Standard Conditions of Sale.[35] These impose an obligation on the seller
to transfer the property in the same physical state as it was at the date of
contract,[36] "which means that the seller retains the risk until completion".
The seller is under no obligation to the buyer to insure and s.47 of the Law
of Property Act is expressly excluded. In principle, this might be thought to
be eminently sensible. However, it would appear that in practice this part
of the standard condition is normally excluded. Practitioners appear to have
decided that time-honoured practices are best and that any overlapping
insurance does not in fact give rise to significant waste or cost.[37]

11.3.2 Effect of section 47 on goods insurance

As far as contracts for sale or exchange of goods are concerned, there is no
doubt that s.47 applies. However, in the case of specific goods where property may well pass at the time of the contract, it is irrelevant simply because
the vendor will have no claim and will have no insurable interest to recover
anything to which the purchaser can claim entitlement, unless, exceptionally,
the risk remains with him. But in this event, the purchaser will not suffer
any loss anyway. Where, however, property does not pass at the date of the
contract, and a loss occurs before it does, there is no reason why the purchaser
should not claim the benefits of any insurance maintained by the vendor, if
he chooses to go ahead with the contract, subject to any consent expressly
required by the insurer and to the other conditions in s.47(2).

11.4   Assignment of the Policy

Prima facie, any insurance policy is freely assignable, being itself a chose
in action. This is statutorily confirmed in respect of life policies, which we
shall consider separately,[38] and marine polices.[39] However, because all other
forms of insurance are regarded as personal to the particular insured, any

---

[35] These replaced the previous "rival" Law Society's General Conditions of Sale and
the National Conditions of Sale. Note, though, that the Standard Commercial
Property Conditions do not alter the common law rule as to the passing of risk and
exclude s.47.

[36] Except for fair wear and tear.

[37] See Silverman, *Law Society's Gazette*, 23 October 1991, at 27. If there were evidence
of waste, the Law Commission might reconsider the position and press for a formal
change in the law. For consideration of other insurance issues, see Harwood (1992)
136 S.J. 408.

[38] See Ch.19.

[39] Marine Insurance Act 1906 s.50. The nature of international trade and standard form international sale contracts necessitate that a marine policy is freely
assignable.

assignment of them requires the consent of the insurers.[40] The result is that, in effect, non-life and non-marine policies are not really assignable, since insurers would consent to an "assignment" to a new insured only in circumstances that would amount to the creation of a new contract or a novation. In *Peters v General Accident Fire and Life Assurance Corp Ltd*,[41] the vendor of a van handed over his insurance policy issued by the defendant insurers to the purchaser. The latter subsequently injured the claimant by the negligent driving of the van and the claimant sued the insurers under what is now s.151 of the Road Traffic Act 1988.[42] It was held that the insurers were not liable to satisfy the judgment awarded against the purchaser, as the insured vendor could not simply assign his motor policy to the purchaser without the insurers' consent.[43] The policy would have lapsed upon the sale of the van for the reasons and under the authorities mentioned earlier.[44]

Further, a valid assignment of a policy must be contemporaneous with the assignment of the subject matter of the insurance. Obviously a non-life policy cannot be assigned in the absence of the assignment of its subject matter; otherwise the assignee would have no insurable interest. The requirement of strict contemporaneity is well established in marine insurance,[45] and there is no reason to doubt that it would apply equally to non-marine policies.

---

[40] Note, though, that the personal nature of insurance contracts does not seemingly preclude undisclosed principals from suing on policies made by their agents: *Siu Yin Kwan v Eastern Insurance Co Ltd* [1994] 1 All E.R. 213; but see the comments made at 4.6.1. As to whether noting the interest of, for example, a purchaser on a vendor's policy could amount to consent, see *Bestquest Ltd v Regency Care Group Ltd* [2003] Lloyd's Rep. I.R. 392.

[41] *Peters v General Accident Fire and Life Assurance Corp Ltd* [1938] 2 All E.R. 267. See also *Bryant v Primary Industries Insurance Co Ltd* [1990] 2 N.Z.L.R. 142.

[42] See 21.5.

[43] It was also held that the clause in the policy extending the cover to a third party driving with the insured's consent was not applicable as the van was the purchaser's property and he was driving it therefore not with the insured's consent, but by virtue of his ownership.

[44] Especially *Rogerson v Scottish Automobile & General Insurance Co Ltd* (1931) 48 T.L.R. 17; see 11.1.3.

[45] *North England Oil Cake Co v Archangel Marine Insurance Co* (1875) L.R. 10 Q.B. 249.

CHAPTER 12

INTERMEDIARIES

12.0

The law concerning insurance intermediaries is of special importance since in effect all insurance business is conducted through the medium of agents of one sort or another. Most insurers are and have to be companies or, in exceptional cases, other corporate bodies or associations[1] and such bodies can, of necessity, act only through agents, ranging from directors and senior management down to junior employees. The only natural person who can be an insurer is a Lloyd's underwriter and by custom, enshrined in statute,[2] that person can act only through the agency of Lloyd's brokers; those brokers recognised by Lloyd's as the people through whom only can a Lloyd's policy be effected. Quite apart from the sorts of intermediary already mentioned, much insurance business is transacted through insurance brokers and other independent agencies, who may act under a title such as "insurance consultants" or "insurance advisers".[3] An insured may act through another intermediary in approaching a Lloyd's broker. Not all intermediaries act full-time in that capacity. There are people such as motor dealers, solicitors, mortgage lenders, travel agents and estate agents, whose principal job is clearly not the selling of or advising on insurance, but who may sell insurance part-time or as an incidental part of their major work, often having pre-existing links with particular insurers. This chapter is concerned in particular with how the general principles of agency law apply to insurance intermediaries, but before that it is necessary to briefly examine how these various types of intermediaries are regulated.

12.1   The Regulation of Intermediaries

The wide variety of types of insurance intermediary raises important questions concerning their suitability and qualifications, and how to respond with conflicts of interest that may arise,[4] and has led over the years to a number

---

[1] See 1.3.

[2] Lloyd's Act 1982 s.8(3).

[3] There are nowadays of course widely-advertised websites through which insurance is sold and which may be intermediaries in law.

[4] For example, where insurance is sold on a commission basis, the intermediary may well try to persuade the client to accept the policy that pays him the best rate of commission, rather than that which is best suited to the client's needs.

of different mechanisms for their regulation. Apart from a statutory scheme for the registration of persons calling themselves insurance brokers, which was repealed in 2000, the oldest form of regulation is of intermediaries advising on life insurance. These were covered by the scheme introduced under the Financial Services Act 1986, which was then replaced by the Financial Services and Markets Act 2000. Independent intermediaries selling most forms of long-term insurance must be authorised by the Financial Conduct Authority (FCA) and an insurer is directly liable for the acts and omissions of one of its appointed representatives.[5] The regulator makes detailed rules governing these intermediaries, which are included in the Insurance: Conduct of Business Sourcebook (ICOBS).

For a relatively short period, intermediaries involved in general insurance business were regulated by a self-regulatory system,[6] but, with some exceptions, in particular for those involved in large risks[7] and reinsurance they too came within the jurisdiction of the Financial Services Authority, now the Financial Conduct Authority, when the Insurance Mediation Directive,[8] which sets minimum standards across Europe for the sale and administration of both general and life insurance, was implemented in 2005.[9] One most important consequence is that all complaints against insurance intermediaries are now within the jurisdiction of the Financial Ombudsman Service.[10]

In many respects the requirements concerning intermediaries are the same as those that apply to insurers, as described briefly in Ch.2. ICOBS draws a distinction between consumers and commercial customers. Consumers are natural persons acting for purposes outside their trade, business of profession. Commercial customers are any other persons, although small businesses do receive some extra protection as regards product disclosure and advice.

The key requirements of ICOBS as it applies exclusively to intermediaries are as follows.[11] They are required to disclose a number of matters, including their name and address, that they are included in the FCA Register and their complaints procedure (including mention of the Financial Ombudsman Service). They must also disclose whether they give advice on the basis of a

---

[5] Financial Services and Markets Act 2000 s.39(3).

[6] Under what was called the General Insurance Standards Council.

[7] As to these, see 2.3.2.

[8] 2002/92/EC. Note that the European Commission published in June 2012 a draft Directive to replace the Mediation Directive.

[9] The Directive was implemented by the Insurance Mediation Directive (Miscellaneous Amendments) Regulations 2002, SI 2004/1473 and the Financial Services and Markets Act 2000 (Regulated Activities) (Amendment) (No.2) Order 2003, SI 2003/1476, which came into force in January 2005.

[10] See 1.9.1.

[11] There are additional requirements for protection policies, which are essentially term life policies and payment protection policies.

fair analysis of the market or are under a contractual obligation to conduct business exclusively with one or more insurers or that they are not under such an obligation nor do they give advice on the basis of a fair analysis of the market. If they do not advise on the basis of a fair analysis of the market, they must inform customers that the latter have the right to request the name of each insurer with which they may and do conduct business. Before the conclusion of an initial contract with a consumer, intermediaries must state whether they are giving a personal recommendation or information. This must all be disclosed clearly, accurately and comprehensibly in a "durable medium" before conclusion of an insurance contract, unless customers require immediate cover or the contract is made by telephone, in which case oral disclosure suffices. Intermediaries must disclose their fees (or the basis for calculating them) before the customer incurs liability to pay them or before conclusion of the contract, whichever is earlier. Commercial customers have the right to be told of the commission that intermediaries receive.

12.2   Agent of Insurer or Insured

As far as general agency principles are concerned, the first question to which we must turn is that of determining whose agent in law a particular intermediary is. This is not something about which it is easy to be dogmatic. As a general rule, only the agent under the direct employment or control of the insurer is the agent of the insurer, and even he may not at all times, when dealing with an insured, be regarded as the insurer's agent.[12] For most purposes, all other agents are in law the agents of the insured, and this is even so in respect of Lloyd's brokers.[13] However, there have been some cases where brokers have, for particular purposes, been regarded as agents of the insurer.[14] The position of the broker[15] in these cases merits further examination.

The question is of particular importance when the broker has notice of certain matters pertaining to the insurance contract, or purports to act on behalf of the insurer. As the broker is, as we have seen, the agent of the insured, the insurer should logically not be deemed to know or be bound

---

[12] See the line of authority of which *Newsholme Bros v Road Transport & General Insurance Co* [1929] 2 K.B. 356 is the leading case, which is discussed below.

[13] *Rozanes v Bowen* (1928) 32 Ll.L.Rep. 98; *Anglo-African Merchants v Bayley* [1970] 1 Q.B. 311; *North & South Trust v Berkeley* [1971] 1 W.L.R. 470; *McNealy v Pennine Insurance Co Ltd* [1978] 2 Lloyd's Rep. 18; *Roberts v Plaisted* [1989] 2 Lloyd's Rep. 341.

[14] *Stockton v Mason* [1978] 2 Lloyd's Rep. 430; *Woolcott v Excess Insurance Co* [1978] 1 Lloyd's Rep. 633 (original trial); [1979] 1 Lloyd's Rep. 231 (Court of Appeal); [1979] 2 Lloyd's Rep. 210 (retrial).

[15] For these purposes broker includes any independent intermediary.

by his actions. It is quite clear that a Lloyd's broker is always the agent of the insured,[16] although there is clearly some judicial unease about this.[17] A broker instructed to find insurance who goes first to reinsurers is the agent of the hitherto unidentified insurers/reinsured, not the agent of the insured.[18] In two relatively modern decisions, however, it was assumed that people who appear to have been independent, non-Lloyd's brokers were agents of the insurer. In *Stockton v Mason*,[19] M's father, the insured, through his wife, instructed his brokers to transfer his existing motor policy from a Ford Anglia to an MG Midget. An employee of the brokers said that this would be all right for a temporary period, which the father naturally assumed meant that the previous policy, which covered the driving of the car by any authorised driver, was thereby transferred to the new car.

Subsequently, the brokers wrote saying that cover on the MG was restricted to the insured only. M was driving the MG when he negligently injured the claimant. The issue was whether, under the Road Traffic Act 1972,[20] the claimant was entitled to sue M's father's insurers[21] and thus it depended on whether the latter were bound by the oral statement of the broker's employee purporting to authorise the MG to be substituted entirely for the Anglia. The Court of Appeal, consisting of three Lords of Appeal, held that the insurers were bound.

> "A broker in non-marine insurance has implied authority to issue on behalf of the insurer, or enter into as agent for the insurer, contracts of interim insurance . . . it seems to me to be quite unarguable that in saying 'Yes, that will be all right. We will see to that, Mrs. Mason', the brokers were acting as agents for the insurance company and not merely acknowledging an order or request by Mrs. Mason to negotiate a contract with the insurance company on his behalf."[22]

In *Woolcott v Excess Insurance Co Ltd*,[23] a case which involved much dispute as to the facts, being referred back by the Court of Appeal to the trial judge

---

[16] *Roberts v Plaisted* [1989] 2 Lloyd's Rep. 341.

[17] Above at 345, where it was commented by Purchas LJ that to the person unacquainted with the insurance industry, it may seem a remarkable state of the law that someone who describes himself as a Lloyd's broker who is remunerated by the insurance industry and who presents proposal forms and suggests policies on their behalf should not be the recipient of full disclosure. The Court of Appeal, echoing the comments of Hodgson J at first instance, thought that the matter should be referred to the Law Commission.

[18] *SAIL v Farex Gie* [1995] L.R.L.R. 116; as a result knowledge obtained by the broker was not imputed to the insured. As to the imputation of knowledge, see 12.4.

[19] *Stockton v Mason* [1978] 2 Lloyd's Rep. 430.

[20] s.149, now replaced by the Road Traffic Act 1988; see 21.5.

[21] The brokers were also sued in the alternative.

[22] *Stockton v Mason* [1978] 2 Lloyd's Rep. 430 at 431–432, per Lord Diplock.

[23] See fn.14, above.

on this issue, it was clearly assumed beyond argument by the Court of Appeal that the knowledge of a material fact by the broker in question was imputed to the insurers, and that the latter's defence of non-disclosure of that fact failed, even if the insured did not know that the insurer had the knowledge or was deemed to know.[24]

These two decisions were clearly to be welcomed as according with the reality of the situation, particularly as that is how it is no doubt perceived by insureds. Where appropriate, the extent of the broker's authority to bind the insurer will depend upon considerations that we shall discuss further, later. It does not seem, however, that the principles of these cases are generally applicable. In both of them there was a close relationship between the brokers and the insurers, the former being actually authorised to conclude at least interim contracts of insurance. More recently, in *Winter v Irish Life Assurance Plc*,[25] it was held that the knowledge of the broker, that both lives insured had cystic fibrosis, was not imputed to the insurers. As a general rule, therefore, it seems safe to say that where an insured negotiates, through a broker or other independent intermediary, with an insurer with whom the broker does not have a close relationship, unless that broker or agent has actual authority from the insurer, the insured is not entitled to rely on principles of apparent authority.[26]

12.2.1 Statutory rules

As part of their general review of consumer insurance law relating to non-disclosure and misrepresentation, the Law Commissions considered various aspects of agency law, including this difficult one, of whose agent a particular intermediary is. In the end,[27] rather than attempting to provide rigid statutory principles, which might rapidly become outdated, they recommended the enactment of more flexible rules to determine the status of insurance agents. As enacted in the Consumer Insurance (Disclosure and Representations) Act 2012, Sch.2, these only apply for the purposes of the Act, that is they are limited to pre-contractual disclosure and misrepresentation in consumer insurances. They are described in 7.4.5.

A consequence of this way of legislating is probably clearly to confirm that, if the insurer is not deemed to know what a particular intermediary

---

[24] *Woolcott v Excess Insurance Co* [1979] 1 Lloyd's Rep. 231 at 241–242 (per Megaw LJ); see also [1979] 2 Lloyd's Rep. 210 at 211 (per Cantley J).

[25] *Winter v Irish Life Assurance Plc* [1995] 2 Lloyd's Rep. 274.

[26] Unless, perhaps, the insurer has previously regarded itself as bound by representations of the broker or agent. For a brief description of apparent or apparent authority, see below.

[27] Consumer Insurance Law: Pre-Contract Disclosure and Misrepresentation, Law Com No.310, Scot Law Com No.219, Cm 7758, Pt 8.

knows in relation to pre-contract information, and does not know because the intermediary failed to pass it on, the latter is in clear breach of duty to the consumer, something that, as discussed below in 12.6.3, was not wholly certain under the previous law.

As regards non-consumer insurance and the duty to make a fair presentation of the risk, the Insurance Act 2015 makes special provision, which applies in place of usual agency principles, for when the knowledge of an intermediary is deemed to be that of the insured or the insurer. These have been considered in 7.5.2 and 7.6.1.

12.3 Relevant Agency Principles

It is not possible, in the space available, to deal by any means comprehensively with all the principles of agency law which may be applicable to the insurance transaction.[28] We must therefore concentrate on those which appear to be of particular relevance, namely, the question of when a principal is bound by his agent's acts in favour of a third party; the question of when an agent's knowledge is imputed to his principal; and the relationship between principal and agent, especially when the principal is the insured.

12.3.1 Principal and third party

A principal is bound by any of the acts of his agent within the latter's actual, apparent (or ostensible) or usual authority and by an unauthorised act which he ratifies. The problems surrounding the concept of usual authority[29] do not appear to have been considered or indeed to be likely to arise in the insurance context, and need not detain us here.

12.3.2 Actual authority

Actual authority may be expressed or implied. What an agent is expressly authorised to do raises no problems. Implied actual authority arises where, in the circumstances, it must be the position that the agent had actual authority, but it was never conferred on him in so many words. If an insurer gives his agent blank cover notes, he impliedly authorises him to effect binding temporary insurance contracts.[30] Similarly, the continuing adoption by the insurer of temporary oral contracts entered into by its agent will confer

---

[28] See, generally, *Bowstead and Reynolds on Agency*, 20th edn (London: Sweet & Maxwell, 2014). There is some discussion of other agency principles in Ch.4.

[29] See, e.g. Markesinis and Munday, *An Outline of the Law of Agency*, at 24–29.

[30] *Mackie v European Assurance Society* (1869) 21 L.T. 102; *Stockton v Mason* [1978] 2 Lloyd's Rep. 430.

implied authority on that agent.[31] An example of the principle where the insured was principal is *Zurich General Accident and Liability Insurance Co Ltd v Rowberry*,[32] where the brokers were instructed to effect a policy in respect of the insured's forthcoming journey to France. The brokers mistakenly inserted in the proposal form that the insured's destination was Paris, whereas, in fact, he was going to Nice. The insured attempted to get out of the policy issued on the grounds of this mistake, but it was held that he was bound by the broker's actions, having given them authority to negotiate the proposal with no specific instructions as to his destination.

12.3.3 Apparent authority

Apparent or ostensible authority arises where the principal, by words or by conduct, holds out his agent as having a particular authority.[33] It is really relevant only when the agent is exceeding his actual authority. The essence of apparent authority is the representation made by the principal to the third party; it matters not what the agent says, nor whether he is acting fraudulently.[34] Thus, apparent authority depends upon an estoppel, usually the representation being the conduct of the principal rather than anything expressly said.[35] Appointing an agent to a particular position confers on him apparent authority to bind his principal in respect of the usual acts which someone in that position would have authority to do, and it is irrelevant, unless the third party is aware of this, in which case there can be no reliance on the representation,[36] that the agent is actually not authorised to do some of the usual acts.

Someone who holds the position of inspector in an insurance company will probably be regarded as having apparent authority to vary the terms of a proposal form.[37] The payment of premiums to an agent will bind the insurer even if he is not authorised to accept them, if, nonetheless, he is held out as having authority to receive them.[38] The receiving of notice of loss by an agent, if he is the person with whom the insured has always dealt, should bind the insurer, unless there is an express indication to the contrary;

---

[31] *Murfitt v Royal Insurance Co* (1922) 38 T.L.R. 334.

[32] *Zurich General Accident and Liability Insurance Co Ltd v Rowberry* [1954] 2 Lloyd's Rep. 55.

[33] See generally, e.g. *Freeman & Lockyer v Buckhurst Park Properties Ltd* [1964] 2 Q.B. 480.

[34] *Lloyd v Grace, Smith & Co* [1912] A.C. 716.

[35] An insurance example is *Eagle Star Insurance Co v Spratt* [1971] 2 Lloyd's Rep. 116.

[36] *Wilkinson v General Accident Fire & Life Assurance Corp Ltd* [1967] 2 Lloyd's Rep. 182.

[37] *Stone v Reliance Mutual Insurance Society Ltd* [1972] 1 Lloyd's Rep. 469; see 12.5.5.

[38] *Kelly v London and Staffordshire Fire Insurance Co* (1883) Cab. & E. 47.

the latter would negate any representation allegedly made by the insurer.[39] An agent held out as having authority to make alterations in a policy or to waive a breach of condition will bind the insurer.[40] Similarly, providing an agent with cover notes gives that agent apparent authority to conclude such temporary contracts, even if the insurer has expressly forbidden this, so that implied actual authority is not available. On the other hand, an agent will never, unless actually authorised, have authority to bind the insurer by the issue of a formal policy,[41] nor will he have authority to fill in a proposal form on behalf of the insured at least if he is a mere canvassing agent,[42] although we shall examine this rather curious rule shortly. An agent of the insurer has no authority to bind his principal as to the meaning or construction of a policy, though this is not so much a result of a lack of authority as of the rule that such a representation would be a representation of law, and in general these are not binding.[43]

12.3.4 Ratification

Even an unauthorised act not binding a principal by virtue of the principles of apparent authority may, however, be ratified by the principal, provided that the agent was purporting to act as an agent[44] and that the principal was in existence and identifiable at the time of the agent's act. Ratification dates back to the time of the original act of the agent,[45] but it is unclear in non-marine insurance whether it is possible to ratify after a loss has taken place. In *Grover & Grover v Mathews*,[46] where a broker effected without authority a renewal of the insured's policy, and the insured suffered a loss before he knew about the broker's actions, it was held that the insurer was not liable even though the insured ratified what the broker had done. It is, however, arguable that this case was wrongly decided and in *National Oilwell (UK) Ltd v Davy Offshore Ltd*,[47] the judge would have refused to follow it.[48]

---

[39] *Brook v Trafalgar Insurance Co* (1946) 79 Ll.L. Rep. 365.

[40] *Wing v Harvey* (1854) 5 De G.M. & G. 265, see 14.11.3.

[41] *Stockton v Mason* [1978] 2 Lloyd's Rep. 430; *British Bank of the Middle East v Sun Life Assurance Co of Canada (UK) Ltd* [1983] 2 Lloyd's Rep. 9. In practice only the directors or someone at least as senior as a branch manager might be actually authorised.

[42] *Newsholme Bros v Road Transport & General Insurance Co* [1929] 2 K.B. 356.

[43] *Re Hooley Rubber & Chemical Manufacturing Co* [1920] 1 K.B. 257; compare, e.g. *Harr v Allstate Insurance Co* 54 N.J. 287 (1969).

[44] An undisclosed principal can sue and be bound only if the agent had actual authority: see generally, *Bowstead* at 51–84. As to the possible use of an undisclosed agent to conclude an insurance contract, see 4.6.1.

[45] *Bolton Partners v Lambert* (1888) 41 Ch D 295.

[46] *Grover & Grover v Mathews* [1910] 2 K.B. 401.

[47] *National Oilwell (UK) Ltd v Davy Offshore Ltd* [1993] 2 Lloyd's Rep. 213.

[48] See 4.6.2.

12.4 Imputing the Agent's Knowledge

Of particular importance in the context of insurance are the rules whereby, in certain cases, the knowledge of an agent is imputed to his principal so that the latter is deemed to know what the agent knows. These will be examined here only in the context of the agent being the agent of the insurer, that is where an insured is seeking to rely upon them, although the same principles will apply when the agent is the agent of the insured.

Most commonly, the issue will relate to material facts of which the insurer alleges non-disclosure or misrepresentation by the insured, but which the latter claims are deemed to be known by the insurer by virtue of its agent's knowledge. The general principles will still be relevant as far as misrepresentation by a consumer insured is concerned because of the provisions of the 2012 Act referred to in 12.2.1, but as regards non-consumer insurance, as also mentioned earlier, the general principles have been replaced by specific provisions in the 2015 Act. Subject to these considerations, the case law contains useful illustrations. *Woolcott v Excess Insurance Co*,[49] which was described earlier, is an example. In general the agent's knowledge will be imputed to the insurer, because he will have been held out as having authority to receive it, but the position may well be different if an incorrect answer is given on a proposal form, even though the agent knows the truth,[50] and it is, it seems, essential that the information is received by a person who is able to appreciate its significance. In *Mahli v Abbey Life Assurance Co*,[51] the insurers had previously been told of material facts (alcoholism and malaria of the life insured) because they had declined an earlier proposal on this basis. However, the person responsible for considering the later application did not know of these facts. It was held by a majority of the Court of Appeal that the insurers had not waived their right to avoid the later policy.[52]

Another illustration would be where the agent knows of something that constitutes a breach of warranty or condition by the insured. The agent's knowledge of the breach may be imputed to the insurer who may therefore, by subsequently accepting premiums, be deemed to have waived the breach.

---

[49] *Woolcott v Excess Insurance Co* [1979] 1 Lloyd's Rep. 231.

[50] *Newsholme Bros v Road Transport & General Insurance Co* [1929] 2 K.B. 356; see below.

[51] *Mahli v Abbey Life Assurance Co* [1994] C.L.C. 615.

[52] McCowan LJ, dissenting, thought that the situation was indistinguishable from the earlier Court of Appeal decision in *Evans v Employers Mutual Insurance Association Ltd* [1936] K.B. 505 on the ground that there the only requirement for imputation of knowledge was that the agent in question was authorised to receive it. With respect, this seems more persuasive. See also the earlier case of *Stone v Reliance Mutual Insurance Association* [1972] 1 Lloyd's Rep. 469, discussed at 12.5.5, which seems to support the broader ground for imputation of knowledge.

In *Wing v Harvey*,[53] a life policy provided that it would become void if the assured travelled beyond the limits of Europe without the insurer's consent. An assignee of the policy subsequently informed an agent of the insurer that the life assured had taken up residence in Canada. For some time after this, before the life assured died, premiums were received by the insurer. It was held that the insurer had waived the breach of warranty; they were deemed to know what their agent knew and having accepted premiums subsequently, could not rely upon the breach.

What knowledge will be imputed depends upon the status of the agent receiving it, in other words, upon his actual or apparent authority. In *Wing v Harvey*, the agent was the local representative of the insurer at a branch office. A mere canvassing or soliciting agent would probably not be regarded as having such a wide authority, which is after all tantamount to varying the terms of the policy, but such an agent probably has authority to receive disclosures of material facts.[54] However, the knowledge of an agent is never imputed when the agent is acting in fraud of his principal.[55]

12.5   Agents and the Proposal Form

It is not uncommon, in an insurance transaction being negotiated through an agent of one sort or another, for the agent actually to fill in the proposal form. Normally this would of course be done in consultation with the proposer, but there are reported cases that show that occasionally this is not the case. If an answer is incorrect due to the fault or with the knowledge of the proposer, then obviously the insurer will be entitled to avoid liability. If, however, the proposer tells the agent the truth, but the latter chooses to falsify an answer, and the proposer does not become aware of what has happened because he does not check what the agent has done, the question arises whether the proposer is bound by what the agent has done. Certainly he is if the agent is in law his agent at all times, and it has even been held that in this case he has no right to sue the agent in damages.[56] If, however, the agent is a full-time agent of the insurer, for example, a canvassing agent or another full-time

---

[53] *Wing v Harvey* (1854) 5 De G.M. & G. 265.

[54] *Ayrey v British Legal & United Provident Assurance* [1918] 1 K.B. 136; *Blackley v National Mutual Life Assurance of Australasia* [1972] N.Z.L.R 1938; see 7.7.1.

[55] See a series of cases arising out of various problems at Lloyd's of London where it was held that the insureds were not deemed to know of their agents' fraud, applying the general principle of *Re Hampshire Land Co* [1896] 2 Ch.743: *PCW Syndicates v PCW Reinsurers* [1996] 1 Lloyd's Rep. 241; *Group Josie Re v Walbrook Insurance Co Ltd* [1996] 1 Lloyd's Rep. 345; *Deutsche Ruckversicherung AG v Walbrook Insurance Co Ltd* [1996] 1 All E.R. 791.

[56] *O'Connor v Kirby* [1972] 1 Q.B. 90, discussed below at 12.6.3. Compare, however, *Dunbar v A & B Painters Ltd* [1986] 2 Lloyd's Rep. 38, which is also discussed later.

employee, it might be argued that his knowledge of the truth should be imputed to the insurer, on the basis of the authorities discussed above.

However, the common law has in general taken the opposite view.[57] This is an area that has given rise to a comparatively large number of reported cases in all common law jurisdictions. We shall here concentrate on the English decisions, but make reference to some particularly apposite Commonwealth cases. It should be noted at the outset that in all the reported cases, the proposal form contained a basis of the contract clause, so that its contents were incorporated as warranties into the contract. This is no longer possible in any insurance contract,[58] so the cases have to be considered with that in mind.

12.5.1 Knowledge imputed

The first authority to be examined is perhaps the earliest in time, a Court of Appeal decision that appears at first sight to be out of line with subsequent cases. *Bawden v London, Edinburgh & Glasgow Assurance Co*[59] concerned a proposal for accident insurance by a proposer who was illiterate and had only one eye. This fact was known to the agent of the insurers who completed the form for him. That form, however, warranted that the proposer had no physical deformity, which was obviously incorrect. Subsequently the insured suffered an accident in which he lost the sight of the other eye. It was held that he could recover under the policy for total loss of sight. The agent's knowledge of the truth at the time of the proposal was imputed to the insurer.

12.5.2 Knowledge not imputed

Bawden was, however, distinguished in a number of subsequent cases[60] and in particular in the leading case of *Newsholme Bros v Road Transport & General Insurance Co.*[61] Here the proposal was for motor insurance and the incorrect answers, which related to previous losses, were warranted to be true. It was found as a fact that the agent who filled in the form knew of the true facts. He was an agent employed by the insurers to canvass for proposals, but he was not authorised to effect insurance whether temporary or permanent. The arbitrator held that the agent's knowledge of the truth was imputed to the insurers who could not therefore repudiate liability, but his decision was overruled by the trial judge and the Court of Appeal. Scrutton LJ, delivering

---

[57] Whether or not statute reverses this in certain cases is discussed below.
[58] See 9.2.1.
[59] *Bawden v London, Edinburgh & Glasgow Assurance Co* [1892] 2 Q.B. 534.
[60] See, e.g. *Biggar v Rock Life Assurance Co* [1902] 1 K.B. 516; *Keeling v Pearl Assurance Co* (1923) 129 L.T. 573.
[61] *Newsholme Bros v Road Transport & General Insurance Co* [1929] 2 K.B. 356.

the leading judgment, gave two principal reasons for the decision. First, he said,[62] if the agent filled in the form at the request of the proposer, for that purpose he must have been acting as the agent of the proposer and not of the insurers. Secondly,[63]

> "I have great difficulty in understanding how a man who has signed, without reading it, a document which he knows to be a proposal for insurance, and which contains statements in fact untrue, and a promise that they are true and the basis of the contract, can escape from the consequences of his negligence by saying that the person he asked to fill it up for him is the agent of the person to whom the proposal is addressed."

Greer LJ also relied upon the agency point,[64] but he laid greater stress upon another reason, namely, that to allow evidence of what the agent actually knew to be introduced would be a violation of the parol evidence rule whereby oral evidence is generally inadmissible to vary the terms of a written contract.[65] Here the proposal form was part of the contract because, as usual, it formed the basis of it and its terms were warranties. Greer LJ was thus able to distinguish the *Bawden* case on the grounds that in the latter, because of the special circumstances of the proposer's illiteracy, the court could rightly ignore the parol evidence rule or put a special meaning on the words used in the contract.[66] In contrast, Scrutton LJ came very close to saying that the *Bawden* case was wrong.[67]

12.5.3 Authority

As to the agency point, the judges seemed particularly impressed by the fact that the agent did not have actual authority to fill in proposal forms. With respect, this should not be conclusive. The fact that agents are armed with such forms and frequently complete them, probably to the knowledge of insurers, must arguably give them apparent authority to do so, unless any such authority is negatived, for example, by a notice on the proposal form,[68] yet the principles of apparent authority were ignored in the *Newsholme Bros* case.

---

[62] Above at 369 and 375.

[63] Above at 376.

[64] Above at 382.

[65] Above at 379–380.

[66] Above at 381.

[67] The *Bawden* case had previously also been subjected to considerable criticism in a number of cases in different jurisdictions. These are cited in the judgment of Scrutton LJ.

[68] See *Facer v Vehicle & General Insurance Co* [1965] 1 Lloyd's Rep. 113. Such a provision might not, though, survive the controls on unfair terms.

Further, even if an agent does become the agent of the proposer, or at least his amanuensis, for the purpose of filling in the form, at that stage the form is merely an offer to enter into an insurance contract and it is not easy to see why the correct knowledge of the agent should not be imputed to the insurer if the facts warrant it.[69] On this basis the strict parol evidence rule could be ignored, as the court has already admitted extrinsic evidence for the insurer that the answer on the form was incorrect.

12.5.4 Signing of form

However, the second reason of Scrutton LJ as described above seems valid and strictly in accordance with the law governing the signature of documents, which holds a person bound by what he has signed, except in the limited circumstances when he can plead non est factum.[70] Therefore, it is suggested that the decision in *Newsholme Bros* is correct, and cases to the contrary must either be wrong or regarded as exceptions, a point to which we shall return.

Whether the result is a fair one is an entirely separate question. The Law Reform Committee[71] certainly thought not and recommended statutory reversal of the rule. However, their recommendation, framed in terms that the agent should be regarded as at all times the agent of the insurer may not have gone far enough. If the analysis of the true ratio for the rule given here is the correct one, the parol evidence rule and the rule relating to the signature of documents would still present problems if the contents of the proposal form are part of the written contract. The need for some reform was also pointed out in a Government White Paper in 1977,[72] and the Law Commissions provisionally proposed reversing both limbs of the *Newsholme Bros* rule,[73] but ultimately the latter simply recommended statutory

---

[69] See Tedeschi, "Assured's misrepresentation and the insurance agent's knowledge of the truth" (1972) 7 Israel L.R. 475.

[70] See *Treitel Law of Contract*, Ch.8. The *Bawden* case might thus be regarded as a case where the insured could plead non est factum because of his illiteracy and consequent inability to check the form.

[71] Fifth Report, 1957 Cmnd. 62.

[72] Insurance Intermediaries, Cmnd. 6715, para.16. The comment here was rather ambivalent. Having supported the Law Reform Committee's recommendation, the White Paper then said: "But it is not the Government's intention that the proposer should be relieved of responsibility for the accuracy of statements made by him in response to questions expressly put to him in the proposal form". The Insurance Ombudsman was prepared to depart from the rule in *Newsholme* when he thought it fair to do so.

[73] See the Consultation Paper, Insurance Contract Law: Misrepresentation, Non-Disclosure and Breach of Warranty by the Insured, LCCP 182/SLDP 134, June 2007.

presumptions regarding agency for the purpose of pre-contractual representations, which have been enacted in the Consumer Insurance (Disclosure and Representations) Act 2012.[74] These have been described in 7.4.5 and clearly could, in a consumer insurance case, affect the agency limb of the *Newsholme Bros* rule. Although, as we have seen, in a non-consumer contract the general principles of imputation are replaced by statutory rules, they could allow knowledge to be imputed in this sort of case. It is thought that the abolition of the basis of the contract clause, in both consumer and non-consumer situations, does not of itself affect the *Newsholme* rule. The relevant provisions[75] only prevent a basis clause from turning proposal statements into warranties. They do not affect a provision simply making a proposal form part of the subsequent insurance contract.

12.5.5 Newsholme Bros overruled?

It was, however, decided in Canada[76] that the decision in *Newsholme Bros* was effectively overruled by the most recent English case, namely the Court of Appeal decision in *Stone v Reliance Mutual Insurance Society*.[77] Here the claimant's fire policy with the defendants had lapsed. An inspector employed by the defendants called on the claimant's wife and persuaded her to effect a new policy. On the proposal form, the answer "none" was put to a question asking for details of lapsed policies and previous claims. This was incorrect. The claimant had made a claim on the defendants and had previously, obviously therefore, insured with them. The inspector had filled in the proposal form as indeed he was instructed to do by the insurers. It was held that the insurers could not avoid liability for loss. Megaw and Stamp LJJ regarded the case as turning on its special facts, namely that the inspector was actually authorised to fill in proposal forms. Lord Denning's judgment could be more widely interpreted, but equally it is suggested that his decision really

---

[74] For an interesting argument that a general regulatory provision reversed the transferred agency aspects of the *Newsholme* rule, see Adams, "More nails for the coffin of transferred agency" [1999] J.B.L. 215. The argument was partly based on the effect of s.39 of the Financial Services Act 1986, now replaced by s.44 of the Financial Services and Markets Act 2000. Adams' argument was largely confined to life insurance cases, which is what the 1986 Act dealt with. Given that the regime now has a wider remit because it covers the selling of general insurance, it might be arguable that this aspect of the rule is affected in all situations.

[75] Section 6 of the 2012 Act and s.9 of the Insurance Act 2015.

[76] *Blanchette v US Ltd* (1973) 36 D.L.R. (3d) 561. This Supreme Court case, in fact, involved the slightly different situation referred to below, namely the agent filling in a blank form after signature by the proposer.

[77] *Stone v Reliance Mutual Insurance Society* [1972] 1 Lloyd's Rep. 469. See also Timmins, "Misrepresentation in insurance proposal forms completed by agents" (1974) Vict. Univ. of Wellington L.R. 217, who is also, it is suggested, over-optimistic.

turned on the authority of the agent, not simply as regards the imputation of knowledge of the agent, but also because he had authority to represent that the form had been correctly filled in, particularly because it was accepted that the claimant's wife with whom he dealt was a person of little education. This is sensible. If an agent is fairly senior within an insurer's hierarchy, the circumstances should be such as to allow the admittance of what he did and said and to regard him as having authority to vary the terms of a written contract.

Another reason for regarding *Stone* as merely an exception to the general rule is that the insurers themselves must have known that the answers were false and what the truth was, because they were the insurers with whom the previous lapsed policy had been held and against whom the previous claim had been made.[78] To have allowed them to repudiate liability in such circumstances would have been ridiculous. This point was not actually taken in the case itself, but it must be correct.

It is suggested therefore, that there is no mandate for regarding the decision in *Stone* as overruling that in *Newsholme Bros*. The latter remains the governing decision, but there are exceptions in the case of illiterate and possibly poorly educated proposers and, possibly, where the agent in question is more than a mere canvassing agent but can be regarded as having some authority to vary the terms of the contract. The latter category might now be wider in consumer insurance cases because of the provisions of the 2012 Act.

12.5.6 Form signed in blank

There is some Commonwealth authority which supports a further exception, namely where the agent fills in the proposal form after it has been signed in blank by the proposer, the latter relying upon the agent's representation that he has the necessary information.[79] This is perhaps tenable, assuming that the proposer acts quite innocently and in the circumstances the agent can be regarded as having the authority to represent that the insurer would be estopped from relying upon a misrepresentation. On the other hand, it is clear that if the proposer signs the form after the agent has filled it in himself without asking any information of the proposer, the latter is bound by what he signs.[80]

---

[78] See Ritchie J, dissenting, in *Blanchette v US Ltd* (1973) 36 D.L.R. (3d) at 572.

[79] *Blanchette v CIS Ltd* 36 D.L.R. (3d) 561. See also *Western Australian Insurance Co v Dayton* (1924) 35 C.L.R. 355.

[80] *Biggar v Rock Life Assurance Co* [1902] 1 K.B. 516.

12.6   Relationship between Principal and Agent

If, for some reason, a principal cannot enforce a contract against a third party
or he is liable to a third party because of the unauthorised acts of his agent, he
may well have a remedy against the agent. Equally, the relationship of principal and agent is a fiduciary one and duties arise as a result. For example, the
insurer bound by a contract which he could have avoided for misrepresentation or non-disclosure had his agent not known the non-disclosed facts and
his knowledge been imputed to the insurer, can sue the agent for damages,
being the amount of money which he has had to pay the insured.[81] Similarly,
if an agent acts beyond his actual authority, but the insurer is liable by virtue
of the principles of apparent authority, the insurer will have a damages
remedy against the agent.

It is more likely in practice, however, that it is the insured seeking a
remedy against his agent, commonly, but not necessarily, his broker or other
independent intermediary. In this context, it is usual and convenient to split
up the heads of liability into two; that arising by virtue of the fiduciary relationship between the insured and his agent, and the duties of care and skill
required of an agent.

12.6.1 Fiduciary duties

A fiduciary relationship carries with it strict duties, in particular the overriding one that the fiduciary, the agent, must not put himself into a position
where his own interests do or may conflict with his duties to his principal.[82]
This means, inter alia, that he must not act for another in a matter relating
to his principal without full disclosure to, and the consent of, his principal. It
appears to be standard practice for Lloyd's brokers to act for the underwriter
in certain matters, despite the fact that, as was mentioned earlier, they are
in law agents of the insured. This practice was condemned in *Anglo-African
Merchants v Bayley*[83] as clearly constituting a breach of fiduciary duty, unless
the insured consented. Shortly afterwards the point arose again in *North and
South Trust v Berkeley*,[84] where a claim by the insured was investigated by
assessors instructed by the brokers.

---

[81] *Woolcott v Excess Insurance Co* [1979] 1 Lloyd's Rep. 231.
[82] *Boardman v Phipps* [1967] 2 A.C. 46. Note that, as confirmed in *Companhia de
    Seguros Imperio v Heath (REBX) Ltd* [1999] Lloyd's Rep. I.R. 571, an action for
    breach of fiduciary duty is subject to the same limitation periods as any action
    in contract or tort. In *Knapp & Knapp v Ecclesiastical Insurance Group Plc and Smith*
    [1998] Lloyd's Rep. I.R. 390, it was held that the cause of action accrues on the
    date of the breach, not on the date that the insurer elects to avoid the policy.
[83] *Anglo-African Merchants v Bayley* [1970] 1 Q.B. 311.
[84] *North and South Trust v Berkeley* [1971] 1 W.L.R. 470.

Their report was handed to the brokers who showed it to the underwriters, but refused to let the insured have sight of it or know what it contained. They were thereupon sued by the insured, who relied upon the earlier decision as establishing that the brokers had acted in breach of duty. Donaldson J again condemned the practice of brokers acting for both parties and held that what had been done was a breach of duty. This was recently confirmed in *Callaghan and Hedges v Thompsons*.[85] Here, the broker instructed and obtained reports from the loss adjusters investigating a claim. The court re-iterated that whilst this practice had been roundly criticised in both the previous cases, there was no doubt that the broker remains the agent of the insured in these circumstances, but is in breach of his duties to his principal because of a conflict of interest. Whether the broker must deliver up the documents to the insured is not clear. In the *Berkeley* case, Donaldson J refused to order the brokers to do so, although he accepted that a remedy in damages would be available to the insured.[86] It may be considered curious that no order for delivery was made,[87] but as it was expressly stated by the learned judge that such a remedy may be available in future cases, this rather unsatisfactory result need not detain us further.

12.6.2 Duties of care and skill

In respect of the duties of care and skill, an agent such as a broker owes a duty to his client, the insured, to take reasonable care and skill.[88] A comparatively high number of cases reported over the last 30 years or so[89] reveals what an important head of liability this potentially is. It should be noted that the insured's cause of action is in damages for breach of duty in contract or tort.[90] If what the insured is claiming is in effect the damages he has to pay to an injured third party, for example, this relates only to the measure of the broker's liability. The claim is not in respect of damages for personal injury, so that the relevant limitation period is six years, not three years.[91]

In advising his client with whom to insure, the broker must take due

---

[85] *Callaghan and Hedges v Thompsons* [2000] Lloyd's Rep. I.R. 125.

[86] Quaere how valuable such a remedy might be in practice.

[87] See the trenchant criticism by Kay and Yates (1972) 35 M.L.R. 78.

[88] It may also be owed to a third party who the broker knows is to become an assignee of the policy: *Punjab National Bank v De Boinville* [1992] 1 Lloyd's Rep. 7.

[89] Too many for them all to be considered in these pages. An excellent survey is contained in Jackson & Powell, *Professional Liability*, 7th edn (London: Sweet & Maxwell, 2015), Ch.7.

[90] *Henderson v Merrett Syndicates Ltd* [1994] 3 All E.R. 506. See also *Osman v J Ralph Moss Ltd* [1970] 1 Lloyd's Rep. 313. It would require significant fault on the part of the insured before a negligent broker could successfully plead the defence of contributory negligence: *Mint Security Ltd v Blair* [1982] 1 Lloyd's Rep. 188.

[91] *Ackbar v Green* [1975] Q.B. 582.

care. In *Osman v J Ralph Moss*,[92] the defendant brokers recommended to the claimant that he effect a motor policy with an insurer already well-known in insurance circles to be in a serious financial situation. The insurer was subsequently wound up, leaving the claimant uninsured. As a result, the latter was convicted of driving without insurance and involved in an accident for which he was liable, with no insurer to foot the bill. The claimant was of Turkish origin and had difficulty in reading and understanding English. The only warning the defendants gave him was a letter asking him simply to insure elsewhere. It was held that the defendants were liable in damages for the amount he was fined and the damages he had to pay the third party. What is not completely clear is how much turned on the fact that the claimant was not really literate in English, so that the letter that the defendants sent could not possibly have been enough to satisfy the duty they owed him. The decision does not actually hold that a broker must always expressly warn his client of the impending insolvency of his insurer, if he is aware or ought to be aware of this, and there are passages in the judgments[93] referring to the particular position of the claimant.

It is suggested that brokers ought to be under a duty at all times to all classes of insured to advise and warn about particular insurers, not just as to their financial stability but also as to the suitability of particular policies and their general record in treating their insureds, for example, as to their generosity in paying claims.[94] It seems clear that a broker who fails to warn the insured of any special terms incorporated on renewal is negligent.[95] There is clearly a duty to obtain effective cover[96] or to warn the insured about the

---

[92] *Osman v J Ralph Moss* [1970] 1 Lloyd's Rep. 313. See also *Bates v Robert Barrow Ltd* [1995] C.L.C. 207, where a broker was held liable for placing insurance with an unauthorised insurer.

[93] Sachs LJ at 315; Phillimore LJ at 319.

[94] There were many successful unreported claims on this basis in 1984 and 1985 against brokers who sold largely worthless life insurance polices issued by Signal Life, a Gibraltar-based concern not authorised to act in the UK.

[95] *Mint Security Ltd v Blair* [1982] 1 Lloyd's Rep. 188. In a similar context, it is incumbent upon the broker to draw to the insurer's attention on renewal any specific changes that the insured is seeking in the terms of the expiring cover and he must obtain confirmation from the insurer that he is willing to accept such changes: *Great North Eastern Railway v Avon Insurance Plc* unreported 2000.

[96] In *FNCB Ltd v Barnet Devanney (Harrow) Ltd* [1999] Lloyd's Rep. I.R. 459, a broker failed to ensure that a policy insuring the interests of both a mortgagor and mortgagee contained a mortgage protection clause. This would have protected the mortgagee bank when the insurers avoided the policy, as they were entitled to do, because of a non-disclosure by the mortgagor. The Court of Appeal held this to be a breach of duty. It was found as a matter of fact that a competent broker at the time the insurance was effected would have ensured that a protection clause was in the policy. The result may be different today in respect of insurance effected after 1997, because of the decision in *New Hampshire Insurance Co v MGN Ltd* [1997]

insurer's particular terms.[97] This includes the significance of any conditions precedent to the insurer's liability in the policy. In *J W Bollom & Co Ltd v Byas Mosley & Co Ltd*,[98] the insured was in breach of a condition precedent to keep the alarm on its premises in working order. The insured, who was also under-insured at the time of loss, reached a settlement with the insurers, but sought to recover the £3 million shortfall from the defendant broker, claiming that the latter was under a duty to inform him both of the consequences of the condition precedent and the consequences of the under-insurance. The court upheld the claim, saying that it was common ground in a case such as this that the broker's duty extended to taking reasonable steps to ensure that his principal was aware of the nature and terms of the insurance and, in particular to drawing to his attention (and if necessary explaining) any terms the breach of which might result in his being under-insured. A breach of the rules in ICOBS is clearly a breach of duty, which can found a claim under s.138D of the Financial Services and Markets Act 2000.[99]

Whether a sub-agent owes duties to the insured is unclear. Clearly, if there is privity between the insured and the sub-agent, then duties will be owed. The Court of Appeal in *Pangood Ltd v Barclay Brown & Co Ltd*[100] were not prepared to find privity between a placing broker (who was instructed by the producing broker to find and place suitable cover) and the principal insured. However, in *Velos Group Ltd v Harbour Insurance Services Ltd*,[101] privity was established. Whether privity exists may depend on whether the producing broker is allowed to go into the market himself and place the cover, which in the latter case he was not.

Another instance of negligent advice arose in *Cherry Ltd v Allied Insurance Brokers Ltd*.[102] Here the defendants had been the claimants' brokers for some 50 years, but the claimants became dissatisfied and proposed to put their business elsewhere. As a result, they wished to cancel all their policies held through the defendants well before their renewal date, and they instructed the defendants to seek to do so. The defendants cancelled most of the policies but advised the claimants that the particular insurer concerned would not

---

L.R.L.R. 24, which confirmed beyond doubt that non-disclosure by one insured does not adversely affect the rights of the other, making the added protection of such a clause unnecessary. As to co-insurance and non-disclosure, see 7.11. See also *Ramco Ltd v Weller Russell & Laws Insurance Brokers Ltd* [2008] EWHC 2202 (QB); [2009] Lloyd's Rep. I.R. 27.

[97] See e.g. *Harvest Trading Co Ltd v Davis Insurance Services* [1991] 2 Lloyd's Rep. 638.

[98] *J W Bollom & Co Ltd v Byas Mosley & Co Ltd* [2000] Lloyd's Rep. I.R. 136.

[99] *Saville v Central Capital Ltd* [2014] EWCA Civ 337. This case concerned the mis-selling of payment protection insurance.

[100] *Pangood Ltd v Barclay Brown & Co Ltd* [1999] Lloyd's Rep. I.R. 405.

[101] *Velos Group Ltd v Harbour Insurance Services Ltd* [1997] 2 Lloyd's Rep. 461.

[102] *Cherry Ltd v Allied Insurance Brokers Ltd* [1978] 1 Lloyd's Rep. 274.

accept cancellation of the claimants' consequential loss policy. The claimants having effected a new policy of this sort thereupon cancelled it to avoid being doubly insured. Subsequently, however, that first insurer did agree to a cancellation of the original policy, but the defendants failed to advise the claimants of this. The latter then suffered a loss for which, because both policies had been cancelled, they were uninsured. It was held that the defendants were negligent in failing to advise the claimants of the first insurer's cancellation, and were liable in damages for the amount which the claimants would have recovered from their insurer had they been insured.

12.6.3 Duty regarding pre-contractual disclosure

Several cases have been concerned with the broker's position in respect of the duty of the insured to disclose material facts and not to make misrepresentations. Although there is no longer a duty of disclosure in consumer insurances and the duty has been rewritten for non-consumer insurances as part of the duty of fair presentation, the principles of these cases will still be relevant to the modern law. This is obviously a crucial area as the insured who is dealing with a broker will not, in practice, have any direct communication with his insurers, and in general any knowledge the broker has will not be imputed to the insurers.[103] Thus the exact nature of the broker's duty with regard to advising his client about such matters is vital. If the broker fails to ask the insured questions about facts that he, the broker, knows are material, he will be liable in damages to the insured if the insurer subsequently avoids liability. In *McNealy v Pennine Insurance Co*,[104] the claimant effected motor insurance through brokers. He was a part-time musician, a fact that, it was held, was material to the risk. The insurance company with which the brokers effected the insurance refused to cover musicians, among other groups, and was not told that the claimant was one. It was held that the brokers were liable in damages in respect of the claimant's liability to a third party, the insurer having avoided their policy. The brokers, with their knowledge that the insurer refused to cover certain risks, were under a duty to the insured to ask him whether or not he was affected by this.

It would seem to follow that the same result would apply if the broker actually knows of material facts that he fails to disclose to the insurer.[105] However, if the broker is unaware of material facts, and there are no special

---

[103] See 12.2.

[104] *McNealy v Pennine Insurance Co* [1978] 2 Lloyd's Rep. 18.

[105] *Woolcott v Excess Insurance Co* [1979] 1 Lloyd's Rep. 231; *Ogden v Reliance Fire Sprinkler Co* [1975] 1 Lloyd's Rep. 52. Exceptionally, as we have seen (at 12.2), the broker's knowledge may be imputed to the insurer; in this situation the insured will, of course, not need a remedy against the broker.

circumstances, as in *McNealy*, requiring him to make express enquiry of the insured, it appears unlikely that the common law would traditionally require the broker to warn the insured of his duty of disclosure. In *Warren v Sutton*,[106] the claimant had an existing motor policy. He was going on holiday to France with a friend with whom he wished to share the driving. So he arranged for the friend to be covered under his policy. However, the latter had an appalling driving record with several convictions, none of which was disclosed to the insurer, so that the latter was able to avoid the policy and not pay in respect of an accident that occurred in France.[107] The claimant had arranged the policy and the extension through the defendant brokers whom he sued for damages. The facts of the case were somewhat complex and there was a crucial conflict of evidence, but it was found that the broker actually said to the insurer that there were "no accidents, convictions or disabilities" when the extension was being arranged. On this basis, the majority of the Court of Appeal held the broker liable. He had made a false representation to the insurance company in breach of his duty to the claimant. Lord Denning MR dissented strongly on the ground that the fault all lay with the claimant who never told the broker or insurer about his friend's record. However, the majority were clearly influenced by the trial judge's much more favourable assessment of the claimant as a witness as opposed to the attitude of the defendant broker. The broker's representation to the insurer was clearly false. He was under a duty to obtain cover for the friend and to make such enquiries as were necessary. Thus, not having made such enquiries, he was solely responsible for the representation he made, and it was this representation that was the cause of the insurer's repudiation. If, however, the broker had not made the representation, and the reason for the insurer's repudiation had simply been non-disclosure by the insured of which the broker was unaware, it appears that the result would have been the other way.[108] This supports the view that the court would not hold a broker under a duty to warn the insured of his duty of disclosure in the abstract.

Further support can perhaps be found in another Court of Appeal decision on a related point.[109] In *O'Connor v Kirby*,[110] the claimant insured his

---

[106] *Warren v Sutton* [1976] 2 Lloyd's Rep. 276.

[107] The friend was driving at the time, though this was legally irrelevant. The insurer was liable in respect of the damages he had to pay for personal injuries, because of restrictions similar to those in the Road Traffic Act 1988 (see Ch.21), but escaped liability in respect of third party property damage. The latter is now prohibited under the Road Traffic Act.

[108] See Browne LJ at 281.

[109] This was relied upon by Lord Denning MR in his dissenting judgment in *Warren v Sutton*; it was not cited by the other members of the Court of Appeal in that case.

[110] *O'Connor v Kirby* [1972] 1 Q.B. 90.

car through the defendant broker. For some reason,[111] the latter incorrectly answered a question on the proposal form relating to the garaging of the car and the insurer subsequently avoided the policy for breach of warranty. The claimant sued the broker for failing to complete the form properly. It was held that he was not liable, as the claimant had signed the form containing the mistake and was solely responsible because it was his duty to see that the information therein was correct.[112] It is suggested that this reasoning is suspect in the light of the consideration that the insured dealing with a broker does place great reliance, and naturally so, on the latter. Far more satisfactory, it is submitted, is the reasoning of Megaw LJ to the effect that a broker who completes a proposal form does owe a duty to the insured to take reasonable care that its contents are correct, but that in the circumstances the broker had fulfilled that duty since the mistake was at most due only to a slip or misunderstanding and the broker had given the form to the insured to check.[113] That this is the better ratio seems to be supported by the more recent decision in *Dunbar v A & B Painters Ltd*.[114] Here brokers who inserted incorrect answers on a proposal form were held liable in damages since it was shown that the answers required fell especially within the broker's knowledge. However, it seems likely that this last factor is crucial. If the broker is not in possession of the relevant information, or, even if he is, but the facts are not especially within his knowledge, then primary responsibility in respect of both non-disclosure of material facts and the answering of questions seems to fall on the insured rather than the broker.[115]

However, later cases indicate a different view, influenced by the introduction of rules made with statutory authority. In *Jones v Environcom Ltd*,[116] David Steel J, after citing the relevant provisions of the Insurance: Conduct of Business Sourcebook, summarised the broker's duty with regard to the proposer's duty of disclosure as requiring that he must (a) advise his client of the duty to disclose all material circumstances; (b) explain the consequences of failing to do so; (c) indicate the sort of matters which ought to be disclosed

---

[111] There was some evidence of collusion between the parties in order to get cheaper cover; this can hardly have disposed the court to look favourably on the claim.

[112] Following the *Newsholme* line of cases discussed earlier in this chapter.

[113] Compare *Reid v Traders' General Insurance Co* (1963) 41 D.L.R. (2d) 148.

[114] *Dunbar v A & B Painters Ltd* [1986] 2 Lloyd's Rep. 38, affirming [1985] 2 Lloyd's Rep. 616. *O'Connor v Kirby* was not cited in this case.

[115] This was confirmed by the Court of Appeal in *Kapur v J W Francis & Co* [2000] Lloyd's Rep. I.R. 361. Here, the incorrect answer was inserted by the broker, but the facts were known to both the broker and the insured. It must be said that in this case the insured was not deserving of much sympathy.

[116] *Jones v Environcom Ltd* [2010] EWHC 759 (Comm); [2010] Lloyd's Rep I.R. 676. See also *Synergy Health (UK) Ltd v CGU Insurance Plc* [2010] EWHC 2583 (Comm); [2011] Lloyd's Rep. I.R. 500. Note also the reference to an earlier Code of Practice in *Harvest Trading Co Ltd v PB Davis Services* [1991] 2 Lloyd's Rep. 638.

as being material (or at least arguably material); and (d) take reasonable care to elicit matters which ought to be disclosed but which the client might think it not necessary to mention.

12.6.4 Measure of damages

If a broker is liable in damages to the insured, the measure of damages will, as has been seen, usually be that sum which the insured would have recovered from the insurer had the latter been liable. If the breach of duty by the broker is a failure to effect insurance at all, the question has arisen whether it is open to him to say that even if he had obtained the cover, the insurer would still not have been liable, and hence he should not be liable, because of some breach by the insured. The point arose neatly in *Fraser v Furman*,[117] where the broker had failed in his duty to effect employer's liability cover for the claimant. The broker argued, however, that the insurer would not have been liable for the loss that subsequently occurred, because the claimant would have been in breach of a condition in the policy to take reasonable precautions to avoid loss. The Court of Appeal held that the broker was liable for the full amount of loss suffered by the claimant. Even if the defence would have been available to the insurer, which was doubted,[118] the fact was that in the circumstances the insurer in question would not have repudiated liability. Therefore, the question depends on the likely attitude of the insurer rather than the strict point as to whether the insurer would have been legally liable.[119]

---

[117] *Fraser v Furman* [1976] 1 W.L.R. 898. See also *Everett v Hogg Robinson* [1973] 2 Lloyd's Rep. 217 and *Dunbar v A B Painters Ltd* [1986] 2 Lloyd's Rep. 38.

[118] See further on this point 13.2.2.

[119] But the position may be different if the insurance which the broker should have effected would have been void: *Thomas Cheshire & Co v Vaughan Bros & Co* [1920] 3 K.B. 240, and if the claimant is in fact virtually uninsurable, the damages payable by the broker are likely to be reduced: *O & R Jewellers v Terry* [1999] Lloyd's Rep. I.R. 436.

CHAPTER 13

CONSTRUCTION AND CAUSATION: RISKS COVERED AND RISKS EXCEPTED

13.0

Many consumer-type or standard-form contracts, such as contracts of sales of goods, for cash or on credit, or for the provision of services, have for some years been subject to a broad range of statutory control of one form or another.[1] In contrast, in insurance contracts, until recently, freedom of contract reigned, and thus the only way to know whether or not a particular loss was within the ambit of a particular policy was to apply to the insurance contract the general principles of construction applicable to all written contracts. It is to the description and illustration of such principles that this chapter is partly devoted. While these principles remain of crucial importance for all types of insurance, as far as individual consumers are concerned, there is now a measure of statutory protection afforded by Pt 2 of the Consumer Rights Act 2015, replacing the Unfair Terms in Consumer Contracts Regulations 1999.[2] The application of these to the questions considered in this chapter is considered shortly.

It should be noted that to refer to the rules of construction as affecting only risks covered and risks excepted is misleading, because these principles may well apply to the other contents of the insurance contract, for example, the meaning of questions and answers on a proposal form, or the warranties and conditions in a policy. It must also be pointed out that in certain respects, it is not strictly accurate to refer to the construction of words; rather the problem is one of describing their scope. For example, what "loss" means in the context of an insurance policy, a question that is considered later in this chapter, is not so much a question of construction, but of description or definition. The same can be said of the word "accident", another word commonly found in insurance policies, which we shall also consider later. The rules of construction do not help in finding out what these words mean, but some principles must be found to assist in explaining or defining them. For this reason we consider those standard words in this chapter.

It is self-evident, given the great range of actual and potential sorts of insurance and the variety of insurers, that the actual number of words or

---

[1] Including the Sale of Goods Act 1979 (as amended), the Consumer Credit Act 1974 and the Unfair Contract Terms Act 1977 controlling contract terms.

[2] SI 1999/2083.

phrases whose meanings may not be immediately apparent in all the insurance contracts that exist may be very large. Here, it is impossible to cover the whole ground, and the general points only can be illustrated. Some further guidance can be found in the later chapters dealing with specific types of insurance. In any event, it is felt that the approach adopted is justified on the ground that this is an attempt to elucidate the principles, not to give a totally comprehensive A-Z guide. Full citation of the authorities actually available on particular wordings can be found in the standard larger works on insurance law.

Although, as a matter of construction, a loss may fall within the risks covered by a particular policy, it may still be necessary for the insured to show that the loss was caused by such a risk and not predominantly by an uninsured risk. Thus the issue of causation is also considered in this chapter. In addition, there are some general considerations regarding the nature of risks under an insurance contract that will be examined.

13.1 General

There are two points that can usefully be made at this stage before we examine the rules of construction in detail. To an extent these follow from comments already made in the introductory remarks, but, as we shall see, they will now be inapplicable to insurance contracts effected by an individual consumer insured. These points are that there is no requirement that an insurance policy is reasonably intelligible in terms of content, and there is no requirement that it be especially legible. Insurance policies are still often notoriously complex documents riddled with jargon, their layout is often muddled to the untrained eye, and the print, or some of it, may be very small. In one marine insurance case, *Koskas v Standard Marine Insurance Co Ltd*,[3] the judge at first instance refused to allow the insurer to rely upon a particular condition on the grounds that the print was so small that it was barely legible. The Court of Appeal,[4] however, overruled this bold attempt to interfere because the print was legible, albeit with difficulty. It is fair to say that even in commercial insurances, such an extreme example is unlikely to be found today and insurers often seek to write all their policies in "plain English". This can, though, still raise difficulties of interpretation and construction.[5]

---

[3] *Koskas v Standard Marine Insurance Co Ltd* (1926) 25 L.I.L.R. 363.

[4] (1927) 27 L.I.L.R. 61.

[5] See, e.g. the case of *Kausar v Eagle Star Insurance Co Ltd* [1997] C.L.C. 129, considered in 7.16.

13.1.1 Consumer Protection

Judges have on occasion railed against insurers for not producing their policies in a form intelligible to the ordinary consumer,[6] and consumer representatives and bodies, including the Insurance Ombudsman, frequently made the same point. The Law Commission clearly intended that conditions and exceptions in insurance contracts should be brought within the ambit of what became the Unfair Contract Terms Act 1977,[7] but pressure from the insurance industry secured their exclusion from that Act[8] in return for their agreeing to promulgate Statements of Insurance Practice.[9] However, many insurers did respond to criticism, in particular by rewording their policies in "plain English". This is clearly to be welcomed, although this does not necessarily mean that the average consumer will read and understand their insurance policies nor, as we have seen, does it necessarily mean that problems of interpretation will not arise.

More recently there have been further significant developments. The first arose from the existence and attitude of the Insurance Ombudsman. He declared that he was prepared to find particular terms in insurance contracts unreasonable, arguing that the spirit, if not the letter, of the Unfair Contract Terms Act applied.[10] Among other things, he refused to allow reliance on provisions producing an unexpected loss of cover secreted in a policy without warning and on exclusions of liability for loss of goods left unattended when those were not highlighted at the outset. He also in effect rewrote the standard provision[11] that suspends cover in the event of a house being unoccupied for more than 30 days, holding that it applied only when the 30-day period has elapsed. While, with respect, the basis for his jurisdiction here was first open to dispute,[12] it was put on a sounder footing in 1992 when his terms of reference were amended to require him to reach a decision in each case which is "fair and reasonable in all the circumstances".[13] This development no doubt resulted in greater clarity of expression and layout in insurance

---

[6] See, e.g. Lord *Wright in Provincial Insurance Co v Morgan* [1932] A.C. 240 at 252.
[7] Second Report on Exemption Clauses (No.69).
[8] Sch.1, para.1(a).
[9] See 1.9.1.
[10] See in particular the Annual Report for 1990, paras 2.4 and 3.9.
[11] See 7.16.
[12] The then Ombudsman stated in his Annual Report for 1990 that the industry agreed to be bound by the spirit of UCTA when they agreed to the Statements of Insurance Practice, but there is no evidence for this in the Parliamentary and ABI statements made at the time of UCTA, when the Statements were first issued and later, when the revised Statements were issued. All these show is a readiness to modify the application of the law in those areas specifically referred to in the Statements. As to the Statements, which are no longer in use, see 1.9.1.
[13] See McGee, (1992) 2 Insurance L. & P. 86.

policies. All the evidence suggests, not surprisingly, that the replacement of the Insurance Ombudsman by the Financial Services Ombudsman[14] has made no difference to this sort of approach, not least because the latter has statutory authority to adopt a similar approach.[15]

A further and, perhaps, more important development was the introduction of the Unfair Terms in Consumer Contracts Regulations, now replaced by Pt 2 of the Consumer Rights Act 2015, to which reference has already been made. It needed EC legislation to produce this measure of consumer protection.[16] Some consideration has already been given to this statutory control of unfair contract terms.[17] In the context of this chapter, there are three points that need to be made. The first is the general requirement of transparency, requiring plain and intelligible language, legibility and prominence.[18] This reinforces the trend toward "plain English" already noted. The second is the enforcement powers given to, among others, the Competition and Markets Authority and the Financial Conduct Authority.[19] The third point is the most important one for present purposes and concerns the question of the application of what can be called the core part of Pt 2 of the Act to the question of the cover provided by an insurance contract.[20]

This core part[21] provides that an "unfair term" is not binding on a consumer. A term is unfair if, contrary to the requirement of good faith, it causes a significant imbalance in the parties' rights and obligations under the contract to the detriment of the consumer.[22] However, it does not apply to any term that "specifies the main subject matter of the contract".[23] It is thought that the provisions concerning the risks covered and excepted under an insurance contract must be within this exception,[24] as these do specify the

---

[14] See 1.9.1.

[15] See above.

[16] The Unfair Contract Terms Directive 93/13/E.C., agreed on 5 April 1993. It must be doubtful whether this would have happened otherwise.

[17] See Ch.5.

[18] Consumer Rights Act 2015 s.64; note also the statutory confirmation of the *contra proferentem* rule, which is discussed below.

[19] Consumer Rights Act 2015 s.70 and Sch.3.

[20] Apart from the requirements of transparency, and prominence which clearly apply. If a term is found to be unclear, it can be adjudged for fairness whether it is a core term or not.

[21] Section 62.

[22] See further at 6.1.

[23] Section 64(1)(a).

[24] Although it is recognised that the Act can quite properly go beyond what the Directive required, the provisions of the Directive must surely nonetheless be an aid to construction. In the preamble to the Directive, it is stated that in insurance contracts, "the terms which clearly define or circumstance the insured risk and the insurer's liability shall not be subject to [assessment of unfair character] since these restrictions are taken into account in calculating the premium paid by the

main subject matter of the contract. This, it is suggested, is also a sensible interpretation. In the result, it is thought that the impact of the Act on the matters under consideration here is limited to the requirements of transparency and prominence, supported by a statutory reinforcement of the *contra proferentem* rule.[25]

13.1.2 American approaches

In quite vivid contrast is the approach to construing insurance policies taken by the courts in many of the States in the United States of America.[26] Here doctrines described as "fulfilling the reasonable expectations of the insured" and "disallowing the insurer any unconscionable advantage" are well established,[27] following early recognition of the contract of insurance as a "contract of adhesion" par excellence,[28] in other words, as one of the classic cases in which there is absolutely no chance of the party which does not produce the standard form bargaining over the terms of the contract.

One interesting example of this approach, which was deemed worthy of being reported in this country, is the decision of the Supreme Court of New Jersey in *Gerhardt v Continental Insurance Companies*.[29] Here a section of a householder's comprehensive insurance policy provided for indemnity against any sums which the insured would become legally liable to pay to a third party for personal injury or property damage arising out of his occupation of his house, but set out on a separate page were certain exclusions to this section, one of which provided that the cover did not apply with respect to bodily injury to a resident employee arising out of and in the course of his employment by the insured. Such an employee was injured in the insured's house and sued the insured, who called upon the insurers to conduct her defence. The latter relied on the exclusion mentioned, but it was held that they were not entitled to do so. Read by itself, the exclusion appears to have

consumer". Assuming that the preamble qualifies the text of the Directive (see Duffy [1993] J.B.L. 67 at 71–72), this is clearly effective to remove from its scope provisions defining the risk and exceptions to it. See *Bankers Insurance Co Ltd v South* [2003] EWHC 380 (Q.B.); [2004] Lloyd's Rep. I.R. 1.

[25] Whether the statutory controls on unfair terms or the other factors discussed here have yet had an effect on all consumer insurance policies may be doubted. There is no doubt that some remain difficult to understand for many who are not lawyers, notably many travel insurance policies.

[26] Perhaps the only real English judgment to similar effect is that of Farwell LJ in *Bradley and Essex & Suffolk Accident Indemnity Society* [1912] 1 K.B. 415.

[27] See especially, Keeton, "Insurance law rights at variance with policy provisions," (1970) 83 Harv.L.R. 961 and 1281.

[28] See generally, Kessler, "Contracts of adhesion-some thoughts about freedom of contract" (1943) 43 Col.L.R. 629.

[29] *Gerhardt v Continental Insurance Companies* [1967] 1 Lloyd's Rep. 380.

been clear and, on ordinary principles of construction, applicable. However, the court said that, on a simple reading of this policy, which was prepared unilaterally by the company and sold on a mass basis as affording broad coverage to homeowners, the average insured, noting the section covering third party liability, would assume that an injury to a domestic employee was covered. The exclusion was not conspicuous, and as in earlier cases[30] the cover was described as comprehensive, and, while the insurer had the right to exclude particular types of liability, the doctrine of honouring the reasonable expectations of the insured required that it did so unequivocally.

Despite the recent modification in approach of the English courts to questions of construction, which we consider below, it seems unlikely that the English common law would adopt an approach like that described.[31] Of course, if a term is not transparent and prominent, it is, as we have seen, subject to being considered for fairness under the Consumer Rights Act. It could be argued that the principles from the American cases are somewhat vague so that it would be difficult, if not impossible, to predict the result on the facts of any particular case, and that, if further interference with policy terms is felt to be justified, it would be better to have a regime of prior approval of policy forms within guidelines laid down by statute.

13.2   Risk

As was pointed out earlier,[32] the essence of insurance is that it provides protection against the risks of uncertain events befalling the insured, normally events that would be adverse to him. The concept of risk is fundamental, and there are a number of general points of universal application that must be made, as they may well apply regardless of whether a loss appears to be covered as a matter of construction.

13.2.1 Intentional and negligent losses

First, as a general rule, the fact that a loss is occasioned by the negligence of the insured is irrelevant, but insurance does not cover losses deliberately caused by him. There are innumerable authorities confirming, for example, that the deliberate arson by the insured of property covered by a fire policy,[33] or the sane suicide of a life insured under a life policy, is not covered.[34] This

---

[30] For example *Bauman v Royal Indemnity Co* 36 N.J. 12 (1961).

[31] Note, though, Clarke's interesting attempt to discover signs of such an approach in English cases; see "The reasonable expectations of the insured-in England?" [1989] J.B.L. 389.

[32] See especially the discussion of the definition of insurance at 1.5.

[33] *Britton v Royal Insurance Co* (1866) 4 F. & F. 905.

[34] *Beresford v Royal Insurance Co* [1938] A.C. 586; see 14.2.

point relates closely to principles of public policy applicable to insurance contracts, which we shall examine in the next chapter. However, leaving these aside for the moment, it is clear that express policy terms can, if appropriately worded, cover deliberate losses, so that the general rule is not an absolute one. In practice, however, this is likely to apply only in respect of suicide under a life policy. In addition, the general rule excludes only losses caused deliberately by the insured him or herself. The fact that his spouse[35] or employee,[36] for example, intentionally destroys property he has insured does not prevent the insured who is not a party to the act from recovering.[37]

A policy may expressly exclude losses deliberately caused by the insured or a member of his or her family. In *Patrick v Royal London Mutual Insurance Society Ltd*,[38] the policy excluded "any wilful, malicious or criminal acts". It was held that "wilful" covered an act that was deliberate and intended to cause damage of the kind in question; it would be enough to show that the insured was reckless as to the consequences of his act. The damage was caused by the insured's co-insured 11-year-old son who had set fire to a den made of pallets which then damaged a neighbouring property and destroyed goods in it. As he was unaware of the risk and there was nothing to show that he did not care whether or not the property burnt down, the exclusion did not apply.

13.2.2 Reasonable care conditions

That the insured who is negligent can recover is subject to the important qualification that a term of the policy may seek to exclude the insurer's liability in this respect, by imposing on the insured an obligation to take reasonable care.[39] This sort of term has been common for some years in liability insurance policies, where, sensibly, a requirement of reasonable care has been construed to be applicable only to reckless acts by an insured; otherwise such policies would not provide the very basic cover, against negligence

---

[35] *Midland Insurance Co v Smith* (1881) 6 QBD 561.

[36] *Shaw v Robberds* (1837) 6 Ad. & El. 75 at 84.

[37] The policy can provide otherwise, of course, and exclude deliberate acts of, for example, employees; see, for example, *KR v Royal & Sun Alliance Plc* [2006] EWCA Civ 368; [2007] Lloyd's Rep. I.R. 368.

[38] *Patrick v Royal London Mutual Insurance Society Ltd* [2006] EWCA Civ 421; [2007] Lloyd's Rep. I.R. 85. See also *Porter v Zurich Insurance Company* [2009] EWHC 376 (HC), where the policy excluded "any wilful or malicious act". It was held that the insured who had recklessly caused the loss would only be able to recover if he could show that he was insane by reference to the M'Naghten rules.

[39] This may be phrased as a warranty or condition (see Ch.9) or as an exception to the risk. Whichever way it is done, the effect will be to relieve the insurer from liability, subject to the application of ss.10 and 11 of the Insurance Act 2015.

liability, for which they are effected.[40] More recently, it seems, such a term has appeared in property and other first party insurances, requiring the insured, for example, to take reasonable care of insured property or to maintain it in a reasonable condition. Following some earlier doubts,[41] it now seems clear that such a term will be construed in the same way as in liability policies, so that mere negligence by the insured will not preclude recovery.

In *Sofi v Prudential Assurance Company Ltd*,[42] conditions requiring the insured to take "reasonable care to avoid loss" in a domestic all risks policy and a travel policy were interpreted in this way. Here, the insured, who was travelling to France, arrived at the Dover ferry with time to spare. He left his car for 15 minutes in the unattended car park at Dover Castle with £50,000 worth of valuables locked in the glove compartment. During that time, the car was broken into and the valuables stolen. The Court of Appeal held that the insured was entitled to recover, not having on the facts acted recklessly. In the light of this decision, insurers who wish to limit their liability without having to prove recklessness have to insert more specific terms in their policies, for example by excluding liability when goods are left unattended.[43]

13.2.3 Perils never insured

A number of perils are never covered by indemnity insurances. Primarily these are wear and tear and inherent vice, in other words, what occurs or happens naturally. Simply, these are not fortuitous and are not therefore

---

[40] See, in particular, *Fraser v Furman* [1967] 1 W.L.R. 898, discussed further at 20.2.5, and as to the effect of such a term in motor policies, see 21.3.4.

[41] See the rather ambiguous dicta in *Stephen v Scottish Boatowners Mutual Insurance Association* [1989] 1 Lloyd's Rep. 535 at 541; *Devco Holder v Legal and General Assurance Society* [1993] 2 Lloyd's Rep. 567 (1988); and the approach of the first Insurance Ombudsman, who took a fairly strict view of the insured's duty particularly in household and travel insurance situations; see his Annual Reports for 1984, 1985 and 1986, at 5–6, 7–8 and 6–8, respectively.

[42] *Sofi v Prudential Assurance Company Ltd* [1993] 2 Lloyd's Rep. 559 (1990); see Birds (1991) 1 Ins. L. & P. 18. *Sofi* was followed in *Paine v Catlins* [2004] EWHC 3043 (TCC); [2005] Lloyd's Rep. I.R. 665. See also *Roberts v State General Insurance Manager* [1974] 2 N.Z.L.R. 312 and *Port-Rose v Phoenix Assurance Co Ltd* (1986) 136 N.L.J. 333. The latter case concerned a situation where the insured under an all risks policy took her eyes off her handbag containing her jewellery at an airport for a brief moment, while she helped a fellow elderly passenger, during which time it was stolen. Hodgson J disallowed the insurer's reliance on a reasonable care provision, although it is arguable that on the facts there was no negligence involved. For discussion of the effect of *Sofi* on the jurisdiction of the Insurance Ombudsman, see the Annual Reports for 1989 and 1991 at paras 2.4 and 2.12, respectively. For a more recent example, see *The Board of Trustees of the Tate Gallery v Duffy Construction Ltd (No.2)* [2007] EWHC 912 (TCC); [2008] Lloyd's Rep. I.R. 159.

[43] As to such provisions, see 13.3.1.

capable of being covered by an insurance contract, the essence of which is to cover uncertain risks.[44] So, for example, decay in food or the rusting of a car or the natural wear of tiles on a roof cannot be insured against. The major exception here, of course, is in the field of contingency insurance, namely life and related contracts. A life contract obviously covers the natural process of dying; a health insurance contract obviously covers what may be inevitable illness.

13.3 Principles of Construction

We now consider the rules of construction applicable to insurance policies. It should be noted that the question of construction is a question of law, and once a word or phrase has been judicially considered, that decision should be followed according to the usual rules of precedent.[45] A good example of this principle is the decision in *Dino Services v Prudential Assurance Co Ltd*,[46] where the Court of Appeal followed long-established authorities[47] in construing cover provided against theft "by forcible and violent means", and denied recovery where the loss had been effected by thieves who used stolen keys to gain entry to the relevant premises without having to resort to "violence", such as breaking down a door or forcing open a window.[48]

The traditional approach to construing insurance contracts involved the elucidation and application of a number of "rules of construction". The most important of these, which will be illustrated shortly by some examples, were probably as follows. Primarily, it was the intention of the parties, as discovered objectively from the whole of the policy, that prevailed. Written parts, if present, prevailed over printed parts as more likely to express the agreement of the parties, and parol evidence was not in general admissible to vary or contradict the written document. The policy was construed according to its literal meaning; only if that was unclear could extraneous circumstances be examined. Words were normally understood in their ordinary meaning, but this was not the case where they had a technical legal meaning; here the latter prevailed. Similarly, the context of a word might dictate a departure

---

[44] But inherent vice will not be conclusive where the proximate or real cause of a loss is an insured peril; see, e.g., *Global Process Systems v Syarikat Takaful Malaysia Berhad, The Cendor MOPU* [2011] UKSC 5; [2011] Lloyd's Rep. I.R. 302.

[45] See, e.g. *W J Lane v Spratt* [1970] 2 Q.B. 480 at 491–492, per Roskill J.

[46] *Dino Services v Prudential Assurance Co Ltd* [1989] 1 All E.R 422. See [1989] J.B.L. 355.

[47] *George and Goldsmiths and General Burglary Insurance Assoc Ltd Re* [1899] 1 Q.B. 595; *Calf and Sun Insurance Office Re* [1920] 2 K.B. 366.

[48] The court did not like the result, though, and urged an ex gratia payment; quaere whether they were not a little hard on the insurers, who rate the risks of simple theft differently from theft involving breaking in to premises.

from its ordinary meaning. Words appearing in the one phrase were prima facie to be construed ejusdem generis. Finally, in the event that there was any ambiguity, the policy was construed *contra proferentem*, that is, against the person who drafted it and in favour of the other. This will normally, of course, be against the insurer and in favour of the insured.

The modern approach to the construction of contracts of all sorts still has as its prime objective the ascertainment of the intention of the parties. Although literal interpretation divorced from the background of facts in which agreements are concluded had already been abandoned,[49] it was still the case that, particularly in standard form contracts, the parties' expressed intention might be interpreted as being rather different from what the parties, or, perhaps one of them, actually intended. What many regarded as a deficiency in the law, not least because the primary rule was founded on the often incorrect premise that the contract was the result of bargaining between parties of equal strength, led to the rules of construction receiving attention in the House of Lords. In *Investors Compensation Scheme v West Bromwich Building Society*,[50] it was said that "a fundamental change . . . has overtaken this area of the law".[51] The result has been

> "to assimilate the way in which such documents are interpreted by judges to the common sense principles by which any serious utterance would be interpreted in ordinary life. Almost all the old intellectual baggage of legal interpretation has been discarded".[52]

Lord Hoffmann set out several principles which judges ought to adhere to when interpreting contracts. In construing contractual documents the aim must be to find the meaning that the document would convey to a reasonable person having all the background knowledge that would reasonably be available to the parties in the situation in which they were at the time of the contract. Previous negotiations and declarations of subjective intent must be excluded, but included is the possibility of ambiguity and the realisation of the possible misuse of words and syntax. The court is not obliged to ascribe to the parties an intention that plainly they could not have had and, in choosing between competing unnatural meanings, it was entitled to decide that the parties must have made mistakes as to meaning. One could add to these

---

[49] See *Prenn v Simmonds* [1976] 1 W.L.R 1381: "The time has long since passed when agreements . . . were isolated from the matrix of facts in which they were set and interpreted purely on linguistic considerations" (per Lord Wilberforce at 1383).

[50] *Investors Compensation Scheme v West Bromwich Building Society* [1998] 1 All E.R. 98. See also *Sirius General Insurance v FAI General Insurance* [2004] UKHL 54; [2004] 1 W.L.R. 3251.

[51] Above at 114, per Lord Hoffmann.

[52] Above.

a further well established principle of commercial contracts, which is that they ought to be construed in a way that makes "good commercial sense".[53] Lord Hoffmann's modern day restatement of the principles of construction certainly has a bearing on the interpretation of insurance contracts,[54] but it is arguable that in reality the impact has been more limited than first appeared likely.[55] The following summary of some of the leading insurance examples of construction must where appropriate be read in this light.

13.3.1 Ordinary meaning

The words in a policy are prima facie to be understood in their ordinary meaning. For example, in *Thompson v Equity Fire Insurance Co*,[56] a fire policy taken out by a shopkeeper exempted the insurers from liability for loss or damage occurring "while gasoline is stored or kept in the building insured". The insured had a small quantity of gasoline for cooking purposes, but no other. It was held that the insurer was liable for a fire that occurred, as the words "stored or kept" in their ordinary meaning implied fairly considerable quantities, and imported the notion of warehousing or keeping in stock for trading. This was not the case and so the exception was inapplicable. In *Leo Rapp Ltd v McClure*,[57] metal was insured against theft "whilst in warehouse". Some of the relevant metal was stolen from a lorry parked in a locked compound surrounded by a wall topped by barbed wire. It was held that the insurer was not liable, as the ordinary meaning of warehouse implied some sort of covered building, and not a yard, however secure.

A number of recent cases have examined the meaning of the word "unattended" in insurances of goods; it is fairly standard for insurers to provide

---

[53] See Lord Diplock in *Antaios Cia Naviera SA v Salen Raderierna AB* [1985] A.C. 191 at 221: "if a detailed semantic and syntactical analysis of words in a commercial contract is going to lead to a conclusion that flouts business common sense, it must be made to yield to business common sense".

[54] Insurance cases considering the principles include *Union Camp Chemicals Ltd v ACE Insurance SA-NV* [2003] Lloyd's Rep. I.R. 487; *Canelhas Comercio Inportacao E Exportacao Ltd v Wooldridge* [2004] EWCA Civ 984; [2004] Lloyd's Rep. I.R. 915; *McGeown v Direct Travel Insurance* [2003] EWCA Civ 1606; [2004] Lloyd's Rep. I.R. 599; *Friends Provident Life and Pensions Ltd v Sirius International Insurance Corp* [2004] EWHC 1999 (Comm); [2005] Lloyd's Rep. I.R. 135 and *Royal & Sun Alliance Insurance Plc v Dornoch* [2005] EWCA Civ 544; [2005] Lloyd's Rep. I.R. 544.

[55] See Clarke, *The Law of Insurance Contracts*, 5th edn (Informa Subscriptions, 2015), para.15–3B1. However, a broad contextual construction to wording in an employers' liability policy was taken by the Supreme Court in *Employers' Liability Policy Trigger Litigation: Durham v BAI (Run Off) Ltd* [2012] UKSC 14. The case is briefly considered at 22.1.

[56] *Thompson v Equity Fire Insurance Co* [1910] A.C. 592.

[57] *Leo Rapp Ltd v McClure* [1955] 1 Lloyd's Rep. 292.

for exemption from liability where goods are unattended. In *Langford v Legal and General Assurance Society Ltd*,[58] it was held that a car was "attended" within the "sensible and practical meaning" of the word where it was left by the insured in her driveway for only a few seconds and was visible from her kitchen window. In *Gordon Leslie Ltd v General Accident Fire & Life Assurance Corporation Plc*,[59] a haulage contracting company's lorries and loads were insured against theft, unless a lorry was locked and the keys removed when it was unattended. In accordance with company practice, to facilitate removal in the event of fire, a driver left the keys in the ignition of his lorry when he locked it in the company's premises over the weekend. The lorry and its load of vodka was stolen. It was held that the exception applied only when the vehicle was actually physically attended by the driver whilst goods were in transit. Once the vehicle was stored overnight, there was no question of it being "unattended" in the context of the exception. However, in *Sanger v Beazley*,[60] it was held that a vehicle was unattended when the owner, feeling unwell, stopped at a motorway service station and went to the lavatory. The judge said that he was not in a position to observe any attempt at interference with his vehicle, nor was he so placed as to have any reasonable prospect of preventing interference. The judge held that the exception required reasonable observation to be kept on the vehicle if a driver left his car for any reason. While some might argue that to leave one's car for what was acknowledged to be only 68 seconds, in such circumstances, could be considered to be outside the scope of the exception, the Court of Appeal has recently confirmed this strict approach. In *Hayward v Norwich Union Insurance Ltd*,[61] the insurer agreed to indemnify Mr Hayward if his Porsche was lost, stolen or damaged. An exception excluded "loss or damage arising from theft whilst the ignition keys of your car have been left in or on the car". The vehicle was stolen from a garage forecourt while the owner paid for petrol at the kiosk. He had left the keys in the vehicle although he had set his immobilising device. The thief entered the car, disabled the immobiliser and drove off. At first instance it was argued that the words "have been left" meant "have been left unattended" and it was held that because the owner was only 20 yards away from the car, the keys had not therefore "been left" in the car within the exception's meaning. The Court of Appeal disagreed, saying that even if this was the true meaning, the fact that the owner had, indisputably, left his keys in the ignition did mean that the keys were left unattended within the ordinary meaning of the word. The court accepted that although Mr Hayward's con-

---

[58] *Langford v Legal and General Assurance Society Ltd* [1986] 2 Lloyd's Rep. 103; see also *O'Donoghue v Harding* [1988] 2 Lloyd's Rep. 281.

[59] *Gordon Leslie Ltd v General Accident Fire & Life Assurance Corp Plc* 1998 S.L.T. 391.

[60] *Sanger v Beazley* [1999] Lloyd's Rep. I.R. 424.

[61] *Hayward v Norwich Union Insurance Ltd* [2001] Lloyd's Rep. I.R. 410.

duct may have been reasonable because he believed the immobiliser would protect the car against theft, nevertheless, the exception had to bite. The results in both *Beazley* and *Hayward* may seem to some a little harsh, but must be considered correct as a matter of strict law.

13.3.2 Technical meaning

In two respects, however, the ordinary meaning of words will not prevail. The first is where a word has a technical legal or other meaning. This will generally be the case in respect of words describing cover or exceptions to it, which are also the names of criminal offences, such as theft, or have acquired a particular meaning.[62] The meaning in the latter respect applies to the word in an insurance policy. The classic example is the decision of the House of Lords in *London & Lancashire Fire Insurance Co v Bolands*.[63] Here a policy on a baker's shop against loss by burglary, housebreaking and theft exempted the insurers from loss caused by, or happening through, or in consequence of, inter alia, "riot". Four armed men entered the shop one day, held up the employees with guns, and stole all the money they could find. There was no actual violence used, and no other disturbance nearby, yet it was held that the event constituted a riot, and thus the insured could not recover. The stated reason for the decision was that "riot" is a technical term which in a criminal context requires only three people executing a disturbance such as might cause alarm to a reasonable person.[64] Applying this meaning to the insurance policy, there was clearly a riot on the facts of the case. However, it may not be entirely insignificant that the shop was in Dublin and the robbery took place at a time of great disturbances involving the IRA and others. It is not impossible that such a body was behind the robbery, and to talk in terms of riot becomes a little more understandable.

It is instructive to compare the views of an American court[65] in holding that riot in an insurance policy meant what ordinary people would normally

---

[62] As to words that are the names of crimes, see Wasik [1986] J.B.L. 45. As to the meaning of "theft" in particular see 13.7.5. See also *Hayward v Norwich Union Insurance Ltd*, above. For an example of the same principle in relation to a word having a statutory and medical meaning, see *Cape Plc v Iron Trades Employers Assurance Ltd* [2004] Lloyd's Rep. 75, concerning the meaning of "mesothelioma" in an employer's liability policy.

[63] *London & Lancashire Fire Insurance Co v Bolands* [1924] A.C. 836. The rule as to technical meaning also seems to have been the basis of the recent House of Lords' decision in *Deutsche Genossenschaftsbank v Burnhope* [1995] 4 All E.R. 717, where it was held that "theft" could not be committed by a company in the absence of the physical presence of someone senior enough to be regarded as the company's directing mind and will.

[64] See, e.g. *Field v Receiver of Metropolitan Police* [1907] 2 K.B. 853.

[65] *Pan Am v Aetna Casualty* [1974] 1 Lloyd's Rep. 232; [1975] 1 Lloyd's Rep. 77.

regard as a riot, distinguishing the decision in *Bolands* for these reasons. In the light of the traditional rules applying to technical words, the decision in *Bolands* was clearly correct. What may be questioned is whether it is a necessary or fair rule to apply to an insurance policy the meaning from another context when such a meaning may be totally different from the ordinary meaning, and it may be that this traditional approach to "technical words" will not survive the restatement of the principles of construction described earlier.[66]

Some support for this can perhaps be found in the decision of the Court of Appeal in *Canelhas Comercio Inportacao E Exportacao Ltd v Wooldridge*.[67] Here it was held that, in the context of a policy issued to cover risks in Brazil, the word "robbery" was to be understood not in any technical English legal sense but in the sense in which ordinary commercial people would understand it. Further detailed examination of the meaning of robbery under either English or Brazilian law was inappropriate. "The proper approach is to interpret the wording of the relevant clause as a whole in the context of the policy as a whole",[68] through the eyes of an ordinary commercial person. Having referred to the principles expressed by Lord Hoffmann in *Investors Compensation Scheme v West Bromwich Building Society*, and described above, he continued,

> "It is of course true that one would expect any ordinary reasonable commercial person obtaining or issuing a policy such as the present to have a general conception of "robbery" which one might also expect to correspond broadly with that used by legislators here and elsewhere. But a proper understanding . . . requires consideration of how such a person would understand the whole clause in its context. That in turn involves considering the aim and purpose of the clause objectively ascertained from the language of the standard wording of this policy".[69]

13.3.3 Context

The second way in which the ordinary meaning of a word may not be adopted is where the context requires otherwise. Frequently, the list of perils covered by, for example, a fire policy does not list each peril individually but groups a few together. This is what happened in *Young v Sun Alliance & London Insurance*.[70] Here, the insured's household policy insured him against

---

[66] But there was no hint of this in *Hayward v Norwich Union Insurance Ltd*, above.

[67] *Canelhas Comercio Inportacao E Exportacao Ltd v Wooldridge* [2004] EWCA Civ 984; [2004] Lloyd's Rep. I.R. 915.

[68] per Mance LJ at 11.

[69] See 12.

[70] *Young v Sun Alliance & London Insurance* [1977] 1 W.L.R. 104.

loss arising from a number of causes, one group of which was "storm,[71] tempest or flood". His house was built on a meadow. Several times water seeped in and caused damage to the ground floor lavatory. On one occasion, the water was three inches deep on the lavatory floor. The insured claimed that this constituted a "flood" and that the insurers were therefore liable to indemnify him in respect of the damage. The Court of Appeal rejected his claim. At least two of their Lordships[72] appeared to accept that in the ordinary sense of the word there was a flood, but they concluded in favour of a contextual approach. As "storm" and "tempest" both import notions of the abnormal, by analogy "flood", appearing in the same phrase, meant a much larger movement of water than natural seepage to a level of three inches. They were almost persuaded, in view of the two possible meanings of "flood", to apply the *contra proferentem* rule. A similar approach was taken in *Computer & Systems Engineering Plc v John Lelliot (Ilford) Ltd,*[73] where Beldam LJ said that a flood "imports the invasion of the property . . . by a large volume of water from an external source, usually but not necessarily confined to the result of a natural phenomenon such as a storm, tempest or downpour".[74]

It has been suggested that the traditional approach should be replaced by an enquiry as to what cover the parties really thought was being provided by the policy and as to the purposes behind the insurance in question.[75] This is certainly the approach taken in a more recent case to deal with this issue, *Rohan Investments Ltd v Cunningham.*[76] Here, the Court of Appeal refused to treat the definitions of flood in *Young* and *Computer & Systems* as akin to statutory ones. In *Rohan*, the damage was caused by an escape of water from the roof, which had built up over a period of nine days during which time there had been prolonged heavy rainfall. The insurance covered damage caused by "storm, tempest and flood". The court had little difficulty in holding that such an ingress of water was a "flood". Although the word carried with it visions of the abnormal, the very fact that had caused the court in the previous two cases such difficulty, both Robert Walker and Auld LJJ thought that the rapid accumulation of water in the present case was abnormal and was exactly the type of event that the insurance was intended to cover. It was, they said, a question of degree in every case. This is perhaps an approach rather similar to the American rules of construction that were referred to

---

[71] As to storm, see *Anderson v Norwich Union* [1977] 1 Lloyd's Rep. 253.

[72] Shaw and Cairns LJJ. Lawton LJ regarded the problem as more straightforward, holding that flood ordinarily meant something violent and abnormal.

[73] *Computer & Systems Engineering Plc v John Lelliot (Ilford) Ltd* [1990] 54 B.L.R. 1. See also *The Board of Trustees of the Tate Gallery v Duffy Construction Ltd* [2007] EWHC 361 (TCC), [2007] Lloyd's Rep. I.R. 758.

[74] Above at 10.

[75] Merkin (1977) 40 M.L.R. 486.

[76] *Rohan Investments Ltd v Cunningham* [1999] Lloyd's Rep. I.R. 190.

earlier. In any event, as *Young* involved a consumer insurance policy, it is likely that the requirement of plainness and intelligibility[77] would now require a description of what the insurers understood by "flood", for example by the use of a glossary of terms used in the policy.[78]

13.3.4 Contra proferentem

The maxim that provides for ambiguities to be construed against the party responsible for drafting them[79] may be brought to the aid of the insured as two leading Court of Appeal decisions show.

In *English v Western*,[80] a motor policy effected by a 17-year-old youth covered his liability for injury to all persons except, inter alia, in respect of "death or injury to any member of the assured's household" travelling in the car with the insured.[81] He negligently injured his sister when she was his passenger. The insurers argued that they were not liable to indemnify the insured against his liability to her by virtue of the above exception. It was held that the expression "any member of the assured's household" was equally capable of meaning "any member of a household of which the assured was the head" as "any member of the same household of which the assured was a member". It was therefore ambiguous and the meaning more favourable to the insured, the former meaning, was adopted, so that the insurers were liable.

Houghton v Trafalgar Insurance Co Ltd[82] also involved an exception in a motor policy, which excluded liability when the car was conveying "any load in excess of that for which it was constructed". Here the insurer argued that the carriage of six persons in a car designed for five was within the exception. It was held that this was not a "load". While the carriage of persons could be so considered, it equally, indeed more naturally, referred to the carriage of goods.

The application of the *contra proferentem* maxim can hardly be said to be free from doubt. It is clear that there must be a genuine ambiguity; ambiguity must not be created simply to apply the maxim. However, whether or not a word or phrase is ambiguous is not always apparent. It could be said that there was ambiguity over the meaning of the word "flood" in the *Young* case, and two of the judges admitted that counsel for the insured had very nearly so persuaded them. A classic illustration of the difficulties, which gave rise to a difference of judicial opinion, is *Alder v Moore*.[83] Here the dispute arose

---

[77] And the statutory *contra proferentem* rule; see 13.1.1.
[78] This is in fact not uncommon.
[79] Now statutorily confirmed in respect of consumer insurances; see 13.1.1.
[80] *English v Western* [1940] 2 K.B. 156.
[81] Such an exclusion is not now permitted under the Road Traffic Act 1988; see 21.2.
[82] *Houghton v Trafalgar Insurance Co Ltd* [1954] 1 Q.B. 247.
[83] *Alder v Moore* [1961] 2 Q.B. 57.

not from the wording of a policy itself, but of an undertaking extracted from an insured following a payment under a policy. The defendant had been a professional footballer and a member of the relevant footballers' union when he suffered an injury to an eye that it was thought would prevent him from playing professionally again. The union had an accident policy under which its members who sustained permanent total disablement would receive £500 from the insurers. The defendant received such a payment, in return for which he agreed that he would not take part "as a playing member" in any form of professional football. Subsequently he recovered sufficiently to take up occasional professional football, though at a much lower level than before. The insurers sued for return of the £500. It was argued for the defendant, inter alia,[84] that the undertaking was ambiguous, because "playing member" could mean either simply "player" or "player who is a member of the union". Moore was not, when he returned to football, a member of the union. The latter interpretation was reinforced by the argument that if the former were correct, the word "member" in the undertaking was superfluous and that in the original policy, "member" was expressly defined as a registered member of the union. Despite this, a majority of the Court of Appeal[85] held that the insurers should succeed and regarded the undertaking as perfectly clear. With respect, the dissenting judgment of Devlin LJ is much more persuasive.[86] For the reasons outlined he held that the phrase was ambiguous, and, although he adopted what he termed a wider rule than *contra proferentem*, he was clearly of the opinion that the phrase should be construed against the insurers. Whichever view is the better on the facts of the case, it does illustrate how even the judges cannot always agree as to whether or not sufficient ambiguity exists.[87]

13.4   Specific Descriptions and Specific Words

It is appropriate to turn now to consider how some of the specific descriptions sometimes applied to insurance policies and some of the standard wordings have been defined in the context of the cover afforded by an insurance policy. Looking first at descriptions, it is well known that insurers, no doubt at least partly for marketing reasons, sometimes attach descriptions such as "Comprehensive", "Invincible", "Homeguard" or "Maxplan" to their appropriate policies. While judges have occasionally commented adversely on such

---

[84] It was also argued that the forfeiture was a penalty clause and void for this reason, but the court held against this argument by a majority.

[85] On this point, Slade J simply agreed with Sellers LJ.

[86] See Goff (1961) 24 M.L.R. 637.

[87] Even in *English v Western*, above, which seems a pretty clear case of ambiguity, Goddard LJ dissented on the grounds that it was not.

descriptions because they give a somewhat misleading picture and may lead an insured to consider that his cover is complete and not subject to exceptions, which it usually will be, it is clear that descriptions of the sort mentioned above are not terms of art and do not carry any legal meanings.[88] The one exception to this is the description "all risks". Frequently, for example, policies on valuables and contractors' policies are "all risks". The nature of an "all risks" policy was explained in the marine insurance case of *British and Foreign Marine Insurance Co v Gaunt*.[89] Basically, it covers all loss to the property insured as occurs through some accidental cause, but not "such damage as is inevitable from ordinary wear and tear and inevitable depreciation"[90] or from inherent vice. The other significant feature of "all risks" cover is that the insured has to show only that a loss is accidental; he need not show the exact nature of the accident or casualty which occasioned the loss.

However, even an "all risks" policy can be subject to exceptions that will be upheld on usual principles of construction if they are clearly stated.

In the Australian case of *Queensland Government Railways and Electric Power Transmission Pty Ltd v Manufacturers' Mutual Life Insurance Ltd*,[91] the insured held a contractors' all risks policy covering the construction of a bridge, but the policy excluded loss or damage arising from "faulty design". The bridge was being constructed to a design that, at the time, was the best available, but nevertheless, its piers were swept away by floodwater after exceptionally heavy rains. It was held that the insurers could rely upon the exception. Even though the design was not negligent, because it was the best available, it was still "faulty" since otherwise the piers would never have collapsed.[92]

13.5 Fire

Insurance against loss or damage by fire is, of course, one of the standard and one of the oldest forms of cover, and the major part of any policy on buildings. As fire does not have a technical meaning like, for example, theft or burglary, and because of its prominence, its meaning is worth exploring. Apart from obvious losses by fire, the actual burning of property insured,

---

[88] Compare the attitude of some American cases; see, e.g. *Gerhardt v Continental Insurance Co* [1967] 1 Lloyd's Rep. 380; at 13.1.2, above, where the fact that the policy was described as a comprehensive one was one of the factors in the decision. Note also the strictures of the Insurance Ombudsman on the use of such titles; see his Annual Report for 1986, at 25–26.

[89] *British and Foreign Marine Insurance Co v Gaunt* [1921] 2 A.C. 41.

[90] Above at 46, per Lord Birkenhead.

[91] *Queensland Government Railways and Electric Power Transmission Pty Ltd v Manufacturers' Mutual Life Insurance Ltd* (1968) 118 C.L.R. 314; [1969] 1 Lloyd's Rep. 214.

[92] This definition of faulty was trenchantly criticised by Merkin (1977) 40 M.L.R. 486 at 489.

the problems that have arisen have been whether it is necessary that there be actual ignition of the property insured and whether loss or damage occurring in or as a result of a "proper" fire is covered. Actual ignition is necessary and damage from excessive heat is not enough. In the old case of *Austin v Drewe*,[93] the stock in a sugar refinery was insured against damage by fire. A flue passed up through all the floors of the refinery from a stove on the ground floor. At the top of the flue was a register that was closed at night to retain heat, but opened when a fresh fire was lit in the morning. One morning an employee of the insured forgot to open the register. The intense heat in the flue damaged sugar being refined on the top floor, but, although there was smoke and sparks, the fire itself was confined to the flue and the sugar did not ignite. It was held that there was no loss by fire.

On the other hand, if there has been actual ignition of some property, the fact that the insured property itself does not catch fire is irrelevant if it is damaged in such a way that the proximate cause of the loss was the fire.[94] We shall return to this point later.

There is no distinction in English law between a "friendly" fire and a "hostile" fire. In other words, the fact that the damage is caused by a fire in its proper place does not matter so long as the loss is accidental. In *Harris v Poland*,[95] the insured's personal property was insured against loss or damage caused by fire. One day, as a security measure, she concealed her jewellery in the grate under coal that was ready for lighting. Later she inadvertently lit the fire without removing the jewellery that, as a result, was damaged. It was held that there had been a loss by fire.

> "[The] risks against which the plaintiff is insured include the risk of insured property coming unintentionally in contact with fire and being thereby destroyed or damaged, and it matters not whether that fire comes to the insured property or the insured property comes to the fire."[96]

Damage caused merely by explosion or lightning is not damage by fire,[97] but explosion caused by fire, or fire following an explosion or lightning will be covered, subject to the rules about causation that will be examined later, because here there has been actual ignition.[98] In practice, lightning damage at least is included in the cover provided by a standard fire policy.

---

[93] *Austin v Drewe* (1816) 6 Taunt. 436.

[94] *Symington v Union Insurance Society of Canton* (1928) 97 L.J.K.B. 646.

[95] *Harris v Poland* [1941] 1 K.B. 462.

[96] Above at 468, per Atkinson J.

[97] *Everett v London Assurance Co* (1865) 19 C.B. (N.S.) 126. As to "explosion", see *Commonwealth Smelting v Guardian Royal Exchange* [1984] 2 Lloyd's Rep. 608.

[98] *Stanley v Western Insurance Co* (1868) L.R. 3 Ex. 71.

13.6   Accident

Loss caused by or arising out of an accident or by accidental means or some similar phrase is a fairly common form of wording in insurance policies, and an essential one in particular types. The considerable problems involved in defining "accident" have occasioned the courts difficulties many times[99] and it is considered worthwhile, therefore, to devote space to this question. Particular policies where these problems arise are policies of personal accident insurance or policies such as motor policies that may well contain a personal accident component, and some policies of liability insurance.

As we have seen, insurance prima facie covers only unintentional acts anyway, so one problem is how the presence of the word "accident" qualifies this. Another is that even a deliberate act by someone may well be accidental from the point of view of the victim. Similarly, an insured may be engaged in a deliberate course of conduct when something happens which he did not intend. Is this an accident? It is suggested that the answers to these and other problems are best considered by a separate examination of first, those first party insurances where the description "accident" is to be found, and secondly, cases of third party or liability insurance where the liability of the insurer to indemnify exists only if the insured acted accidentally. It must be pointed out, however, that the cases do not necessarily adopt this distinction.

13.6.1 First party insurances

In the first sort of case policies of personal accident insurance predominate.[100] Leaving aside for the present the issue of causation, which can be of importance in this field, it would appear that injury arising from accident can be defined as injury which arises from some unexpected or unintended event, which is not natural. So, for example, in *Hamlyn v Crown Accidental Insurance Co Ltd*,[101] the insured bent down to pick up a marble dropped by a child. In doing so, he wrenched his knee. As he had no history of knee trouble it was held that his injury was accidental. Although obviously he intended to bend down, he did not intend or expect to hurt his knee.[102] The fact that the

---

[99] The classic illustration is perhaps the decision in *Trim Joint District School Board of Management v Kelly* [1914] A.C. 667, a workmen's compensation case where the House of Lords split 4–3.

[100] Common also at one time were policies issued under the Workmen's Compensation Acts, which gave birth to a considerable amount of litigation; see below.

[101] *Hamlyn v Crown Accidental Insurance Co Ltd* [1893] 1 Q.B. 750. See also *Voison v Royal Insurance Co of Canada* (1989) 53 D.L.R. ON 299.

[102] It is not certain that the result in *Hamlyn* would be the same today, because the policy required "accidental means" (see below), but it is clearly still a good illustration of an "accident".

insured is negligent is by itself irrelevant, so that being knocked down by a train when crossing a railway line without due care will be covered by a personal accident policy.[103] Death or injury from sunstroke or exposure would not normally be regarded as accidental, being the result of natural events.[104]

In *Marcel Beller Ltd v Hayden*,[105] a company insured its employees against death consequent upon "accidental bodily injury" being the sole cause. An employee having consumed alcoholic drink to the extent that he had much more than the permitted level of alcohol in his blood, was driving his car too fast when approaching a corner; he lost control, crashed and was killed. One of the points for decision was whether this was an accident. It was argued for the insurers that it was not, because the death was a reasonably foreseeable consequence of a deliberate act by the employee, that is, the consumption of a considerable quantity of alcohol. The judge rejected this argument and distinguished the difficult case of *Gray v Barr*,[106] a decision on liability insurance that will be examined shortly. In his view, accident should be interpreted in its ordinary sense as an ordinary person would understand it. As, on the facts, an ordinary person would have said that the employee's death was an accident, because he did not intend to kill himself nor expose himself to deliberate risk, the death was prima facie covered by the policy.

If the insured does take a deliberate risk, a resulting injury may fairly be said not to be accidental. In one Canadian case,[107] cited in *Marcel Beller Ltd v Hayden*, the insured stood on the coping of a hotel patio 13 floors above the street in order to demonstrate to a friend that he had not lost his nerve. Unfortunately he lost his balance and fell to his death. This was held not to be an accident. In the words of the learned judge in *Marcel Beller Ltd v Hayden*, "It seems to me that a clear distinction can be drawn between cases where the predisposing cause is the deliberate taking of an appreciated risk and the cases such as the present where the predisposing cause, although it leads to the taking of risks, involves risk which was neither deliberately run nor actually appreciated".[108]

Sometimes, though probably rarely, cases are found where property

---

[103] *Cornish v Accident Insurance Co* (1889) 23 Q.B.D. 453.

[104] *Sinclair v Maritime Passengers' Assurance* (1861) 3 E. & E. 478, followed in *De Souza v Home and Overseas Insurance Co Ltd* [1995] L.R.L.R. 453 (1990).

[105] *Marcel Beller Ltd v Hayden* [1978] Q.B. 694.

[106] *Gray v Barr* [1971] 2 Q.B. 554.

[107] *Candler v London & Lancashire Guarantee & Accident Co of Canada* (1963) 40 D.L.R. (2d.) 408.

[108] *Marcel Beller Ltd v Hayden* [1978] 2 Q.B. at 705. Modern policies will probably contain an exception excluding liability if there is "wilful exposure to needless peril". This has the same effect. In *Morley v United Friendly Insurance Plc* [1993] 1 Lloyd's Rep. 490, it was held that this did not exclude the situation where the insured jumped on to the bumper of a car as a prank and fell off.

damage is covered under a first party policy only if caused by or arising out of accident. In the Australian decision of *Lombard Australia Ltd v NRMA Insurance Ltd*,[109] an approach similar to that of the personal injury cases was taken. There a car, the subject of a hire purchase agreement, was jointly insured against loss by accident by the hirer and the owner. The hirer deliberately committed suicide by driving it into a tree. It was held that the loss of the car was accidental so far as the owner was concerned and thus covered, as the latter certainly did not intend the loss.

13.6.2 Accidental means

One final, but very important, point to consider in this context is whether subtle changes in wording can affect the interpretation of words. For example, a personal accident policy may not simply cover death or injury "caused by accident", but one "caused by accidental means" or, in the fuller phrase often employed, "by violent, accidental, external and visible means".[110] Here it could be argued not just that the final event or injury must be accidental, but also the "means", in other words, the prior act of the insured or whoever is responsible for the act, so that if a deliberate act led to the final "accident", the insured is not covered. An argument along these lines seems to have been rejected in the *Hamlyn* case, which we have already examined, where the wording was of this sort and the bending over of the insured was clearly deliberate, but it has prevailed in the intervening years in decisions in some other jurisdictions, including a leading American case,[111] and was adopted by the Court of Appeal in *Dhak v Insurance Company of North America (UK) Ltd*,[112] where recovery was denied in circumstances where the insured died from asphyxiation due to vomiting while under the influence of alcohol; she had drunk in order to control severe back pain. It is submitted that the earlier English approach is to be preferred. As that great American judge, Cardozo J, dissenting, said[113]: "The attempted distinction between accidental results and accidental means will plunge this branch of the law into a Serbian bog". It is to be hoped that in a future case, the Court of Appeal or Supreme Court

---

[109] *Lombard Australia Ltd v NRMA Insurance Ltd* [1969] 1 Lloyd's Rep. 575.

[110] The continuing use of this antiquated phrase is perhaps surprising, and it is thought that it could not now, in a consumer policy, survive the statutory requirement of transparency (see 13.1.1).

[111] *Landress v Phoenix Insurance Co* 291 US 491 (1933); see also, the Scottish case of *Clidero v Scottish Accident Insurance Co* (1892) 19 R. 355 supporting the distinction between means and results.

[112] *Dhak v Insurance Company of North America (UK) Ltd* [1996] 1 Lloyd's Rep. 632. See also the analysis of *Hamlyn* in *De Souza v Home and Overseas Insurance Co Ltd* [1995] L.R.L.R. 453 (1990).

[113] In *Landress v Phoenix Insurance Co* 291 US 491 (1933).

steers English law back away from this particular bog.[114] Such an approach has been taken in Scotland in the case of *MacLeod v New Hampshire Insurance Co Ltd*.[115] The policy provided cover for bodily injury caused by "accidental, violent, visible and external means". The insured injured his back when throwing a tyre into the back of his pick-up truck. The insurers argued that the injury had been caused by an intentional act and, as such an injury was a foreseeable consequence of the act it could not have been caused by accidental means. Giving judgment for the insured, Lord Nimmo Smith held that the qualifying words were there to distinguish accidental injury from general sickness or degenerative illnesses and that the word "accidental" must be given its natural meaning. Taking a broad constructive approach, he said that the determining factor was not whether the act was intentional but whether the outcome was intended.[116]

13.6.3 Liability insurances

As far as the meaning of accident in a liability policy is concerned, it is convenient to examine separately cases on property damage and those on personal injury or death. Here a particular problem is that even an intended act by an insured will almost always be accidental from the point of view of the third party victim, but it is clear that this is irrelevant and indemnity will not be provided if what the insured did was not from his point of view an accident.[117] However, in considering the degree of foresight necessary to

---

[114] Other jurisdictions have generally done so: see, e.g. the Scottish Court of Session case of *Glenlight Shipping Ltd v Excess Insurance Ltd* 1983 S.L.T. 241 (where the decision in *Clidero*, above was ignored; see Davidson [1984] J.B.L. 391), the decision of the High Court of *Australia in Australian Casualty Co Ltd v Federico* (1986) 66 A.L.R. 99; the Canadian case of *Tracey-Gould v Maritime Life Assurance Co* (1992) 89 D.L.R. (4th) 726; and the decision of the New Zealand Court of Appeal in *Groves v AMP Fire & General Insurance Co (NZ) Ltd* [1990] 1 N.Z.L.R 122. The judgment of Hardie Boys J in the last case, where recovery was given when the insured had died as a result of an unforeseeable consequence of the proper administration of anaesthetic prior to an operation, contains a very clear and relatively brief summary of the leading common law authorities on this question.

[115] *MacLeod v New Hampshire Insurance Co Ltd* [1998] S.L.T. 1191.

[116] See also *Sargent v GRE (UK) Ltd* [2000] Lloyd's Rep. I.R. 77, where, in a case involving a personal accident policy, but not concerned with the meaning of accident in any sense, the Court of Appeal said that a purely linguistic interpretation of words could produce conflicting conclusions and that a broad constructive approach was necessary in such cases.

[117] If, however, the insured is a company that is responsible for the actions of someone who acted deliberately, then it will still be able to recover if the knowledge of the actual perpetrator is not attributed to it; as far as the insured is concerned, the conduct is still accidental: *Hawley v Luminar Leisure Plc* [2006] EWCA Civ 18; [2006] Lloyd's Rep. I.R. 307.

prevent the insured from recovering, it appears that the courts have taken a stricter view in the case of injury to third parties than in the case of property damage.

13.6.4 Personal injury

The classic decision concerning personal injury is *Gray v Barr*.[118] The insured's wife had been having an affair with the claimant's husband, which the insured was led to believe had ended, which indeed may have been the case. However, on discovering one day that his wife was not at home, he suspected her to be with Gray and he set off for the latter's house with a loaded shotgun in order to frighten him. When he arrived there, he and Gray were involved in a struggle on the stairs as the result of which two shots were fired from the gun, the second one killing Gray. The insured was acquitted of murder and manslaughter, but was sued in tort by Mrs. Gray. He brought in his insurers as third parties, claiming that they were liable to indemnify him. The relevant liability aspect of his policy provided such an indemnity if the loss was "caused by accident". Tied up very much with the question of defining accident in the context were questions of causation and public policy which will be considered later, but it does appear that the majority of the Court of Appeal held that what happened was not an accident within the policy, on the ground that the death of Gray was a foreseeable consequence of Barr's intentional act of taking a loaded shotgun into the deceased's house.[119]

With great respect, it is submitted that the opinions of the trial judge[120] and Salmon LJ to the contrary are to be preferred.[121] On the facts as found there was no intention to fire a shot nor to kill. Most people would surely regard what happened as an "accident" therefore, and to introduce questions as to prior acts is arguably to bring in that confusing distinction between means and results upon which we have already commented. It may still be the case that the result in *Gray v Barr* was correct, but here we are only concerned with the meaning of the word "accident", not with the inevitable issues of causation and public policy that also arose in that case.

---

[118] *Gray v Barr* [1971] 2 Q.B. 554.
[119] This was clearly the view of Phillimore LJ. Lord Denning MR seemed to base his decision more on the ground of causation, as to which see below, at 13.9.4.
[120] [1970] 2 Q.B. 626; see also the comments in *Marcel Beller Ltd v Hayden* [1978] Q.B. 694.
[121] Compare the Australian decision of *S & Y Investments (No.2) Pty Ltd v Commercial Union Assurance Co of Australia Ltd* (1986–87) 85 F.L.R. 285.

13.6.5 Property damage

So far as property damage is concerned, the Australian decision of *Robinson v Evans*[122] is a good example of the use of what, it is suggested, is a sensible test, that the event must be unintended and unexpected from the point of view of the insured. Here the claimant sued the defendant company in tort for damages for the destruction of his crop of brussel sprouts. The claimant was a market gardener, the defendant owned a neighbouring brick works. The claim, which involved two separate incidents, was settled and the dispute concerned the defendant's claim to be indemnified by its public liability insurers, the terms of the policy providing such indemnity in respect of accidental damage only.[123] The court found that the damage to the crop was caused by the emission of fluoride. In respect of the first incident, the defendant's managing director knew about the danger. It was held that this claim was not for accidental damage. While it may have been unintended by the defendant, it could not be said to be wholly unexpected because of the managing director's knowledge. The test to be applied was whether an ordinary reasonable sensible man, in the position of the insured (or, in this case, its responsible officers), would or would not have expected the occurrence. The second incident arose after the defendant had built a much higher stack on its chimney, which it was genuinely believed would cure the problem, but which did not. It was held that the defendant's insurers were liable to indemnify it in this respect. This damage was unintended and unexpected and hence accidental.

In contrast, the decision of the Canadian Supreme Court in *Canadian Indemnity Co v Walkem Machinery & Equipment Ltd*[124] is rather surprising.[125] W Ltd was the agent and distributor for a company that manufactured a special type of crane. It negligently sold to a customer a crane which had been inadequately repaired and which was in a dangerous condition. This crane collapsed and W Ltd was held liable to pay damages to a third party. Its comprehensive business liability policy, issued by the appellant insurer, indemnified it against liability to third parties arising from accident. It seems clear that W Ltd took a calculated risk in selling the crane, so that the subsequent collapse could hardly be said to be quite unexpected, even if unintended, but the court held that the liability of W Ltd arose from accident. It followed in particular some of the English workmen's compensation cases[126] in holding

---

[122] *Robinson v Evans* [1969] V.R. 885.

[123] The policy's actual wording was "damage caused by accidental means", but the court sensibly rejected the distinction between means and results.

[124] *Canadian Indemnity Co v Walkem Machinery & Equipment Ltd* (1975) 52 D.L.R. (3d) 1.

[125] See Hasson, (1976) 14 OHLJ 669.

[126] *Fenton v Thorley & Co Ltd* [1903] A.C. 443 and *Clover, Clayton & Co Ltd v Hughes* [1910] A.C. 242.

that accident meant "any unlooked for mishap or occurrence", thus deciding that an unintended occurrence, however risky, was within the cover. The court laid great stress upon the fact that the policy was a comprehensive business liability policy and that a narrower construction of accident would deny the insured recovery if an occurrence were the result of a calculated risk or of a dangerous operation. With great respect, this misses the point. Of course an insured can be covered against a calculated risk; a third party policy which indemnifies simply against legal liability to third parties, without any limitation by reference to accident, will cover all except deliberate risks. However, the inclusion of "caused by accident" must make a difference, especially it might be thought where the insured is a well-advised commercial concern. It is suggested that this case would not and should not be followed here. It contrasts most strongly with the decision in *Gray v Barr*, which, it has already been suggested, goes to the other extreme.

13.6.6 Natural causes

An important point in this context concerns the relevance of natural causes to a third party policy insuring against liability caused by accident. As has been seen, in the context of personal accident policies, if the real cause of the loss is natural, it will not be covered, indeed it will usually be expressly excepted, and of course it is a general principle that insurance does not cover natural wear and tear. In *Mills v Smith*,[127] a householder's liability policy indemnified the insured against liability for "damage to property caused by accident". The insured was held liable in damages to a neighbour for settlement damage to the neighbour's house caused by the root action of a tree in the insured's garden taking water from the soil on the neighbour's land. It was held that this was caused by accident. The learned judge was clearly disposed to give a wide meaning to these words in a householder's policy and the insured obviously did nothing that was intended or expected in any way. On the other hand, it could be argued that the real cause of the insured's liability was entirely natural, namely the action of the tree roots, albeit there was an "accident" when the neighbour's foundations dropped. Paul J regarded it as significant that the insurers had chosen to use the same words as used to appear in the Workmen's Compensation Acts and felt able to rely on leading decisions under those Acts with appropriate adjustments. That led him to the conclusion that there were two questions to be answered on the facts. The first was whether there had, at any moment in time, been some unexpected event leading to damage. Here the settlement was this event, being more than the natural movement of foundations. The second question involved determining the cause of this. His answer was that it was

[127] *Mills v Smith* [1964] 1 Q.B. 30.

the action of the roots of the tree and that this meant that the insurers were liable.

With respect, this reasoning is difficult to follow. If the real cause of the loss was the action of the tree, that was surely natural and not "caused by accident". If the proximate cause rule means anything in this sort of case, a question to be discussed later in this chapter, the decision can hardly be supported on this ground. If it can be supported, it must be on the ground that the event must be looked at solely from the point of view of the insured, ignoring underlying "natural" factors. If, so far as he was concerned, the event was unexpected and unintended, then the loss was caused by accident. Perhaps underlying this is a rationale of providing broad support to the individual insured without too much regard to narrow principles of definition and causation.

Two further points can be made. The first is that changes in wording might make a difference to the result in a case like *Mills v Smith*. If, for example, the policy had provided an indemnity in respect of damage "caused by an accident" or "caused by accidental means", it would have been more difficult to reach the same result.[128] Accident by itself is much more capable of a wide meaning than "an accident", and the use of "accidental means" according to the latest English authority requires that the entire causal history must be accidental.[129]

The second point concerns the relevance of workmen's compensation cases, which, as we have seen, have been relied on in some of the third party policy cases.[130] Clearly these cases may be useful when the wording of a policy is the same as that used in the Workmen's Compensation Acts, in other words "injury or damage caused by accident". But it is also true that workmen's compensation policies were construed more liberally than other insurance contracts because they were the system of first party insurance established for the benefit of employees before the days of state insurance under the social security system. For example, death or injury from natural phenomena has been held covered under a workmen's compensation policy, whereas it would not be so regarded under a personal accident policy. Workmen's compensation cases are therefore no more than useful and are certainly not binding in this context.[131]

---

[128] See the judgment of Paull J [1964] 1 Q.B. 30 at 36.

[129] *Dhak v Insurance Company of North America (UK) Ltd* [1996] 1 Lloyd's Rep. 632; see 13.6.2. On the other hand it has been argued above that the distinction between means and results should not be adopted and this was certainly the case in the property damage case of *Robinson v Evans*, as we have seen.

[130] Particularly *Mills v Smith* [1964] 1 Q.B. 30 and *Canadian Indemnity Co v Walkem Machinery & Equipment Ltd* (1975) 5 2 D.L.R. (3d) 1.

[131] See especially the comments in *De Souza v Home and Overseas Insurance Co Ltd* [1995] L.R.L.R. 453 (1990).

13.6.7 Conclusions

The cases that have been reviewed here illustrate, if nothing else, that "accident" is a difficult concept to define accurately. The following tentative conclusions can perhaps be drawn. The meaning of accident is wider in the context of personal accident cover than in third party cover. In the former, the event need be only either unexpected or unintended, provided that the insured does not expose himself to a deliberate risk. In the latter it should be both unexpected and unintended. However, the degree of foresight that is relevant to determining whether or not an event is unintended is not clearly established. *Gray v Barr* suggests that not a great deal of foresight of an event is needed before it is so regarded as intended for these purposes, whereas *Robinson v Evans* held that the insured as a reasonable man must have foreseen the event before he is denied indemnity. It may be that *Gray v Barr* should be regarded as incorrect on this point and treated solely as an authority on causation and public policy. What is clear is that disputes over the meaning of accident will continue to be the subject of litigation.

13.7   Loss

The word "loss" appears frequently throughout this book and in policies of insurance, for obvious reasons. It is the risk of loss that is central to the concept of insurance. In some contexts, "loss" appears merely as a part of a wider phrase, such as, for example, "loss by fire". In this sort of case, the meaning of loss itself is not important. Whether or not the insured can recover depends upon the meaning of fire and on whether his loss was caused by that insured peril. However, in other contexts, particularly perhaps in insurances of goods, "loss" is itself one of the forms of cover provided. A standard description is insurance against "loss, damage or destruction". The latter two words raise no problems of construction or definition, but the meaning of "loss" does, and it has exercised the courts on a number of occasions. A rather special case, which merits separate consideration, is loss by theft.

13.7.1 Constructive total loss

In marine insurance law, there is a doctrine of "constructive total loss" whereby, even if a ship or other property insured is not actually lost or cannot be proved to be so lost, the insured can, by giving notice, claim as for a total loss, the insurer thereafter becoming entitled to the ship or property if it should turn up.[132] This is because traditionally marine insurance has been regarded as insurance of the adventure as much as of the ship or other

---

[132] See the Marine Insurance Act 1906 ss.60–63.

property insured. The same result can be achieved in non-marine insurance by agreement between insurer and insured, for example, an insurer might agree to pay in respect of a stolen car even if it cannot be shown to have been actually lost on the tests to be examined shortly, but it is well-established that there is no automatic doctrine of constructive total loss in non-marine insurance[133]; if necessary, the insured must prove an actual loss.

13.7.2 Missing goods

Obviously, if goods are actually destroyed, they are lost, but cover in this respect falls more naturally under the "destruction" part of the standard phrase quoted above. If goods are mislaid or are missing or have disappeared, then they become lost if after a reasonable time and a diligent but fruitless search, recovery of them is uncertain or unlikely. In *Holmes v Payne*,[134] an insured necklace was mislaid and could not be found despite all the insured's efforts. The insurers agreed to replace it. Some months later the necklace was found in the insured's cloak, having probably fallen into the lining. It was held that it had been truly lost. The insurers were therefore bound by the replacement agreement, although, of course, the insured was not entitled to keep the necklace as well as the replacement jewellery. Indeed, she had, before the action brought by the insurers, offered it to them as salvage.

13.7.3 Irrecoverable goods

A rather different situation is where the insured knows where his property is, but he is unable to recover it. If it remains his property and is safely in the hands of parties who are bailees of it for him, then it is not lost even if physically he is temporarily deprived of possession. In *Moore v Evans*,[135] just before the First World War, the insured jewellers sent a quantity of pearls to trade customers in Frankfurt and Brussels on sale or return. When war broke out, the Germans occupied Brussels. Thus for some four years, both sets of pearls were irrecoverable. However, the available evidence showed that they were being safely kept for the insured and had not been seized or interfered with by the German authorities. The House of Lords held that the goods were therefore not lost.

If, however, the insured property has been interfered with or taken by someone without authority, then it may well be lost even if in theory the insured might have a legal remedy that would entitle him to reclaim the property. The test would seem to be whether, after all reasonable steps have

[133] *Moore v Evans* [1918] A.C. 185.
[134] *Holmes v Payne* (1930) 37 L.I.L.R. 41.
[135] *Moore v Evans* [1918] A.C. 185.

been taken, recovery is uncertain. In *London & Provincial Leather Processes Ltd v Hudson*,[136] skins bought by the insured were as usual shipped from the seller directly to a German firm which was accustomed to process them for the insured before sending them to the UK. The German firm entrusted some of the skins to a sub-agent who retained them in purported exercise of a lien for money owed to them by the firm. The firm then went bankrupt, whereupon the equivalent of its trustee in bankruptcy sold more of the skins for the benefit of the estate. It was held that the insurers of the skins were liable for both losses, even though in theory the insured might have had remedies in respect of them in the German courts. The policy here was an all risks policy, but that would appear to make no difference in principle.

In *Webster v General Accident Fire and Life Assurance Corporation Ltd*,[137] the insured's car was stolen and passed through the hands of a number of people before it reached a purchaser who probably, but not necessarily, received good title to it under the provisions of the Factors Acts.[138] On discovering his loss, the insured had taken all reasonable steps to recover the car by contacting the police and the motoring organisations. It was held that the car was lost within the meaning of his insurance policy.

13.7.4 Loss of proceeds

Finally, it must be the insured property itself that is lost and not, for example, a sum of money received for it. If, then, the insured voluntarily hands over his property to another, intending to part with ownership, he cannot claim to have suffered a loss of it if the cheque that he receives in return for it subsequently bounces. What has been lost is the proceeds of sale, not the property.[139] This contrasts neatly with the facts of the *Webster* case to which we have already referred. There, the circumstances were that the insured entrusted his car to an auctioneer, when bidding for it had not reached the reserve price, upon the latter's saying that he had a private buyer. This statement was a lie, and the auctioneer intended at the time to deprive the insured of the car. He subsequently sent several cheques that were dishonoured. Here there was a loss of the car because, apart from the point already mentioned, the insured did not voluntarily part with property in the car. The auctioneer's dealings amounted to conversion and theft of the car.

---

[136] *London & Provincial Leather Processes Ltd v Hudson* [1939] 2 K.B. 724.

[137] *Webster v General Accident Fire and Life Assurance Corp Ltd* [1953] 1 Q.B. 520.

[138] The point was not decided. It was held that the insured did not have to sue to find out, having taken legal advice to the effect that he would probably not succeed, and thus having acted reasonably.

[139] *Eisinger v General Accident Fire and Life Assurance Corp Ltd* [1953] 2 All E.R. 897. Compare the decision in *Dobson v General Accident Fire & Life Assurance Corp Plc* [1990] 1 Q.B. 274, discussed below.

13.7.5 Loss by theft

Rather than simply insuring goods against loss (as well as damage or destruction), it seems that modern policies on goods sometimes specify the risk more precisely, in particular by describing one of the particular relevant perils as "loss by theft". One issue here is whether there must therefore be a loss of the property in the sense just considered as well as a loss by theft, the latter clearly bearing its technical criminal law meaning in accordance with the principle described earlier.[140] The decision in *Dobson v General Accident Fire & Life Assurance Corporation Plc*[141] raised these points and gave what could be regarded as somewhat controversial answers. It was another case of an insured being induced to part with property by a rogue. The claimant had advertised a watch and diamond ring for sale and parted with them in return for what proved to be a worthless forged building society cheque. The Court of Appeal held that he could recover the value of the goods under his household insurance policy, their having been lost by theft.

It could be argued that there are difficulties with this decision. The reasoning of the Court of Appeal was concerned almost exclusively with whether there had been a theft in the criminal law sense, a matter which has caused some degree of difficulty since the enactment of the Theft Act 1968.[142] In so deciding, the court followed the House of Lords' decision in *Lawrence*[143] rather than interpretations of the later decision of the same court in *Morris*[144] and held that there had been a theft because the insured had merely consented to the rogue having his property, rather than giving an express authorisation by his parting with the property. While it is not within the province of this book to give an authoritative view of the criminal law distinction between theft and obtaining property by deception, it has been argued that the Court of Appeal's decision confuses or even obliterates this distinction in an unnecessary way.[145] However, the House of Lords, in the criminal law case of *Gomez*,[146] approved the decision in *Dobson* and confirmed the decision in *Lawrence*. The matter is therefore clearly settled in criminal law terms.

However, it seems difficult to reconcile *Dobson* with the earlier insurance cases just examined, at least if the presence of the word "loss" is meaningful.

---

[140] See 13.3.2.

[141] *Dobson v General Accident Fire & Life Assurance Corp Plc* [1990] 1 Q.B. 274.

[142] As to the distinction between theft and robbery in an insurance context, see *Hayward v Norwich Union Insurance Ltd* [2001] Lloyd's Rep I.R. 410, discussed in 13.3.1.

[143] *Lawrence* [1972] A.C. 626.

[144] *Morris* [1984] A.C. 320.

[145] See Smith and Hogan, *Criminal Law*, 7th edn (Butterworths, 1994) especially at 509–510; Clarkson (1992) 55 M.L.R. 265.

[146] *Gomez* [1993] 1 All E.R. 1.

The facts are in reality indistinguishable from those in *Eisinger*.[147] Was there really a loss of the property, as opposed to a loss of the proceeds? It seems unlikely that the insurers intended the risk of being duped by a rogue to be covered by the wording they adopted. Perhaps the answer to this latter point is that the presence of the word "loss" here is of no significance and that the matter is to be determined solely by what is the proper meaning of theft; as we have seen, that is now abundantly clear. This suggestion is not, however, put forward with any degree of conviction, but if insurers do not wish to cover the risk of their insured being duped by a rogue, to be safe they will have to draft their policies accordingly.

13.8   Cover Provided—Consequential Issues

Having considered the principal rules of construction applicable to determining the cover provided by an insurance policy, and examined some of the common wordings used, it is convenient to look now at three points which are nothing directly to do with these questions, but which follow neatly from them. The first point concerns the timing of the insured peril, the second the question of consequential losses, and the third the question of whether an insured peril must actually operate upon property insured and costs incurred in preventing an insured peril running.

13.8.1 Timing of the insured peril

We have seen earlier[148] that indemnity insurance policies are conventionally of a limited duration, typically for one year at a time.[149] It may often happen, particularly in the context of claims under insurances of land and buildings for loss arising from such matters as subsidence and heave, that the damage caused by a particular event may not evidence itself for some considerable time. It seems self-evident that, in the absence of express provision to the contrary, the insured cannot claim unless he can show that an insured peril occurred during the term of the policy and this was confirmed in *Kelly v Norwich Union Fire Insurance Society Ltd*.[150] Here, leaks from water mains caused the clay under the insured's property to expand and after a period this "heave" caused damage to the property. The crucial leak[151] occurred

---

[147] *Eisinger* [1953] 2 All E.R. 897.

[148] See 5.7.

[149] In contrast life policies are usually entire and the problem dealt with here will not arise in connection therein.

[150] *Kelly v Norwich Union Fire Insurance Society Ltd* [1989] 2 Lloyd's Rep. 333; see [1990] J.B.L. 145.

[151] There was a subsequent leak that occurred after the claimant had taken out the insurance with the defendant, but he accepted that it was impossible to apportion

before the insured effected the insurance with the defendant, which provided that the latter would indemnify the insured "in respect of events occurring during the period of the insurance". The Court of Appeal held that the insurers were not liable. The most likely situation where in practice this principle will not apply is in the context of professional indemnity insurance, where the standard wording generally provides for retrospective cover.[152]

13.8.2 Consequential losses

Insurance of property prima facie covers that property only in respect of the loss attributable to its own value. How that value is measured will be considered in Ch.15. In other words, consequential losses are not recoverable unless they are separately insured. So, for example, in *Maurice v Goldsborough Mort*,[153] where consignees of wool insured it as trustees for the owners, so that they were liable to account to them for the insurance money received following a loss, they could not recover in respect of their loss of commission. Similarly, in the old case of *Re Wright and Pole*,[154] an insured inn was destroyed by fire, but the insured was unable to recover in respect of the loss of custom and the hire of other premises, and in *Theobald v Railway Passengers Assurance Co*,[155] loss of business profits were not recoverable under an accident policy.

It is possible to effect insurance against loss of profits arising as the result of loss of property, and such cover, now known commonly as Interruption Insurance, is popular with businesses.

13.8.3 Must the risk run? Prevention costs

The question that arises here is perhaps partly a matter of cover provided and partly a matter of causation. Traditionally, it is considered under the latter heading, but it is suggested that it is better examined on its own.

The problem simply stated can be put in the following way. If property is insured against a specific loss, can the insured recover if that loss does not actually operate upon the insured property, but it is lost or damaged in

---

blame between the two leaks and that, unless it was shown that the first leak was within the policy, he could not succeed in his claim. Perhaps there should be some mechanism for apportionment in such cases, as claims in respect of events like subsidence and heave are likely to involve events occurring over a substantial period of time.

[152] That is, in respect of claims made against the insured during the policy period, whether or not the negligence occurred earlier.

[153] *Maurice v Goldsborough Mort* [1939] A.C. 452.

[154] *Re Wright and Pole* (1834) 1 A. & E. 621.

[155] *Theobald v Railway Passengers Assurance Co* (1854) 10 Exch. 45.

circumstances when the insured peril was imminent? Furthermore, if there is no loss, but only because the insured incurs expenditure in preventing what would have been a certain loss, can the insured recover this expenditure? We shall deal with these questions separately.

13.8.4 Insured peril imminent

As regards the first, there is clear authority in marine insurance cases that if the peril insured against has happened, and is so imminent that it is about to operate upon the insured property, loss to the property caused by measures necessarily taken to avert the risk happening to the insured property is covered. It can be said that the proximate or real cause of the loss is a peril insured against. In *Symington v Union Insurance of Canton*,[156] cork insured against loss by fire and stored on a jetty was jettisoned by being thrown into the sea to prevent an existing fire from spreading. It was held that the loss was covered, the real cause of it being the fire, an insured peril. It was stated clearly that the peril must have happened and be so imminent that the action was immediately necessary to avert the danger. Although there appear to have been very few non-marine cases on the point,[157] there is no reason to doubt that the same principle would apply, so that if, for example, house contents are insured against fire and are damaged by water to prevent an existing fire spreading, such damage would be covered even if water damage was not covered or was an excepted peril.

13.8.5 Costs of prevention

The answer to the second question is more problematical, there being a clear distinction in that property insured is not actually damaged in any way. Suppose, for example, the case of a house by a river insured against damage by flood. Following heavy storms, the level of the river is rising and it is as certain as it can be that unless measures are taken, the house will be flooded. The insured incurs expenditure in buying equipment that successfully prevents such a flood. Can he recover such costs from his insurer? It might be regarded as a little strange if he could not, if he could prove that had he done nothing, the house would have been damaged by an insured peril and the insurer would have been liable. In marine insurance, a "sue and labour" clause would permit recovery,[158] and by analogy the same principle was applied to the case of a charter party involving marine risks: "sums paid

---

[156] *Symington v Union Insurance of Canton* (1928) 97 L.J.K.B. 646.

[157] One such is *Glen Falls Insurance v Spencer* (1956) 3 D.L.R. (2d.) 745.

[158] *Integrated Container Service Inc v British Traders Insurance Co Ltd* [1984] 1 Lloyd's Rep. 154.

to avert a peril may be recovered as upon a loss by that peril".[159] But in the absence of an express clause, it is not clear whether prevention costs are recoverable in marine insurance.

In *The Knight of St Michael*,[160] a cargo of coal from Newcastle, Australia, to Valparaiso was insured against loss by fire under a marine policy. Because of the overheating of part of the coal, some was discharged in Sydney. This was clearly necessary to prevent its spontaneous combustion. It was held that the consequent loss of freight was within the policy, and it was suggested that it was a "loss by fire", as there was an "actual existing state of peril of fire and not merely a fear of fire", although there was no actual fire. The problem with regarding this decision as clear authority is that there were also general words of cover in the policy covering "other losses" and the learned judge stated the opinion that if the loss was not by fire, it was within the other cover provided. In the United States of America there is clear authority that prevention costs can be recovered under a non-marine policy even in the absence of express coverage.[161] It is thought that this principle could usefully be followed here, and that such costs should be recoverable provided that there is an actual existing state of the peril insured, in other words that loss by a peril insured against is certain; mere danger of such loss would clearly not be sufficient.[162] However, in a fairly recent liability insurance case,[163] the Court of Appeal refused to imply a term that would have permitted the insured to recover such prevention costs,[164] and it must be admitted that this approach seems likely to prevail in English law.

---

[159] *Pyman Steamship Co v Admiralty Commissioners* [1919] 1 K.B. 49 at 53.

[160] *The Knight of St Michael* [1898] P. 30.

[161] *Leebov v United States Fidelity & Guaranty Co* 401 Pa. 477 (1960) (Pennsylvania Supreme Court). A contractor caused a landslide, but, before it could do much damage, incurred expense in preventing it from causing certain further damage. It was held that his liability insurer was liable in respect of this expense. See further, note (1971) 71 Col.L.R. 1309.

[162] *Becker, Gray & Co v London Assurance Corp* [1918] A.C. 101.

[163] *Yorkshire Water Services Ltd v Sun Alliance & London Insurance Plc* [1997] C.L.C. 213. See also *Corbin v Payne, The Times*, 11 October 1990 and *Liverpool London & Globe Insurance Ltd v Canadian General Electric Co Ltd* (1981) 123 D.L.R. (3d.) 513, where the Supreme Court of Canada refused to permit the recovery of prevention costs where the insured risk had not actually begun to operate. It should also be noted that, if prevention costs were claimed under a fire policy, and it was a loss by fire that had been prevented, there is the old authority of *Austin v Drewe* (see 13.5), requiring that there must be actual ignition, which would have to be distinguished.

[164] One reason was that the policy contained a express term requiring the insured to take reasonable care and this made it clear that any prevention costs were to be at the insured's expense, but in addition the Court of Appeal ruled out the possibility of implying the equivalent of a sue and labour clause.

13.9   Causation

As has been noted several times in the course of this chapter, it is not sufficient, in order that an insured should recover for a loss, that the loss falls within the cover provided as a matter of construction or definition. He must also show that the loss was proximately caused by an insured peril.[165] The proximate cause does not, however, mean the last cause, but the effective, dominant or real cause.[166] Working out what is the proximate cause in any situation is strictly a question of fact, so that decided cases cannot be binding but are merely illustrations. It should be noted that the doctrine can be excluded by appropriate wording.[167]

It has already been seen how the doctrine can operate to find an insurer liable where the insured peril is the real cause but not the actual instrument of the loss.[168] Otherwise it seems most relevant, and indeed it has been said to be relevant only really at all, in a case where, on the facts, there can genuinely be said to be competing causes of a loss, one of which is specifically covered by the policy and the other of which is excepted.[169] Whether the doctrine can be at all relevant where there can be no question of an excepted peril is a matter to be considered later.

13.9.1   Determining the proximate cause

It has been said that determining the proximate cause of a loss is simply the application of common sense, and in many of the cases that would appear to be so. In *Marsden v City & County Insurance*,[170] for example, a shopkeeper insured his plate-glass against loss or damage arising from any cause except

---

[165] For a useful review, see Clarke [1981] CLJ 284.

[166] The classical explanation of the doctrine of proximate cause is the judgment of Lord Sumner in *Becker, Gray & Co v London Assurance Corp* [1918] A.C. 101.

[167] For an example in a household policy, see *Oei v Foster* [1982] 2 Lloyd's Rep. 170; see [1982] J.B.L. 516.

[168] *Symington v Union Insurance of Canton* (1928) 97 L.J.K.B. 646; see 13.8.4.

[169] Lord Dunedin in *Leyland Shipping Co v Norwich Union Fire Insurance Society* [1918] A.C. 350 at 363. This point is supported by *JJ Lloyd (Instruments) Ltd v Northern Star Insurance Co Ltd* [1987] 1 Lloyd's Rep. 32, where there were found to be two proximate causes of the damage suffered by a cruiser; adverse weather conditions and defective design. It was held that, as defective design was not an excepted peril and adverse weather was not required to be the sole cause, the insurers were liable. See also *Global Process Systems v Syarikat Takaful Malaysia Berhad, The Cendor MOPU* [2011] UKSC 5; [2011] Lloyd's Rep. I.R. 302, where the insured property was an oil rig and fatigue failure and consequent cracking led to loss of three of its legs during an ocean voyage. It was held that the real cause of the loss was the perils of the sea (the classic insured peril in marine policies) and not any inherent vice in the property, even where the actions of wind and waves were foreseeable.

[170] *Marsden v City & County Insurance* (1865) L.R. 1 C.P. 232.

fire. Fire broke out in a neighbour's property, as the result of which a mob gathered. The mob then rioted and broke the plate-glass. It was held that this riot, not the fire, was the cause of the loss and thus the insured recovered. In effect, the fire merely facilitated the subsequent loss rather than caused it. In *Winicofsky v Army & Navy Insurance*,[171] goods were stolen from a building during an air raid. It was held that the theft not the air raid was the real cause of the loss; the latter merely facilitated it.

13.9.2 Two real causes

If it truly can be said that there are two real causes of a loss, discovering the cause which is the proximate cause is not always an easy matter. In a leading marine insurance case, *Leyland Shipping Co v Norwich Union Fire Insurance Society Ltd*,[172] a ship was insured against loss from perils of the sea, with an exception in respect of loss due to hostilities. The ship was torpedoed by an enemy boat during the First World War. It was towed to Le Havre and moored in the harbour where it was quite safe. Subsequently, the harbour authorities required that it be moved to just outside the harbour. There, because of the action of the sea, it sank. It was held that the loss was not covered, the real cause being the torpedoing and not the perils of the sea. Yet had the ship not been moved outside the harbour, it would have been all right. The point is that the original cause predominates and is regarded as the real cause of the loss unless it was merely facilitating a subsequent cause that totally changed matters.

This analysis, however, does not appear to fit very well with some of what have been called the accident cases. There has been a great number of cases on questions of causation in accident policies, two of which will suffice here for detailed illustration. In *Winspear v Accident Insurance Association*,[173] the policy covered death or injury "caused by accidental, external and visible means" and excluded "any injury caused by or arising from natural disease". While crossing a stream, the insured suffered a fit, fell in and was drowned. It was held that the cause of death was accidental, namely the drowning, and not the fit, even though had it not been for the latter the insured would not have died as the stream was very shallow. *Lawrence v Accidental Insurance Co*[174] is even stranger in that the policy, while including the same wording, also required that accidental injury be the "direct and sole cause" of death. There the insured suffered a fit while standing on a railway platform. This caused him to fall on to the track, whereupon he was run over by a train.

---

[171] *Winicofsky v Army & Navy Insurance* (1919) 88 L.J.K.B. 111.
[172] *Leyland Shipping Co v Norwich Union Fire Insurance Society Ltd* [1918] A.C. 350.
[173] *Winspear v Accident Insurance Association* (1880) 6 Q.B.D. 42.
[174] *Lawrence v Accidental Insurance Co* (1881) 7 Q.B.D. 216.

It was held that the accident of being run over was the proximate cause of death.

Decisions like these can be interpreted in different ways. For example, it might be said that the natural cause, the fit, merely facilitated the real, accidental cause, but if that is so, surely it could be said of the *Leyland Shipping* case that the torpedoing merely facilitated the sinking by the perils of the sea. Alternatively, the judges[175] may have been interpreting "proximate" as meaning latest, which subsequent cases[176] revealed clearly to be wrong. A further possibility is that the cases can be justified on the ground that the accident superseded the prior, excluded, cause, to such an extent that it constituted a totally fresh cause,[177] but, with respect, this is difficult to understand on the facts. Perhaps the best explanation is the generosity of the English judges who decided these cases. Needless to say, insurers have been astute to draft changes in wordings so as to attempt to gain a more favourable result in this sort of case and more recent case law reveals that they have succeeded.

In *Jason v Batten*,[178] the policy provided benefits to the insured if he sustained "in any accident bodily injury resulting in and being—independently of all other causes—the exclusive, direct and immediate cause of the injury or disablement". There was an exception in respect of "death, injury or disablement directly or indirectly caused by or arising or resulting from or traceable to . . . any physical defect or infirmity that existed prior to an accident". The insured suffered a coronary thrombosis after being involved in a motor accident, the clot blocking a coronary artery that had been narrowed by disease existing before the accident. It was held that the insurers were not liable. Stress associated with the accident had precipitated the thrombosis, but, assuming that the clot was an injury sustained in the accident, it was not "independently of all other causes" the exclusive cause of the insured's disablement. Equally efficient was the pre-existing disease. In addition, it was said, the loss fell clearly within the exception. It would appear therefore, that with the phrase "independently of all other causes" insurers should ensure that they are liable under their personal accident policies only when there is an accident and nothing else. This view is supported by the Court of Appeal decision in *Blackburn Rovers Football & Athletic Club Ltd v Avon Insurance Plc*.[179]

---

[175] See, especially, Watkin Williams J in *Lawrence v Accidental Insurance Co*, above, at 229.

[176] Especially the leading House of Lords cases of *Becker, Grey & Co v London Assurance Corp* [1918] A.C. 101 and *Leyland Shipping Co v Norwich Union Fire Insurance Society* [1918] A.C. 350. See also *Wayne Tank Co v Employer's Liability Assurance Corp* [1974] 1 Q.B. 57 at 66 (Lord Denning MR) and 72 (Roskill LJ).

[177] See the explanation in *Jason v Batten* [1969] 1 Lloyd's Rep. 281 at 291.

[178] *Jason v Batten* [1969] 1 Lloyd's Rep. 281.

[179] *Blackburn Rovers Football & Athletic Club Ltd v Avon Insurance Plc* [2005] EWCA Civ 423; [2005] Lloyd's Rep. 447.

A policy provided cover in respect of accidental bodily injury which solely and independently of any other cause occasioned disablement, but excluded "permanent total disablement attributable either directly or indirectly to arthritic or other degenerative conditions, in joints, bones, muscles, tendons or ligaments". The claimants had obtained the policy to cover one of their employees, a professional footballer, who suffered an injury to his back while taking part in a practice match. The injury effectively ended his professional career. The insurers rejected a claim under the policy on the ground that disablement had not been caused by the injury alone but resulted directly or indirectly from a degenerative condition of the lower spine. It was held that the exclusion had to be construed as potentially applicable to degeneration experienced by the majority of footballers (although it would still be open on the medical evidence to conclude that the degree of degeneration did not fall within the phrase "arthritic or other degenerative conditions"). Further following *Jason v Batten*, it was arguable that the degeneration was a proximate cause of the injury and that, because it contained the phrase "attributable either directly or indirectly", the exclusion applied.[180]

13.9.3 Two proximate causes

It may be that in a case without such a clause qualifying the proximate cause rule, the court cannot genuinely say that one cause is more effective than another, so that an excepted cause and a covered cause are equally strong. This was a possible view of the facts in *Wayne Tank and Pump Co Ltd v Employers' Liability Insurance Corporation Ltd*.[181] Wayne Tank was held liable to pay damages to Harbutt's "Plasticine" Ltd for breach of a contract under which they installed new equipment in Harbutt's factory.[182] The equipment was defective and a resultant fire gutted the factory. Wayne Tank were insured by the defendants under a public liability policy which excluded

---

[180] As to the sequel, where the insurers' rejection was upheld, see *Blackburn Rovers Football and Athletic Club Ltd v Avon Insurance Plc (No.2)* [2006] EWHC 840; [2007] Lloyd's Rep. I.R. 1.

[181] *Wayne Tank and Pump Co Ltd v Employers' Liability Insurance Corp Ltd* [1974] 1 Q.B. 57. See also *Midland Mainline Ltd v Eagle Star Insurance Co Ltd* [2004] EWCA Civ 1042; [2004] Lloyd's Rep. I.R. 739; *Tektrol Ltd v International Insurance Co of Hanover Ltd* [2005] 1 All E.R. (Comm) 132 and *ENE Kos 1 Ltd v Petroleo Brasileiro SA, The Kos* [2012] UKSC 17 (which concerned an indemnity clause in a charterparty).

[182] *Harbutt's "Plasticine" Ltd v Wayne Tank and Pump Co Ltd* [1970] 1 Q.B. 447. Had this case been decided correctly (see *Photo Production Ltd v Securicor Transport Ltd* [1980] 2 W.L.R. 283), the subsequent insurance case would not have arisen. Harbutt's insurers rather than one of Wayne Tank's insurers would have borne the loss. It is clear that the insurance case was in substance a battle between two of the latter's insurers.

indemnity for liability arising from damage caused by the nature or condition of any goods supplied by the insured. One cause of Wayne Tank's liability was the defective nature of the equipment used, but another cause was the fact that one of its employees negligently and quite without authority turned on the equipment and left it on all night. Had this not happened, it was likely that the loss would not have occurred, as the equipment would have been tested under supervision and found to have been defective before any damage could be done.

However, the Court of Appeal was unanimous in holding that the real cause of the loss was the defective nature of the equipment, a conclusion clearly in accordance with authority such as the *Leyland Shipping* case, whereby the original cause predominates unless it merely facilitates the subsequent cause and the latter totally alters the situation. The Court commented obiter, though, on the result if it could not genuinely be said that one of the two causes was predominant, and held that the insurers would still be protected, on the ground that they had provided for exemption from liability for one of the causes and the only way to ensure this was to exempt them totally. It is perhaps unfortunate that they did not consider the possibility in such a case of apportionment of the loss.[183]

13.9.4 Cause not expressly exempted

One final point remains to be discussed. As was seen earlier, it was stated in one of the leading cases that the question of competition between causes becomes relevant only when there are two causes and one of them is expressly covered and the other is expressly exempted. In the case of *Gray v Barr*,[184] however, which we have already discussed,[185] Lord Denning MR introduced the causation point where there was no express exclusion of a possible cause of the loss. In his view the proximate cause of the liability of the defendant Barr was not the shooting of the gun, whether that was an accident or not, but his deliberate conduct in approaching and grappling with the deceased while holding a loaded shotgun. Although neither of the other judges mentioned the causation point, and thus it cannot form part of the ratio of the case, consideration of it is logical. It seems unlikely though, that it will matter in practice if it is considered.[186] In a case like *Gray v Barr*, the same result can be, and indeed was, reached simply on the construction of "accident" and/or the application of principles of public policy. This would seem

---

[183] See Ahmed (1974) 124 N.L.J. 592.

[184] *Gray v Barr* [1971] 2 Q.B. 551.

[185] See 13.6.4.

[186] Compare the case of *JJ Lloyd (Instruments) Ltd v Northern Star Insurance Co Ltd* [1987] 1 Lloyd's Rep. 32, described in fn.169, above.

likely to be the position in most cases, that is, that the same result can be achieved by considering whether the loss came within the cover provided as a matter of construction or definition.

There is one type of case, though, where consideration of the causation rule, even though there is no question of an expressly excepted peril, might make a difference. This is where a possible cause of the loss is natural, whether from wear and tear or from the natural actions of living objects. An example, as pointed out earlier, is *Mills v Smith*.[187] The learned judge in that case considered the matter as simply one of construction of the words "caused by accident", but if his attention had been directed towards the discovery of the proximate cause of the loss, the result might have been different.

---

[187] *Mills v Smith* [1964] 1 Q.B. 30.

CHAPTER 14

CLAIMS UNDER THE POLICY

14.0

Claiming for a loss under an insurance policy may be considered to involve not simply the formal requirements usually imposed upon the insured, but also the question of the possible application of the rules of public policy and the law regarding the making of fraudulent claims. It is convenient also to examine some of the issues that may arise when claims are settled.

14.1   Public Policy

In a famous dictum,[1] a judge once referred to public policy as an "unruly horse", and it is clear that in the insurance field as much as in any other, care is needed in assessing the relevance of public policy considerations.[2] There seem to be two relevant basic maxims which apply throughout the law, first, a ex turpi causa non oritur actio (no action can arise from a wrongful cause) and secondly, people may not profit from their own wrongs or crimes, the latter probably being merely a particular application of the former.[3] The very application of these maxims to claims on insurance policies may be questioned in some instances, but, even assuming that it is sensible to apply them, how they actually apply is not always clear. It is convenient to subdivide the insurance cases into two basic groups, namely first and third party insurance. It should be noted that insurers often put in express exclusions in respect of

---

[1] Burrough J in *Richardson v Mellish* (1824) 2 Bing. 229 at 252.

[2] In so far as the application of public policy in any of the insurance cases rests on the "public conscience", it may perhaps have to be reconsidered in the light of *Tinsley v Milligan* [1994] 1 A.C. 340. However, it is thought that the views of the House of Lords in *Tinsley v Milligan* should affect only cases where a contract is unlawful from its inception. What we are concerned with here is simply where performance of a contract may be denied on public policy grounds. See generally, Clarke, "Illegal insurance" [1987] L.M.C.L.Q. 201 and Clarke, "Insurance of wilful misconduct: the court as keeper of the public conscience" (1996) 7 Ins. L.J. 173.

[3] For a useful brief summary in an insurance case, see the judgment of Kerr LJ in *Euro-Diam Ltd v Bathurst* [1988] 2 All E.R. 23 at 28–30. Although aspects of this judgments were commented on adversely in *Tinsley v Milligan*, above, it is thought that this ignored the different situation in insurance cases; see fn.2. The ex turpi causa rule has been the subject of a number of non-insurance recent cases, especially *Gray v Thames Trains Ltd* [2009] UKHL 33; [2009] 1 A.C. 1339 and *Safeway Stores Ltd v Twigger* [2010] EWCA Civ 1472; [2011] 1 Lloyd's Rep. 462.

losses that the general public policy rules would probably cover and may well
rely on these rather than those general rules.[4]

14.2   First Party Insurances

If an insured is claiming in respect of a loss suffered solely by him, then
it is clear, as we have already seen,[5] that he cannot recover if the loss was
caused by his deliberate act. This may be simply the true construction of an
insurance contract,[6] or it may alternatively be regarded as the application of
a principle of public policy.[7] In *WH Smith v Clinton*,[8] an indemnity granted
to a publisher against libel was held to be unenforceable, at least where the
libel was intentional. In addition, there is a general principle flowing from
the maxims mentioned, that an insured cannot recover in respect of a loss
caused by his own criminal or tortious act. This was neatly applied in the case
of *Geismar v Sun Alliance and London Insurance*.[9] Here the insured smuggled
certain items of jewellery into Britain without declaring them and paying
the legally required excise duty on them. As a result, they were liable to be
forfeited. They were among items subsequently insured by him with the
defendant and later stolen. It was held that the insured could not recover
in respect of this jewellery, as to allow such recovery would enable him to
profit from his deliberate criminal act, even though the profit was sought
indirectly under the insurance policy. In contrast, the ex turpi causa rule did
not prevent recovery in *Euro-Diam Ltd v Bathurst*,[10] where diamonds sent by
the insured on sale or return to a customer in Germany were stolen from the
latter's warehouse. At the latter's request, the insured had supplied an invoice
understating the price of the diamonds. This was to enable the customer to
deceive the German tax authorities. Even though the insureds probably knew
this, they were not precluded from recovering on their policy since they were
not relying on any illegality and the only person who stood to benefit from
it was the customer.[11]

---

[4] See, for example, the cases discussed in 13.2.1.

[5] See 13.2.1.

[6] *Beresford v Royal Insurance Co* [1938] A.C. 586.

[7] Shand, "Unblinkering the unruly horse: public policy in the law of contract" (1972)
30 C.L.J. 144 at 161.

[8] *WH Smith v Clinton* (1908) 99 L.T. 840. See also Defamation Act 1952 s.11
confirming that indemnity or insurance against unintentional defamation is
enforceable.

[9] *Geismar v Sun Alliance and London Insurance* [1977] 2 Lloyd's Rep. 62.

[10] *Euro-Diam Ltd v Bathurst* [1988] 2 All E.R. 23.

[11] As mentioned in fn.3, above, some of the reasoning in this case attracted unfavourable comment in the House of Lords decision in *Tinsley v Milligan* [1994] 1 A.C.
340. The latter decision would seem to suggest that if the insured stands to profit
from his own illegal act that is an end to it; there is no question of then considering

Public policy will debar someone who has murdered a life insured from claiming the proceeds of the policy as beneficiary under the life insured's will,[12] on the latter's intestacy or as co-insured or nominee under the policy.[13]

It would seem that the commission of a crime or tort must be deliberate. It has often been recognised that insane suicide, when a crime, did not prevent recovery under a life policy.[14] So, for example, an insured might unintentionally commit a crime of strict liability in circumstances giving rise to a claim on his policy, but it is suggested that he would not be debarred from recovery. A nice question arises concerning the interrelationship of the two principles mentioned. The rule that deliberate acts per se are not covered can, because it is not an overriding requirement of public policy, be expressly excluded. The usual example is the inclusion of suicide, sane or insane, in the cover provided by a life policy, although normally only after the policy has run for a period of one or two years. If the commission of such an act, however, is also criminal or tortious, the question arises whether the maxims of public policy debar recovery. The answer would appear to be in the affirmative, following the leading case of *Beresford v Royal Insurance Co.*[15] Here the life insured deliberately took his own life at a time when suicide was still a crime. It was arguable, and indeed was held, that on the construction of the policy death by suicide was covered, but the House of Lords nevertheless denied the insured's representative recovery. The principal ground for the decision was that recovery would permit a benefit to result to the insured from his criminal act,[16] although it was recognised that an assignee for value of the policy would have been entitled to recover, because then there could not be said to be such benefit. However, there must be a public policy in favour of enforcing contractual obligations which one party has freely undertaken. If the insurer had contracted to pay on the suicide of the life insured, why should they not have been held to that promise? This point was discussed by Lord MacMillan who concluded that the public policy considerations had to be weighed, finally concurring with the result in this way:

whether or not recovery would offend the "public conscience", as was reasoned in *Euro-Diam Ltd v Bathurst*. It is suggested that the public conscience test is still useful in insurance cases, for the reason given in fn.2. In any event, the decision in *Euro-Diam Ltd v Bathurst* must still be good since, as indicated in the text, there was no question of the insured benefiting from their illegal act.

[12] *Cleaver v Mutual Reserve Fund Life Association* [1892] 1 Q.B. 147.

[13] See, e.g. *Davitt v Titcumb* [1989] 3 All E.R 417, where the defendant, who had murdered his partner, had no claim to a share of the proceeds of the endowment policy effected by them jointly to cover their mortgage.

[14] *Beresford v Royal Insurance Co* [1938] A.C. 586.

[15] Above. See also *Husak v Imperial Life Assurance Co of Canada* (1970) 9 D.L.R. (3d.) 602.

[16] As will be seen, Lord Atkin referred also to other public policy principles.

"I feel the force of the view that to increase the estate which a criminal leaves behind him is to benefit him . . . And no criminal can be allowed to benefit in any way by his crime."[17]

It may be thought that this is slightly unreal, a point to which we shall return when assessing the public policy question in general. There can be little doubt now that the actual result of the *Beresford* case would be different, not least because suicide is no longer a crime.[18] Further, in respect of life assurance, account must now be taken of the provisions of the Forfeiture Act 1982.[19] Section 2 of this Act gives the court a wide discretion to allow a claim by someone who has unlawfully killed another to the benefits of, inter alia, a life insurance policy. It cannot apply where the claimant is guilty of murder[20] nor does it apply to cases of suicide,[21] but it would be apt to cover a case of manslaughter where there was no intention or recklessness.[22]

14.3   Third Party Insurances

Turning to consider the cases involving third party policies, the same general principles apply.[23] Thus, the intentional commission of a crime against the third party for which the insured is liable in damages in tort will not be covered by the insured's liability insurance. However, it is not clear what degree of deliberation is required, and it can be said again that there are competing public policy considerations involved.[24] In a sense, the idea of the insured benefiting from his own wrong in this sort of case is ridiculous, as any indemnity received goes to his third party victim. Furthermore, there is surely an important public policy consideration in attempting to ensure that the victims of tortfeasors receive any damages awarded to them, which in practice means in the majority of cases that the tortfeasor ought to be allowed to enforce his insurance policy.[25] This has at least been recognised in the context of compulsory motor vehicle insurance, and there are four important cases that support this line of argument. These cases will be

---

[17] *Beresford v Royal Insurance Co* [1938] A.C. 586 at 605.

[18] Suicide Act 1961; see the comment of Salmon LJ in *Gray v Barr* [1971] 2 Q.B. 554 at 582.

[19] See generally, Kenny (1983) 46 M.L.R. 66.

[20] Section 5.

[21] Because it only applies where the beneficiary has killed "another" (s.1).

[22] See *Re S (deceased)* [1996] 1 W.L.R. 235.

[23] The Forfeiture Act is of no relevance here because of the requirement in s.2(4) that the claimant has an "interest in property".

[24] See generally the excellent analysis by Shand in the article referred to in fn.7.

[25] Public policy will not prevent a liability insured from being indemnified against liability to pay exemplary damages, at least where the insured did not act criminally: *Lancashire County Council v Municipal Mutual Insurance Ltd* [1996] 3 All E.R. 545.

examined first, before we consider whether there are any differences in any other contexts.

14.3.1 Motor insurance

Tinline v White Cross Insurance Association[26] and *James v British General Insurance Co*[27] arose out of similar situations. The insured in both cases had third party cover in respect of injury or death arising out of the use of their cars, although this was not actually compulsory at the time. They were both involved in accidents resulting in the deaths of pedestrians in circumstances that led to their convictions for manslaughter. In *Tinline*, the insured was driving at an excessive speed; in *James*, he was drunk. Clearly both insureds were more than merely negligent, but on the other hand did not intend death or injury. In both cases it was held that their insurers were liable to indemnify them against the damages they were liable to pay in tort, despite the fact that, in the sense that the courts have used elsewhere, they would thereby profit from their own criminal actions.

If the insured acts deliberately, however, it appears that public policy is still against his recovering. This was made clear in the judgments in *Hardy v Motor Insurers' Bureau*.[28] This case involved the deliberate injury of the claimant by an uninsured car thief. The claimant's claim against the defendant was resisted on public policy grounds. The Court of Appeal made it quite clear that, had the tortfeasor himself been seeking to enforce a motor policy, he would have been denied, but fortunately the Road Traffic Act 1988[29] permits a third party victim to sue the tortfeasor's insurer directly and, where the tortfeasor is uninsured, there is a right of action against the Motor Insurers' Bureau.[30] Thus, on the facts of the case, there was no question of the ex turpi causa maxim applying, and this will be the case in respect of all victims of car accidents. In what is perhaps the most lucid rationalisation by an English judge[31] of the place of public policy in the insurance context, Diplock LJ referred to the importance of weighing up the different considerations:

> "I can see no reason in public policy for drawing a distinction between one kind of wrongful act, of which a third party is the innocent victim, and another kind of wrongful act; between wrongful acts which are crimes on the part of the perpetrator and wrongful acts which are not crimes; or between wrongful

---

[26] *Tinline v White Cross Insurance Association* [1921] 3 K.B. 327.

[27] *James v British General Insurance Co* [1927] 1 K.B. 311.

[28] *Hardy v Motor Insurers' Bureau* [1964] 2 Q.B. 745. See now also *Charlton v Fisher* [2001] All E.R.(D.) 20.

[29] s.151; see 21.5.

[30] See Ch.21.

[31] Followed in Australia in *Fire & All Risks Co Ltd v Powell* [1966] V.R. 513.

acts which are crimes of carelessness and wrongful acts which are intentional crimes. It seems to me to be slightly unrealistic to suggest that a person who is not deterred by the risks of a possible sentence of life imprisonment from using a vehicle with intent to commit grievous bodily harm would be deterred by the fear that his civil liability to his victim would not be discharged by his insurers."[32]

The decision in *Hardy* was approved and followed by the House of Lords in *Gardner v Moore*,[33] where the facts were indistinguishable and it was held that the proper construction of the Road Traffic Act 1988 and the Motor Insurers' Bureau agreements, and the policy underlying them, required the MIB to satisfy the motorist's liability to the innocent claimant.[34]

14.3.2 Other compulsory insurances

The immediate question that arises is how far this sort of reasoning can be applied outside the motor insurance field. It is suggested that it will be applied wherever else third party insurance is compulsory in respect of personal injury or death, and particularly therefore to employers' liability insurance.[35] The fact that an employee is injured in circumstances involving a criminal offence, for example under health and safety legislation, should not entitle his employer's insurer to invoke the defence of public policy, if the employer is liable in tort to the employee, however great the degree of negligence or recklessness. Considerations as to the insured's profiting from his wrong or not being deterred if insurance moneys are available, are outweighed by the consideration that Parliament deemed it of the utmost importance that injured employees should be compensated by making this insurance compulsory.

If, however, the crime or tort was intentionally committed by the employer or someone for whom he is responsible, then it is possible that the claim for insurance indemnity could be denied, because there is no machinery equivalent to the Road Traffic Act provisions for the injured employee to sue the insurer directly, and thus any litigation would necessitate the insured employer directly enforcing the policy to recover in respect of a deliberate wrong, something which even under *Hardy v Motor Insurers' Bureau* and *Gardner v Moore*, the courts would not permit.

---

[32] *Hardy v MIB* [1964] 2 Q.B. at 769–770.
[33] *Gardner v Moore* [1984] A.C. 548.
[34] In the words of Lord Hailsham LC above at 561–562: "To invoke, as [the MIB] now do, the well-known doctrine of public policy that a man may not profit by the consequences of his own wrongdoing seems to me to stand the principle of public policy on its head."
[35] See Ch.22.

14.3.3 Other third party insurances

Outside these areas where the countervailing public policy considerations can be invoked, it seems that the courts will, despite the more liberal tenor of the judgments in *Hardy*, adhere to the traditional approach. In *Haseldine v Hosken*,[36] for example, a solicitor sought to enforce his professional indemnity policy in respect of a loss he had suffered by entering into a champertous agreement. Despite his claim that he had not known that he was committing a criminal offence, a claim that in any event it might be difficult to believe, the Court of Appeal held that he was unable to recover.[37] Scrutton LJ commented:

> "It is clearly contrary to public policy to insure against the commission of an act, knowing what act is being committed, which is a crime, although the person committing it may not at the time know it to be so."

These are very wide words, appearing to make no distinction between negligent and intentional crimes.[38]

Whether such a distinction can be drawn must depend on the effect of the decision in *Gray v Barr*,[39] although it is not easy to formulate precisely from the judgments here exactly what principles of public policy are to be applied. This case was also considered in Ch.13.[40] It will be recalled that it concerned the man who shot and killed his wife's lover. Although he was acquitted of both murder and manslaughter by a jury in a criminal trial, the Court of Appeal held in the civil action that he was in fact guilty of manslaughter, a conclusion that cannot itself be faulted. It was also held that, apart from any questions as to the construction of his insurance policy, public policy required that he could not recover from his insurers the damages he was liable to pay in tort to the deceased's widow. All three judges regarded as of the utmost significance the fact that Barr carried a loaded shotgun and threatened violence with it, thus engaging in a wilful and culpable act. The public conscience would be shocked, it was said, if he were allowed to enforce his insurance contract. Yet it may be noted that the public conscience of

---

[36] *Haseldine v Hosken* [1933] 1 K.B. 822. See also *Charlton v Fisher*, fn.28 above.

[37] Another reason for the decision was that on its true construction the policy did not cover the loss in question.

[38] In fact the court doubted the correctness of the decisions in *Tinline* and *James*, doubts that were not finally removed until the decision in *Gray v Barr* [1971] 2 Q.B. 554.

[39] *Gray v Barr* [1971] 2 Q.B. 554. See also, *Co-operative Fire & Casualty Co v Saindon* (1975) 56 D.L.R. (3d) 556, justly criticised by Hasson in (1976) 14 OHLJ 769 and *Meah v McCreamer (No.2)* [1986] 1 All E.R. 943 at 950–951.

[40] See 13.6.4.

the 12 of the public who sat as the jury in the criminal trial can hardly have been shocked by Barr's actions as the "wronged husband". Can it really be said that permitting him to recover would have encouraged the greater use of violence and guns, which is implicit in the court's reasoning? These more general questions will be returned to shortly. *Gray v Barr* did at least recognise that the motor manslaughter cases were correctly decided, but the problem is whether these are sui generis, or whether there are other distinguishing features. The stress laid in the judgments on the intentional aspects of Barr's conduct, that is the use of a loaded gun quite deliberately, does support the view, perhaps, that genuinely negligent criminal acts by an insured will not invoke the defence of public policy if committed in the course of perfectly lawful behaviour. If, for example, a sportsman with an appropriate liability policy negligently shoots someone mistaking them for a deer, it is suggested that he should be able to enforce the policy in respect of any damages he has to pay.

The present public policy rules can therefore probably be summarised in this way. In motor insurance on the personal injury side, and probably in employers' liability insurance, only deliberate criminal conduct could possibly prevent an insured from enforcing a claim on public policy grounds. In all other cases, mere negligence in the commission of a crime or tort would not matter, but public policy will be a good defence where the act causing the loss was deliberate or reckless and where the insured deliberately, or possibly recklessly, engaged in a criminal course of conduct, even if the final act causing the loss was accidental. It should be noted that there is also clear authority that insurance against the consequences of crime is strictly unenforceable for reasons of public policy.[41] Indeed, such insurance may itself be void, rather than merely a claim made under it. So, for example, insurance against parking fines would be against public policy. The same must apply to what used to be a common form of insurance, namely that offered to motorists against the consequences of being "breathalysed".[42] It is a criminal offence to drive with more than the permitted level of alcohol in the blood. Policies offering chauffeur services, or an equivalent, for the period of the mandatory year's disqualification following such a conviction, must have fallen within this prohibition. In 1988, the Government threatened to outlaw such insurance by statute. It appears that insurers have voluntarily ceased to offer such insurance.

---

[41] *Hardy v MIB* [1964] 2 Q.B. 745 at 760.
[42] This was the subject of the decision in *DTI v St Christopher's Motorists' Assurance Ltd* [1974] 1 All E.R. 395, discussed at 1.6.5.

14.4   Some General Comments

Running through these cases appear to be a number of justifications for these principles of public policy. Some of these we have already briefly examined and they have all been the subject of detailed scrutiny elsewhere,[43] but it is appropriate here to make some general comments. The principles appear to rest particularly upon three points. First, there is the idea that refusing to allow indemnity will deter others. Secondly, there is the theme that it is right to punish an insured in this way. Thirdly, there is what has been called the absolute rule, that, simply, the courts should not allow someone to profit from their wrong. With great respect, it is suggested that deterrence and punishment should have no place in the civil law. While Mr Barr was no doubt punished as a result of the Court of Appeal's ruling, which was tantamount to the imposition of a fine on him, is this proper when at a criminal trial he had been acquitted? Can it really be said that someone in his position would be deterred from using a gun when the prospect of life imprisonment did not do so? Furthermore, as has already been argued, the idea that insurance being available means that the insured will profit from his wrong is curious, at least in cases of suicide and third party insurance.

> "In most cases of insurance . . . the people most likely to be harmed by withholding indemnity are the innocent victims of the fault insured against, who more likely than not will be left with an empty judgment against a man of straw."[44]

As has already been noted, there were signs of a more rational approach in *Hardy v Motor Insurers' Bureau*, but the effect of this, other than in the motor insurance field, appears to have been quite overlooked in *Gray v Barr*. It is submitted that in all these cases, all the factors should be weighed, in other words, the particular gravity of the conduct of the insured against the likely real consequences of refusing to enforce the insurance.[45] However, the prospect of the courts' doing this without legislative intervention appears remote.[46]

---

[43] See, in particular, the articles by Clarke (fn.2) and Shand (fn.7) and the note by Fleming (1971) 34 M.L.R. 176 on the first instance decision in *Gray v Barr* which, on public policy, was to the same effect as that of the Court of Appeal.

[44] Shand (1972) 30 C.L.J. 144 at 160.

[45] Applying these sorts of considerations to the facts of *Gray v Barr*, Shand (above at 164) suggests that the result would and should have been different.

[46] Furthermore, the notion of using a "public conscience" test to determine the issue, as suggested in *Euro-Diam Ltd v Bathurst* [1988] 2 All E.R. 23 has been expressly disapproved in *Tinsley v Milligan* [1994] 1 A.C. 340.

14.5 The Claims Procedure

In the absence of any specific term in an insurance policy, it is undecided whether, upon suffering a loss, an insured is bound to claim for it within a reasonable time on pain of the claim being denied, or whether it is sufficient merely to claim before the statutory limitation period expires.[47] In practice, this is a purely academic question, as all policies contain conditions regarding such matters as when notice of a loss is required to be given and what claims procedure and what proofs, etc. are required. Commonly such conditions will be conditions precedent to the liability of the insurer, a breach of which will entitle the insurer to avoid liability for the particular loss, or, possibly, conditions precedent to the validity of the policy.[48] If such a condition is not made precedent to liability, a breach will simply entitle the insurer to claim damages for such loss as it has suffered.[49]

In general, as with any other part of the insurance contract, an insurer is free to insert whatever conditions it chooses in this regard. The Statement of General Insurance Practice used to state that an insured would not be asked to report a claim and subsequent developments except "as soon as reasonably possible", but, as we have seen,[50] the Statement was withdrawn when the Financial Services Authority (now the Financial Conduct Authority) took over the regulation of general insurance business. The Insurance Conduct of Business Sourcebook does not contain this requirement, but it does require that an insurer must not unreasonably reject a claim[51] and imposes various requirements with regard to the handling of a claim. Further, any term regarding the claims procedure in a consumer insurance policy which is "unfair" will be struck down under Pt 2 of the Consumer Rights Act 2015.[52]

The matters that are usually contained in conditions governing the claims procedure can be examined under a number of heads.

---

[47] *MacGillivray on Insurance Law*, 13th edn, para.20–037, suggests that there would be such an obligation as part of the insured's duty to act with good faith.

[48] See 9.11. A condition making the giving of notice a proviso, as in "provided that the insured shall give notice", has been held to be precedent to liability: *Millichap v Pontrillas Timber and Builders Merchants Ltd*, unreported, November 1992.

[49] See above. It may be difficult to show a causal link between the breach and any loss suffered by the insurer: *Porter v Zurich Insurance Co* [2009] EWHC 376 (QB).

[50] See 1.9.1.

[51] ICOBS 8.1.1. See 9.12.

[52] See generally 6.1 and the decision in *Parker v NFU Mutual Insurance Society Ltd* [2012] EWHC 2156 (Comm), which is considered in 14.7.

14.6   Notice

The first basic obligation is to give notice of a loss. If the policy is a third party policy, the condition may well require that notice be given of any event that is likely to give rise to a claim against the insured in addition to an actual claim.[53] Oral notice is sufficient unless the policy provides otherwise.

Such conditions are strictly construed against the insurer. In *Verelst's Administratrix v Motor Union Insurance Company*,[54] a motor policy that covered the insured against death by accident required his representative to give notice in writing of a claim "as soon as possible" after it had come to his knowledge. This was construed subjectively so that the fact that notice was given nearly one year after the accident was irrelevant, as the existence of the policy was unknown until just before notice was given and all the circumstances of the representative had to be taken into account. It is suggested that a similar interpretation should be given to common modern notice conditions requiring notice to be given "as soon as reasonably possible", so that this means as soon as the insured (or his representative) could be expected to give notice taking all the circumstances into account.

14.6.1 Time limits

It is unlikely that, in those situations where they are not constrained by the statutory controls on unfair terms, insurers retain conditions as generous to the insured as that in *Verelst*. Far more likely are those requiring notice within a specific time limit. If such a condition is clear, and is precedent to the insurer's liability, a failure to comply, however inadvertent or excusable, will entitle the insurer to avoid liability. A relatively old example is *Cassel v Lancashire & Yorkshire Accident Insurance Company*,[55] where an accident policy required notice within 14 days. It was not until eight months after an accident that the insured became aware that he had been injured as a result of it, and he then gave notice, but it was held that the insurer was not liable. The term was clear and, simply, was not complied with. Similarly, in *Adamson v Liverpool London & Globe Insurance Company*,[56] a cash in transit policy had the following condition:

---

[53] In *Layher v Lowe* [2000] Lloyd's Rep. I.R. 510, the Court of Appeal held that the word "likely" in a policy meant at least a 50 per cent chance that a claim would eventuate and that the onus of proof of such lay with the insurer. This was confirmed in *Jacobs v Coster* [2000] Lloyd's Rep. I.R. 506. It was also made clear that the fact that a person had suffered injury did not necessarily, without more, mean that an eventual claim in respect of that injury against the insurance was "likely".

[54] *Verelst's Administratrix v Motor Union Insurance Co* [1925] 2 K.B. 137.

[55] *Cassel v Lancashire & Yorkshire Accident Insurance Co* (1885) 1 T.L.R. 495.

[56] *Adamson v Liverpool London & Globe Insurance Co* [1953] 2 Lloyd's Rep. 355.

"The insured shall, immediately upon the discovery of any loss, give notice thereof to the company . . . The company shall be under no liability hereunder in respect of any loss which has not been notified to the company within 15 days of its occurrence."

Over a period of two years before the loss was discovered, an employee of the insured embezzled money entrusted to him for the purchase of National Insurance stamps. When the loss was discovered, the insured immediately notified his insurers. It was held that the latter were liable only in respect of the losses that occurred within the 14 days prior to notification, by reason of the last part of the condition. It does seem though that there was an element of ambiguity in the condition, the first part of which referred to the giving of notice immediately upon discovery. The insured had done this and indeed had done all that he could do in the circumstances. The decision can only be regarded as a little harsh.

Modern commercial policies often require the giving of immediate notice of, for example, "any cause, event or circumstance which has given or is likely to give rise to a claim" or "on the happening of any injury or damage in consequence of which a claim is or may be made". These phrases are construed objectively.[57]

The result of conditions such as these, if strictly relied upon, and it is not suggested that they always are, may be that an insured is treated harshly without real justification. There appears to be an unanswerable case for giving a court power by statute to relieve a breach of such a condition in favour of an innocent insured, or to prescribe that a breach can be relied upon only when the insurer can show that it has been prejudiced thereby, or alternatively that a breach can never be used to defeat a claim per se, but entitles the insurer to counterclaim for such loss as it can show that it has suffered as the result of the breach.[58] An alternative approach, recently suggested obiter by the Privy Council,[59] would be to hold that a time limit was not of the essence of the contract and that a failure to comply would not necessarily relieve the insurer of any liability. It will be interesting to see if this possibility is taken further in future cases. In *Milton Keynes BC v Nulty*,[60] the insured failed to give notice of a claim within the time required under a liability policy, but

---

[57] See those phrases and the comments on them in, respectively, *Laker Vent Engineering Ltd v Templeton Insurance Ltd* [2009] EWCA Civ 62; [2009] Lloyd's Rep I.R. 704 at [82] and *Loyaltrend Ltd v Creechurch Dedicated Ltd* [2010] EWHC 425 (Comm) at 31.

[58] Provisions such as these are common in other jurisdictions, e.g. the US and Australia.

[59] *Diab v Regent Insurance Co Ltd (Belize)* [2006] UKPC 29; [2006] Lloyd's Rep. I.R. 779 at 13–17.

[60] *Milton Keynes BC v Nulty* [2011] EWHC 2847 (TCC).

the relevant condition was not made precedent to liability. It was held that the insurers were entitled to damages for breach. Their loss was of a chance to prove that the insured had not been negligent and they were entitled to deduct 15 per cent from the sum due under the policy.

14.6.2 Place of notice

In addition to stipulating time limits, a condition as to notice may require that it is given to a particular place, for example, the insurer's head office. This will be upheld and a local agent will not have authority to waive the requirement,[61] but some power to relieve against technical reliance on a breach here seems desirable. In the absence of a specified destination, notice to any agent with usual authority to receive it will suffice. Notice need not be given by the insured himself, but by an agent of his authorised to do so. Whether or not a condition as to notice is satisfied if an unconnected third party informs the insurer of a loss depends on whether the decision in *Lickiss v Milestone Motor Policies*[62] is followed. This will be discussed in 14.7.1.

14.7   Particulars

The giving of notice of a loss is usually fairly informal, in the sense that it does not comprehend full details of a claim. These are normally separately required by a condition and frequently in practice consist of the filling in of a claim form sent by the insurer upon receipt of notice. In the absence of such a condition, the insured would simply have to prove his loss in the normal way if the matter were litigated.

The standard conditions imposing the legal obligation with respect to particulars appear to be of two types. One requires the insured to give full particulars of the loss, which has been defined as the best particulars he can reasonably give which must be sufficient to enable the insurer to ascertain the nature, extent and character of the loss.[63]

The other standard condition requires the insured to give such proofs and information as may reasonably be required by the insurer.[64] What an insurer reasonably requires must be a question of fact, but it will be virtually impossible for an insured to resist anything of relevance to his claim, and, if he is a businessman, he may well have to submit matters of general relevance to his

---

[61] *Brook v Trafalgar Insurance Co* (1946) 79 Ll.L.R. 365.
[62] [1966] 2 All E.R. 972.
[63] *Mason v Harvey* (1853) 8 Ex. 819 at 820.
[64] "Proofs satisfactory to the insurer" will be interpreted in the same way; *Braunstein v Accidental Death Insurance Co* (1861) 1 B. & S. 782. For a recent decision involving a similar condition, see *Widefree Ltd v Brit Insurance Ltd* [2009] EWHC 3671 (QB).

business. In *Welch v Royal Exchange Assurance*,[65] the claimant insured his stock in trade against fire. Following a claim, the insurers denied liability, and the dispute was referred to arbitration. The insurers, relying upon a condition of the sort mentioned, requested to see bank accounts which the insured used for the purpose of his business, but which were in his mother's name. The insured refused this until under cross-examination in the arbitration proceedings. The arbitrator held that these details were reasonably required, and the Court of Appeal upheld that decision, the argument having centred on whether the condition was precedent to the insurers' liability. Having decided that it was,[66] the insured's claim was lost, as he had failed to comply before pursuing his claim to law, albeit, as it turned out, the bank accounts contained nothing of any relevance. In *Parker v NFU Mutual Insurance Society Ltd*,[67] a condition to this effect, requiring the insured to provide all written details and documents the insurer asked for, which must be exercised reasonably,[68] was held not to be an unfair term within what is now Pt 2 of the Consumer Rights Act.

14.7.1 Personal compliance unnecessary?

An interesting point exists with regard to the insured's obligation to give full particulars, and a similar point could also arise with respect to the giving of notice. In *Lickiss v Milestone Motor Policies*,[69] the insured motorcyclist was involved in an accident on 17 May in which he negligently damaged a taxi. His policy covered him against such third party liability and required him to provide his insurers with full particulars of any accident as soon as possible and to forward immediately any summons, writ or similar matter relating to the accident. The insured never himself informed his insurers of the accident, but they learnt of it from the taxi driver. Neither did he forward a summons that he received, but the police on 18 June sent full details to the insurers. The main reason for the decision turned upon a point of waiver which will be examined later, but Lord Denning MR, with whom Danckwerts LJ agreed, held that the insured was not in breach of the condition mentioned on the ground that, although he himself did not comply, the insurers received all the necessary information, in particular from the police, within the necessary time.

---

[65] *Welch v Royal Exchange Assurance* [1939] 1 K.B. 294.

[66] The condition provided for no liability "unless" it was complied with; compare the construction of "until" in a similar context in *Weir v Northern Counties Insurance* (1879) 4 L.R.Ir. 689.

[67] *Parker v NFU Mutual Insurance Society Ltd* [2012] EWHC 2156 (Comm).

[68] See *The Vainqueur Jose* [1979] 1 Lloyd's Rep. 557; *Gan Insurance Co Ltd v Tai Ping Insurance Co Ltd* [2001] 1 Lloyd's Rep. 667.

[69] *Lickiss v Milestone Motor Policies* [1966] 2 All E.R. 972, reported as *Barrett Bros (Taxis) Ltd v Davies* [1966] 1 W.L.R. 1334.

This aspect of the decision is difficult to justify as a matter of strict law, as the condition did expressly provide that *"the insured* shall give full particulars . . .",[70] although it is impossible to deny its justice, as the insurers were in no way prejudiced by the insured's failure. Assuming that the decision is followed, and there has as yet been no subsequent directly relevant case, its logic must apply to any condition concerning the claims procedure, including the giving of notice, even if such a condition expressly appears to require personal compliance by the insured (or his duly authorised agent).[71]

14.7.2 Further co-operation

In addition to the requirement of particulars, conditions in appropriate policies sometimes require further co-operation by the insured. Examples of this will be seen in the context of liability policies in Ch.20, but a particular example is worth citing at this stage. In *London Guarantee Co v Fearnley*,[72] a fidelity policy taken out by an employer covered him against the risk of embezzlement by an employee. A condition precedent provided that, if a claim was made, the insured should prosecute the employee concerned if the insurer so required. Following a particular claim, the insured refused to comply with such a request and it was held that the insurer was thereby entitled to avoid liability.

14.8   Proof of Loss

A condition may also require the insured to provide proof of his loss. This differs from particulars in that it means documentary proof of the loss, not merely a description of it. Sometimes the insured will be required to make a statutory declaration. Even though the proofs may show prima facie that the loss is covered by the policy, the burden of proving this, should the matter be litigated, still rests upon the insured.[73]

---

[70] Emphasis added; see, on this point, the dissenting judgment of Salmon LJ.

[71] See in a similar context the Scottish case of *Horne v Prudential Assurance Co Ltd* [1997] S.L.T. (Sh. Ct.) 75; (1997) S.C.L.R. 1151, where it was held that a company that had been wound up before any claim was made against the insurers by an injured third party by virtue of rights conferred by s.1(1) of the Third Party (Rights against Insurers) Act 1930 was not in breach of a condition requiring it to report any claims against the insurance "as soon as possible". The company was not in a position to know of any such claims once it was dissolved. As to the 1930 Act, see Ch.20.

[72] *London Guarantee Co v Fearnley* (1880) 5 App. Cas. 911.

[73] *Watts v Simmons* (1924) 18 Ll.L.R. 177.

14.9   Contesting the Insurer's Denial of Liability

Finally, a condition may require the insured, if the insurer disputes liability for a loss, to contest this denial by legal proceedings within a stated period, on pain of liability being totally avoided. Such a condition has been upheld in a case that involved a claim against third party liability.[74] The insured failed to contest the insurer's denial of liability within the year stated and his claim was thus totally defeated, even though his actual liability to the third party was not established until long after the year after the insurers repudiated. The only course for an insured in this position will be to seek a declaration that his insurers are liable to indemnify him, if he should be adjudged liable to the third party.

14.10   Arbitration

Despite the undertaking that will be referred to shortly, it is still usual to find in insurance policies of most sorts a condition precedent to the insurer's liability to the effect that any disputed claim must go to arbitration before a court of law. Such arbitration clauses can refer to disputes over liability, but more likely now they will cover only disputes over the quantum of a loss.

While arbitration may be cheaper than litigation, it naturally does not attract the attention that court action does, so that insurers might thereby be able to rely upon "technical defences" without public opprobrium. Furthermore, legal aid is not available to a party to arbitration. Reporting in 1957, the Law Reform Committee[75] expressed concern and said that they had evidence that insurers had abused their position in certain cases against honest and careful insureds by insisting upon arbitration. However, they recommended no change in the law because at the time of their enquiry, the British Insurance Association and Lloyd's stated that their members had agreed not to enforce arbitration against the wishes of an insured in cases of disputes over liability. Excepted from this undertaking were reinsurance, marine insurance and certain aspects of aviation insurance where arbitration is specially negotiated and where the parties are perfectly capable of looking after themselves.[76] In many cases, therefore, the law surrounding the use of

---

[74] *Walker v Pennine Insurance Co* [1980] 2 Lloyd's Rep. 156. Recent authorities concerning similar terms are *Super Chem Products Ltd v American Life and General Insurance Co Ltd* [2004] UKPC 2; [2004] 2 All E.R. 358 and *Fortisbank SA v Trenwick International Ltd* [2005] EWHC 399 (Comm); [2005] Lloyd's Rep. I.R. 464.

[75] Fifth Report on Conditions and Exceptions in Insurance Policies, Cmnd. 62, para.13.

[76] In a consumer policy situation, an arbitration clause might well be regarded as unfair under Pt 2 of the Consumer Rights Act 2015.

arbitration clauses is of practical importance only at all in respect of disputes over the amount of a loss, and even here it seems unlikely that arbitration is used in consumer insurance disputes.

The leading case of *Scott v Avery*,[77] which concerned an arbitration clause in an insurance policy, decided that such clauses in contracts generally are enforceable as conditions precedent provided that they do not purport ultimately to oust the jurisdiction of the court, and that they can cover disputes over liability as well as over quantum. If legal proceedings are brought by an insured in respect of a matter covered by an arbitration clause, the court has a discretion under the Arbitration Act 1996 to stay the proceedings and thus enforce the clause. Obviously the onus is on the party seeking to keep the dispute out of arbitration. A number of insurance cases have considered the exercise of this discretion, and it seems that the legal proceedings will usually be stayed unless the dispute concerns difficult points of law or involves an allegation of fraud.[78]

14.10.1 Independent validity of arbitration clauses

The final question here concerns what has been termed the independent validity of arbitration clauses.[79] It is clear that if the insurer is seeking to deny the validity or very existence of the policy in question, it cannot rely on any of its terms to enforce arbitration,[80] unless the arbitration clause itself is worded widely enough to cover the reference of a dispute as to the validity of the contract.[81] There are, it seems, three clear instances in the insurance context where, for this reason, an arbitration clause cannot be relied upon. These are

(i) where the existence of the contract is disputed[82];

(ii) where the insurer alleges that the contract is void or illegal, for example, for lack of insurable interest required by statute[83]; and

(iii) where it is alleged that the policy has been avoided ab initio for non-disclosure or misrepresentation.[84]

---

[77] *Scott v Avery* (1856) 5 H.L.C. 810.

[78] See *Clough v County Livestock Insurance Assurance* (1916) 8 5 L.J.K.B. 1185 and *Smith v Pearl Assurance Co* [1939] 1 All E.R. 95, holding that the cost of arbitration for the insured and the unavailability of legal aid are not valid grounds for disallowing it.

[79] Powell [1954] C.L.P. 75.

[80] *Heyman v Darwins* [1942] A.C. 356.

[81] Above, at 385 (Lord Wright) and 392, 398 (Lord Porter).

[82] *Toller v Law Accident Insurance Society* [1936] 2 All E.R. 952.

[83] But not where the insured merely fails to have the interest required by the contract: *Macaura v Northern Assurance Co* [1925] A.C. 619 (see 3.11).

[84] *Stebbing v Liverpool & London & Globe Insurance Co* [1917] 2 K.B. 433.

Where, however, an insurer is simply relying on the terms of the contract to deny liability, then the contract, and hence the arbitration clause, still stand. Thus, an allegation of breach of warranty or condition, or that a loss is not within the cover provided, does not affect the validity of an arbitration clause.[85] Repudiation of the policy alleging a fraudulent claim also does not now do so.[86]

14.11 Waiver and Estoppel

It is in connection with conditions regarding the claims procedure that the insured is most often likely to argue that the insurer is in some way precluded from relying upon a breach. Insurers may be so precluded by application of the doctrines of waiver and estoppel. The use of the description "waiver" in this and similar contexts has been criticised, but it is well established and will be followed here.

While waiver and estoppel may have a common base, they are essentially different.[87] Waiver is a form of election. The insurer that has the right to avoid liability may elect not to do so or may be deemed to have so elected, provided that it has knowledge of the breach and either expressly so elects or else acts in such a way as would induce a reasonable insured to believe that it is not going to insist upon its legal rights. Thus, waiver requires a conscious act by the insurer or its agent, but it does not require the insured to act in response in any way. Estoppel on the other hand requires a representation by words or conduct to the insured that the insurer will not rely upon a breach of condition, which the insured relies upon and acts upon to his detriment. It does not depend upon the knowledge of the person estopped and is a doctrine of much wider significance, although it is clear that the representation must be unequivocal; the mere continuation of negotiations, for example, does not amount to an unequivocal representation.[88] Waiver and estoppel may very well arise upon the same facts, but in certain cases the distinction may be crucial, as will be seen.

The doctrine of waiver by election does not apply to a breach of a condition

---

[85] As to the effect of a breach of warranty or condition, see Ch.9.
[86] *Super Chem Products Ltd v American Life & General Insurance Co Ltd* [2004] UKPC 2; [2004] 2 All E.R. 358, finally overruling the much-criticised dictum to the contrary in *Jureidini v National British & Irish Millers' Insurance Co* [1915] A.C. 499 per Viscount Haldane; the other members of the House of Lords decided the latter case on other grounds.
[87] See especially the judgment of Lord Goff in *Motor Oil Hellas (Corinth) Refineries SA v Shipping Corporation of India, The Kanchenjunga* [1990] 1 Lloyd's Rep. 391.
[88] *Super Chem Products Ltd v American Life and General Insurance Co Ltd* [2004] UKPC 2; [2004] 2 All E.R. 358; see also *Fortisbank SA v Trenwick International Ltd* [2005] EWHC 399 (Comm); [2005] Lloyd's Rep. I.R. 464.

precedent, just as it does not apply to a breach of warranty.[89] In *Kosmar Villa Holidays Plc v Trustees of Syndicate 1243*,[90] after a full review of the authorities, the Court of Appeal decided that waiver by estoppel was the only form of waiver applicable to a condition precedent, breach of which affords a defence to all claims that originated after the breach.

> "I do not think that we have been shown any case where the doctrine of election has been applied, in the context of a merely procedural condition precedent, to the conduct of a claim on behalf of an insured by an insurer, nor do I think it would be consistent with the paradigm examples of election, or with the nature of the doctrine, which requires unequivocal conduct which has irrevocable effect, to treat that doctrine as being by its rationale applicable to this situation. The doctrine is ill-fitting in these circumstances, and unneeded. For there remains the doctrine of estoppel: in circumstances where it can be said that the handling of a claim by an insurer is an unequivocal representation that the insurer accepts liability and/or will not rely on breach of some condition precedent as affording a defence, and there has been such detrimental reliance by the insured as would make it inequitable for the insurer to go back on his representation, the insured will have all the protection he needs."[91]

The cases that are examined in the following sections can clearly be regarded as concerned with waiver by estoppel. They are all cases where the relevant condition was a condition precedent. Clearly the decision in *Kosmar Villa Holidays* does not apply to situations where a claims condition is not made precedent to liability, as is more likely these days in at least some consumer contracts. Here, waiver by election might still be available.

14.11.1 Evidence of waiver

It is clear that for waiver to operate, the insurer must know of the breach, but that knowledge may be the knowledge of an agent that is imputed to the insurer under general principles.[92] Apart from express affirmation, the conduct of the insurer that can amount to waiver may be constituted by the acceptance of a renewal premium, but perhaps the most likely form in this context will arise simply from its handling of the claim. If, with knowledge of the breach, the insurer does anything such as writing for further particulars or continuing to process the claim without denial of liability or without reserving its position, that will amount to waiver and waiver by estoppel if

---

[89] See 9.2.
[90] *Kosmar Villa Holidays Plc v Trustees of Syndicate 1243* [2008] EWCA Civ 489; [2008] Lloyd's Rep. I.R. 489.
[91] Per Rix LJ at [70].
[92] See Ch.12.

the insured acts in reliance. The facts of *Lickiss v Milestone Motor Policies*,[93] examined above, provide a good illustration. The insured failed to forward any information to his insurers, but the police did so. Subsequently, the insurers wrote to the insured referring to the summons and indicating that they wished to arrange for his defence to it. It was held unanimously that this constituted waiver of their right to avoid liability. The insurers knew of the breach, yet had ignored it and written in terms indicating that they accepted liability.

On the other hand, a letter or an oral representation indicating that the insurers are still enquiring into the matter, without any indication that they regard themselves as bound, cannot amount to a waiver.[94]

The insurers may, knowing of a breach, continue to rely upon the policy to exercise a right given to them thereunder. If they do so without reserving their position, this may amount to waiver. In *Craine v Colonial Mutual Fire Insurance Co*,[95] a fire policy required the insured to deliver particulars of loss within 15 days of the loss as a condition precedent to recovery. The insured failed to do so. In the meantime, however, under another condition in the policy, the insurer took possession of the premises and remained there for four months. It was held that by reason of this action, the insurer was precluded from relying upon the breach. By its conduct in taking possession of the premises, the insurer represented that it would not rely upon the breach. The insured relied upon this to his detriment by being deprived of possession of his premises for the period stated.

14.11.2 Waiver of future performance

Just as an insurer may waive an existing breach, it may also waive future performance of a condition. In *Burridge v Haines*,[96] a policy on horses contained a condition providing that in the event of death by accident, the insured should obtain the certification of a qualified vet to the effect that death was caused by a peril insured against. Following the death of one horse, the insurer's own vet examined the animal, and the insurer told the insured that this was acceptable and that it would accept evidence of the horse's death other than that prescribed in the policy. It was held that the insurer had waived its right to rely upon a breach of the condition, because by its conduct it had implied that it would not enforce it, and it had rendered it impossible for the insured

---

[93] *Lickiss v Milestone Motor Policies* [1966] 2 All E.R. 972.

[94] See, e.g. *Farrell v Federated Employers' Insurance Association* [1970] 1 W.L.R. 1400.

[95] *Craine v Colonial Mutual Fire Insurance Co* (1920) 28 C.L.R. 305 (High Court of Australia). The decision was affirmed by the Privy Council, sub nom. *Yorkshire Insurance Co v Craine* [1922] 2 A.C. 541, but rather on the construction of the condition in question.

[96] *Burridge v Haines* (1918) 87 L.J.K.B. 641.

to comply by appointing its own vet who dissected and destroyed the horse before a vet chosen by the insured had the chance to examine it.

14.11.3 Agent's authority

Just as insurers may be deemed to have knowledge of a breach through an agent, so also in appropriate circumstances an agent may have authority actually to waive a breach. This will turn on the extent of the agent's actual or ostensible authority. An agent who has authority to accept premiums or settle claims will probably have at least ostensible authority to waive a breach of condition.[97] A mere canvassing agent will not. In *Brook v Trafalgar Insurance Co*,[98] the policy required notice of loss to be given to the company's head office, and it was held that a mere local agent had no authority, by accepting notice himself, to waive breach of that condition.

14.11.4 Delay as waiver

Mere delay by the insurers in dealing with, for example, a late claim does not amount to waiver. In *Allen v Robles*,[99] a motor insured was obliged to notify his insurer of a claim against him within five days of the claim being made. Following an accident, he did not notify the insurers that a claim was made against him until two months later. However, the insurers did not deny liability to the insured for four months, although they had informed the third party and had warned the insured one month after the claim that they reserved their position. It was held that the insurers had not lost their right to avoid liability merely by lapse of time. In the words of Fenton Atkinson LJ:

> "The lapse of time would only operate against [the insurer] if thereby there was prejudice to the defendant or if in some way rights of third parties intervened or if the delay was so long that the court felt able to say that the delay in itself was of such a length as to be evidence that they had in truth decided to accept liability."[100]

14.12   Fraudulent Claims

The topic of fraudulent claims merits its own special treatment. While there can never be any doubt that recovery by making a fraudulent claim is and never has been permissible, there were traditionally different bases for that

---

[97] See 12.3.3.
[98] *Brook v Trafalgar Insurance Co* (1946) 79 Ll.L.R. 365.
[99] *Allen v Robles* [1969] 1 W.L.R. 1193.
[100] Above at 1196.

result. One was the duty of the insured to act with the utmost good faith,[101] which clearly survives beyond the time of effecting the policy.[102] Although it was not entirely clear whether the remedy for breach expressed in s.17 of the Marine Insurance Act as originally enacted—avoidance of the policy ab initio—would apply to a fraudulent claim, this will soon be an academic question as that part of s.17 is abolished by the Insurance Act 2015.[103] Quite apart from that, however, many policies contain express terms to the effect that a fraudulent claim will lead to the policy becoming void and all benefits being forfeited, and it is clear that there is a separate common law principle, founded on public policy, to the effect that fraud defeats a claim in its entirety. The exact relationship of these various principles was the subject of much case law in recent years and the legal position remained somewhat confusing.[104] It might be argued that this is still the case, notwithstanding the introduction of specific statutory provisions in the Insurance Act 2015, which in any event will only apply to contracts entered into, varied or renewed on or after 12 August 2016. For this reason an account of the previous law is retained before the new provisions are explained.

As far as the standard express term is concerned, one important issue is as to the effect of a fraudulent claim, which is a matter of construing the words used. However, it seems fairly safe to assume that while the fraudulent claim itself and any future claim are barred, any reference to the policy becoming void does not mean that it is retrospectively avoided.[105] In effect the insurer is entitled to repudiate the contract from the date of the breach.[106] Although it has long been clear that an express term was probably not necessary by virtue of the common law principle already mentioned, it is only relatively recently that the exact scope and effect of that principle was clarified. In *Galloway v*

---

[101] See Ch.7.

[102] *Britton v Royal Insurance Co* (1866) 4 F. & F. 905 is an old authority to this effect.

[103] Section 14(1) and (3)(a). This is only the case as regards contracts entered into, varied or renewed on or after 12 August 2016.

[104] For useful reviews, see Clarke, "Lies, damned lies and insurance claims" [2000] N.Z.L.Rev. 233; Thomas, "Fraudulent insurance claims: definition, consequences and limitations" [2006] L.M.C.L.Q. 485; Swaby, "The price of a lie: discretionary flexibility in insurance fraud" [2013] J.B.L. 77 and Hjalmarsson, "The law on fraudulent insurance claims" [2013] J.B.L. 103. In addition, the Law Commissions' Papers referred to in 14.12.4 contain excellent descriptions of the law.

[105] Although this was left open in *Insurance Co of the Channel Islands v McHugh* [1997] L.R.L.R. 94, it is clearly the case under the common law rule, as will be seen shortly, and was confirmed with regard to the standard term in *Direct Line Insurance Plc v Fox* [2009] EWHC 386 (QB); [2009] 1 All E.R. (Comm) 1017.

[106] It is thought that there is no scope for the insured to validate a claim by retracting the fraud; see the views of His Honour Judge Richard Seymour QC in *Direct Line Insurance Plc v Fox* [2009] EWHC 386 (QB); [2009] 1 All E.R. (Comm) 1017.

Royal Guardian Royal Exchange (UK) Ltd,[107] the claimant claimed for losses following a burglary. The amount was probably a fair estimation of his total loss, but he claimed for a computer that had not in fact been lost, and the receipt for its purchase had been forged. He signed a declaration that the particulars given on the claim form were true and complete. Despite being convicted of fraud, the claimant sued the insurers, but the latter's rejection of the claim was upheld, the Court of Appeal holding that, although there was no express clause in the policy barring all recovery in the event of a fraudulent claim, the policy would be treated as if there were such a clause, "in accordance with legal principles and sound policy".[108] Lord Woolf MR said that the purpose of the law must be to discourage fraudulent claims and although the fraud must be "substantial", a fraudulent claim representing 10 per cent of the whole, as in this case, satisfied such a test. Millett LJ went even further and said that "substantial" ought not to be tested by reference to the proportion of the entire claim represented by the amount of the fraudulent claim on the ground that this would lead to the absurd result that the greater the genuine loss, the more fraudulent the claim could be without penalty.[109] In *The Star Sea*,[110] Lord Hobhouse confirmed the existence of the common law principle,[111] and in *Axa General Insurance Ltd v Gottlieb*,[112] the Court of Appeal clarified the position further. Here four claims were made and paid under a household policy but the insurers later discovered that false documents had been submitted in connection with two of the claims and claimed repayment of all they had paid, relying solely on the common law principle. It was held that the principle did not result in the forfeiture of sums paid in response to honest claims and before the perpetration of any fraud, but that an entire claim was forfeited for fraud, so that interim payments made under that claim could be recovered, even though the fraud was committed after the interim payments and in order to obtain payment of a final sum.

What was still somewhat unclear as regards the common law principle was the extent that it would allow the insurers to treat the whole contract as avoided or repudiated for the future.[113] In *Orakpo v Barclays Insurance*

---

[107] *Galloway v Royal Guardian Royal Exchange (UK) Ltd* [2000] Lloyd's Rep. I.R. 209.

[108] Above.

[109] Subject to the "de minimis" principle.

[110] *Manifest Shipping Co Ltd v Uni-Polaris Co Ltd* [2001] UKHL 1; [2003] A.C. 469, at [62].

[111] See also Mance LJ in *Agapitos v Agnew, The Aegeon* [2002] EWCA Civ 247; [2003] Q.B. 556 at 45.

[112] *Axa General Insurance Ltd v Gottlieb* [2005] EWCA Civ 112; [2005] Lloyd's Rep. I.R. 369. See also *Yeganeh v Zurich Plc* [2011] Lloyd's Rep. I.R. 75; affirmed as to the law in the Court of Appeal ([2011] Lloyd's Rep. I.R. 540).

[113] This was not in issue in *Axa General Insurance Ltd v Gottlieb*, above.

Services Co Ltd,[114] the common law principle was analysed as an implied term incorporated in order to give effect to the overriding principle of utmost good faith and it was held that fraud went to the root of the contract and therefore entitled the insurers to repudiate it for the future. However, this approach was not endorsed in *The Star Sea*[115] and in *Agapitos v Agnew*,[116] the tentative view was expressed that the common law principle fell outside the scope of s.17.

However, this still left open the question of the extent to which the general principle of utmost good faith applies as distinct from the common law principle. Once the 2015 Act is in force, this becomes academic, as we have seen, as s.17 is amended to remove the remedy of avoidance for breach.[117] It was clear from the House of Lords' decision in *The Star Sea* that non-disclosure or misrepresentation at the claims stage did not lead to retrospective avoidance of the contract,[118] but their Lordships did not rule clearly on the relationship between s.17 and a fraudulent claim. Two subsequent Court of Appeal decisions provided further guidance. In *The Mercandian Continent*,[119] the right to avoid was restricted to a case where (a) the fraud would have an effect on the insurers' ultimate liability and (b) the gravity of the fraud or its consequences would entitle the insurers, if they wished to do so, to terminate the contract for breach. In *Agapitos v Agnew (The Aegeon)*,[120] a distinction was drawn between "material fraud" and "fraudulent devices". The former meant claims where there was no loss or the loss was exaggerated. The latter referred to any device which was used to promote what was in essence an honest claim.[121] Mance LJ described "fraudulent devices" as when "the insured believes that he has suffered the loss claimed, but seeks to improve or embellish the facts surrounding the claim by some lie".[122] He addressed the issue as to whether the s.17 duty of utmost good faith could apply "in the event of use of fraudulent means or devices to promote a claim, which claim may prove at trial to be in all respects valid". His conclusion was that the common law principle, namely forfeiture of the claim as described above, should be applied in a case where fraudulent devices are used but that

---

[114] *Orakpo v Barclays Insurance Services Co Ltd* [1994] C.L.C. 373.
[115] Above.
[116] Above at [45].
[117] See 7.3.
[118] Overruling the decision to the contrary in *The Litsion Pride* [1985] 1 Lloyd's Rep. 437, at 514–516.
[119] *K/S Merc-Scandia v Certain Lloyd's Underwriters* [2001] EWCA Civ 1275; [2001] 2 Lloyd's Rep. 563.
[120] *Agapitos v Agnew (The Aegeon)* [2002] EWCA Civ 247; [2003] Q.B. 556.
[121] *Agapitos v Agnew, The Aegeon* [2002] EWCA Civ 247 at [4].
[122] Above at para.30. See also *Eagle Star Insurance Co Ltd v Games Video Co SA* [2004] EWHC 15 (Comm); [2004] Lloyd's Rep. I.R. 867.

s.17 was inappropriate and no question of avoidance of the whole contract should ever arise in these circumstances.[123]

The removal of the remedy of avoidance from s.17 and the introduction of specific statutory provisions dealing with fraudulent claims ought to mean that the general duty of good faith will become no more than background. There is nothing in the Insurance Act that affects express terms so, subject to what is said below, it would seem that an insurer could still rely on breach of such a term. This though ought to become unnecessary given the provisions of ss.12 and 13 of the Act. It seems as though these are intended to replace the common law principle, which they mirror and expand, although that is not actually spelt out. Simply, s.12 provides that if an insured makes a fraudulent claim, the insurer is not liable to pay it, may recover any sums already paid in respect of it and may by notice to the insured treat the contract as having been terminated from the time of the fraud, with no obligation to return any of the premium paid. Termination means that the insurer is under no liability in respect of any "relevant event" occurring after the time of the fraud but does not affect any "relevant event" occurring before the time of the fraud. "Relevant event" means whatever gives rise to the insurer's liability, which includes, for example, the occurrence of a loss, the making of a claim and the notification of a potential claim. Section 13 contains provision to deal with group insurance and to ensure that the fraud of one co-insured does not affect the position of an innocent co-insured.

As with most of the other provisions of the 2015 Act, ss.12 and 13 can be excluded in a non-consumer contract, subject to the transparency requirements of s.17. In theory therefore an insurer could provide for this and rely on either an express term or, if it survives, the common law principle. However, there seems little point as far as the latter is concerned as ss.12 and 13 effectively enact the common law principle. The only possible advantage of an express term is that it could be drafted to have retrospective effect, but whether that would be upheld as a matter of construction remains to be seen.

14.12.1 Meaning of fraud

The 2015 Act does not define what is a fraudulent claim, so that the meaning as elaborated in the case law will apply both to the Act and to any express term.[124] Clearly a claim is fraudulent if it can be shown that the insured intended to defraud the insurer by, for example, maliciously damaging insured property, or put forward false evidence when in fact there was

---

[123] Above at [45(d)].

[124] It has been held that a fraud by an agent of the insured acting within the scope of his authority will bind the insured: *Savash v CIS General Insurance Ltd* [2014] EWHC 375 (TCC).

no loss.[125] It is also fraudulent if an otherwise honest claim is supported by fraudulent devices, namely:

> "any lie, directly related to the claim, . . . which is intended to improve the insured's prospects of obtaining a settlement or winning the case, and which would, if believed, tend, objectively . . . to yield a not insignificant improvement in the insured's prospects."[126]

This is in line with the Court of Appeal's earlier approach in *Galloway v Royal Guardian Royal Exchange (UK) Ltd.*[127] Otherwise, a fraudulent claim usually consists of an exaggeration by the insured of the amount of his loss. The decisions referred to above cast some doubt on the traditional position that mere exaggeration is not fraud. An insured may well claim higher than he knows he is entitled to as a bargaining device and in some cases has been regarded as acting fraudulently only, it seems, if he had a specific intent to recover more than he was entitled to. In *Central Bank of India v Guardian Assurance Company,*[128] a claim figure of nearly one hundred times the actual value of the goods destroyed was, naturally, held to be fraudulent.[129] However, in *Ewer v National Employers' Mutual General Insurance Association,*[130] the insured under a fire policy claimed the current market price of goods destroyed, whereas he probably knew that all he was entitled to was their second-hand value. This was held not to be fraudulent. The figure claimed, which was "preposterously exaggerated", was held to be merely a bargaining figure. This may be regarded now as doubtful.[131]

---

[125] The burden of proof in the insurers is a high one: *S & M Carpets (London) Ltd v Cornhill Insurance Ltd* [1982] 1 Lloyd's Rep. 423, affirming [1981] 1 Lloyd's Rep. 677. See also *Diggens v Sun Alliance and London Insurance Plc* [1994] C.L.C. 1146.

[126] *Agapitos v Agnew, (The Aegeon)*, above at [45(c)], per Mance LJ, endorsed in *Stemson v AMP General Insurance (NZ) Ltd* [2006] UKPC 30; [2006] Lloyd's Rep. I.R. 852.

[127] Above.

[128] *Central Bank of India v Guardian Assurance Co* (1936) 54 Ll.L.R. 247. For more recent examples, see *Orakpo v Barclays Insurance Services Co Ltd* [1994] C.L.C. 373 and the cases cited in Clarke, *The Law of Insurance Contracts*, Ch.27.

[129] See the comments of Millett LJ on this point in *Galloway v Guardian Royal Assurance (UK) Ltd* [2000] Lloyd's Rep. I.R. 209, discussed generally above. His Lordship was disapproving of exaggerated or, worse, genuinely fraudulent claims, saying, "The making of dishonest claims has become all too common. There seems to be a widespread belief that insurance companies are fair game, and that defrauding them is not morally reprehensible." He clearly thought the opposite.

[130] *Ewer v National Employers' Mutual General Insurance Association* [1937] 2 All E.R. 193; compare *Norton v Royal Life Assurance Co, The Times*, 12 August 1885 where the finding at first instance ((1885) 1 T.L.R. 460) that a claim for £274 in respect of a loss of £87 was not fraudulent was reversed.

[131] However, the idea that mere exaggeration is not of itself fraudulent was accepted in *Danepoint Ltd v Underwriting Insurance Ltd* [2005] EWHC 2318 (TCC); [2006] Lloyd's Rep. I.R. 429.

14.12.2 Assignees and joint insureds

It appears that an assignee of the policy would not be defeated by the insured's fraudulent claim,[132] but that does not apply to the insured's trustee in bankruptcy,[133] nor to the case of a joint insurance where one insured's fraud will taint the whole claim.[134] However, joint insurance is only properly found where insurance is effected as regards property jointly owned by the insureds.[135] Insurance under one policy of composite interests, that is the different interests of the different insureds, for example, landlord and tenant or mortgagor and mortgagee, is not joint insurance, and fraud by one insured will not prevent the other who is innocent from recovering.[136] As we have seen, this is confirmed by s.13 of the 2015 Act.

14.12.3 Insurer's remedy

The insurer who has paid out on what turns out to have been a fraudulent claim may recover the money, both at common law and under the 2015 Act, but it has been clearly decided that it was not entitled to recover as damages for breach of contract the costs incurred in investigating the claim.[137] An action in the tort of deceit might lie.[138] More recently, in *Parker v National Farmers Union Mutual Insurance Society Ltd*,[139] the insurer was awarded damages to cover its costs in investigating the fraudulent claim, but both parties accepted that this would be the case and the basis for the award was not clarified.

---

[132] *Central Bank of India v Guardian Assurance Co*, above, at 260.

[133] *Carr and Sun Insurance Re*, (1897) 13 T.L.R. 186.

[134] *P Samuel & Co Ltd v Dumas* [1924] A.C. 421 at 445; *Central Bank of India v Guardian Assurance Co*, above; *State of the Netherlands v Youell* [1997] 2 Lloyd's Rep. 440 at 445.

[135] *Central Bank of India v Guardian Assurance Co*, above. Compare, though, the New Zealand view in *Maulder v National Insurance Co of New Zealand* [1993] 2 N.Z.L.R. 351, holding that even insurance effected by joint owners may not be joint insurance. See the examination of this and other authorities by Campbell, "Wilful misconduct, fraud and the innocent no-insured" [2000] New Zealand Law Review 263.

[136] *General Accident Fire & Life Assurance Corp v Midland Bank* [1940] 2 K.B. 388.

[137] *London Assurance v Clarke* (1937) 57 Ll.L.R. 254.

[138] *London Assurance v Clarke* (1937) 57 Ll.L.R. 254, per Goddard J at 270.

[139] *Parker v National Farmers Union Mutual Insurance Society Ltd* [2012] EWHC 2156 (Comm) at [204].

14.13 Settlement of Claims

Consideration of the precise legal rules governing the amount of compensation an insured is entitled to, following an insured loss, is deferred until the next chapter, but at this point, it is convenient to consider some general points surrounding the settlement of claims other than the question of quantum. Frequently, of course, claims are settled following negotiations between insured and insurer, or parties acting on their behalf such as assessors and loss adjusters. The reported cases have been concerned with whether an insurer can reopen a settlement, but it is conceivable that an insured could do so on the ground of misrepresentation or undue influence by the insurer; this, though, would be difficult to show.[140]

A simple promise by the insurer to pay is not binding unless the insurer is actually legally liable, but once an insurer has actually made a payment, it may be recoverable if the claim was fraudulent or if the payment was made under a mistake of fact or of law. This is a matter of the law of restitution or unjust enrichment.[141] For example, in *Kelly v Solari*,[142] a life policy provided for the quarterly payment of premiums, and that in default the policy would lapse. The life insured died when one such payment had not been made, but the insurers paid the sum insured to his widow. It was held that, if the payment was made in ignorance or genuine forgetfulness of the facts, the insurers were entitled to recover it, and a new trial was ordered to ascertain this. "I think that the knowledge of the facts which disentitles the party from recovering must mean a knowledge existing in the mind at the time of payment."[143] The fact that the insurers may have been careless did not deprive them of their right to recovery.

14.13.1 Contracts of compromise

Somewhat different is the case where the insurer and insured enter into a contract of compromise.[144] This might take the form of a replacement agree-

---

[140] It is more likely when an insurer acting for its liability insured negotiates with the latter's victim as in *Horry v Tate & Lyle Refineries Ltd* [1982] 2 Lloyd's Rep. 416; see Merkin (1983) 46 M.L.R. 99 and 20.4.

[141] See especially *Kleinwort Benson Ltd v Lincoln City Council* [1998] 4 All E.R. 513, where the House of Lords abolished the previous distinction between mistakes of fact and mistakes of law.

[142] *Kelly v Solari* (1841) 9 M. & W. 54.

[143] Above at 58, per Lord Abinger C.B.

[144] It would seem that such a contract is not itself one of the utmost good faith: *Baghbadrani v Commercial Union Assurance Co Plc* [2000] Lloyd's Rep. I.R. 94 at 118; *Direct Line Insurance Plc v Fox* [2009] EWHC 386 (QB); [2009] 1 All E.R. (Comm) 1017, at [31], but note the comments on the latter case in *Aviva Insurance Ltd v Brown* [2011] EWHC 362 (QB) at [78].

ment, as in *Holmes v Payne*,[145] where jewellery that was lost was replaced by the underwriters with jewellery of a similar value. Such a contract is binding unless one of the general grounds for rescission of a contract exists, such as misrepresentation or mistake. As far as mistake is concerned, there has never been any basis for saying that such a contract was void at common law because that can apply only where there is a fundamental common mistake affecting the subject matter of the contract.[146] A contract of compromise following an insurance claim could hardly ever be void on such grounds. The fact that an insurer entered into it under a mistaken impression that it was liable to the insured is a mistake as to the quality of the contract, the rights in respect of it. There is no mistake as to the nature of the contract. So, for example, the fact that an insurer need not have entered into it because it could avoid liability by reason of a right to avoid the policy for misrepresentation (in consumer cases) or breach of the duty of fair presentation (in non-consumer cases) or because the policy had lapsed would not render the contract of compromise void. Needless to say, the insurer could not possibly claim mistake if it compromised knowing of its right to avoid liability. For some years there was authority that a contract of compromise could be voidable in equity,[147] although the cases were of doubtful status. They have in effect now been overruled[148] and it is clear that this basis for challenging an insurance settlement has now disappeared.[149]

14.13.2 Ex gratia payments

If an insurer consciously pays out on a claim for which, in fact, it is not liable, then it is acting ex gratia. Such payments though are perfectly proper and not ultra vires an insurance company,[150] but it is established that they do not bind an insurer in the sense that the insurer who pays ex gratia is not bound to pay in subsequent, similar, or even identical circumstances.[151]

---

[145] *Holmes v Payne* [1930] 2 K.B. 301; see 13.7.2.

[146] *Bell v Lever Bros* [1932] A.C. 161. See generally, *Treitel Law of Contract*, Ch.8.

[147] *Magee v Pennine Insurance Co* [1969] 2 Q.B. 507, following *Solle v Butcher* [1950] 1 K.B. 671.

[148] *Great Peace Shipping Ltd v Tsavliris Salvage (International) Ltd* [2002] EWCA Civ 1407; [2003] Q.B. 679.

[149] See also *Kyle Bay Ltd v Certain Lloyd's Underwriters* [2006] EWHC 607 (Comm); [2007] Lloyd's Rep. I.R. 460.

[150] *Taunton v Royal Insurance Co* (1864) 2 H. & M. 135.

[151] *London & Manchester Plate Glass Co v Heath* [1913] 3 K.B. 411. For a powerfully argued case against the use in certain circumstances of ex gratia payments by life insurance companies, see Selmer (1966) 33 U. Chicago Law Rev. 502.

CHAPTER 15

PAYMENT UNDER THE POLICY—THE MEASUREMENT OF LOSS

15.0

This chapter is concerned with the question of how much the insured will be entitled to recover following an insured loss and with one or two related matters. This involves first a consideration of the nature of the insurer's liability, and then an examination of the legal principles that determine the actual assessment of an insured loss in respect of insurance contracts that are contracts of indemnity.

15.1 The Insurer's Liability as Damages for Breach of Contract

It is well established that a claim under an insurance contract is a claim for damages for breach of contract,[1] even where the insurer admits liability. Although the term "damages" may have been used historically in a different sense from the modern meaning of compensation for breach of contract,[2] the modern cases have ignored any distinction, with, perhaps, unfortunate consequences. They categorise the insurer's promise to pay as a promise to prevent the insured from sustaining loss, so that an action for damages for breach of contract arises upon the occurrence of the loss.[3] The most commonly cited dictum is that of Lord Goff in *The Fanti and The Padre Island*[4] that the promise of indemnity in an insurance contract is simply "a promise to hold

---

[1] *Jabbour v Custodian of Israeli Absentee Property* [1954] 1 W.L.R. 139 at 143, per Pearson J; *Edmunds v Lloyds Italico & L'Ancora Compagnia di Assicurzioni & Riassicurazione SPA* [1986] 1 Lloyd's Rep. 326 at 327 per Donaldson MR; *The Fanti and The Padre Island* [1991] 2 A.C. 1.

[2] See the comments of Pearson J in the *Jabbour* case, above.

[3] See the authorities cited in fn.1, above and *The Italia Express (No.2)* [1992] 2 Lloyd's Rep. 281; *The Kyriaki* [1993] 1 Lloyd's Rep. 137; *Callaghan v Dominion Insurance Co Ltd* [1997] 2 Lloyd's Rep. 541. See the excellent analysis and critique by Campbell, "The nature of an insurer's obligation" [2000] L.M.C.L.Q. 42, arguing that in property insurances there is both a primary obligation to indemnify and, where relevant, a secondary liability to pay damages for breach. See also Campbell, "An insured's remedy for breach" (1994) 5 New Zealand Business Law Quarterly 51, where he examines the New Zealand cases that have taken a different view from the English cases and awarded damages for consequential loss, especially *NZ Insurance Co Ltd v Harris* [1990] 1 N.Z.L.R. 10.

[4] *The Fanti and The Padre Island* [1991] 2 A.C. at 35.

the indemnified person harmless against a specified loss or expense".[5] There are two consequences of this that we must examine.[6]

The first concerns when the insured's right to damages arises and will be of importance to determine the period within which the insured must claim before the period of limitation expires.[7] Here there is a distinction between liability insurances and all other types of insurance. Under a liability policy, the cause of action does not accrue until the liability of the insured is established, whether that is by judgment, arbitration or agreement.[8]

> "However, in respect of other types of insurance policy, including property, life, marine and other forms of insurance, the law has long been that, because an insurance policy is to be construed as insurance against the occurrence of an insured event, the occurrence of that event is treated as equivalent to a breach of contract by the insurer. Accordingly, in the absence of policy terms affecting the matter, the limitation period begins to run as soon as the insured event occurs, even though no claim has been made."[9]

So, an action on a fire policy commenced more than six years after the date of the fire was statute-barred.[10] It is irrelevant that the insured may be bound by policy conditions to give notice or particulars of loss only within a period after loss,[11] although a term that has the effect of postponing the

---

[5] Emphasis added. It is arguable that this dictum has been misinterpreted; see the critical comments in Clarke, *The Law of Insurance Contracts*, para.30–7A, the analysis by Campbell (fn.3, above) and *MacGillivray on Insurance Law*, 13th edn, para.20–076.

[6] It looked possible that the House of Lords would re-examine this question in the case of *Pride Valley Foods Ltd v Independent Insurance Co Ltd* [1999] Lloyd's Rep. I.R. 120, where the Court of Appeal gave leave to appeal in a case where the facts were similar to those in *The Italia Express (No.2)*, above and *Sprung v Royal Insurance (UK) Ltd* [1997] C.L.C. 70; [1999] Lloyd's Rep. I.R. 111 (described below), but unfortunately the appeal was not pursued. The Law Commissions examined this question in detail and, pointing out that the law is different in Scotland and in many common law jurisdictions, and in the light of recent developments regarding damages for breach of contract in general, considered that in fact this categorisation was incorrect; see Issues Paper 6 – Damages for Late Payment and the Insurer's Duty of Good Faith (March 2010) and their Consultation Paper, *Insurance Contract Law: Post Contract Duties and Other Issues*, LCCP 201/SLCDP 152, December 2011. For the end result of their review, see 15.1.1.

[7] The limitation period for an action for breach of contract is six years: Limitation Act 1980 s.6.

[8] *Bradley v Eagle Star Insurance Co* [1989] A.C. 957; *The Fanti* and *The Padre* Island [1991] 2 A.C. 1. As to these decisions, see further Ch.20.

[9] *Virk v Gan Life Holdings Plc* [2000] Lloyd's Rep. I.R. 159 at 162, per Potter LJ.

[10] *Callaghan v Dominion Insurance Co Ltd*, above.

[11] As to such terms, see 14.5 and following.

insurer's liability until after a stated period will stop time running until the end of that period.[12]

The second consequence of categorising an insurance claim as a claim for damages of breach of contract is that recovery is limited to an indemnity calculated in the ways described later in this chapter. This is because there is a general principle that damages are not awarded for a failure to pay damages.[13] The leading case is *Sprung v Royal Insurance (UK) Ltd*.[14] This case illustrates the harshness of the rule, a fact admitted by the Court of Appeal who reached their decision "with undisguised reluctance".[15] The claimant owned a small business dealing in animal waste products. He had insurance providing an indemnity against the cost of making good sudden and unforeseen damage to the plant which necessitated immediate repair or replacement before it could resume working.[16] In April 1986 vandals entered the claimant's premises and wrecked his machinery. The insurers denied liability on what proved to be wholly spurious grounds and it was not until three and a half years later that the claimant received any substantial payment under the policy, namely an indemnity in respect of the machinery. It was found at first instance that he should have been paid by October 1986. The substance of the case was his claim for damages, assessed by the judge at £75,000, to compensate him for the fact that he was out of pocket for so long, his business collapsed and he was unable to sell it. The Court of Appeal had no difficulty in dismissing the claimant's claim for damages for late payment, following the authorities already referred to. These same authorities had already led Hirst J in *The Italia Express (No.2)*[17] to dismiss a damages claim on a marine insurance policy,[18] and *Sprung v Royal* confirmed that the same principle must apply in non-marine insurance.[19]

---

[12] See *Virk v Gan Life Holdings Plc* where the policy was one of critical illness insurance and the insurer's liability arose only when the insured had survived such an illness for 30 days.

[13] *President of India v Lips Maritime Corp* [1988] A.C. 395.

[14] See fn.6, above, noted [1997] J.B.L. 368 (Birds); [1998] L.M.C.L.Q. 154 (Hemsworth).

[15] *Sprung v Royal Insurance (UK) Ltd* [1997] C.L.C. at 79, per Evans LJ.

[16] Under the policy conditions, the insured was permitted to proceed with minor repairs "without prejudice to the liability of the [insurers]", provided that the latter were given notice and particulars. However, other repairs could be effected only with the consent of the insurers.

[17] *The Italia Express (No.2)* [1992] 2 Lloyd's Rep. 281.

[18] He also relied on the statutory rules as to recovery in the Marine Insurance Act 1906.

[19] See also *Normhurst Ltd v Dornoch Ltd* [2004] EWHC 567 (Comm); [2005] Lloyd's Rep. I.R. 27 and *Tonkin v UK Insurance Ltd* [2006] EWHC 1120 (TCC). The decision in *Grant v Co-operative Insurance Society* (1984) 134 N.L.J. 81, where damages representing consequential loss were awarded to an insured must now be regarded as wrongly decided.

It was clearly unfortunate that damages were not recoverable from an insurer who unjustifiably delays in paying, although, unless the Supreme Court reversed the view that a claim under an insurance policy is an ordinary claim for damages for breach of contract, it was difficult to see how this could be done at common law. It is worth noting that North American courts regularly award damages in contract or tort (including punitive damages) against an insurer who has acted in bad faith[20] and the decision of the Canadian Supreme Court in *Whiten v Pilot Insurance Co*[21] provides a dramatic example. There, where the insurers repudiated a claim for fire damage on the basis of a wholly unfounded allegation of arson, and a consequence of the fire was that the insured and her family had to flee the house in the middle of an Ontarian winter night wearing only their night clothes in a temperature of minus 18 degrees Celsius, the court upheld an award of punitive damages in the sum of $1 million.[22] On the other hand, the fact that the Insurance Conduct of Business Sourcebook provides detailed rules regarding the handling of claims[23] ought to admit the possibility of an action for breach of statutory duty[24] against an insurer who unjustifiably delays in paying.[25]

15.1.1 Statutory reform

However, there is now the prospect of significant statutory reform. The Law Commissions, in an extremely valuable and carefully-argued Issues Paper (no.7) published in March 2010, provisionally recommended the reversal of *Sprung*, which they regard as wrongly decided anyway, and the introduction of a clear statutory duty on an insurer, breach of which would, in appropriate cases, allow the award of damages in addition to the basic measure of an insured's loss. They confirmed this view in their December 2011 Consultation Paper[26] and in their 2014 Report.[27] However, the provision

---

[20] The principles are admirably summarised in Clarke, *The Law of Insurance Contracts*, para.30–10.

[21] *Whiten v Pilot Insurance Co* [2002] S.C.C. 18.

[22] The award was in contract and it seems most unlikely that an English court would follow this approach, not least because of the rejection by the House of Lords in *Banque Financière de la Cite v Westgate Insurance Co Ltd* [1991] 2 A.C. 249 of the availability of damages for a breach by an insurer of its duty of utmost good faith (see Ch.8). Equally a remedy in tort is likely to fail on the eastern side of the Atlantic.

[23] See ICOBS 8—Claims Handling.

[24] Under s.138D of the Financial Services and Markets Act 2000.

[25] For example, ICOBS 8.1.1 requires an insurer to settle a claim promptly.

[26] See fn.6.

[27] *Insurance Contract Law: Business Disclosure; Warranties; Insurers' Remedies for Fraudulent Claims; and Late Payment* (Law Com No.353, Scot Law Com No.238, 2014, CM 8898).

in the draft Bill therein was regarded as too controversial for the Bill that became the Insurance Act 2015, but it is included in the Enterprise Bill before Parliament at the time of writing. If this becomes law, which looks fairly certain to happen at some time in 2016, then the relevant provision will come into force one year later and apply to contracts entered into, renewed or varied after then.

The Bill inserts new ss.13A and 16A into the Insurance Act 2015. It would be an implied term of every contract of insurance that if the insured makes a claim, the insurer must pay any sums due within a reasonable time, this including a reasonable time to investigate and assess the claim. What is reasonable would depend on all the relevant circumstances, but there are examples of things that might need to be taken into account, these being (a) the type of insurance, (b) the size and complexity of the claim, (c) compliance with any relevant statutory or regulatory rules or guidance and (d) factors outside the insurer's control. If the insurer shows that there are reasonable grounds to dispute the claim either completely or as to the amount, it does not breach the term merely by failing to pay the claim while the dispute is continuing, but its conduct in handling the claim might be relevant to whether the term was breached. The remedies available for breach of the term, for example damages, would be in addition to and distinct from any right to enforce payment of the claim and any right to interest.

It would not be possible to contract out of this regime in a consumer insurance contract. As far as a non-consumer insurance contract is concerned, there would be a right to contract out, but it is a qualified right as compared to the right to contract out of other provisions of the 2015 Act.[28] Essentially any contracting-out here would be of no effect where an insurer deliberately or recklessly acted in breach of the implied term. Otherwise any contracting-out has to satisfy the same transparency requirements as applicable to other provisions of the 2015 Act. It is perhaps a little strange that any contracting-out is permitted, given that the case that has caused the most concern, namely *Sprung v Royal Insurance*, was a non-consumer case.

Nonetheless, if it reaches the statute book, this will clearly be a welcome reform. There remains the possibility of the Supreme Court at some time putting right the exact nature of an insurance claim, which would render any contracting out of the statutory provisions otiose. It might also be argued that an insurer's reliance on a contracting-out where it was negligent in taking an unnecessary length of time to settle a claim was a breach of its duty of good faith; however, it is not clear that this would entitle the insured to any damages.

---

[28] As to these, see especially 7.10.

15.2 The Measure of Indemnity

We now consider how the insured's entitlement is to be calculated. It is possible first of all largely to exclude certain categories of insurance from consideration here, in particular all contingency policies, in other words, those of life and accident and their variations. These are not generally speaking contracts of indemnity, or contracts to pay the insured strictly only what he loses.[29] In these cases, there are no difficulties as to the basic measurement of loss, because the policies themselves will provide the fixed sums that are payable in the event of a loss. Similarly, although third party liability policies are contracts of indemnity, the amount recoverable raises no real problems, since that is simply the amount of the insured's liability,[30] subject to any maximum sum insured and to any excess clauses, as to which more will be said below.

Therefore we are largely concerned hereafter with insurances on property of whatever sort, including both goods and land. The presumption is that such insurances are contracts of indemnity. This follows from the requirement of insurable interest at the time of the loss that is necessary in all such contracts unless it is waived.[31] It is only in the case of valued policies that the principle of indemnity is strictly irrelevant, and these will be examined separately. The modern "new for old" policies whereby insurers agree to pay the cost of replacing goods insured, are still indemnity policies, albeit of a different sort, despite the fact that they do not raise the same problems in calculating the measure of indemnity, as will be seen.

15.2.1 Sum insured

One overriding point is that the insured can never recover more than the maximum expressly stated in the policy.[32] This is usually referred to as the "sum insured", and in property insurance, and to a lesser extent in liability insurance, the premium payable is calculated very largely according to that figure. The problems that can arise from that figure being inaccurate, in the sense of being below or above the actual value of the property insured, will be considered later. For the present it is assumed that there are no such problems of under or over insurance.

---

[29] See Ch.3. An accident or sickness policy may be a contract of indemnity (see 17.1), but even where this is the case, the measure of the insured's loss will not give rise to any legal problems.

[30] This can include exemplary damages: *Lancashire County Council v Municipal Mutual Insurance Ltd* [1996] 3 All E.R. 545.

[31] See Ch.3.

[32] In some cases of liability insurance there is no such maximum. The most common is motor insurance, where statute prohibits a limit in respect of liability for personal injury; see Ch.21.

15.3 Total and Partial Loss

Property may be totally or partially lost, in other words it may be totally destroyed or lost, or it may only be damaged. The measure of recovery may well differ according to this distinction. Total loss need not necessarily mean, in this context, complete destruction, although it is obviously included. A total loss includes cases where "the subject matter is destroyed or so damaged as to cease to be a thing of the kind insured".[33] For example, a house may, after a fire, be left with walls and foundations standing, but if none of it is usable, it must be regarded as totally lost. The same will apply to the car that is a genuine "write off". It may be in practice that cars are written off because it is regarded as uneconomic to repair them, even though they may not be so damaged as to cease to be cars, because they could be repaired comparatively easily. Whether in law these would strictly be regarded as totally lost must be open to doubt, even though in practice they may be so treated. It is, of course, perfectly permissible for insurers to adopt this attitude, provided that the insured agrees. One or two problems that may flow from this sort of case will be discussed later.

15.4 Total Loss in the Case of Goods

It is convenient to deal separately with the two classes of relevant property, namely goods and land, assuming for the present a genuine total loss.[34] In respect of goods, the measure of what the insured has lost will prima facie be the market value of the property lost at the time[35] and place[36] of loss, in other words, its second-hand or resale value.[37] This is because it is that sum that it will cost him to obtain equivalent goods.

In *Richard Aubrey Film Productions Ltd v Graham*,[38] a film producer effected a policy against loss of negatives and films. A film that was almost completed

---

[33] *Halsbury's Laws of England*, 4th edn (London: Butterworths, 2005), Vol.25, para.298.

[34] We are only concerned here with the determination of the measure of indemnity in respect of the insured property itself. Many property insurances will also provide for the insured to be indemnified against additional costs, for example in the case of insurance of a motor vehicle, the cost of hiring a replacement, in the case of insurance of a house, the cost of alternative accommodation, surveyors' charges, etc.

[35] *Wilson and Scottish Insurance Corp Re*, [1920] 2 Ch.28; see below.

[36] *Rice v Baxendale* (1861) 7 H. & N. 96.

[37] In assessing market value, latent defects in the goods can be ignored if the evidence shows that the appropriate reasonable buyer would not have detected the defects: *State Insurance Office v Bettany* [1992] 2 N.Z.L.R. 275. See also *Scottish Coal Co Ltd v Royal & Sun Alliance Insurance Plc* [2008] EWHC 880 (Comm); [2008] Lloyd's Rep. I.R. 718 at [119].

[38] *Richard Aubrey Film Productions Ltd v Graham* [1960] 2 Lloyd's Rep. 101.

was stolen. The evidence showed that on completion it would have had a market value of about £20,000 but that finally to complete it would have cost between £4,000 and £5,000. The insured therefore recovered the difference between those sums. This measure ignores feelings of lost effort and concentrates purely on loss in material terms. Similarly, in an appropriate case, nothing is recoverable to compensate for what can be called sentimental value or hurt feelings. A family "heirloom", for example, will only attract its market value even though its owners may have felt that it was worth much more than that to them.[39]

15.4.1 Value at time of loss

It is value at the date or time of loss that is recoverable, which, of course, may or may not correspond to the value at the date of commencement or renewal of the policy. In *Wilson and Scottish Insurance Corp Ltd*,[40] a car was insured in November 1915 for £250, which was its purchase price at the time and which was stated by the insured to represent his estimate of present value. The policy was renewed in subsequent Novembers until the car was destroyed by fire in June 1919. It was then worth £400. The policy covered the car "up to full value". The arbitrator reserved for the court the question whether the insured was entitled to £250 or £400, and Astbury J held that it depended upon when the increase in value took place. If it was even partly before the last renewal, the insured was entitled to only £250, but if it occurred totally since the renewal, he was entitled to £400.

There are a number of difficulties surrounding this decision. First, it is a little difficult to see how the insured could in any event be entitled to more than £250, as one would have thought that that figure, as it had never been changed, operated as the sum insured, the maximum recoverable. The answer to this must be that, on the construction of the policy, there was no such sum insured, as none was expressly stated and the policy undertook to pay "full value". Assuming this to be the case, there is an inconsistency in the reasoning. At one point in his judgment, Astbury J suggested that on each renewal, "the insured must be deemed to have continued or repeated his 'estimate of present value' at £250", and he implied that if this was incorrect on the renewal in November 1918, the policy was voidable.[41] Whether this was because of a non-disclosure of a material fact under the law at the time, that is, the increase in value, or a breach of warranty of value, is not made

---

[39] The strictness of the usual indemnity measure has no doubt astonished individual insureds from time to time; see the comments of MacKinnon J in *Ewer v National Employers' Mutual General Insurance Association Ltd* (1937) 157 L.T. 16 at 21.

[40] *Wilson and Scottish Insurance Corp Ltd* [1920] 2 Ch.28.

[41] Above at 31, citing Creswell J in *Pim v Reid* (1834) 6 Man. & G. 1 at 25.

clear. It is suggested that it can only be the former, there being no authority and no reason for holding that statements in a proposal form not referable to the future are automatically warranted again upon renewal; indeed there is a clear dictum to the contrary;[42] in any event this could no longer be the case given the abolition of the basis clause.[43] If, then, the increase in value occurred before renewal and non-disclosure of it amounted to non-disclosure of a material fact, the policy was voidable and there was no basis for holding that the insured was entitled to anything as a matter of strict law. However, the insurers had agreed to pay £250 in any event, and must therefore be deemed to have waived any right to avoid the policy. If, as has been seen, there was no sum insured in this case, so that the figure of £250 in the proposal form was not to be taken as the maximum recoverable, the insured should have been entitled to the value of his car at the date of loss, namely £400, regardless of when the increase in value took place.

It is suggested therefore, that the decision itself in *Wilson* is open to question. However, the principle of value at the time of loss is clearly correct, and it would seem unlikely that the sort of facts there could recur, simply because estimates of value in a proposal form do usually correspond to the sum insured.[44]

15.4.2 Replacement value

As the basic principle of indemnity is only contractual, it can be contractually varied. Policies on goods can, and very often do, undertake to pay replacement value rather than market value,[45] and indeed there may be cases where this is impliedly the measure, even if not actually spelt out.[46] Policies containing express undertakings to pay replacement value are increasingly common, and there can be no doubt that, subject to the sum insured, the insured is entitled to what it actually costs to replace the lost property by equivalent new property. These "new for old" policies were no doubt a major inroad into the traditional principle of indemnity, but it goes without saying that insurers demand higher premiums for such cover.

---

[42] Winn LJ in *Magee v Pennine Insurance Co* [1969] 2 Q.B. 507 at 517.

[43] See 9.2.1.

[44] It would also be most unusual now for a car to increase in value anyway, unless it is a vintage car.

[45] See e.g. *Kuwait Airways Corp v Kuwait Insurance Co SAK* [2000] Lloyd's Rep. I.R. 439. Here insurers of aircraft spares undertook to pay "full replacement value" and this was held to be the cost of buying in a replacement regardless of any betterment accruing to the insured.

[46] Particularly insurances of plant and equipment: *Roumeli Food Stores v New India Assurance Co* [1972] 1 N.S.W.L.R. 227 at 236–238.

15.5 Total Loss in the Case of Land

Until relatively recently, there was very little real authority determining what the insured whose house or office or factory is totally destroyed is entitled to claim, possibly because a total loss here is not that common. Logic might favour the market value approach as for goods, for the same reason that this measure should enable the insured to purchase an equivalent. In fact, an insured would not usually choose to do this; he would wish to be able to rebuild or reinstate. In some cases he may be compelled so to do.[47] For most of the time that insurance has been available, this probably did not matter, as the market value of property would cover the cost of rebuilding. Now it is notorious that this is less likely. Hence, whether or not an insured is entitled to the cost of reinstatement may be vital.

In most cases there will be such an entitlement as a result of the decision in *Leppard v Excess Insurance Company*.[48] Here the Court of Appeal stressed that the insured is entitled to an indemnity against the amount of his loss and no more. There is no general principle dictating market value or cost of reinstatement. It is a question of fact, and all the relevant facts of the particular case must be examined in order to ascertain the actual value of the loss at the relevant date. In the case itself, the insured had purchased a cottage which was worth some £4,500, including the site value, when it was burnt, but which would cost some £8,000 to rebuild. On the evidence the insured never intended to live in the cottage. He had purchased it from his in-laws solely for resale. It was held therefore that his loss was the market value of the cottage, that is what he lost by not being able to sell it. The judgments indicate, however, that in the normal case of the insured who lives in or otherwise occupies his house, office or factory, the measure of indemnity will be the cost of rebuilding, because otherwise his actual loss will not be made good.

In *Leppard*, the insured had argued in the alternative that his policy contractually provided that he was entitled to the cost of reinstatement. He placed particular reliance upon facts that are probably fairly standard. These were, first, that in the proposal form he warranted that "the sums to be insured represent not less than the full value (the full value is the amount which it would cost to replace the property in its existing form should it be totally destroyed)", and secondly, that the policy contained a declaration by him that the sum insured represented and would at all times be maintained at not less than the full value of the buildings. The court held, no doubt correctly as a matter of law, that these could not affect the basic nature of the policy, which was otherwise in normal indemnity form. Such declarations

---

[47] See Ch.16.
[48] *Leppard v Excess Insurance Co* [1979] 1 W.L.R. 512. Noted in (1980) 43 M.L.R. 456 (Birds).

were promissory warranties, on breach of which the insurer would have been discharged from liability.[49] The insured had, in fact, complied with them and had insured the cottage for, eventually, £14,000. More about the effect of such warranties will be said later. All that remains to be said here is that the insured may have felt somewhat aggrieved, and understandably so, at being required to pay a premium calculated on £14,000 worth of insurance on pain of the insurer being able to avoid all liability, when he was entitled to substantially less.[50]

15.6   Partial Loss under an Indemnity Policy

In respect of a partial loss, there can be no case for treating goods and land any differently. A measure based on market value is generally inappropriate, since the insured cannot go into the market and restore himself to his pre-loss position, and payment based on the difference in market value before and after loss may well not compensate him. Therefore, the basis for an indemnity ought, where the property is capable of repair, to be the cost of repair,[51] less perhaps any amount by which the insured is better off than before the loss[52]; the technical term for the latter is "betterment".[53]

15.6.1 Some potential difficulties

Before examining some of the cases, it must be pointed out that there may be difficulties arising from the adoption of the above measure. In the main, these stem from the problem in deciding whether or not a loss is to be regarded as partial or total. If a car is dented, however badly, or the roof of a house is damaged, these are clearly partial losses. But in practice a car may be so badly damaged that, although it is capable of repair and can be still properly termed a car, it is regarded as uneconomic to repair it; it may then

---

[49] See Ch.9.

[50] Quaere whether he might have had a remedy against the broker who advised him.

[51] This is implied in *Scottish Amicable Heritable Securities Association v Northern Assurance Co* (1883) 11 R. (Court of Session) 287 at 295 and *Westminster Fire Office v Glasgow Provident Society* (1888) 13 App. Cas. 699, although the actual decisions turned on other points. It has been held in Scotland that the insured is not entitled to interim payments in a situation where he is obliged to pay stage payments to the builder who is repairing the property: *Anderson v Commercial Union Assurance Co Plc* 1998 S.L.T. 826.

[52] If it is not capable of repair, then the court has to attempt to work out the difference in value pre and post loss: see, e.g. *Quorum v Schramm* [2001] EWHC 494 (Comm); [2002] Lloyd's Rep. I.R. 292, which concerned damage to a valuable painting.

[53] In *Reynolds v Phoenix Assurance Co* [1978] 2 Lloyd's Rep. 440, (see below) Forbes J held that the principle of betterment was well established.

be written off. Similarly, the top floor of a house might be damaged to such an extent that, although the bottom half is more or less intact and usable, in order to restore the house to its original condition, it is necessary to demolish the surviving part and start again. In *Leppard v Excess*, if Leppard's cottage had been so damaged, would he have been entitled to the costs of repairing it, which may well have been more than the market value of the cottage? It must be likely that the law would follow what is presumably insurance practice and look at what the insured actually loses, so that Leppard would have recovered no more than he did get, the fact of his non-occupation being crucial. However, in the case of a car or similar consumer durable, or any goods which tend to depreciate in value, the problem may be more complex simply because such depreciation is usual.

A more complex illustration will demonstrate the point further. Imagine a modest family car some ten years old but in very good condition for its age with low mileage and sound bodywork. Its market value will be reflected, however, primarily by its age, and, although it may attract the top price for a model of its kind of that age, this will hardly reflect its true worth to its owner. This top market price is £500. In an accident, the car is damaged on one side so that a wing and a door need replacement, there is some general tidying-up necessary, but the mechanics and the rest of the bodywork are sound. The work of restoring the car will cost £700 in total. Fairly clearly, the car is only partially lost, but is the insured entitled to £700, assuming this to be less than the sum insured, bearing in mind that this is more than the market value of the car, which is all he would get if the car had been totally lost? It is suggested that he is and that the courts would in such a case follow the principles adopted in respect of insurance of buildings in fairly recent cases, namely that a partial loss is assessed on the cost of repair or reinstatement save where the insured does not genuinely intend to reinstate.

15.6.2 Legal authorities

In *Reynolds v Phoenix Assurance Co Ltd*,[54] the claimants in 1969 bought an old maltings that they insured for £18,000, which was a little more than they had paid for it. Subsequently, on the advice of their brokers and valuers, the sum insured was increased to cover the likely cost of reinstatement in the event of a total loss, and at the material time that sum insured was £628,000. The claimants had a sound business reason for purchasing the maltings. A fire occurred which destroyed about 70 per cent of the buildings. This was clearly a partial loss. There was some dispute in subsequent discussions involving assessors employed by the claimants and loss adjusters acting for

---

[54] *Reynolds v Phoenix Assurance Co Ltd* [1978] 2 Lloyd's Rep. 440. See also *Pleasurama Ltd v Sun Alliance & London Insurance Ltd* [1979] 1 Lloyd's Rep. 389.

the insurers as to the cost of reinstatement and as to the claimants' intention in this respect. The insurers elected not to reinstate as they were entitled to under the policy,[55] but it was accepted that the claimants intended to do so, although the insurers were unwilling to pay over a provisionally agreed settlement figure except in stages as the rebuilding progressed. The claimants were unwilling to proceed on this basis, the settlement fell through, and the matter came to trial.

Forbes J outlined three possible bases for indemnity. The first was market value, which would be difficult to assess, there being no ready market for buildings such as maltings, but which would probably be far less than the cost of reinstatement. The second was described as equivalent modern replacement value, namely the cost of building afresh a modern building for the purposes of the claimants when commercially it would not be sensible to retain the original building. Again this would be considerably less than reinstatement cost. The third was the cost of reinstatement, which worked out at something more than £200,000. The learned judge held that the policy was an ordinary indemnity policy, and, as in *Leppard v Excess Insurance Company*,[56] this meant that the claimants were not automatically entitled under the contract to the costs of reinstatement. However, the claimants were entitled to a genuine indemnity and the basis of that indemnity was the cost of reinstatement where, as on the facts, the claimants did have the genuine intention to reinstate. The test to be adopted on this latter point was taken from an Irish case on compensation under statute[57]: "Would [the owner], for any reason that would appeal to an ordinary man in his position, rebuild [the property] if he got replacement costs, or is his claim for these a mere pretence?" Forbes J held, therefore, that the claimants were entitled to the largest sum, less an allowance for betterment which, he held, was a principle too well established in insurance cases of this kind to be upset.

Frequently insurers will have an option under the policy to reinstate or repair rather than pay money. The different considerations that may arise if this option is exercised are considered in the next chapter.

15.7   The Insured with a Limited Interest

The preceding discussion has assumed that the insured is the sole unencumbered owner of the property insured, but this may not be the case, and indeed the insured may not own the property at all but be, for example, a tenant or mortgagee of real property or a bailee, as under a hire-purchase contract, of goods. In certain exceptional cases, an insured may recover more than the

---

[55] See Ch.16.
[56] *Leppard v Excess Insurance Co* [1979] 1 W.L.R. 512; see above.
[57] *Murphy v Wexford CC* (1921) 2 Ir.R. 230.

value of his interest and hold the balance above his own loss for another. These circumstances were examined earlier in Ch.4. The measure of recovery here will be the value of the loss calculated in accordance with one or other of the ways already discussed.

Where someone with a limited interest insures or is entitled to recover in respect of only his own interest, problems may arise concerning the value of his interest and the amount of indemnity to which he is entitled. If a number of different interests in the same property are insured by the persons with those different interests, for example by different mortgagees, each insured is entitled to recover the value of his loss regardless of the position of the others and regardless of whether the total amount recovered by all the insureds exceeds the value of the property in question.[58]

In respect of certain insureds with limited interests, no problem will arise. For example, the indemnity claimable by a mortgagee will be the amount of his outstanding debt, and the same may be said of the hirer under a hire-purchase contract, unless the insured contracted for full value in order to cover his own and the owner's interests together. The case, though, of a tenant who insures the property that he has leased raises the problem quite neatly. If he has, in fact, covenanted to insure or to make good fire damage, he is only fully indemnified if he receives the full value of the property, which would normally, as has been seen, be the cost of reinstatement, regardless of the market value of his lease. Even if the tenant has not covenanted to insure or repair, it has been said that he is entitled to more than market value, since he will have been deprived of his home.[59] In the Australian case of *British Traders' Insurance Co v Monson*,[60] it was said that the market value of a lease coupled with an option to purchase of which the tenant had the benefit would prima facie determine the amount of the tenant's loss, though that would not be all he was entitled to. The actual calculation, apart from that, would no doubt be somewhat speculative.

15.8   Loss under a Valued Policy

Although, as a general rule, a contract of property insurance is a contract of indemnity, the parties are free to contract out of this by agreeing conclusively that a certain sum is payable in the event of loss. If this occurs, the policy is a valued policy and, unless the value is hopelessly excessive, it is enforceable.[61] Valued policies are more commonly found in marine than non-marine insur-

---

[58] *Westminster Fire Office v Glasgow Provident Society* (1888) 13 App. Cas. 699.
[59] *Castellain v Preston* (1883) 11 Q.B.D. 380 at 400.
[60] *British Traders' Insurance Co v Monson* (1964) 111 C.L.R 86 at 92, 103–104 and 104–105.
[61] Excessive over-valuation might be non-disclosure of a material fact (see Ch.7).

ance, but no doubt there are some non-marine policies.[62] A policy is a valued policy only if the parties expressly agree that the property is assumed to have the value attached to it. The mere existence of a sum insured does not mean that a policy is valued.[63]

In the case of a total loss, the amount recoverable is obviously the agreed value, whether that is more or less than the insured's actual loss.[64] In the case of a partial loss, the formula worked out in *Elcock v Thomson*[65] is applied, the insurer being liable for that proportion of the agreed value as is represented by the depreciation in the actual value of the property, that is the difference between market value before and after loss. A property insured for £100,000 that is worth £50,000 before loss and £30,000 afterwards, will attract a recovery of £40,000, that is, two fifths of the agreed value. It does not matter what it actually costs to repair the property, except that it was suggested in that case[66] that if, in fact, the insurers had exercised their option to repair, they would have been liable for those costs whether that sum was more or less than that produced by the formula.

15.9 Under-Insurance

Hitherto, it has been assumed that the sum insured is not less than the value of the property insured or the cost of its reinstatement. There will frequently be an obligation on the insured to keep to the latter, as is evident from the facts of *Leppard v Excess Insurance Co*,[67] as described earlier. Some nice questions arise if, in fact, the sum insured is less than either of these, that is, if there is under-insurance. Under-insurance is a problem that concerned the insurance industry very much since high inflation became a problem for the British economy from around the early 1970s.[68]

---

[62] A valued policy on a building would be difficult to justify if the Life Assurance Act 1774, especially s.3, applies, but as we have seen (at 3.9.1), the modern tendency is to treat the Act as inapplicable to property insurance. A recent non-marine case where a policy on a valuable painting was unsuccessfully argued to be a valued policy is *Quorum v Schramm* [2001] EWHC 494 (Comm); [2002] Lloyd's Rep. I.R. 292.

[63] It is a question of construing all the relevant parts of the policy as a whole. For a recent example of a marine policy where the reference to a "sum insured" was held fatal to the insured's argument that the policy was valued, see *Kyzuna Investments Ltd v Ocean Marine Mutual Insurance Association (Europe)* [2000] Lloyd's Rep. I.R. 513. See also *Thor Navigation Inc v Ingosstrakh Insurance* [2005] EWHC 19 (Comm); [2005] Lloyd's Rep. I.R. 490.

[64] This is also treated as the loss for subrogation purposes: *Burnand v Rodocanachi* (1882) 7 App. Cas. 333.

[65] *Elcock v Thomson* [1949] 2 K.B. 755.

[66] Above at 764.

[67] *Leppard v Excess Insurance Co* [1979] 1 W.L.R. 512.

[68] To such an extent that there was a great deal of inertia selling of index-linked policies, and much publicity and exhortations to insured persons to check their

15.9.1 Insurer's right to avoid

The first point to note is that the insurers may well in such a case be entitled to avoid the policy or liability, or else to use a right to avoid to compel the insured to settle for a sum less than his actual loss. This may arise by virtue of the pre-contractual duties of the insured or by virtue of a breach of warranty. Failure upon renewal to disclose a change in the value of the property insured could be regarded in a non-consumer case to amount to a breach of the duty of fair presentation,[69] as most renewals amount to the making of a new contract.[70] In a consumer case it could be a breach of the duty under the 2012 Act. Alternatively, the initial estimate of value by an insured may well be warranted and if incorrect entitle the insurer to be discharged from liability upon this basis, although, if that is the only warranty, and it is not of a continuing nature, there is, it is suggested, no basis for repudiation simply because upon subsequent renewals the sum insured has not been increased.[71] Perhaps more likely nowadays is an express continuing warranty of the sort that existed in the policy in *Leppard v Excess Insurance Co.*[72] In such a case, there is a clear basis for repudiation of liability if the sum insured does not keep pace with the value or cost of replacement of the property.

15.9.2 Average

Quite apart from this, the insurer in a case of under-insurance may be able to rely upon the principle of average. This is irrelevant to a total loss, because the sum insured is the maximum recoverable. But an insured may suffer a partial loss below the sum insured where the property is under-insured. If so, and the policy is subject to average, he will recover only that part of the loss which the sum insured bears to the value of the property; the insured is deemed to be his own insurer with respect to the balance. For example, if a house worth £60,000 is insured, subject to average, for £40,000, the insured will be entitled to only two thirds of any loss.

Commercial policies generally contain average clauses and it has been suggested that the principle of average would be implied, if not expressed,

---

sums insured. The sum insured in most standard property insurances is now automatically index-linked.

[69] This seems to be implied in *Re Wilson and Scottish Insurance Corp* [1920] 2 Ch.28, discussed above at 15.4.1 In the case of buildings, where the problem of under-insurance has been especially acute, it might perhaps be possible to argue that the facts were common knowledge and hence, not required to be disclosed; see (1976) 126 N.L.J. 482.

[70] See 5.7.

[71] See 15.4.1.

[72] *Leppard v Excess Insurance Co* [1979] 1 W.L.R. 512; see 15.5.

in commercial policies on goods.[73] However, average clauses are unusual, it seems, in household policies, except those issued by Lloyd's underwriters, and there is clear authority that the principle of average will not be implied in such a case.[74] Thus, in the absence of a breach of a relevant warranty, the insured in this case is entitled to recover fully up to the amount of the sum insured.

15.10   Excess and Franchise Clauses

It is convenient to mention here two devices often adopted which, if applicable, will limit the amount an insured recovers, although they raise few legal difficulties. Excess clauses or deductibles are common in motor, household and third party policies, among others. They provide that the insured is to bear the first amount of any loss, expressed either as an amount of money or as a stated percentage of any loss. The effect of an insured acting as a self-insurer in this way is considered later.[75]

Franchise clauses are perhaps less common in non-marine insurance. These take the form of relieving the insurer from liability completely in the respect of losses below a certain figure or percentage, and at this level operate in the same way as excess clauses, whereas losses above the specified figure or percentage are fully covered.[76]

15.11   Payment of Interest

A question of importance in some contexts is whether or not an insured is entitled to claim interest on the policy moneys payable to him. This can only arise, of course, if there has been some delay in payment. There is no rule that interest is payable as a matter of course from the date when the money becomes payable, but the court has a discretion under s.35A of the Senior Courts Act 1981 to award interest if it thinks fit.

Interest will be so awarded when the insurer has wrongfully detained money that ought to have been paid. There was some authority that, in an ordinary indemnity policy, interest would normally be awarded from the date when the loss has been quantified, in other words when the insured called upon the insurer to pay, to the date of judgment.[77] A similar principle

---

[73] *Carreras Ltd v Cunard Steamship Co* [1918] 1 K.B. 118.
[74] *Sillem v Thornton* (1854) 3 E. & B. 868.
[75] See 17.4.1.
[76] *Paterson v Harris* (1861) 1 B. & S. 336; a number of truly separate losses on separate occasions, each falling below the figure or percentage, cannot be added together so as to bring the loss above the figure or percentage: *Stewart v Merchants' Marine Insurance Co* (1885) 16 Q.B.D. 619.
[77] *Burts & Harvey Ltd v Vulcan Boiler & General Insurance Co* [1966] 1 Lloyd's Rep. 354.

has been applied to life policies.[78] Interest was not due from the date of loss because, for a period after that, it was reasonable for the parties to negotiate to find out exactly how much money was due in respect of a claim.[79] However, it would appear that the courts today are likely to take a view more favourable to the insured and award interest from the date of loss, unless the insured unreasonably delayed in pursuing his claim.[80] The normal practice is to award interest at one per cent above base rate.

Somewhat different considerations may apply in the case of an insurer claiming interest when suing by virtue of subrogation rights. These will be examined in Ch.17 in the general context of subrogation.

---

[78] *Webster v British Empire Mutual Life* (1880) 15 Ch D 169; *Re Waterhouse's Policy* [1937] Ch.415.

[79] *Burts & Harvey Ltd v Vulcan Boiler & General Insurance Co*, above.

[80] *Adcock v Co-operative Insurance Society Ltd* [2000] Lloyd's Rep. I.R. 657; *Kuwait Airways Corp v Kuwait Insurance Co SAK* [2000] Lloyd's Rep. I.R. 678; *Quorum A/S v Schramm (No.2)* [2001] EWHC 505 (Comm); [2002] Lloyd's Rep. I.R. 315.

CHAPTER 16

REINSTATEMENT

16.0

In certain circumstances an insurer may be entitled or bound to reinstate[1] insured property that has been damaged or destroyed, rather than pay a sum of money to the insured. In so far as insurers may have a right to reinstate rather than pay money, this may arise under the terms of the policy or by statute. Reinstatement by contract will be permitted only if the policy expressly refers to it; if it does not, the insurers must pay money.[2] Insurers may become bound to reinstate under statutory provision. In this chapter, contractual and statutory reinstatement will be examined separately, together with one or two related matters. Of necessity, reinstatement is relevant only to property insurances.

16.1   Contractual Reinstatement

Clauses giving insurers the option to reinstate or repair have been common for a long time, particularly in insurances of real property,[3] but they are equally common nowadays in goods policies where they will often refer to replacement as well as to reinstatement or repair. Their purpose is to protect insurers against excessive demands and fraudulent claims.

The option depends upon the insurer's election to reinstate, repair or replace rather than pay money, and it is a general principle that if a party with the benefit of such an option wishes so to elect, he must give unequivocal notice to the other party, that is the insured in this context, within a reasonable time or within the time, if any, fixed by the policy. Once the election is made, the insurer is bound by it, and it is therefore important to know when it occurs. There are two rather conflicting Scottish decisions on the point. In the first, *Sutherland v Sun Fire Office*,[4] after investigation of a claim, the insurer offered a money payment, which the insured refused, and then offered to go to arbitration over the amount of the loss. This was also refused, whereupon the insurer elected to reinstate. It was held that this

---

[1] Reinstatement is the conventional term; it comprehends rebuilding, replacement or repair, as appropriate.

[2] Brett LJ in *Rayner v Preston* (1881) 18 Ch D 1 at 9–10.

[3] An early example appears from the facts of *Sadler's Co v Badcock* (1743) 2 Atk. 554.

[4] *Sutherland v Sun Fire Office* (1852) 14 D. (Ct. of Sess.) 775.

was a good election. By contrast, in *Scottish Amicable v Northern Assurance*,[5] following the loss there were prolonged negotiations. The insured claimed money or reinstatement; the insurers ignored the latter claim but disputed the amount of the loss and prepared for arbitration over it. Only when the insured commenced proceedings 18 months after the fire did the insurers purport to elect to reinstate. It was held that this was too late. The distinction between the cases is, it seems, that in the latter the parties had agreed on a money payment, although the amount was disputed. Once this form of indemnity is agreed, it is too late for the insurer to elect to reinstate. In the former case, however, there had been agreement on nothing and therefore the election was still available.

16.1.1 Effect of election

At common law, once the insurer has made an effective election to reinstate, it is bound to restore the property to its original condition. In the old case of *Alchorne v Favill*,[6] the premises when rebuilt were smaller than before the fire that caused the loss and, as a result, worth less. This was because of planning restrictions that prevented the insurer from rebuilding in the same manner. It was held, however, that having made their election, the insurers were bound by it and were liable to compensate the insured for the difference in value between the old and new buildings. It is likely nowadays that insurers protect themselves against the dangers of such planning restrictions by providing in the policy to the effect that reinstatement will be "as circumstances permit and in reasonably sufficient manner". Clearly they would still be liable in damages if the actual construction work were done badly, and the amount recoverable would be the cost of putting right the work and any foreseeable consequential losses, such as loss of rent or profit.

The effect of the election to reinstate is that the contract becomes a building or repair contract.[7] The correct legal analysis seems to be that the insured's claim is an offer which is accepted by the insurer's election to reinstate. The insurer is bound to complete the work regardless of cost, unless this contract is discharged by frustration. However, there is authority that the insured's only remedy against a defaulting insurer is in damages; specific performance will not lie.[8] Prima facie it does not matter that reinstatement costs more than was originally estimated, that it costs more than the sum insured in the policy, nor that the insured receives a better building as a result, unless there is a clause in the policy whereby the insured is bound to

---

[5] *Scottish Amicable v Northern Assurance* (1883) 11 R. (Ct. of Sess.) 287.
[6] *Alchorne v Favill* (1825) 4 L.J. (O.S.) Ch. 47.
[7] *Home District Mutual Insurance Co v Thompson* (1847) 1 E. & A. 247.
[8] *Smith v Colonial Mutual Fire Insurance Co Ltd* (1880) 6 Vict.L.R 200.

pay towards the costs in this sort of situation. Because the insurers who have elected to reinstate are in the position of building contractors, they must bear any loss or damage occurring while they are in possession for that purpose. In *Anderson v Commercial Union Assurance Co*,[9] the insurers elected to reinstate the insured house following a partial loss. While they were in possession, and when they had partly reinstated, a second fire occurred. The insurers claimed that they were entitled to deduct from the cost of reinstatement after the second fire the amount spent before that, but it was held that they could not do so. Having elected to reinstate, they had to complete the job properly, and were their own insurers while the work was in progress.

16.1.2 Impossibility

If it is impossible to reinstate before the insurers have made their election, for example, because planning permission will not be given, the insurers will be liable simply to pay the insured the amount of his loss.[10] If it becomes impossible after the election, there is authority that the insurers are nonetheless bound by their election and liable in damages for not reinstating despite the impossibility. Thus the insured might be entitled to compensation for the full value of the property, even if originally the loss was only a partial one. In *Brown v Royal Insurance Co*,[11] the only case directly in point, after the election to reinstate a partial loss, the Commissioners of Sewers under statutory authority ordered that the premises be totally demolished as being in a dangerous condition. It was held that the insured was entitled to the full value as damages for breach of the contract to reinstate. This case was decided, however, before the courts developed the doctrine of frustration,[12] under which a contract may be discharged where performance becomes impossible due to an unforeseen supervening event that is not the fault of either party. In circumstances such as the *Brown* case, or where, for example, following the election the local authority compulsorily purchases the property, a plea of frustration might well succeed. It would not necessarily be successful, however, if, for example, the insurers could have discovered what was going to happen.

If the contract to reinstate is frustrated, the insurers would not be liable in damages, but they would not be relieved of their original liability under the insurance contract to pay for the loss.[13] Thus the insured should still recover

---

[9] *Anderson v Commercial Union Assurance Co* (1885) 55 L.J.Q.B. 146.

[10] *Brown v Royal Insurance Co* (1859) 1 El. & El. 853 at 858–859.

[11] *Brown v Royal Insurance Co* (1859) 1 El. & El. 853 at 858–859.

[12] The founding case was *Taylor v Caldwell* (1863) 3 B. & S. 826.

[13] *Anderson v Commercial Union Assurance Co* (1885) 55 L.J.Q.B. 146. See [1960] J.B.L. at 276–279.

monetary compensation in full, even though the insurers may have incurred expenditure before the frustrating event.[14] It is arguable that the insurers might claim from the insured under s.1(1) of the Law Reform (Frustrated Contracts) Act 1943. Although that Act does not apply to contracts of insurance,[15] as we have seen, the contract here has become a contract to reinstate. Therefore the Act should apply. Section 1(3) provides that the party who has received a "valuable benefit" before the frustrating event may be ordered to pay such sum as the court considers just to the other party. However, it cannot really be said that the insured has received a valuable benefit if, in fact, he is deprived of his property by demolition or compulsory purchase.

16.2   Statutory Reinstatement

Section 83 of the Fires Prevention (Metropolis) Act 1774 is a potentially important, but perhaps relatively little used, provision. In essence it provides two things. Following a loss by fire, and only such a loss, it requires an insurance company, but not a Lloyd's underwriter,[16] to apply the policy moneys, so far as they will go, towards rebuilding or reinstating an insured building at the request of any person or persons interested in the building. Secondly, it authorises an insurance company so to act if they have grounds for suspecting that the insured was guilty of fraud or arson. The second point is obviously a useful protection to insurers, though it seems to add little to the usual contractual right they reserve which has just been examined. Of more interest is the obligation arising under s.83.

It should be noted first that the section applies only to fire policies on buildings,[17] but that it is not limited to buildings in London. There is clear authority that it applies throughout England and Wales,[18] but it does not

---

[14] See further Clarke, *The Law of Insurance Contracts*, para.29–2C.

[15] See s.2(5)(b).

[16] *Portavon Cinema Co v Price* [1939] 4 All E.R. 601. Quaere whether it could apply to an EU insurer selling fire insurance directly from its country of establishment.

[17] See, e.g. *Ex p. Gorely* (1864) 4 De G.J. & S. 477, where s.83 was held inapplicable to insurance of a tenant's trade fixtures.

[18] Above. It also applies to much of the Commonwealth. The New Zealand Law Commission (Report No.46, 1998, para.55) examined the section and recommended its repeal. The Law Commissions examined it as part of their general review of insurance contract law; see the Briefing Paper issued in March 2009, in which it invited views on whether it should be left alone, repealed or replaced. It is submitted that the last option would be the best one as a statutory right to reinstatement given to third parties interested in the property seems in principle unobjectionable; see also *MacGillivray on Insurance Law*, 13th edn, para.22–025. However, the Commissions concluded that it was best left alone: see the Summary of Responses (February 2010), available at *http://www.lawcom.gov.uk/wp-content/uploads/2015/03/ICL_s83_Fires_Prevention_Act_responses.pdf* [Accessed 1 January 2016].

apply to Scotland or Ireland.[19] Under s.83, reinstatement need only be to the extent of the policy moneys available, which should be compared with the position under contractual reinstatement. However, this does mean the whole of the money potentially available under the policy, even if the "person interested" has, in fact, only a limited insurable interest in the building.[20]

16.2.1 Request to reinstate

The obligation on an insurer under s.83 arises only upon a clear and distinct request to reinstate by a "person interested" (see below) before the insurer settles with the insured. A mere request not to pay the insured, for example, is not enough. In *Simpson v Scottish Union Insurance Co*,[21] the tenant of premises insured them, as he was obliged to do under his lease. Following a fire, the landlord wrote to the insurers asking them not to pay anything to the tenant and claiming that he was entitled to the benefit of the policy. Despite this, the insurers settled with the tenant. The landlord then proceeded to rebuild the premises and claimed that the insurers were liable to him. It was held that his claim was ill founded. His request to the insurers was not sufficient to invoke the section; it was not a request to reinstate but rather a claim to the money, and he had no other right to the benefit of the policy. In any event, s.83 does not authorise a person to perform the rebuilding himself and then claim the cost.

16.2.2 Remedy against insurer

If an insurer fails to comply with a proper request under s.83, it is likely that the appropriate remedy is a mandatory injunction to compel them to do so. This was the opinion of Page-Wood VC in the *Simpson* case, and although, in the later case of *Wimbledon Golf Club v Imperial Insurance Co*,[22] it was said that the only remedy is an injunction to restrain the insurers from paying the insured, it is submitted that the former opinion is the better one and certainly the one more in accord with the purpose of the section.

16.2.3 Person interested

The most interesting question is who is a "person interested" for the purposes of using s.83 to compel an insurer to reinstate. As has been seen, it is not

---

[19] *Westminster Fire v Glasgow Provident* (1888) 13 App. Cas. 699; *Andrews v Patriotic Assurance Co* (1886) 18 L.R.Ir. 355.
[20] *Simpson v Scottish Union Insurance Co* (1863) 1 H. & M. 618 at 628.
[21] *Simpson v Scottish Union Insurance Co* (1863) 1 H. & M. 618.
[22] *Wimbledon Golf Club v Imperial Insurance Co* (1902) 18 T.L.R. 815.

necessary that such a person has a full insurable interest in the property, nor is it necessary that the person has any contractual relationship with the insurer. On the other hand, the insured must be entitled to enforce the policy. The insured, however, is not such a person interested, so that he cannot compel reinstatement,[23] but otherwise it appears that anyone with a legal or equitable interest in the property can do so. In *Sinnot v Bowden*,[24] the mortgagee of the property, whose debt was considerably less than the amount of the loss, was held entitled to insist that the mortgagor's insurers reinstate. There have also been several cases where a landlord was held entitled to use s.83 against his tenant's insurer.[25]

Conversely, a tenant can compel his landlord's insurer to reinstate.[26] This can provide a practical solution to some problems raised by the requirement of insurable interest.[27] In *Lonsdale & Thompson Ltd v Black Arrow Group Plc*,[28] it was held that a tenant was entitled to use s.83 against the landlord's insurers even where the landlord had contracted to sell the freehold before the fire and thus no longer had any insurable interest. Although the benefit of the insurance did not pass to the purchasers of the freehold,[29] the policy was construed as inuring for the benefit of the tenant,[30] whose entitlement clearly survived the sale of the freehold.[31]

It may also be the case that the purchaser of real property between contract and completion can invoke s.83 against his vendor's insurers. This was clearly stated, obiter, in *Rayner v Preston*[32] and logically seems correct,

---

[23] *Reynolds v Phoenix Assurance Co* [1978] 2 Lloyd's Rep. 440, especially at 462.

[24] *Sinnot v Bowden* [1912] 2 Ch 414.

[25] For example *Vernon v Smith* (1821) 5 B. & Ald. 1.

[26] *Wimbledon Golf Club v Imperial Insurance Co* (1902) 18 T.L.R. 815; *Lonsdale & Thompson Ltd v Black Arrow Group Plc* [1993] 3 All E.R. 648. As standard commercial leases often provide for the landlord to insure, but also for the tenant's benefit (see 17.14), this is the more likely scenario today.

[27] See 4.7.

[28] *Lonsdale & Thompson Ltd v Black Arrow Group Plc* [1993] 3 All E.R. 648. See [1994] J.B.L. 188.

[29] See *Rayner v Preston* (1881) 18 Ch D 1, discussed at 11.1.1.

[30] The judge applied the analogy of the "bailee cases" (see 4.2.1). This disposed of the arguments of the insurers, following *Castellain v Preston* (1883) 11 Q.B.D. 380 (see 17.4), to the effect that allowing the tenant to benefit would result in the insured vendor profiting from his loss. In line with the modern trend (see 3.9.1), the question of the possible applicability of the Life Assurance Act 1774 was ignored.

[31] The same would apply to the facts of a case like *British Traders' Insurance Co v Monson* (1964) 111 C.L.R. 86 (see 4.7), where a tenant who has insured for full value is entitled only to the value of his interest and cannot claim the full value for the benefit of his landlord. If the landlord invokes s.83 in time, the result contended for by the tenant on such facts would in practice be achieved.

[32] *Rayner v Preston* (1881) 18 Ch D 1 at 15; see 11.1.1. See also *Royal Insurance Co Ltd v Mylius* (1926) 38 C.L.R. 477.

provided that the insured vendor has not received the full purchase price, in which case he will have suffered no loss.[33] If so, some of the difficulties surrounding the insurance position in this situation and the true meaning of s.47 of the Law of Property Act 1925 can be circumvented if, as is common, the new standard contract provision keeping the risk with the vendor is not adopted.[34]

16.3   The Insured's Duty to Reinstate?

Finally, there arise a number of questions not concerned with the position as between insured and insurer, but with those cases where the insured has recovered money from his insurer which a third party claims should be spent by the insured on reinstatement.

By s.108(2) of the Law of Property Act 1925, the mortgagee of property has the right to compel the mortgagor, who has insured and received money, to use it on reinstatement. Trustees who have received insurance money may reinstate trust property with it, but there is no obligation to do so.[35]

Apart from these cases, it is likely that the insured and the third party are parties to a contract that, it is argued, expressly or impliedly, provides for reinstatement at the third party's option. A hire-purchase contract may, for example, contain such an express term for the benefit of the owner in respect of insurance the owner requires to be effected by the hirer. Another common example would be a covenant to reinstate in a lease. However, in the absence of an express covenant to reinstate, the court will not usually imply one even where the insured covenanted to insure.[36] It may be, however, that the circumstances, including the imposition of a covenant to insure, show that the insurance was intended to be a joint one for the benefit of both parties, so that the third party may insist upon reinstatement.[37] In *Mumford Hotels Ltd v Wheeler*,[38] the tenant of property covenanted to pay what was called a "yearly insurance rent" equal to the premium necessary for a comprehensive policy on the premises. The landlord covenanted to effect such an insurance but did not covenant to reinstate. It was held that no such covenant could be

---

[33] See the decision of the High Court of Australia on an equivalent provision in *Kern Corp Ltd v Walter Reid Trading Pty Ltd* (1987) 61 A.L.J.R. 319 and the discussion in Derham, *Subrogation in Insurance Law*, at 61–64. The proviso mentioned is essential to overcome the decision in *Rayner v Preston*, above, because it is unlikely that any insurance effected by a vendor could ordinarily be construed as effected also for the benefit of the purchaser.

[34] See 11.1.2.

[35] Trustee Act 1925 s.20(4).

[36] *Lees v Whitely* (1866) L.R. 2 Eq. 143.

[37] This question is discussed further in the next chapter at 17.14.

[38] *Mumford Hotels Ltd v Wheeler* [1964] Ch 117.

implied, but the true inference from the circumstances was that the insurance was to be treated for the joint benefit of the insured landlord and the tenant, so that the latter had an interest in the policy moneys and could oblige the former to use them for reinstatement. On appropriate facts, this provides for an alternative route for such a tenant to achieve the same result as is available under s.83, as discussed, if, for example the section is no longer available because the insurer has settled with the landlord, or if s.83 does not apply at all.[39]

---

[39] For example because the insurer is a Lloyd's underwriter; see above. See also the discussion of insurance of third parties' interests in Ch.4.

CHAPTER 17

SUBROGATION

17.0

This chapter is concerned with the fundamental correlative of the principle of indemnity, namely, the insurer's right of subrogation.[1] Although often in the insurance context referred to as a right, it is really more in the nature of a restitutionary remedy. The "fundamental rule of insurance law" is

> "that the contract of insurance contained in a marine or fire policy is a contract of indemnity, and of indemnity only, and this contract means that the assured, in the case of a loss against which the policy has been made, shall be fully indemnified, but shall never be more than fully indemnified".[2]

A number of points arise simply from that oft-cited dictum and the doctrine of subrogation has many ramifications that must be examined. It is convenient first, though, to consider some general points.

17.1   Application of Subrogation

Subrogation applies to all insurance contracts which are contracts of indemnity, that is, particularly to contracts of fire, motor, property and liability insurance. It does not apply to life insurance[3] nor prima facie to accident insurance.[4] However, although payments under an accident policy are usually of a fixed stated sum or according to a fixed scale, it is possible to have such policies whereby payments are made on an indemnity basis, in other words are related to specific heads of loss suffered by the insured. This might well also be the case in, for example, a health insurance policy or a medical expenses section of a larger policy. There can be no real doubt that these policies are indemnity policies and therefore should attract the right of subrogation.[5] It

---

[1] An exhaustive and most useful monograph, although now somewhat dated, is R. Derham, *Subrogation in Insurance Law*, (Sydney: Law Book Company, 1985). See also Mitchell, *The Law of Subrogation* (Oxford, 1994).

[2] Brett LJ in *Castellain v Preston* (1883) 11 Q.B.D. 380 at 388.

[3] *Solicitors & General Life Assurance Society v Lamb* (1864) 2 De G. J. & S. 251.

[4] *Theobald v Railway Passengers Assurance Co* (1854) 10 Exch. 45.

[5] See various North American authorities: *Glyn v Scottish Union & National Insurance Co* (1963) 40 D.L.R. (2d) 929, where subrogation was held applicable to medical payments cover under a motor policy, and *Gibson v Sun Life Assurance Co of Canada* (1985) 7 C.C.L.I. 65, where it was held applicable to a disability insurance policy;

has indeed been argued[6] that many forms of life insurance have indemnity intentions, a point discussed earlier and reinforced by the requirement of s.3 of the Life Assurance Act 1774.[7] Notable examples are "keyman" policies effected by employers on the lives of their employees, and policies by creditors on the lives of their debtors. The only real purpose of such insurance is to indemnify against the risk of a loss. However, whatever the attractions of such an argument, it seems safe to assume that the law would not regard any form of life insurance as attracting the right of subrogation.

17.2   Origins of Subrogation

There has been some dispute as to the true origins of the doctrine of subrogation. Some claim to have found traces in Roman law. It was probably first developed in this country in the Courts of Chancery and Admiralty,[8] and a number of authorities refer to it as a creature of equity.[9] On the other hand, some modern cases, particularly in judgments delivered by Lord Diplock, refer to it as a common law doctrine arising out of a term implied into every contract of indemnity insurance.[10]

The matter was considered by the House of Lords in *Napier v Hunter*.[11] Here the question arose in an acute form. The insureds were members of a Lloyd's syndicate who in effect reinsured the risks they had agreed to bear by insuring with "stop loss" insurers. Claims on the insurance were made and paid by the insurers and subsequently money was recovered from a third party whose negligence had caused the loss to the insureds.[12] This money was held by a firm of solicitors. There was no dispute as to the entitlement

---

Michigan Medical Services v Sharpe 339 Mich. 574, 54 N.W. (2d) 713 (1954), where there was an express term providing for subrogation; compare *Michigan Hospital Services v Sharpe* 339 Mich. 375, 63 N.W. (2d) 638 (1954), a case which arose out of the same facts, where the absence of such a term was fatal. See generally, Kimball and Davis, "The extension of insurance subrogation" (1962) 60 Mich. L.R. 841, especially at 860–861.

[6] Kimball and Davis, (1962) 60 Mich. L.R. 841.

[7] See Ch.3, especially at 3.4.

[8] Goff and Jones, *The Law of Restitution*, 6th edn (London: Sweet & Maxwell, 2002) at 523.

[9] See, e.g. *Burnand v Rodocanachi* (1882) 7 App. Cas. 333 at 339; *Morris v Ford Motor Co Ltd* [1973] 1 Q.B. 792 at 800–801.

[10] Especially, *Yorkshire Insurance Co v Nisbet Shipping Co* [1962] 2 Q.B. 330 at 339; *Morris v Ford Motor Co*, above, at 809–812; *Hobbs v Marlowe* [1977] 2 All E.R. 241 at 254–255.

[11] *Napier v Hunter* [1993] 2 W.L.R. 42. The views of Lord Diplock were treated with scant respect: see especially Lord Browne-Wilkinson at 65. Another important aspect of this decision is considered at 17.4.1.

[12] In fact, the third party was the syndicate's managing agent who had negligently committed the insureds to the risks.

of the insurers to at least some money back,[13] but the question was whether
the insurers had merely a personal claim pursued by means of an action
for money had and received, that is a common law right only, or whether
they also had an equitable proprietary claim to part of the fund held by the
solicitors.[14]

Their Lordships were unanimous in holding that insurers have an equitable interest in money received by the insured (or someone acting for him).
The opinions contain reviews of the history of the doctrine of subrogation
that indicate that at the very least it developed in equity as well as at
common law.[15] In the words of Lord Templeman:

> "The principles which dictated the decisions of our ancestors and inspired their
> references to the equitable obligations of an insured person towards an insurer
> entitled to subrogation are discernible and immutable. They establish that such
> an insurer has an enforceable equitable interest in the damages payable by the
> wrongdoer."[16]

The equitable interest of the insurers was to be satisfied by saying that
they had a lien or charge over the money in question, rather than by saying
that the money was impressed with a trust.[17] Thus, if the insured who has
received the money goes bankrupt or, if a company, goes into insolvent liquidation, the insurers can recover the money without regard to the claims of

---

[13] By virtue of the first aspect of subrogation described below. The issue as to how
much is considered at 17.4.1.

[14] Differing views were expressed on the question of whether insurers would have
an equitable claim to use the insured's name in litigation, the second aspect of
subrogation described below. Lord Templeman thought that they would have (at
52–53), but reserved the question (at 56) in the light of the views expressed by
Lord Goff (at 61). The latter was inclined to support the view expressed by Lord
Templeman, but referred to decisions indicating the contrary and preferred not
to reach a firm conclusion without full consideration of the authorities. This may
be important in the light of the decision in *Morris v Ford Motor Co Ltd* [1973] 1
Q.B. 792, where Lord Denning denied the use of this aspect of subrogation on
"equitable" grounds. See further, at 17.16. In *Ballast Plc* [2006] EWHC 3189
(Ch); [2007] Lloyd's Rep. I.R. 742, Lawrence Collins J held that there is no such
equitable interest.

[15] Particular reliance was placed on the decisions in *Randal v Cockran* (1748) 1 Ves.
Sen. 98; *White v Dobinson* (1844) 14 Sim. 273; *Commercial Union Assurance Co v Lister*
(1874) L.R. 9 Ch. App. 483 and *Re Miller Gibb & Co Ltd* [1957] 1 W.L.R. 703,
showing that equity enforced rights of subrogation against an insured as well as
intervening to enable the insurer to sue in the name of the insured. A very persuasive argument to this effect is also made by Derham, above, Ch.1.

[16] *Napier v Hunter* [1993] 2 W.L.R. at 64.

[17] The imposition of a trust would, it was felt, impose too great a burden on the
person actually holding the money.

other creditors.[18] Money paid into court for the benefit of the insured may also be subject to a lien in favour of the insurers, which can take priority over any claim under the Legal Aid Board's statutory charge.[19] The insurers' proprietary interest cannot be defeated by any inequitable conduct on their part, although if the insured suffered any loss or prejudice from such conduct, he would have a right to claim damages for breach of an implied term that the insurers will not exercise subrogation rights to the prejudice of the insured.[20]

Although it has been clearly held that subrogation in insurance is governed by equitable as well as common law principles, it may be more proper to classify it as a legal doctrine supported by equity.[21] Further, it is clear that its application can be modified, excluded or extended by contract. The extension of subrogation rights by express terms in insurance policies is commonplace, and examples of this appear throughout this chapter.

It should also be noted that the doctrine of subrogation applies more widely than simply to insurance.[22] However, it is probably safe to proceed upon the understanding that, although the essential nature of subrogation applies in all cases, each is self-contained, and in examining insurance subrogation, these other contexts may be ignored. Indeed it has been said in the House of Lords that it should not be assumed that principles that grew up in one area can be transplanted to another.[23]

---

[18] *Re Miller, Gibb & Co* [1957] 1 W.L.R. 703, approved by the House of Lords in *Napier v Hunter*. This aspect of the decision in *Napier v Hunter* is in line with other modern authorities extending the range of equitable proprietary remedies. Discussion of the appropriateness of this trend is outside the scope of this book, but is much considered in the restitution law texts and other writings. For a very useful critical comment, see Mitchell, [1993] L.M.C.L.Q. 192.

[19] *England v Guardian Insurance Ltd* [2000] Lloyd's Rep. I.R. 404.

[20] See above.

[21] For more detailed discussion, see *MacGillivray on Insurance Law*, 13th edn, at 22–013 to 22–023. See also the dictum of Lord Hoffmann in *Banque Financière de la Cité v Parc (Battersea) Ltd* [1998] 1 All E.R. 737 at 744–745, where he said that, although *Napier v Hunter* had rejected the idea that subrogation was exclusively a common law doctrine and assigned a larger role to equitable principles, "there was no dispute that the doctrine of subrogation in insurance rests upon the common intention of the parties and gives effect to the principle of indemnity embodied in the contract".

[22] For a full description, see Goff and Jones, *The Law of Restitution*, Ch.27 and Mitchell, above fn.1.

[23] *Orapko v Manson Investments* [1977] 3 W.L.R. 229 at 234 (Lord Diplock). See also Lord Hoffmann in *Banque Financière de la Cité v Parc (Battersea) Ltd*, above, where he pointed out that subrogation arising out of contract and subrogation to prevent unjust enrichment are "radically different institutions".

17.3   The Two Aspects of Subrogation

The passage cited earlier from the leading case of *Castellain v Preston*[24] by itself gives a picture of only one aspect of the doctrine of subrogation, namely that the insured cannot make a profit from his loss and that for any profit he does make he is accountable in equity to his insurer. Later passages, though, in the judgments in that case, describe the second aspect of the doctrine. This is the right of the insurer who has indemnified his insured to step into the shoes of the insured—the literal meaning of "subrogation"—and in his name pursue any right of action available to the insured which may diminish the loss insured against. Typically, the insured's right will be to sue a third party liable to pay damages in tort or for breach of contract or under a statutory right or liable to provide an indemnity to the insured, the third party's liability being in respect of the event for which the insured has recovered from his insurer. As already noted, the insured can, if necessary, be compelled to lend his name for the purposes of the action.[25]

Although the purposes of these two aspects of subrogation are the same, namely, the prevention of the unjust enrichment of the insured, they are essentially different and, to some extent, different principles are relevant and different qualifications surround each aspect. They will therefore be examined separately.

17.4   The Insured Cannot Make a Profit

The leading illustration here is still the case of *Castellain v Preston*.[26] This was the sequel to the decision in *Rayner v Preston*,[27] which was examined in Ch.11.[28] It will be recalled that the insured vendor of a house, which was burnt down between the contract and completion, recovered money from his insurer for which he was held not accountable to his purchaser. The latter subsequently completed the purchase, as he was bound to do despite the fire, and paid the agreed price. It was held that the vendor was therefore bound to account to his insurer for the money the latter had paid. The Court of Appeal followed the slightly earlier decision in *Darrell v Tibbits*,[29] where the owner of a house that was let to a tenant insured it against fire. The local authority caused an explosion that damaged the house, and paid compensation to the tenant. The insurers paid the insured, but then sought to recover this sum.

---

[24] *Castellain v Preston* (1883) 11 Q.B.D. 380.
[25] *King v Victoria Insurance Co Ltd* [1896] A.C. 250 at 255–256; *Edwards v Motor Union Insurance Co* [1922] 2 K.B. 249 at 254.
[26] *Castellain v Preston* (1883) 11 Q.B.D. 380.
[27] *Rayner v Preston* (1881) 18 Ch D 1.
[28] See 11.1.1.
[29] *Darrell v Tibbits* (1880) 5 Q.B.D. 560.

It was held that they were entitled to succeed, as the insured had already been compensated by virtue of the tenant's receiving the compensation that had been used to repair the house. In both cases, to have allowed the insured to keep the insurance money would have meant that he would have been doubly indemnified, and would have profited from his loss. In *Darrell v Tibbits*, the tenant had covenanted to repair the house in the event of losses such as occurred. It was made clear that the same result would in effect have happened had the insurers, upon payment to the landlord, used his name to sue the tenant under this covenant. This, of course, would have involved the other aspect of the doctrine of subrogation.

The rule that the insured cannot profit from his loss is subject to three limitations. First, he is accountable only when he has been fully indemnified. Secondly, if he receives a gift following the loss, this may not necessarily be taken into account. Thirdly, if a surplus results after the insurer has recovered back its money, it seems that the insured is entitled to keep it. These three points must now be examined in detail.

17.4.1 Full indemnity

In *Scottish Union & National Insurance Co v Davis*,[30] the defendant insured's damaged car was handed to a garage for repair with the consent of the insurers. After three attempts at repair by the garage, the insured was not satisfied with their work and took the car elsewhere. The garage nonetheless sent their bill to the insurers who paid it without getting a satisfaction note signed by the insured. The latter then recovered compensation from the party originally responsible for the damage and used this money to have his car properly repaired. The insurers claimed this latter sum, but the Court of Appeal had no difficulty in rejecting their claim. "You only have a right to subrogation in a case like this when you have indemnified the assured, and one thing that is quite plain is that the insurers have never done that."[31]

It was not clear from this decision whether the insured must merely be fully indemnified within the terms of the policy before the duty to account arises or whether he must be fully compensated. This is an issue that is likely to arise commonly in practice. Three simple illustrations can be given for the purposes of discussion. In the first, property insured for £100 may be worth £200 or cost £200 to replace; that is, it is under-insured.[32] If the property is destroyed, and the insured recovers £100 from his insurers and then subsequently receives £100 from the party responsible for the loss, must he account to his insurers for the latter sum, on the grounds that they have fully

---

[30] *Scottish Union & National Insurance Co v Davis* [1970] 1 Lloyd's Rep. 1.
[31] Per Russell LJ, above at 5.
[32] As to under-insurance generally, see 15.9.

indemnified him under the terms of the insurance?[33] The second illustration is where the policy contains an excess or deductible, so that the insured bears the first part of any loss.[34] If he recovers that from the party responsible for the loss, is he accountable to the insurers?

For the third illustration, suppose the case of a motor insured whose car is damaged in an accident. His insurers pay the costs of repair, but have no interest in pursuing their right to sue the person responsible for the accident. The insured recovers from the third party a sum that includes compensation for what we can term consequential losses in respect of which he was not insured; these might include the cost of hiring a substitute car while his was being repaired,[35] and, if the insured needs his car for business purposes, loss of profits while he was without his car. Can the insurers claim that he has profited because he was fully indemnified by them, even though he was not fully compensated by them?

Until recently, there were no clear answers to these questions in any decided English case.[36] In *Napier v Hunter*,[37] the House of Lords gave an authoritative answer at least to the second one. The facts of this case have been briefly described earlier. A relatively simple set of figures was used for the purposes of argument and decision. The loss suffered by the insured was £160,000. The limit of the insurers' liability, that is the sum insured, was £125,000, and there was an excess of £25,000. The sum recovered from the third party responsible for the loss was £130,000. The insurers paid the insured £100,000, namely the sum insured less the excess. The question was whether the insured was entitled to £60,000 of the sum recovered from the

---

[33] This assumes that the insured acted properly in accepting only £100 from the other party. If he did not, he will have failed to act in good faith and prejudiced his insurers' right of subrogation and be liable to the insurers accordingly; see 17.8. However, it may be that the insured was able to recover only £100, e.g. because of the third party's impecuniosity.

[34] See 15.10.

[35] See the facts of *Hobbs v Marlowe* [1977] 2 All E.R. 241, discussed in 17.15. It is now common for this sort of loss to be insured.

[36] A decision of the Canadian Supreme Court, *Ledingham v Ontario Hospital Services Commission* (1974) 46 D.L.R. (3d) 699 seemed to support a general view that an insured had to be fully compensated before the insurers obtained rights of subrogation, and was cited and discussed in earlier editions of this book as authority for that (at 241 of the 2nd edn). There are other Commonwealth authorities to similar effect, admirably summarised in Derham, *Subrogation in Insurance Law* (1985), Ch.12. However, except in respect of genuinely uninsured losses, this no longer seems supportable in the light of *Napier v Hunter*, considered below.

[37] *Napier v Hunter* [1993] 2 W.L.R. 42. The lower courts' decisions are reported, sub nom. *Napier v Kershaw Ltd*, at [1993] 1 Lloyd's Rep. 10. Saville J at first instance held in favour of the insured, but the Court of Appeal's decision on this point was the same as that of the House of Lords.

third party, so that he would recover the whole of his loss, and the insurer would therefore receive £70,000 back; or whether the insurer was entitled to a greater proportion of the £130,000, so that the insured would be under-compensated.

It was held that the latter approach was the correct one. The effect of the excess was that the insured was deemed to be his own insurer for the amount of that excess, namely £25,000. Further, he must be assumed to have agreed to bear any loss over the sum insured, namely over £125,000. The result was that the insured was entitled to only £35,000 of the sum of £130,000 recovered from the third party, that is his uninsured loss of £60,000 less the amount of the excess, and the insurers were entitled to the balance of £95,000.

Only Lords Templeman and Jauncey considered this aspect of the decision in *Napier v Hunter* in detail. The former[38] rationalised the position by assuming that there were in fact three insurances, the first for the first £25,000 of any loss, the second for the next £100,000 and the third for any payment in excess of £125,000. On the loss of £160,000, the insured would recover £25,000, £100,000 and £35,000 from the respective insurers. On the recovery of £130,000, £35,000 would first go back to the third insurers and the remaining £95,000 would go back to the second insurers. The latter were, of course, the actual insurers in the case. The reasoning of Lord Jauncey is summed up in this dictum[39]:

"When an insured loss is diminished by a recovery from a third party, whether before or after any indemnification has been made, the ultimate loss is simply the initial loss minus the recovery and it is that sum to which the provisions of the policy of assurance apply including any provision as to an excess."

Thus, on the assumed figures, the ultimate loss was £30,000, namely the initial loss of £160,000 less the recovery of £130,000, and the excess of £25,000 applied to the £30,000 so that the insured recovered from the insurers only £5,000. Although no previous authority pointed unequivocally to this result, dicta were cited[40] which, in the words of Lord Jauncey[41] were significant because of:

"the emphasis they place upon the fact that in the context of recoveries subrogation is concerned only with the loss against which the assured is insured rather than any general loss. If an assured has suffered an insured loss and an uninsured

---

[38] Above at 46–48.
[39] Above at 64.
[40] Especially from *Castellain v Preston* (1883) 11 Q.B.D. 380 at 386, 393 and 395 and *Burnand v Rodocanachi* (1882) 7 App. Cas. 333 at 339.
[41] *Napier v Hunter* [1993] 2 W.L.R. at 63.

loss full indemnification of the former subrogates the insurers irrespective of the fact that the assured has not yet recovered the uninsured loss."

The logic of the reasoning here is difficult to fault, and it is hard to disagree with the result in a situation involving commercial insurance where it must perhaps be assumed that the parties are fully aware as to the significance of an excess. However, it may not be so easy in other contexts to rationalise the result by saying that the insured agreed to bear the amount of the excess. At least some insureds do not in reality so agree. In many classes of insurance, they have no choice as to whether or not there is to be an excess, although in some they may have a choice as to the amount of the excess.

Strictly perhaps, *Napier v Hunter* was concerned only with the effect of an excess on subrogation recoveries. However, it seems clear that the same reasoning would apply to a case of under-insurance. Indeed, Lord Templeman expressly stated[42] that the insured is deemed to be his own insurer of any loss above the sum insured. This suggests that, in the example given above, the insured would be bound to account to the insurer for the £100 received from the third party responsible for the loss. Again, this result might work harshly on some insureds.

However, the case of consequential losses that are uninsured, illustrated by the third example given above, seems quite different. They are simply not covered by the policy and it can hardly be said that the insured is deemed to be his own insurer in respect of them. Another way of putting it is to say that, as mentioned earlier, the purpose of subrogation is to prevent unjust enrichment, and it can hardly be said that an insured is unjustly enriched until he receives full compensation for his loss, including compensation for such consequential losses.

What does seem quite clear is that the insured is entitled to deduct from any sum to which the insurer is entitled any legal or other reasonably incurred expenditure arising in reasonable attempts to recover the loss that has been insured.[43]

17.4.2 Gifts

If the insured has been fully indemnified, but he also receives a gift from another to mitigate the effects of his loss, he will normally have to account to his insurers for the amount of the gift. In *Stearns v Village Main Reef Gold Mining Co*,[44] the South African Government commandeered the defendant's insured gold. The insurers paid the defendant for a total loss. The

---

[42] Above at 47.
[43] *England v Guardian Insurance Ltd* [2000] Lloyd's Rep. I.R. 404.
[44] *Stearns v Village Main Reef Gold Mining Co* (1905) 10 Com. Cas. 89.

Government then returned a sum of money to the insured in return for the latter's agreeing to keep the mine open. It was held that the insurers were entitled to recover the equivalent of that money because it had been given in order to diminish the insured's loss. This decision can be compared with the earlier marine insurance case of *Burnand v Rodocanachi*.[45] Here, during the American Civil War, the insured ship was destroyed by a Confederate cruiser. The insurers paid the agreed value. The insured subsequently received a gift from the United States Government. The House of Lords held that as, according to the construction of the relevant statute authorising the payment, this money was paid purely as a gift and intended to benefit the insured over and above any insurance money, the insurers were not entitled to claim it. It is clear that this case establishes the exception rather than the rule, and that the insured will be entitled to retain the gift only when it was intended as extra compensation for him.

17.4.3 A surplus

If, somewhat unusually perhaps, there happens to be a surplus after the insurers have recovered their money, the insured is entitled to keep it, in other words the insurers' subrogation rights extend only to the amount they actually paid to the insured. In *Yorkshire Insurance Co v Nisbet Shipping Co*,[46] the point arose in a neat form. An insured ship was lost in 1945 as the result of a collision and the insurers paid its agreed value of £72,000. With the latter's consent, the insured started proceedings against the Canadian Government, owners of the other ship, and in 1955 the Government was eventually found liable. The damages awarded were some £75,000, which were properly converted into Canadian dollars at the rate of exchange prevalent at the time of the collision. That sum was paid to the insured in 1958, but when it was transmitted to this country and converted into sterling, it produced a sum of some £126,000, because the pound had been devalued in 1949. The insured could not of course deny the insurers' entitlement to £72,000, but disputed that they were entitled to the surplus of nearly £55,000. Diplock J held that the subrogation rights of the insurers extended only to the sums they had paid out. Although he was construing s.79 of the Marine Insurance Act 1906, there can be no doubt that the decision is generally applicable. Although logically unimpeachable,[47] the result is somewhat unfair. After all, the insured had the benefit of prompt payment of the money in 1945. It was the insurers who were out of pocket for some 13 years or more. Had the

---

[45] *Burnand v Rodocanachi* (1882) 7 App. Cas. 333.

[46] *Yorkshire Insurance Co v Nisbet Shipping Co* [1962] 2 Q.B. 330.

[47] But note the comments of Megaw LJ in *Lucas v ECGD* [1973] 1 W.L.R. 914 at 924, and the possible effects of express subrogation terms; see 17.13.

insurers actually exercised their right to sue the Canadian Government in the insured's name, they would probably have been better off because they would have been entitled to claim interest on the money for their own benefit.[48]

17.5   The Insurer's Right to Take Action

The insurer's right to bring proceedings in the name of the insured is long established, being referred to as a commonplace occurrence as long ago as 1782 in *Mason v Sainsbury*.[49] It is important to remember, however, that the action remains the insured's and that the defendant, if he is adjudged liable, gets a good discharge only if he pays the insured. If the insured should refuse to allow his name to be used, the insurer can, as an alternative to compelling it, bring proceedings against the wrongdoer and join the insured as second defendant.[50]

A classic illustration of the insurer's right is the decision of the House of Lords in *Lister v Romford Ice and Cold Storage Ltd*.[51] There an employee of the respondent negligently injured another employee; in fact, they were son and father respectively. The respondent was therefore vicariously liable to pay damages to the father, an award satisfied by the respondent's liability insurers, who then used the respondent's name to sue the negligent employee to recoup the loss. The claim was that the employee had failed to exercise the reasonable care and skill impliedly expected as part of an employee's duty to his employer, and, by a majority, the House of Lords held that the claim succeeded. The majority regarded the fact that the action was in reality brought by the insurers as irrelevant. There was such an implied term in the employee's contract of employment and he had broken it. The main defence of the appellant was that, even if he should have acted with reasonable care and skill, if in fact his employer had insured against the consequences of a breach to a third party, there was equally to be implied in his contract of employment a term that he would be entitled to the benefit of that insurance. This persuasive reasoning was adopted by the dissenting judges, in particular by Lord Radcliffe, whose judgment is, it is suggested, much more realistic than

---

[48] *Cousins v D & C Carriers* [1971] 2 Q.B. 230; see 17.11.

[49] *Mason v Sainsbury* (1782) 3 Doug. K.B. 61 at 64 (Lord Mansfield)—"Every day the insurer is put into the shoes of the assured". Note that if the insured is a company which has been wound up, the insurers have no rights since the insured's name no longer exists to be used: *M H Smith (Plant Hire) Ltd v D L Mainwaring* [1986] B.C.L.C. 342.

[50] In special circumstances the reality of the situation, i.e. that the action is really being brought by the insurers, may be recognised, as, e.g. in *Graham v Entec Europe Ltd* [2003] EWCA Civ 1177; [2004] Lloyd's Rep. I.R. 660, construing the meaning of knowledge for the purposes of s.14A of the Limitation Act 1980.

[51] *Lister v Romford Ice and Cold Storage Ltd* [1957] A.C. 555.

those of the majority.[52] Although, as will be seen later, employers' liability insurers have as a result of this decision, agreed to forgo their subrogation rights in this sort of case,[53] the decision does illustrate that the consequences of this aspect of the doctrine of subrogation can be wasteful.[54]

A more recent example of the second aspect of subrogation in a different context is *Caledonia North Sea Ltd v British Telecommunications Plc*.[55] Here, the matter arose as a consequence of the Piper Alpha disaster, when fire on a North Sea oil rig killed many people thereon. The insured's legal liability to the dependants of the victims had been satisfied by their insurers, who then successfully claimed by way of subrogation against various contractors engaged on the project to build the oil rig who had given indemnities to the insured against their liability.[56]

There are a number of very important limitations surrounding, and consequences of, this aspect of the doctrine of subrogation. These will be examined under the following heads.

---

[52] See also Parsons, "Individual responsibility versus enterprise liability" (1956) 29 A.L.J. 714, a comment on the Court of Appeal decision which was decided the same way but again only by a majority.

[53] See Gardiner (1959) 22 M.L.R. 652.

[54] See also 17.17, and compare *Morris v Ford Motor Co* [1973] Q.B. 792 discussed at 17.16. A more recent straightforward example is *Bee v Jensen (No.2)* [2007] EWCA Civ 923; [2008] Lloyd's Rep. I.R. 221, where the claimant, which in reality was his insurers, was held entitled to recover the reasonable costs of hiring a replacement vehicle, which had been paid by his insurers, when his car was damaged by the negligence of the defendant. In reality the action was against the latter's insurers, for the sum of just over £610! This does appear somewhat wasteful, although it was concerned with an important principle so far as motor insurers are concerned, namely whether if they provide a replacement hire care under arrangements already made, and which might cost more than their insured would be liable to pay by shopping around, they can nonetheless recover the actual costs. The Court of Appeal confirmed that they can do so as long as those costs are reasonable.

[55] *Caledonia North Sea Ltd v British Telecommunications Plc* [2002] UKHL 4; [2002] Lloyd's Rep. I.R. 261; affirming the decision reported sub nom. *Caledonia North Sea Ltd v London Bridge Engineering Ltd* [2000] Lloyd's Rep. I.R. 249; for a comment on the Inner House decision, see [2000] J.B.L. 347.

[56] The particular significance of the case lies in the fact that the House of Lords and the Inner House of the Court of Session, in allowing subrogation, overturned the decision of the judge at first instance. He had held that the contractors were indemnifiers in a similar position to insurers and that the doctrine of contribution (discussed in the next chapter) rather than subrogation should apply. This would have upset the basis of the carefully agreed scheme for liabilities between the various contractors, reflecting what is a standard commercial arrangement in many construction projects.

17.6   The Insured Must Be Indemnified

As with the first aspect of subrogation, the insured must be indemnified by the insurer before the latter's right arises, and this is in respect of all claims made by the insured in respect of the particular event. In *Page v Scottish Insurance Corp*,[57] P, while driving F's car, negligently collided with and damaged T's car, as well as damaging F's car. F's insurers instructed P to have F's car repaired, but refused to pay these costs and, before indemnifying P against the claim of T, claimed to have the right to sue P in the name of F for damages for negligently driving F's car, and to be able to set off against the repair costs the damages payable to T. The Court of Appeal held that the insurers' exercise of their subrogation rights in F's name was premature: "The underwriter [has] no right to subrogation unless and until he [has] fully indemnified the insured under the policy".[58]

The question again arises whether it is enough for the insurer fully to have indemnified the insured under the policy, or whether the insured must be fully compensated. Similar examples to those given earlier[59] can be used to illustrate this point. Most apt, because of its likely occurrence, is the case of the insured car driver fully indemnified for car damage but with a claim for uninsured losses against the tortfeasor, which might be for consequential loss and/or the sum not recovered from his insurer because of an excess clause in his policy. In *Page v Scottish*, Scrutton LJ expressly reserved the question whether full compensation is necessary.[60] There is some authority that it is,[61] but it now seems certain that the courts would hold that only a full indemnity is necessary.[62] If, as the result of a subrogation action, the insurer recovered more than it had paid the insured, the latter would be entitled to the surplus in so far as it represented an uninsured loss. In any event, as will be seen, if the insurer declines to sue, the insured can himself bring proceedings.

In practice, this question may be a rather academic one. This aspect of the doctrine of subrogation is frequently covered by an express clause in the policy vesting subrogation rights in the insurer upon indemnification under the policy or even, sometimes, before that.[63]

---

[57] *Page v Scottish Insurance Corp* (1929) 98 L.J.K.B. 308.

[58] Above, at 311, per Scrutton LJ.

[59] See 17.4.1.

[60] *Page v Scottish Insurance Corp* (1929) 98 L.J.K.B. 308 at 312.

[61] For example the Canadian decision in *Globe & Rutgers Fire Insurance Co v Truedell* [1927] 2 D.L.R. 659.

[62] As a result of the decision in *Napier v Hunter* [1993] 2 W.L.R. 42, discussed at 17.4.1. Although the decision was not concerned with this aspect of subrogation, the thrust of the reasoning dictates that there can be no distinction on this point between the two aspects.

[63] See 17.13.

17.7   Who Controls the Proceedings?

It follows from the points just discussed that, until the insured is indemnified and in the absence of anything to the contrary in the policy, as a matter of general law he has the right to sue the wrongdoer and control the proceedings. In *Commercial Union Assurance Co v Lister*,[64] the insured's mill was damaged by an explosion for which, it was alleged, the local authority was liable. He was insured for £33,000 but the damage was estimated at £55,000. The insured wished to sue the authority, but the insurers sought a declaration that they were entitled to the benefit of any such action. It was held that, as he would not be fully indemnified by his insurers, the insured was entitled to bring and control the action, provided he acted bona fide and sued for the whole loss.[65] In addition, before the insurers have the right to control, they must agree to indemnify the insured in respect of costs. It is also clear that even if the insured has been fully indemnified, he can if he wishes, sue the third party and control the proceedings if the insurer declines. The insurer has no right to stop the insured.[66]

In practice, though, many of these points may be redundant. Express subrogation clauses will often give the insurers the right to control the proceedings regardless of indemnification. One important question may then arise as to the position of the insurers who elect not to take control, in particular as to their liability for costs, as the standard term provides that if the insurers do take control, it is at their expense. Again the typical case may involve an under-insured insured who has been paid by his insurers and has a claim against a tortfeasor that he wishes to exercise to recover his uninsured loss. The insurers are not interested, save in the possibility of recovering anything if the insured is successful. The insured, as has been seen, must sue for his whole loss. Can he claim that the insurer must bear the costs of his action on the ground that, if he succeeds, it will be partly to the benefit of his insurers, and had they taken control, they would have been responsible for the costs? These facts arose in the New Zealand case of *Arthur Barnett Ltd v National Insurance Co of New Zealand*,[67] where the Court of Appeal held that the insurers were not responsible. This result is also implied by the course of events in *Hobbs v Marlowe*,[68] a case on similar facts which will be examined later, but where the point was not actually in issue.

---

[64] *Commercial Union Assurance Co v Lister* (1874) L.R. 9 Ch.483.
[65] The requirement on the insured to act in good faith in the interests of the insurer was confirmed in *Napier v Hunter*, above.
[66] *Morley v Moore* [1936] 2 K.B. 359; *Hobbs v Marlowe* [1977] 2 All E.R. 241.
[67] *Arthur Barnett Ltd v National Insurance Co of New Zealand* [1965] N.Z.L.R. 874.
[68] *Hobbs v Marlowe* [1977] 2 All E.R. 241. See 17.15.

17.8   The Insured Must Not Do Anything to Prejudice the Insurer

It has just been seen that the insured who takes proceedings against a wrong-doer must sue for his whole loss, even if he has been partly indemnified by his insurers who decline to exercise their subrogation rights. This is perhaps one aspect of the general principle that, once rights of subrogation exist or potentially exist for the benefit of the insurers, the insured must not do any-thing which might prejudice those rights on pain of his being liable to repay to the insurers as damages the amount which the insurers have paid or, where appropriate, of the insurers being able to avoid liability. If the insured does so act, he will have broken the duty of good faith imposed on him.[69]

Therefore, while a compromise entered into between the insured and the wrongdoer will normally bind the insurers, such a compromise, whether agreed before or after indemnification by the insurers, will amount to a breach of this duty of the insured. However, the insured must actually prej-udice the insurers' position, so that if his claim against the third party is a doubtful one and he acts bona fide in the interests of the insurers as well as himself, he will not suffer. In *West of England Fire Insurance Co v Isaacs*,[70] the defendant insured property of which he was the sub-tenant. Following a fire, he recovered money from the insurers, which he paid to the tenant of the property who had covenanted with both him and the head landlord to insure. He undertook also not to sue the tenant for breach of this covenant, it appearing that the latter had not adequately insured. It was held that the insured was liable to return the equivalent money to the insurers, having prejudiced their potential right to use his name to sue the tenant for breach of the insuring covenant. There are a number of other illustrations in the cases of the same point, involving insureds who compromised a statutory claim or a claim in tort against a wrongdoer.[71] The principle will obviously apply if the insured actually sues the wrongdoer and recovers only his uninsured loss.[72]

---

[69] As confirmed in *Napier v Hunter* [1993] 2 W.L.R. 42. See the discussion in the recent decision in *Horwood v Land of Leather Ltd* [2010] EWHC 546 (Comm) at [56] to [70].

[70] *West of England Fire Insurance Co v Isaacs* [1897] 1 Q.B. 226.

[71] For example *Phoenix Assurance Co v Spooner* [1905] 2 K. B. 753; *Re Law Fire Assurance Co* (1888) 4 T.L.R. 309; *Horse, Carriage & General Insurance Co v Petch* (1916) 33 T.L.R. 131. In *Horwood v Land of Leather Ltd* [2010] EWHC 546 (Comm); [2010] Lloyd's Rep. I.R. 453 at [67], Teare J was prepared to accept, obiter, that there was an implied term that the insured must act reasonably and in good faith with regards to the interests of the insurer and its right of subrogation, but it is not thought that he would have imposed a duty on the insured to take positive steps in this regard.

[72] That this is probably a fairly common occurrence is illustrated by the facts of a case like *Hayler v Chapman* [1989] 1 Lloyd's Rep. 490.

It seems that this principle could unjustifiably penalise an innocent insured not aware of the intricacies of subrogation and tort claims. For example, following a car accident, an insured who was the innocent party might well, because his insurance is comprehensive, agree quite reasonably with the other driver that he will not pursue any claim against her. If that were a binding agreement, it would prejudice the insurers' subrogation rights and yet it seems a harsh application of the principle. This is not to suggest, of course, that an insurer would necessarily take the point, but the question remains as to whether it should be there to be taken.

17.9 The Wrongdoer's Position Vis-à-vis the Insurer

A wrongdoing defendant cannot claim in defence that, in reality, the claimant is actually an insurer and that the nominal claimant has already been fully compensated for the defendant's wrong.[73] The proceeds of insurance are ignored in assessing damages,[74] a principle that operates by way of exception to the rule against double recovery.[75] Equally, it is no defence for the defendant to claim that the insurer satisfied the claimant's claim when in law it was not bound to, for example, because the insurer had the right to avoid liability under the policy.[76] He can, however, rely on a prior agreement between himself and the insured that the latter would limit his rights. This would have been the result in *Lister v Romford Ice and Cold Storage Ltd*,[77] if the reasoning of the minority had been accepted. There is county court authority,[78] which appears correct in principle, that the defendant cannot rely upon a purported waiver by the insured after he knows of the insurer's payment to the insured and thus, that the insurer's subrogation rights have crystallised.

If, however, the insured, bringing proceedings by himself, has received judgment against the wrongdoer, the insurers will not normally be able sub-

---

[73] The form of the insurer's indemnification does not matter; see, e.g. *Brown v Albany Construction Co* [1995] N.P.C. 100, where it took the form of the insurers purchasing the insureds' house from them at full market value. The same result will apply as regards litigation funding arrangements adopted by the insurers: *Sousa v London Borough of Waltham Forest Council* [2011] EWCA Civ 194, although note the critical comment of Ward LJ at [39].

[74] See *Hunt v Severs* [1994] A.C. 350 at 358, per Lord Bridge.

[75] For applications of this principle, see *Bristol and West Building Society v May May & Merrimans* [1998] 1 W.L.R. 336, and *Arab Bank Plc v John D Wood Commercial Ltd* [2000] Lloyd's Rep. I.R. 471, and the other cases cited in the judgments in these cases, concerning the claims of mortgage lenders, who had been indemnified against shortfalls on mortgage debts, against various parties including solicitors and valuers, who were legally responsible for the mortgage lenders' losses.

[76] *King v Victoria Insurance Co* [1896] A.C. 250.

[77] *Lister v Romford Ice and Cold Storage Ltd* [1957] A.C. 555; see 17.5.

[78] *Haigh v Lawford* (1964) 114 L.J. 208 (Salisbury County Court).

sequently to reopen the judgment on the grounds that the insured did not claim for his insured losses from the wrongdoer.[79] Further, if insurers exercising subrogation rights settle their insured's claim against the wrongdoer and sign a form of discharge of the claim which refers to all claims which might arise out of the relevant event, they will be bound by that discharge and unable to reopen the claim.[80]

Whether or not a defendant can rely upon what is commonly referred to as a "subrogation waiver clause" in the policy is also a question of some importance. Such a clause may provide, for example, that insurers will not exercise rights of subrogation against companies that are subsidiaries of or associated with the insured or against an employee of the insured or someone who is a co-insured. Co-insurance situations are considered further below.[81] Outside these, the better view was probably that the defendant could not rely on such a clause, unless he was properly a party to the insurance contract; otherwise the defence would contradict the principle of privity of contract.[82] However, there are authorities to the contrary,[83] and in any event, the defendant should now be able to rely on such a clause by virtue of the provisions of the Contracts (Rights of Third Parties) Act 1999.[84]

17.10   Subrogation Applies Only When the Insured Has a Right of Action

If, quite apart from agreement or compromise, the insured has no right of action that he could pursue, the insurer can be in no better position. The leading illustration of this point is the decision in *Simpson v Thomson*.[85] The insured owned two ships that collided due to the negligence of one of the masters. In respect of the ship that was negligently sailed, the insured paid money into court, as he was statutorily bound to do, in order to compensate the various parties involved. The insurers paid for the other ship and then claimed the right to use the insured's name as owner of this ship to claim against the

---

[79] *Hayler v Chapman* [1989] 1 Lloyd's Rep. 490. As indicated above, the insured who acts in this way without the sanction of his insurers will be in breach of his duty to act in good faith and not to prejudice the insurers' subrogation rights.

[80] *Kitchen Design and Advice Ltd v Lea Valley Water Co* [1989] 2 Lloyd's Rep. 333.

[81] See 17.14.1.

[82] *National Oilwell (UK) Ltd v Davy Offshore Ltd* [1993] 2 Lloyd's Rep. 582.

[83] See the Canadian decision in *Clark & Sons v Finnamore* (1973) 32 D.L.R. (3d) 236 and *Enimont Supply SA v Chesapeake Shipping Inc (The Surf City)* [1995] 2 Lloyd's Rep. 242. In the latter case, Clarke J also relied on equity to defeat the insurers' claim; see further at 17.14.2.

[84] These have been briefly examined at 4.5.

[85] *Simpson v Thomson* (1877) 3 App. Cas. at 279. See also *Buckland v Palmer* [1984] 1 W.L.R. 1109, where the principle was applied when the insured had lost her right of action because of rules of court. See [1985] J.B.L. 54.

fund. It was held that the insurers had no such right, as it would be tantamount to the insured suing himself, which, of course, is impossible. It would have been different had the ships been owned by different companies, albeit they were both owned or controlled by the same person.[86]

17.11   The Insurer's Claim For Interest

The question may often arise whether insurers suing in their insured's name are entitled to claim interest for their own benefit. Nominally, that award would go to the insured, the nominal claimant, but it is now clear that the insurers' subrogation rights include the right to appropriate interest under s.51A of the Senior Courts Act 1981.[87] In *H Cousins & Co Ltd v D & C Carriers Ltd*,[88] it was argued in an action for damages for breach of a contract of carriage that the claimant was entitled to interest only in respect of the period that he really suffered, namely until he was indemnified by his insurers. It was held that there was no reason why the claimant should not be awarded interest to the date of judgment on the usual basis, because the appropriate part of it would rightly inure to the benefit of the insurers.[89]

17.12 Assignment as an Alternative to Subrogation

The essence of subrogation is, of course, that the insurers sue in the name of the insured. It is, however, possible for the insurers to seek to adopt an alternative, namely, to persuade the insured to assign his cause of action to them. A bare cause of action, that is the right to sue another, is not assignable, but one enforced by an insurer is legitimate because it is supported by the insurer's interest in recouping for himself the amount of the loss he has paid out as a result of the wrong of the defendant.[90] Provided that the assignment is complete, that is that notice is given to the defendant in accordance with s.136 of the Law of Property Act 1925, the insurer/assignee can sue in his own name.

Such assignments are probably rare. Insurers prefer to use the names of their insureds because of the consequent lack of publicity. However, assignment does have advantages over subrogation. In particular, there will be no requirement that the insured be fully indemnified before the insurer can sue, and it must be the position that the insurers can keep everything they recover

---

[86] *Simpson v Thomson* (1877) 3 App. Cas. at 294 (Lord Blackburn).
[87] See further 15.11.
[88] *H Cousins & Co Ltd v D & C Carriers Ltd* [1971] 2 Q.B. 230.
[89] The contrary views expressed in *Harbutt's "Plasticine" Ltd v Wayne Tank & Pump Co* [1971] 1 Q.B. 447 were clearly based on a misunderstanding. See (1970) 96 L.Q.R. 513.
[90] *Compania Columbiana de Seguros v Pacific Steam Navigation Co* [1965] 1 Q.B. 101.

from the action. The principle of *Yorkshire Insurance Co v Nisbet Shipping Co*[91] will not apply simply because the cause of action is entirely the insurers' and the insured has forfeited all interest in it.

17.13   The Effect of Express Terms[92]

It has already been seen in certain respects how express conditions in a policy may refer to subrogation rights. Such terms appear common and there is no doubt that they can exclude or modify some of the conditions surrounding the exercise of subrogation rights at common law.[93] If a policy does contain such a term, the correct approach is to consider it first for a determination of the parties' rights and to refer to general subrogation principles only if there is ambiguity in the term or if it is not all embracing. In *Lucas v Exports Credit Guarantee Department*,[94] the courts were faced with a subrogation term in a policy issued by the Department.[95] The issue concerned a question very similar to that in *Yorkshire Insurance Co v Nisbet*,[96] and it was held that whether or not the insurer was entitled to an excess resulting after the wrongdoer had paid, and arising because of a variation in the Exchange Rate, depended entirely on the construction of the relevant term. Indeed, in the House of Lords, general principles of subrogation were not considered at all.

Express terms will commonly entitle the insurers to take proceedings before or after indemnifying the insured, and may well entitle them to control or take over proceedings taken by the insured in which they have hitherto taken no interest. It has been seen how, under the general law, even if the insured has been fully indemnified, he is perfectly entitled to proceed against the wrongdoer if the insurers choose not to. In practice express terms may well permit the insurers to take control and thus abandon such an action. It is suggested that this should only be permissible if the insurers act in good faith and with due regard to the interests of the insured, and that in practice insurers would not be so acting if the insured has suffered uninsured loss for which he seeks compensation.[97]

An express term may also purport to give subrogation rights in the name

---

[91] *Yorkshire Insurance Co v Nisbet Shipping Co* [1962] 2 Q.B. 330; see 17.4.3.

[92] See further, Birds, "Contractual subrogation in insurance" [1979] J.B.L. 124.

[93] However, for an interesting argument that contractual subrogation has in fact nothing to do so with general subrogation, see Brown, "An insurer's rights in litigation or contractual subrogation: an oxymoron?" (1997) 8 Ins. L.J. 60.

[94] *Lucas v Exports Credit Guarantee Department* [1974] 1 W.L.R. 909.

[95] Which at the time was a government department.

[96] *Yorkshire Insurance Co v Nisbet* [1962] 2 Q.B. 330; see 17.4.3.

[97] See further (1978) 41 M.L.R. 201 at 204 and Birds, "Contractual subrogation in insurance" [1979] J.B.L. 124 at 134–136.

of a party who is not the insured.[98] In certain circumstances,[99] the insured may recover on a policy for the benefit of a third party. If that third party has a claim in respect of the loss against a wrongdoer, the insurer would probably not be subrogated to this right of action at common law simply because the third party has no direct right to sue the insurer. An express term of the sort mentioned is clearly an attempt to cure this problem, and ought now to be enforceable under the Contracts (Rights of Third Parties) Act 1999.

17.14   Two or More Persons Interested in the Same Property

Some nice subrogation questions may arise where two or more people have interests in the same property. This may happen, for example, where the people are landlord and tenant or mortgagor and mortgagee of real property, and it may well also involve questions of contribution to which we shall return in the next chapter. The parties may be separately insured, only one of them may be insured, or they may be jointly insured.

Where the parties are separately insured, the loss will fall on the party legally liable, and hence on that party's insurer. The other party's insurer alone can have subrogation rights if it indemnifies its insured first. If a bailor and bailee of goods are both insured and the goods are lost in circumstances whereby the bailee is responsible, the bailee's insurer bears the loss.[100] Similarly, if landlord and tenant are both insured, but the latter covenanted to insure or to repair in the event of a loss, the latter's insurer will bear the loss.[101] The converse will apply if the landlord covenanted appropriately.[102]

Even where only one of the parties is insured, it may be that the insurance inures to the benefit of the other so that the insurer can have no recourse against the latter. The point arose for the first time in this country in the important case of *Mark Rowlands Ltd v Berni Inns Ltd*,[103] where property leased to the defendant was damaged by the negligence of the defendant.[104] Under the terms of the lease, the landlord covenanted to insure and the defendant covenanted to pay a sum (an "insurance rent") of approximately one quarter of the premium. Further the defendant was relieved from its

---

[98] Birds, "Contractual subrogation in insurance" [1979] J.B.L. 124 at 129–130.

[99] See Ch.4.

[100] *North British & Mercantile Insurance Co v London, Liverpool & Globe Insurance Co* (1877) 5 Ch. D 569, discussed further at 18.2.2.

[101] *Darrell v Tibbitts* (1880) 5 Q.B.D. 560; see 17.4.

[102] For example *United Motor Services v Hutson* [1937] 1 D.L.R. 737.

[103] *Mark Rowlands Ltd v Berni Inns Ltd* [1986] Q.B. 211; see 3.9.1 for the insurable interest issues decided in this case and for a detailed note, Birds (1986) 6 Oxford J. Legal Stud. 304. The subrogation point was the primary issue.

[104] The defendant was insured but against third party liability, not under an insurance of the property itself, so that this was not the sort of case discussed above.

covenant to repair in respect of "damage by or in consequence of any of the insured risks". The Court of Appeal held that the landlord's insurers could not exercise subrogation rights against the defendant[105]:

> "An essential feature of insurance by fire is that it covers fires caused by accident as well as by negligence. This was what the plaintiffs agreed to provide in consideration of, inter alia, the insurance rent paid by the defendants. The intention of the parties, sensibly construed, must therefore have been that in the event of damage by fire, whether due to accident or negligence, the landlord's loss was to be recouped from the insurance monies and that in that event they were to have no further claim against the tenants for damages in negligence."[106]

It was clearly crucial to the result of the *Mark Rowlands* case that the terms of the lease made it clear that the insurance was for the benefit of both parties. Not all leases will be so worded, and a simple covenant by the landlord to insure is unlikely to be construed as being for the benefit of the tenant.[107] The principle of the *Mark Rowlands* case has been applied to the parties to a contract to repair a ship[108] and it may be that the reasoning can be extended to other relationships between persons interested in the same property, for example vendor and purchaser of land where the vendor's policy expressly inures to the purchaser's benefit between contract and completion,[109] and owner and hirer of goods where the owner has insured pursuant to a term of the contract of hire.[110] It will not apply to the normal case where a mortgagee

---

[105] An odd feature of the case is the fact that it was openly admitted that the real claimant was the insurer. It could so easily have been fought as simply a landlord and tenant case, although it is not suggested that this would have made any difference to the result. The principle of *Mark Rowlands* was applied, obiter, in *Quirkco Investments Ltd v Aspray Transport Ltd* [2011] EWHC 3060 (Ch), where there was also a waiver of subrogation clause.

[106] per Kerr LJ at 232. The learned judge relied on a number of Commonwealth and American decisions on the same point, especially three cases in the Canadian Supreme Court: *Agnew Surpass Shoe Stores Ltd v Cummer-Yonge Investments Ltd* (1973) 55 D.L.R. (3d) 248; *Ross Southwood Tire Ltd v Pyrotech Products Ltd* (1975) 57 D.L.R. (3d) 248; *T Eaton Co Ltd v Smith* (1977) 92 D.L.R. (3d) 425. See Hasson, (1976) 14 OHLJ 769 at 779–782 and (1985) 5 Oxford J. Legal Stud. 416 at 430–433. See also *Marlborough Properties Ltd v Marlborough Fibreglass Ltd* [1981] 1 N.Z.L.R. 464, commented on by Yates (1983) 3 Oxford J. Legal Stud. 431. Note that Canadian law does not excuse the actual negligent employee of the tenant; *Greenwood Shopping Plaza v Beattie* (1980) 111 D.L.R. (3d) 257.

[107] See *Lambert v Keymood Ltd* [1999] Lloyd's Rep I.R. 80.

[108] *Talbot Underwriting Ltd v Nausch, Hogan & Murray Inc* [2006] EWCA Civ 889; [2006] Lloyd's Rep. I.R. 531; see also *Scottish & Newcastle Plc v GD Construction Ltd* [2003] EWCA Civ 809; [2003] Lloyd's Rep. I.R. 809.

[109] cf. *Rayner v Preston* (1881) 18 Ch D 1 (see 11.1.1) and *Castellain v Preston* (1883) 11 QBD 380 (see 17.4).

[110] See further Birds, above.

effects mortgage indemnity insurance against the risk of the mortgagor not repaying his debt, even if the mortgagor in effect pays the cost of the insurance.[111]

17.14.1 Co-insurance cases

A different situation is where both parties are insured under the same policy, namely a situation of co-insurance or composite insurance.[112] This point arose first in *Petrofina Ltd v Magnaload Ltd*,[113] where it was held that the insurers under a contractors' all risks insurance policy could not use the name of the principal insureds, the owners of the property and main contractors working thereon, to sue the negligent subcontractors responsible for the loss. The latter were held to fall within the definition of "the insured" in the policy and to have an insurable interest in the whole of the contract works, with the result that the insurer's right was defeated by circuity of action.[114] Underlying this conclusion were reasons of "commercial convenience", which also featured strongly in the Canadian Supreme Court decision in *Commonwealth Construction Co Ltd v Imperial Oil Ltd*,[115] a decision upon which the judge relied heavily.

Petrofina Ltd v Magnaload Ltd was followed in the slightly different circumstances of a shipbuilding contract in *Stone Vickers Ltd v Appledore Ferguson Shipbuilders Ltd*.[116] Here subrogation was refused to the insurers of the head contractor who sought to use the latter's name to sue a subcontractor

---

[111] *Woolwich Building Society v Brown* [1996] C.L.C. 625. Whether or not this is always a fair result is another matter. Many cases arising out of shortfalls in mortgage debts, where the lender has been indemnified by an insurer, have come before the courts, sometimes involving a subrogated claim against the mortgagor, as in *Woolwich v Brown*, at other times involving a claim against a third party whose negligence caused the loss, as in the cases mentioned in fn.75, above.

[112] Note that this is not joint insurance in the strict sense since this arises only where the parties' interests in the property insured are the same: see, e.g. *Re King* [1963] Ch.459, where a policy in the joint names of landlord and tenant was not a joint insurance.

[113] *Petrofina Ltd v Magnaload Ltd* [1984] 1 Q.B. 127; see [1983] J.B.L. 497. As we have seen (in 4.2.2), part of the basis for this decision seems flawed, but in terms of the subrogation aspects of it, it is clearly far too well-established to be upset. However, as discussed below, recent case law tends to proceed on an alternative basis anyway.

[114] See [1984] 1 Q.B. at 139–140 and the same judge's (Lloyd J) earlier comment in *The Yasin* [1979] 2 Lloyd's Rep. at 54–55.

[115] *Commonwealth Construction Co Ltd v Imperial Oil Ltd* (1977) 69 D.L.R. (3d) 558.

[116] *Stone Vickers Ltd v Appledore Ferguson Shipbuilders Ltd* [1991] 2 Lloyd's Rep. 288. Although the decision was reversed by the Court of Appeal, [1992] 2 Lloyd's Rep. 578, this was on a point of construction and does not affect the reasoning of the judge at first instance on the point under consideration here.

who had supplied a defective propeller. On the assumption that the sub-contractor was a co-insured under the policy,[117] it was held that they had an insurable interest, and were sufficiently interested, in the whole of the contract works to be able to resist the insurer's claim.[118] The legal basis for this result was, however, slightly different from that in *Petrofina*. In the judge's view, the exercise of subrogation rights would be so inconsistent with the insurer's obligation to a co-insured that there must be implied into the contract of insurance an exclusion of those rights.[119] A similar view was taken in the subsequent decision in *National Oilwell (UK) Ltd v Davy Offshore Ltd*,[120] but here the supplier's claim to be a co-insured fell at the first hurdle.[121] More recently, in *Co-operative Retail Services Ltd v Taylor Young Partnership Ltd*,[122] the Court of Appeal has favoured the implied term basis, rather than the circuity of action basis, for denying subrogation rights against a co-insured.

In *Co-operative Retail Services Ltd v Taylor Young Partnership Ltd*, the question arose in the context of a claim for contribution under the Civil Liability (Contribution) Act 1978 by two parties involved in a building project against the principal contractor and a sub-contractor, where the latter were co-insured under the all risks policy insuring the contract works. Part of the decision was concerned with the proper construction of s.1 of the above Act, but of interest here is the Court of Appeal's rejection of the notion of circuity of action, which, it was held, was an inappropriate plea in the co-insurance context.[123] "As Colman J observed,[124] it is an inappropriate plea if the insurer has provided a full indemnity to one co-assured because it will have discharged its liability under the policy in respect of the losses in question and a second co-assured cannot look to it to pay him those losses

---

[117] It was on this point that the Court of Appeal differed from the judge at first instance.

[118] On the insurable interest point, see 4.2.2.

[119] See [1991] 2 Lloyd's Rep. at 302.

[120] *National Oilwell (UK) Ltd v Davy Offshore Ltd* [1993] 2 Lloyd's Rep. 583, decided by Colman J who was also the judge at first instance in *Stone Vickers*.

[121] See also 4.6.2, where the important agency aspects of the case are considered.

[122] *Co-operative Retail Services Ltd v Taylor Young Partnership Ltd* [2000] 2 All E.R 865; [2001] Lloyd's Rep. I.R. 122.

[123] See also the learned treatment of this issue (and of *Petrofina* and other relevant authorities) by Brownie J "Co-insurance and subrogation" (1991) 3 Ins. L.J. 48. He concludes that there is no fundamental rule of law preventing one co-insured, i.e. the insurer exercising subrogation rights, suing another, but that the contract between them may be construed to have that effect. See also Mead, "Of subrogation, circuity and co-insurance: recent developments in contract works and contractors' all risks policies" (1998) 10 Ins. L.J. 125, examining recent Australian authorities.

[124] In the *Stone Vickers* and *National Oilwell* cases referred to above.

a second time."[125] Although this decision has clearly now laid this basis for denying subrogation to rest, it was arguably not a case where co-insurance was the real reason for the result. The building contract here[126] quite clearly excluded the right of the employer, and hence the insurers in the employer's name, to claim against the principal contractor and the sub-contractor in question in respect of loss arising from the perils insured. It is thus really an application of the principle we have already examined that comes from *Mark Rowlands Ltd v Berni Inns Ltd* and not, or at least not just, a co-insurance case.[127] In effect that was the decision of the House of Lords,[128] which upheld the decision of the Court of Appeal but on different grounds.

It is arguable, with respect, that the courts have reached what seem clearly the right results in the co-insurance cases by unnecessarily straining the concept of insurable interest. This aspect of them has been considered earlier.[129] It must also be noted that the Court of Appeal decision in *Deepak Fertilisers Ltd v ICI Chemicals & Polymers Ltd*[130] appears to restrict the extent of an insurable interest that a co-insured can have in these sorts of cases,[131] and thus implicitly restricts the basis for denying the insurer subrogation rights.

It has been suggested that there are three possible bases for denying subrogation in the context of co-insurance.[132] One is what has been described as the "fiction" of one assured. In essence it is that which was adopted in *Stone Vickers*, and now approved in *Co-operative Retail Services*, although dressed up in the language of implied terms.[133] The second basis is circuity of action, favoured in *Petrofina*, but now clearly out of favour. The third basis is a broader "equitable" approach that has been adopted in the United State of America.

---

[125] per Brooke LJ [2001] Lloyd's Rep. I.R. 122 at 137.

[126] Unlike the contracts in the earlier English cases cited above.

[127] See further Birds, "Denying subrogation in co-insurance and similar situations" [2001] L.M.C.L.Q. 193. The confusion may have arisen because all parties accepted the existence of what was described as the "Petrofina principle" on the pervasive interest of the various parties involved in a building project. See also *Talbot Underwriting Ltd v Nausch, Hogan & Murray Inc* [2006] EWCA Civ 889; [2006] Lloyd's Rep. I.R. 531.

[128] *Co-operative Retail Services Ltd v Taylor Young Partnership Ltd* [2002] UKHL 17; [2002] 1 W.L.R. 1419.

[129] See 4.2.2 and Birds, "Insurable Interests", Ch.4 in Palmer and McEndrick (eds) *Interests in Goods*, 2nd edn (Oxford: OUP, 1998).

[130] *Deepak Fertilisers Ltd v ICI Chemicals & Polymers Ltd* [1999] 1 Lloyd's Rep. 387 at 399.

[131] See 4.2.2. Note that the *Deepak* decision was not cited in *Co-operative Retail Services*, but it was in the more recent *Tyco Fire* case discussed below.

[132] See Derham, *Subrogation in Insurance Law*, Ch.7.

[133] See also *National Oilwell*. This was the basis of the reasoning of the Canadian decision in the *Commonwealth Construction* case, above, which was heavily relied on by Anthony Coleman QC in *Stone Vickers*. See also *The Board of Trustees of the Tate Gallery v Duffy Construction Ltd* [2007] EWHC 361 (TCC); [2007] Lloyd's Rep. I.R. 758.

It is thought that there is merit in considering further such an equity based on commercial convenience and business efficacy, as described below.[134]

In the context of a construction project where there are detailed terms regarding insurance obligations,[135] none of these bases is likely now to be adopted. This was perhaps implicit in the *Co-operative Retail Services* case and now seems absolutely settled following the Court of Appeal decision in *Tyco Fire & Integrated Solutions (UK) Ltd v Ross-Royce Motor Cars Ltd*.[136] From this, the proper basis for determining the issue as between co-insureds in construction cases is now clearly the express terms of the construction contract.[137] Here the terms of the relevant contract were quite different from those in *Co-operative Retail Services* and could not be read in any sense as excluding the liability of the contractor to the employer for loss caused by their negligence. This perhaps means the death of the idea using an implied term in the insurance contract to deny subrogation, certainly where there are detailed and comprehensive terms, and it certainly avoids stretching the concept of insurable interest too far.[138] Further the Court of Appeal here was clearly against the idea of there being any automatic principle or rule of law that a provision for insurance in joint names, which was found in this case as well as many of the others concerned with this question, overrides the other terms of the contract in order to exclude rights of subrogation by itself.[139] On the other hand, in a more recent Court of Appeal case, *Rathbone Brothers Plc v Novae Corporate Underwriting Ltd*,[140] which concerned professional indemnity insurance rather than a construction project, two of the judges, Elias and Sharp LJJ, relied on both an implied term in the insurance contract and an implied term in the underlying contract to deny subrogation. Beatson LJ, on the other hand, was firmly of the view that the proper basis was on the basis of the underlying contract and not the insurance contract. Another, yet more recent, Court of Appeal decision, *Gard Marine & Energy Ltd v China National Chartering Co Ltd*,[141] which concerned a charterparty, was very firmly based on the same basis as that of Beatson LJ, albeit here the view was obiter.

---

[134] This may perhaps have motivated the court in the different context of the decision in *Mark Rowlands Ltd v Berni Inns Ltd*, above. See 17.14.

[135] At least there will be in large commercial projects—there might not be in, say, a contract to extend a house.

[136] *Tyco Fire & Integrated Solutions (UK) Ltd v Ross-Royce Motor Cars Ltd* [2008] EWCA Civ 286; [2008] Lloyd's Rep. I.R. 617.

[137] This supported by comments in the *Co-operative Retail Services* case; see above at [75] and [76].

[138] See the comment of Rix LJ at [63], where he raises a doubt about the extent of the contractor's insurable interest by reference to the *Deepak* decision.

[139] See above at paras [74] to [82].

[140] *Rathbone Brothers Plc v Novae Corp Underwriting Ltd* [2014] EWCA Civ 1464.

[141] *Gard Marine & Energy Ltd v China National Chartering Co Ltd* [2015] EWCA Civ 16.

However, outside situations like projects where there is a detailed contract, subrogation against a co-insured may have to be denied, if it is to be denied at all, on something like the following basis. When in the circumstances, that is on a proper construction of the relationship between the parties (the contract between them if the relationship is contractual) and the terms of the contract of insurance, it can fairly be assumed that one policy of insurance was effected to benefit more than one "insured", it must be inferred that there can be no liability between them in respect of losses insured by the policy, at least in the absence of deliberate causing of the loss by one, when the right to benefit is forfeited.[142] In this way, the same result is reached as that achieved in the *Petrofina* and *Stone Vickers* cases,[143] but without perhaps straining the concept of insurable interest. Such an analysis could be applied to other co-insurance situations, for example, an insurance by both hirer and owner of goods under a hire purchase contract or insurance of a domestic building project. If a building contract wording follows the words used in the *Co-operative Retail Services* case, an alternative route would be to follow the principle demonstrated by *Mark Rowlands Ltd v Berni Inns Ltd*, which perhaps, as already noted, provides a sounder basis for the denial of subrogation and is the one most favoured in the most recent decisions of the Court of Appeal, as noted above.

17.14.2 Express waiver of subrogation in co-insurance cases

In some co-insurance situations, the policy may contain a provision expressly waiving the insurer's subrogation rights against a co-insured, although such a provision does not seem to have been in place in most of the reported English cases. There was such a clause, though, in the *National Oilwell* case, providing that subrogation would not lie against "any assured and any person, company or corporation whose interests are covered by this policy". It was held that this only applied where the co-insured had an interest in the loss in question.[144] On the other hand, a more broadly worded waiver provision could seemingly be effective as a matter of construction.[145] In contrast, the

---

[142] *Samuel v Dumas* [1924] A.C. 431 at 445–446; *Lombard Australia Ltd v NRMA Insurance Ltd* (1968) 72 S.R. (N.S.W.) 45.

[143] And as would have been achieved in *National Oilwell*, had it been a case of co-insurance.

[144] On this basis, it is irrelevant that the Contracts (Rights of Third Parties) Act 1999 gives a co-insured the right to enforce the term. Compare the decision in *The Surf City* [1995] 2 Lloyd's Rep. 242, where the presence of a waiver provision was the basis for both parties' agreeing that the exercise of subrogation would not be equitable. See also *BP Exploration Operating Co Ltd v Kvaerner Oilfield Products Ltd* [2004] EWHC 999 (Comm); [2005] 1 Lloyd's Rep. 307.

[145] And here the 1999 Act would, if necessary, provide a basis for enforcement of it.

Western Australian Court of Appeal has adopted a much broader approach to a waiver of subrogation clause in a co-insurance policy that was worded in a similar way to the one in the *National Oilwell* case.[146]

17.15   Waiver of Subrogation Rights in General

Insurers may voluntarily agree not to exercise rights of subrogation in certain circumstances. As we have seen, this may arise in the context of an agreement between insured and insurer; for example, it could be a term of the policy or of an agreement of settlement. Alternatively, insurers may simply undertake in general not to exercise their rights. The classic illustration of this is the undertaking by members of the British Insurance Association and Lloyd's that, as employer's liability insurers, they would not pursue claims in an employer's name against a negligent employee to recoup money paid out to indemnify the employer against a third party claim by a fellow employee based on the negligence of the employee.[147]

Insurers may also agree amongst themselves to waive their subrogation rights. The prime example used to be the "knock for knock" agreements between motor insurers, under which, following an accident in which both damaged cars were insured against first party damage, that is, under the usual comprehensive motor policy, each insurer indemnified its own insured regardless of the strict legal position as to liability in tort. Although in practice "knock for knock" agreements have been abandoned, for the time being at least, there is still merit in discussing the legal consequences of such agreements between insurers.[148]

The existence of such an agreement does not prevent the innocent insured from pursuing his tort claim, at least unless and until his insurer takes it over and abandons it, a question which was discussed earlier. In *Hobbs v Marlowe*,[149] the innocent car owner did indeed pursue this course because he wished to recover his uninsured loss, namely, his uninsured excess and damages for having to hire a substitute car while his was being repaired. He was supported by the Automobile Association. The House of Lords had no difficulty in rejecting the argument for the negligent driver, in reality

---

[146] *Woodside Petroleum Development Pty Ltd v H & R-E & W Pty Ltd* (1999) 10 A.N.Z. Ins. Cas. 61–430. For further discussion, see Birds, [2000] J.B.L. 350.

[147] See fn.53, above This undertaking followed the decision in *Lister v Romford Ice & Cold Storage Ltd* [1957] A.C. 555, discussed earlier in 17.5.

[148] Although "knock for knock" had some advantages, in particular by eliminating costly and wasteful subrogation actions, there were disadvantages for the "innocent" driver, in particular the possible impact on any "no claims" bonus and the discouragement of actions to pursue uninsured losses; see further (1978) 41 M.L.R. 201.

[149] *Hobbs v Marlowe* [1978] A.C. 18.

the latter's insurer, that the existence of the "knock for knock" agreement between the two insurers concerned removed the victim's right of action. In practice the damages recovered by the plaintiff would largely have to be repaid to his insurer, which was then under the agreement bound to pay them to the defendant's insurer. It was held, however, that the claimant (or really the AA) was entitled to only those costs appropriate to an action to recover his uninsured loss and as these were below the limits of the County Court Arbitration Scheme, he was not entitled to his own solicitor's costs.[150] The claimant had sued for his whole loss, and the result is somewhat harsh in the light of the fact that, had he not done so, he could have been penalised by his insurer.[151] On the actual facts of *Hobbs v Marlowe*, it appears that this was no real danger because of the attitude of the claimant's insurer, but in another case, an insurer might not be so unconcerned. If an insurer did indeed insist upon the insured's suing for full damages, it is to be hoped that the court would exercise the discretion permitted to award full costs.[152]

17.16   Denial of Subrogation Rights

It may be that the court has a general power to deny an insurer its subrogation rights in certain contexts. In *Morris v Ford Motor Co*,[153] Cameron Industrial Services Ltd (Cameron) contracted to clean at Ford's works. A term of this contract provided that Cameron would indemnify Ford in respect of any liability attaching to Ford for the negligence of the employees of either of them. Morris was injured by an employee of Ford for whom Ford was vicariously liable. Ford claimed an indemnity from Cameron under the term described and Cameron in return claimed upon indemnifying Ford to be subrogated to Ford's right to sue its employee for failing to take reasonable care and skill. Although Cameron was not an insurer as such, though no doubt it was backed by one, its position was analogous to that of an insurer and in particular to the position of the insurer in *Lister v Romford Ice and Cold Storage Ltd*.[154] The undertaking given by insurers following the latter case, which has been referred to, was not relevant as that applies only when the injury in question is caused by one employee to another employee of the

---

[150] Under the former County Court Rules Ord.47, r.5(4).

[151] Upon the principles discussed earlier in 17.8.

[152] This point remains valid notwithstanding the general abandonment of the "knock for knock" agreements.

[153] *Morris v Ford Motor Co* [1973] Q.B. 793. See Powles (1974) 90 L.Q.R. 34. For another example, as well as the recent English cases mentioned below, where the wrongdoer was the son of the insured and subrogation was denied at least partly on moral grounds, see *Morawietz v Morawietz* (1984) 5 C.C.L.I. 11; see the useful comment thereon by Baer, above.

[154] *Lister v Romford Ice and Cold Storage Ltd* [1957] A.C. 555.

same employer. On the authority of the *Lister* case, Cameron should have succeeded in its claim. However, by a majority, the Court of Appeal held that subrogation would not be permitted. If the decision is correct, then its principles must apply to insurers directly and it cannot be written off simply as "not an insurance case".

One of the principal difficulties with *Morris v Ford* is that the judges in the majority gave different reasons for their decisions, so that it is virtually impossible to say what the ratio is. Lord Denning MR claimed a broad jurisdiction to refuse to allow the enforcement of subrogation rights where it would not be "just and equitable". In his view, subrogation is an equitable remedy whose exercise is therefore subject to general equitable principles. That subrogation was, if not exclusively, recognised by equity is not in doubt[155]; but there are objections to this line of reasoning. First, there is no precedent for such a broad ground for dispensation, and secondly, even if there were, the "equity" ought strictly to refer to the position between insured and insurer, that is the merits of the insurer's claim as between them. The "equity" or rather "inequity" here was much more general, being the potentially harmful effects of permitting subrogation on industrial relations at Ford's. In the alternative, Lord Denning said that if subrogation depended on an implied term, the circumstances showed that such a term should not be implied.

The reasoning of James LJ is somewhat more convincing. In his view, subrogation, which would normally attach to such a contract of indemnity, was excluded by an implied term in the contract between Cameron and Ford, because that contract was made against the background of the decision in *Lister v Romford Ice and Cold Storage Ltd* and the possible implications of that decision. This is not really the same reasoning as Lord Denning's alternative. The latter held that subrogation should not be implied in the first place to a contract of this sort. James LJ held that it would normally be so implied, but the circumstances negated that implication. While the reasoning of James LJ, that it is possible to exclude a normal incident of a contract by implication, is no doubt legally sound, there is a difficulty in relating this to the facts of the case. As the dissenting judge, Stamp LJ, pointed out, to imply such a term in law the court must conclude that both parties would have said—"we did not bother to express it, it is too clear"—and there was no evidence to do so, the trial judge having found that Cameron did not know of the circumstances of the *Lister* case and the agreement resulting from it.

Despite this criticism, it is difficult not to sympathise with the result of the case. There are, it is suggested, sound reasons for not allowing risks of this sort to fall on individual employees when insurers have been paid to take them, a point of more general application that will be made again shortly.

---

[155] See 17.2.

Further, there are increasing signs that the courts may follow this approach and deny subrogation on equitable grounds.[156] In *Woolwich Building Society v Brown*,[157] it was said that the case "may be some support for asserting that equity will in certain circumstances not assist by compelling a party to use its name for the benefit of another so as to enforce a subrogated claim",[158] but it was pointed out that this would only apply in extreme cases.[159]

While there is no doubt that the decision in *Morris v Ford* has effectively stymied the application of subrogation in the area of employer's liability insurance as a matter of practice, at least until a party is prepared to take the matter to the Supreme Court, legally, the reasoning of James LJ and the alternative reasoning of Lord Denning, cannot stand if an insurer inserts an express term conferring subrogation rights in its policy, although a solution might be found in a doctrine which requires the insurer to exercise its rights under the policy in good faith in the interests of itself and the insured.[160] Otherwise, we must await future cases for any further development.

17.17   Some General Comments on Subrogation

It is appropriate to conclude this chapter with some very brief general comments about the role of subrogation. There can be no doubt that, to the extent that it prevents an insured from making a profit from a loss, it is an eminently sound principle. However, in the context of subrogation actions, the doctrine has attracted criticism. First, it must be rare for an insurer to exercise subrogation rights except against a defendant who is also insured, simply because there is little point otherwise. If so, this can be said to be wasteful and expensive in resources; it unnecessarily promotes multiple insurance, requiring that the same risk be covered both by first party and third party policies. Secondly, if the defendant is not, in fact, insured, throwing liability on him relieves the insurer who has been paid to assume the risk in question and who is able to distribute the cost among the premium-paying

---

[156] Note that *Morris v Ford* was cited in *Commonwealth Construction v Imperial Oil* (1976) 69 D.L.R. (3d) at 566, which influenced the English cases on co-insurance. As already explained, they have often "denied" subrogation on more traditional grounds although it has been argued that these are somewhat tortuous on occasion, and a broader "equitable" approach might be sounder in at least some instances; see 17.14.1.

[157] *Woolwich Building Society v Brown* [1996] C.L.C. 625.

[158] per Waller J at 629.

[159] See also *Enimont Supply SA v Chesapeake Shipping Inc (The Surf City)* [1995] 2 Lloyd's Rep. 242, where it was common ground that subrogation would not be equitable in circumstances where the insurer had expressly agreed to "waiver of subrogation" (see 17.15).

[160] See further Birds, "Contractual subrogation in insurance" [1979] J.B.L. 124 at 134–136.

public. In a sense, therefore, subrogation may work to curtail the very essence of insurance, which is risk distribution. The arguments are, of course, political ones encompassing the whole question of individual responsibility for civil wrongs in the legal system. For reasons which have been merely outlined here, and have been much more cogently and more fully argued elsewhere,[161] it is suggested that no harm would be done, and a great deal of resources would be saved, if we followed the Scandinavian practice[162] of permitting insurers to exercise subrogation rights only against a wrongdoer who was guilty of real misconduct. At the very least it is thought that the law should be amended to deny subrogation against a member of the insured's family residing with them, against employees of an insured employer and against persons with whom the insured has a close relationship.[163]

---

[161] See especially the forceful critique by Hasson, "Subrogation in insurance law—a critical evaluation" (1985) 5 Oxford J. Legal Stud. 416. See also *Harper, James and Gray on Tort*, 3rd edn (Aspen: 2006), para.25–23; Fleming (1966) 54 Calif.L.R. 1478 at 1533–1542; Young, *Cases and Materials on Insurance*, at 342. For a contrary view, see Horn, *Subrogation in Insurance Theory and Practice* (SS Huebner Foundation, 1964).

[162] See Hellner, *Forsakringsgivarens regressatt* (The Insurer's Right of Subrogation) (1953) 257 and following (English summary).

[163] This is broadly the approach adopted in the *Principles of European Insurance Contract Law* (as to which see 1.10.2), based on the majority of the national laws of other EU member States. See Article 10:101 of the *Principles*.

CHAPTER 18

CONTRIBUTION AND DOUBLE INSURANCE

18.0

Like subrogation, contribution is a principle designed to prevent unjust enrichment. It too applies only to those insurance contracts that are contracts of indemnity. Unlike subrogation, however, contribution applies not as between insured and insurer[1] but as between insurers.[2] There is nothing wrong in an insured taking out as many policies as he wishes on the same property or against the same risk, so that he may be doubly insured. If he suffers a loss, he is, of course, by virtue of the doctrine of subrogation, entitled to no more than a full indemnity, but he can at common law choose from which insurer to claim. The insurer that pays, unless it pays voluntarily,[3] is entitled to claim a contribution from the other insurer or insurers, as otherwise the latter would be unjustly enriched. The insurer claiming a contribution must sue in its own name.[4]

18.1   Rateable Proportion Clauses

In practice contribution is most unlikely to arise in quite the way described because of a standard term in all indemnity insurances. This will provide that if there is any other insurance on the property or the risk covered by the policy, the insurer will not be liable to pay or contribute more than its rateable proportion of any loss or damage. Such a rateable proportion clause does not affect the basic legal principles of double insurance, but it simply prevents the insured from recovering all his loss from one insurer. He is

---

[1] Except in the very special situation concerning liability arising from exposure to asbestos, as briefly discussed in 22.1.

[2] The doctrine of contribution can also apply to contracts of indemnity that are not insurance contracts and to contracts of suretyship, among others. In all cases it recognises "the obvious justice of requiring that a common liability should be shared between those liable" (per Lord Bingham in *Royal Brompton Hospital National Health Service Trust v Hammond* [2002] UKHL 14; [2002] 1 W.L.R. 1397 at 1399). However, it will not normally apply as between an insurer and someone who has agreed to provide an indemnity to the insured under a standard contract term, e.g. in a construction contract: *Caledonia North Sea Ltd v British Telecommunications Plc* [2002] UKHL 4; [2002] Lloyd's Rep. I.R. 261; see 17.5.

[3] See below.

[4] *Austin v Zurich General Accident & Liability Insurance Co* [1945] K.B. 250 at 258, per MacKinnon LJ; *Sydney Turf Club v Crowley* (1972) 126 C.L.R. 420.

compelled to claim the appropriate proportion from each and the insurers are relieved of the burden of having to claim contributions inter se. In the words of Rix LJ "if the insured is forced to involve both his insurers, then there will be no need for contribution and the need for the application of the doctrine is excluded as a matter of fact".[5]

It may be, though, that, notwithstanding a rateable proportion clause, one insurer does pay the whole of the insured's loss, perhaps because it is at the time unaware of the other insurance, and it subsequently claims a contribution from the other insurer. If the latter insurer would in fact have been entitled to reject a claim made upon it by the insured, the question arises as to whether this precludes the first insurer's claim. This question has produced conflicting authorities in recent years.

In *Legal and General Assurance Society Ltd v Drake Insurance Co Ltd*,[6] the claimant insurer paid a motor insured's claim, discovering only some ten years later that the defendants had also insured the insured. Both insurance policies contained a standard rateable proportion clause and a condition precedent requiring the giving of immediate written notice of an event giving rise to a claim. The insured had obviously failed to comply with this provision as regards the second insurer. It was held first by the Court of Appeal[7] that the right to contribution, being dependent on a principle of equity, dictated that prima facie, when there was double insurance, the burden of any loss should be shared between the insurers. The breach of a notice provision did not modify or exclude the equitable right to contribution, because the unfairness to the defendant of being deprived of the defence and of being unable to investigate the claim itself had to be balanced against the unfairness in making the claimant liable for the whole loss when the insured might as easily have claimed and recovered against the defendant instead; the balance of equity was clearly in favour of enforcing the right to contribution.

However, because of the rateable proportion clause in its policy, the claimant had been legally liable to indemnify the insured as to only half of the third party's claim. The policy with the defendant was clearly "any other insurance". The claimant's payment of half of the loss therefore amounted to a voluntary payment and because contribution arose only where an insurer had been obliged under its policy to pay more than

---

[5] *Drake Insurance Plc v Provident Insurance Plc* [2003] EWCA Civ 1874; [2004] 2 W.L.R. 530, at para.114. This was the implication of the decision of the Privy Council in *Eagle Star Insurance Co Ltd v Provincial Insurance Plc* [1993] 3 All E.R.1, examined below, contrary to views expressed in *Legal and General Assurance Society Ltd v Drake Insurance Co Ltd* [1991] 2 Lloyd's Rep. 36.

[6] *Legal and General Assurance Society Ltd v Drake Insurance Co Ltd* [1991] 2 Lloyd's Rep. 36.

[7] Lloyd and Nourse LJJ, Ralph Gibson LJ dissenting on this point.

its rateable proportion, the claim for a contribution from the defendant failed.[8]

The decision on the general point[9] was not entirely persuasive. What is the equity in making liable an insurer who, if a claim had been made against it, would have had a cast iron defence?[10] Considerations like this led the Privy Council to take a different view in *Eagle Star Insurance Co Ltd v Provincial Insurance Plc*.[11] Here it was held that that the right to contribution was to be determined at the date of any judgment against the insurer which pays. Although, of course this decision could not technically overrule the decision in *Legal and General*, if it is followed, the insurer that has a cast iron defence to the insured's claim will be able to resist the other insurer's claim for a contribution.[12] On the other hand, in the recent first instance decision in *O'Kane v Jones*,[13] the judge refused to follow the decision in *Eagle Star*, preferring the Court of Appeal's view that the right to contribution must be determined as at the date of loss and regarding himself in any event as bound by it.

Whatever view the law will ultimately take on this general point, which may require resolution by the Supreme Court, the result of the decision in *Legal and General* on the voluntary payment point must strictly be correct. Since invariably, as we have seen, policies contain a standard rateable proportion clause, the first insurer's claim for a contribution will be met by the argument that they paid more than they were legally liable to pay and that contribution does not apply to voluntary payments. In this context, however, the payment must be genuinely voluntary and it seems as though relatively

---

[8] This result was not affected by provisions of the Road Traffic Act. Although under s.151 of that Act a motor insurer is liable to settle a third party's claim in full (see 21.5), where there was double insurance and a rateable proportion clause in its policy, it could recover the proportion above its strict legal liability back from its insured, and so the excess payment remained a voluntary one. See also *Bovis Construction Ltd v Commercial Union Assurance Plc* [2000] W.L. 33148637. However, the Court of Appeal in *Drake Insurance Plc v Provident Insurance Plc* [2003] EWCA Civ 1874; [2004] 2 W.L.R. 530 (see below) clearly found this point somewhat difficult to accept and it is quite likely that it would not survive detailed re-examination in a future case.

[9] Curiously the subject of only one previous reported case: *Monksfield v Vehicle and General Insurance Co Ltd* [1971] 1 Lloyd's Rep. 139. This was to the opposite effect and was overruled.

[10] It seems that even the majority in *Legal and General* would have exempted the second insurer from liability if they had a good defence based on non-disclosure or breach of warranty; see the judgment of Nourse LJ [1991] 2 Lloyd's Rep. at 42.

[11] *Eagle Star Insurance Co Ltd v Provincial Insurance Plc* [1993] 3 All E.R. 1.

[12] Thus reinstating the decision in *Monksfield v Vehicle and General Insurance Co Ltd*, above. On the facts of *Eagle Star*, both insurers were in fact held liable to pay, because of provisions in the Bahamian Road Traffic Act similar to those in the British statute (see Ch.21).

[13] *O'Kane v Jones* [2003] EWHC 2158 (Comm); [2004] 1 Lloyd's Rep. 389.

little will be required to challenge that view on the facts of typical cases where the issue arises, especially road traffic accidents where the liability of a driver appears prima facie to be covered by more than one policy. The issue arose in the decision in *Drake Insurance Plc v Provident Insurance Plc*.[14] The facts have been described earlier[15] because one aspect of the decision was the rather novel holding of the Court of Appeal that an insurer's right to avoid for non-disclosure or misrepresentation could be restricted by application of the doctrine of utmost good faith. Here the insurers who had settled the claim protested and continued to protest at the attitude of the other insurers and attempted to recover a share from them. This was sufficient for the court to find that they were not volunteers.

It is also notable that, in the course of reaching their decision in *Drake v Provident*, the court also indicated its general disapproval of rateable proportion clauses. Rix LJ commented[16]:

> "It is a matter of concern that an insurer who takes a premium to cover 100 per cent of a risk may only be liable for 50 per cent of a loss, on the basis that the insured can obtain the other half elsewhere, in circumstances where the insured finds that he cannot contractually do so."

This indicates that future decisions may take a very robust view on these standard terms.[17]

18.2   The Meaning of Double Insurance

Whether the issue arises as a matter of general law or under such a rateable proportion clause, the same conditions must be fulfilled before it can be said that there is double insurance. Essentially these are that the same property or liability is covered against the same risk under policies which are both or all legally enforceable. A number of points require further elucidation.

18.2.1 Policies with different scopes

Whether the policies cover the same property or liability is fairly easily established. It is not required, though, that the scope of the policies as a whole

---

[14] *Drake Insurance Plc v Provident Insurance Plc* [2003] EWCA Civ 1874; [2004] 2 W.L.R. 530.

[15] See 7.10.

[16] See para.120.

[17] As they have done in respect of terms that purport to oust the liability of an insurer entirely if there is other insurance; see 18.4.1. In a consumer policy one basis for challenging the validity of such clause ought to be under Pt 2 of the Consumer Rights Act 2015; see also fn.40, below.

be the same. There may be an overlap between a motor and an employer's liability policy that can give rise to double insurance.[18] Similarly, a household policy may cover certain property owned by the insured when it is taken outside the house. This would be regarded as a small part of the total cover. For example, the insured under such a policy might take his watch, which is one of the items so covered, to be repaired, and while it is at the repairers, it might be covered by a policy held by the latter. This would also be a small part of the repairer's cover. Prima facie, there would be double insurance, though it may well be that the position is affected by policy conditions.

18.2.2 Same risk

The requirement that the risk be the same means essentially that the same interest is covered by or on behalf of the same insured. In *North British & Mercantile Insurance Co v London, Liverpool & Globe Insurance Co*,[19] grain that belonged to a bailor was in the possession of a bailee, a wharfinger. The grain was lost in circumstances whereby in law the bailee was liable for the loss. Both parties had insured this grain, the owner under an ordinary property policy, the bailee under a floating policy. The bailee recovered from their insurers who then claimed a contribution from the bailor's insurers. The Court of Appeal held that there was no right to a contribution because the policies covered different interests. The loss in the circumstances fell on the bailee and hence their insurers; had the bailor's insurers paid their insured, they would have been subrogated to the latter's right to sue the bailee. Therefore, whenever in law the loss should be borne by only one of the insureds, there is no contribution.

It should be noted, however, that in practice this legal rule is often ignored. The most notable instance is by virtue of one of the rules of the Fire Offices' Committee whereby contribution is applied by agreement between

---

[18] For example the Australian case of *Albion Insurance Co v Government Insurance Office of New South Wales* (1969) 121 C.L.R. 342. This is much less likely to happen now in the UK because of changes to the compulsory insurance requirements; see Ch.21.

[19] *North British & Mercantile Insurance Co v London, Liverpool & Globe Insurance Co* (1877) 5 Ch D 569, followed in *Caledonia North Sea Ltd v British Telecommunications Plc* [2002] UKHL 4; [2002] Lloyd's Rep. I.R. 261 (see 17.5). See also *Dawson v Bankers' & Traders' Insurance Co* [1957] V.R. 491, where it was held that there was no double insurance between a motor policy and an employer's liability policy where the former policy covered a negligent employee directly, i.e. he was included as one of the insured, and the latter covered only his employer's vicarious liability; see also *Zurich Insurance Co v Shield Insurance Co Ltd*, an unreported decision of the Irish High Court, 29 July 1985. Compare the *Albion* case (fn.18), where only the employer's vicarious liability was covered under both policies and there was therefore double insurance.

insurers wherever real property[20] is, in fact, insured by different people with different interests, regardless of questions of legal liability.[21]

18.2.3 Same insured?

The judgments in the *North British* case appear at times to imply not just that the same interest must be doubly insured, but that the insured actually be the same person. It was thought, though, that this is not required and this view was confirmed in *O'Kane v Jones*.[22] Double insurance arises wherever an insured is entitled to recovery under another policy, even if he is not the insured under that policy and hence not legally entitled to sue upon it, if in fact he recovers from that insurer. If, in what is likely to be the most common practical application, the bailor and bailee of goods both insure and a loss occurs in circumstances which attach no legal liability to either party, as in *Hepburn v Tomlinson*,[23] and on the construction of the bailee's policy, he is entitled to claim for the benefit of the bailor, as also was the position in that case, there is double insurance. Otherwise, the problem would be insoluble, neither party having rights against the other and thus neither party's insurer having rights to which they could succeed by virtue of subrogation to throw the loss on the other. If the bailee is entitled to recover only in respect of his own loss or only when he is legally liable to the bailor, then the position is quite different. The bailor has no claim against the bailee and hence against his insurer, and there is no double insurance.

As far as land is concerned,[24] double insurance might arise by virtue of one party having the right to call upon the other's insurer to reinstate the property under s.83 of the Fires Prevention (Metropolis) Act 1774.[25] In one case involving a landlord and tenant who were both insured,[26] it was argued by the tenant's insurer that, because the tenant had the right to require reinstatement under the Act by the landlord's insurer, the tenant was therefore doubly insured and the landlord's insurer was liable for a contribution. This argument was easily rejected. It was clear that the tenant had not exercised his statutory right and hence there could be no question on the facts of the case of his having a right under the two policies. The judgment implies that

---

[20] There is no agreement regarding goods, but in practice contribution may be applied ad hoc.

[21] For consideration of all the relevant insurers' agreements, including one which had the effect of making the *Albion* case (fn.18) inapplicable in Britain, see Lewis (1985) 48 M.L.R. 275 at 286–289.

[22] *O'Kane v Jones* [2003] EWHC 2158 (Comm); [2004] 1 Lloyd's Rep. 389.

[23] *Hepburn v Tomlinson* [1966] A.C. 451; see 4.2.1.

[24] Assuming that the Life Assurance Act 1774 does not apply; see 3.9.1.

[25] See 16.2.

[26] *Portavon Cinema Co v Price* [1939] 4 All E.R. 601.

the result would have been the same even if he had made a demand for reinstatement but, with respect, this may be doubted. Following a proper demand, the landlord's insurer would have had to comply, thus indemnifying the tenant. As contribution is an equitable principle to prevent unjust enrichment, it must be flexible enough to allow that the tenant's insurer is liable for its share, otherwise the insurer with the primary liability might escape quite unjustifiably. The same would apply if the position of the parties was reversed or if their relationship was that of mortgagor and mortgagee or vendor and purchaser.

18.3   The Ratio of Contribution

Whether an insurer is seeking to claim a contribution from another insurer or deciding how much it should pay under a rateable proportion clause, the question will arise as to how the contributions of the different insurers are worked out. This can be a very complex question,[27] but for present purposes the basic principles only will be examined and it will be assumed that there are only two insurers involved. There has been a noticeable lack of case law on this question, and the ratios to be applied may depend as much on the practices of insurers as on binding legal authority.

The real problems arise when the sums insured by each insurer are not the same or where the policies in question have different ranges so that it is difficult properly to compare the sums insured. It may be necessary here to distinguish between property and liability insurances, the reason being that in property insurance, the premium is calculated with particular reference to the sum insured, whereas there is not necessarily the same relationship in liability insurance. In property insurance where the cover provided under both policies is more or less the same, the contribution of each insurer can most fairly be assessed simply by reference to the sum insured. The proper result, therefore, should be that each insurer pays that proportion of a loss that his sum insured bears to the total of the sums insured. For example, if property is insured for £10,000 with insurer A and for £20,000 with insurer B, A will bear one-third and B two-thirds of any loss.

This approach is termed the "maximum liability" approach, because it always takes account of the maximum of the two insurers' liabilities. The alternative standard approach is that based on "independent liability". Here, following a loss, it is asked what each insurer would independently have been liable for and the contributions are assessed according to the proportions that each such figure bears to the total of the figures. For example, X suffers a loss of £5,000. His policy with insurer A has a sum insured of £10,000; his

[27] For more detail, see *MacGillivray on Insurance Law*, 13th edn, paras 25–032 to 25–053.

policy with B a limit of £50,000. Each insurer would independently have been liable for the full amount of the loss. Their contribution is therefore equal because £5,000 plus £5,000 divided by £5,000/£10,000 is £5,000. If X's loss were £11,000, A would be liable independently for £10,000, B for £11,000. Therefore, A bears 10,000/10,000 + 11,000, that is 10/21, of the loss and B 11/21. On this basis, wherever the loss is smaller than the lesser of the sums insured, the insurers will bear it equally. A loss falling between the sums insured will attract a ratio whereby the insurer with the larger sum insured will gradually attract more liability. Only when the loss is the same as, or greater than, the total of the sums insured will the calculation be the same as under the maximum liability approach.

18.3.1 Liability insurances

It was conclusively settled in *Commercial Union Assurance Co v Hayden*[28] that the independent liability approach is the legal basis in liability insurance. The principal reasons for this were first that liability insurance premiums are not calculated pro rata according to the sum insured; in the case itself the plaintiff had charged £6 for cover of £100,000, whereas the defendant had charged £5 for only £10,000 of identical cover. Secondly, the bulk of claims in liability insurance fall within a low limit.

> "Each limit of liability and each premium may be taken to be fixed without knowledge of the limit under any other policy . . . it is difficult to suppose that when a limit of £10,000 was fixed by the defendant, it could have been intended that if there happened to be another policy with a limit of £100,000, the defendant should be liable for only one-eleventh of the claim, however small. The independent liability basis is much more realistic in its results . . . The obvious purpose of having a limit of liability under an insurance policy[29] is to protect the insurer from the effect of exceptionally large claims: it seems to me artificial to use the limits under two policies to adjust liability in respect of claims which are within the limits of either policy."[30]

Finally, some stress was laid upon the fact that certain liability policies are unlimited; in these cases the maximum liability approach would simply be impossible to apply.

---

[28] *Commercial Union Assurance Co v Hayden* [1977] Q.B. 804.
[29] This must mean in respect of liability policies only.
[30] per Cairns LJ [1977] Q.B. at 815–816.

18.3.2 Policies with different ranges

There remains the question of which method of assessment applies where the policies have different ranges.[31] We can use the example of the insured watch that was referred to earlier.[32] Imagine that the owner's household policy has a sum insured of £10,000, but there is no specific sum for the watch, which is worth £20. The repairer has a floating policy covering all goods in his possession from time to time, which is a goods policy and not a liability policy. His sum insured is £3,000. The watch is stolen, neither party being responsible, so that both insurers are prima facie liable. It could hardly be right here, albeit that it is a case of property insurance, to apply the maximum liability ratio, so that the owner's insurer should bear 10/13 and the repairer's insurer 3/13 of £20. That would ignore the fact that both policies cover many other items and are essentially quite different. In this case the independent liability approach is the only realistic one so that each insurer is liable for half the loss up to the lesser of the sums insured. This was the method adopted in *American Surety Co of New York v Wrightson*[33] in relation to fidelity insurance effected by an employer against the dishonesty of his employees, where one of the policies also had a much wider scope, and it is submitted that it is the only workable approach.[34]

18.4   Conditions Regarding Double Insurance

Apart from the rateable proportion clauses already discussed, most policies of indemnity also contain other important conditions relevant to double insurance. These fall into two categories. The first sort purports to oust the liability of the insurer if the liability is covered elsewhere. The second requires notification of double insurance.

18.4.1 Conditions ousting liability

Examples of this sort of condition are as follows:

---

[31] "Non-concurrent policies" is the usual jargon.
[32] See 18.2.1.
[33] *American Surety Co of New York v Wrightson* (1910) 103 L.T. 663.
[34] In *O'Kane v Jones* [2003] EWHC 2158 (Comm); [2004] 1 Lloyd's Rep. 389, the judge declined to decide between the different approaches in a case where the result of either was the same. He rejected a third alternative, described as the common liability approach, as inconsistent with s.80 of the Marine Insurance Act 1906, which strictly governed the case as a marine case. As that section, like many others, simply expresses the common law, no doubt the same view would be taken in a non-marine case. *MacGillivray*, 13th edn, para.25–050, suggests that the independent liability basis is the fairest to adopt in all cases.

"There shall be no liability under this insurance in respect of any claim where the insured is entitled to indemnity under any other insurance except in respect of any excess beyond the amount which would have been covered under such other insurance had this insurance not been effected."

"There shall be no liability hereunder in respect of any claim for which the assured are entitled to any indemnity under any other policy."

"This policy does not cover liability which forms the subject of insurance by any other policy."

Problems will arise if one or both of the insurers covering the same risk have this sort of clause. If one insurer does have it, but the other does not, then the latter should be solely and wholly liable. The first insurer's liability is excluded and so far as the second is concerned, there is, therefore, no double insurance. If both insurers have such a clause, the position is more complex. It has arisen in a number of cases.

In *Gale v Motor Union Insurance Co*,[35] L was driving G's car when he caused an accident. Prima facie L was insured both by his own motor policy, because that had an extension covering the driving of cars other than his own with the owner's consent, and by G's policy on G's car, because that had a permitted driver extension.[36] However, both extensions had qualifications which in effect provided that they were not applicable if the person concerned was otherwise insured. Both policies also had rateable proportion conditions. Roche J held that the conditions purporting to oust liability were not clear, and that the only way to read them was as referring to cases where the other cover gave complete and full indemnity. Here, because of the rateable proportion clauses, neither policy, when looked at from the point of view of the other one, gave complete cover. Therefore, neither clause applied and the insurers were both liable rateably. According to this reasoning, the presence of rateable proportion clauses in both policies was vital.

Weddell v Road Transport & General Insurance Co[37] involved similar facts in that a negligent driver was prima facie covered by both his own and the relevant car owner's policies. His own policy had a rateable proportion clause and a clause excluding liability if there was other insurance. The owner's policy was more subtly worded; under the extension, liability was excluded if there was other insurance. There was a rateable proportion clause but this had a proviso whereby it was declared not to impose on the insurer any liability from which, but for it, the insurer would have been excluded under the extension. In other words, the rateable proportion clause was not to apply to a situation of double insurance, and, as has been seen, the presence of a rateable proportion clause was crucial to the ratio in *Gale*. In fact, the driver's

---

[35] *Gale v Motor Union Insurance Co* [1928] 1 K.B. 359.
[36] See 21.3.2.
[37] *Weddell v Road Transport & General Insurance Co* [1932] 2 K.B. 563.

own insurer repudiated liability for breach of condition, so the question was whether the driver was entitled to half or all of his loss under the owner's policy. The owner's insurer did not seek to argue that it was not liable at all. Rowlatt J went somewhat further than the judge in *Gale* had gone and held that it would be unreasonable to suppose that these extensions would cancel each other out.

> "The reasonable construction is to exclude from the category of co-existing cover any cover which is expressed to be itself cancelled by such co-existence, and to hold in such cases that both companies are liable, subject of course in both cases to any rateable proportion clause which there may be."[38]

Thus, on the facts, the owner's insurers, because they had a rateable proportion clause, were liable for half the loss.

The judgment seems to admit that logically, if neither policy had a rateable proportion clause, neither insurer would be liable, and, further, that this ought to have been the result on the facts because of the proviso in the owner's policy whereby the rateable proportion clause should not have operated. There was "other insurance", namely, the driver's own, albeit this was not enforceable in respect of this loss, and therefore this should have excluded liability under the owner's policy. However, the insurer did not argue this and the ratio of the case appears wide enough to exclude this sort of possibility. Indeed, this must be the legal position because the Court of Appeal has approved the decision in *Weddell*.[39] Here it was said:

> "The court should invoke the equitable principle of contribution between co-insurers to avoid the absurdity and injustice of holding that a person who has paid premiums for cover by two insurers should be left without insurance cover because each insurer has excluded liability for the risk against which the other has indemnified him."[40]

It is clear, therefore, that the courts have not taken kindly to these clauses and it is probably safe to assume that, whatever forms of wording are adopted, they will be construed in such a manner that, where there is genuine double insurance, they will cancel each other out.[41] However, an exclusion of liability in one policy in the event of there being other insurance

---

[38] Above at 567.

[39] *National Employers' Mutual v Hayden* [1980] 2 Lloyd's Rep. 149; see also *Austin v Zurich General Accident & Liability Insurance Co* [1945] K.B. 250 and *Structural Polymer Systems Ltd v Brown* [2000] Lloyd's Rep. I.R. 64 at 75.

[40] Above at 152, per Stephenson LJ. See also Bridge LJ at 154 and Templeman LJ at 156.

[41] It is also possible, where the insured is a consumer, that such clauses would be regarded as unfair under Pt 2 of the Consumer Rights Act 2015; as to this, see 6.1.

will override a rateable proportion clause in the other policy, so that there is no double insurance.[42]

18.4.2 Conditions requiring notification

Another standard condition, which may be found particularly in fire and other property policies, requires the insured to notify the insurer if he effects double insurance during the currency of the policy. Generally the sanction for non-disclosure will be forfeiture or repudiation of the policy. Obviously, insurers insert such conditions to protect themselves against the possibility of fraud, although their use is much less common than was formerly the case.

A mere accidental overlap between policies does not bring such a condition into operation. In *Australian Agricultural Co v Saunders*,[43] the insured effected a fire policy on some wool while it was in storage, in transit by land to Sydney, Australia, or in storage in Sydney until shipped. The policy contained the relevant condition. Subsequently, some wool was carried by ship to Sydney and a marine policy was effected to cover this. When this wool was in store in Sydney, it was destroyed by fire. It was held that the fire insurer was liable. The court rejected the argument of the insurers that they should have been notified of the marine policy, as the risks covered were not the same and there was no double insurance. Even if the policies had overlapped in their coverage for a brief period, it was made clear that such accidental overlap would not have required notification, though presumably if the loss had taken place during the overlap, there would have been double insurance.

An insured can only really be prejudiced by this sort of condition if it appears in both of the policies. If it is in only one, that one will be ineffective but the other will stand, unless, of course, the insurer can avoid liability for some other reason. Even if it is in both policies, it will be only rarely, it seems, that the insured will lose out completely. In *Equitable Fire & Accident Insurance Co v Ching Wo Hong*,[44] a fire policy contained the relevant condition. The insured effected a second policy, about which it did not inform the first insurer, but this policy provided that it was not effective until the first premium was paid. No premium was ever paid on it. It was held by the Privy Council that the second policy never, therefore, came into existence and the obligation to disclose it to the first insurer never arose, so that the first insurer could not avoid its policy. The same result must apply if the second policy is void, for example, for lack of insurable interest.

---

[42] *National Farmers Union Mutual Insurance Society Ltd v HSBC Insurance (UK) Ltd* [2010] EWHC 773 (Comm); [2011] Lloyd's Rep. I.R. 86.

[43] *Australian Agricultural Co v Saunders* (1875) L.R. 10 C.P. 668.

[44] *Equitable Fire & Accident Insurance Co v Ching Wo Hong* [1907] A.C. 96; see also *Steadfast Insurance Co v F & B Trading Co* (1972) 46 AJ.L.R.10.

However, the second policy may be valid but the insurer is entitled to avoid liability under it for the particular loss by virtue of a breach of condition, such as the failure to give notice in time. Here non-notification of the second policy to the first insurer will entitle it to avoid its policy and the second insurer will not be liable for the reason stated.[45] The same would apply if the second insurer could avoid liability, but not avoid the policy ab initio, that is for breach of a continuing warranty. In this case, therefore, the insured will be prejudiced by a failure to comply with a notification condition.

---

[45] See Walsh J in the *Steadfast* case, above, at 14.

CHAPTER 19

LIFE INSURANCE

19.0

Life insurance is the first area where we examine principles peculiar to particular types of insurance rather than of general application. The modern forms of life policies are numerous, ranging from the traditional whole life policy, which simply pays an agreed sum of money on the death of the life insured, and the term policy, which pays on death within a stated time, through endowment policies, often linked to mortgages effected for house purchase, to annuities and policies linked to investment in securities or property.[1] Many of these types of policy can be "with profits", so that the insured expects to receive a bonus over and above the stated sum insured.[2] The fact that many life policies of the latter sort are in reality also investments has been recognised for some years, with additional regulatory measures being adopted for the protection of consumers.[3] Detailed consideration of this is outside the scope of this book, but there is one aspect concerning insurance contract law, namely the cancellation provisions, which will be examined shortly.

There are a number of other respects in which life insurance has its own principles. Two such broad areas of principle, the assignment of life policies and the law relating to trusts of life policies, will be considered here because of their particular practical importance and because they have thrown up problems for life insurance, even though questions of assignment and trusts are, of course, of much more general application. Detail on questions such as mortgages of life policies, the law of succession or the bankruptcy of the life

---

[1] A contract which contains provision for life cover is still a contract of life insurance, especially for the purposes of the Life Assurance Act 1774 and the Financial Services and Markets Act 2000, where the amount of life cover is variable and no more than the amount for which the policy might be surrendered at any time: *Fuji Finance Ltd v Aetna Life Insurance Co Ltd* [1994] 4 All E.R. 608.

[2] Although whether the amounts of bonuses and other benefits in recent times are what policyholders were led to believe is open to question and has been publicly much debated. As to the duty of the directors of the insurer when allocating bonuses, see *Equitable Life Assurance Society v Hyman* [2000] 3 W.L.R. 529.

[3] In particular, the Financial Services Act 1986 included most life policies within its definition of "investments". The regulatory scheme now in force under the Financial Services and Markets Act 2000 does not distinguish to the same extent between life and non-life insurance, because, as we have seen (Ch.2), its scope is wider.

insured is felt to be unnecessary here, as there are no principles peculiar to life insurance or problems raised by these in this area. Furthermore, there are certain technical questions, no doubt of great importance in practice, which are more than adequately dealt with elsewhere.[4] Examples of these would be the law relating to proof of death and proving title to a life policy.

19.1   Formalities—Disclosure and Cancellation

In addition to the many general disclosure requirements imposed by the Financial Conduct Authority on life contracts along with other forms of investment,[5] there are particular requirements for pre-contractual disclosure in life insurance introduced as a result of the EC Directive on life insurance.[6] These apply to contracts entered into by a UK or EU company or a member of Lloyd's which constitute the carrying on in the UK of long term business which is not reinsurance business or the provision in the UK of long term insurance.[7] Before entering into such a contract the insurer must provide the prospective insured with the following information in a durable medium or make it available on a website[8]:

(a)   the name of the undertaking and its legal form, the name of the EEA State in which the head office and, where appropriate, the agency or branch concluding the policy is situated and the address of the head office and, where appropriate, of the agency or branch concluding the policy;

(b)   a definition of each benefit and option;

(c)   the term of the contract and the means by which it may be terminated;

(d)   the method of paying premiums and the duration of the payments;

(e)   the method of calculating bonuses and the distribution of bonuses;

(f)   an indication of surrender and paid-up values and the extent to which these values are guaranteed;

(g)   an indication of the premiums for each benefit;

---

[4] See especially, *MacGillivray on Insurance Law*, 13th edn, Ch.25.
[5] Discussion of these is outside the scope of this book.
[6] See the Conduct of Business Sourcebook (COBS). As to the Directive, see generally Ch.2 and, for the equivalent provisions regarding non-life insurance, see Ch.5.
[7] They thus catch insurance sold from an establishment in the UK and insurance sold directly from another Member State.
[8] As to the information that an intermediary advising on life insurance must provide, see COBS 7.

(h) in respect of unit-linked policies, a definition of the units and an indication of the nature of the underlying assets;

(i) the arrangements with respect to the period within which the policy holder may cancel the contract;

(j) the tax arrangements applicable to the policy;

(k) the arrangements for handling complaints; and

(l) the law applicable to the contract where the parties do not have a free choice or, where the parties are free to choose the law applicable, the law which the insurer proposes to choose.

In addition to the disclosure of information before the contract is entered into, there are requirements for disclosure of information by the insurer during the contract. These apply to the same categories of insurers and primarily require the disclosure in writing of any changes to most of the information described above. In addition, if the policy provides for the payment of bonuses, information in writing as to the amount of bonuses which has become payable must be given once a year.

Because the life insurance contract is a long-term contract, and because individuals may be persuaded by high pressure salesmanship to enter into contracts which may not be entirely appropriate for them, the law has for some years provided for a cooling off period, that is policy-holders are given a period within which they can change their minds and cancel an already legally binding contract without penalty.[9] In essence, an individual customer has a right of cancellation for a minimum of 30 days from their receipt of the appropriate notice sent by the insurer.[10]

19.2   Assignment of Life Policies

Life insurance policies are undoubtedly a valuable piece of property, normally attracting a surrender value after the payment of a number of premiums. They can be sold or otherwise disposed of or used as security, features which are assisted by the fact that the requirement of insurable interest exists only at the date the policy is effected.[11] Many dealings of this sort with life policies will in law be assignments of the policies, and there are a number of

---

[9] These rules were introduced originally on the recommendation of the Scott Committee on Property Bonds and Equity Linked Life Assurance, 1973, Cmnd.5281, and have their equivalent in the hire purchase and consumer credit legislation.

[10] The rules, which apply to some other investments as well as life insurance, are contained in COBS 15.

[11] See 3.3.

special rules. The description "assignment" covers any case where the insured disposes entirely of his interest in the policy, whether by way of sale, gift or mortgage. If a policy is used as security, some of the statutory formalities as to assignment may be used even where the insured does not dispose entirely of his interest. The use of a life policy in such circumstances may very well attract some of the provisions of the Consumer Credit Act 1974, that is, if it is used in connection with a regulated consumer credit agreement.[12]

19.2.1 Assignment as mortgage

If a transaction with a life policy appears to be an absolute assignment, but in reality is a mortgage as security for a debt, the insured is entitled to redeem the mortgage on repayment of the debt and recover his policy, notwithstanding any provision to the contrary. In deciding whether or not a transaction with a life policy is an outright assignment or a mortgage, the court will look at the surrounding circumstances and parol evidence is admissible. For example, in the Irish case of *Murphy v Taylor*,[13] a policy for £999 was assigned for a consideration of £144. The evidence showed that the assignor in fact borrowed the £144 from the assignee. The assignee later recovered £600 from the insurer. It was held that the substance of the transaction was that of a mortgage to secure a debt. Therefore, after allowing for the debt of £144, the assignor was entitled to redeem the mortgage and recover from the assignee the remainder of the £600 that the latter had recovered from the insurer.

The rule allowing the insured to redeem what is in substance a mortgage of a life policy is part of the general law relating to mortgages whereby clogs or fetters on the equity of redemption or equitable right to redeem are void. Detailed consideration of this body of law can be found elsewhere,[14] but an interesting example in the life insurance context is the decision in *Salt v Marquess of Northampton*.[15] Here, X borrowed £10,000 from an insurer and secured this by a charge on his reversionary interest in certain property. In addition, he agreed to pay the premiums on a policy for £34,000 taken out by the insurers against the possibility of the interest not vesting. It was agreed that if X paid off the loan before the interest was vested, the policy would be assigned to him, but if he died before repayment and vesting, the policy would belong to the insurers. The latter event occurred. It was held that, despite the agreement, the transaction was in substance a mortgage,

---

[12] For the detail see Pt VIII of the 1974 Act and Hill-Smith, *Consumer Credit: Law and Practice*, (London: Sweet & Maxwell, 1985) Ch.8.

[13] *Murphy v Taylor* (1850) 1 Ir.Ch.R. 92.

[14] For example Megarry and Wade, *Law of Real Property*, 5th edn (London: Sweet & Maxwell, 1984), at 964–971.

[15] *Salt v Marquess of Northampton* [1892] A.C. 1.

and the personal representatives of X were entitled to redeem and recover the proceeds of the policy, after deducting the loan and interest.

19.2.2 Statutory assignment

Prior to the Policies of Assurance Act 1867, a life policy was not assignable at law. Although equity always permitted such assignments, the assignee could only sue to enforce the policy if he joined the assignor in the action, and an insurer could not obtain a good discharge against payment from the assignee alone. The 1867 Act permits legal assignments so that the assignee of a life policy can, if the requirements of the Act are complied with, enforce it in his own name.[16] Furthermore, a life policy is a chose in action,[17] one of the forms of intangible personal property, so that an alternative procedure for assignment lies under s.136 of the Law of Property Act 1925. In addition, an assignment that is incomplete according to statutory requirements may well still be valid as an equitable assignment.

There is one essential difference between the two statutory procedures. Under the 1867 Act, an assignment is valid if it is of the assignor's whole interest in the policy or of merely a part of it, by way of mortgage. Under s.136, an assignment must be absolute, that is it must be of the assignor's whole interest. Therefore, a mortgage whereby the whole interest in a life policy is charged can be effected under s.136, but one whereby only part is charged has to be effected under the 1867 Act.

An assignment under the 1867 Act must be in the form prescribed in the Schedule to the Act or in words with a similar effect and it must be endorsed on the policy or contained in a separate instrument.[18] Written notice of the assignment must be given to the insurer at its principal place of business.[19] An assignment under s.136 must simply be in writing but again notice must be given to the debtor, that is the insurer. In neither case is the consent of the insurers necessary, but a condition in the policy making it non-assignable is effective to prevent a legal assignment, although it cannot prevent an effective equitable assignment.[20]

In most cases, therefore, the statutory procedures are alternative devices for achieving the same result, and which one is used must simply be a matter of preference. Even if one of the statutory procedures is not complied with, as we have seen, an assignment may be effective in equity. This may be

---

[16] s.1.
[17] *Re Moore* (1878) 8 Ch D 519.
[18] See s.5.
[19] See s.3.
[20] *Re Turcan* (1888) 40 Ch D 5.

because there was a failure to give notice to the insurer,[21] because there was merely an agreement to assign, or because the policy was simply delivered to the assignee, for example, as security. If there have been more than one purported assignments of the same policy, the well-established rules as to priority apply. Briefly,[22] a legal assignee has priority over anyone except an earlier equitable assignment of which he has notice or an earlier legal assignment. Equitable assignments generally rank in order of creation, except that the first such assignee to give notice to the insurers will take priority over any prior assignments of which he had no notice. If there is any doubt as to who is entitled to the policy moneys, in this or any other context, the insurer may pay them into court under the Life Assurance Companies (Payment into Court) Act 1896.[23]

19.3 Trusts of Life Policies

A life policy may often be held by the insured on trust for someone else. This will normally arise only on an own-life policy. If such a trust can be shown to exist, it has two distinct advantages. The first is that on the death of the life insured, the monies will belong to and go directly to the beneficiary, thus avoiding and not being counted as a part of the insured's estate.[24] Secondly, if the insured becomes bankrupt, the beneficiary can claim the policy without its being subject to the claims of the insured's creditors, provided that the trust itself was not created in order to defraud creditors.[25] A further reason for seeking to show that a life policy was held on trust used to be that this would avoid the problem of the doctrine of privity of contract for a third party who claimed that the policy was taken out for his benefit. This should no longer be a problem in respect of policies effected on or after 11 May 2000.[26]

19.3.1 Section 11 trusts

The easiest way to establish such a trust is under the provisions of s.11 of the Married Women's Property Act 1882, although this section is limited in its application. Under it, a policy effected on his or her own life by a married man or woman, and expressed to be for the benefit of his or her spouse and/

---

[21] For example *Williams v Thorp* (1828) 2 Sim. 257.

[22] The detail can be found in *MacGillivray*, 13th edn, paras 26–087 to 26–098.

[23] Above at paras 26–059 to 26–063.

[24] This can help in avoiding, or paying for, inheritance tax.

[25] Insolvency Act 1986 ss.423–425; proviso to Married Women's Property Act 1882 s.11.

[26] By virtue of the Contracts (Rights of Third Parties) Act 1999, described at 4.5.

or children,[27] creates a trust in favour of the spouse and/or children, and the money payable under the policy does not form part of the insured's estate. Section 11 applies also to insurances effected by civil partners.[28] A joint life policy effected by a husband and wife may in reality create two separate policies, each within s.11.[29] However, such a policy must refer to the Act or contain other words indicating that each effected it for the benefit of the other.[30]

It should be noted first that s.11 applies only to policies effected by a married man or woman on his or her own life. Thus, for example, a policy by a father on the life of his son, even if legal, which must be doubtful,[31] cannot fall within s.11.[32] If the section does apply, the insured is a trustee and must therefore act with respect to the policy in the best interests of the beneficiaries. For example, if he or she has an option to surrender the policy, that may properly be exercised only in the interests of the beneficiaries; it is not exercisable in order to defeat the trust, and if the policy is surrendered, the money received will probably be held for the ultimate benefit of the beneficiaries.[33]

Section 11 applies to any policies securing benefits payable on the death of the life insured, including an accident policy covering only death by accident,[34] and an endowment policy that provides for payment if the insured dies before the expiry of the stated period.[35] If the policy names the beneficiary or beneficiaries, then the latter acquire an immediate vested interest in it.[36] In *Cousins v Sun Life Assurance Society*,[37] a wife was the named beneficiary of a policy effected by her husband whom she predeceased. It was held that the policy monies belonged to the wife's estate, even though the husband had remarried. It should be noted that divorce does not of itself change any rights under a s.11 policy, but that these can be varied as part of a general settlement of property rights under s.24 of the Matrimonial Causes Act 1973.

If the policy does not name the beneficiaries but is merely expressed to be for the benefit of the insured's wife and children, for example, the beneficiaries have only a contingent interest, and only those people who fit the description on the death of the life insured will be entitled to benefit.

---

[27] "Children" includes adopted and illegitimate children; Adoption and Children Act 2002 ss.66 and 67; Family Law Reform Act 1969 s.19.

[28] Civil Partnership Act 2004 s.70.

[29] *Re S (deceased)* [1996] 1 W.L.R. 235.

[30] *Rooney v Cardona* [1999] 1 W.L.R. 1388.

[31] See 3.4.1.

[32] *Re Engelbach* [1924] 2 Ch. 348.

[33] *Re Fleetwood's Policy* [1926] Ch. 48.

[34] *Re Gladitz* [1937] Ch. 588.

[35] *Re Loakimidis' Policy Trusts* [1925] Ch. 403.

[36] So if the beneficiary becomes bankrupt before the death of the life insured, the policy vests in the trustee in bankruptcy, and only he can give a good receipt for the proceeds: *Rooney v Cardona* [1999] 1 W.L.R. 1388.

[37] *Cousins v Sun Life Assurance Society* [1933] Ch. 126.

19.3.2 Other trusts

If s.11 is inapplicable, to establish a trust of a life policy it is necessary to comply with the well-established principle of trusts law that a person will not be regarded as having declared himself a trustee of property in the absence of words showing a clear intention to do so.[38] In addition, many of the cases dealing with trusts of life policies reveal deficiencies in the law relating to life insurance. If A effects a policy on his own life for the benefit of B, there are no problems if a trust is created, the point to which we shall shortly return, and provided that B's name is inserted in the policy.[39] But often the point arises because it appears that A has effected a policy on B's life for the benefit of B.

The law is clear that A must therefore have an insurable interest in the life of B,[40] quite apart from whether or not there is a trust in B's favour. Many of the policies in the relevant cases took a form which it appears is quite common, whereby a parent insures the life of his child for the latter's benefit. It may well be an endowment policy, perhaps taken out for the purposes of paying school fees. Whether or not such a policy is lawful must be open to great doubt, as a parent does not usually have an insurable interest in the life of his child.[41] The question is rarely raised in this context, usually because the insurer will have already handed over the money, so that the sole question is whether A or B is entitled to it, and insurers who did raise lack of insurable interest as a defence would attract unfavourable publicity. Nevertheless, the point should be recognised as a consequence of the narrowness of the law governing insurable interest, and perhaps also as a factor which should encourage the court to find a trust. If this is so, the position is not so much that A is insuring B's life for the benefit of B, as that A is acting for B in insuring B's life, perhaps because, as a minor, B is unable to do so himself.

The more recent cases appear to reveal more willingness to find that a trust has been created, but two things are clear.[42] First, the mere fact that A takes out a policy which is expressed to be for the benefit of B or on behalf of B does not constitute a trust for B. Secondly, the mere fact that the policy provides that the policy monies are to be payable to B does not create a trust in favour of B. For example, in *Re Engelbach*,[43] a father proposed "for his daughter" an endowment policy whereby she was to receive £3,000 if she should reach the age of 21. If she died before then, her father was entitled to recover the premiums paid. It was held that the father's estate, on his death, was entitled

---

[38] e.g. *Jones v Lock* (1865) 1 Ch App 25.
[39] Life Assurance Act 1774 s.2; see 3.6.
[40] Life Assurance Act 1774 s.1; see 3.2.
[41] *Halford v Kymer* (1830) 10 B. & C. 724.
[42] Plowman J in *Re Foster* [1966] 1 W.L.R. 222 at 227.
[43] *Re Engelbach* [1924] 2 Ch. 348.

to the £3,000 when the daughter became 21. Simply, there was not sufficient evidence to create a trust. Similarly, in *Re Sinclair*,[44] the insured was godfather to a baby of six months. He effected an endowment policy wherein the baby was referred to as "the nominee" and the moneys were payable to the child at 21. Again no trust arose because there was insufficient evidence. In both these cases, and indeed in the other ones to the same effect,[45] the policies must strictly have been illegal for want of insurable interest.

It should be noted, though, that if on similar facts, the "beneficiary" is, in fact, paid the insurance money, he will normally be entitled to keep it, even if there was no trust in his favour. The only situation where this would not be the case is if the policy compels the conclusion that he was to receive it merely as nominee or agent for the insured.[46] A court is most unlikely to conclude this nowadays, unless the wording of the policy compels it, so that if the insurer pays the "beneficiary", the result is a useful way around the decisions just discussed.

19.3.3 Modern cases

Modern policy wordings and more modern cases evince in any event a greater willingness to find a trust. In *Re Webb*,[47] a father took out policies on the lives of his two children. He was described as "the grantee" and in the proposal form as wishing to effect insurance "on behalf of and for the benefit of the person . . . named as the life assured". Each policy provided (1) that on the child's death at or after the age of 21, the money would be paid to his representatives, and, on his 21st birthday, all the father's interest in the policy would cease; until then the father had power to surrender, assign and otherwise deal with the policy, and the father would recover the premiums paid if the child died before the age of 21; (2) that if the father, having paid all the premiums due, died before the child reached 21, the policies would remain in force until the child's 21st birthday. The father did die before the children were 21, and the question was whether the policies, which survived by reason of the term mentioned, belonged to his estate or to the children. It was held that they belonged to the children, having been effected by the father on trust for them.

According to Farwell J there was more than the mere taking out of a policy for the benefit of another as in the earlier cases. The terms of the

[44] *Re Sinclair* [1938] Ch. 799.
[45] For example *Cleaver v Mutual Reserve Fund Life Ass* [1892] 1 Q.B. 147; *Re Foster* [1938] 3 All E.R. 357.
[46] *Re Schebsman* [1944] 1 Ch. 83, approved in *Beswick v Beswick* [1968] A.C. 58, where the House of Lords disapproved of *Re Engelbach* above, in so far as it held to the contrary.
[47] *Re Webb* [1941] Ch. 225.

policies were sufficient to establish a trust, especially that providing that the father's interest in them would cease completely when the children were 21 and that providing that the policy moneys themselves were never payable until the children reached the specified age, thus making it clear that the father had no interest in these. This is logically sound, since such provisions are inconsistent with the father or nominal insured having the whole beneficial interest in the policy. A beneficial interest must lie elsewhere, that is with the children, and hence there must be a trust.

Re Webb was followed in *Re Foster*,[48] where the policy was not quite in the same form. It provided that upon the child becoming 21, the rights vested in the father (the grantee) to surrender or charge the policy until the child reached that age were to be vested in the child. Plowman J held that the fact that these rights were vested absolutely in the child at 21 was inconsistent with the father thereafter retaining any beneficial interest, so that, although this latter point was not expressly spelt out, as it had been in *Re Webb*, it was necessarily impliedly provided, and the same result followed.

As a result of these cases, it appears likely nowadays that the court will strive to find a trust where policies are taken out for children, not least because it avoids any insurable interest problems. In effect, therefore, the children in these cases were insuring their own lives through a trustee. At all times, the trustee must act in accordance with the responsibilities surrounding that position. For example, although he will probably until a stated age have the right to surrender or assign the policy, he can properly do so only if it is in the best interests of the child. When the latter reaches the specified age, he has full powers over the policy and, if the trust still exists, will be able to terminate it.[49] He will also, if necessary, be able to enforce it through the trustee, and, now, as mentioned earlier, under the provisions of the Contracts (Rights of Third Parties) Act 1999.[50] It must be stressed, though, that all cases must turn on their particular facts and on the provisions in the policies, and it is by no means impossible that a case will occur when these are not sufficient to establish a trust.

---

[48] *Re Foster* [1966] 1 W.L.R. 222.

[49] *Saunders v Vautier* (1841) Cr. & Ph. 240.

[50] The relevant provisions are briefly described at 4.5. The Act applies only to policies taken out on or after 11 May 2000. In respect of a policy effected before then, the child will be able to enforce it directly only if he becomes legal owner or if there is a new agreement arising by virtue of his paying and the insurer accepting from him, the premiums due. It was suggested by the Law Revision Committee (6th Interim Report, at 32) that s.11 of the Married Women's Property Act be extended to cover these child policies, but the Law Commission recommended (Law Com No.242, 1996, especially at paras 12.22 to 12.26.) that s.11 be left alone, noting that its recommendations to reform the doctrine of privity of contract, now implemented in the 1999 Act, would enable the third party beneficiary to sue on the contract.

19.3.4 Group insurance

The trust question has hitherto been considered solely in the context of family arrangements. The other equally common area where the same problems can arise is that of group insurance policies, for example, taken out by an employer on the lives of his employees or a group of them for the benefit of the latter. The circumstances may make it clear that the employees are beneficiaries under a trust, as in *Bowskill v Dawson (No.2)*,[51] where the employer entered into a trust deed with the trustee company that effected the policy for the employees. There were clear references to the fact that, inter alia, any sums received by the trust company were to be held on trust for the employees and the court had no difficulty in holding that the latter were therefore beneficiaries under the trusts of the deed.

By contrast, there were no such references in *Green v Russell*,[52] where an employer, called the insured, effected a group accident policy for the benefit of his employees named in a schedule to the policy. The policy expressly provided that the insurer was entitled to treat the insured as absolute owner and was not bound to recognise any equitable or other claim or interest in the policy. In the light of this, it was held that the employees had no legal or equitable claim to the policy, in spite of the fact that one of the employees covered, or rather his widow, had received a sum of money paid under the policy.[53] There was clearly no basis for implying a trust on the authorities already mentioned. It must therefore be doubtful whether the policy was strictly legally enforceable, as the employer may not have had an insurable interest in the lives of his employees, or at least not to the extent of the amount for which each employee was insured.[54] It seems in practice that group policies of this nature are not always effected with terms that would enable the court to find a trust, but, of course, employees may now have a statutory right to enforce them under the Contracts (Rights of Third Parties) Act 1999.[55]

---

[51] *Bowskill v Dawson (No.2)* [1955] 1 Q.B. 13.

[52] *Green v Russell* [1959] 2 Q.B. 226.

[53] The case arose under the Fatal Accidents Acts, the question being whether the third party who caused the death of the employee in question could deduct the insurance money from the damages he was liable to pay to the widow.

[54] See also the comments at 3.4.2.

[55] See 4.5.

CHAPTER 20

LIABILITY INSURANCE

20.0

Insurance against the insured's potential legal liability to a third party, whether in contract or tort, is of course commonplace. In a number of instances, such insurance is required to be effected by statute, most notably in the fields of motor vehicle and employer's liability insurance. The additional requirements and restrictions imposed in these instances will be considered in Chs 21 and 22. This chapter will concentrate upon aspects common to all liability insurances, which range from those effected by householders to public liability and professional indemnity policies. Here we consider in detail those matters that appear genuinely to be common to all such insurances, rather than points that arise as the result of detailed policy wordings concerning the risks covered and excepted.[1]

Having said that, a few general comments on the scope of liability insurance are appropriate. Standard market practice has led to some standard words of basic cover and indeed basic exclusions. For example, a public liability or a products liability policy will generally seek to cover tortious, but not contractual, liability.[2] Although the opening words may refer to indemnity against sums that the insured is legally liable to pay, words which by themselves are wide enough to cover contractual liability, there will normally be an express exclusion of contractual liability. However, the use of the tautologous phrase "liable at law" in "all sums which the insured shall become liable at law to pay as damages" does not by itself exclude contractual liability.[3] Provided that the insured is legally liable to the third party, amounts paid under an ex gratia settlement are covered.[4] The fact that the insured has

---

[1] For detail, see, for example, the excellent book, published in Australia, Derrington and Ashton, *The Law of Liability Insurance* (Sydney: Butterworths, 1990). See also, Enright, *Professional Indemnity Insurance*, 2nd edn (London: Sweet & Maxwell, 2007) and *MacGillivray on Insurance Law*, 13th edn, Ch.29.

[2] See, for example, *Tesco Stores Ltd v Constable* [2008] EWCA Civ 362; [2008] Lloyd's Rep. I.R. 636.

[3] *MIS Aswan Engineering Establishment Ltd v Iron Trades Mutual Insurance Co Ltd* [1989] 1 Lloyd's Rep. 289. If there is concurrent liability in contract and tort, any exclusion for contractual liability is inapplicable as cover for tort liability takes priority: *Jan de Nul (UK) Ltd v Axa Royale Belge SA* [2002] EWCA Civ 209; [2002] Lloyd's Rep. I.R. 589.

[4] *Peninsular & Orient Steam Navigation Co v Youell* [1997] 2 Lloyd's Rep. 136; *Structural Polymer Systems Ltd v Brown* [2000] Lloyd's Rep. I.R. 64. Professional indemnity

been adjudged legally liable to the third party is not of itself determinative of the insured's rights against his liability insurer.[5]

There are four parts to this chapter: first, the statutory protection given to a third party in the event of the insured's insolvency; secondly, the important questions that arise from standard conditions to be found in all liability insurance policies; thirdly, some questions that can arise concerning the sums insured and costs; and fourthly, the insurers' duty to the victim of the insured.

20.1   Insolvency of the Insured

At common law, if an insured went bankrupt, or, if a company, went into liquidation, after a claim arose against him by a third party, any money paid by his insurers to indemnify the insured against the claim after the commencement of the bankruptcy or liquidation went towards the general assets of the bankrupt or insolvent company, and were not entitled to be claimed by the third party.[6] The latter had merely the right to prove in the bankruptcy or liquidation as an ordinary creditor along with all the other ordinary creditors of the insured, because he had no rights in respect of the contract between insured and insurer. This was clearly unjust and in 1930, the Third Parties (Rights Against Insurers) Act was passed to remedy the situation.[7] In essence, the Act statutorily subrogates the third party to the position of the insured, although, as we shall see, the protection afforded to the third party can prove somewhat illusory. On the other hand, the 1930 Act must be regarded as part of the statutory scheme governing insolvency, and this may give the third party the right to claim that an insolvency procedure would unfairly prejudice his claim.[8]

Section 1(1) of the 1930 Act, as amended,[9] provides:

policies often refer to cover against any "negligent act, error or omission", but the word "negligent" does not qualify the words "act" and "omission": *Wimpey Construction UK Ltd v Poole* [1984] 2 Lloyd's Rep. 499.

[5] *Omega Proteins Ltd v Aspen Insurance UK Ltd* [2010] EWHC 2280 (Comm); [2011] Lloyd's Rep. I.R. 186.

[6] *Re Harrington Motor Co* [1928] Ch 105; *Hood's Trustees v Southern Union General Insurance Co of Australasia Ltd* [1928] Ch. 793.

[7] It was passed at the same time as compulsory motor insurance was introduced and the two cases referred to in fn.6 both arose out of road accidents. It seems clear that at the time the Act was primarily envisaged as applying to such situations. It is not perhaps surprising that later developments, including the expansion of liability insurance, have led to situations where the Act does not seem to give sufficient protection to third parties and, as explained in 20.1.5, the Act will be replaced in the near future.

[8] *Sea Voyager Maritime Inc v Bielecki* [1999] 1 B.C.L.C. 133.

[9] By the Insolvency Acts 1985 and 1986 and by the Enterprise Act 2002 (Insolvency) Order 2003, SI 2003/2096.

> "Where under any contract of insurance a person (hereinafter referred to as the insured) is insured against liabilities to third parties which he may incur then,
>
> (a)—in the event of the insured becoming bankrupt or making a composition or arrangement with his creditors; or
>
> (b)—in the case of the insured being a company, [being wound up[10] or entering administration or receivership or a voluntary arrangement][11]
>
> if, either before or after that event, any such liability as aforesaid is incurred by the insured, his rights against the insurer under the contract in respect of the liability shall, notwithstanding anything in any Act or rule of law to the contrary, be transferred to and vest in the third party to whom the liability was so incurred."

The same applies where the insured dies insolvent.[12] Section 1(3), relating to exclusions of the Act, is considered separately below. "Liability" in s.1(1) includes contractual liabilities, in debt as well as in damages, as well as tortious liabilities. In *Re OT Computers Ltd*,[13] the Court of Appeal, in laying down this principle, held that the Act was apt to apply to liabilities under extended warranties sold by the insured. The Act can still apply after the bankrupt insured has been discharged from bankruptcy.[14]

Section 2 casts upon the insured who becomes insolvent the duty to inform the third party who has a claim of any relevant insurance. This duty arises on the occurrence of one of the insolvency events covered by s.1(1) and is not dependent on the insured's liability being established.[15] Section 3 provides that settlements made between the insurer and the bankrupt or liquidated insured are of no effect as regards the third party, but applies only to settlements made after bankruptcy or liquidation, and does not affect a prior settlement even in respect of a liability already incurred by the insured.[16] A claim under the 1930 Act is a claim for indemnity under a contract of

---

[10] Other than a voluntary winding up merely for the purposes of a reconstruction or amalgamation: s.1(6).

[11] Under the Insolvency Act 1986.

[12] See s.1(2).

[13] [2004] EWCA Civ 653; [2004] Lloyd's Rep. I.R. 669; overruling the decisions restricting "liability" to tortious liability in *Tarbuck v Avon Insurance Plc* [2001] 2 All E.R. 503 and *T & N Ltd v Royal & Sun Alliance Plc (No.2)* [2003] EWHC 1016 (Ch); [2004] Lloyd's Rep. I.R. 106.

[14] *Law Society of England and Wales v Shah* [2007] EWHC 2841 (Ch); [2008] Lloyd's Rep. I.R. 442.

[15] *Re OT Computers Ltd*, above, overruling the decisions to the contrary in *Nigel Upchurch Associates v Aldridge Estates Investment Co Ltd* [1993] 1 Lloyd's Rep. 535 and *Woolwich Building Society v Taylor* [1995] 1 B.C.L.C. 132. See further below.

[16] *Normid Housing Association Ltd v Ralphs* [1989] 1 Lloyd's Rep. 265. Section 3 does not apply to a scheme of arrangement under the Companies Act: *Re T & N Ltd (No.4)* [2006] EWHC 1447 (Ch); [2006] Lloyd's Rep. I.R. 817.

insurance and not, even where it arises out of an accident causing personal injury, a claim for damages for personal injury.[17]

Over the years there were a number of decisions on the Act that, in varying degrees, tended to restrict its effectiveness so far as third parties were concerned. In some respects the position has improved following the decision in *Re OT Computers Ltd* already referred to and discussed again below. Otherwise, some of the decisions simply confirm that the 1930 Act has a relatively narrow impact and certainly cannot put the third party in a better position than the insured.[18] The Law Commissions engaged in a lengthy review of the Act, culminating in a Report in 2001.[19] Eventually this led to the Third Parties (Rights against Insurers) Bill being presented to Parliament in November 2009. The Bill received royal assent in March 2010 but contained some crucial omissions. It has been amended by Pt 6 of the Insurance Act 2015 and, at the time of writing, is awaiting commencement. Given that, in any event, the 1930 Act will continue to apply for some time to situations where either the alleged liability or the insolvency of the insured occurs before commencement, this account deals first with the position under the 1930 Act and considers the new scheme subsequently in 20.1.5.

20.1.1 Liability must be established

The Act does not give the third party any right actually to sue the insurer until the liability of the insured has been established by judgment or settlement, although, as will be seen below, it does confer what can be described as a contingent transfer. In *Post Office v Norwich Union Fire Insurance Co*,[20] the insureds were contractors engaged in road works. In the course of their excavations they damaged a cable belonging to the Post Office. The latter claimed that this was the fault of the contractors, though this was denied, the contractors claiming that it was the fault of a Post Office engineer. The contractors having gone into liquidation, the Post Office sued their insurers under the 1930 Act before the insured's liability was established. It was held that the action was premature, the third party being able to sue the insurers only when the insured's liability has been determined or agreed.[21] The

---

[17] *Burns v Shuttlehurst Ltd* [1999] 1 W.L.R. 1449. This can be important with regard to questions of procedure and limitation.

[18] See especially the House of Lords' decisions in *Bradley v Eagle Star Insurance Co Ltd* [1989] A.C. 957 and *The Fanti* and *The Padre Island* [1991] 2 A.C. 1, both of which are considered in detail below. For a detailed critical examination, see Mance, "Insolvency at sea" [1995] L.M.C.L.Q. 34.

[19] Third Parties—Rights against Insurers, Law Com No. 272, Scot Law Com No.184, Cm. 5217.

[20] *Post Office v Norwich Union Fire Insurance Co* [1967] 2 Q.B. 363.

[21] This was the ratio of Lord Denning MR and the principal ratio of Salmon LJ.

correct procedure in this sort of case is for the third party to obtain the leave of the court to bring proceedings against the insolvent insured. Only when these proceedings have been determined can the insurer be liable under the 1930 Act. The *Post Office* case was followed and approved by the House of Lords in *Bradley v Eagle Star Insurance Co Ltd*.[22] Here, the insured had been the company employing the plaintiff, Mrs Bradley, against which the latter was assumed to have the right to claim damages as a result of her having contracted byssinosis while working in circumstances which involved the inhalation of cotton dust. The company had been dissolved in 1976 and so, there being no other possible defendant, Mrs Bradley commenced proceedings directly against her employer's insurers. It was held that this action had to be struck out as disclosing no cause of action. No liability had been incurred by the insured employer that could bring s.1 of the 1930 Act into operation.

While the decisions in *Post Office v Norwich Union* and *Bradley v Eagle Star* cannot logically be faulted,[23] they are nonetheless somewhat artificial as almost inevitably in such cases the insurers will in practice be the real defendants and, once the insured's liability is established, will normally immediately satisfy it. However, insurers have their own good reasons for not wishing to appear as the defendants in civil actions, principally the fear that it would gain them bad publicity,[24] and these are clearly legitimate reasons within the context of the tort/liability insurance system. Further, Parliament has enacted what in many cases, because the insolvent defendant would be a registered company, will in practice amount to a reversal of the decision in *Bradley v Eagle Star*. Since 1989, an application to the court for a declaration that the dissolution of a company is void may be made at any time if it is for the purpose of bringing proceedings against the company for damages for personal injury or under the Fatal Accidents Act.[25] Claimants like Mrs Bradley can now use this procedure to find a defendant to sue, and then use the 1930 Act to claim against the latter's insurers.[26]

However, the latter also relied upon the fact that the third party takes subject to any conditions in the policy, one of which forbid the insured from admitting liability in any way without the insurer's consent (as to this, see below). Harman LJ relied on this latter reason only.

[22] *Bradley v Eagle Star Insurance Co Ltd* [1989] A.C. 957.

[23] Notwithstanding Lord Templeman's vigorous dissent in *Bradley*.

[24] See Salmon LJ in *Post Office v Norwich Union* [1967] 2 Q.B. at 378.

[25] Companies Act 2006 s.1029.

[26] This is still not foolproof, of course. For example, there will still have to be evidence that a particular insurer was the relevant insurer at the appropriate time.

20.1.2 Transfer of rights

However, the decisions in the *Post Office* and *Bradley* cases did not directly address the issue of the issue as to when the insured's rights are transferred to the third party, namely whether it is on the insolvency of the assured or when liability is established. In *Re OT Computers Ltd*,[27] it was held that the rights are transferred on the occurrence of one of the insolvent events specified in the Act.

> "The 1930 Act makes no reference to the need to establish the insured's liability before the transfer takes place. It is therefore more natural to read the Act as envisaging that the transfer to and vesting in the third party of the rights of the insured occurs on insolvency whether the establishment of the right occurs before or after the insolvency. The rights so transferred may be contingent or inchoate in the sense that the rights may not give rise to legal liability on the part of the insurer until the existence and amount of the liability is established but the transfer nevertheless takes place on the insolvency."[28]

In the context of this case, the effect was to give the third party the information rights under s.2.[29]

20.1.3 Third party's rights no better than insured's

One of the reasons for the decision in *Post Office v Norwich Union* was that the plaintiff/claimant obtains his rights under the 1930 Act subject to the conditions of the policy. There a condition forbade the insured from making any admission of liability without the insurer's consent[30]; the third party's statutory rights were subject also to this term. This point is of general application, so that, except in compulsory motor insurance and, to a lesser extent in employer's liability insurance, where insurers' rights are more circumscribed by statute,[31] any defence which the insurers have against the insured under

---

[27] *Re OT Computers Ltd* [2004] EWCA Civ 653; [2004] Lloyd's Rep. I.R. 669.

[28] Above per Longmore LJ at [28]. Support for that view was found in, inter alia, the dissenting speech of Lord Templeman in *Bradley v Eagle Star*, which in this respect was not contradicted by anything in the majority speeches, and in the earlier Court of Appeal decision in *Cox v Bankside Members Agency Ltd* [1995] 2 Lloyd's Rep. 437 (per Saville LJ at 467).

[29] The same approach was adopted in the subsequent Court of Appeal decision in *Centre Reinsurance International Co v Freakley* [2005] EWCA Civ 115; [2005] Lloyd's Rep. I.R. 303; which related in particular to s.1(3), discussed below, and in *Financial Services Compensation Scheme Ltd v Larnell* [2005] EWCA Civ 1408; [2006] Lloyd's Rep. I.R. 448; where it was held that the rule that limitation periods ceased to run at the date of winding up applied to a claim under the Act.

[30] As to such terms, see 20.2.1.

[31] See Chs 21 and 22.

the insurance contract is available against the third party. This might be the right to avoid the policy for non-disclosure or misrepresentation[32] or to avoid liability for a fraudulent claim,[33] the right to avoid liability for breach of warranty or condition, or the right to insist upon arbitration.

In *Freshwater v Western Australian Assurance Co*[34] and *Smith v Pearl Assurance Co*,[35] the insurers' right in motor policies to insist upon arbitration as a condition precedent to liability was upheld against the injured third party. In fact these decisions have probably been overruled by statute so far as motor insurance is concerned,[36] but the principle holds good for other liability insurances.[37] In *Farrell v Federated Employers' Insurance Association Ltd*,[38] a breach of condition precedent by an employer who was insured against liability to his employees was held effective against an injured employee,[39] and in *Pioneer Concrete (UK) Ltd v National Employers Mutual General Insurance Association Ltd*,[40] a breach of a condition precedent requiring immediate notification by the insured of legal proceedings instituted against it could be relied upon against the innocent third party. However, if compliance with a particular condition is impossible because the insured is insolvent, the third party will not be prejudiced by this.[41]

Further, the third party will be bound by any limitations in the policy regarding the amount of indemnity provided,[42] and if the total insurance fund available is insufficient to pay all the claims made by third parties, the fund is distributed on a first come, first served basis.[43]

However, insurers cannot simply claim to set off against the amount due to the third party any premiums due but unpaid by the insured. In *Murray v Legal & General Assurance Society*,[44] it was held that the rights and liabilities of the insured transferred to the third party are only those rights and liabilities

---

[32] e.g. *McCormick v National Motor and Accident Insurance Union Ltd* (1934) 43 Ll.L.R. 361.

[33] *Total Graphics Ltd v AGF Insurance Ltd* [1997] 1 Lloyd's Rep. 599.

[34] *Freshwater v Western Australian Assurance Co* [1933] 1 K.B. 515.

[35] *Smith v Pearl Assurance Co* [1939] 1 All E.R. 95.

[36] By s.148(5) of the Road Traffic Act 1988; see *Jones v Birch Bros* [1933] 2 K.B. 597 and 21.4.2.

[37] See *Socony Mobil Oil Co Inc v West of England Ship Owners Mutual Insurance Association (London) Ltd* [1984] 2 Lloyd's Rep. 408, noted [1985] J.B.L. 403.

[38] *Farrell v Federated Employers' Insurance Association Ltd* [1970] 1 W.L.R. 1400.

[39] The actual decision in the context of employers' liability insurance is over-ruled by the Employers' Liability (Compulsory Insurance) Regulations: see 22.1.3.

[40] *Pioneer Concrete (UK) Ltd v National Employers Mutual General Insurance Association Ltd* [1985] 1 Lloyd's Rep. 274; see [1985] J.B.L. 333.

[41] *Horne v Prudential Assurance Co Ltd* 1997 S.L.T. (Sh. Ct) 75; *Saunders v Royal Insurance Inc* 1999 S.L.T. 358.

[42] *Averando (UK) Ltd v National Transit Insurance Co Ltd* [1984] 2 Lloyd's Rep. 613.

[43] *Cox v Bankside Members Agency Ltd* [1995] 2 Lloyd's Rep. 437.

[44] *Murray v Legal & General Assurance Society* [1969] 3 All E.R. 794.

in respect of the liability incurred by the insured to the third party. The right to claim premiums was a general right, not dependent on any term of the policy. It would appear that the effect of this decision would be reversed if there were an express term in a liability policy that it was a condition precedent to the liability of the insurer for any particular claim that all premiums owing under the policy before the claim arose were duly paid.

20.1.4 Exclusions of the Act

Section 1(3) provides that in so far as any insurance contract purports, whether directly or indirectly, to avoid the contract or to alter the rights of the parties in the event of the insured's insolvency, it shall be of no effect. The relatively limited effect of this provision, and the fact that in theory the application of the 1930 Act can be avoided quite easily, was demonstrated in the House of Lords' decision in two cases heard and decided together, *Firma C Trade SA v Newcastle Protection and Indemnity Association (The Fanti)* and *Socony Mobil Oil Co Inc v West of England Ship Owners Mutual Insurance Association (London) Ltd (The Padre Island)*.[45]

These concerned the standard provisions in the rules of ship owners' mutual insurance clubs which provide that the clubs, the insurers, do not pay an indemnity to their members, the insureds, until the latter have paid the third party making a claim against them; these are commonly referred to as "pay to be paid" clauses.

Both insureds in the cases had been wound up after their liability to third parties had been established but before the third parties' claims had been paid. It was held that the third parties did not have direct rights against the insurers under the 1930 Act. First it was held that s.1(3) was of no assistance to the third parties. The pay to be paid clause was a provision imposing a condition necessary to be fulfilled before any liability of the insurers could arise and was not a provision which applied on the happening of an insolvency. What were affected or altered by insolvency were not the rights of the insureds themselves but the ability of the insureds to exercise them. Thus, the provision applied equally before and after a winding up order and was not rendered ineffective by s.1(3). With this reasoning, it is submitted, there can be no quarrel. As worded, the subsection strikes down only provisions clearly aimed at affecting the rights of an insured in the event of its becoming insolvent in an attempt to contract out of the statutory assignment.

[45] *Socony Mobil Oil Co Inc v West of England Ship Owners Mutual Insurance Association (London) Ltd (The Padre Island)* [1991] 2 A.C. 1. These were followed in *Centre Reinsurance International Co v Freakley* [2005] EWCA Civ 115; [2005] Lloyd's Rep. I.R. 303, where a claims control clause in a reinsurance agreement did not fall foul of s.1(3) as it did not purport to alter the rights of the parties under the contract of insurance.

Two other arguments were, however, put forward by the third parties as to why the pay to be paid clauses should be regarded as ineffective. The first[46] was that there were transferred to the third parties rights to be indemnified by the insurers, subject to a condition that the third parties first paid to themselves the amounts of the liabilities to them which had been incurred by themselves. Such a condition precedent was impossible or futile for the third parties to perform and thus performance should be excused. This argument was easily rejected. What the 1930 Act transfers is the insured's right that, in the circumstances of the case, was a contingent right to indemnity, conditional on the insured having paid the third party's claim. If that condition was not satisfied, the insured had no present right to be indemnified. The statutory transfer could not put the third party in any better position than the insured.

The other argument was in effect that a principle of equity could override the "pay to be paid" provisions. It ran as follows. At common law the only remedy against an indemnifier under a contract of indemnity was an action of assumpsit by the person entitled to the indemnity, a condition of prior payment by him being implicit in the contract. Equity, however, intervened where reliance on that condition would defeat the indemnity altogether, by requiring the indemnifier to pay the third party directly or pay the indemnified person before he paid the third party, and the equitable remedy prevailed over the common law. While accepting that this principle was in substance as had been argued, the House of Lords rejected its application essentially on the ground that it could not be applicable in the face of the express "pay to be paid" provisions in the contracts of insurance.

The reasons given by the House of Lords cannot easily be faulted as a matter of strict law. The interpretation of the 1930 Act is logical and the rejection of the argument based on equity convincing. On the other hand, an instant reaction might well be to say that the result looks like yet another blow to an innocent third party who has lost out simply because he had the misfortune to have a sound claim against an insured who happened to go into liquidation. This looks like the sort of situation against which the 1930 Act was directed. This point was directly addressed by Lord Goff and it is thought that his arguments supporting the result are ultimately persuasive.[47] All that the 1930 Act was ever intended to do was to transfer to a third party such rights as the insured had under the contract of insurance.

> "[I]t is very difficult to see how it could be said that a condition of prior payment would drive a coach and horses through the Act, for the Act was not directed to giving the third party greater rights than the insured had."

[46] In effect this was the basis of the decision of the Court of Appeal ([1989] 1 Lloyd's Rep. 239), which the House of Lords overruled.

[47] See especially [1991] 2 A.C. at 38–39.

In sharp contrast, where liability insurance is compulsory, especially in respect of motor and employer's liability insurance, Parliament has expressly provided that provisions in contracts defeating the purpose of the insurance will be ineffective.[48] Further, Lord Goff recognised that the *Fanti* and *Padre Island* litigation was in substance fought between insurers. The third parties, the cargo owners, were no doubt insured as is customary, so in substance the plaintiffs were their insurers exercising subrogation rights. In the light of this, sympathy for an unfortunate third party is rapidly lost and it can be argued that there is little real merit in a first party insurer seeking to transfer the risk he has undertaken to a liability insurer.[49] It also seems likely that provisions like the "pay to be paid" clauses are to be found only in contracts like those of mutual insurance clubs. The only weak and uninsured third parties likely to be at risk of being prejudiced by them are those injured or killed as the result of a shipping accident. The evidence was that in such cases the clubs do not rely on the condition of prior payment to defeat a claim. If they did, or indeed if other insurers sought to use the device to evade the 1930 Act, there can be little doubt that legislation restricting their freedom would follow. In effect the 2010 Act has done this.

20.1.5 Reforming and replacing the 1930 Act

Until the important decision in *Re OT Computers Ltd*, which has been discussed earlier, it was clear that no one with an interest in the operation of the Act was totally content with it, and that it was not entirely apt to deal with the very different circumstances that exist today from those existing in 1930. Then probably the only significant instance in practice of liability insurance was motor vehicle insurance. Now there are many forms of such insurance, including employers' liability, public liability, products liability and professional indemnity insurance, reflecting the growth of civil liability over the twentieth century. For some years the Law Commissions examined the operation of the Act. They issued a Consultation Paper in 1998[50] and a Report, with a draft Bill appended, in 2001.[51] Despite the Lord Chancellor's Department issuing its own Consultation Paper in 2002[52] indicating that

---

[48] See Chs 21 and 22.

[49] See 17.17.

[50] Third Parties (Rights against Insurers) Act, Law Com Consultation Paper No.152, Scot Law Com Discussion Paper No.104. For an argument in favour of an alternative and simpler approach, based on that in Australia, which would give the third party a judgment creditor's priority over the insurance money, see Jess, "Reform of direct rights of action by third parties against non-motor liability insurers" [2000] L.M.C.L.Q. 192.

[51] Law Com No.272, Scot Law Com No.184, 2001, Cm. 5217.

[52] CP 08/02.

it was minded to implement the recommendations by way of a Regulatory Reform Order,[53] eventually the Third Parties (Rights against Insurers) Bill 2009 emerged.[54] This became the Third Parties (Rights against Insurers) Act 2010 but, because its date of commencement is still unknown, this account merely highlights the reforms that it will introduce when brought into force.

As well as completely redrafting what is s.1(1) of the 1930 Act, the Act reflects changes in insolvency law by widening the scope of the application of the scheme to include situations where an insured facing financial difficulties enters into various voluntary arrangements with his or its creditors. Perhaps, in practice, most importantly, it removes the need for the third party to issue proceedings both against the insolvent insured and then against the latter's insurers. This will remain an option but alternatively the third party will be able to sue the insurer for a declaration as to either or both the insured's liability to him or the insurer's potential liability to him. This will become the second situation[55] where the law will permit an "action directe" against an insurer, something that is more widespread in civil law jurisdictions. It will also remove the need for the third party to apply to have an insured company restored to the register.[56] The Act expressly covers voluntarily incurred liabilities and it gives the third party much greater rights to information about the insurance, which are set out in detail in Sch.1.

In line with the Law Commissions' recommendations, although the Act continues to allow the insurer to raise defences such as non-disclosure, misrepresentation or breach of warranty by the insured, to set off against the third party the amount of any liability of the insured to it, and to apply any excess to the third party's claim, it does reform the current law in other important respects. So, s.9 applies where transferred rights are subject to a condition, whether under the contract of insurance or otherwise, that the insured has to fulfil. Anything done by the third party which, if done by the insured, would have amounted to or contributed to fulfilment of the condition is treated as if done by the insured. This will allow the third party, among other things, to give notice and particulars of a claim. Further, transferred rights are not subject to a condition requiring the insured to provide information (other than giving notice of a claim) or assistance to the insurer if it cannot be fulfilled because the insured is a body corporate that has been dissolved or an individual who has died. Transferred rights

---

[53] Under the Regulatory Reform Act 2001.

[54] No doubt the delay was at least partly because the decision in *Re OT Computers Ltd* removed any urgent need for reform by holding that the statutory transfer of rights occurs on the insolvency of the insured, so that the third party acquires the information rights under s.2, and that the Act covers all liabilities and not just tortious liabilities.

[55] The other is in respect of compulsory motor insurance, as described in 21.5.1.

[56] See 20.1.1.

are not subject to a condition requiring the prior discharge by the insured or the insured's liability to the third party, although in marine insurance this applies only to the extent that the insured's liability is in respect of death or personal injury. Thus the ratio of the decisions in *The Fanti* and *The Padre Island* is reversed except where, as in that case, the third party's claim is for property damage.

20.2   Contractual Provisions in Liability Policies

There are basically two common form conditions of relevance for present purposes. They concern first admissions of liability and the conduct of proceedings, and secondly the obligation of the insured to take reasonable care.

20.2.1 Admissions of liability and the conduct of proceedings

The standard term reads something like the following[57]:

> "No admission of liability or offer or promise of payment, whether expressed or implied, shall be made without the written consent of the insurer, which shall be entitled at its own discretion to take over and conduct in the name of the insured the defence or settlement of any claim."

Professional indemnity policies may have in addition a clause providing that proceedings by the third party are not to be contested unless a Queen's Counsel so advises (the "QC clause").[58]

20.2.2 Control of proceedings—duty of insurer

The clause cited contains two elements, that prohibiting unauthorised admissions of liability and that giving the insurer the right to control proceedings against the insured. In respect of the latter, it would seem from the standard wording that the insurer has an absolute discretion as to what is done, but it is clear that this discretion is controlled. The insurers have "the right to decide upon the proper tactics to pursue in the conduct of the action,[59]

---

[57] This standard form of wording is unlikely to be used in liability policies sold to individual consumers and indeed should not be, as it is likely to fall foul of the Pt 2 of the Consumer Rights Act 2015.

[58] As to this, see *West Wake Price & Co v Ching* [1957] 1 W.L.R. 45.

[59] Including the appointment of solicitors to represent the insured. However, the insurers cannot compel the insured to accept legal representation: *Barrett Bros v Davies* [1966] 1 W.L.R. 1334.

provided that they do so in what they bona fide consider to be the common interest of themselves and their assured".[60]

A blatant ignoring of the interests of the insured occurred in *Groom v Crocker*[61] where, quite without foundation and knowing of its inaccuracy, the solicitors acting for the insurers admitted to the third party claimant that the insured had been negligent. It was held that this was a clear breach of duty and the insured was entitled to damages for breach of contract and to damages in tort for libel. The contract damages, however, were only nominal, as the insurers had paid the third party the sum he claimed, and the court declined to award damages for the injury to reputation or feelings.[62] That *Groom v Crocker* did not, however, establish a very strict limit on the insurer's discretion is evident from the later case of *Beacon Insurance Co v Langdale*.[63] Here the insurers did not admit that their motor insured was negligent, but without his knowledge they settled the third party's claim with a strict denial of liability. They then sued the insured for the £5 excess provided for by the policy, and it was held that they were entitled to succeed. They had acted quite properly, had made an advantageous settlement and denied liability. With respect, the niceties of paying up but with a denial of liability may be lost on some insureds. The defendant in the case continued to deny that he was liable and would not therefore see why he should have to pay anything until the contrary were proved. Furthermore, such evidence as there is from the report suggests that the third party recovered sufficient to cover him only for his out of pocket expenses and not for the fairly severe injuries he received, implying that it was by no means certain that the insured was liable.

Despite any sympathy that might be felt for such an insured, it can safely be said that in law the insurer can settle with the third party so long as they do not unjustifiably admit liability, and, possibly, so long as they do not unjustifiably settle beyond the policy limits or refuse a settlement offer by the third party within these limits. There is no English authority on this latter point, but the question has been much litigated in the United States of America where there are decisions holding that if a liability insurer refuses an offer of settlement by the third party within the policy limits, and the latter subsequently recovers more than the sum insured in a civil action against the insured, the insurer is liable for the whole amount.[64] It is suggested that such conduct on the part of an insurer here should also entail civil liability as a breach of the duty to act in good faith laid down by *Groom v Crocker*. The

---

[60] Lord Greene M.R. in *Groom v Crocker* [1939] 1 K.B. 194 at 203.

[61] *Groom v Crocker* [1939] 1 K.B. 194.

[62] But see now, e.g. *Heywood v Wellers* [1976] 1 All E.R. 300.

[63] *Beacon Insurance Co v Langdale* [1939] 4 All E.R. 209.

[64] See especially, *Crisci v Security Insurance Co* 66 Cal. (2d) 425, 426, P. (2d) 173 (1967). The action was categorised as tortious. It has been followed on numerous occasions in the US.

American cases have often also awarded the insured punitive damages, but it is not suggested that the English courts would, or should, do so.

On the other hand, it is clear that the standard condition in English policies does not oblige the insurers to take over the insured's defence,[65] so that there can be no basis for any liability on the insurer if it chooses not to do so, other than to indemnify the insured within the limits of the policy if the latter is adjudged legally liable to the third party. In practice, a refusal by the insurer to conduct the defence is unlikely, since it would hardly wish to be without a say in negotiations.[66]

20.2.3 No estoppel

If an insurer does take control of proceedings under the standard condition, it is not necessarily thereby prevented from subsequently denying liability to indemnify the insured. This may arise because of a non-disclosure or breach of warranty or condition by the insured discovered only at a later date. If, however, the insurer does discover such a right to avoid liability, it will be deemed to have waived its right if it continues to act for the insured.[67]

Another situation where the insurer might seek to avoid liability is on the grounds that the event that occurred was not within the cover provided by the policy. Provided that the insurer does not clearly admit to liability, the question arises whether the mere fact that it conducted the defence is sufficient ground for holding that it cannot subsequently deny liability. The only conceivable legal basis for such a conclusion would be by application of the doctrine of estoppel. That such an estoppel could operate in this context was denied in the case of *Soole v Royal Insurance Co*.[68] The insured effected a policy to indemnify himself against the possible successful enforcement by his neighbours of a restrictive covenant on his property. The insurers conducted his unsuccessful defence against the action by his neighbours, but they subsequently denied that they were liable to indemnify him. In fact they were held liable, but the court also held that, if they had not been, their conduct in defending the insured would not have estopped them from denying liability. That conduct did not amount to an unequivocal representation that they would indemnify the insured regardless, because no insurer, when it takes over the defence of its insured, can be sure that it will be liable in the long run. For example, the third party's claim might fail. The insurer's conduct

---

[65] As US policies often do; see the discussion by Stephen J in *Distillers Co v Ajax Insurance Co* (1974) 48 A.L.J.R. 136, especially at 147.

[66] But compare the attitude of the insurers in *Distillers v Ajax*, above, discussed below.

[67] *Evans v Employers' Mutual Insurance Association* [1936] 1 K.B. 505.

[68] *Soole v Royal Insurance Co* [1971] 2 Lloyd's Rep. 332. Compare the Australian case of *Hansen v Marco Engineering (Aust) Pty Ltd* [1948] V.L.R. 198, where it was held that the insurer was estopped.

of the defence is merely an indication that the proceedings may give rise to a liability to indemnify the insured.

20.2.4 Admissions of liability

The part of the standard condition which prohibits admissions of liability, etc. without the insurer's consent is obviously very important, and is no doubt regarded by insurers as essential for the protection of their interests. There can be no doubt as to the validity of such a condition,[69] and it should not matter on principle whether or not the insurer has been prejudiced by an admission by its insured, for example if there can be no doubt whatsoever as to the latter's legal liability.[70] What is perhaps slightly disturbing about this standard condition is its width and the fact that an insurer could rely on a fairly casual "it's my fault" said or written to the third party by the insured to avoid liability, despite the lack of any real prejudice to their position. It must be admitted though that a case with no prejudice at all might not be so likely, as the insurer could always argue that it might well have persuaded the third party to accept a smaller settlement.

20.2.5 Insurer's refusal to defend

The question may arise whether an insurer is still entitled to rely upon this condition if it elects not to have anything to do with the insured's defence against the third party. The essence of the condition is that it prohibits the insured from settling without consent. If the insurer refuses to consent, the insured will be compelled to let the matter go to litigation, unless he can argue that by refusing to have anything to do with his defence, the insurer has forfeited its right to rely upon the condition. This question, which appears never to have been considered in the English courts, produced a difference of opinion in the High Court of Australia in *Distillers Co Ltd v Ajax Insurance Co Ltd*.[71]

The dispute arose out of the manufacture of drugs containing thalidomide, which the insured, a subsidiary of the UK company, had distributed in Australia. These drugs were taken by pregnant women and, allegedly owing to the negligence of Distillers, caused severe damage to their unborn foetuses. Distillers had public liability cover with Ajax, the policy containing the relevant condition. Upon being sued for negligence, Distillers wished to consider compromising with the third parties, but Ajax refused to consent to this, at the same time refusing to conduct Distillers' defence. By a majority,

---

[69] See, e.g. *Terry v Trafalgar Insurance Co* [1970] 1 Lloyd's Rep. 524.
[70] Above.
[71] *Distillers Co Ltd v Ajax Insurance Co Ltd* (1974) 48 A.L.J.R. 136.

it was held that the insurers were entitled to refuse consent without incurring any liability. Gibbs J dissenting, preferred to follow an Irish case,[72] and held that the two aspects of the standard condition were linked, so that the right to rely upon no admissions without consent applied only where the insurer conducted the insured's defence.

The decision of the majority appears correct in principle, but Stephen J, one of the majority, in an important judgment which, it is suggested, should be followed, made it clear that the decision would not confer upon an insurer an arbitrary power to refuse consent. He referred in particular to the sort of case where a conflict between insured and insurer might arise, where the claim against the insured is above the sum insured under the policy and the insured is anxious to settle below that figure whereas the insurer would gain little from a settlement close to the limit and might prefer to fight the case. He said that in such a case, the insurer must exercise its powers under the policy with due regard to the interests of the insured, following *Groom v Crocker*[73] on the analogous point already discussed. The position must depend on a reasonable estimate of the third party's claim. If that has every chance of succeeding, it would be improper for the insurer to refuse to consent to a settlement substantially within the policy limits. If, on the other hand, the third party's claim is doubtful, and the only or principal reason why the insured wishes to settle is to avoid the bad publicity attendant on being sued, the insurer would be justified in refusing its consent. The result is that if the insurer refuses its consent and leaves the insured to act alone, but the latter enters into a quite reasonable settlement, the insurer will be liable to indemnify him regardless of the breach of condition.

20.2.6 The obligation to take reasonable precautions

The second standard condition requires the insured to take reasonable precautions or care to avoid loss. This sort of condition has already been considered generally.[74] Such a clause construed literally would negate a large part of the cover intended to be effected, since one of the major purposes of a liability policy is to insure the insured against liability in negligence, and negligence is a failure to take reasonable care when a duty of care is owed. So the courts have adopted a common sense construction of this condition. In *Woolfall & Rimmer Ltd v Moyle*,[75] the insured employer was vicariously liable for the acts of a foreman who had failed to ensure that certain scaffolding was safe. The court rejected the insurer's argument that the insured had therefore failed to

---

[72] *General Omnibus Co Ltd v London General Insurance Co Ltd* [1936] I.R. 596.

[73] *Groom v Crocker* [1939] 1 K.B. 194; see 20.2.2.

[74] See 13.2.2.

[75] *Woolfall & Rimmer Ltd v Moyle* [1942] 1 K.B. 66.

take reasonable precautions. The insured had complied with that condition by selecting a competent foreman and reasonably delegating to him certain tasks. The insured was not personally negligent, which was the circumstance when the condition might apply. The Court of Appeal went further than this in the later case of *Fraser v Furman*,[76] so that only recklessness or worse on the part of the insured will now amount to a breach of this condition. Reasonable care does not mean reasonable as between the insured and third party, but as between insured and insurer having regard to the commercial purpose of the contract, which includes indemnity against the insured's own negligence. The insured's omission or act

> "must be at least reckless, that is to say, made with actual recognition by the insured himself that a danger exists, and not caring whether or not it is averted. The purpose of the condition is to ensure that the insured will not, because he is covered against loss by the policy, refrain from taking precautions which he knows ought to be taken".[77]

20.3 Sums Insured and Costs

It has already been noted how the sum insured in a liability policy may be of great importance in the context of an admission of liability condition. More generally, while the sum insured obviously puts the limit of the insurer's liability, and is commonplace except in relation to personal injury aspects of motor insurance where statute does not allow it, it may be expressed in different ways. For example, the policy may have a limit applying to any one contractual period, regardless of the number of claims made, or the limit may apply to each accident or each occurrence or each claim, with no global maximum. The first sort of limit causes no problems, and it has been held that where the limit is per accident, each separate claim by a third party arises out of a separate incident. For example, in *South Staffordshire Tramways Co v Sickness and Accident Assurance Association*,[78] a policy indemnifying the insured against liability for accidents caused by vehicles had a limit of "£250 in respect of any one accident". One of the insured's trams over-turned injuring 40 passengers. It was held that each passenger had an accident and therefore the insurer was potentially liable for 40 x £250.

If, however, the limit is expressed to be per occurrence, then it seems that the number of occurrences is the number of times the insured is negligent. If there is only one negligent act, there is only one occurrence, and the policy

---

[76] *Fraser v Furman* [1967] 1 W.L.R. 898.

[77] Above at 906, per Diplock LJ. See also *Aluminium Wire and Cable Co Ltd v Allstate Insurance Co Ltd* [1985] 2 Lloyd's Rep. 280.

[78] *South Staffordshire Tramways Co v Sickness and Accident Assurance Association* [1891] 1 Q.B. 402.

limit will apply regardless of how many individual claims may be made by third parties as a result. In *Forney v Dominion Insurance Co Ltd*,[79] a solicitor's professional indemnity policy had a limit of £3,000 per occurrence. His assistant was negligent in advising a client about a cause of action in tort. The matter involved a motor accident when a man driving negligently injured some of his family and caused the death of himself and his father in law. The survivors, including the driver's widow, were advised to sue the driver's estate, which was quite proper, but the assistant failed to issue the writs in time. In addition, she advised the widow to act as the driver's administratrix, which was also negligent, because it meant that the widow would effectively lose her damages, not being able in her personal capacity to sue herself as representing the driver's estate. It was held that the two acts of negligence were two occurrences, and the insurer's maximum liability was therefore £6,000. It seems that the same construction applies where the limit applies per claim, that is, that claim means claim by the insured against the insurer rather than claim by each third party against the insured. This is certainly the construction adopted in a case where the relevant limit was contained in an excess clause in a liability policy.[80]

Liability policies invariably include in their cover any costs incurred by the insured, in addition to the damages he is liable to pay. This would not usually include the costs of the insured in successfully defending a claim as the provision as to costs normally applies only where the insurer is liable to indemnify the insured,[81] but the insured will in general recover these from the claimant third party. Costs though will normally be limited; for example, by being included together with damages in the sum insured, or by being limited to the same proportion which the indemnity provided bears to the insured's loss where the latter exceeds the former because it is greater than the sum insured by the policy.

---

[79] *Forney v Dominion Insurance Co Ltd* [1969] 1 W.L.R. 928.

[80] *Trollope & Colls Ltd v Haydon* [1977] 1 Lloyd's Rep. 244. See also the Privy Council decision in *Haydon v Lo & Lo* [1997] 1 W.L.R. 198. Although the actual words used may differ in different policies, for example they may refer to "cause" or "event", the same principle applies: see, e.g. *Caudle v Sharp* [1995] L.R.L.R. 80; *Cox v Bankside Members Agency Ltd* [1995] 2 Lloyd's Rep. 437. As to the construction of the phrase "single act or omission" in the context of an excess or deductible, see *Lloyds TSB General Insurance Holdings v Lloyds Bank Group Insurance Co Ltd* [2003] UKHL 48; [2003] Lloyd's Rep. I.R. 623. In other contexts, especially in determining the cover under a policy written on a "claims made" basis, the word "claim" means claim by a third party against the insured: *Thorman v New Hampshire Insurance Co* [1988] 1 Lloyd's Rep. 7. Professional indemnity policies are usually written on this basis, with the insurer being obliged to indemnify in respect of a claims made on the insured during the policy period, irrespective of when the negligence occurred. See also *Robert Irving & Burns v Stone* [1998] Lloyd's Rep. I.R. 258.

[81] *Cross v British Oak Insurance Co* [1938] 2 K.B. 167 at 174.

20.4 Insurer's Duty to the Victim

Frequently, in practice, liability insurers will negotiate directly on their insured's behalf with the latter's victim. For obvious reasons, but to the potential detriment of the victim, they will seek to keep their liability as low as possible and may well induce the victim to agree to a settlement for an amount below his legal entitlement. Where the victim so relies on the insurers, it is likely that a fiduciary relationship will arise and that the settlement will be voidable on the ground of undue influence unless the insurers either inform the victim of the desirability of seeking independent advice or make an offer that is realistic in respect of the victim's loss.[82]

---

[82] *Horry v Tate & Lyle Refineries Ltd* [1982] 2 Lloyd's Rep. 416, applying *Lloyds Bank Ltd v Bundy* [1975] Q.B. 326; see Merkin (1983) 46 M.L.R. 91. The contract of settlement may also be voidable for misrepresentation: see *Saunders v Ford Motor Co Ltd* [1970] 1 Lloyd's Rep. 379.

CHAPTER 21

MOTOR VEHICLE INSURANCE

21.1 Introduction

Some form of motor vehicle insurance has been compulsory since 1930. What the law requires at present is essentially that anyone who uses or causes or permits another to use a motor vehicle on a road or other public place must be insured against liability to pay damages for death or bodily injury or property damage caused by or arising out of the use of the vehicle.[1] The detail of this requirement will be considered shortly. The requirement in respect of property damage was introduced only at the end of 1988, pursuant to the Second EC Directive on Motor Insurance,[2] although in practice most motor policies have long covered third party property damage. This area of insurance contract law has been substantially affected by EU law. The five separate Directives were consolidated in 2009.[3] Note that they only require that civil liability in any Member State is covered by insurance and do not affect the nature of that liability, which in the UK is of course based on fault.[4] As well as the provisions derived from EU law that are described throughout this chapter, and European Court of Justice cases construing aspects of the Directives, which continue to indicate that UK law is not fully compliant with them, we should note the establishment, pursuant to the Fourth Directive,[5] of the Motor Insurers' Information Centre, which is required to keep information about all vehicles normally based in the UK and the insurance arrangements applying to them, so that information can be provided to victims of accidents.[6]

It has long been conventional to sell motor policies under particular labels, although these have no legal significance. Thus, a "comprehensive" policy

---

[1] Road Traffic Act 1988 ss.143 and 145.

[2] Directive 84/5, O.J. L8/17. This was implemented first by regulations and then consolidated in the Road Traffic Act 1988. Part VI of the latter contains the provisions regarding compulsory motor vehicle insurance. The history of these provisions since 1930 is usefully set out in *Norman v Aziz* [2000] Lloyd's Rep. 1. R. 52 at 54–6.

[3] See Directive 2009/103/EC.

[4] In contrast in some Member States there is some form of strict liability for example where passengers are injured. As to the requirements of EU law in this respect, see *Ferreira v Companhia de Seguros Mundial Confianca SA* [2000] All E.R. (D.) 1197.

[5] Implemented by the Motor Vehicles (Compulsory Insurance (Information Centre and Compensation Body) Regulations 2003, SI 2003/37.

[6] There are equivalent institutions throughout the European Economic Area.

will generally, in addition to what is compulsory, cover first party property damage, that is insurance of the vehicle as goods against loss, and first party injury, that is in effect a personal accident insurance under which the insured who is killed or injured when involved in an accident in his vehicle will receive a stated sum. It often also covers personal effects in the vehicle.[7] The other common form of motor policy which does not just cover third party liability is the third party, fire and theft policy; in addition to third party liability, this covers insurance of the vehicle itself but limited to those losses caused by fire or theft.

In practice a motor policy may not just cover the insured or policyholder himself. The policy may extend either to named others or possibly to anyone driving the car with the insured's permission, and may also cover the insured driving other vehicles.[8] In addition, there are various categories of use, for example, "social, domestic and pleasure purposes" and "business purposes", adopted by insurers, which determine the uses to which the vehicle can be put while remaining covered.[9]

Other insurance practices, including excesses and no claims and loyalty bonuses, are of special importance in the field of motor insurance. No claims bonuses provide for specified reductions in premiums if no claim, or no relevant claim, is made during the previous year.[10] "Knock for knock" agreements used to be common in the motor insurance industry, but have fallen out of favour in recent years.[11]

---

[7] In addition, there are usually special provisions regarding windscreen damage whereby the insured may be able to have a broken windscreen replaced and only claim later, and without prejudice to his no claims bonus. Some policies now provide for the insured to be entitled to claim the cost of hiring an alternative vehicle while his is being repaired, and there are special policies available to people over particular ages.

[8] For the double insurance problems that can arise as a result of these extensions, see 18.4.1.

[9] See 21.3.3.

[10] The practice of offering no claims bonuses has spread to other forms of insurance in recent years. Loyalty bonuses tend to allow for an unlimited number of claims over a longer period without their being lost. Technically, there may be difficulties in showing a legal entitlement to such bonuses since motor policies, like other indemnity policies, are of limited duration and each renewal is a separate contract. As to possible arguments around these difficulties, see 5.7.3.

[11] See 17.15. There are still other agreements that operate within the industry; see Lewis (1985) 48 M.L.R. 275.

21.2   The Scope of Compulsory Cover

Part VI of the Road Traffic Act 1988,[12] which governs the compulsory aspect of motor insurance, as well as defining these obligations, also provides special protection to the injured third party from the strict contractual rights of the insurer as against the insured. The basic obligations will be examined at this stage and the latter aspect will be considered later.

Subject to the exceptions in s.144,[13] s.143 provides that a person must not use, or cause or permit any other person to use, a motor vehicle on a road or public place, unless there is in force a policy which complies with the Act covering the required third party risks or a security in relation to those risks.[14] The requirements are stated in s.145. First, the policy must be issued by an authorised insurer; for this purpose this means a person carrying on motor insurance business in Great Britain who is a member of the Motor Insurer's Bureau.[15] The required risks are:

(1) Insurance against liability[16] in respect of death or bodily injury to any person[17] or damage to property caused by or arising

---

[12] This consolidated earlier legislation dating originally from 1930.

[13] Particularly in respect of vehicles owned by public bodies and vehicles owned by a person who has deposited £500,000 in court.

[14] Securities, which it seems are rarely used, are governed by s.146. This requires first that they are given by either (1) an authorised insurer or (2) by some body of persons which carries on in the UK the business of giving securities of a like kind and has deposited and keeps deposited with the Accountant General of the Supreme Court the sum of £500,000 in respect of that business. Secondly, subject to the limits that the amount secured need not exceed £5,000 or £25,000 in respect of an undertaking relating to the use of public service vehicles, the security must consist of an undertaking by the giver of it to make good, subject to any conditions specified in it, any failure by the owner of the vehicle or such other persons or classes of persons as may be specified in the security duly to discharge any liability which may be incurred by him or them which is a liability required under s.145 to be covered by an insurance policy.

[15] As to the Motor Insurers' Bureau, see 21.7. It is now perfectly lawful for a motor policy to be issued by any EU insurer, subject only to the requirement of MIB membership. Note that cessation of MIB membership does not affect policies issued or obligations arising before such cessation: s.145(6).

[16] For this purpose liability includes liability intentionally caused: as regards personal injury, see *Hardy v MIB* [1964] 2 Q.B. 745 and *Gardner v Moore* [1984] A.C. 548, which are discussed in 14.3.1. As far as property damage is concerned, see *EUI Ltd v Bristol Alliance Ltd Partnership* [2012] EWCA Civ 1267, which is considered further in 21.5.

[17] But not the driver: *R. v Secretary of State Ex p. National Insurance Guarantee Corp Plc, The Times*, 3 June 1996. So far as passengers are concerned, it does not matter that the vehicle is not designed to carry passengers: *Farrell v Motor Insurers Bureau of Ireland* C356/05 [2007] Lloyd's Rep. I.R. 525, where the European Court of

out of, the use of the vehicle on a road or public place in Great Britain[18];

(2)   Insurance against any liability in the other EU Member States which those states require; and

(3)   Insurance against liabilities in respect of emergency treatment.[19]

Where a vehicle is normally based in one EU Member State, and used in another, the compulsory insurance cover must be in accordance with the law requiring the greater cover.[20]

Heading (1) does not, however, require insurance in respect of the following:

(a)   The liability of an employer to an employee in respect of death or bodily injury arising out of and in the course of his employment, provided that in respect of someone carried in or upon a vehicle or entering or getting on to or alighting from a vehicle,[21] the

Justice so held, construing art.1 of the Third Motor Insurance Directive (90/232/ EEC).

[18] This does not mean that the user has to be insured against his potential liability to the driver, e.g. because he has negligently let him drive an unsafe vehicle: *Cooper v Motor Insurers' Bureau* [1985] Q.B. 575. See also, *Limbrick v French* [1990] C.L.Y. 2709. See also *Bretton v Hancock* [2005] EWCA Civ 404; [2005] Lloyd's Rep. I.R. 454, which is discussed at 21.2.5.

[19] This liability arises under s.158. Where medical or surgical treatment is immediately required as a result of bodily injury (including fatal injury) to a person caused by or arising out of the use of a motor vehicle on a road and such emergency treatment is effected by a legally qualified medical practitioner, the person who was using the vehicle at the time of the event out of which the injury arose must, on a claim being made under s.159, pay to the practitioner (1) a fee of £15 per person treated and (2) travelling expenses of 29 pence per mile (or part of a mile) for every mile over two miles that he had to travel. If the treatment is first effected in a hospital, the fee goes to the hospital. If the person using the vehicle was not the tortfeasor who caused the accident, he can recover the money paid from the tortfeasor. The claim under s.159 may be made orally at the time when the emergency treatment is effected; if not so made, it must be made by written request served on the user of the vehicle within seven days of the treatment. Note also the separate liability on insurers to pay for hospital treatment under s.157, although this is not part of the compulsory insurance provisions, and the effect of the Road Traffic (National Health Service Charges) Act 1999 and Pt 3 of the Health and Social Care (Community Health and Standards) Act 2003.

[20] Amendments made to s.145 by the Motor Vehicles (Compulsory Insurance) Regulations 1992, SI 1992/3036, implementing the Third EC Directive on Motor Insurance 90/232.

[21] This does not cover someone such as a policeman trying to stop a vehicle by opening the door: *Miller v Hales* [2006] EWCA 1529 (QB); [2007] Lloyd's Rep. I.R.

exception does not apply unless there is effective cover under the Employers' Liability (Compulsory Insurance Act) 1969[22]; because employers' liability policies are no longer required to cover these risks,[23] in practice they are likely to be covered by a motor policy[24];

(b)   Cover in respect of property damage of more than £1 million "caused by, or arising out of, any one accident involving the vehicle"[25];

(c)   Liability in respect of damage to the vehicle;

(d)   Liability in respect of damage to goods carried for hire or reward in or on the vehicle or in or on any trailer drawn by the vehicle[26];

(e)   Liability of a person in respect of damage to property in his custody or under his control[27]; and

(f)   Any contractual liability.[28]

The basic obligation arising from the words of s.143 cited above has been the subject of considerable case law. One problem used to be the meaning of the word "road", when the obligation to insure was limited to use of a vehicle on a road. In particular, this would not normally include a car park.[29]

---

54. In *Axa Insurance Plc v Norwich Union Insurance Ltd* [2007] EWHC 1268 (QB); [2008] Lloyd's Rep. I.R. 122, it was held that an employee in a hoist incorporating an elevating platform was not being carried in on upon the vehicle, which was stationary at the time. As the employer had operative employers' liability insurance covering the employer's potential liability, the exception applied.

[22] The requirement of effective employers' liability cover, rather than a blanket exemption of employers' liability risks, was inserted as s.145(4A) by the 1992 Regulations.

[23] The Employers' Liability (Compulsory Insurance) Regulations 1998, SI 1998/2573, Sch.2, para.14.

[24] A policeman is not an employee: *Miller v Hales*, above.

[25] See s.161(3), which provides that any reference to an accident includes a reference to two or more causally related accidents. The limit, which was raised by SI 2007/1426 in order to implement the fifth EC Directive, was adopted in order to mitigate the effect on the Motor Insurers' Bureau (see below) in cases of uninsured drivers. Note that there is a broad construction of "accident" in this sort of context; see *South Staffordshire Tramways Co v Sickness and Accident Assurance Association* [1891] 1 Q.B. 402, described at 20.3.

[26] This does not exclude liability in respect of goods carried gratuitously, although the next exception may do so.

[27] For example, the belongings of passengers. It is unclear how far this exception goes. It would probably apply to luggage in the boot of a car, although it can hardly apply to items of clothing or other things on the person of a passenger.

[28] See s.145(4).

[29] See the decision of the *House of Lords in Cutter v Eagle Star Insurance Co Ltd* [1998] 4 All E.R. 417. A hotel forecourt habitually used by the public as a road was

However, s.143[30] has been amended by the insertion of "public place", which clearly includes a car park.[31] Insurance is required when part of a vehicle is on a public road after being driven from private property.[32]

21.2.1 Use of a vehicle

The major problem has been the meanings of the words "use" and to "cause" or "permit" use in s.143. "Use" includes the leaving of a car on a road or other public place, even though it is incapable at present of being mechanically propelled.[33] It has also been held to cover the case of someone who left their car because it had run out of fuel and caused an accident when they crossed the road for help.[34] On the other hand, the word is not so wide as to include, for example, the normal case of someone being a passenger in a motor vehicle,[35] or asking another to transport some goods in his car, even though it could perhaps be said colloquially that that person was using the other's car. In the context of the Road Traffic Act, use implies an element of controlling, managing or operating the vehicle at the relevant time.[36] In *Brown v Roberts*,[37] the passenger in a car was negligent in opening her door and thereby injured a pedestrian. It was held that she was not using the car in the statutory sense, because she had no control over the vehicle, so the driver was not therefore causing or permitting her to use it and thus not liable in damages for breach of statutory duty in not insuring her against her potential liability. Use does not cover a situation where a vehicle has stopped to pick up a passenger who is injured when crossing the road in an attempt to reach the vehicle.[38] The

---

held to be a road: *Bugge v Taylor* [1941] 1 K.B. 198, but compare *Thomas v Dando* [1951] 2 K.B. 620. See also *Evans v Clarke* [2007] Lloyd's Rep. I.R. 16.

[30] And other relevant provisions of the 1988 Act.

[31] The Motor Vehicles (Compulsory Insurance) Regulations 2000, SI 2000/726, effective as from 3 April 2000. The Regulations were made under the European Communities Act 1972 in order to comply with the EC Motor Insurance Directives. Difficult questions as to what is a "public place" might still arise though, and it is arguable that this limit is in breach of EU law; see the decision of the ECJ in *Vnuk v Zavarovalnica Triglav*, Case C-162/13, where it was held that liability for injury caused by a tractor being driven on a farm was compulsorily required, when the use of a vehicle was consistent with its normal function.

[32] *Randall v Motor Insurers' Bureau* [1968] 2 Lloyd's Rep. 553.

[33] *Elliott v Grey* [1960] 1 Q.B. 367. It is otherwise if the vehicle is totally immovable: *Thomas v Hooper* [1986] R.T.R. 1.

[34] *Dunthorne v Bentley* [1999] Lloyd's Rep. I.R. 560, construing "arising out of" as contemplating more remote consequences than "caused by".

[35] *B (A Minor) v Knight* [1981] R.T.R. 136; *Hatton v Hall* [1999] Lloyd's Rep. I.R. 313.

[36] *Brown v Roberts* [1965] 1 Q.B. 1 at 15, per Megaw J.

[37] *Brown v Roberts* [1965] 1 Q.B. 1.

[38] *Slater v Buckinghamshire County Council* [2004] Lloyd's Rep. I.R. 432.

drugging and commission of serious sexual assaults on female passengers by a taxi driver in his vehicle did not arise out of the use of the vehicle.[39]

There can, though, be more than one person using a vehicle at any given time within the statutory meaning. So, in *Leathley v Tatton*,[40] it was held that a passenger involved in a criminal adventure with others to steal and take away a car was using the car for the purposes of s.143, and in *O'Mahony v Joliffe*,[41] in respect of a passenger who was enjoying a joint escapade with the unlicensed and uninsured driver of a motor cycle that was untested and untaxed.[42] In *Bretton v Hancock*,[43] a passenger who had an interest in a car was held to be a user.

21.2.2 Causing or permitting use

Whether someone causes or permits another to use a vehicle is a question of fact. Clearly it is so if, for example, X allows Y to drive his car. The word "cause" involves an express or positive mandate to use a car in a particular way, whereas "permit" is looser, and merely denotes an express or implied licence to use a vehicle.[44] In *McLeod v Buchanan*,[45] a man appointed his brother as manager of his farm and bought him a car that was insured for business and private use. The car having proved unsatisfactory, the man authorised his brother to buy a van instead; this was insured for business use only, but was in fact used for private purposes. It was held that the man had permitted his brother to use the van while uninsured. The van was given to him for the same purposes as the car, and the brother was not told not to use it for private purposes. In *Lyons v May*,[46] a garage owner was driving a car back from the garage after repair, at the request of the car's owner. It was held that the latter had caused or permitted the use of the car. In contrast, in *Watkins v O'Shaughnessy*,[47] an auctioneer sold a car which the purchaser drove away immediately without, to the auctioneer's knowledge, being insured. It was held that the auctioneer had not caused or permitted the use of the car because, having sold it, he no longer had any control over it. In *Thompson v*

---

[39] *AXN v Worboys* [2012] EWHC 1730 (QB).

[40] *Leathley v Tatton* [1980] R.T.R. 21. See also *Cobb v Williams* [1973] R.T.R. 113 and *Stinton v Stinton* [1995] R.T.R. 167; compare *B (A Minor) v Knight* [1981] R.T.R. 136.

[41] *O'Mahony v Joliffe* [1999] Lloyd's Rep. I.R. 321.

[42] This point is especially important in the context of the MIB Agreements where the same words are construed in the same way; see 21.8.1.

[43] *Bretton v Hancock* [2005] EWCA Civ 404; [2005] Lloyd's Rep. I.R. 454, discussed at 21.2.5.

[44] Lord Wright in *McLeod v Buchanan* [1940] 2 All E.R. 179 at 187.

[45] *McLeod v Buchanan* [1940] 2 All E.R. 179.

[46] *Lyons v May* [1948] 2 All E.R. 1062.

[47] *Watkins v O'Shaughnessy* [1939] 1 All E.R. 384.

Lodwick,[48] a driving instructor was held not to have caused or permitted his pupil to use the vehicle when the latter owned it.

21.2.3 Policy required

Section 143 requires that there be in force a "policy" of insurance.[49] A policy exists for these purposes even though it is voidable,[50] and it has been held that avoidance does not amount to avoidance ab initio for criminal law purposes.[51] Policy includes a cover note.[52] However, it has been decided that the existence of a contract of insurance by itself is not enough to satisfy the statute. In *Roberts v Warne*,[53] the relevant policy did not cover the particular driver who was using the car, although a cover note had been arranged to effect this and when this expired, the insurers clearly regarded the driver as covered.[54] The driver was convicted for using the car without insurance and the owner for causing or permitting this. It was held that, even if the insurers were contractually bound to cover the driver, which may well have been the case, the policy did not cover him and hence there was no policy as s.143 requires. It is thought that this decision is wrong.[55] There seems no reason to read the word "policy" as meaning anything other than a legally enforceable contract of insurance. Even an enforceable oral contract should suffice.[56]

21.2.4 Certificate of insurance

In addition to the requirement under s.143 to have a policy, s.147 provides that the policy is of no effect unless and until the insurer delivers to the insured a certificate of insurance.[57] Notwithstanding this wording, it has

---

[48] *Thompson v Lodwick* [1983] R.T.R. 76.

[49] Unless there is a security; see above.

[50] For example for non-disclosure or misrepresentation: *Adams v Dunne* [1978] R.T.R. 281 (now this would be for misrepresentation under the terms of the Consumer Insurance (Disclosure and Representations) Act 2012, where the insured is a consumer or for breach of the duty of fair presentation under the Insurance Act 2015, where the insured is a non-consumer).

[51] *Goodbarne v Buck* [1940] 1 K.B. 771.

[52] See s.161(1), although it must be contractually binding, see *Taylor v Allon* [1966] 1 Q.B. 304, discussed in 5.6.2.

[53] *Roberts v Warne* [1973] R.T.R. 217.

[54] There were severe communication difficulties at the time because of a postal strike.

[55] See also (1973) Crim. L.R. 244.

[56] Compare *Scher v Policyholders Protection Board* [1993] 3 All E.R. 384, where the Court of Appeal held that there was no magic in the word "policy" in the Policyholders Protection Act 1975; see especially at 396 per Lord Donaldson MR.

[57] See s.147(2) for the certificate of security when the obligation is satisfied by a security rather than by insurance. Where a policy or security is cancelled, the insured must, within seven days, surrender the certificate or, if it is lost or destroyed, make

been held by the Privy Council[58] that the substantially identical words in the equivalent Barbadian statute[59] did not operate to prevent the third party from suing the insurers under the equivalent of s.151,[60] where a certificate was issued subsequently to the accident but expressed to be retrospective to a time before the accident, and a cover note, which is ordinarily an effective insurance contract,[61] had been issued before the accident. Although this looks like a fairly generous interpretation of the equivalent of s.147, it nonetheless seems an entirely sensible decision. It is thought that it should also apply to the basic obligation under s.143,[62] so that someone with a fully effective contract of insurance should not be guilty of the offence under the section notwithstanding that a certificate may not have been issued.

Certificates constitute the easily checkable evidence of compliance with the insurance obligation; in particular they are the evidence that must exist in order to obtain a road fund licence for a vehicle.[63] While the certificate or parts of it may be incorporated into the contract of insurance or policy, for example, concerning the permitted user of the vehicle, if there is any conflict between the two, the policy prevails, and the certificate itself is not a contract of insurance.[64] Certificates may now be issued electronically and in such cases are regarded as delivered when they have been electronically transmitted to the insured or made available on a website.[65]

21.2.5 Sanctions for failure to insure

The consequences of a failure to comply with the obligation to insure under s.143 are potentially two-fold. First, it is a criminal offence of strict liability.[66]

---

a statutory declaration to that effect: s.147(4). The forms of certificates are prescribed by the Motor Vehicles (Third Party Risks) Regulations 1972 SI 1972/1217, as amended.

[58] *Motor and General Insurance Co v Cox* [1990] 1 W.L.R. 1443.

[59] Motor Vehicles Insurance Act ss.4(7), 9(1).

[60] As to s.151, see 21.5.

[61] See 5.6.

[62] And also to the other relevant section of the Road Traffic Act, especially s.148, which is discussed at 21.4.1, where the same requirement is stated.

[63] See s.156. As to the police powers regarding certificates, see ss.165 and 165A and *Pryor v Chief Constable of Greater Manchester Police* [2011] EWCA Civ 749; [2011] R.T.R. 33.

[64] *Biddle v Johnston* [1965] 2 Lloyd's Rep. 121.

[65] S.147(1A)-(1E), inserted by the Motor Vehicles (Electronic Communication of Certificates of Insurance) Order 2010 (SI 2010/1117) art.3.

[66] Subject to the defences in s.143(2), which provide for no liability if a person proves (1) that the vehicle did not belong to him and was not in his possession under a contract of hire or loan, (2) that he was using the vehicle in the course of employment or (3) that he neither knew nor had reason to believe that there was no valid insurance or security.

Secondly, commission of the offence is a breach of statutory duty and anyone who suffers loss as a result can sue in tort for damages. The importance of this is not against the negligent driver, who would be liable in negligence anyway, but against someone who used the car with him or caused or permitted him to use it. The meanings of these expressions, as already discussed, may therefore be of importance in this context as well as in the criminal context.

In *Monk v Warbey*,[67] the defendant owner of a car lent it to a friend who permitted another to drive. Neither of the latter was insured. It was held that the plaintiff, who had been injured by the negligence of the driver, could sue the owner.[68] It would appear that the owner's insurer, assuming that he has one, might be liable in such circumstances to indemnify him against this liability, as the standard policy wordings do not require the insured to be driving, but indemnify him against "legal liability . . . arising from an accident caused by, through or in connection with the insured car". Since 1946, the Motor Insurer's Bureau indemnifies such uninsured drivers,[69] but it has been held that this does not remove the action for breach of statutory duty. In the case in question, *Corfield v Groves*,[70] judgment was awarded against the owner subject to the proviso that if the MIB did satisfy the judgment, it could not be enforced against the owner. In practice, therefore, this action is really only relevant if for some reason the MIB is not liable, for example because of a failure to comply with one of the conditions precedent to their liability.[71]

However, a claim under the principle of *Monk v Warbey* does not comprehend a claim for pure economic loss.[72] Here the claimant B had an ownership interest in the vehicle being driven by her uninsured fiancé, in which she was a passenger. An accident for which the latter was found 25 per cent to blame and the other driver 75 per cent caused the death of the fiancé and injury to the other driver, the defendant H, who brought a counterclaim against B for breach of statutory duty. It was held that although B, because of her interest, had been using the car within the meaning of s.143, a user was not bound to insure against the liability of one tortfeasor to contribute with another tortfeasor in respect of their joint liability to the user. Because the Road Traffic Act was only concerned with third party risks, the principle operated only when the victim was the claimant and there was an essential difference

---

[67] *Monk v Warbey* [1935] 1 K.B. 75.
[68] This action is "in respect of personal injuries" and therefore the limitation period under the Limitation Act 1980 s.11, is three years: *Norman v Ali* [2000] Lloyd's Rep. 395.
[69] See 21.8.
[70] *Corfield v Groves* [1950] 1 All E.R. 488.
[71] In *Norman v Aziz* [2000] Lloyd's Rep I.R. 52, an attempt to argue that *Corfield v Groves* was wrongly decided was rejected.
[72] *Bretton v Hancock* [2005] EWCA Civ 404; [2005] Lloyd's Rep. I.R. 454.

between the claim of the primary victim and the claim of the joint tortfeasor, which was only in respect of the other tortfeasor's right of indemnity or contribution.

21.3 Common Terms and Exceptions in Motor Policies

The standard terms and conditions that are found in motor vehicle policies are important to compulsory and non-compulsory insurance alike, because, even though, as will be seen, some of them may not be enforceable against a third party victim where insurance was compulsory, they may remain of effect between insurer and insured so that the insurer who has had to pay the third party may be entitled to recover this sum of money from the insured. The standard terms will be considered under three headings: standard extensions; limitations on use; and terms relating to the condition of the insured vehicle.

21.3.1 Standard extensions

It is common for motor policies to insure people other than the insured or policyholder driving the car or vehicle in question. For example, cover may extend to the spouse of the insured, to particular named drivers or drivers identified by a class, or, most widely, to anyone driving the vehicle on the insured's order or with the insured's permission. Only the last sort of extension can give rise to legal problems, but before examining these, one important point of general interest relates to the status of the other driver in terms of the contract between insured and insurer.

At common law, the insured can enforce the contract in so far as it confers a benefit on a third party, there being in effect a waiver of any requirement of insurable interest.[73] The latter though cannot enforce the contract himself.[74] Now, however, the common law seems redundant in this context, for two reasons. First, s.148(7) of the 1988 Act provides:

> "Notwithstanding anything in any enactment, a person issuing a policy of insurance under section 145 of this Act shall be liable to indemnify the persons or classes of persons specified in the policy in respect of any liability which the policy purports to cover in the case of those persons or classes of persons."

Thus, the third party can enforce the contract directly, subject, of course, to any right in the insurer to avoid liability,[75] and he is not dependent on the

[73] *Williams v Baltic Insurance Association of London* [1924] 2 K.B. 282; see 4.3. It would seem that the insured holds any money recovered on trust for the third party; see above.
[74] *Vandepitte v Preferred Accident Insurance Corp of New York* [1933] A.C. 70; see 4.5.
[75] *Guardian Assurance v Sutherland* [1939] 2 All E.R. 246.

owner insuring as his trustee or agent.[76] In effect, he is by statute a party to the contract.[77] Secondly, the third party can now in the alternative rely on the Contracts (Rights of Third Parties) Act 1999.[78]

21.3.2 Permitted drivers

The question of whether someone is driving with the insured's permission, other than in obvious cases, has occasioned some difficulty. It seems that the law would not sanction a permitted driver himself giving effective permission to another so that the other is covered, in the absence of the insured's direct consent. In the Canadian case of *Minister of Transport v Canadian General Insurance*,[79] a son of the insured who was permitted to drive the car in question purported to give permission to a friend. It was held that the friend was not insured. It seems likely that an English court would reach the same conclusion.[80] In *Morgans v Launchberry*,[81] the permitted driver, the husband of the insured, gave permission to another to drive the car. The latter was negligent and injured or killed the passengers in the car. Strictly the case involved only the point of tort law as to whether the insured as owner of the car was vicariously liable for the acts of the driver, and the House of Lords held that she was not. However, a passage in Lord Denning's judgment in the Court of Appeal[82] indicates that, if the insured was not liable, the insurers would not be liable to indemnify the driver because the latter did not have her permission. That is why the case was fought as one of vicarious liability.[83]

That the insured can become the third party and recover as such if injured by the negligence of someone whom he permitted to drive the car is well established. In *Digby v General Accident Fire and Life Assurance Corp*,[84] the

---

[76] *Tattersall v Drysdale* [1935] 2 K.B. 174.

[77] It was undecided, before it was compulsory to insure against property damage liability, whether the statute covered only the compulsory aspects of a motor policy. For discussion of the point, see the second edition of this book at p.299. It is now an academic point except where a policy provides more cover than s.145 requires, e.g. unlimited cover in respect of property damage cover rather than the £1 million limit allowed. Even here, it is thought that where a policy satisfies s.145, it will be enforceable by a third party because of the reference in s.148(7) to "any liability which the policy purports to cover".

[78] See 4.5.

[79] *Minister of Transport v Canadian General Insurance* (1971) 18 D.L.R. (3d) 617.

[80] See *Sands v O'Connell* [1981] R.T.R. 42.

[81] *Morgans v Launchberry* [1973] A.C. 127.

[82] [1971] 2 Q.B. 245 at 253.

[83] At the time of the case, liability to passengers was not within the compulsory requirements, which is another reason why the case was argued as it was. Now, the injured parties would receive compensation from the MIB in such a situation if all other claims failed.

[84] *Digby v General Accident Fire and Life Assurance Corp* [1943] A.C. 212.

insured's policy covered anyone driving with her permission. She gave such permission to her chauffeur and was then, as a passenger, injured by his negligent driving. It was held that the insurers were liable to indemnify the chauffeur in respect of his liability to the insured. Permission may be expressly or impliedly limited to a particular class of use of the vehicle.[85] In *Singh v Ratour*,[86] the driver had borrowed a van belonging to an association of which he was a member, the representative of the association believing that he had borrowed it for the purposes of the association. In fact he had borrowed it to attend a private social function. The driver sought an indemnity against the consequences of his negligence from his own insurers under a term in the policy that permitted him to drive vehicles belonging to another "provided he [had] the consent of the owner". The Court of Appeal held that he was not entitled to recover, as the consent was impliedly limited to use for the purposes of the association.

Permission once given can obviously be revoked. In the absence of such revocation, it appears that permission continues even when the insured dies. In *Kelly v Cornhill Insurance Co*,[87] the insured gave permission to his son to drive the insured car and soon afterwards died. Some eight months later the son was involved in an accident, the policy period not having expired. By a bare majority, the House of Lords held that the son was entitled to sue under the policy, the permission of his father not having been revoked by his death. It is noteworthy that there was little merit in the insurers' defence, as under the policy the father was expressly precluded from driving; it had been effected solely for the son's benefit. While there are obvious difficulties in saying that permission continues in such a case in the absence of its renewal by the insured's personal representatives, in whom the ownership of the car and policy will have vested, the result is sensible, since otherwise a permitted driver could automatically and without his knowledge become uninsured, even for example in the course of a particular journey. The decision implies that the insured's personal representatives in such a case would have the power to revoke the permission. Otherwise it must continue only until the expiry of the policy. It would appear that revocation of permission is effective only when actually communicated to the person given permission.

A purchaser of a car, however, cannot be claiming to drive with the former owner, the insured's, permission, unless the insurers expressly consent. Here the insured ceases to have any insurable interest in the car, his policy lapses and is not assignable.[88]

---

[85] As to limitations on use, see below.
[86] *Singh v Ratour* [1988] 2 All E.R. 16.
[87] *Kelly v Cornhill Insurance Co* [1964] 1 All E.R. 321.
[88] *Peters v General Accident Fire & Life Assurance Corp* [1938] 2 All E.R. 267; see 11.4.
The insurer's consent would in law amount to the creation of a new contract.

21.3.3 Limitations on use

As was mentioned earlier, insurers have well-established categories of permitted use of an insured vehicle, and these are enforceable even against a third
party.[89] These vary from, for example, use covering only social, domestic and
pleasure purposes and use by the insured for travel to and from his place of
business, to use by the insured in person or use by others in connection with
the insured's or his employer's business. Few legal difficulties can arise over
some of the distinctions adopted, but in one respect there is a body of case law.

If an insured is covered for social, domestic and pleasure purposes and
not for business use, or at least only for travelling to and from work,[90] the
distinctions become important and not always easy to apply. As Roskill LJ
pointed out,[91] there will be cases falling each side of the line when a phrase
such as social, domestic and pleasure purposes is used, and it is impossible to
state any firm principle under which it can be predicted on which side of the
line a particular case will fall. It must depend on the facts of the particular
case and the "essential character"[92] or "primary purpose"[93] of the journey. In
Jones v Welsh Insurance Corp,[94] the policy covered social, etc. purposes and use
in connection with the insured's business, which was stated in the schedule
to be that of motor mechanic. In addition, the insured farmed a few sheep,
really as a hobby but with the aim of making a small profit. He was carrying some sheep when the relevant accident occurred. It was held that the
insurers were not liable. The insured was carrying on the business of sheep
farming; this was not stated in the schedule and thus the cover did not apply.
In *Wood v General Accident Fire & Life Assurance Corp*,[95] the relevant accident
happened when a garage proprietor was being driven in his own car by one of
his drivers to a firm with which he intended to negotiate a business contract.
It was held that, though it was convenient and comfortable for him to make
the journey like this, the car was not being used for social, etc. purposes. In
Seddon v Binnions,[96] a father—who helped his son occasionally on Sundays in

---

[89] As will be seen below, many provisions in contracts of motor insurance cannot be
relied upon against a third party.

[90] Travelling to work is not a social, domestic or pleasure purpose; it must be separately covered (see *Seddon v Binions* [1978] 1 Lloyd's Rep. 381), although in practice
it probably always is.

[91] *Seddon v Binions*, above, at 384–385.

[92] Per Roskill LJ above.

[93] Per Megaw LJ above at 387.

[94] *Jones v Welsh Insurance Corp* [1937] 4 All E.R. 149.

[95] *Wood v General Accident Fire & Life Assurance Corp* (1948) 65 T.L.R. 53.

[96] *Seddon v Binnions* [1978] 1 Lloyd's Rep. 381. This decision was followed in *Killick
v Rendall* [2000] Lloyd's Rep. I.R. 581, construing a similar term in a personal
accident policy, and in *Caple v Sewell* [2001] EWCA Civ 1848; [2002] Lloyd's Rep.
I.R. 626, a marine case.

the latter's business of carpet layer—was driving home in his son's car, with his son's only employee who had toothache. Having delivered the latter, the father intended to go home for his lunch. The father's own policy covered his driving of other cars but only for social, etc. purposes. The son's insurers had paid in respect of the accident that occurred and were claiming a contribution from the father's insurers. It was held that the latter were not liable, the essential purpose of the journey being a business one, namely the father transporting his son's employee back from work. On the other hand, in *Keeley v Pashen*,[97] where a mini-cab driver had dropped off his last passengers of the day and was driving home, the purpose of his journey became for social, etc. purposes.[98] The fact that he reversed towards the passengers after they had alighted in order to frighten them, because they had seemingly been drunk and abusive towards him, was merely an incidental episode and could not be classed as a separate journey; the essential purpose was still to return home.[99]

Use of driving for purposes connected with the motor trade may be excluded, as in *Browning v Phoenix Assurance Co Ltd*,[100] where a garage employee was authorised by the insured to drive his car in order to warm the engine oil before it was drained at the garage. It was held that the insurers were not liable in respect of an accident, which occurred when the employee was driving the car for pleasure the day after the oil had been drained, although the principal ground for the decision was that the employee was not a permitted driver in this respect.[101] It was also clear that the car would not have been insured while the oil was being warmed. The exclusion, though, may be qualified so that cover is provided while the vehicle is merely in the custody or control of a motor trader for the purposes of repair, that is, so long as it is not being driven by someone other than the insured or a permitted driver.[102]

---

[97] *Keeley v Pashen* [2004] EWCA Civ 1491; [2005] Lloyd's Rep. I.R. 289.

[98] Which under the policy included travelling to and from work.

[99] The insured in fact killed one of the passengers and pleaded guilty to a charge of manslaughter, but this was not criminal conduct of the sort that altered the essential purpose of the journey; see the comments of Brooke LJ at [19].

[100] *Browning v Phoenix Assurance Co Ltd* [1960] 2 Lloyd's Rep. 360.

[101] This aspect of the decision was approved by the Court of Appeal in *Singh v Ratour* [1988] 2 All E.R. 16, discussed in 21.3.2.

[102] See the Court of Appeal's construction of somewhat difficult terms to this effect in *Samuelson v National Insurance Guarantee Corp Ltd* [1985] 2 Lloyd's Rep. 541. The actual decision was concerned with whether or not the insured vehicle was being driven by or in the charge of a person other than an authorised driver. It was made clear that once someone has completed his present journey, he is no longer in charge of the vehicle for insurance purposes. Thus, although the car had not been insured while being driven by a repairer on his way to collect spare parts, cover reattached once his journey was completed and the insured could recover for the theft of the car from where the repairer had parked it.

A case may arise when the purposes of a journey are mixed. For example, an insured covered for social, etc. purposes but not for business purposes might be travelling to a business meeting followed by a social dinner. In *Seddon v Binnions*,[103] the view of the trial judge was that there was a mixed purpose; the father was driving for social, etc. purposes in going home for lunch, not being an employee of his son and hence not strictly travelling from work, and for business purposes in taking his son's employee home. It was held, and the Court of Appeal confirmed this, that in this event the policy would not apply since the car was partly being used for an unauthorised purpose.

21.3.4 Conditions regarding the condition of the insured vehicle

Motor policies generally provide that the insurers are not to be on risk or liable when the insured vehicle is being driven in an unsafe or unroadworthy condition and/or if the insured fails to maintain the vehicle in an efficient or roadworthy condition.[104] Such provisions may be drafted as exceptions to the risk or found under the heading "conditions", in which case they may be warranties or conditions precedent. It is more common now for them to appear as conditions or warranties.[105] In both cases, although the insurers will not be able to rely upon a breach as against an injured third party, because of the provisions of the Road Traffic Act which will be examined shortly, if they are warranties or conditions, they may well be able to recover from the insured, as damages for breach of condition, the money they have to pay to the third party.[106]

21.3.5 A marine analogy?

Application of the standard exception or condition has occasioned some difficulty. In *Barrett v London General Insurance*,[107] Goddard J held that, because of the verbal similarities, roadworthiness was to be interpreted in an analogous way to the standard requirement of seaworthiness in a marine policy. In a marine policy, seaworthiness is required only at the commencement of a voyage. The learned judge applied the same reasoning to a car journey in deciding that a car whose foot brake failed at the time of the relevant acci-

---

[103] *Seddon v Binnions* [1978] 1 Lloyd's Rep. 381; see above.
[104] This is not interpreted in the same way as "reasonable care" provisions (see 13.3.2 and 20.2.5). Negligence on the part of the insured will be a breach of such a provision: *Amey Properties Ltd v Cornhill Insurance Plc* [1996] C.L.C. 401.
[105] As to these, see Ch.9.
[106] Under s.148(4) of the Road Traffic Act or, it seems, at common law; see below.
[107] *Barrett v London General Insurance* [1935] 1 K.B. 238.

dent was not unroadworthy in the absence of proof that it was not working when the insured set out on his journey. He may have been influenced by the fact that had the injured third party's claim arisen slightly later, the insurer would not have been able to take the point because of the imminent introduction of the statutory provisions which are now s.148 of the Road Traffic Act 1988.[108] This reasoning was expressly disapproved by the Privy Council in *Trickett v Queensland Insurance Co*,[109] though the exception in question there did not concern roadworthiness as such, but applied if the car was being driven in "a damaged or unsafe condition". The insured was involved in an accident at night at a time when the lights on his car were not working. It was held that this was sufficient to render the car damaged or unsafe. The knowledge of the insured was irrelevant, as was the question whether or not the lights were working at the beginning of the journey. The question was simply one of fact to be judged objectively.

More recently, it has been suggested that the marine analogy may be useful, but it appears unlikely that the decision in *Barrett* would be followed. The usual wording of this sort of exception is "while the car is being driven", and this must include anything that happens during a journey and not just at the start of it.[110] In *Clarke v National Insurance Corp*,[111] a car intended to seat four people was driven with nine people in it. The Court of Appeal held that it was thereby rendered unroadworthy, although, with the normal number of people in it, it would have been quite safe. Unroadworthiness does not relate to just the mechanical condition of a vehicle, but can include any other relevant factors. In marine cases, overloading can render a ship unseaworthy, and the analogy was apt to this extent.

21.3.6 The term as a warranty or condition

In the cases just discussed, the term in question was an exception and phrased in such a way that, fairly clearly, it should be properly read in a continuing objective sense. As noted above, modern policies tend to have replaced this exception by a condition or warranty requiring the insured to maintain the vehicle in a roadworthy or efficient condition. It has been suggested that these alternatives mean the same,[112] but it would seem that a term is narrower if phrased as a condition or warranty. This is because, as a condition or warranty, it cannot be read wholly objectively. If a car's lights or brakes,

---

[108] Goddard J referred (above at 240) to the imminent introduction of the Road Traffic Act 1934.

[109] *Trickett v Queensland Insurance Co* [1936] A.C. 159.

[110] *Clarke v National Insurance Corp* [1963] 2 All E.R. 375 at 377.

[111] *Clarke v National Insurance Corp* [1963] 2 All E.R. 375.

[112] Sellers J in *Brown v Zurich General Accident and Liability Insurance Co* [1954] 2 Lloyd's Rep. 243 at 246.

for example, fail quite unexpectedly in the course of a journey, it may not be possible to say that the insured has failed to maintain the car in a roadworthy or efficient condition, whereas it can be said that the car is being driven in an unroadworthy condition. An insured's failure to maintain imports the notion of his knowing or being in a position where he ought to know that something is wrong, which requires the insurer to show more than a simple fact. This view is supported by the decision in *Conn v Westminster Motor Insurance Association Ltd*.[113] Here the insured's taxi was defective in two ways: the tyres were badly worn and illegal and the brakes were dangerous. Although the insured should have known that his taxi's tyres were no good, as this was easily visible, the same did not apply in relation to his braking system.[114]

21.3.7 Insured's liability in damages

One question remains in this context. If a condition or warranty concerning the condition of the insured vehicle is broken, the insurers cannot rely upon the breach as against a third party, but, if they have to compensate such a person, they have a statutory right to recover this money from the insured.[115] It may be, however, that they also have a common law right, which would be important when the event was not required to be insured under s.145 of the 1988 Act.[116]

In *National Farmers' Union Mutual Insurance Society v Dawson*,[117] the insured caused an accident when unfit to drive through drink. This was clearly a breach of a term of the policy requiring the insured to use all care and diligence to avoid accidents and prevent loss. Having paid the third party, the insurers sought to recover this sum from the insured. Their argument, which was based on what is now s.148(4) of the 1988 Act, failed; it was held that they could in fact have avoided liability to pay the third party. However, they succeeded in their claim to recover the money as damages for breach of contract. One may question whether this is a correct result where the insurers are not compelled by statute to pay the third party.[118] What, then, is their loss? In addition, if, as is usual, the term is a warranty or condition precedent

---

[113] [1966] 1 Lloyd's Rep. 407. See also *Lefevre v White* [1990] 1 Lloyd's Rep. 569 and *Amey Properties Ltd v Cornhill Insurance Plc* [1996] C.L.C. 401.

[114] The aspect of the decision that held that the insurers could rely on the breach of warranty regarding the state of the tyres even though that did not cause or contribute to the relevant accident becomes an academic one under the terms of s.11 of the Insurance Act 2015, unless the insured is a non-consumer and the effect of that section is excluded (see 9.7).

[115] Road Traffic Act 1988 s.148(4).

[116] Principally in a case of property damage exceeding the £1m statutory minimum.

[117] *National Farmers' Union Mutual Insurance Society v Dawson* [1941] 2 K.B. 424.

[118] See 21.5.

in the insurance sense,[119] it is arguable that it is not the same as a condition in other contracts. Its purpose is simply to relieve the insurers from liability, and it is thought that there is no merit or logic in allowing the insurers to recover from the insured.

21.4   Third Parties' Rights

As well as making motor insurance compulsory, as we have already seen, the Road Traffic Act 1988 interferes with the contractual rights of insurers for the benefit of third parties to whom the insured is legally liable. The 1988 Act has now been supplemented by additional protection for third parties introduced pursuant to the Fourth EC Directive, as explained below. Because this additional protection was introduced without amending the provisions of the Act, we will explain the provisions of the Act first and then consider the additional rights.

21.4.1 Invalid terms

Section 148(1) provides that, where a certificate of insurance has been delivered to the policyholder,[120] so much of the policy as purports to restrict the insurance of the persons insured by reference to any of a list of specified matters is of no effect as regards insurance required under s.145. This invalidates certain terms in policies regardless of their exact legal status, i.e. whether they are warranties, conditions or exceptions. Section 148(2) lists the matters as follows:

(a)   the age or physical or mental condition of persons driving the vehicle;

(b)   the condition of the vehicle;

(c)   the number of persons that the vehicle carries;

(d)   the weight or physical characteristics of the goods that the vehicle carries;

(e)   the times at which or the areas within which the vehicle is used;

(f)   the horsepower or cylinder capacity or value of the vehicle;

(g)   the carrying on the vehicle of any particular apparatus; and

---

[119] See the discussion in Ch.9.

[120] This requirement of delivery of a certificate should perhaps be ignored in circumstances such as those in *Motor and General Insurance Co v Cox* [1990] 1 W.L.R. 1443, which is discussed at 21.2.4.

(h) the carrying on the vehicle of any particular means of identification other than any means of identification required to be carried by or under the Vehicle Excise and Registration Act 1994.

In most respects the sorts of warranties, conditions or exceptions avoided by s.148(1) are clear. For example, conditions or exceptions relating to road-worthiness, etc. will be of no effect; they fall within (b) above. A breach of warranty as to the value or size of engine of a vehicle will fall within (f). On the other hand, a condition requiring the insured to use all care and diligence to avoid accidents and prevent loss is not covered by the list,[121] and a limita-tion as to use is always effective as against third parties,[122] unless it relates to the use of a private vehicle under car-sharing arrangements.[123]

Given that, if a term is enforceable, the third party will have recourse against the Motor Insurers' Bureau, as will be seen below, it is curious that the list in s.148(2) does not catch all provisions.[124] Why should an insurer be liable to a third party even if, say the insured has failed in the most deliberate and dangerous way to keep his vehicle roadworthy, whereas it could avoid liability for the slightest infringement of a limitation as to use? The logic of having an incomplete list as against a complete list or even no list at all is not easy to follow. As has already been noted, s.148(4) entitles the insurer com-pelled to pay the third party, but who would otherwise have avoided liability, to recoup this money from the insured.

21.4.2 Breaches of condition

Section 148(5) invalidates other breaches of condition by an insured so far as the third party is concerned. The conditions covered are those providing that no liability shall arise under the policy, or that any liability so arising shall cease, in the event of some specified thing being done or omitted to be done after the happening of the event giving rise to the claim. This clearly covers a breach by the insured of a condition regarding notice or particulars of loss, and it must also cover an admission of liability in breach of the standard condition.[125] Whether an arbitration clause is caught by s.148(5) is an open question if it has the *Scott v Avery* addition making it precedent to the insur-er's liability.[126] The majority of the Court of Appeal in *Jones v Birch Bros*[127]

---

[121] *National Farmers' Union Mutual v Dawson* [1941] 2 K.B. 424. See 21.3.7.

[122] *Jones v Welsh Insurance Corp* [1937] 4 All E.R. 149.

[123] See s.150 of the 1988 Act.

[124] The list has never been amended since its introduction in the Road Traffic Act 1934.

[125] See 20.2.4.

[126] See 14.10.

[127] *Jones v Birch Bros* [1933] 2 K.B. 597.

inclined to the view that such a clause would be caught, although it was held that one which did not provide that it was a condition precedent to liability was valid. In view of the unlikelihood of arbitration ever being used in motor vehicle disputes,[128] the question is probably totally academic now.

Section 148(6) allows insurers to insert in their policies provisions allowing them to recover back from the insured money which they have had to pay to a third party only by virtue of subs.(5). There is no automatic right given to insurers as there is under s.148(4), although it must be arguable that insurers would have that right in restitution, as there is a general principle that a claimant compelled by law to make a payment discharging the defendant's liability to a third party can recover that sum from the defendant.[129]

21.5   Insurer's Duty to Satisfy Judgments Under Section 151

The key provision so far as third parties are concerned is s.151,[130] although an alternative to using s.151 is now available in certain circumstances, as we shall see in 21.5.1. In effect, provided that a certificate of insurance has been delivered to the insured and a third party has obtained a judgment against any person insured by the policy, the whole of the judgment, in respect of liability for death or bodily injury, and up to £1 million of it in respect of liability for damage to property, must be satisfied by the insurer, notwithstanding that the insurer may be entitled to avoid or cancel, or may have avoided or cancelled, the policy.[131] Further, this obligation applies in respect of persons not insured by a policy, for example, persons not within the category of permitted drivers or even a thief of the vehicle,[132] except that, in respect of liability for death or personal injury, it does not apply if the third party was allowing himself to be carried in or upon the vehicle knowing or having reason to believe that the vehicle had been stolen or unlawfully taken.[133] Although it has been held[134] that this covers the situation where a third party passenger possessed sufficient information to afford him good

---

[128] See 14.10.

[129] See Goff and Jones, *The Law of Restitution*, 6th edn, Ch.14.

[130] The equivalent provision formed the basis for denying the need for a certificate to be delivered for the purposes of s.147 in *Motor and General Insurance Co v Cox* [1980] 1 W.L.R. 1443; see 21.2.4.

[131] See s.151(1), (2), (5) and (6). The award that must be satisfied includes costs and interest awarded. Where a property damage judgment exceeds £1 million, s.151(6)(b) provides as to how the insurer's exact liability is to be assessed.

[132] As to the potential impact of the liability to indemnify a thief on an innocent insured's no claims bonus, see Birds (1998) 148 N.L.J. 1672.

[133] Unless he did not realise this until after the journey commenced and could not reasonably be expected to have alighted from the vehicle: s.151(4).

[134] *McMinn v McMinn* [2006] EWHC 827 (QB); [2006] Lloyd's Rep. 802.

reason to believe that the vehicle had been stolen or unlawfully taken, it is submitted that this is too broad a construction of the statute in the light of the approach taken by the European Court of Justice.[135] In all cases, any term in a policy that purports to restrict its operation by requiring a driver to hold a licence to drive is invalid.[136] The section does not prohibit a policy from having a term excluding the liability of the insurer for deliberate damage, which is therefore enforceable against the insurer of property damaged by the insured where that insurer, having indemnified its own insured (the third party), is seeking to be subrogated to the rights of the third party to sue the insurers under s.151.[137]

Where an insurer is liable to indemnify a person not insured by the policy, s.151(8) provides that it can recover the amount paid to the third party from the driver or from an insured who caused or permitted the use of the vehicle.[138] This is another provision that has caused difficulties in the light of EU law and it was held not to apply when the insured was a passenger in the vehicle and also a victim, as the insurer's obligation to satisfy a judgment in his favour and then have the right to recover that back under the subsection was incompatible with the provisions of the Second Directive protecting third parties who are passengers.[139] Subsequently it has been held by the Court of Appeal that, in order to construe s.151(8) to accord with the Directive, it must be read as including the qualification that where the person insured by the policy may be entitled to the benefit of any judgment to which the sec-

---

[135] See especially *Candolin v Vahinkovakuutusosakeyhtio Pohjola Case* C-537/03 [2006] Lloyd's Rep. I.R. 209 construing national legislation in the light of art.2(1) of the second Directive and art.1 of the third Directive and see the authorities on the equivalent phrase in the MIB agreement, discussed at 21.8.

[136] See s.151(3). The insurer can recover from the driver what he has paid out: s.151(7)(a).

[137] *EUI Ltd v Bristol Alliance Ltd Partnership* [2012] EWCA Civ 1267. Although the decision may look inconsistent with the views of the ECJ on the scope of the compulsory insurance requirement, it may be thought sensible in the context of property damage claims and is consistent with the position under the MIB agreement which also, when a driver is uninsured, precludes subrogated claims in a situation like this.

[138] As to the meaning of permission in this context, see *Lloyd-Welper v Moore* [2004] EWCA Civ 766; [2004] Lloyd's Rep. I.R. 730.

[139] *Churchill Insurance Co Ltd v Wilkinson, Evans v Equity Claims Ltd* Case C-442/10. Here the European Court of Justice ruled on issues referred to it by the Court of Appeal [2010] Lloyd's Rep. I.R. 591 which provisionally had come to the same conclusion, approving the first instance decision in *Wilkinson v Fitzgerald* [2009] EWHC 1297 (QB). The English case law was yet another example (others have arisen largely in the context of the MIB agreements and are referred to below) illustrating how difficult in part it is to construe the hotchpotch of provisions governing compulsory motor insurance law consistently with the requirements of EU law.

tion refers, any recovery by the insurer in respect of that judgment must be proportionate and determined in the basis of the circumstances of the case.[140]

The insurer's obligation to satisfy judgments is qualified, however, by the provisions of s.152, in four respects:

(1) It arises only where the insurer was given notice, formally,[141] of the proceedings against the insured before or within seven days of their commencement[142];

(2) It is not exercisable where execution of a judgment has been stayed pending an appeal;

(3) It does not apply if the insured's policy was cancelled before the relevant accident, either by mutual consent or under a term in the policy, and the certificate of insurance was surrendered or the insured made a statutory declaration that it was lost or destroyed within 14 days of the cancellation, or within the same period the insurer commenced proceedings in respect of the failure to surrender the certificate; and

(4) It does not apply if the policy was obtained by non-disclosure or misrepresentation of a material fact and the insurer, within three months of the commencement of the proceedings against the insured, obtains a declaration of the court that it is entitled to avoid it under either the Consumer Insurance (Disclosure and Representations) Act 2012 or the Insurance Act 2015, and the third party receives notice of the action for a declaration and the particulars of the non-disclosure or misrepresentation within seven days of its being commenced.[143]

The fourth qualification does not remove the insurer's right to avoid for non-disclosure or misrepresentation, but it limits the effectiveness of that

---

[140] *Churchill Insurance Co Ltd v Wilkinson, Evans v Equity Claims Ltd* [2012] EWCA Civ 1166. The reference to proportionality etc is designed to reduce recovery where, for example, in the tort claim, the victim is regarded as contributorily negligent and hence damages would be reduced accordingly.

[141] *Herbert v Railway Passengers Assurance Co* [1938] 1 All E.R 650. A solicitor's letter to the insurers stating merely that the third party is being advised to issue proceedings is not sufficient to satisfy the requirement: *Harrington v Link Motor Policies* [1989] 2 Lloyd's Rep. 310, but the notice does not have to be in writing or take a specific form: *Desouza v Waterlow* [1999] R.T.R. 71. See also *Wylie v Wake* [2001] R.T.R. 291 and *Nawaz v Crowe Insurance Group* [2003] EWCA Civ 471; [2003] Lloyd's Rep. I.R. 471.

[142] This includes a counter claim by an injured defendant against an insured claimant, where appropriate: *Cross v British Oak Insurance Co* [1938] 2 K.B. 167.

[143] The third party has the right to be a party to this action.

right. However, it appears not to include an insurer denying liability on the grounds of breach of warranty. Section 152(2) refers expressly to the insurer's right to avoid apart from any provisions contained in the policy, meaning only the general right to avoid given now under the relevant statutory provisions.[144] Warranties arise from express provisions.[145] Thus, an insurer can avoid liability for breach of warranty as against the injured third party, without using the s.152 procedure, unless of course, the warranty relates to one of the matters in s.148(1), in which case the breach cannot be relied on at all.

If insurers are liable under s.151 to satisfy a judgment awarded to a third party, but could have avoided liability as between themselves and the insured, but chose not to do so, they can recover from the insured the amount paid to the third party.[146]

By s.153, the fact that the insured goes bankrupt or dies insolvent or, if a company, goes into liquidation, administration or receivership, does not affect the liability of the insured in respect of compulsory insurance, notwithstanding anything in the Third Parties (Rights against Insurers) Act 1930.[147] In other words, the sections in the Road Traffic Act regarding the third parties' rights continue to apply, but otherwise s.153 incorporates the statutory assignment of the 1930 Act.

21.5.1 The alternative right to sue insurers

There is now an alternative way in which third parties may proceed, introduced by the European Communities (Rights against Insurers) Regulations 2002.[148] These Regulations implement part of the EC Fourth Directive, but in fact go further than that Directive requires. The critical point is that, subject to the requirements explained below, a third party may proceed directly against the insurers without first having to obtain a judgment against the negligent driver, although the insurers will of course be able to defend the claim on the basis that the driver was not in fact liable in tort. The Regulations provide that an "entitled party" can, without prejudice to his right to issue proceedings against the insured person, issue proceedings against the insurer, which "shall be directly liable to the entitled party to the extent that he is liable to the insured person".[149] An entitled party is someone

---

[144] *Merchants' & Manufacturers' Insurance Co v Hunt* [1941] 1 K.B. 295.

[145] See, generally, Chs 5 and 8. In any event, a breach of warranty does not give rise to a right of avoidance of the policy.

[146] See s.151(7).

[147] As to the 1930 Act, see Ch.20.

[148] SI 2002/3061, in force from 19 January 2003, but seemingly irrespective of the date on which the accident occurred.

[149] Reg.3(2). As to the effect of the Directive and EC Regulation 44/2001 (the

who is a resident of the UK or any other EEA Member State,[150] so, for example, a tourist from outside Europe will not be able to use this right.

In addition, the entitled person must have a cause of action in tort against an "insured person", which arises out of an accident caused by or arising out of the use of a vehicle on a road or other public place in the UK.[151] For these purposes an insured person is a person insured under a policy fulfilling the requirements of s.145 of the 1988 Act.[152] The requirement for an "accident" is not one that appears anywhere else in the compulsory motor insurance requirements. Theoretically it could limit the application of the right, or at least raise the issue of whether or not a deliberate or reckless running down could be regarded as an accident, which would require a decision as to whether an event was to be looked at from the point of view of the insured driver or the victim.[153] In practice it seems unlikely to matter, since under the Regulations the victim has no better rights than the insured, and it is clear that, on public policy grounds, the insured would not be entitled to an indemnity in such a case.[154] In contrast, public policy would not prevent an action brought under s.151 of the 1988 Act. There are other limits to this right, in contrast to the position under s.151. While the restrictions in s.148 would also apply to an action brought under the Regulations, there is no other restriction on the insurer's contractual rights. There is no right under the Regulations to sue in respect of a tort committed by someone not insured under the policy nor when the insurance has actually been cancelled. In the latter case, s.151 will still apply if the insured is in possession of the certificate of insurance.

21.6 Information Regarding Insurance

Finally, under s.154, the driver against whom a claim is made in respect of damage compulsorily insurable is under a duty, enforceable by criminal penalties, on the demand of the third party, to give him information as to whether or not he was insured and, if so, such details of his insurance as are specified in his certificate of insurance.

Rome II Regulation), see *FBTO Schadeverzekeringen NV v Odenbreit* Case C-463/06, [2008] Lloyd's Rep. I.R. 354.
[150] Reg.2(1).
[151] The vehicle must be normally based in the UK.
[152] See 21.2.
[153] See the discussion of the word "accident" in 13.6 and following.
[154] See Ch.14.

21.7   Third Parties' Rights Against the Motor Insurers' Bureau

The provisions just examined concerning third party rights under the Road Traffic Act have given rise to relatively few reported cases in recent years. This probably illustrates their relative unimportance since the Motor Insurers' Bureau (MIB) was established. In 1937, the Cassel Committee[155] recommended that a central fund be established to protect the victims of road accidents who received no compensation despite the protection afforded by the Road Traffic Act. Obviously the Act could not cover the situation of the driver who did not have insurance cover, nor was it really relevant when an insurer went into liquidation. Furthermore, as has been seen, there are occasions when an insurer can rely on terms in the policy to avoid liability to the third party despite provisions in the Act. Finally, the statute cannot of necessity protect the victim of an untraced or "hit and run" driver. In this last respect, the Cassel Committee did not consider it practicable to give such victims rights against the fund and this remained the position until 1969, although they did have a discretionary entitlement before then.

It was probably fears of possible nationalisation of motor insurance business that led the motor insurers to conclude, on 31 December 1945, the first agreement between their creation, the MIB, and the Minister of Transport. It is now a condition of authorisation to transact motor insurance business that the insurer is a member of MIB Ltd,[156] and the MIB agreements are now required by EU law.[157] UK residents injured in an accident within the European Economic Area[158] now have a statutory right to claim from the MIB pursuant to the Consolidated EC Directive[159] in the situations covered by the MIB agreements.[160] There are two agreements between the MIB and the Secretary of State covering, respectively, the victims of uninsured and untraced drivers. Until recently, the latest uninsured agreement was dated August 1999, and applies to accidents occurring on or after 1 October 1999. It was amended by a short supplementary agreement dated November 2008. This replaced the agreement dated December 1988. Both the 1988 and 1999 agreements were in substance the original 1945 agreement with a number of amendments. In July 2015 a new uninsured agreement was

---

[155] Cmnd.5528, paras 151–168.

[156] s.145(5) of the Road Traffic Act 1988.

[157] Under the second Motor Insurance Directive.

[158] And other countries that are party to the "Green card" scheme for mutual recognition of motor insurance.

[159] See the Motor Vehicles (Compulsory Insurance) (Information Centre and Compensation Body) Regulations 2003, SI 2003/37.

[160] In the case of an accident outside the UK, the MIB has the right to claim indemnity from the insurers or its equivalent in the appropriate country.

made, which applies to accidents occurring on or after 1 August 2015. Since the 1999 agreement is likely to apply to accidents for a number of years, we retain an account of it alongside the 2015 agreement.

The untraced agreement, dated February 2003,[161] replaced earlier agreements dating from 1969, 1972 and 1996.[162] It is supplemented by an agreement of November 2008.

A matter of some importance was the extent to which this method of providing compensation to the victims of uninsured and untraced drivers complied fully with the requirements of the second Motor Insurance Directive. This was raised in some cases concerning the untraced drivers agreement[163] and a reference was made to the European Court of Justice.[164] The principal questions raised were that the use of a non-statutory body was insufficient compliance, that provisions in the former untraced drivers' agreement allowing for no payment of interest and costs were in breach of the Directive and that the procedure did not confer the right to a full and fair hearing, in breach of the European Convention on Human Rights. The ECJ gave its decision in December 2003,[165] ruling, to the surprise of at least some,[166] almost entirely in favour of the MIB and the UK Government. Interest on awards and costs were held in effect to be a matter for national law and courts.[167] The arguments on procedure were largely rejected. On the more fundamental constitutional question, the court held that the use of the MIB rather than a statutory system was sufficient compliance

> "provided that [the agreements are] interpreted and applied as obliging that body to provide victims with the compensation guaranteed to them by the Second Directive and as enabling victims to address themselves directly to the body responsible for providing such compensation".[168]

It should be noted that the MIB agreements apply only if insurance was compulsorily required so that if, for example, the accident in question did

---

[161] And applying to accidents occurring on or after 14 February 2003.

[162] Both the 1996 and 2003 agreements incorporate a supplementary agreement dating from 1977. Before 1969, the victims of "hit and run" accidents were compensated only on an ex gratia basis, an unsatisfactory state of affairs illustrated by the decision in *Adams v Andrews* [1964] 2 Lloyd's Rep. 349.

[163] In particular *Mighell v Reading* [1999] Lloyd's Rep. I.R. 30.

[164] *Evans v Secretary of State for the Environment, Transport & the Regions* [2002] Lloyd's Rep. I.R. 1.

[165] Case C-63/01 [2004] Lloyd's Rep. I.R. 391.

[166] And substantially contrary to the views of the Advocate General.

[167] The 2003 untraced drivers agreement does now in fact make some provision in this regard, although the earlier agreement will cover cases for some time to come.

[168] In *McCall v Poulton* [2008] EWCA Civ 1263; [2009] Lloyd's Rep. I.R. 454, there was a further reference to the ECJ, but it seems that the case was settled and thus not pursued at that level.

not happen on a road or public place, the MIB can, and does, take the point in defence.[169]

21.8   The Uninsured Agreement

This provides, in essence, that if a person injured or killed in a road accident, or whose property is damaged therein, obtains a judgment in respect of a liability that should have been insured against, and if that judgment is not satisfied in full within seven days, the MIB will satisfy it.[170] Thus, the agreement covers the case of the uninsured driver, the driver without effective insurance and the driver whose insurer is unable to indemnify him, although in the latter case the compensation will normally be paid under the Financial Services Compensation Scheme,[171] and the MIB will be in effect exempt under cl.17 of the 1999 agreement or cl.6 of the 2015 agreement. However, where a claim is made in respect of property damage, the MIB's liability is limited to £1 million.[172]

Under cl.17 of the 1999 agreement, in respect of claims for either personal injury or property damage, the MIB may deduct from the sum it pays an amount equal to compensation received by the third party from the Financial Services Compensation Scheme, from an insurer "under an insurance agreement or arrangement" or from any other source. As far as property damage is concerned, this is likely to apply in respect of damage to the third party's vehicle recovered under his own insurance and in respect of damage to other property that was separately insured. As far as personal injury claims are concerned, it might be argued that it is only compensation received from the Financial Services Compensation Scheme or possibly social security payments that are likely to be relevant. Money received by the third party (or his dependents) under his personal accident or life insurance policy is surely not "compensation" in the proper sense; they are not "indemnities"[173] and are not taken into account when tort damages are assessed. On the other hand, it might be that payments received under, for example, a

---

[169] See, e.g. *Buchanan v MIB* [1955] 1 W.L.R. 488; *Randall v MIB* [1968] 1 W.L.R. 1900.

[170] Clause 5(1) of the 1999 agreement, cl.3 of the 2015 agreement. The MIB can be required to make interim payments: *Sharp v Pereira* [1999] 1 W.L.R. 195.

[171] See 2.6.

[172] Clause 16 of the 1999 agreement, cl.11 of the 2015 agreement. This, of course, is the limit permitted by s.145 of the 1988 Act. Until the 2008 supplementary agreement (back-dated to 11 June 2007) there was an excess of £300 in the 1999 agreement restricting MIB's liability but that had to be removed to comply with the fifth EC Directive.

[173] The notes to the agreement state that "claims for loss and damage for which the claimant has been compensated or indemnified may be deducted".

medical insurance policy, which are assessed on an indemnity basis, might be deductible.

The equivalent provision in the 2015 agreement is cl.6. Under this, the MIB is not liable for any claim, or any part of a claim, in respect of which the claimant has received, or is entitled to receive or demand, payment or indemnity from any other person (including an insurer) other than the Criminal Injuries Compensation Authority.[174] A claimant will not recover when they have failed to make a claim or a valid claim on its own insurance. This mirrors the position under the 1999 agreement, as described above.

There are a number of conditions precedent to the MIB's liability in both agreements.

21.8.1 Other exceptions

There are a number of other exceptions to MIB's liability contained in cl.6 of the 1999 agreement and clauses 4, 5, 7, 8 and 9 of the 2015 agreement. First they cover some fairly straightforward cases, namely:

(1) in respect of liabilities arising out of the use of vehicles owned or possessed by the Crown, unless there was in fact insurance;

(2) cases where insurance was not compulsory by virtue of s.144 of the Road Traffic Act,[175] unless, in fact, there was insurance in such a case;

(3) vehicle damage claims where the claimant had failed to insure as required by the Road Traffic Act and either knew or ought to have known of this; in the 2015 agreement, the last phrase is "had reason to believe that that was the case"[176]; and

(4) something that is new to the 2015 agreement, claims where injury or death was caused by or in the course of an act of terrorism.

In the 1999 agreement, there are then some complex exceptions where the victim was a passenger, which both mirror, and go further than, the provisions in s.151 of the 1988 Act.[177] The equivalent in the 2015 agreement is considered separately below. They exclude claims where the claimant knew or ought to have known (a) that the vehicle had been stolen or unlawfully

---

[174] There are exceptions covering a claim to meet a liability to reimburse an employer, provided the employer is not insured for that loss and covering the claimant's legal costs.

[175] The provision as to deposits; see 21.2.

[176] The reason for this is explained below.

[177] See 21.5.

taken, (b) that the vehicle was being used without there being such insurance in force as required by the Road Traffic Act, (c) that the vehicle was being used in the course or furtherance of a crime,[178] and (d) that the vehicle was being used as a means of escape from, or avoidance of, lawful apprehension.[179] The burden of proof as to the claimant's knowledge is on the MIB, but there are presumptions of knowledge where (a) the claimant was the owner or registered keeper of the vehicle or had caused or permitted its use, (b) the claimant knew that the driver was under the lawful driving age, (c) the claimant knew that the driver was disqualified, and (d) the claimant knew that the user was not the owner or keeper of the vehicle nor an employee of the latter nor the owner or keeper of any other vehicle. Further, knowledge for these purposes includes knowledge of matters that the claimant could reasonably be expected to have been aware of had he not been under the self-induced influence of drink or drugs.[180] For the purpose of these exceptions, a "claimant" includes a person bringing an action under the Fatal Accidents Act 1976 as a dependent so that they only apply if that person had the appropriate knowledge and it is irrelevant that the deceased passenger would have been precluded from making a claim.[181]

While few would quarrel with the exclusion of claims from persons who clearly knew of the various illegalities within this exception, the fact that it also covers claimants who "ought to have known" is both more difficult to justify and was arguably in conflict with the requirements of the second EC Directive. Article 1(4), in requiring the establishment by Member States of a body to ensure compensation for the victims of uninsured or untraced drivers, only allows them to exclude the payment of compensation by that body "in respect of persons who voluntarily entered the vehicle which caused

---

[178] This exception was held to apply even where the crime was not that serious: *Delaney v Pickett* [2011] EWCA Civ 1532; [2011] R.T.R. 16, where the claimant was in possession of a relatively small amount of cannabis for supply as well as personal use. However, it is not contained in the Motor Insurance Directive and it was arguable that it is incompatible with the ECJ's rulings regarding the protection of passengers, especially that in *Churchill Insurance Co Ltd v Wilkinson, Evans v Equity Claims Ltd* Case C-442/10; see fn.139, above. However, the point was not argued. With respect, the dissenting view of Ward LJ that, in the light of the Directive, the exception should be read as applicable only to serious crimes, seemed more convincing than the reasoning of the majority. In any event, the victim then sued the Secretary of State for Transport (*Delaney v Secretary of State for Transport* [2015] EWCA Civ 172; affirming [2014] EWHC 1785 (QB)) and succeeded on the basis that the UK had failed properly to implement the second Directive, under the *Francovich* principle (*Francovich v Italy* Case C-6/90).

[179] (c) and (d) were new in the 1999 agreement.

[180] These presumptions and the "intoxification" provision were new in the 1999 agreement.

[181] *Phillips v Rafiq* [2007] EWCA Civ 74; [2007] Lloyd's Rep. I.R. 413.

the damage or injury when the body can prove that they knew it was uninsured". After the question had arisen in two cases[182] heard by the Court of Appeal together, it appeared that this might have to be subject of a reference to the European Court of Justice.[183] However, the House of Lords in *White v White*[184] produced a neat solution, the majority construing the words in the agreement to accord with the Directive and not exclude a claim by a merely negligent claimant. Knowledge means either actual knowledge or "blind eye" knowledge, that is that the passenger was aware of a problem but deliberately shut his eyes to it.[185]

In the 2015 agreement, cl.8 deals with the question of passenger claims. The first principal difference from the 1999 agreement is that there is no longer any reference to vehicles being used in the course or furtherance of a crime or as a means of escape from, or avoidance of, lawful apprehension.[186] The second is the use of the phrase "had reason to believe" rather than "ought to have known", which better reflects the consequences of the decision in *White v White*.

21.9 The Untraced Agreement

This agreement is necessarily much more complex than the first, because there will of course be no judgment against a tortfeasor for the MIB to satisfy. This account seeks to highlight the significant aspects of the agreement but does not purport to give a comprehensive account and does not consider the detailed procedures laid down for handling the claim, investigations and reports, the making of payments and appeals. It should be noted that the earlier agreements did not cover claims for property damage at all.[187] The 2003 agreement does allow these in the limited situation where the responsible vehicle has been identified and proves to have been stolen by an unknown driver,[188] but not if the property was insured under a first party policy nor,

---

[182] *Mighell v Reading* and *White v White* [1999] Lloyd's Rep. I.R. 30.

[183] Other questions of EU law were raised. For a stringent criticism of the Court of Appeal's judgment on these, see Davey and Richards [1999] J.B.L. 157.

[184] *White v White* [2001] UKHL 7; [2001] 1 W.L.R. 481.

[185] See also *Akers v Motor Insurers' Bureau* [2003] EWCA Civ 18; [2003] Lloyd's Rep. I.R. 427 and *Pickett v Motor Insurer Bureau* [2004] EWCA Civ 6; [2004] Lloyd's Rep. I.R. 513. The same point must apply as regards s.151(4) of the Road Traffic Act; see 21.5.

[186] This seems to reflect the decision in *Delaney v Secretary of State for Transport*, as described in fn.178.

[187] There are also problems regarding whether the earlier agreements were compliant with EU law; see *Moore v Secretary of State for Transport* [2007] EWHC 879 (QB) and *Byrne v Motor Insurers' Bureau* [2008] EWCA Civ 574; [2008] Lloyd's Rep. I.R. 705.

[188] This is subject to an excess of £300 per claimant.

in the case of damage to a motor vehicle, if the vehicle was not compulsorily insured to the knowledge of the person suffering the damage. A significant change from the earlier agreements is the provisions that allow the payment of interest and costs.[189] A number of requirements must be satisfied by an applicant for an award, including[190]:

(1) The applicant must be unable to trace the person responsible for the death, injury or damage or a person partly so responsible.

(2) The death, injury or damage must have been caused in circumstances such that on the balance of probabilities the untraced person would have been liable to the applicant in damages.

(3) That liability must have been one required to be insured against under the 1988 Act; this is assumed in the absence of evidence to the contrary.

(4) The application must be made in writing within three years of the accident for personal injury claims (nine months for property damage claims).

There are exceptions[191] that are very similar to the exceptions to the first agreement already mentioned, including claims from passengers involved in a crime.[192] Injury or loss resulting from terrorist acts is also excluded.[193] The amount of compensation awarded to the applicant is assessed on the same basis as a court would assess damages in a tort action, except that the MIB does not award damages for loss of earnings in so far as they have been paid by the applicant's employer.[194]

There are special provisions dealing with the cases where an untraced driver was only partly to blame for the accident.[195] Here the applicant may be required to obtain judgment against the known driver or the known principal of an unidentified driver, or the applicant may have obtained such judgment without being required to do so. If this judgment is not satisfied at all within three months, the MIB awards an amount equal to the untraced

---

[189] Clauses 9 and 10. Interest was not payable under the earlier agreements: *Evans v MIB* [1999] Lloyd's Rep. I.R. 30.

[190] Clause 4.

[191] Clause 5.

[192] This is subject to knowledge on the same basis as in the uninsured drivers agreement (see 21.8.1).

[193] This exclusion replaces one in the earlier agreement that excluded any liability for death or injury caused deliberately.

[194] Clause 8.

[195] Clauses 12 to 15.

person's contribution to a full award, namely, that proportion which a court would have awarded if proceedings had been taken against all the tortfeasors. If this judgment is only partly satisfied within three months, the MIB awards an amount equal to either the unsatisfied part of the judgment or the untraced person's contribution, whichever is the greater. If the applicant has not obtained, and is not required by the MIB to obtain, judgment against the known driver, and has not received any payment as compensation from any such person, the amount the MIB awards is an amount equal to the untraced person's contribution to a full award.

21.10 Procedural Issues

A number of procedural issues have over the years been relevant in the context of the MIB agreements. The most important, in theory at least, related to their enforcement, because technically they are only contracts between the Secretary of State and the MIB. However, since the implementation of the EC Fourth Directive,[196] which confers a statutory right on victims to claim from the Bureau, this appears to be an academic question.[197] In addition, it has been held that, as the second agreement was entered into after the Contracts (Rights of Third Parties) Act 1999 came into force, a victim can rely on that Act to sue the MIB directly.[198]

---

[196] By the Motor Vehicles (Compulsory Insurance) (Information Centre and Compensation Body) Regulations 2003, SI 2003/37.

[197] As to the effect of reg.13(2)(b) of these Regulations, see *Jacobs v MIB* [2010] EWCA Civ 1208; [2011] 1 W.L.R. 2609.

[198] *Carswell v Secretary of State for Transport* [2010] EWHC 3230 (QB); [2011] Lloyd's Rep. I.R. 644.

CHAPTER 22

EMPLOYERS' LIABILITY AND OTHER COMPULSORY
INSURANCES

22.0

This chapter is concerned with those liability insurances other than motor insurance that are compulsory. Foremost among these is employers' liability insurance.

22.1   Employers' Liability Insurance

An employee injured at work has, broadly speaking, the right to claim compensation from the State, regardless of questions of fault, under the legislation dealing with industrial injury benefit.[1] This replaced workmen's compensation insurance, which was an important class of insurance business for many years. The employee who can show that his employer, or someone for whom the latter is responsible, was at fault in some way will also have the right to claim damages in tort from him. This may be in negligence or it may be for breach of statutory duty. Statistically, work accidents rank with road accidents as the most common source of tort actions. Against an employer who is not insured or not effectively insured this tort action may be worthless. Some notorious instances of employers being without cover led to the enactment of the Employers' Liability (Compulsory Insurance) Act 1969.[2]

Section 1(1) provides that, subject to some exceptions which will be considered later, every employer carrying on any business in Great Britain shall insure and maintain insurance under one or more approved policies with an authorised insurer against liability for bodily injury or disease sustained by his employees, and arising out of and in the course of their employment in Great Britain in that business, but except in so far as regulations otherwise provide, not including injury or disease suffered or contracted outside Great Britain.[3]

---

[1] Strictly this legislation covers "employed earners" which is wider than "employees". See generally Wikeley, Ogus and Barendt's *Law of Social Security*, 5th edn (Oxford: OUP, 2002) Ch.20.

[2] Considerable concern has been expressed about the cost of employers' liability insurance, but it would seem that there is nonetheless a high level of compliance with the requirement: see the survey conducted for the Health and Safety Commission, December 2003.

[3] The Act was brought into force on 1 January 1972 by the Employers' Liability

However, such an employers' liability policy is not required to cover risks that must be insured under the Road Traffic Act.[4] Thus, in practice, although an employers' liability policy could cover such risks, this is not now likely. An employers' liability policy, and the underlying tort claim, is transferred on the sale of a business under the Transfer of Undertakings (Protection of Employment) Regulations 1981.[5]

A policy effected by an employer can be wider than the statute prescribes. For example, it might not be limited to liability "arising out of and in the course of employment". In practice, though, this phrase does appear as the standard limit in employers' liability policies. Its meaning is thus important both for this reason and because it defines the scope of the statutory requirement. The phrase also appears in the Road Traffic Act 1988, and it was the classic formula used in the workmen's compensation legislation to determine eligibility.[6] It is clear that it has the same meaning in any of these contexts where it survives unchanged, but the fact that its meaning has been enlarged in the social security context[7] must be ignored.[8] On the other hand, the formula is still the basic one for industrial injury benefit purposes, and it must be the case that decisions on its interpretation in the statutory context, which are not concerned with the statutory extensions, are of relevance to its meaning in an employers' liability policy and s.1 of the 1969 Act. There is a very large number of decisions on its meaning in social security legislation, but this is not the place where those decisions can be considered in any detail.[9] One or two will, however, be referred to.

In *BAI (Run-Off) Ltd v Durham*,[10] the Supreme Court held that s.1 requires an employer to insure against liability for disease caused during the period of the policy, even if the disease manifests itself only later. It did not matter whether the policy referred to injury or disease "sustained" or injury or disease "caused" during the policy period. In the test cases that were the

---

(Compulsory Insurance) Regulations, SI 1971/117. The operative Regulations, hereafter referred to as the "Regulations", are now the Employers' Liability (Compulsory Insurance) Regulations 1998, SI 1998/2573, as amended by SI 2004/2882, SI 2008/1765 and SI 2011/686.

[4] The Regulations Sch.2, para.14.
[5] *Martin v Lancashire County Council* [2000] Lloyd's Rep. I.R. 665. See now the 2006 Regulations.
[6] That legislation also required an "accident"; see 13.6 and following.
[7] See, e.g. Social Security Contributions and Benefits Act 1992 s.99.
[8] *Vandyke v Fender* [1970] 2 Q.B. 292.
[9] See, e.g. Wikeley, Ogus and Barendt, *The Law of Social Security*, 5th edn.
[10] *BAI (Run-Off) Ltd v Durham* [2012] UKSC 14; [2012] 1 W.L.R. 867, reversing the majority decision in the Court of Appeal ([2010] Lloyd's Rep. I.R. 1) and restoring the decision at first instance ([2009] Lloyd's Rep. I.R. 295). The case is often referred to as "the trigger litigation". The judgment of Burton J gives a very detailed and useful account of the history and development of employers' liability insurance.

subject of the litigation, some policies had one form of wording and others the other form, but the Court was adamant that the phrases had to be given a purposive construction, that is in the light of the requirement for employers to insure against their liability in contexts where, as in the present case which concerned exposure to asbestos, the symptoms of disease manifested themselves years later than the time of exposure. This very important decision, the effect of which was to ensure the benefit of insurance to employees whose employers had the "sustained" policy wordings, is probably to be confined to situations where liability insurance is compulsory, rather than applying to, for example, public liability policies that use the "sustained" wording.

An important consequential issue arose in the subsequent Supreme Court decision in *Zurich Insurance Plc v International Energy Group Ltd*.[11] This concerned the situation where an employer did not have insurance over the whole period of exposure of the employee to asbestos and on the facts the particular insurer provided insurance for only eight of the 27 years of the exposure. By a bare majority, it was held that this insurer was liable for the whole of the damages awarded to the employee, but had a right of contribution[12] against any other insurer(s) at risk during the period and against the employer itself for any period where there was no insurance. While this result apparently reflected practice in the insurance industry, it is not, it is thought, free from difficulty as a matter of both law and policy, especially in deciding that an employer is to be regarded as "self-insured" for the period where it has no cover, so that the equitable doctrine of contribution could be applied against it regardless of the contractual relationship between it and the insurer.[13]

22.1.1 Out of and in the course of employment

Broadly, the formula covers two different principles. "In the course of employment" means that

> "the accident must arise when the employee is doing what a man so employed might reasonably do during a time during which he was employed and at a place where he may reasonably be during that time to do that thing".[14]

---

[11] *Zurich Insurance Plc v International Energy Group Ltd* [2015] UKSC 33.

[12] As to contribution, see Ch.18.

[13] But note that Lord Mance at [1], giving the principal judgment of the majority, emphasised that the decision was concerned only with situations falling within the special rule developed (by the House of Lords in *Fairchild v Glenhaven Funeral Services Ltd* [2003] 1 A.C. 32 and the Compensation Act 2006) to deal with exposure to asbestos dust (see also Lord Hodge at [109]).

[14] Lord Loreburn in *Moore v Manchester Liners Ltd* [1910] A.C. 498 at 500–501.

Therefore, employees travelling to and from work are not in the course of their employment, even if travelling in vehicles provided by their employers, unless their terms of employment oblige them so to travel.[15] In *Vandyke v Fender*,[16] V and F were employees of R. They worked some distance from home and R agreed to provide a car in which F would drive himself and V to work. R also paid an amount towards petrol costs. While they were driving to work one day, V was injured owing to F's negligence. One of the questions for decision was whether R's employers' liability insurers were liable to pick up the bill or whether the relevant motor insurer[17] was liable. It was held that the employers' liability insurer was not liable as the accident did not arise in the course of employment, V not being obliged to travel in the car.

In contrast, in *Paterson v Costain & Press (Overseas) Ltd*,[18] the claimant employee was injured due to the negligence of his employer's driver while being taken from the office to the construction site where the claimant had been told that he was required. It was the defendant employer's practice to transport their employees to the site. It was held that the accident did arise in the course of the claimant's employment as he was in the vehicle under an obligation to go to the site in obedience to what he had been told. The defendant's employers' liability insurers were therefore liable to indemnify them against their liability to the claimant.[19]

Even an accident at work is not necessarily in the course of employment. A policeman playing football for his force in a match against another force at the force sports ground was held not to be covered for state compensation when he was injured during the match even though participation was expected of him.[20] The Court of Appeal rejected the argument that "in the course of employment" includes matters reasonably incidental to employment, except where the accident occurs at the place of work during an interruption, for example, for a tea break.

If an employee is injured outside his strict hours of work, this may still be

---

[15] Note, however, that in an industrial injury benefit case, the test of obligation to travel has been held inapplicable: *Nancollas v Insurance Officer* [1985] 1 All E.R. 833. Doubt was raised by Donaldson MR on the interpretation of old workmen's compensation cases put forward in *Vandyke v Fender* (see below). It may be therefore that when the opportunity arises in a dispute on an employers' liability policy, the courts will adopt the view of the *Nancollas* case that there is no overriding principle concerning whether or not travel is in the course of employment.

[16] *Vandyke v Fender* [1970] 2 Q.B. 292.

[17] In fact, it was the MIB, as the motor insurer had gone into insolvent liquidation.

[18] *Paterson v Costain & Press (Overseas) Ltd* [1979] 2 Lloyd's Rep. 204.

[19] As an employers' liability policy is no longer required to cover motor risks (see above), it is unlikely that cases with facts like those of *Vandyke v Fender* and *Paterson v Costain & Press (Overseas) Ltd* will arise in the future.

[20] *R. v National Insurance Commissioner Ex p. Michael* [1977] 1 W.L.R. 109.

in the course of employment. A reasonable period at the beginning and end of work will usually be included.[21]

The other limb of the formula, namely, "out of employment", is somewhat looser. Essentially it requires a causal connection between the employment and the accident. It seems unlikely that it can give rise to any problems in the employers' liability insurance field. If an employer has been adjudged or has agreed to be legally liable in tort to an employee, a necessary precondition of the insurers' liability, it must follow that the liability of the employer arose out of the employee's employment.

22.1.2 Employees covered

Section 2 of the 1969 Act defines "employee" for the purposes of the obligation to insure under s.1. It means anyone who works under a contract of service or apprenticeship, express or implied, written or oral, thus excluding any obligation to insure against liability to the self employed, those who work under a contract for services. The distinction between a contract of service and a contract for services can be a fine one. It has caused problems in many areas of the law and reference should be made elsewhere for details.[22] Section 2(2) also excludes the obligation to insure in respect of employees who are close relatives within the list specified and employees not ordinarily resident in Great Britain, except in so far as regulations provide otherwise.[23]

22.1.3 Prohibited conditions

There is one further and very important point arising under s.1(1) of the Act. This requires that insurance be by "approved policies", defined as policies of insurance "not subject to any conditions or exceptions prohibited for these purposes by regulations".[24] The regulations duly list four prohibited conditions "in whatever terms" which will be examined shortly. It is clear that the prohibited conditions may not be conditions in the strict sense; they may be warranties. However, they are only prohibited if they are conditions precedent to liability under the policy, either generally (i.e. as warranties) or in respect of a particular claim (i.e. as conditions precedent).[25] Thus it is perfectly permissible to have conditions which are not precedent to liability, but merely give the insurer the right to claim damages for breach. This is

---

[21] See, e.g. *R. v National Insurance Commissioner Ex p. East* [1976] I.E. 206.
[22] See, e.g. Smith & Baker, *Smith & Wood's Employment Law*, 12th edn (Oxford: OUP, 2015), Ch.2.
[23] See the definition of "relevant employee" in reg.1(2).
[24] See s.1(3).
[25] See generally Chs 6 and 8.

confirmed by reg.2(3), whereby a policy can expressly provide for the insured to pay or contribute any sum to the insurer in respect of the satisfaction of any claim made under the contract of insurance by a relevant employee or costs and expenses incurred in relation to any such claim. This wording[26] is strange in referring to "a claim made under the contract of insurance by a relevant employee". Employees do not make claims on employers' liability policies, their employers do.

The conditions prohibited are any that provide "that no liability (either generally or in respect of a particular claim)[27] shall arise under the policy, or that any such liability so arising shall cease if:

> "(a) some specified thing is done or omitted to be done after the happening of the event giving rise to a claim under the policy."

This is analogous to s.148(5) of the Road Traffic Act 1988,[28] and covers such matters as failure to give notice or particulars of loss in time and unauthorised admissions of liability. Thus, it reverses *Farrell v Federated Employers Insurance Co*,[29] although it is doubtful whether it prohibits a condition making the prior payment of due premiums by the insured precedent to liability, as it only covers things "after the happening of the event. . ."[30]:

> "(b) the policy holder does not take reasonable care to protect his employees against the risk of bodily injury or disease in the course of their employment."

As has been seen earlier,[31] the courts have interpreted conditions in liability policies generally which require the insured to take reasonable care as broken only if the insured is more than merely negligent, so in this sense the prohibition changes nothing. Even recklessness would not entitle an insurer to avoid liability, it is suggested, if it relies merely upon a condition to take reasonable care, for such a condition is prohibited.[32] However, a condition expressly providing that recklessness debars liability would arguably be enforceable.

> "(c) the policy holder fails to comply with the requirements of any enactment for the protection of employees against the risk of bodily injury or disease in the course of their employment."

---

[26] It is not identical to that in the earlier Regulations.

[27] Thus confirming that terms may be warranties or conditions precedent.

[28] See 21.4.2.

[29] *Farrell v Federated Employers Insurance Co* [1970] 1 W.L.R. 1400; see 20.1.3.

[30] See *Murray v Legal & General Assurance Co* [1969] 3 All E.R. 794, discussed at 20.1.3.

[31] See 20.2.5.

[32] Contra Hasson, "The Employers' Liability (Compulsory Insurance) Act—A broken reed" [1974] I.L.J. 79 at 84, especially fn.32.

The meaning of this is evident.

> "(d) the policy holder does not keep specified records or provides the insurer with or makes available to him information from such records."

It is not uncommon for premiums for employers' liability policies to be adjusted by reference to wages and salaries actually paid by the employer, and for the policy to provide for the keeping of records for this purpose. Failure to comply cannot defeat an employee's claim.[33]

22.1.4 Sums insured

Employers are not required to maintain policies with no limit on the maximum liability of the insurer, but policies must have a sum insured of £5 million in respect of claims relating to any one or more of their employees arising out of any one occurrence.[34]

22.1.5 Exceptions

Section 3 of the 1969 Act exempts certain employers altogether from the requirement to insure. Basically these are certain local government councils, nationalised industries and any employer specifically exempted by regulations. The latter[35] list a number of other public bodies that are exempt.[36]

22.1.6 Enforcement

Enforcement of the 1969 Act is effected first by ensuring the display of certificates of insurance, secondly by permitting inspections of certificates and policies, and thirdly by criminal penalties.[37]

Section 4(1) requires insurers to issue certificates in the form prescribed in the Regulations, and reg.5 requires these to be displayed at any place of business where an employer employs any person whose claims may be the subject

---

[33] With respect, Hasson, [1974] I.L.J. 79 at 85, is wrong to suggest that this "merely restates the common law rule". Although such a condition was held not to be precedent to liability in *Re Bradley and Essex & Suffolk Accident Indemnity Society* [1912] 1 K.B. 415 (see 9.11), this was as a matter of the construction of the policy in question, not as a general rule.

[34] See s.1(2) and reg.3. As to "occurrence", see 20.3.

[35] Sch.2.

[36] See also the Employers' Liability (Compulsory Insurance) Amendment Regulations 2004 SI 2004/2882, exempting any employer that is a company with only one employee who also owns 50 per cent or more of the issued share capital in that company.

[37] As to the penalty, see s.5.

of indemnity under the insurance. Employers must produce their certificates, or copies, to an officer of the Health and Safety Executive on being served with notice to do so.[38] In addition, any inspector authorised by the Secretary of State can demand to inspect any policy of employer's liability insurance on reasonable notice.[39]

22.1.7 Comment[40]

When compared with the Road Traffic Act provisions relating to third party motor insurance, the 1969 Act and the associated regulations appear paltry and inadequate.[41] There is no mechanism whereby the injured employee can recover directly from the insurer, save where his employer becomes insolvent so that he can use the provisions of the Third Parties (Rights against Insurers) Act 1930.[42] There are no restrictions on the right of the insurer to avoid liability or the policy for breach of the duty of fair presentation or breach of warranty, and it is conceivable, though perhaps unlikely in practice, that policies could contain quite wide-ranging exceptions which do not fall foul of the prohibitions in reg.2. Further, it has been held by the Court of Appeal that the directors of a company that has failed to insure as required by the 1969 Act are not personally liable in tort for breach of statutory duty.[43] Perhaps most importantly, if an employer is not insured or not effectively insured, there is no equivalent of the Motor Insurers' Bureau.[44] These deficiencies seem all the stranger when it is considered that the event which gave the final impetus to the enactment of the Act was a fire in Glasgow when the employer's insurers successfully avoided liability for non-disclosure and injured employees were uncompensated. It can hardly be denied that the compulsory insurance scheme for employers is a half-hearted system.[45]

---

[38] Reg.6.

[39] Reg.7.

[40] See also Hasson, [1974] I.L.J. 79; Simpson (1972) 35 M.L.R. 63 and Parsons, "Employers' liability insurance—how secure is the system?" (1999) 28 I.L.J. 109.

[41] This is particularly strange given the review that the Government engaged in, which led to minor changes in the 1998 Regulations.

[42] See Ch.20.

[43] *Richardson v Pitt-Stanley Ltd* [1995] 1 All E.R. 460.

[44] A private members' Bill, the Employers Liability Insurance Bureau Bill, was presented to Parliament in 2010, but, not surprisingly, did not get very far through the legislative process.

[45] Another problem in practice in the "long tail" nature of much employers' liability business, that is claims may be made by employees, and hence by employers on their insurers, many years after the event. The ABI recommends that employers' liability policies are retained for 40 years.

22.2   Other Compulsory Insurances

There are a number of other instances where third party insurance is in effect compulsory although in none of these are there any provisions affecting the contractual position between insurer and insured. The most important of these are the following. Professional indemnity insurance may be required, not by statute, but by the rules of the profession. If, as for example is the case with the legal profession, one has to be a member of the body concerned in order to practice, insurance is effectively compulsory. Insurance is required by statute or by rules made under statutory authority in an increasing number of similar cases.[46]

Riding establishments are required to insure against their liability to those who hire and use their horses and against the liability of the latter for injury to third parties.[47] Owners of oil tankers and other vessels must insure against liability for oil pollution under the Merchant Shipping Act 1995. The operator of a nuclear establishment is required to effect insurance under the Nuclear Installations Act 1965–1969, though this is done in a rather special way with a committee of insurers. As far as aviation is concerned, subject to some exemptions, insurance covering liability in respect of passengers, baggage, cargo and third parties is compulsory under Regulation 785/04 of the European Parliament and Council.[48] The Regulation applies to all air carriers and aircraft operators flying within, into, out of or over the territory of a Member State. The insured risks must include acts of war, terrorism, hijacking, acts of sabotage, unlawful seizure of aircraft and civil commotion and there are detailed provisions regarding the minimum amount of cover that must be obtained.

---

[46] For example under the Credit Unions Act 1979, the Estate Agents Act 1979, the Financial Services and Markets Act 2000 and the Chiropractors Act 1994.

[47] Riding Establishments Act 1964 s.1.

[48] [2004] O.J. L138, as supplemented by the Civil Aviation (Insurance) Regulations 2005 SI 2005/1089.

INDEX

LEGAL TAXONOMY
FROM SWEET & MAXWELL

This index has been prepared using Sweet and Maxwell's Legal Taxonomy. Main index entries conform to keywords provided by the Legal Taxonomy except where references to specific documents or non-standard terms (denoted by quotation marks) have been included. These keywords provide a means of identifying similar concepts in other Sweet & Maxwell publications and online services to which keywords from the Legal Taxonomy have been applied. Readers may find some minor differences between terms used in the text and those which appear in the index. Suggestions to *sweetandmaxwell.taxonomy@thomson.com*.